CHRISTIAN THEOLOGY

John Macquarrie

SCM PRESS LTD · LONDON

TO THE REVEREND JOHN KNOX
Baldwin Professor of Sacred Literature
in Union Theological Seminary New York 1943–1966

334 01300 3

First British edition 1966
published by SCM Press Ltd
26–30 Tottenham Road, London N1
reprinted four times
Revised edition 1977
Fifth impression 1984

Typeset in the United States of America
and printed and bound in Great Britain by
Redwood Burn Limited, Trowbridge, Wiltshire

PRINCIPLES OF
CHRISTIAN THEOLOGY

REVISED EDITION

PRINCIPLES OF

REVISED EDITION

Preface

Christian theology seeks to think the Church's faith as a coherent whole. It aims not only at showing the internal coherence of the Christian faith, that is to say, how the several doctrines constitute a unity, but also at exhibiting the coherence of this faith with the many other beliefs and attitudes to which we are committed in the modern world. Only if these tasks are accomplished can the faith be held intelligently and be integrated with the whole range of human life.

The theological task needs to be done over and over again, as new problems, new situations, and new knowledge come along. But there are many pitfalls along the way. Sometimes the theologian gets lost in academic speculations that are far removed from the living faith of the Church; sometimes he clings tenaciously to the myths and symbols of a bygone age; sometimes, in a pathetic desire to be "contemporary" and "relevant," he reduces the Christian faith to a pale reflection of whatever happens to be the currently popular philosophy. No theologian can hope to avoid all the pitfalls. Yet the fact that every theology will have some flaws is not a reason for turning away from the theological task, or for underestimating the place of theology in the Church's life. Theology is indispensable to the Church, and where theology fails, we must take this as a demand for better theology and certainly not as an excuse for turning away from it or for imagining that the Church can get along without it. It is foolish, for instance, to suggest that we need devote ourselves only to the practical tasks of Christianity, or that theology can be replaced in the Church by such sciences as psychology and sociology. However important these matters may be—and certainly I have no wish to deny their importance—they do not in the slightest degree take away the need for fundamental theological thinking. Christian action itself will become aimless and sporadic unless it is illuminated by clear theological understanding.

Every theologian must write from his own perspective, and this will be limited in various ways. I hope, however, that the presentation offered in this book will be helpful to readers from a wide range of Christian traditions, for I do not think that I have taken up many "extreme" or "sectarian" positions, but have tried to bring to expression the broad mainstream of Christian thought and experience. The founders of the Seminary in which I teach aimed at making it one "around which all men of moderate views and feelings, who desire to live free from party strife, and to stand aloof from all the extremes of doctrinal speculation, practical radicalism, and ecclesiastical domination, may cordially and affectionately rally." The Christian communion to which I belong has for long been celebrated for the *via media Anglicana*. Of course, it would be absurd to imagine that the truth is always midway between the extremes, and perhaps some of my positions will seem extreme enough to some readers. Nevertheless, there is a kind of dialectic that operates in theology and that arises, I believe, out of the polarities of human existence itself. The effect of this dialectic throughout the history of theology has been to exclude extreme and exaggerated points of view. The Church needs both stability and flexibility in its theology if it is to go forward, and not be either disintegrated or petrified.

Let me say frankly, however, that I have not tried to please everyone. I have no use for that mistaken kind of ecumenism which glosses over genuine differences and seems to suggest that every point of view is equally valid, so long as it is sincerely held. Those who think in this way are really saying that there is neither truth nor untruth in theology; and this implies, in turn, that the whole theological enterprise is a waste of time. We have to face the fact that there are many controversial and divisive issues in theology, some more important, others less so. Natural theology or no natural theology? A genuine knowledge of God in the non-Christian religions, or no such knowledge? Infant baptism or adult baptism only? Bishops or no bishops? Women in the ministry, or men only? These are issues about which the theologian has got to decide, or else to become evasive. I have tried to deal frankly with these and other controversial questions; but in each case I have sought to give reasons for the position taken, to show how this position is implied and supported by the total theological structure, and, I hope, to show also some understanding for alternative points of view.

By far the most important ecumenical development in recent years has been the new outreach of the Roman Catholic Church to Christians of other communions. I have been very much aware of this development while writing this book, and have tried to respond to it by discussing openly and, I hope, constructively, such supposedly divisive issues as mariology, the papacy and transubstantiation.

Equally important are the increasing contacts of Christianity with other faiths in a world where we are all living more closely together. It seems to me that the time has come for the abandonment of some of the old exclusive attitudes, and for a new openness and generosity of spirit on the part of Christians toward the other great world-religions. I have accordingly tried to present the truths of Christian theology in a way which will encourage such openness.

For many of the philosophical categories employed in this book, I am indebted to the writings of Martin Heidegger. As it seems to me, his way of philosophizing and the concepts he has developed provide the basis for a viable twentieth-century philosophical ("natural") theology, and can be used further for the articulation and elucidation of the whole body of Christian truth in a contemporary way. This does not mean in the very slightest that our theology is being made subservient to a philosophy; but it does mean that, like theologians of the past, we can avail ourselves of such current philosophical work as will best serve to express the faith in terms that communicate with the secular culture of our time.

Among contemporary theologians, I have found Karl Rahner the most helpful. In saying this, I am acknowledging that the leadership in theology, which even ten years ago lay with such Protestant giants as Barth, Brunner, and Tillich, has now passed to Roman Catholic thinkers. Among them, Karl Rahner (himself a penetrating student of Heidegger) is outstanding. He handles in a masterly way those tensions which constitute the peculiar dialectic of theology mentioned above: faith and reason, tradition and novelty, authority and freedom, and so on.

Rudolf Bultmann has remained my principal guide in the understanding of the New Testament, though I have never been uncritical of some of his positions. In New Testament theology, I am indebted also to my colleague, John Knox, especially for his profound insights into the nature of the Church; and I owe him so much in other and more personal ways that I have ventured to dedicate this book to him, in gratitude and affection.

Four years have passed since the publishers invited me to undertake this work. I wish to thank their editors for their patience and courtesy, and their readers for some useful suggestions.

JOHN MACQUARRIE

Union Theological Seminary,
New York

Preface to the New Edition

It is ten years since this book was first published, and I have felt it a duty both to my readers and to myself to make a thorough revision. The revised edition contains a great deal of new material; indeed, there is scarcely a topic on which I have not felt obliged to think afresh and to take note of new theological developments.

I wish to thank the many reviewers, critics, commentators, and friends who have stimulated me to produce what I hope will be a more adequate book, and also the publishers for their encouragement.

JOHN MACQUARRIE

Christ Church,
Oxford

CONTENTS

PART THREE APPLIED THEOLOGY 371

PRINCIPLES OF
CHRISTIAN THEOLOGY

REVISED EDITION

1 | Introduction

1. WHAT IS THEOLOGY?

Theology may be defined as the study which, through participation in and reflection upon a religious faith, seeks to express the content of this faith in the clearest and most coherent language available.

Definitions can be misleading, but they are not unimportant, for our approach to any study or investigation whatsoever is guided by our initial assumptions about what we are seeking and how we are to seek it, and it is an advantage to make these assumptions explicit in a definition. There are several possible approaches to theology, and therefore the definition given above already points us (as any other definition would also do) to a definite avenue into the matters which we are to study. The justification for taking this approach and for the definition in which it is made explicit can come only with the working out of the complete theology; yet, as the result of a kind of two-way traffic, the definition itself has been shaped and modified and brought to its explicitness because some of the areas of theology that lie ahead have already been explored, and some approaches have been found more fruitful than others.

However, some provisional remarks ought to be made here, by way of commenting on our definition and drawing out some of its content that may not yet be fully explicit.

A comment may be made first on the assertion contained in our definition that theology proceeds "through participation in and reflection upon a religious faith." This phrase is intended to indicate that theology is both continuous with and yet distinct from faith. Theology is continuous with faith because it participates in faith and speaks from the standpoint of faith. In theology, faith is bringing itself to a certain kind of expression, though of course it expresses itself in other ways as well. Furthermore, it is some specific faith that expresses itself in theology, not just faith in general but the faith of an historic community. This book contains Christian theology, but there could equally well be books of Jewish theology or Muslim theology. Theology, however, will always speak from a specific faith. This means also that theology implies participation in a community. No doubt theologians have their individual styles and to some extent they grapple with the problems which they themselves have found especially challenging. But if they remain theologians, they are not expressing a private faith, but have become spokesmen for their community, charged with a special responsibility within it.

These remarks on participation serve also to distinguish theology from the philosophy of religion. Probably even the philosopher of religion needs to have some degree of participation if he is to understand the matter which he is studying, but the nature of his study demands a measure of detachment which would not be looked for in the theologian. Moreover, while the philosopher of religion may be himself involved in some particular faith, we rightly expect him to take account of all the forms of faith and to study the universal phenomenon of religion rather than any specific manifestation of it. Again, whereas the theologian speaks out of the community of faith, the philosopher of religion is an individual investigator.

But our definition stresses reflection just as much as participation in theology's relation to faith. While theology participates in a specific faith and does not speak from outside of this faith, it has nevertheless taken a step back, as it were, from the immediate experiences of faith. In theology, faith has been subjected to thought. This may even be critical thought, though more often it is descriptive and interpretative. When St. Thomas says, "My Lord and my God!" [1] this is indeed faith expressing itself in language, but it is not yet theology, for there is still no reflection upon it, and indeed the language is not even, grammatically speaking, a sentence. Yet an immediate expression of faith, such as we find in St. Thomas' words, becomes a kind of *datum* for theology and through reflection it might be brought to the level of theological expression.

These remarks point us now to the dimension of theology in which it operates as an intellectual discipline. The second part of our definition declares that it is the intention of theology to express the content of its particular faith "in the clearest and most coherent language available." Whereas faith is an attitude of the whole man and expresses itself in many

[1] John 20:28.

fashions, notably in action and in a way of life, theology, as the very name implies, is discourse, and although it is rooted in the total life of faith, it aims at verbal expression. In intending that its language shall be the clearest and most coherent possible, theology shares the character of all intellectual enterprises, for they all aim at intelligibility and consistency. It may be that somewhere along the line, theology will come up against something that eludes or surpasses comprehension, but it can never relinquish its aim of attaining the highest possible degree of intelligibility. Also, the consistency or coherence at which it aims is not only an internal consistency but a coherence, so far as this is required, with all the other intellectual enterprises of the human mind. For in aiming at the verbal expression of faith and in employing our common language, theology implicitly claims to have its place in the total intellectual endeavor of mankind, and it is continuous on this side with other disciplines of the mind, just as on the other side we found it to be continuous with faith.

Our definition spoke noncommittally of theology as a "study," but now we must face the question whether it is (as it has often been described) a science. St. Thomas Aquinas, author of the greatest systematic theology ever constructed, asks whether Christian theology (*sacra doctrina*) is a science, and he pronounces that it is.[2] Yet he immediately goes on to point out that sciences are not all of the same kind, and to define more clearly what he means by calling theology a "science." Since the days of St. Thomas, the conception of what constitutes a science has undergone many changes, and in modern English the word "science" tends to get more and more restricted to the natural sciences. In view of this common usage, it is probably misleading to talk nowadays of theology as a "science." If, however, one were to follow Wilhelm Dilthey in recognizing that alongside the natural sciences there are sciences that have to do with the mental or spiritual life of man, sometimes called the "human sciences" (*Geisteswissenschaften*), then one might still want to call theology a "science," especially as Dilthey considered that participation in the very matter with which these human sciences deal is the peculiar characteristic that differentiates them from the detached attitude of the natural sciences. Yet even though one can see that theology stands closer to such a "human" science as history (if this is indeed a science) than it does to a natural science such as zoology, yet it would still differ from the human sciences because of its relation to faith, and because of the remarkable claim, implicit in its very name, to be somehow a "divine" science.

[2] *Summa Theologiae*, Ia, I, 2.

Whether or not we call theology a "science" is perhaps not of very great importance, provided that we remain aware of both the difference between theology and other disciplines, arising from its continuity with a religious faith, and the kinship of theology with all other intellectual disciplines in that it shares their common aim of striving for intelligibility and coherence.

2. FORMATIVE FACTORS IN THEOLOGY

Many books of theology contain a section near the beginning on what are called the "sources" of theology. But one finds that many disparate items get included under this description, and that they cannot all be considered "sources" in the same sense of the word. So I propose instead to talk about "formative factors" in theology, recognizing that these are not all on the same level or of equal importance. There are probably many formative factors, and some of them may operate unconsciously, so that we are not even aware of them. Here we shall briefly consider six factors that seem to call for special notice, though, as already indicated, these six are not to be regarded as all on the same level. They are: experience, revelation, scripture, tradition, culture, reason. These would seem to be almost universally operative in theology, and although w. are concerned here with Christian theology, parallels in the theologies of other religious faiths will readily suggest themselves, and I may occasionally allude to them.

Though parts of this discussion of the formative factors may seem somewhat elementary, I do not think we should be misled into supposing that we are dealing here with merely preliminary questions that are to be got quickly out of the way. Actually, it is at this "elementary" stage that fundamental decisions are made, and these decisions may well determine the whole character of the theology that is subsequently worked out. If one were to attempt to construct something like a typology of theologies, this could be done on the basis of inquiring about the dominating role assigned to one or other of the formative factors. There are theologies of experience and theologies of revelation, rational theologies and biblical theologies, theologies oriented to the traditional teaching of the Church and theologies that seek the maximal degree of accommodation to prevailing cultural forms. In every case too, the characteristics of the individual theologian will exert their influence, sometimes hiddenly, sometimes overtly.

If distortions and exaggerations are to be avoided, or at least minimized, this can best be done by setting out plainly at the beginning the major factors that have to be reckoned with in the construction of a theology and resolving to give to each of them its due weight. This does not mean that one decides on a kind of recipe: "Take a little experience, a little revelation, a little reason, and shake well together . . ." Rather, one tries to be exposed to the genuine tensions among the factors that go into the making of theology, and avoiding such one-sided simplifications as traditionalism, modernism, biblicism and the like, tries to allow for a dialectical interplay among these factors. Only so can there be built a theology that can meet the demands that may be fairly made upon it, and especially the demands that it should be loyal to the faith which it seeks to express, yet pertinent to the cultural environment which it seeks to address.

1. *Experience* appeared first on our list, not because it is to dominate the other factors as it has done in so-called "empirical" theologies, but because theology implies participation in a religious faith, so that some experience of the life of faith precedes theology and may indeed be said to motivate it. In this area of experience, as in every other, we seek to "make sense" of our experience, and the process of bringing the content of the faith-experience to clear expression in words embarks us on the business of theology.

Our experience of the life of faith comes, in turn, from participation in a community of faith. The form of this experience, however, varies widely from individual to individual and even from one particular community to another. For some, it is associated with a moral struggle; for others, with an intellectual quest; for a few, perhaps, with mystical awareness or with esthetic sensibility. Again, the personal quality of such experience varies widely, from the dramatic and emotional to the quiet and contemplative. Here we meet what William James taught us to call the "varieties of religious experience." We see too the danger attending theologies that place an exaggerated emphasis on experience, for they can easily become distorted by the particular types of experience out of which they come, and at the worst they may try to erect individual idiosyncrasies into universal spiritual principles.

Running through the many varieties, however, there may be discerned certain basic elements common to them all. In the community of faith, there is met what seems to be a quest inherent in the very constitution of our human existence. The quest is met by the opening up of the dimension of the holy, which is experienced as addressing, judging, assisting, renewing, and so on. Unless it does have its roots in experience of this kind, theology deals in abstractions and becomes a mere scholasticism. Yet if the theology that speaks out of such experience of the life of faith is not to become subjective, introspective, and individualistic, it must keep in view the experience of the whole community of faith, and even this experience must be kept in closest relation with other formative factors of a more objective kind.

In these paragraphs I have had in view specifically religious experience, and such experience is certainly important. But theology draws on the whole range of human experience, and especially in a secular age when many people might disclaim any explicitly religious experience, theologians have drawn attention to what might be called "religious dimensions" in everyday experience. The specifically religious experience concentrates, as it were, elements which can then be recognized as diffusely present in wide areas of experience, such as awareness of finitude, freedom, creativity, transcendence, and so on. J. G. Davies goes so far as to say that "it is misleading to speak of religious experience as something distinct from ordinary experience" for the latter "possesses a dimension of holiness." [3] He cites evidence from interpersonal relations, political commitment, esthetic enjoyment, and other areas of experience. Sociologist Peter Berger claims in a rather similar fashion that we can recognize "signals of transcendence within the empirically given human situation," that is to say, phenomena that "belong to ordinary everyday awareness" but appear to point beyond the empirical situation.[4] He instances experiences of order, play, and hope, among others.

In the broadest sense, then, it is the experience of existing as a human being that constitutes a primary source for theology; not just explicitly religious experience, but all experience in which a religious dimension is discernible. This was implied in my remark that faith meets "what seems to be a quest in the very constitution of our human existence." But this remark implies further that although it is only in experience that we become conscious of the quest, the roots of the quest are, in a sense, prior to experience since they belong to the very structure or form of human experience. The point is well expressed by Langdon Gilkey, another theologian who has sought to show that elements of what he calls "ultimacy" and "sacrality" are present in secular experience. Acknowledging that for the secular man an explicitly religious experience of the ultimate is lacking, he claims that "ultimacy has not thereby vanished—and could not

[3] *Every Day God*, p. 80.
[4] *A Rumor of Angels*, pp. 65–66.

vanish—from modern experience; on the contrary, it is present, as it always has been in human life, as a base, ground and limit of what we are, as a presupposition for ourselves, our thinking, our deciding and our acting." [5] The quest of which I have spoken is then present in experience from the beginning. In the broadest sense it is a quest for self-understanding and it has theological significance to the extent that it comes to grips with the religious dimensions of experience.

2. Next we consider *revelation*. This is the primary source of theology, and is also a basic category in theological thinking. Precisely what is the structure of revelation, and what grounds we may have for supposing that anything like revelation ever occurs, are questions that will be studied later. For the present, we may notice that essential to the idea of revelation is that what we come to know through revelation has a gift-like character. If, in general terms, we say that what is disclosed in revelation is the dimension of the holy, then, in the revelatory experience, it is as if the holy "breaks in" and the movement is from beyond man toward man.

It would seem that almost anything in the world can be an occasion for revelation. Natural phenomena may take on the dimensions of a revelatory situation, and in primitive and archaic religions especially, the holy is believed to manifest itself in nature. At a more sophisticated level, nature is replaced by history and personal relationships as the locus wherein the holy discloses itself; or in some cases, the revelatory experience is entirely interiorized, and the holy is encountered in the depths of the human mind itself. In the Christian religion, a person, Jesus Christ, is the bearer of revelation.

Because of its gift-like character, revelation is of a different order from our ordinary matter-of-fact knowing of the world. Thus it is not surprising that recipients of revelatory experiences, when they try to describe them, have to stretch our ordinary language beyond the limits of normal usage, and may even seem to be using quite fantastic talk as they try to communicate to us the ecstatic experience in which, as they believe, a holy reality broke in upon them. But in spite of the astonishing variety of such experiences and the extravagant language in which they are sometimes described, a perfectly definite pattern runs through them all, and this basic pattern of revelation seems to be common to all the religions of the world. It can be clearly seen in such widely separated examples as the revelation granted to Moses in the desert,[6] to the Gnostic writer who

[5] *Naming the Whirlwind*, p. 296.
[6] Exodus 3:1ff.

receives the gospel of Poimandres,[7] to Arjuna who receives a theophany of the god Krishna,[8] and in numerous other cases. The basic pattern may be summarily analyzed as follows: a mood of meditation or preoccupation; the sudden in-breaking of the holy presence, often symbolized in terms of the shining of a light; a mood of self-abasement (sometimes terror, sometimes consciousness of sin, sometimes even doubt of the reality of the experience) in face of the holy; a more definite disclosure of the holy, perhaps the disclosure of a name or of a purpose or a truth of some kind (this element may be called the "content" of the revelation); the sense of being called or commissioned by the holy to a definite task or way of life.

What is here described as "revelation" has obviously much in common with what was described above under the term "experience." Revelation is a mode of religious experience, while our experiences of the holy as judging, assisting, addressing, and the like, all have a revelatory element. One cannot therefore draw a hard and fast line between experience and revelation, but in practice it is desirable to keep these two formative factors distinct in our theological thinking. We do not normally dignify our day-to-day experiences of the holy by the name of "revelation," and no theology properly so called could be founded on private revelations, for, as has been stressed already, theology expresses the faith of a community. Yet on the other hand we would never believe that anyone had been the recipient of a revelation unless we ourselves had had some experience of the holy. Indeed, the very notion of revelation would be completely unintelligible to us unless we knew at first hand some experience that bears some analogy to revelation.

The practical distinction between what is to be called "revelation" and what we would normally include under the term "religious experience," and their interdependence as formative factors in theology, can be best set out as follows. A community of faith, within which a theology arises, usually traces its history back to what may be called a "classic" or "primordial" revelation. This classic revelation, a definite disclosive experience of the holy granted to the founder or founders of the community, becomes as it were the paradigm for experiences of the holy in that community. A revelation that has the power to found a community of faith becomes fruitful in that community, and is, so to speak, repeated or reenacted in the experience of the community, thus becoming normative

---

[7] *Poimandres*, Introduction.
[8] *Bhagavadgita*, xi.

for the experience of the community. Yet only because the primordial revelation is continually renewed in present experience can it be revelation for us, and not just a fossilized revelation (though this indeed would have ceased to be a revelation and would be a mere unintelligible curiosity from the past). In the construction of a theology, a proper balance must be maintained between the two formative factors of experience and revelation. It is present experience within a community of faith that gives rise to theology and that enables us to recognize the primordial revelation as revelation; but if theology is to be saved from the dangers of subjectivism, the varieties of experience within the community must be submitted to the relatively objective content of the classic revelation on which the community is founded.

If, however, the classic revelation was given at the origin of the community, how can we have access to it today? This question leads us to consider the next two factors, scripture and tradition, for these together mediate the primordial revelation to us. These factors are not coordinate with revelation, but subordinate to it.

3. *Scripture,* or the sacred writings of the community of faith, have played a large part in the Christian religion, but the possession of scriptures is characteristic of most of the major religions, and there is a good reason for this. Just as the brain provides storage cells on which the memory of the individual depends, so scriptures or written accounts provide for the community a kind of memory, by which it can reach back to and recall its past.

Scripture is not itself revelation, but it is one important way (not the only one) by which the community of faith keeps open its access to that primordial revelation on which the community has been founded. The scriptures do not indeed automatically lay this revelation before us but, in conjunction with a present experience of the holy in the community of faith, the scriptures come alive, so to speak, and renew for us the disclosure of the holy which was the content of the primordial revelation. This power of bringing again or re-presenting the disclosure of the primordial revelation so that it speaks to us in our present experience is what is meant when we talk of the "inspiration" of scripture. Such inspiration does not lie in the words (it is not "verbal inspiration"), but belongs to the scriptures only as they are set in the context of the whole life of faith in the community. Once more our attention is being directed to the close but puzzling relation between present experience and the past occasion of the community's classic revelation, but a fuller understanding of this relation can be gained only after we have formed a clearer idea of the structure of the life of faith.

Scripture, as bringing again the disclosure given in the primordial revelation, has a stability and even a certain kind of objectivity as over against the vagaries of individual experiences in the community. The scriptures of a community are a major factor in maintaining stability and a sense of continuing identity in the community itself. We find therefore that scriptures become a norm in the theology of the community, and along with tradition provide a safeguard against the subjectivist excesses that arise from placing too much emphasis on the deliverances of present experience. In the Christian community, any theology which claims to be Christian theology (as distinct from someone's private philosophy of religion) must maintain close and positive relations with the Bible.

The danger that theologians might slight the Bible is probably less common than the danger that the Bible may get absolutized as a formative factor in theology. The belief that the Bible is infallible is one that dies hard in some parts of the Christian world. As was asserted above, the Bible is not itself revelation. The Christian revelation comes in a person, not in a book. But the Bible is not even an infallible record of or witness to this revelation. The very fact that there are textual variants destroys at once the old idea of an infallible book, providentially preserved intact. This is only a beginning in demolishing the idea of biblical infallibility. There are in the Bible divergencies and discrepancies—and not merely on relatively trivial questions of detail, as how many animals went into the ark or what women went to the tomb on Easter morning, but on questions of theology and of ethics. Again, critical research has shown that traditional views about the authorship and dates of composition of various books of the Bible are in many cases false or doubtful, so that instead of having an eyewitness account of the exodus by Moses, or of the ministry of Jesus by St. Matthew, we have in fact anonymous accounts of these matters, written so long after they happened that their historical accuracy is open to grave question. But enough of this. I am not trying to impugn the Bible (far from it!), but only that misuse of the Bible which absolutizes it and then makes it (or tries to make it) the exclusive formative factor in theology. As over against this exaggerated regard for the Bible, it must be claimed that the critical study of the Bible, and the recognition that other factors too have their place in theology, will in the long run do more justice to the biblical teaching and will not run counter to any reasonably conceived doctrine of inspiration; for such a critical attitude accepts our own responsibility in face of the Bible.

While these remarks have been directed against ultra-conservative biblicists, something must also be said about the biblical theology that has so greatly flourished in recent times. This movement in theology has vastly increased our understanding of biblical concepts and images and has had the further value of calling us back to serious theological study of the Bible, as distinct from merely historical and critical study. But sometimes one encounters extravagant pretensions among the exponents of biblical theology. There is a tendency to expand biblical theology to take in all theology, to imply that only biblical categories are proper to theological thinking, and one even gets the impression from some writers that to understand the Christian faith, one would need to cultivate an archaic Hebrew mentality. If this were true, it would surely mean that Christianity was entirely a local and temporary phenomenon. Actually, the Christian faith has extended itself both in time and space because of its ability to interpret itself in ever new categories. We are all agreed that theology must keep in close touch with its biblical sources, but to try to exclude non-biblical categories is absurd.

4. *Tradition* has long been a bone of contention in Christian theology; Catholics have held that the revelation in Christ has been transmitted to us both in scripture and tradition, while Protestants have acknowledged scripture alone. Nowadays, however, it would seem that many Protestants are willing to acknowledge some positive role for tradition. But whether acknowledged or not, the fact is that tradition always has had its place in helping to determine the doctrine and practice of the Christian community, and that, properly understood, tradition is no rival to scripture but is its necessary complement. For scripture is not a frozen or petrified record, but something that comes alive only in the ongoing life of the community which first gave birth to scripture and has since proclaimed and interpreted the teaching of scripture.

The earliest Christian scriptures were preceded by and based upon the tradition that was handed down and in turn received in the primitive Christian community, as is made clear by St. Paul.[9] Again, Jesus was recalled or remembered not only in the scriptures, when these came to be written, but in the sacraments of the Church, above all in the eucharist which is said to be explicitly for the "remembrance" (ἀνάμνησις) of him;[10] and of course, as Dom Gregory Dix has written, "eucharistic worship from the outset was based not on scripture at all, but solely on *tradition*." [11]

---

[9] I Cor. 11:23; 15:3.
[10] I Cor. 11:24.
[11] *The Shape of the Liturgy*, p. 3.

It was the community which eventually decided about the canon of the New Testament, thereby settling what writings were to be regarded as authoritative Christian scripture, and this decision was based on the traditional usage of the Church. Doctrines that are stated only obscurely or implicitly in scripture were eventually (and this took several centuries) brought to explicitness in the dogmatic pronouncements of the Church, so that today we do not come to the scriptures cold, as it were, but read them in the light of the traditional interpretation.

Hence tradition, like scripture itself, is another bulwark against individualism and enthusiasm in theology. Scripture needs the complement of tradition in order to guard against private interpretations of scripture, for almost anything can be read into scripture, and some control has to be exercised by the mind of the Church as expressed in received interpretations. Actually, nobody could so rid his mind of received interpretations that he could go to the scriptures free from the influence of tradition; but even if this were possible, no sensible theologian would want to do it. On the contrary, he will be only too glad to have his mind enlightened and his thoughts directed by the communal wisdom and experience of the Church, for these must be far beyond anything that he could hope to attain with his own limited powers or from his own very restricted perspective.

Sometimes there are enthusiasts who break with tradition either for the sake of being modern or for the sake (as they imagine) of going right back to the New Testament, as if all the intervening development could be left out. Sometimes both of these errors occur in the same person. Tradition is meant to guard against this, for in either case there is a break in the life of the community, or rather, the community has been abandoned and a new one set up. A Christian theology can no more fly in the face of the mainstream of tradition than it can in the face of scripture. To deny fundamental doctrines, like that of the Trinity; to reject the creeds; to set aside the beliefs of the early councils of the still undivided Church—these may be actions to which individuals are impelled by their own thinking on these matters, but they cannot take place in Christian theology, for they amount to a rejection of the history and therefore of the continuing identity of the community within which Christian theologizing takes place. "That which has been believed everywhere, always and by all," in the famous formula of St. Vincent of Lérins,[12] cannot be set aside without abandoning the community itself.

[12] *Commonitorium*, II, 3.

But just as we saw in the case of scripture, so with tradition there can be an uncritical and excessive regard that leads to bad theology. Tradition, as everyone knows, can become dead and mechanical, so that all growth and healthy development are inhibited. I have argued the case for tradition alongside scripture precisely on the ground that a living tradition lends its life to scripture. But if tradition itself becomes dead, then we get a rigid fixity of the theological (as well as the other) expressions of a religious faith that is just as harmful as any rigid biblicism. But this need not happen. The function of tradition that has been stressed here is interpretation, and interpretation needs to be done over and over again. Ancient interpretations of the faith that have become part of the very texture of the community's identity, such as the Apostles' Creed or the doctrine of the Trinity, cannot be set aside without destroying the community, but they need continual reinterpretation. Everything of this kind is historically conditioned in respect to its language and even its very concepts, and if it is passed on in a merely mechanical way, it becomes a mere lifeless tradition. Each generation must appropriate the tradition, and in order to do this it has to interpret the ancient formula, or whatever it may be, into its own categories of thought. This means that one has to ask what the formula was trying to express in its own historical context, or what error it was trying to guard against, and then rethink this in our own situation. This needs more insight and patience than the simple rejection of the tradition, but such reinterpretation is needed if the tradition is to be carried on critically and responsibly as a living and growing tradition.

5. These remarks about the need for ever-renewed interpretation bring us to the next formative factor in theology, *culture*. The factors considered so far have all belonged to the life of faith, and represent that element in our definition of theology which spoke of theology's "participation" in faith. Now, however, we are turning to factors that have to do with theology's character as an intellectual discipline, and with its intention of finding expression "in the clearest and most coherent language available," to use the expression employed in our definition. If theology is to be intelligible, it has to use the language of the culture within which it is undertaken. Actually, no one can escape sharing in the mentality or intellectual climate of his own culture, so that even the theologian who would try to exclude from his thinking all secular influences is deceiving himself, for these influences will operate unconsciously. The commonest words that we use have gathered around them connotations which imply a whole cultural background. It is better that the theologian should ex-

plicitly recognize the cultural factor in this thinking, and come to terms with it.

Recognition of the cultural factor is equivalent to acknowledging that there is no final theology. The work of theology needs to be done again and again, for its formulations are culturally conditioned, and therefore need reinterpretation as cultural forms change. Many expressions in the New Testament were intelligible in the cosmology or psychology or social conditions of the first century of our era, but have become unintelligible in terms of our modern understanding of these matters. Such a word as "person," as used in formulations coming from the patristic age, had a quite different connotation from that which it now bears. While indeed the primordial revelation remains and, as we have seen, scripture and tradition together act as checks to prevent wanton and irresponsible theological innovations, there is also a variable element in theology as it addresses itself to its own day and generation in terms of the prevailing cultural forms. It may even be the case that in the use of ideas taken over from the contemporary culture, deeper insights are gained into the revelation that has been passed on.

Of course, the great temptation in all this is for the theologian to try to be modern for the sake of modernity, to accommodate the revelation to the mood of the time, to merge its content into the cultural forms so that it is subordinated to the culture and is perhaps used to throw a kind of glamorous sanctity over the institutions and ideals of the culture. It was against this prostitution of theology that Karl Barth protested so vigorously in his early writings: "Form believes itself capable of taking the place of content. Man has taken the divine into his possession; he has brought it under his management." [13] But over against this entirely necessary warning from Barth, one may set the words of his contemporary, Paul Tillich, in defense of his procedure of stating theology in forms derived from the prevailing culture: "I am not unaware of the danger that in this way the substance of the Christian message may be lost. Nevertheless, this danger must be risked, and once one has realized this, one must proceed in this direction. Dangers are not a reason for avoiding a serious demand." [14] The problem becomes one of maintaining a fine balance. If the demand for relevance and intelligibility is to be met, then there will always be a danger of infringing the autonomous—and even judgmental

[13] *The Word of God and the Word of Man*, p. 68.
[14] *Systematic Theology*, vol. III, p. 4.

—character of the primordial revelation; but this must be weighed against the other danger of so insulating the revelation against all contact with the changing forms of secular culture, that it becomes encapsulated, and shut off from everything else in life. It should not prove impossible to find a way between these dangerous extremes. But this can best be done if we frankly acknowledge the cultural factor in theology, and try to handle it in full awareness of its potentialities. If we try to exclude this factor, then it will work unconsciously, for it is inescapable.

6. The last formative factor to be considered is *reason*. Again, this is a factor that has to do with theology's character as an intellectual discipline. There have been sharp differences of opinion over the role of reason in theology. Broadly speaking, the mainstream of Christian thinking in the Fathers, in Roman Catholic theology, in Anglican theology, and also in much Protestant theology, has maintained a positive attitude toward reason and seen it as an ally of revelation. But a very influential counter-current has coursed through the Fathers and the Middle Ages, and found its most vigorous spokesmen in some of the schools of orthodox Protestant theology. This counter-current either has assigned a very minor role to reason or, in a few extreme cases, has actually denounced reason as the enemy of revelation. A discussion of these matters can be only provisional, until we have looked at the relation of theology to philosophy, and, above all, studied the problem of a natural or philosophical theology. However, I think we can reject right away the extreme position of the theologian who tries to exclude human reason altogether, and to rely entirely on the biblical revelation. Such an attitude seems tantamount to abandoning any claim that theology is an intellectual discipline. Immanuel Kant rightly observed: "Were biblical theology to determine, wherever possible, to have nothing to do with reason in things religious, we can easily foresee on which side would be the loss; for a religion which rashly declares war on reason will not be able to hold out in the long run against it." [15]

Almost all theologians would be prepared to allow some place to reason, and the question at issue concerns the extent to which reason may enter as a formative factor. Reason may be broadly divided into speculative reason and critical reason. In its speculative exercise, reason endeavors to construct a metaphysic or theory of reality. Within speculative reason, we have to distinguish further between *a priori* theories (such as St. Anselm's famous ontological proof of the existence of God) based on the

[15] *Religion within the Limits of Reason Alone*, p. 9.

pure reason alone and on the concepts which belong to it apart from any experience of the world; and *a posteriori* theories (such as the equally famous "five ways" of St. Thomas) where reason constructs its theories on the basis of experience of the world. Some theologies have held that metaphysics constructed in this way offer confirmation of the content of revelation; while in some cases a rational metaphysic has been allowed to determine the entire shape of a theology, notably in some of the nineteenth-century theologies which relied on speculative idealism. Since the time of Hume and Kant, however, metaphysics has been placed more and more in question as a legitimate exercise of reason, and in contemporary philosophy there is a strong anti-metaphysical spirit. Theologians too have sought to disentangle themselves from dependence on the metaphysicians. Thus it would be true to say that nowadays there is widespread suspicion of any speculative role for reason in theology. The fact that there is such suspicion does not, of course, settle the question about the legitimacy of rational speculation, and we shall have to look at these matters more closely in due course. But in so far as we have to pay attention to the cultural factor and to the prevailing anti-speculative climate of thought, a theology addressed to our time would seek to avoid any heavy dependence on speculative reason.

It may be noticed however that there would seem to be a function of reason somewhat akin to its speculative exercise, yet in some respects quite distinct from it. I have in mind a constructive use of reason in which we build up rational wholes, theories, or interlocking systems of ideas, but do so not by deductive argument but rather by imaginative leaps which, so to speak, integrate the fragmentary elements in inclusive wholes. Of course, such imaginative leaps need to be immediately tested and subjected to scrutiny, yet something of this kind goes on in most intellectual disciplines, including the natural sciences. This might be called the "architectonic" function of reason, and it would seem to have something in common with esthetic sensibility. Clearly a well-constructed theology aiming at coherent expression, even if it eschews the speculative reason, will owe something of its shape and general structure to the architectonic reason. Even theologians who in theory allow very little place to reason are sometimes builders of a theological fabric of such design and complexity that they must themselves be gifted with an imaginative reason comparable to that of a great architect. Karl Barth is the obvious example.

Reason is not opposed to the use of imagination and indeed demands it. Both reason and imagination have their place in the intellectual quest for understanding and each needs the other. In theology, sometimes rational deduction can expand our understanding of the truths of faith, as when, for instance, a peripheral doctrine is inferred from one or more central doctrines. But the central doctrines themselves may come to be better understood through the deployment of imaginative metaphors, analogues, and symbols which point us beyond the range of rational concepts. Then, however, the exuberance of the imagination and its mythologizing tendency may need to be held in check by rational criticism.

Now we must turn to the second of the two broad divisions that were assigned to reason, to the critical reason. This may itself be subdivided into the elucidatory and the corrective exercises of reason. The elucidatory reason would be admitted into theology even by theologians who are fairly negative in their attitude to reason. In its elucidatory function, reason sifts, analyzes, expounds and, generally speaking, brings into the light the content of the revelation. This use of reason would not, according to those theologians who reduce reason to its most lowly status, be an autonomous exercise, but would always be subject to the revelation itself and perhaps even to divine illumination, so that reason here is entirely ancillary to revelation; but other theologians would hold that reason must interpret revelation according to the same canons and hermeneutic principles that it works out for the guidance of interpretation in general. The corrective use of reason assigns to the rational factor in theology a much larger role, though one that still falls far short of the speculative reason. Corrective reason (which would be rejected by those who restrict reason to an ancillary function) is directed upon the revelation or alleged revelation itself, questioning its credentials, submitting it to scrutiny and criticism, removing from its content whatever may be involved in irreconcilable conflict with other well-founded convictions that may be held. The corrective use of reason will be strongly upheld in this book, for without it, we would seem to be potential victims of the pretensions of any supposed revelation that might seek to impose itself upon us. The ideal of a *rational* religion, in the sense of one founded on a rational metaphysic, may be an impossible and perhaps undesirable one, but we should never relinquish the ideal of a *reasonable* religion, in the sense of one whose content has been subjected to the scrutinizing and corrective exercise of critical reason. I am in hearty agreement with Archbishop William Temple's remark when, in criticizing the meager place given to reason by the early Barth, he asserted that "revelation can, and in the long run must, on pain of becoming manifest as superstition, vindicate its claim by satisfying reason." [16] It is true that Barth in his later writings seems to have accorded a higher place to reason, so that Temple's criticism perhaps applies nowadays more forcibly to some of Barth's disciples than to himself. But wherever it is found, any excessive depreciation of reason is to be deplored. We shall have more to say about this later.

In the meantime, a claim has been staked for reason among the formative factors in theology—and not merely for elucidatory reason, but also for corrective and architectonic reason. The question of speculative reason, though we have seen that it is suspect, must be deferred for further discussion. As is the case with the other formative factors, reason can sometimes play an exaggerated role in theology, and can even subordinate revelation and experience to rigid theories that have been laid down in advance. But in the current mood of theology, this overprizing of reason seems to be less of a danger than that reason's place should be underestimated.

3. THE DEVELOPMENT OF DOCTRINE

This survey of the principal formative factors in theology lets us see the complexity of the subject, and also shows us how such widely differing styles of theologizing have been practiced at various times, though this variety has to do also with the question of method, still to be considered. Exaggeration of one or other of the formative factors must lead to theological distortion. Too much stress on experience is the cause of individualism, enthusiasm and, at the worst, fanaticism. A too rigid emphasis on revelation, and on the scripture and tradition which mediate it, leads to obscurantism, antiquarianism, ultra-conservatism. Those who lean too far in the direction of accommodating theology to the mood of the culture or of trying to exhaust its content in terms of what can be rationally established apart from religious experience and revelation end up with a shallow modernism or rationalism from which the distinctive religious content has been eliminated. Heresy (the word seems to have meant originally "taking for oneself," that is to say, "individual preference") is just the distorted kind of theology that arises from the exaggeration of one element at the expense of others.

It seems then theology must hold a nice balance or tension among the formative factors, and this in turn might seem so difficult as to be almost

---

[16] *Nature, Man and God*, p. 396.

impossible. But awareness of the dangers is a big step toward avoiding them. Moreover, there is theological freedom, the right, within limits, to stress viewpoints and use methods which, in the situation, seem to need stressing. This freedom is quite a wide one, even in the relatively authoritarian churches, though, as has been indicated above, there are some points which theology can transgress only if it is resolved to cease being Christian theology and becomes some private individual's philosophy of religion, though still in the main a Christian philosophy of religion. It is in the discussion that goes on between the points of view that theological freedom is exercised and theological advance achieved.

We have quoted the words of St. Vincent of Lérins about "that which has been believed everywhere, always and by all," and these words might suggest that Christian doctrine is static and unchanging. But the same writer claimed that "there should be a great increase and vigorous progress in the individual man as well as in the entire Church as the ages and the centuries march on, of understanding, knowledge and wisdom." [17] There is general agreement that even if there is some initial given or basic revelation, nevertheless there is doctrinal development or theological advance as that given is continually being reformulated and expressed anew in words. But there is considerable disagreement about the nature of such development.

Do genuinely new truths come to light in the course of doctrinal development, or is it only a matter of making explicit the truths already contained in the original given? Can one rightly speak of "development" or do we simply see theologians striving to adapt themselves to the advances in secular knowledge by abandoning the old dogmas and reformulating them or even redefining them in ways more likely to gain acceptance? Or is it perhaps an exercise in rationalization by providing theological justification for beliefs and practices that have sprung up unreflectingly in the community?

There are no simple answers to these questions. Often doctrine seems to have developed in haphazard ways, and these have sometimes looked like cultural adaptation, sometimes like mere rationalization. But on the question of rationalization, it must be remembered that the relation of practice and belief in the community of faith is a reciprocal one. Sometimes an insight is gained on the practical level before the theological grounds for it are clearly understood, and the fact that these grounds may

[17] *Commonitorium*, XXIII, 28.

be understood only subsequently cannot mean that therefore they are merely rationalizations. It cannot be claimed that there has been a straightforward development of Christian doctrine in the sense of an uninterrupted progressive deepening of theological understanding, but it can be argued that the development has been due as much to the inner dynamic and creativity of the given revelation as to the pressure of external influences, and that the more bizarre developments called forth by such influences have tended in time to wither away.

On the question of whether the genuinely new emerges in the course of theological development, one could hardly speak of "development" unless there were some thread of continuity. As Maurice Wiles has remarked, "The idea of radical discontinuity in doctrine is not strictly conceivable." [18] Such fundamental theological concepts as God, sin, grace, salvation need constantly to be rethought, but there are limits to the possibility of reformulation and redefinition if one claims still to be speaking in the tradition of Christian or any other theology. Within these limits, however, it is legitimate to acknowledge that genuinely novel insights can appear. The community of faith has itself eventually to decide what are legitimate developments of its belief and what is inacceptable.

When one looks at the history of theology the impression is often that of a pendulum which swings all the way from one position to its opposite and then perhaps a generation later swings back again. Also, there seems to be as much forgetting as learning, so that the same old controversies get fought out again, though tricked out in new terminologies. All this is, in a way, inevitable. A theologian may firmly believe that he is holding in balance the various factors that contribute to the fullness of a theology, yet in spite of himself he may be overstressing some point because it has seemed to him to be understressed in the theology to which he is reacting. These stresses and strains that go on in theology serve to remind us once more that there can be no final theology in which we can rest once and for all—not biblical theology, nor the system of St. Thomas, nor the thoughts of Luther and Calvin, though indeed these may all contain permanent and indispensable insights. But every theology is historically and culturally conditioned, so that the best it can hope to do is, through its participation in the faith that has persisted from the community's beginning, to express the content of that faith without undue exaggeration, omission, or distortion, in "the clearest and most coherent language available" for its own time.

---

[18] *The Making of Christian Doctrine*, p. 167.

4. THEOLOGY IN RELATION TO OTHER DISCIPLINES

As an intellectual discipline, theology is part of the whole intellectual enterprise of mankind, and must therefore stand in relation to other disciplines. The ideal of the unity of knowledge may be unrealizable, but we should not cease to strive for an approach as near to the ideal as possible. The days are certainly past when an encyclopedic genius, such as Aristotle or Leonardo da Vinci, could embrace the knowledge available in his time, and it seems that as knowledge expands, it becomes increasingly fragmented and specialized. We often hear it said that ours is a split culture, and nobody claims that this is a healthy state of affairs. The split is very obvious when we consider theology in relation to other disciplines, for often it seems to have lost touch with secular studies altogether and to have become compartmentalized and esoteric. We have, so to speak, a Sunday mentality and an everyday mentality. We may succeed in keeping them apart and in this way we prevent latent conflicts between them from flaring up, but this is done at the expense of restricting religion to a special and somewhat rarefied sector of life. To explore the borders between theology and other disciplines with a view not only to removing conflicts but, more positively, in the hope of gaining reciprocal illumination, is a task that cannot be avoided if we are dissatisfied with the fragmentation of life and culture.

The question of theology and other disciplines is an extension of the theme already introduced when we considered culture and reason among the formative factors in theology. Now we are selecting for closer study some particularly sensitive points at which the interaction between theology and cultural factors may go on. Four such points will be briefly discussed—those at which theology comes into relation with philosophy, history, the sciences of man (anthropology, psychology, sociology), and the natural sciences.

1. Let us begin with theology's relation to *philosophy*, for of all the disciplines, philosophy seems to be the one that stands nearest to theology. On the basis of the faith which it explicates, theology expounds convictions about God, man, and the world. During most of its history, philosophy has treated of the same themes, though it does so not on the basis of faith; rather it claims reason and ordinary experience for its guides. How are the two strands of thinking related, if indeed they are related at all?

From the beginning, theologians have held divergent views on the nature of the relationship, and even on whether it is desirable that any common ground between their own discipline and philosophy should be recognized. The two points of view on the place of reason in theology, noted above, have typically found expression on the specific issue of the relation of theology to philosophy. In the early days of the Church, we find on the one side advocates of an alliance between theology and sympathetic philosophies. For instance, St. Justin Martyr, speaking of Plato and the Stoics, claims that they shared in the Word (λόγος) that was in Jesus, and that "whatever things were rightly said among all men are the property of us Christians"; [19] and Clement of Alexandria holds that philosophy "assists towards true religion as a kind of preparatory training for those who arrive at faith by way of demonstration." [20] On the other hand; Tatian ridicules and abuses the philosophers, sometimes in a crude fashion,[21] while Tertullian equates their ideas with "the world's wisdom, that rash interpreter of the divine nature and order." [22] When we discussed reason in theology, I claimed that the mainstream of the Church's thinking had favored the alliance with reason and therefore with philosophy, but conceded that there has always been a lively opposition. Although my own view goes along with the mainstream in advocating a positive relationship toward reason and philosophy, let me say that the opposition has performed a necessary task in keeping the relationship under critical scrutiny and in fighting against bad forms of the relationship, which can get distorted so as to be injurious sometimes to theology, sometimes to philosophy.

The trouble is that in such an alliance one partner tends to overshadow the other, and may deprive the other of its legitimate freedom. In the medieval synthesis, theology was the dominant partner and philosophy tended to become her handmaid and supporter. In the great days of idealist philosophy, however, the situation was reversed and theology became just one department of the all-embracing system of thought. Theologians have been afraid, and sometimes not without reason, that the distinctive revelation communicated in faith may be swallowed up and thus be neutralized or distorted in an alien metaphysic.

The present mood between theologians and philosophers tends to be one of suspicion and standoffishness, as each remembers the injuries which his discipline has received or is supposed to have received at the hands of the other. Both theology and philosophy are determined to maintain their

---

[19] *Second Apology*, xiii.
[20] *Miscellanies*, I, v.
[21] *To the Greeks*, ii–iii, xxv, etc.
[22] *On Prescription against Heretics*, vii.

autonomy. Karl Barth talks of theology's having escaped from the Egyptian bondage of philosophy, while a typical philosophical viewpoint is expressed by Gilbert Ryle who sees in the laicizing of our culture the freeing of philosophy from the leading-strings of theology, so that now philosophy can get on with its own work. But there is something rather chauvinistic in these declarations of independence. The fact that there may have been distorted relations in the past does not mean that there cannot be healthy relations, or that the two disciplines must go their separate ways in sulky isolation. This, I believe, would be most unfortunate, and would heighten still more the fragmentation of modern culture.

When we look at the present situation, there is ground for hoping that a better relation between the two disciplines can be established. We have already seen that metaphysics has fallen into disrepute, and new forms of philosophizing have appeared. Thus the old fear of the theologian that his theology might get drawn into the meshes of a metaphysic should no longer be a barrier in the way of a positive relation to philosophy. There are nowadays few philosophers engaged in the construction of all-embracing systems, and the prevailing tendency is analysis rather than synthesis. While indeed some of the traditional schools still have their following, the philosophical movements that belong distinctively to the twentieth century stand off from metaphysics. *Logical analysis* contents itself with the critical scrutiny of our different modes of discourse; it does not profess to say anything about the substance of what used to be regarded as the great problems of philosophy, but considers itself a formal discipline, aiming at the detection and removal of confusions in our discourse about any themes whatsoever. *Existentialism* is similarly analytic, but it admits a more substantial content for philosophy; what is analyzed is human existence in its manifold modes of being, and the aim of this philosophy is that man should attain to self-understanding. But all the existentialists agree about the limitation of man's powers, and they agree that it belongs to the very essence of his existence that he must live without that comprehensive knowledge that was sought in metaphysics. Some philosophers do indeed develop an *ontology*, or philosophy of being, but nowadays this is usually claimed to rest on existential foundations and to be different from a metaphysic constructed by the speculative exercise of reason. Mention should be made also of the influential school of *phenomenology*, but this again is something far removed from metaphysics and is indeed a methodology, a technique of description designed to provide a new inroad into philosophical problems.

The theologian should not back away from this field of philosophical endeavor, for there is much here that can be of the greatest value in his own theological work. English theologians, such as Ian Ramsey, are showing how logical analysis can help toward cleaner and better theology. Rudolf Bultmann's interpretations of the New Testament have amply demonstrated how much theology can profit from attending to existential analysis. Ontology and phenomenology are prominent in the work of Paul Tillich, though in his case it must be conceded that several of his critics claim that he remained an old style metaphysician at heart and that his work was given shape by the German idealist tradition.

It has been mentioned that some metaphysical types of philosophy still have a following. Since there are important theologians of our time who are still influenced by them, these metaphysical styles of thinking deserve some mention. *Process philosophy*, based mainly on the work of Whitehead and having close affinities with empiricism and natural science, has been specially influential among American theologians and has made significant contributions toward the rethinking of theism. The *dialectical philosophy*, stretching from Hegel through Marx to such modern thinkers as Bloch and Marcuse, is renewing its influence in Germany, and its strongly social emphasis can be seen as a corrective in such theologians as Moltmann and Metz to the alleged individualist bias of existentialism. Finally, the *perennial philosophy* of St. Thomas has revived in recent times, especially in the dynamic form known as transcendental Thomism which has been powerfully operative in the new style Roman Catholic theology associated with the Second Vatican Council. We shall have to take note of all of these at later stages of our study.

Has philosophy on its side anything to gain from keeping in touch with theology? Perhaps it is presumptuous for a theologian to venture any remark on this. But I believe that theology keeps the philosopher aware of dimensions of experience that tend to get overlooked in our technological age. No one wants to make philosophy subservient to theology or to take away its freedom, for its very independence is necessary if it is to maintain that critical pressure which the theologian needs to have exerted on him if he is to seek clarity and consistency. Yet at the same time the theologian would hope that the philosopher might take theology seriously. The tendency toward positivism could mean that philosophy has indeed cast away the leading-strings of theology but has fallen into a new servitude in which it is dominated by natural science.

So I am claiming that a positive relationship between theology and philosophy is certainly good for theology, and probably good for philosophy as well. This relationship may well differ from what it customarily was in times past, and we must think of it as much in terms of a healthy tension as in terms of an alliance. But I do not believe that any theology can stand without philosophically defensible foundations, and so, no worthwhile theology can be delivered from the duty of conversing with philosophy. More will be said about these matters when we come to the theme of philosophical theology.

2. *History* is another discipline with which theology stands in relation, and this relation would seem to be specially important in the case of Christian theology which takes its origin from a revelation given in an historical person rather than in a dateless myth or a timeless corpus of laws or of philosophical truths. But the relation between theology and history seems to be a very complex one and to have many ramifications.

Just as philosophers have turned away from metaphysics, so the historians of our day are suspicious of any speculative interpretations of history. They recognize that our view of history is always too limited for us to be able to claim with any confidence that we can discern in historical events some great pattern, such as the working out of a providential scheme or the movement of events toward some goal of divine perfection. All-embracing interpretations of history, especially those with theological implications, as we find them proposed by thinkers from St. Augustine to Hegel, no longer command interest. Even the more modest schemes of Spengler and Toynbee still go far beyond what most contemporary historians are prepared to regard as legitimate interpretation of history. Thus the theologian of today would not look to the historian to provide him with some comprehensive metaphysic of history, but would think of the areas where theology and history interact as quite definitely limited and circumscribed. There are several such areas.

First may be mentioned the general *history of religion* and the comparative study of religion that has been made possible on the basis of this history. Only in relatively recent times has there been opened up to research the panorama of the world's faiths, both living and extinct. Since theology explicates the particular faith within which it arises and continues to move, it cannot, like the philosophy of religion, relate itself to the whole spectrum of the world's faiths. Nevertheless, it must take note of those parallels to its own faith which the history of religions has shown to abound in other faiths. This history shows that the faith of one's own community is not an isolated phenomenon. The impact of history upon theology at this point is that it puts in question the claim of any revelation to have an exclusive or normative status. The study of history in any field has a broadening effect, and not least in the field of religion. Here it might even seem to point in the direction of a relativism, but this in turn might seem to conflict with the ultimate claim of a divine revelation and the faith founded upon it. The question of Christianity's relation to other faiths, and whether the Christian revelation has a unique status or one that is analogous to the status of other revelations or alleged revelations, will come up for discussion in due course. Meanwhile we notice that one relevant factor in settling this question will be the evidence offered by history.

The *history of Christian origins* is another area of historical inquiry that has a bearing upon theology. We have already glanced at this in noticing how historical research and criticism has resulted in a changed attitude to the Bible. One might claim that just as a direct result of historical research, theology can never again be constructed by the citing of so-called "proof-texts," chosen more or less at random from the Bible as a whole, as one finds the practice in some of the confessions of faith produced in the period after the Reformation. But historical research has gone so far in eroding the record of events contained in the New Testament that much more than an attitude to the Bible is at stake. What is left of our knowledge of the historical Jesus, after form-criticism has done its work? How important *for theology* is it that we should know something about the historical Jesus? Is it of any *theological* importance that, as many historical scholars now claim, Jesus may never have thought of himself as Messiah? These questions and others like them will have to be deferred until we come to the proper place for discussing them. But they are mentioned here to show again how theology and history are bound to find areas of common concern, where the theologian will have to take note of what the historian is saying.

Relevant too is what may be included under the general heading of the conception of *historical existence*. Although speculative interpretations of history have been left aside, no one can study history without having some conception of the historical; and just as in philosophy we see metaphysics being replaced by analytical styles of philosophizing, so the old speculative interpretations of history have been replaced by attempts of a more critical and analytical kind to determine what we mean by "historical happening," and how this relates to or differs from what we call "natural process." What is meant by recognizing that all human existence is historical existence? How do we relate to the past that is disclosed in history? What does it mean to say that all human thinking and talking is historically conditioned? The way in which such questions get answered obviously has a bearing on matters that are of great importance in theology, especially Christian theology; for in the Christian faith, an actual historical existence is claimed to be the bearer of the revelation, and this claim raises the further question of how events of long ago can be relevant for persons living today—how the so-called "salvation-history" (*Heilsgeschichte*) can still be understood as effecting salvation, now that it has slipped so far into the past. Some understanding of history seems to underlie the Christian teaching on these matters, and this implicit understanding needs to be brought out into the open and tested alongside what students of history have learned about the nature of historical existence.

These questions cannot be carried further for the present, but even to have raised them in this provisional way shows us that theology, if it talks about history and historical happenings as Christian theology does, cannot disregard what the historians have to say, any more than it can turn its back on the philosophers. Theology must be open to these secular disciplines.

3. Theology must come to terms also with the *sciences of man*, especially with such studies as anthropology, psychology, and sociology. These studies investigate the phenomena of human life scientifically. Whether they can ever become as purely scientific as the natural sciences is a debatable point, but their aim is certainly to be scientific, and in so far as they proceed by observation, measurement (statistical and other), and even by experiment, it is clear that to a remarkable degree they do offer us something like a scientific account of the life of man. Among the phenomena of human life they find religion, so that each of these sciences offers us, from its own point of view, its account of religion. How, if at all, do these scientific accounts of religion relate to theology?

Anthropology, through the patient labors of many investigators, has shed much light on the origins of religion and on the early stages of its evolution. It shows us a process of gradual development, marked, it is true, by leaps forward from time to time, yet on the whole continuous. It leaves no doubt that the great religions of today have descended from primitive faiths, and in the case of some particular features in them, the course of this evolution can be traced in detail. Primitive religion itself is shown to be shot through with ignorance, error, superstition, childish fantasy and self-centeredness. Sometimes it is concluded without further ado that the humble origins of religion are sufficient to discredit it. This, however, would be a hasty verdict. After all, every human activity goes back to very lowly origins. Probably science itself originated in part out of magic and occult practices, but this in no way discredits it. Both science and religion deserve to be judged by what they now are, and it is as justifiable to read the whole process of development from above downward as from below upward; that is to say, in the case of religion to recognize even in the practices of primitive religion the beginnings of higher things, as well to recognize in developed religion the legacy of savage times. Anthropology, as a science, brings facts and connections of facts to our notice, but as soon as we begin to interpret these facts, we have to introduce factors which the anthropologist cannot judge on the basis of his science. But the theologian must be prepared to offer some interpretation from his theological point of view, and he must try to show that this is as legitimate a point of view as the positivistic and naturalistic one that is held by some anthropologists. In trying to see these matters in a theological perspective, the theologian may find—as we noted already in connection with the history of religion—that he has to reconsider what he means by "revelation," especially if this has been customarily thought of not in connection with a continuous process of development but as a discontinuous and isolated phenomenon.

Psychology has had much to say about religion, and has offered theories about such phenomena as conversion and mysticism. It has shown that strange though these phenomena are, it is possible to go far toward accounting for them in terms of factors immanent within man's mental life without positing any supernatural or even transhuman factor at work. Psychology shows, moreover, that religious attitudes and beliefs originate, at least in part, to satisfy certain needs. The extreme development of this point of view is found in Freud, who thinks of religion as the last stronghold of the pleasure principle, providing us with an illusion that promises satisfaction and shields us from the harshness of reality. Here again, however, interpretation has outrun the empirical evidence, for it is not from psychology that Freud learns that "reality" has this harsh and unbearable character. This is not to minimize the psychological critique of religion, to which we must return later. The theologian may well believe that he can make a reasonable reply to this critique, and that, while psychology can give an account of the origin and history of religious beliefs, we must go outside of psychology when it is a question of deciding about the value of these beliefs and their claim to be true. But the theologian is bound to acknowledge that the psychologist makes clear to him that a great deal which is infantile and immature can mask itself under religion, and that theology must be purged of such elements.

Beyond this, the theologian can learn not only from psychological studies of religion but from the light which psychology has thrown on man's mental life as a whole, and consequently on his behavior. This may be summed up by saying that psychology has made clear to us that we are less rational than we like to believe; and again the work of Freud has been of special importance in exploring the unconscious and in showing how its demands can shape even our very thinking. In so far as theology talks about man, sin, freedom, and responsibility, it must take account of what modern psychology has discovered on these themes.

Sociology too has its points of contact with theology. In the community of faith, attention is directed upon the faith which has created the community, and this faith is thought of as having some transcendent character; but viewed from outside, the same community appears as a community within the world, subject to all the usual laws of social dynamics, responding to pressures, needs, fears, the desire for security, and other purely immanent factors. Some writers, notably Marx and, in a different way, Durkheim, have believed that religion itself is capable of being explained simply as a social phenomenon. This thesis is again an exaggerated one and goes far beyond the limits of a scientific sociology. Yet, as with anthropology and psychology, sociology takes the lid off, so to speak, and reveals through its scientific approach aspects of the community of faith that should be noticed by the theologian. Any doctrine of the Church, for instance, must have regard not only to the Church as the fellowship of those called into the life of faith, but also to its status as a social phenomenon.

Spokesmen for the three sciences briefly discussed above have often been hostile toward theology and have claimed that their own scientifically conducted investigations of religion have done away with the mystifications of theology and shown religion to be a purely immanent phenomenon, entirely accessible to this kind of approach. The theologian on his side has been suspicious of these sciences, and has felt them to be rivals. Certainly, if they claim that their accounts of religion are exhaustive—and such a claim means that they have gone beyond the assertions of science to embrace a positivistic or naturalistic philosophy—then the theologian must combat these claims. He replies that a positivistic account of religion is abstract and one-sided, and in particular is devoid of that participation in religious faith which theology itself knows and which, so it would be maintained, opens up dimensions that are inaccessible to the outside observer.

But if the theologian is compelled to resist exaggerated claims for what we have called the "sciences of man," he ought nevertheless to be prepared to hear what they have to say and to take this into account in his own work. These sciences show him that the phenomena of religion have an ambiguous character. What to the eye of faith is revelation can also be seen as just an ordinary event. When he pays attention to what anthropologists, psychologists, and sociologists say about religion, the theologian is forced to consider more penetratingly what he means by faith, what is this extra dimension in the phenomena of religion that faith perceives and the scientific observer does not, what intelligible account can he give of it; for if he is unwilling or unable to consider these matters, then it might seem indeed that the positivist had won the day.

4. Finally, something has to be said about theology's relation with the *natural sciences*—the theme popularly called "science and religion."

Everyone knows the story of the great battles of the past between scientists and theologians. The new theory of the universe developed by Copernicus and Galileo pushed the earth out of the center of things and set it in motion, and this was bitterly contested by the theologians who believed that a geocentric universe was part of their revelation. Then the discovery of the geologists that the earth had been in existence for millions of years led to a new dispute, for this stretching of the time-span completely upset the scheme of so-called "sacred history" that claimed to trace the course of events from the creation down to our Christian era. Perhaps the greatest battle of all was fought with Darwin and his followers over the question of man's evolution from lower forms of life, for in the eyes of the theologians this was a further blow to the Christian faith.

Everyone knows too how these disputes ended. They all ended with the retreat of the theologian. The scientific findings, backed by irrefragable evidence, were accepted, and most theologians adjusted themselves as well as they could to the new situation.

Sometimes it is said that we should not think of these disputes as leading to the victory of one party and the defeat of the other, but rather in terms of both sides coming to a clearer understanding of where the boundary between the two disciplines lies. This is a face-saving kind of statement, but up to a point it is true. The old quarrels ostensibly had to do with the scientist's contradiction of the revealed truths set forth in scripture. The theologian of today would say that the statements in the Bible that conflict with the findings of modern science are not part of the revelation to which the Bible bears witness, but simply reflect the current scientific thinking of biblical times. He would accept that on empirical matters of fact we must be guided by science and that neither theology nor the revelation which it professes to explicate can have anything to say on such matters. On the other hand, it is claimed that science cannot pronounce on matters of faith, which are not based on the empirical world.

To some extent science and theology have thus been insulated from each other. It is unlikely that they will again quarrel over empirical matters of fact. Even such a question as whether the world had a beginning in time is one that nowadays would be turned over to scientific cosmology, and with the development of the radio telescope by which we can perceive events that took place billions of years ago, this question is one that in principle can be settled empirically.

But to conclude from such considerations that the battle between science and religion is over or that the two have arranged terms for coexistence would be premature. Future quarrels may not be so crude as those in the past, but the underlying tension could be even more severe. Although ostensibly the old battles had to do with the Bible and the contradiction of alleged truths of revelation, there was a much deeper cleavage. I believe that the real shock of the Copernican revolution was not just that it challenged the scriptural cosmology, but that on a more fundamental level it offered the greatest challenge to his sense of security man has ever experienced, and inflicted on him a traumatic experience with which he has still not fully come to terms. By dislodging man from the center, it began that process whereby he has gradually been stripped of his privileges and driven into a wilderness. The expansion of the time scale and the theory of evolution have simply gone further along the same road and increasingly stressed the apparent insignificance of man in the universe. Hence the likelihood that he should be the concern of such powers as there may be, or that they should grant him a special revelation, fades away. The old idea that the cosmic process is to be understood as centering in God's dealings with man, in the sacred biblical history of creation, fall, redemption, and final consummation, becomes pathetically improbable. It may indeed be the case that the essential truths of faith can be restated in the context of a modern world view, but they can hardly fail to be profoundly modified in the process. Whether or not we accept Bultmann's way of doing it, some kind of "demythologizing," to use his expression, has got to be carried out.

Not only has science destroyed man's ancient and infantile illusion that the world had been built around his needs, it has also taught him to understand the universe as a self-regulating mechanism where each event that takes place is adequately accounted for in terms of other events within the system. The scientist regards it as neither necessary nor permissible to appeal to alleged "supernatural" forces to keep the universe moving or to intervene from time to time to achieve special effects. We all live from day to day as if this point of view of the scientist were indeed correct. This clearly presents new problems for the theologian, for the old ways of conceiving divine action in the world in miracle, providence, and the like, were frequently infected with the discredited idea of a supernatural power breaking into and disrupting the natural course of events. Nowadays the theologian will respond to this situation by acknowledging that all events can be seen as belonging to the immanent sequence of happenings within the world, but he will claim that it is possible also to see in events a dimension that science misses. Here, however, we come against the most stubborn problem in the science-theology relation, the problem of reconciling the two underlying attitudes. Is there indeed a dimension which science misses, and which religion or theology perceives? When the theologian renounces the world of empirical fact to the scientist, has he himself anything else left to talk about? This is once again the challenge of positivism. It would seem that the theologian has to respond to it by prefacing his actual theology with as careful an exposition as he can give of the experiences, concepts, and modes of discourse on which his theology is based. In this way he will hope to show that his theological way of seeing matters may be regarded as a legitimate approach to the world, alongside the scientific one. This is the procedure which will be followed in due course in this book.

It has become clear that the relations of theology and science are not so simple as they were once taken to be, and that the contacts are indirect rather than direct, in so far as both science and religion can give rise to different attitudes to our world and our life in it. There are still some writers who try a more direct approach and who argue to religious conclusions either from specific scientific findings or from the general scientific view of the world. Such approaches are not very successful, for it is very hard to see the logical path that leads from a starting point in the empirical findings of science to the convictions of religion, which do not seem to belong within the world of empirical fact. Nevertheless, these essays to relate science and religion, even if they fail in constructing a "religious world view," have their use in removing conflicts and in trying to show that the two points of view are compatible. Theology cannot be content to be in conflict with science, either with particular findings of science or with its spirit of inquiry.

We conclude then by reiterating that theology has a duty to maintain contact with the disciplines discussed in this section, both by learning from them and by sharpening and defining its own point of view in relation to theirs.

5. THEOLOGICAL METHOD

From all that has already been said about the nature of theology, the formative factors which enter into it, and its relations to the disciplines which seem to stand nearest to it, there follow some fairly obvious principles that would guide our method of study. It is worthwhile, however, to devote a short section to stating more explicitly what these methodological principles are.

According to Bernard Lonergan, method can be understood as "a normative pattern of recurrent and related operations yielding cumulative and progressive results." [23] In his own wide-ranging study, he covers not only the method of theology proper, but the methods of the whole complex of theological studies, beginning with researches of the biblical scholar as he seeks to establish the text and to place it in its historical setting, and ending with the preacher and teacher as they seek to communicate the Christian faith to different types of people. Clearly, some of these methods are not peculiar to theology; the biblical scholar uses the same methods of textual criticism as the classicist and the historian of doctrine the same methods as any other historian. From the point of view of theology proper, that is to say, the kind of exposition of doctrine with which we are concerned in this book, biblical and historical studies constitute a preliminary to the work of theology and provide some of its material; while teaching and preaching are specialized skills which are subsequent to theology and communicate its insights in highly specific situations. The distinctive methods of theology lie in the middle of this route that leads from the establishment of the text to the act of communication in a concrete situation, but it is worth noting that theology is closely associated on both sides with these related studies and that it is partly dependent on methods which are common to many intellectual disciplines. It is, however, to the core of theological method that we must address our attention.

It should be noted that in theology, as in other disciplines, the method of study is a complex one, or perhaps one should better say that several methods are employed together. Even though we may associate particu-

---

[23] *Method in Theology*, p. 5.

lar theologians with distinctive methods—Bultmann with demythologizing, Tillich with correlation, Barth with dialectic, and so on—these distinctive procedures by no means exhaustively constitute the methods of
these theologians. They are emphases within the whole texture of theological method, rather than complete methods in themselves. Thus, whatever
the differences among the three theologians mentioned, we can see also
that there is something common in their approaches when we set them
over against the German liberal theologians of the previous generation.

In theological method, as indeed in the method of any discipline, there
is (explicitly or implicitly) an overriding *rationale* which coordinates the
various avenues of approach and assigns to each its proper degree of emphasis. This is in accordance with the constructive role of reason, in its
imaginative or architectonic function, to which allusion was made at an
earlier stage in this chapter.[24] We are not to think of this methodological
rationale as an arbitrary presupposition, or as entirely *a priori*. It must indeed be sketched out at the beginning, if the inquiry is to proceed on
consistent lines and is to be properly articulated; yet it will have been
formulated in the light of dealing with theological problems, almost, one
might say, by a process of trial and error, and it should remain as flexible
and adaptable as possible. Further, the vindication of any particular
method can be found only in the kind of theology to which it conduces.
If it leads to a coherent and intelligible presentation of what is recognizably the genuine content of the revelation, as that has been held in the
community of faith, then a theological method vindicates itself. This is
simply to say that method and content are inseparable in theology. Any
discussion of method in abstraction can be only provisional.

In this work, the *rationale* underlying the methodology recognizes and
seeks to coordinate three major avenues of approach to the content of
theology. Let me say briefly what these are.

1. An important role is assigned in this book to *description* as an element in theological method. The kind of descriptions offered may be
called "phenomenological," since I learned the value of this method from
Husserl and his followers in the school of phenomenology. This does not
mean that we are going to be bound too closely to any particular technique of phenomenology, but it does recognize the valuable contributions
that this school of philosophy offers to theology, as well as to various
other disciplines.

[24] See above, p. 16.

Phenomenology is careful analytic description; or, to express the same idea in another way, it is letting us see that which shows itself (the phenomenon) by removing, as far as possible, concealments, distortions, and whatever else might prevent us from seeing the phenomenon as it actually gives itself. This phenomenological procedure would seem to have at least three major advantages.

The first advantage is that it begins at the right place, with the phenomena themselves. It is only too easy for us to have made up our minds already, before we study the phenomena. We bring along some ready-made idea, either on the basis of our own previous history or on the basis of what we have learned of the earlier history of reflection on these matters. This is not to say that we can rid our minds of all the ideas we have picked up on a subject or that we can start entirely anew, or even that we should try to do this. No thinking can be without presuppositions, or entirely uninfluenced by previous thinking. We have indeed already maintained that tradition has its place among the formative factors in theology, and that no Christian theology can reject the mainstream of tradition. But we stressed also that what is handed down must be appropriated, or made our own, and that it must be continually subject to criticism and fresh interpretation. What is required is that we should not allow presuppositions or ideas taken over from the history of philosophy or theology to dominate our minds to such an extent that we never really face the phenomena but remain content with some ready-made interpretation. A ready-made interpretation passively and thoughtlessly taken over is not genuinely appropriated, and may conceal instead of illuminating the phenomena. It may well be that eventually we shall decide to accept some interpretation that is already available, but we ought to do so only because we see that it really does interpret the phenomena; and we can decide about this only if, so far as possible, we let ourselves be confronted by the phenomena. So we look at the phenomena as they show themselves, trying as far as possible to see and describe them as they are, without distorting prejudices.

The second advantage of phenomenology is that it conduces to clarity. In any subject, it is useful to know what one is talking about. It is possible to plunge into theology and to discourse about man, sin, God, revelation, history, and all the rest without having taken the time and trouble to see what these words mean, or how they refer, or in what context of experience they have their home, so to speak. A careful description of the phenomena to which these words are intended to point can first of all help to make the discourse which employs these words intelligible, and as a consequence can enable us to judge whether such discourse is likely to be true or not.

The third advantage of phenomenology is that in proceeding by description rather than by deduction, it moves upon a more secure ground. In any deductive argument there is, at every step, the possibility of falling into a logical fallacy. However strong an argument may appear, it may have some logical defect. A good illustration of this point is afforded by the classical arguments (they were called "proofs") for God's existence. They once seemed convincing, but now all kinds of logical defects have been exposed. No doubt description too is fallible, and as we have already seen, it can be distorted by uncritically accepted presuppositions. But phenomenological description (the expression is almost pleonastic) at least aims at a degree of care and precision which would seem to lay a firm foundation for any study. And although phenomenology does not "prove," in the sense of offering a demonstration, it does bring into the light the conditions that have to be satisfied in order that our assertions on some matter or other could be true, and it does enable us to judge how likely it is that these conditions are in fact satisfied.

The descriptive method will be especially prominent in the earlier part of this book, where we are trying to lay the foundations of the theological inquiry. To some extent, however, the phenomenological approach will continue to be used throughout the book.

2. A second methodological strand that calls for mention is *interpretation*. Among the formative factors that we have noted in theology, an important place was assigned to revelation. The primordial revelation, we have seen, has been mediated through scripture and tradition, and all three of these have come down to us from a past that in many ways is strange to us, so that revelation, as it comes to us in scripture and tradition, needs to be continually reinterpreted. Even our present experience may call for interpretation. So too does history, and likewise the mood of the contemporary culture. It would seem that wherever there is understanding, there is also interpretation. As well as the formal kind of interpretation that goes on when we try to penetrate into the meaning of, let us say, an ancient poem, there seems to be an informal and scarcely explicit kind of interpretation going on all the time in our everyday life. We interpret other people's actions, we interpret the weather signs, and so on.

When interpretation becomes a deliberate and explicit task, as it does in theology, then, if it is to be carried out in a more than haphazard way, we need some definite principles. There is indeed a science of interpretation, the science of hermeneutics, and one hears a good deal of it nowadays. For the present, a few preliminary remarks on interpretation will suffice, for once again, it will be in the actual task of interpretation that any particular approach will be vindicated.

The first point to notice about interpretation is the considerable complexity of the process, which seems always to involve some kind of circular movement. Roughly, we could say that this movement is from the known to the unknown, and back to the known. Dilthey has neatly expressed the point by saying: "Interpretation would be impossible if expressions of life were completely strange. It would be unnecessary if nothing strange were in them. It lies, therefore, between these two extremes." [25] What is implied in saying this is that we could never interpret anything unless we have some initial understanding of it, from which we set out. We bring this prior understanding to the task, and if we could not relate what is to be interpreted to what we already understand, then we could only gape at it in mute incomprehension. Yet while a prior understanding of the matter is necessary to open up for us that which is to be interpreted, once this has been opened up we make a gain, and come back with a widened and deepened understanding, which may correct and enlarge or even in some ways contradict the initial understanding from which we set out.

To give a concrete illustration will be useful. Let us suppose I am confronted with an ancient love poem. Only some understanding of love gained from my own experience could make it possible for me to interpret the meaning of the poem. But if the poem has something important to say, then once I have entered into the meaning of it, my insight into the nature of love and even my understanding of my own experience may have been very much sharpened.

A further point about interpretation is that it seems to require ability to use two different modes of expression (these may be language or something else) in parallel, as it were. One mode of expression does not supplant the other, and perhaps cannot take its place, or express all that the other expresses. However, it throws light on the other, and brings out its meaning. But in accordance with the circular character of interpretation, this is again a reciprocal process, so that each mode of expression throws light on the other and has light thrown on it by the other. For instance, when a composer sets a poem to music, the music interprets the poem, and equally the words of the poem interpret the music. Neither com-

[25] *Pattern and Meaning in History*, p. 77.

pletely expresses what the other expresses, but each helps to bring out the meaning of the other. We shall later be discussing the language of theology, but here let it be said that the method of interpretation to be employed will try to illuminate the symbolic language of revelation with an existential-ontological language drawn from contemporary philosophy, though this language will in turn be illuminated by the symbols of faith.

A third point about interpretation is that one has to have regard to the content of that which is to be interpreted, so that the illuminating language is an appropriate one, and is capable of expressing the kind of matter that has found expression in the language to be interpreted. Thus it will be necessary to show why, in the case of theology, an existential-ontological language is an appropriate one for the kind of content that is expressed in the symbols of a religious revelation.

A final point about theological interpretation is its dialectical character. By this I mean that whatever has been said, something more remains to be said; or again, that whatever doctrinal formulation has been offered will be susceptible to correction by a new formulation—and will indeed demand such correction. I do not agree with those theologians who have gloried in the "paradoxes" of Christianity, but one can admit that they were correct in recognizing that there can never be one tidy final interpretation. The reasons for this have already been partly made clear in our remarks on the development of doctrine but at the deepest level they lie in the subject-matter of theology itself. There is in both God and man an inexhaustibility that no verbal formulation can finally grasp.

The kind of interpretation described here will be most in evidence in the middle part of this book. The interpretative language, itself founded upon the descriptive analysis in the earlier part of the book will be brought into confrontation with the symbols in which faith has expressed itself.

3. The last methodological strand that I want to mention needs only a word or two. It is *application*. Theology takes its rise within the life of the community of faith, and it seeks to bring this faith to clear and coherent expression. But then it comes back to the life of faith, for theology as a whole may be considered as an interpretation and thus shows the kind of movement that belongs to any interpretation. A theology that becomes an end in itself can easily degenerate into rarefied academic speculation that has lost sight of the existential realities out of which it arose, and which it was intended to bring to expression. As has already been stressed more than once, a theology is not a disinterested philosophy of religion. Thus even as theology proceeds from existence in faith, it comes back

to this existence so that the community of faith can better understand itself and can better order its life. How this is to be done in detail will not be a matter for theology, but the general principles must be theologically informed.

6. THE DIVISIONS OF THEOLOGY

Systematic theology is the total theological enterprise as this has been unified by the architectonic reason. The preceding pages have given us an idea of the manifold tasks that have thus to be coordinated within the structure of a systematic theology. The word "systematic" should not be taken too strictly. It is the traditional word, and there are no good reasons for dropping it, but it should not be taken to mean something like a metaphysical system in which everything from God to the electron is given its place. Systematic theology has more modest aims, but it does claim to be systematic in the sense that it seeks to articulate all the constituent elements of theology in a coherent whole, and that it seeks to articulate this whole itself with the other fields that go to make up the totality of human knowledge, and especially with those disciplines which stand in a specially close relation to theology.

The preceding section on method has already made it clear that I consider that systematic theology can best be divided into three major divisions, and this threefold division of the subject determines the pattern of the remainder of the book.

The first division is *philosophical theology*. This may be considered as roughly corresponding to the *natural theology* of older treatments of the subject. Philosophical theology, as we shall see in due course, differs from the old style natural theology in being descriptive rather than deductive, but it performs the same function of providing a link between secular thought and theology proper. It lays bare the fundamental concepts of theology and investigates the conditions that make any theology possible. In doing this it also provides a defense of theology against its detractors, by showing that theology can claim to have foundations in the universal structures of human existence and experience. Hence it has an *apologetic* function, though this is incidental to its primary function as foundational theology. Apologetics is not a branch of theology, but rather a style of theology, namely that style which defends faith against attacks. There is also a difference between philosophical theology and the *philosophy of religion*, for whereas the latter is a general and disinterested study of religion, philosophical theology belongs within the theological enterprise and is indeed a necessary part of any theology that claims to be reasonable.[26]

The second great division is *symbolical theology*. I have chosen this name only after considerable thought about the matter, and of course it is not to be understood in the narrow sense of "symbolics," as this term has been used, to mean the study of creed, confessions of faith, and the like. By "symbolical" theology I mean the unfolding and interpretation of the great symbols or images in which the revealed truths of faith are set forth—the triune God, creation, the fall of man, incarnation, atonement, eschatology, and whatever else belongs to the specific faith of the Christian Church. Only after we have considered the logic of theological language will the full reason for talking about "symbolical" theology become apparent. This, however, is the core of theology, and corresponds, to a large extent, to what has customarily been called *dogmatic theology*. It seems to me, however, that the adjective "dogmatic" has acquired such a pejorative connotation in ordinary usage that theology ought to get rid of it, even if it may be convenient to keep the noun "dogma" for some restricted technical use. In any case, dogmatic theology has usually had a wider scope than the symbolical theology to be developed here, for dogmatic theology also dealt with the Church, the sacraments, and other matters, which in this book will be assigned to a distinct division.

This third division is *applied theology*. It will be concerned with the expression of faith in concrete existence, in the institutional, cultic, and ethical aspects of the life of faith. It will not indeed pursue these matters in detail, for this belongs to *practical theology* (with its many branches such as *pastoral theology, ascetical theology, homiletics*, and so on), to *liturgics*, and to *Christian ethics*, or, it may be, *moral theology*. But applied theology will provide the theological principles from which these specialized studies will move into their particular fields.

Like apologetics, *biblical theology* and *historical theology* are not distinct branches of theology, but special ways of considering theological questions, and clearly the pronouncements of both biblical and historical theology must be carefully considered over the whole areas of symbolical and applied theology.

It should perhaps be added that the lines of demarcation separating the different branches and modes of theology should not be considered as rigid. One area merges into another, and indeed it is the conviction that they all belong together that makes possible the unified structure of a systematic theology.

[26] See above, p. 2.

PART ONE

PHILOSOPHICAL THEOLOGY

2 | The Tasks of Philosophical Theology

(THEO - GOD): OLOGY - SCIENCE OF.)

7. PHILOSOPHICAL THEOLOGY AND NATURAL THEOLOGY

All theology proceeds upon assumptions, of which some may be readily seen on examination, others may be more or less concealed. For instance, any talk about revelation assumes that there are truths concerning ourselves or the world or perhaps something beyond the world, and that these truths are not to be learned as we learn truths concerning ordinary matters of fact, but that they are communicated to us in a special way. Again, belief in the immortality of the soul has its implications about what constitutes a self, the nature of death, and many other difficult matters. The business of philosophical theology, as understood in this book, is to bring these assumptions out into the open, to express them in a precise philosophical language (so far as this may be possible), and then to subject them to scrutiny to see whether they can stand up. Since the basic theological ideas—"revelation," "God," "sin," "grace" and the like—are not the private property of any particular religion, though no doubt the content of these ideas varies considerably from one religion to another, philosophical theology may be thought of as an inquiry into the possibility of any theology whatsoever. It tries to show us what are the foundations of theological discourse—how this talk arises, how it refers, what are its presuppositions. To express this in another way, philosophical theology seeks to show us what is the logic of theological discourse, or perhaps to show us whether it has a coherent logic at all. Only when these matters have been explored can we judge about the claims of theology, and have some reliable grounds for assessing whether it does in fact speak of matters that are of paramount importance for our human life, or whether it is a tissue of confusions and errors, or whether it is baseless and illusory, like the pseudo-science of astrology.

The questions on which we have just touched are sometimes discussed under the heading of "faith and reason." To be sure, there is no objection to this, though there are some dangers. There is, I believe, the very real danger that such a formulation leads us to think of reason and faith as parallel activities which lead to the same kind of result, that is to say, propositions about man or the universe or whatever it may be; and this is too intellectualized a view of faith, for although we have not yet studied the structure of faith in any detail, we have perhaps seen enough to suggest strongly that faith is not a merely cognitive activity but an attitude of the whole self. As such, it is more than belief, though undoubtedly it implies some beliefs. But since these beliefs are rooted in a total existential attitude, they have a different character from beliefs that we reach by rational deduction. An associated danger is one that we have noted already when discussing theology's relation to philosophy, namely, that everything gets subordinated to an all-embracing rationalistic metaphysic.

Because of such dangers, it is possible to understand why some theologians have always been so zealous to uphold the autonomy of faith that they have gone much too far in depreciating reason, though we have seen that they can hardly deny some role to reason, even if only an ancillary one.

As against extreme positions that seem to allow either too much or too little to reason, I indicated that this book will adhere to the ideal of a reasonable faith, that is to say, one which is not indeed purely rational, in the sense that it could be demonstrated by reason—for faith, as already indicated, is more broadly based—but one which has exposed itself to the scrutiny and testing of critical and corrective reason and has survived. Faith will not be subordinated to reason or regarded as simply an enlargement of reason; it must be shown to be compatible with reason and perhaps even supported by reason. To show this belongs to the function of philosophical theology.

When philosophical theology was mentioned as the first major division of systematic theology, it was said that this philosophical theology would correspond roughly to the natural theology which formed the initial part of many older systems. Natural theology provided the traditional way of formulating the relation between faith and reason. This suggests that in order to develop the philosophical theology which will be the theme of the next few chapters, a good point of departure would be a brief consideration of the traditional natural theology. We shall then be able to see how the philosophical theology to be presented in this book preserves some continuity with the old style natural theology, though departing from it in some major respects.

There is nowadays considerable discussion about what exactly the traditional natural theology was trying to do. We shall come back to this point shortly. Here we simply note what natural theology is commonly supposed to do, and that is to supply rational proof of the reality of those matters with which theology deals. It allowed theological discourse to get started, so to speak. Beginning from universally accepted premises, it sought to establish some basic truths, such as that God exists, that he is beneficent, that the soul is immortal, and perhaps some other matters. This provided a basis on which revealed theology could take over and lead into a fuller understanding of these matters—for instance, while natural theology might show that God is, and that he is beneficent, only revealed theology could go on to expound his triune nature.

Within natural theology, it is important to distinguish the kind of *a)* argument that proceeds in terms of rational concepts alone and the kind *b)* which sets out from the facts of common experience. The first type of *a.* argument is represented by the ontological proof of God's existence, as stated by St. Anselm,[1] Descartes,[2] and others; and something like an ontological argument for the immortality of the soul is put forward by Plato when he argues that since it is the very nature of the soul to be the life-giving principle, the notion of a dead soul is self-contradictory.[3] Arguments of this kind carry rationalism to its furthest lengths, though perhaps in doing so they defeat themselves. The ontological argument for God's existence assumes that we have the concept of a perfect being, that existence is an essential constituent of this idea of perfection, and hence that we can proceed from the idea of such a being to the assertion of the being's reality.

Somewhat more modest than these *a priori* arguments are the ones *b.* which begin from our experience of the world and seek to argue from certain features of this experience to the existence of God. The classic statement of these *a posteriori* arguments is given by St. Thomas,[4] and perhaps this is natural theology proper, as distinct from the purely rational

[1] *Proslogium*, II–IV.
[2] *Meditations*, V.
[3] *Phaedo*, 100–106.
[4] *Summa Theologiae*, Ia, 2, 3.

theology of the ontological proof. St. Thomas' "five ways" have been
i) developed along two major lines, the cosmological argument which tries
to argue back from the finite and dependent status of everything in the
world to a self-subsistent Ground from which everything proceeds, and
ii) the teleological argument which claims to find evidences of a wise and
purposeful creative Intelligence in the ordering and arrangements of the
world. These arguments have at least the advantage of beginning from
concrete empirical facts that are open to observation rather than from
abstract ideas, though whether they are any more successful we need not
judge for the moment.

We do see, however, that natural theology played a very useful and
perhaps even indispensable part in the whole theological enterprise. It
linked the theologian's world with the world of ordinary experience, or,
to put the same thing in another way, it showed the connection between
theological discourse and everyday discourse. It provided a foundation for
theology, and this should not be despised. Moreover, if it could indeed
be shown that there is a God, that he is beneficent, and that man has an
immortal destiny, then one would think it almost highly probable that this
God would reveal himself more fully, and so revealed theology gets a
flying start; whereas if natural theology is wiped out, revealed theology
is left as a very odd and isolated phenomenon, and the probability that it
is mere illusion becomes vastly increased. The trouble is that natural theology has been pretty nearly wiped out, and its present sorry plight will
be the theme of our next section.

8. PHILOSOPHICAL CRITICISMS OF NATURAL THEOLOGY

For a long time now the carefully constructed fabric of natural theology
has been under heavy fire, and it is perhaps not an exaggeration to describe its present state as ruinous. Few philosophers believe any more that
the existence of God, or whatever else may be required as a basis for
theology, can be rationally demonstrated. Many theologians have come
to share this view.

We do not propose to offer here a detailed philosophical discussion of
the classical proofs of the existence of God. There are already many
such discussions.[5] Since the time of Hume and Kant, the traditional argu-

---

[5] Recent philosophical criticisms of the proofs can be found in H. J. Paton, *The
Modern Predicament*, pp. 174–221; R. W. Hepburn, *Christianity and Paradox*,
pp. 155–185; John Hick, *Philosophy of Religion*, pp. 15–30.

ments have been subjected to critical scrutiny, and many defects and weaknesses have been exposed. In turn, however, new and more subtle statements of the arguments have been devised. It would be impossible to follow out the many variations and ramifications of the arguments, and we must be content with a brief consideration of what I take to be the decisive points.

The ontological argument for God's existence is better called "rational theology" than "natural theology," for it depends solely on the analysis of concepts. We believe God to be, in St. Anselm's famous phrase in the treatise cited above, "something than which nothing greater can be thought." But, it is argued, if God had his being only in our thought, then we could think of something greater or more excellent, namely, this same being existing in reality. Thus the very concept of God, when defined as Anselm defines it, appears to entail his existence. Alternatively, it is argued that existence belongs necessarily to the very concept of God, just as three-sidedness belongs to the concept of a triangle.

The decisive objection to the argument was put forward by Kant [6] when he pointed out that existence or being is not a predicate describing the characteristics of something. To claim that something exists is not to ascribe to it a property like three-sidedness, but to posit it as something real. Incidentally, the point that being is not a property will prove to be important in our later discussion of being and God.

Turning from rational theology to natural theology proper, we consider first the cosmological proof of God's existence. The argument begins from the fact that everything in the world seems to call for explanation in terms of something else, and concludes that the world itself has to be explained in terms of God. It is said, for instance, that everything has a cause, but as we trace back the chain of causes, we cannot go on for ever, and must eventually come to a first cause which is itself uncaused or the cause of itself, and this is at least part of what we mean by "God." Alternatively, it is said that whatever we observe exists only contingently; it might not have been, or it might have been otherwise. But it is claimed that nothing at all could exist contingently unless there was something that existed necessarily, and this necessary being is what we call "God."

These arguments raise many difficulties. If the first cause is of the same order as the subsequent causes, why should it be called "God"? On the other hand, if it is of a different order, does not the whole argument

[6] *Critique of Pure Reason*, B626.

from causation lose its force? Again, while we may agree that everything in the universe seems to exist contingently and to call for explanation, is this true of the universe itself? But the most thoroughgoing rejection of the argument has come in recent times from those philosophers of radical finitude such as Nietzsche and Camus. They see no reason for denying that the universe just is an endless conglomeration of contingent beings and events, with neither beginning nor end nor center.

2. That brings us to the teleological arguments for the existence of God. These hold that there is in fact evidence of purpose, intelligence, and even benevolence in the way the universe is ordered. David Hume acknowledged that the "argument from design," as it was called, was the strongest argument of all for the existence of God; and so it must have seemed, as its proponents pointed to the suitability of the earth for life, the regularity of the heavens, the remarkable adaptations of plants and animals.

But it was Hume who made one of the most telling criticisms when he pointed out that the universe is more like an organism than an artifact— that is to say, that the principle of order seems to be immanent in nature itself rather than derived from a designer.[7] Since his time, the advance of the natural sciences has shattered some of the most cherished evidences of design. Not divine purpose, but random mutations and natural selection appear to be the agencies that have brought about the adaptations of living things to the multitude of environments. And the whole process seems to have been one of trial and error, confirming Hume's speculation that "many worlds might have been botched and bungled throughout an eternity ere this system was struck out, much labor lost, many fruitless trials made." [8]

When one considers the philosophical criticisms briefly set out in the last few paragraphs, then my remark that the state of natural theology is ruinous seems to be confirmed. Of course, if the arguments for theism seem to be in disarray, this does not mean that atheism has triumphed. The proofs have failed, but so have any attempted disproofs. Furthermore, valiant efforts have been made and are still being made [9] to reformulate the arguments in ways that might avoid some of the defects of the older

[7] *Dialogues Concerning Natural Religion,* pt. VI.

[8] *Op. cit.,* pt. XII.

[9] For the ontological argument, see Charles Hartshorne, *The Logic of Perfection;* for the cosmological argument, Austin Farrer, *Finite and Infinite,* and E. L. Mascall, *He Who Is;* for the teleological argument, in conjunction with other arguments, F. R. Tennant, *Philosophical Theology,* and Pierre Teilhard de Chardin, *The Phenomenon of Man.*

versions. But even those who have been most successful in restating the arguments usually make it clear that they do not claim for them the cogency of proofs, and that the conclusions to which the arguments point fall far short of the full content of religious faith. Nevertheless, there remains some value in the arguments. The ontological argument shows that an idea of God or perfect being is somehow native to the human mind, so that man has, in Schleiermacher's expression, a "sense and taste for the infinite." [10] The cosmological argument articulates an awareness of the mystery of existence and proceeds from what E. L. Mascall has called "the capacity for contemplative wondering." [11] The teleological argument draws our attention to the amazingly complex structure of the universe and its potentialities for bringing forth living and even personal beings; and Hume's point about the immanence of these potentialities in nature, made at a time when God was conceived in starkly transcendent terms, seems less important in a time when we have to some extent recovered a sense of God's closeness to the world.

Thus, even if the proofs fail as proofs, they may retain enough residual value as to form a cumulative argument for the reasonableness of belief in God. "What has been taken as a series of failures when treated as attempts at purely deductive or inductive argument," writes Basil Mitchell, "could well be better understood as contributions to a cumulative case." [12]

9. THEOLOGICAL CRITICISMS OF NATURAL THEOLOGY

I have passed quickly over the philosophical criticisms of the traditional natural theology, but it is right that I should spend more time over the theological criticisms of it. For theologians as well as philosophers have largely turned away from natural theology. Some theologians have done this joyfully, others reluctantly, but for the most part they have done it not only because they have been impressed by the damaging criticisms of the philosophers but also because there are grave theological objections to some elements in natural theology, or at least in natural theology as this has come to be commonly understood.

One theological objection that has been urged from Calvin to Barth l. ought, I believe, to be firmly rejected, and I will begin with it in order to get it out of the way. This is the objection that man's fallen or sinful

10 *On Religion*, p. 39.
11 *The Openness of Being*, p. 141.
12 *The Justification of Religious Belief*, p. 39.

condition has stripped him of "sound intelligence" as well as of moral integrity and that his corruption extends to the intellect as well as to the will.[13] Hence even if there were some way by which our minds could attain to the knowledge of God from the evidence accessible within the world, we would be unable to get through to this knowledge, for our very reasoning is so perverted that we would fall into error and arrive at an idea of God so false and distorted that we could not be said to have any knowledge of him at all. There is of course a measure of truth in this point of view. We do have a tendency to believe whatever fits in with our wishes and ambitions and whatever will gratify our own ego. Calvin and Barth can get support here too from psychological theory, though in the end this support would react against their own position, for Freud and those who follow him tell us that all our ideas of God, whether they are supposedly "natural" or "revealed," are illusions to which our minds are led by the desire to shelter ourselves from the harshness of reality. But to hold that our intellect is so perverted that we just cannot think straight is to fall into a skepticism so bottomless that further discussion becomes pointless. The Calvinist believes that he himself, as one of the elect, has been rescued from this sea of error and that his mind has been enlightened by the Holy Spirit. However much he may insist that this is God's doing and not his own, his claim is nevertheless one of the most arrogant that has ever been made. It is this kind of thing that has rightly earned for theology the contempt of serious men. Actually, everyone knows that thinking can be easily distorted by selfish and unworthy desires—the masters of propaganda know this only too well. But even to know that this happens is already to be struggling against it. There need not be a skeptical resignation of the possibility of trustworthy thinking (this would be a kind of intellectual suicide); rather, there needs to be an effort to think more strictly and more rationally. In the case of natural theology, then, the objection that points to the perversion of our reasoning as an insuperable obstacle is one that cannot be sustained. It does indeed alert us to dangers, and the history of religion affords plenty of instances of the distortion of the knowledge of God. But to make this the whole story is a one-sided exaggeration that must be resisted.

2. A much more convincing theological objection to the traditional natural theology takes its stand on the finitude of our human existence. Finitude and sin are certainly related and they often get confused; later

---

[13] Calvin, *Institutes of the Christian Religion*, II, iii.

we shall have to clarify the distinction between them, and more than once we shall find this distinction to be of importance. For the present, however, let us notice that contemporary theology probably reckons more seriously with the finitude of human existence than many theologies of the past have done, and this may reflect the similar emphasis on finitude in much of our contemporary philosophy. Thus theologians who would not go along with Calvin in rejecting natural theology on the ground that man's intellect is fallen may very well reject it on the ground that it tries to do something that is incompatible with man's finitude. To be finite is to live in risk and uncertainty, and that this is our life is clear to us from everyday experiences in which we have to commit ourselves to policies of action without complete knowledge of all the relevant circumstances and still less of all the consequences that will flow from the action. Our life in this world is not one that can be based only upon the certitude of knowledge—the man who tries to live this way, without risk, never really lives at all—but one that must go out in faith. This is true about the understanding of our life as a whole—we see it only from our own limited standpoint and cannot know the ultimate truth about it. Thus to demand the guaranteed certitude of rational demonstration (that there is a God, that God is good, that the soul is immortal, and so on) is to refuse to acknowledge one's own finitude, or to refuse to accept oneself. As St. Paul reminds us, we do not see "face to face," but "in a mirror dimly." [14] Of course, as has been urged several times already, our faith must be a reasonable faith that takes into account all relevant factors, one that submits itself to the scrutiny of the critical reason; and this point has been reinforced by the refusal to reject natural theology on the grounds that reason is corrupted. But we must still recognize that man's life *in via* proceeds on the basis of faith, not of demonstrable certainty, so that the attempt to provide a rational demonstration is open to the objection that it attempts to escape from the radical finitude and risk of an existence such as ours.

Another theological objection to natural theology in the old style 3. questions the propriety of talking about God within the terms that are available in a deductive argument. This theological objection is perhaps the counterpart of the philosophical objection that questions the logic of a move from the empirical to the allegedly transempirical. In any case, the theological objection makes, like Pascal, a sharp distinction between the God of religious faith and the God of the philosophers. The God who is

---

[14] I Cor. 13:12.

the conclusion of an argument, we are told, is not the God who is worshipped in religion. A God whose existence is deduced from the existence of the objects we perceive within the world, it is felt, must be regarded himself as another object, or a God who is posited as a hypothesis to account for the observed phenomena must be considered as himself part of the phenomenal nexus. Champions of natural theology protest against such criticisms. They deny that God is treated like an object or manipulated like a hypothesis in the theistic proofs. Jacques Maritain, for instance, claims that the five ways of St. Thomas, so far from attempting to grasp God with the intellect or to subject him to it, "make God known only by kneeling before him." [15] At the same time, however, he claims that the arguments really are proofs or demonstrations. There would seem to be some disagreement among Roman Catholic scholars about the precise nature of the arguments. Karl Adam holds with Maritain that the theistic proofs are different from any "profane inquiry" and have a specific "mental attitude" characterized by reverence and humility.[16] On the other hand, we find Etienne Gilson saying that natural theology belongs "to the order of the things that are of this world and are, in the proper acceptation of the word, profane." [17] Now the difference between the two points of view seems to be an important one. If we accept the view that the arguments proceed in a spirit of reverence and admiration, then this may overcome the objection that God is being treated like another object, but it makes it hard to see how we can still talk of "proof" or "demonstration." If there is a "specific difference" between the procedure of natural theology and that of a "profane" demonstration, the logician will want to know just what this difference is and whether it is such a difference that we cannot properly talk of "proof" or "demonstration" in the case of natural theology. On the other hand, if we accept the view that the theistic proofs are nowise different from "profane" argumentation, how can it be denied that God is indeed treated as an object or a hypothesis? And how, in turn, can it be denied that this infringes his transcendence?

4. We shall return to the question of how precisely the arguments of natural theology are to be taken, but meantime let us notice one further theological objection to the old style natural theology—an objection which underlies all the others. The objection is, that in our knowledge of God, the initiative lies with God. He makes himself known to us, so

15 *The Degrees of Knowledge*, p. 225.
16 *The Spirit of Catholicism*, p. 54.
17 *The Spirit of Thomism*, p. 23.

that the movement is from his side to us, not from our side to him. Natural theology, in opposition to this, seeks to find a way from man to God.

This objection has, I believe, been very much exaggerated by some Protestant theologians, yet there is an important truth in it. It becomes exaggerated when the distance between God and man has been made so great that man becomes the purely passive recipient of the knowledge of God, and there is no room left for reciprocity or appropriation. It is exaggerated to the point of depressing man below the level of rational, responsible, personal being. Nevertheless, such exaggerations aside, it seems clear that our knowledge of God could never be like our knowledge of some fact in the world. Our knowledge of facts in the world is gained by our own active discovery of them, but since God is himself the supremely active principle, he does not await our discovery but presents and manifests himself in an active manner. More will have to be said about this also, but if we think of God as active and taking the initiative in making himself known, the boundaries between the "natural" and the "revealed" knowledge of God become blurred.

The stress laid by Barth and other theologians on God's initiative in any knowledge of himself is correct and justified as a protest against the idea that God can be discovered like a fact of nature, and as an assertion that he *gives* the knowledge of himself; but the position of these theologians becomes distorted when they try to narrow the knowledge of God to a single self-revealing act on his part (the biblical or Christian revelation), and as against them at this point, the traditional natural theology was correct and justified in claiming a wider and indeed universal possibility for knowing God. There are objections to the expression "general revelation" because of its abstractness. The knowledge of God comes always in particular concrete revelations. However, the notion of "general revelation" is justified in so far as it seeks to express the claims both of "natural" and "revealed" theology, and in so far as it is understood not as a body of highly abstract truth common to all particular revelations but rather the universal possibility of revelation, which is in turn the condition that there may be any particular occasions of revelation whatsoever. The structure of such a general possibility of revelation will be expounded later.

We have seen then how the old style natural theology has sustained some shattering blows. The philosophers have found it to be in various ways logically defective, while many theologians have claimed that from the point of view of Christian faith, it conflicts both with the recognition of man's finitude and the acknowledgment of God's transcendence. Yet we were not persuaded by some of the more extravagant railings against natural theology. Let it be agreed that it does not demonstrate the reality of God, immortality, and whatever else was supposed to be implied in the basic presuppositions of theology. Does this mean that we can just abandon all natural theology, and content ourselves with revealed theology alone? Many theologians take this point of view, but it seems to me that they are in a very unenviable position. They have been left with a revelation which, now that the old support of natural theology has been pulled out, is left suspended in mid air, so to speak, as an arbitrary and isolated phenomenon. Let us remind ourselves that apart from what it tried to prove, the old style natural theology acted as a bridge between our ordinary everyday knowledge and experience of the world, and that knowledge which is the content of faith and which is made explicit in theology. This particular bridge is now shaky or even collapsed, but some bridge there must be if our ideal of a *reasonable* faith is to be attained and if theology is to have solid intellectual foundations. Otherwise it can be only an isolated segment, with no protection against illusion and superstition.

In this situation we have to consider how there may be constructed a philosophical theology which will take over some of the basic functions of the old style natural theology but will try to avoid its weaknesses. Such a philosophical theology might be called a "new style natural theology." Actually this name might be misleading in so far as it would suggest too close a connection with what has traditionally been called "natural theology," but on the other hand it would make clear both our recognition that there was something of indispensable importance in natural theology, and our unflagging opposition to those who go to the extreme length of recklessly rejecting all natural theology and rely on a supposedly revealed theology alone.

10. PRINCIPLES OF A PHILOSOPHICAL THEOLOGY OR NEW STYLE NATURAL THEOLOGY

Many contemporary writers have suggested that we should try to understand the traditional natural theology, especially its theistic proofs, in a new way. They point out, for instance, that the "five ways" of St. Thomas appear in the context of a whole theological system, and that it is wrong to lift them out and treat them in isolation. Instead of going to them cold, as it were, and asking whether they are cogent demonstrations from premises universally acceptable among rational men, we should try to place them in the context of medieval debate; not least, we should remember that St. Thomas may well have had in mind those theologians who, then as now, were distrustful of reason and philosophy, and who would not seek to establish any accord between these and faith.[18] Once we begin to consider the theistic proofs in relation to the situations that called them forth, we see that in every case the person offering the proof had already been himself convinced of God's reality on grounds quite other than those mentioned in the proof; we see also that the proof arises from his subsequent meditation upon his conviction, perhaps in order to meet the objections of skeptics, perhaps to allay his own doubtings, or to raise his convictions to the status of reasonable faith, or to demonstrate the compatibility of faith and reason. It is rather like the procedure outlined by John Wisdom in his well-known essay, "Gods," [19] where the theist goes over the details of his world, tracing and emphasizing patterns and connections that support his conviction, and presumably also trying to explain the gaps and recalcitrant facts that count against his belief. The very conviction from which he begins perhaps causes him to notice connections that would not otherwise have been noted, or to be painfully aware at other points of a seeming lack of connections. In the long run, the picture must be acknowledged to be ambiguous, in the sense that no finally conclusive proof in support of his conviction can be offered by the theist or, for that matter, by the atheist who has been calling attention to other elements in the picture. Yet it has been important that the theist has exposed his conviction to a confrontation with the observable facts of our world, and has shown that it is at least not incompatible with them.

We are, however, left with the question about where the conviction came from in the first place. If it was not produced by the argument, but was already there before the argument so that this argument only served to clarify or confirm the conviction, then what are we to say of the conviction? Are we perhaps to turn to psychology and trace the natural history of the conviction in terms of irrational demands and wishes that lie deep within us, so that we would then see the arguments as only attempted rationalizations of a fantasy-created wish-world? Or are we to push back the inquiry into the fundamental ways in which we come to know anything, and try to elucidate the basic structures and patterns of experience that might seem to offer valid credentials for a religious con-

[18] See Edward Sillem, *Ways of Thinking about God*, pp. 31, 97.
[19] *Philosophy and Psychoanalysis*, pp. 149ff.

viction? Even if we did these things, would we still be faced with a radically ambiguous situation? From the stress already laid on human finitude, we may suspect that there will be no escape from ambiguity into a certain conclusive understanding of the world. Yet we could at least strive toward ascertaining the conditions that would have to obtain if a religious conviction were to be valid, so that we could judge how reasonable or unreasonable such a conviction is, or how big and how risky the leap of faith may be.

The philosophical theology envisaged in this book would therefore be more fundamental than the old style natural theology, in so far as it would press back beyond the traditional arguments to examine the conviction that lay behind them. It would also have a different method, for it would be *descriptive* instead of *deductive*. This is entirely in line with what was said above [20] about the place of phenomenology in theological method. This descriptive type of philosophical or natural theology does not *prove* anything, but it *lets us see*, for it brings out into the light the basic situation in which faith is rooted, so that we can then see what its claims are. Incidentally, it may well be that this kind of procedure will be far more effective as an apologetic than the old attempts to demonstrate by rational argument. It is not likely that too many people have become Christians through the abstract and theoretical considerations adduced by the traditional arguments, but if we proceed by way of description rather than demonstration, we are asking the person addressed to *look with us* at the phenomena. There is a measure of participation here which is more likely than an abstract argument to lead into a genuine understanding of a religious faith, for this latter is never in any case a merely theoretical belief.

A further point about the new style natural theology has already become apparent in these remarks—this approach is *existential* rather than *rationalistic*. It may well be, of course, that the word "rational" had much wider connotations in the Middles Ages than it has now so that, as we have already seen suggested,[21] St. Thomas went about the formulation of the "five ways" in a spirit of humility and reverence that was not just an accompaniment of the enterprise but an integral element in it. But nowadays we think of rationalism in a fairly narrow sense, as the abstract theoretical operation of the intellect, with mathematics as the paradigmatic case. This purely abstract kind of thinking misses some of the di-

[20] See above, pp. 34–36.
[21] See above, p. 52.

mensions of our human experience; but these, as we shall see, are not just to be dismissed as emotive. There is a broader understanding than that which belongs to the purely theoretical reason, and it is this broader understanding, arising out of the whole range of our existence in the world, that can alone help us to penetrate into the meaning of religious faith.

So far, attention has been drawn to three differences between the new style philosophical theology and the old style natural theology, namely, that the former is more fundamental in going to the very sources of religious conviction, that it is descriptive in its method rather than deductive, and that it is existential rather than rational. But are these differences not so great that it is misleading to think of this philosophical theology as continuing the work once done by natural theology, and still more misleading to talk, as we have sometimes done, of a "new style natural theology"? It is true that the differences are very marked. The first of the three mentioned means the virtual abandonment of the old distinction between "natural" and "revealed" knowledge of God, for the appeal is going to be to a general possibility of revelation (this expression is to be preferred to "general revelation") rather than to a "second route" to God, such as a speculative metaphysic, that would stand alongside his self-manifestation; though it should be clear from what has already been said that there is no desire to rule out rational reflection as a way of testing or even confirming what has been given in revelatory experience. The second and third differences mentioned mean the abandonment of any attempt at a "profane" science of God, if this means a purely rationalistic and theoretical approach, though here we have already noticed that some acute Catholic commentators deny that natural theology was ever intended to be taken as a profane inquiry.

Yet in spite of these differences, the philosophical theology to be developed here will perform the same basic function as the old natural theology. It will provide a bridge between our everyday thinking and experience and the matters about which the theologian talks: it will relate religious discourse to all the other areas of discourse. It will do this by setting out from ordinary situations that can be described in secular language, and will seek to move from them into the situations of the life of faith. In the course of these descriptions, distinctively religious words such as "God," "sin," "revelation," "faith," will be given their meanings. It is true that we have already used all of these words, and this was necessary if we were to get started at all. Their meanings have up till now been indicated only in a provisional way, if at all, but an important task of philosophical theology will be to show how these words find their places on the map of meaning, so to speak, and this will be done by a procedure of description that starts off from familiar and universally known situations—just as the traditional natural theology tried to make its beginning from premises accepted by all reasonable persons.

The starting point of philosophical theology is man himself, the common humanity that is known to each of us men existing in the world. This analysis of our own existence will draw attention especially to those structures and experiences which lie at the root of religion and of the life of faith. An attempt will be made to describe the revelatory situation and to determine what we mean when we talk of "God." Something will be said here too about the modes of thinking and knowing. An attempt will then be made to offer an analysis of theological language and to show what is its basic logic and how it "makes sense." Since these considerations are all of a general nature, and investigate the universal conditions that make any religion or theology whatsoever possible, something must finally be said about the general possibility of revelation in relation to particular occasions of revelation, and so the way will be prepared from foundational philosophical theology into the special symbolic theology of the Christian faith.

These themes will occupy the remaining chapters of the part of this work devoted to philosophical theology.

3 | Human Existence

11. HUMAN EXISTENCE AND ITS POLARITIES

We turn to man, for it is man who lives in faith (or without faith) and it is man who pursues theology as the explication of faith, so that if we are to reach any understanding of the foundations of faith and theology, it might seem that we must seek it through a study of man, in whom alone (so far as we know) the phenomena of faith and theology show themselves. Moreover, since both the man of faith and the man without faith have in common their humanity, it would seem that any attempt to say what faith is and to present its claims as not just arbitrary must proceed from the common ground of a shared humanity, so that faith can be seen as something that is rooted in the very constitution of our human existence, and the centrality of its claim be seen at the same time.

But how are we to know what man is—or, to express it more concretely, who we are? From the earliest times, men have indeed sought to know themselves, but they have acknowledged that this is very difficult. True self-knowledge would seem to be the hardest knowledge to acquire. It should be the easiest, for nothing is closer to man than himself; yet because of this very closeness, such knowledge can never be a matter of indifference or an abstract theoretical knowledge, and so what is closest in existence may be furthest in understanding. In modern times we seem to be as far as ever from an agreed understanding of what man is or who we are, and the great conflicting ideologies of our time reflect different understandings of what constitutes a genuinely human existence—the understandings that we find in humanism or Christianity or Marxism or Buddhism or in plain unsophisticated and unthinking hedonism.

In face of these conflicting views, we can only try to follow the phenomenological method, that is to say, to put aside so far as we can presuppositions and interpretations, so that we are confronted with the phenomena of human existence as they show themselves; and when we have tried to expose ourselves honestly to the phenomena, and to describe them as they give themselves, being especially careful not to omit what we may not want to see, then we can turn to the problem of interpretation. Yet even the task of description here is fraught with possibilities of error. Human existence is not only variable, it is also ambiguous and polar, so that even what professes to be only description of the phenomena is in danger of becoming one-sided.

A starting point is afforded by the question of what differentiates man from other beings in the world. The existentialists answer this question in terms of man's "existence," where the term "existence" is understood not in its traditional sense as whatever may be found occurring in the world, but rather in its root sense of "standing out." In the traditional sense, men, cats, trees, and rocks all alike exist; but in the more restricted sense, while men, cats, trees, and rocks all *are*, only man is said to exist. Of course, so long as we merely say that "existing" is to be understood as "standing out," then to say that existence is what differentiates man from other beings in the world seems to be little more than a tautology. We have at once to ask how man stands out.

Men, cats, trees, rocks all *are;* they have being, we come across them in the world. But so far as we know, only man is open to his being, in the sense that he not only is, but is aware *that* he is, and aware too, in some degree, of *what* he is. He has his being disclosed to him, and this disclosure, as will be shown, comes not only in understanding but also over the whole range of his affective and conative existing in a world. The expression "in a world" is to be noted. It is not man's inner life that is disclosed to him in some kind of subjective introspection, but his life as already involved in a world of things and persons; without some world, there could not be an existence such as man's. If the word "existence" then points to the characteristics of human life just mentioned, the denial of "existence," in the special sense defined, to rocks, trees, and the like is clear. It has of course nothing whatever to do with an "idealist" point of view or with the assertion that the mental has more reality than the physical. A rock, or any other inanimate object, does not exist only in the sense that it does not have its being disclosed to it. It *is* just as certainly as we *are*, but its mode of being is different. Cats presumably come somewhere between rocks and men, but even they do not exist as we exist, and this will become clearer as the notion of existence gets filled out in the analysis. In a paradoxical way, while man in modern times has become more than ever conscious of his kinship with the lower animals and with all nature, of which he can be for certain purposes regarded as a part, at the same time he has become more than ever conscious of the gulf that separates him from nature. The same science that has brought to light man's animal origins has also secularized nature and divested it of every vestige of animism, so that whereas primitive man projected his thoughts and feelings upon the world around him and supposed natural forces to be motivated by a life like his own, the man of modern times understands the processes of nature to be alien and indifferent to him. Some philosophers seem not far removed from a thoroughgoing dualism, in which man's existence (history) stands in the sharpest opposition to cosmic process (nature).

Let us try to clarify further what is meant by "existence." This has already been characterized as a mode of being in which the existent has its being disclosed to it. Such disclosure is not just the passive receiving of an impression. The existent is concerned with the existence that is disclosed and becomes, within limits, responsible for it. Man's unique status in nature arises from the fact that in him the evolutionary process has for the first time (at least, on earth) become transparent to itself and capable to some extent of self-direction. This peculiarity of existence may be expressed in another way, by saying that man has a relation to himself. We continually use such expressions as "I hated myself for doing it," or "I feel pleased with myself," or even "I was not myself when I said that," and we understand well enough what is meant by these expressions, yet if we think about them, we see that they are something of a puzzle. Just who is the "I" that is distinguished from "myself"? What complex structure of existence do we have to envisage to explain this language? Something will need to be said later about how we are to understand selfhood, but for the moment it will be enough to make two points that follow from the conception of existence as the existent's responsible relation to himself. The first point is that selfhood is not ready-made, so to speak, but is always on its way, and always incomplete at any given moment. Objects in nature have their properties given to them, but what is "given" to man is an existence that stands before different possibilities of being, and among these it must responsibly discriminate. This brings us to a further point. Because selfhood is not a ready-made "nature," or collection of properties, but a potentiality that has to be responsibly actualized, man can either attain to authentic selfhood or miss it, and so fall below the kind of being that can properly be called "existence" in the fullest sense.

What we have here called "existence," following the terminology of the existentialist philosophers, is the same phenomenon that other modern philosophers call the "transcendence" of man. In some respects this notion of "transcendence" better expresses the dynamic character of man's being—it is his very nature to be always transcending or passing beyond any given stage of his condition. Also the traditional word "spirit" expressed something of the same idea, for it was the endowment with spirit that allowed man to be creative and responsible and to rise above the lower levels of life. But whether we speak of existence, transcendence, or spirit, we have in mind humanity as an unfinished, open kind of being, moving into possibilities that have still to be unfolded.

While the concept of "existence" differentiates man's being from the being that belongs to objects in nature, and so sets up a certain tension between man and nature, further analysis of what is involved in "existence" reveals that existence itself contains tensions or polarities, and that the opposition between existence and nature is paralleled by oppositions within existence itself—some of them so sharp that man, as the bearer of such existence, is almost torn apart by them.

Among the polarities of existence, we may notice first that of *possibility* and *facticity*. The provisional exposition given above of the idea of existence stressed man's possibility, as the existent who stands before potentialities for being and for action, and who responsibly decides among them and commits himself to some definite policy. These points were stressed because the freedom and the responsibility of an existence that is not ready-made, but stands before possible ways of being, is distinctive of man. However, in talking of man's possibility, conceived as his freedom to decide among ways of being, I was careful to use such qualifying expressions as "within limits" and "to some extent." Man, it is perfectly obvious, never faces unrestricted possibility. He exists in a world, and his possibilities relate to his world and, more than that, to the particular situation in which he already finds himself in the world. In any situation, the area of freedom may be very small indeed. At the opposite pole of existence from possibility is facticity, and this includes all the "givens" of any particular existence—intelligence, race, temperament, and many other factors that no one chooses for himself. Environment and heredity, our place in history and society, these contribute so much to making us what we are that the area of the possible is cut down, sometimes, it would seem, almost to vanishing point. Every freedom is balanced against a limitation, perhaps a limitation of power that prevents us from carrying out a policy, or perhaps a limitation of knowledge that frustrates our intention. So existence is always characterized by the tension between possibility and facticity, between man's freedom and his manifold finitude.

A closely related polarity is that between *rationality* and *irrationality*. Rationality has often been taken as the distinguishing mark of man, so that he has been defined as the "rational animal." Certainly the ability to judge, discriminate, sift, understand, interpret, is a striking characteristic of man, and I have already defended his rationality against those who would depreciate it. If we deny man's rationality then there is no point in saying anything further, for rationality has to be assumed as the postulate for any discussion. Yet we must qualify man's rationality just as much as his freedom. The researches of Freud in particular have made clear the almost frightening extent to which our lives are ruled by dark irrational forces. We never fully understand our own motives, and we do things sometimes in ignorance of why we do them, sometimes deceiving ourselves about why we do them. Our minds move in the light of truth, and yet at the same time they move in untruth, error, and deception. So again we find a tension set up in existence. While man's rationality seems to afford a ground for the right ordering of life and for almost unlimited progress in improving its conditions and deepening its quality, his irrationality, as we know only too well, keeps breaking in and threatening to disrupt all order.

A further polarity is the opposition between *responsibility* and *impotence*. The notion of responsibility has already been mentioned. It belongs to the disclosedness of existence, for this is not a passive disclosedness but an opening up that demands decision. Our existence is disclosed by our rationality and understanding, and also, as will be shown, by some affective states of mind. But the mode of disclosure which has to do most closely with responsibility is conscience. This phenomenon is sometimes explained in terms of factors outside of the individual who experiences conscience, either in terms of a divine influence which warns or approves, or of social convention which has been built in, so to speak, as a superego and which likewise warns or approves. Both of these theories may have some truth in them and may account for some forms of conscience, but neither of them strikes the central phenomenon of conscience which, as the name "conscience" implies, is a kind of synoptic self-understanding, the self's own awareness of how it measures up to itself, that is to say, how far it is failing or succeeding in bringing to actualization its own potentialities for being. But it is well known that while the summons of conscience may be clear enough, the will to obey this summons may be too weak. We recognize responsibility and even the "oughtness" of a situation, yet we cannot bring ourselves to do what is demanded. The factors of facticity, irrationality, and individuality may all be involved here, but impotence in the face of responsibility seems sufficiently distinctive to need a mention of its own. Such impotence seems to make nonsense of the moral life (where "ought" must imply "can") and challenges the value of any aspiration.

I have spoken of "polarities" and "tensions" in existence, but perhaps this language has been too neutral. As is well known, there are philosophers who would say bluntly that man's existence, as finite possibility thrown into the world, is self-contradictory. Man in Sartre's famous phrase is "a useless passion," [1] for his very existence is such as to make nonsense of his aspirations and potentialities. And indeed, we have still to add the final touch to the picture—death. This existence of man, an existence that is throughout subjected to the tensions between its opposing poles, will terminate in any case in death, and this looks like the triumph of finitude and negativity over whatever sparks of positive and affirmative being show themselves in man. An existence of contradictions, coming finally to nothing in death—this is an absurdity. Yet it is very hard for us to accept that our existence is just absurd and futile. Even philosophers who talk this way are soon found to be trying to get beyond it. The very fact that we go on living seems to testify to a deeply rooted conviction that existence does make sense, or can make sense.

Nevertheless, the fact that the viability of human existence can be so radically put in question brings us to still another polarity, that of *anxiety* and *hope*. In a sense, this one sums up all the others. A life lived amid the tensions generated by the polarities we have described can never be quite free from anxiety, that is to say, from a sense of the threat of absurdity and negativity. On the other hand, such a life can be lived only on the basis of the hope that it is somehow worthwhile. Anxiety and hope are both moods or feelings, and we shall have something to say about the role of such affective states later.[2] For the moment, it will be enough to claim that they are not merely subjective emotions but ways of being related to our environment such that they light up its character for us. In Sartre's words: "The affected subject and the affective object are bound in an indissoluble synthesis. Feeling is a certain way of apprehending the

---

[1] *Being and Nothingness*, p. 615.
[2] See below, pp. 86–87, 96–100.

world. . . . What a feeling signifies is the totality of the relationships of the human reality to the world." [3]

But anxiety and hope seem to contradict one another. If they rule each other out, how can they tell us anything about human existence? Or is one of them more fundamental and disclosive than the other? It is true that some writers (Heidegger and Sartre are examples) seem to make anxiety fundamental in their phenomenological analysis, but others stress hope, even in the face of death. Thus Pannenberg can write: "It is inherent in man to hope beyond death, even as it is inherent in man to know about his own death." [4] Both anxiety and hope seem to be very deeply rooted in the being of man. Paul Ricoeur suggests that these seemingly contradictory moods might be understood as two ways of experiencing the same relation. Anxiety is the sense of the *difference* between the finite being and the mysterious totality in which he has, so it seems, an insignificant place; hope or joy arises from the sense of *belonging* to that totality and having some affinity with it. Ricoeur himself believes that the second, more affirmative kind of mood, is the more fundamental and significant.[5]

Both in the life of an individual and in the experience of a generation moods may come and go almost unpredictably. Hope and anxiety may alternate almost like the perceptions of an ambiguous figure in a textbook of psychology. The twentieth century has seen many oscillations between hope and anxiety—even between a brash unthinking optimism which lacks the humility of true hope to an apocalyptic despair that has nothing of the subtlety of ontological anxiety. And there are other moods, ranging from what Camus called "metaphysical rebellion" to sheer boredom. Affirmative and negative tendencies both show themselves, fundamental questions about the significance of human existence are raised by both, and it would seem that only a thoroughly dialectical interpretation can be adequate to the complexity of the phenomena.

Perhaps after all it has been wise to keep to the neutral language of "polarities" and "tensions" rather than to rush immediately to the conclusion that human existence is a self-contradictory absurdity. It certainly has an ambiguous character, and because of the finite reach of human understanding which sees existence only from within and from a limited point of view, presumably we could never conclusively resolve the ambi-

[3] *The Emotions*, pp. 52, 93.
[4] *What Is Man?*, p. 44.
[5] *Fallible Man*, p. 161.

guities. But we cannot hastily conclude that ambiguity is to be equated with absurdity. Even death, in spite of its apparently utter negativity, may turn out to have an ambiguous character. We who find ourselves thrown into existence are impelled to try to make sense of it. By existing, we are involved in the question of existence, and this question is certainly no speculative or theoretical one, but a question with which we are very much concerned and to which our very mode of existence gives an answer, even if only implicitly. Of course, it may be said this impulsion to "make sense of existence," as I have expressed it, is just the beginning of wish-fantasy, a desperate subterfuge to conceal the unbearable truth that existence is indeed absurd. This may be the case. But at least let us give the matter a hearing before we make up our minds to dismiss it. For it cannot be denied that this quest for a sense to existence is so universal as to be a constituent element in existence itself; yet this quest is at the root of religion and faith.

12. THE INDIVIDUAL AND SOCIETY

There is still another polarity in human existence, but as it is of a different order from those considered so far, it deserves a separate and more extended treatment. In all human existence there is both an *individual* and a *social* pole, and these are sometimes in acute tension.

No human being exists in isolation. We have already noted that man exists in a world, and the world is constituted by persons as well as things. Any human existence constitutes itself and realizes its possibilities only in interaction with other human existents. According to Ludwig Feuerbach, "where there is no 'thou' there is no 'I' " [6]—an insight which has been more fully developed in Martin Buber's philosophy of interpersonal relations. Sociality then is intrinsic to human existence; it is not just something that gets added on when a number of individuals come together, as was supposed in, for instance, the old social contract theories. The existent emerges as already a social being.

Feuerbach mentioned sexuality as one of the fundamental characteristics of human existence making it essentially a social existence. For in respect of his or her body, every human being is incomplete as far as the reproductive function is concerned, and needs a partner of the opposite sex. Of course, as Feuerbach was well aware, sex is much more than just

---

[6] *The Essence of Christianity*, p. 92.

a physical or biological difference. Sexuality permeates every area of human existence, and this means that sociality does so too.

Language is another basic human characteristic; indeed, it is the capacity for language that most decisively distinguishes mankind from the animals. But there are no private languages, for one function of language is to communicate. Thus, if to use language is essential to humanity, and if any language is shared by a number of interlocutors, then we have another evidence of the essentially social character of man.

Perhaps even at the simplest stages of economic life, as in the hunting of animals, the cooperation of a group of people was necessary. Certainly, as soon as economic life begins to develop any complexity, it leads to an increasingly close interdependence among human beings, and to the paradox that as their functions become more and more differentiated their unity also is heightened for they cannot do without one another. Modern technological developments have brought the interdependence of all human beings and groups of human beings to a level hitherto unprecedented.

But the fact that sociality is intrinsic to human existence does not mean that an ideal society or a genuine community grows up automatically. There is another side to the human existent, and this other side is just as fundamental. Every existence is unique; it is someone's own, unrepeatable and irreplaceable. Each human being looks out on the world from the point of view of a particular ego and constitutes, as it were, a microcosm. There is a privacy about each existence which cannot be quite penetrated even by the most sympathetic friend or companion, and which more often than not is veiled or perhaps even misunderstood. Within limits, at least, the privacy and autonomy of the individual deserve to be respected, and his uniqueness recognized and protected.

But this polarity, like the others we have considered, sets up a tension that threatens to become destructive. Belonging in an equally primordial way to the very structure of existence is the need for community and an inescapable interdependence, together with the privacy and separateness of each existent, who in some regards cannot be other than lonely and isolated. In Reinhold Niebuhr's words, "the community is the frustration as well as the realization of individual life." [7] If individuals tend to disrupt community by self-seeking, societies tend to oppress individuals through collective egoism and institutional injustice.

When we ask about "making sense" of human existence, "fulfilling" its

---

[7] *The Nature and Destiny of Man*, vol. II, p. 320.

potentialities, seeking "wholeness" or even "salvation," we must keep in mind the problem posed by the polarity of the individual and the social, as well as the other polarities. But in saying that this one is of a different order from the others, I was meaning that the problems that arise for theology have always to be seen on two levels, the individual and the social. There can be no wholeness for individuals apart from their fellows and apart from supportive social structures; but there can be no healthy society without the integrity of its members. Sometimes religious thinkers have emphasized the individual, sometimes society. Kierkegaard, for instance, in reaction against a false collectivism, made faith and salvation a matter for individual decision. In our own time, conscious as we are of the interdependence of mankind, we are more concerned with the social implications of faith.

The relation of the individual to the social is a complex one. Some broad parallels can be established. Existence and transcendence in the individual correspond roughly to history and progress in society. The attainment of selfhood in the individual is related to the achievement of authentic community in society. Even the death of the individual has a parallel in those apocalyptic situations in which a society or even all mankind faces the possibility of its end. But the society is always more than the sum of its members and the parallels are not simple.

It is interesting to note that in the Bible the boundaries of individual existence are sometimes blurred, so that it is hard to tell whether an individual or a community is intended. Abraham, the first man of faith, appears sometimes to be clearly delineated as an individual, but sometimes the name seems to denote a community, and in a sense he is both. In the New Testament, Christ is not always to be simply identified with the individual, Jesus of Nazareth. He merges into the community and the history which he initiated, and, as St. Augustine said, "the head and body is one Christ." [8]

Sometimes in this book we shall be thinking primarily of individual existence, sometimes of social existence, sometimes of both together, but finally neither aspect can be ignored.

13. THE DISORDER OF EXISTENCE

So far the description of human existence has presented man's possible ways of being rather than his actual condition. We have seen the polarities of existence, and even this view of the matter has suggested the possibility

[8] *De Trinitate,* IV, 9.

that this existence may be an absurdity of which it is impossible to make sense. But what do we find when we turn our attention to the actual instances of existing that present themselves for inspection?

A question like this can, of course, be answered only by a broad empirical generalization, and such generalizations can always be challenged. Yet perhaps no one would deny that when we do look at actual human existing, we perceive a massive disorder in existence, a pathology that seems to extend all through existence, whether we consider the community or the individual, and that stultifies it. Because of this prevalent disorder, the potentialities of existence are not actualized as they might be, but are lost or stunted or distorted. If, as has been claimed above, selfhood is disclosed to us not only as it has actually come about but also in its authentic potentiality, then we cannnot fail to be aware of the gulf separating the two, both in ourselves and in the human race generally. This disclosure, as we have seen, belongs peculiarly to conscience as a kind of synoptic self-knowing.

The disorder of human existence can be defined more precisely as *imbalance*, and in calling it "pathological" I have implicitly compared it to imbalances in the physical organism. But here we are thinking of existential imbalance. The tension between the polar opposites in existence is not maintained, but one overcomes the other and pulls it out of place, so to speak, so that the whole structure is thrown out of joint. The possibilities for such distortion are presumably infinite. In general, however, we can perceive two main directions in which the imbalance takes place, though both may well be present together in a single person or in a single society, in different regards or alternating with each other. On the one hand are such disorders, individual or social, as pride, tyranny, angelism, utopianism, with all their variations and intermixings. Individualism belongs here too. These disorders arise from reluctance or refusal to give full acceptance and acknowledgment to the facticity, finitude, and, generally, the limitation of human existence, and also from the desire to have a superhuman or godlike existence, free from the restraints that are inseparable from a genuinely human life. Of course, although men may try to get away from the limitations of existence, they cannot escape them, and so their attempted flight results in some such distortion as those that have been mentioned. On the other hand, there are disorders such as sensual indulgence, insensitivity to others, despair, and the irresponsibility of collectivism. These disorders represent the retreat from possibility, decision-making, responsibility, individual liability and even from rationality. They move in the direction of a subhuman mode of being, that of the animal which is free from care and lives in and for its present. Of course, here again man cannot really relinquish the being that is his own; he cannot attain pure irresponsibility or animality or rid himself of care, but he distorts his being in the attempt. The two kinds of disorder are found side by side in the same society or even in the same individuals, but by and large the second kind is characteristic of the masses while the first reaches its pitch in the relatively few who become intoxicated and bewitched with the sense of their own power. This first kind of disorder, though no doubt present to some extent among all kinds of people, has shown its most frightening manifestations in the great tyrants of history, and in them perhaps we see existence at its most disordered. Hence it is understandable that interpreters of man from St. Augustine to Reinhold Niebuhr should have seen in pride the typical perversion of human life.

While perhaps few would deny that there is indeed this massive and manifold disorder of human existence, there would probably be considerable debate as to the extent to which the perversion of existence prevails. Once again, the picture is ambiguous. Calvin, as is well known, taught a doctrine of total depravity, and bluntly characterized "everything proceeding from the corrupt nature of man damnable." [9] This point of view seems to conflict with ordinary experience, for surely anyone who is not a misanthrope will acknowledge that many things proceeding from the "natural man" are not in the slightest degree "damnable": that the view is also unsound theologically will be shown in due course. Yet although Calvin exaggerates the disorder of human existence, such exaggeration may have had some excuse as against tendencies to underestimate the disorder in man's life and to take too facile a view of the matter and too optimistic a prospect of human capacities. Although we must reject as false the idea that human existence is *totally* disordered, we must acknowledge that the disorder runs pretty deep, and in acknowledging this, we are following not only the belief of the most thoughtful analysts of the human condition but the Christian belief about man from the New Testament on.

Less debatable than the question about the totality of the disorder of existence is that of its universality, understood in the sense of its horizontal spread. Every society acknowledges its injustices and imperfections, and every individual, when pressed, acknowledges his own disorder and his share in the wider disorder. Such an individual is thrown into a situation where disorder is already prevalent, and thus from the beginning he is

[9] *Institutes of the Christian Religion*, II, iii.

wrongly oriented, and whatever decisions he makes or policies he adopts are relative to the disordered situation. So we can assert that the disorder is universal in human existence.

Can something be said to define more closely the character of the disorder that afflicts our existence? It has already been described as an "imbalance," in terms of the polarities of existence, and perhaps this model of imbalance is the best available and, as we shall see, one that can be further developed in connection with the idea of selfhood. But other models are useful in lighting up aspects of the disorder. It can be described as "falling," and although this particular term has its origins in religion and myth, it has been brought into secular philosophy by Martin Heidegger [10] and has an obvious usefulness. It suggests failure to attain, falling short of actualization, or falling away from an authentic possibility, without of course implying that one had first arrived there, and then only subsequently fallen away. Another model is that of "alienation," also used by Heidegger and by many other writers. The description of the various modes of imbalance showed these as a turning away from one or other of the poles of human existence, so that this imbalance becomes an alienation within existence itself. The basic alienation is really from oneself, in the full range of one's possibility and facticity. This in turn leads to alienation from other existents, for, as we have seen, individualism at one extreme and collectivism at the other take the place of authentic community. Is it not the case, however, that there is still a third level of alienation, a deeper level where one feels alienated from the whole scheme of things? Perhaps this could be called "lostness." It is the sense of being cut off not only from one's own true being or from the being of others, but from all being, so that one has no "place" in the world. This is surely the deepest despair that can arise out of the disorder of existence.

At this point it is appropriate to introduce the word "sin." It will be remembered that one part of the purpose of this philosophical theology is to describe the situations in which theological or religious words and assertions have their meaning. So far we have been discussing the human condition in secular terms. "Sin" is a religious term, and it has connotations that differentiate it from notions like "guilt" or "wrongdoing," though presumably "sin" includes these notions. What is distinctive in sin, however, is the last point to which we came in our discussion of models of human disorder—the notion of "lostness," of being alienated not only

[10] *Being and Time*, p. 175.

from oneself and from other existents but, at a still deeper level, from all being. The religious man would say that this lostness is separation from God, but until we can study the word "God" more closely, this assertion can be left aside. For the meantime, in accordance with the method of a philosophical theology that proceeds descriptively, we can only ask whether the situation described is one that can be recognized as typical of our human existing in the world. That sin can be understood as "separation" or "missing the mark" or "falling away" in respect of one's relation to oneself or to one's neighbor would perhaps be universally conceded. That it is understood as alienation at a still deeper level is what is asserted in the distinctively religious connotation of the word, and I have tried to show that this religious connotation is firmly grounded in a common and widely recognizable element in man's awareness of his own existence in the world, or, more briefly, in his self-understanding. There is of course much that has still to be unfolded and examined before this as yet vague awareness of being cut off at the deepest level can be properly evaluated.

In the meantime, however, it would seem that our discussion of the disorder in human existence has led us still further in the direction of despairing about man and concluding that his existence cannot make sense. Already when we had taken note of the polarities and tensions that enter into the constitution of existence, we noted the possibilities for frustration and the frankly despairing views of some philosophers. Now that we have seen how, in actual existing, frustration and distortion do come about and how there is universal disorder, imbalance, falling, alienation, or however it may appear to us, have we not already reached the stage at which we must simply say that it is hopeless to try to make sense of this strange kind of being that we call "existence" and that we know in the phenomenon of man? At least, we have seen enough to show us that Sartre and those who think like him are far nearer to a realistic appraisal of the human condition than those complacent humanists who believe that with more science and education, better social conditions and the like, the ills of humanity can be cured and a fuller existence enjoyed. These men just have not faced the radical character of existential tension and disorder, and this becomes increasingly clear as the problems of the affluent society show themselves to be just as intractable as those of the impoverished society. Our analysis has rather shown that because of the universality and solidarity of human disorder, there is within the human situation no remedy to hand that will be adequate to overcome the problems of that situation.

We can say then that the alternatives confronting us have been sharpened. Either we must go along with Sartre and company, and acknowledge that life is indeed a useless passion, so that the best we can hope for is to reduce its oppressiveness at one point or another, to patch up the situation here and there, without any hope or possibility of really overcoming the absurdity and frustration that belong intrinsically to human existence, as thrown possibility; [11] or, if we are seeking to make sense of life and to bring order into existence so that its potentialities can come to fulfillment, we have frankly to acknowledge that we must look for support beyond humanity itself, pervaded as this is with disorder. To put the disjunction in another way: either we acknowledge the absurdity of a situation in which we find ourselves responsible for an existence which we lack the capacity to master, and have just to make the best of a bad job; or else we look for a further dimension in the situation, a depth beyond both man and nature that is open to us in such a way that it can make sense of our finite existence by supporting it and bringing order and fulfillment into it. We see then that the quest for meaning and sense in existence, for order and fulfillment, now takes on a more definitely religious character. Whether there is any support from beyond man such as would make sense of his existence and overcome its frustrations, we cannot yet say. But at least we can see that the idea itself is not an empty one. Our descriptive analysis of the human situation has provided a frame of reference within which this idea can be located, that is to say, assigned its meaning. The term in the religious vocabulary which denotes the idea described is "grace," so it is permissible for us now to introduce this word, in addition to "sin" which appeared earlier in the section.

Of course, in the famous words of St. Thomas, "grace does not abolish nature but perfects it." [12] This point has to be stressed lest anyone should get the mistaken idea that we are saying that man's quest for grace (which is finally identical with the quest for God) arises only from his lack, disorder, and frustration. The condition of his being conscious of any lack is that he already seeks a fulfillment. We have already seen that in the human being anxiety and hope are intertwined. The quest for grace is ultimately rooted in the openness of human existence or the transcendence of the human spirit toward a whither that attracts. All this will become clearer in the section which follows.

[11] For the use of the word "thrown" in this and similar expressions, see my book *An Existentialist Theology*, p. 83.
[12] *Summa Theologiae*, Ia, I, 8.

14. SELFHOOD AND FAITH

I have talked about "making sense" of human existence, bringing "order" into it, "overcoming" its frustrations, "fulfilling" its potentialities. These somewhat mixed expressions need to be examined. Can we say more definitely what is meant by them? Can we see what conditions would have to be fulfilled if this "making sense," "bringing order" and the like were to come about? Can we show how this leads into a religious interpretation of life?

Our discussion will turn on the notion of "selfhood." Existence fulfills itself in selfhood. An authentic self is a unitary, stable, and relatively abiding structure in which the polarities of existence are held in balance and its potentialities are brought to fulfillment. The expression "self" should not mislead us into thinking of the solitary individual, for authentic selfhood is possible only in a community of selves, and we have seen already that among the polarities to be held in tension are community and individuality. Although we talk about the self, this is not to be understood in an individualistic way.

How then is this structure of the self constituted? We may begin by recalling that in Greek philosophy there were various theories about the self or soul, and that Plato and Aristotle present us with an interesting contrast. Plato may be taken as an exponent of the "substantial" soul. On this view, the soul is regarded as capable of existing apart from the body. In Plato's teaching, the soul is represented as having existed prior to its union with the body, and as continuing to exist after the dissolution of the body. It might, moreover, become conjoined with many bodies one after the other. Aristotle, on the other hand, thinks of the soul as the "form" of the body, that is to say, as the proper functioning of a bodily existence in the world. Though he seems to have believed that reason, the highest part of the soul, could continue in existence apart from the body, the soul as a whole (the whole range of living and personal being) was thought to be inseparable from the body, so that man was conceived as a psychosomatic unity.

For most of its history, Christian theology has tended to follow the Platonic doctrine. The soul has been conceived as a substance, and this has been considered as guaranteeing the unity, stability, and abidingness (or even immortality) of the self. For just as we see a rock persisting through time as the same rock, so it was supposed we must posit a substantial self (though admittedly an immaterial substantial self) as the bearer of personal existence. Such a self or soul gets "implanted" in the body, probably at conception, and remains united with the body until death, after which, because of its substantial character, it can continue in existence apart from the body.

But this whole doctrine of a substantial soul has, like the natural theology considered earlier, been subjected to destructive criticism in modern philosophy. The conception of a disembodied soul or self is very difficult, since it is precisely through being embodied that we are in a world and with other selves, and as we have already noted, there can be no selfhood apart from a world and other selves. Moreover, on the empirical level, we never have experience of souls apart from bodies and we see plainly from the effects of injuries, drugs, and the like how closely linked are the mental and physical sides of man's being. By a "person," we do not mean an invisible, intangible and immaterial soul-substance, but always an embodied self in the world. Not only is no purpose served by imagining a ghostly soul "inhabiting" the body, but the very idea is superfluous and confusing.

In any case, as some philosophers have pointed out, the attempt to understand the self as substance is really an example of reductionist naturalism at its most abstract. The model or paradigm underlying the notion of substance is that of the solid enduring thing, like the rock cited above as an illustration. But thinghood cannot be an enlightening model for selfhood. What is distinctive in selfhood is personal being, and we cannot hope to get a proper conception of selfhood in terms of subpersonal being, indeed of inanimate being, although this is precisely what we are trying to do when we seek to explicate the self as substance. This is to reify the self, to treat it as a thing, however refined that thing may be thought to be. This is at bottom a materialistic understanding of selfhood that cannot do justice to it. The self, as personal existence, has a dynamism, a complexity, a diversity-in-unity, that can never be expressed in terms of inert thinghood, even if we refine this conception as far as we can and dignify it with the name of "substantiality."

The overthrow of the idea of substantial selfhood has been a somewhat traumatic experience for theologians, for many of them seem to have thought that this philosophical idea was an essential presupposition of certain Christian doctrines. On the other hand, the blow has been somewhat softened by the revival of biblical theology and its rediscovery of the fact that the Bible does not seem to work much with the idea of a substantial soul that may be either conjoined with or separated from the body, but thinks rather of man as a psychosomatic unity—as is clear, for instance, from the doctrine of the resurrection of the body.

Actually the decline of the idea of a substantial soul does not mean that we have to conclude that the soul is simply an epiphenomenon of the material body, or that it is, as Hume supposed, simply a concatenation of experiences. We can look again at the doctrine which Aristotle offered as an alternative to the Platonic one, and see whether the notion of the soul as the form of the body can be developed in such a way as to give us a more adequate conception of selfhood. And right away, we can discern one advantage in the Aristotelian over the Platonic point of view. Whereas the idea of a substantial self that gets inserted or implanted into the body at the beginning of life suggests something ready-made that has only to grow as, let us say, the organs of the body do, the notion of the self as form suggests much better the thought that the self is not given ready-made but has to be made in the course of existence, and that indeed authentic selfhood may never be attained at all. What is given at the outset is not a fixed entity but a potentiality for becoming a self.

The model for such an understanding of the self is not substantiality or thinghood but rather temporality. It is temporality, with its three dimensions of past, present, and future that makes the kind of being called "existence" possible. We have already seen that basic to the constitution of existence are possibility (the openness of the future) and facticity (the heritage of what has been), and that the existent stands in the tension between these, which is the present. The disorder or imbalance of existence can be understood as at bottom an imbalance among the temporal dimensions; for instance, of the disorders mentioned in an earlier analysis,[13] those such as angelism, utopianism, and the sins of pride generally, arise from a dwelling in the future that fails to relate to the actual situation inherited from the past, while the sins of irresponsibility dwell in the past, shunning the openness and risk of the future.

What constitutes existence or personal being is a peculiar and complex temporal nexus in which the three dimensions of past, present, and future are brought into a unity. Man differs from a thing or even from an animal in so far as he is not only aware of the present but remembers the past and anticipates the future. The basically temporal structure of existence was clearly understood by St. Augustine, who says of the mind that "it both expects and considers and remembers" and that "that which it expects, through that which it considers, may pass into that which it remembers." [14] In an existence that is scattered and disrupted, the existent has

---

[13] See above, pp. 69–70.
[14] *Confessions*, XI, xxviii.

cut himself off from one or other of the temporal dimensions of existence, and his existence declines toward the kind of being that belongs to things or animals, though of course he can never lose himself, as it were, in an entirely dehumanized way of being. On the other hand, in an existence that is fulfilling its potentialities, the three dimensions are held together in unity. Their balance and tension are maintained. This is the "moment" of which existentialist philosophers from Kierkegaard to Heidegger have written, the authentic present that does not shut out either past or future but, through its openness to both, forges them into a unity.

Authentic selfhood implies the attaining of a unified existence, in which potentialities are actualized in an orderly manner and there are no loose ends or alienated areas. The attaining of selfhood is therefore a matter of degree. It is clear however that this selfhood can never be something ready-made, and clear also that its unity is quite different from that of a thing. A thing endures through time and is the same thing, and moreover what it is now is both determined by what it has been and is determinant for what it will be. But the unity through time that belongs to a thing is one in which past, present, and future are only externally and causally related, and this is quite different from that intimate and intrinsic relationship of the three dimensions of temporality when these are gathered up into the moment of personal existence.

Can we see more clearly what is this unity that belongs to authentic selfhood? It might perhaps be thought of as being like the unity of perspective in painting, a unity in which the various strands of existence in its aspects both of possibility and facticity converge upon a point so that the picture makes sense. The conditions that this kind of unity may be brought into existence and authentic selfhood attained would seem to be that there should be both *commitment* and *acceptance*. Commitment is the prospective view of this unity, for it has to do with the future, with the possibilities of existence. A committed existence is one that has in view some master possibility. In consistently directing itself on this master possibility, the other possibilities of life are subordinated to it and the movement is toward unified selfhood. The absence of such a commitment results in an existence that jumps from one immediate possibility to the next, an existence that may be very much at the mercy of chance circumstances or changing desires and that has only the lowest degree of selfhood and unity. But acceptance is just as necessary as commitment. Acceptance is the retrospective view of the self's unity, for it has to do with what has been, with the situation that already obtains and in which we find ourselves. If anything like unified selfhood is to be reached, the facticity of the situation has to be accepted in its entirety, with no loose ends rejected. Only if there is this frank and total acceptance can the commitment in turn be a realistic one. For not just any commitment can lead to unified selfhood. A fantastic commitment that was not related to an acceptance of the factical situation could be utterly disruptive.

What has to be taken into consideration if there is to be anything like a complete acceptance of the factical situation of human existence is death. For it is death that more than anything else brings before us the radical finitude of our existence, and it is in the light of this that every possibility must be evaluated. But is this not equivalent to saying that death nullifies everything? If death, as the ending of existence, is to be given a central place in the understanding of existence, are not all the strivings and aspirations of existence stultified? We may recall that when death was briefly mentioned earlier [15] as the last and most formidable obstacle in the way of making sense of human existence, it was said that in spite of its seemingly utter negativity, even death might turn out to have an ambiguous character. This is indeed the case, for death can have a positive, or affirmative, role in existence. Even on the level of everyday thinking and judging, death is recognized to have the potentiality for becoming an achievement, where it is willingly accepted for some cause greater than the individual's own well-being; and in exceptional cases, the manner of a person's death can even be understood as in some measure redeeming the blameworthy actions of his life.

The positive potentialities in death have long been recognized, but they are expounded with especial insight, and in a philosophical language, by Heidegger.[16] Death appears in his analysis as both the most significant element in the factical heritage of every existent and also as the horizon that closes off the future, so that all our possibilities can be seen as set out in front of death. Death becomes the *eschaton*, and as such it brings into existence a responsibility and seriousness that it could scarcely have otherwise. Death, in one sense destructive, is in another sense creative of unified, responsible selfhood, the concerns of which become ordered in the face of the end. Furthermore, death also becomes a criterion for judging our concerns. Death exposes the superficiality and triviality of many of the ambitions and aspirations on which men spend their energies. What Heidegger calls "everyday" existence is frequently the escape from respon-

[15] See above, p. 64.
[16] *Being and Time*, p. 236ff.

sibility, the covering up of death and finitude, the jumping from one immediate concern to the next without any thought that our existence, as bounded, has the potentiality for some measure of unity and wholeness. Often enough too it is the quest for illusory security. Our consideration of the polarities of human existence has already made it clear that to make, let us say, sensual pleasure or self-aggrandizement the leading concern of one's existence would be to distort that existence, but the fact of death makes clear in a more dramatic fashion the transient and nugatory character of the achievements of the man who does not take into account the full range of possibility and facticity.

These remarks suggest something further, namely, that selfhood is attained only in so far as the existent is prepared to look beyond the limits of his own self for the master concern that can create such a stable and unified self. He must be prepared to accept the factical aspects of his existence, his finitude, transience, and mortality, and take these up into the potentiality which he projects for himself into the future. This means in effect that by looking beyond himself or, as we may say, dying to himself, he becomes himself. This is the paradox well known to the religions, and expressed in such sayings as that one must "die to live" and that "whoever would save his life will lose it; and whoever loses his life for my sake and the gospel's will save it." [17] The contrast between the genuine fulfillment of selfhood attained by looking beyond the self and the illusory fulfillments sought within the narrow limits of self-regarding concern is well expressed in the question: "What does a man gain by winning the whole world at the cost of his true self ($\tau\grave{\eta}\nu$ $\psi\upsilon\chi\grave{\eta}\nu$ $\alpha\grave{\upsilon}\tau\hat{o}\hat{\upsilon}$)?" [18]

But while these considerations do let us see that death can be understood in ways that are positive and creative, they do not in the slightest degree remove the negativity of death or the ambiguity of the phenomenon. If death shows up the futility of so many of our concerns, does it not stultify them all? Are we not driven to a kind of nihilism in which every human aspiration is devalued so that, as Sartre goes so far as to suggest, the life of the solitary drunkard and that of the great statesman are equally pointless? [19] This assertion of the absurdity of human existence helps us to understand by way of contrast what the religious attitude in face of the situation is. It involves no less radical an acceptance of the facticity of existence than does Sartre's view, and just as much as he, does it see the gulf between human resources (the heritage that is factically

[17] Mark 8:35.
[18] Mark 8:36. (N.E.B.)
[19] *Being and Nothingness*, p. 627.

given) and the demands to which we are responsible (the potentialities that are disclosed). It seeks sense in this situation, and it sees that the condition that there is sense in it is that the being which we are given (the factical pole of existence) is of a piece with the being to which we are summoned (the pole of possibility); that these are not accidentally conjoined or destined to be in perpetual and frustrating conflict with each other, but that they are both rooted in the wider context of being within which man has his being. Human existence can make sense if this wider being supports and supplements the meager heritage of our finite being as we strive to fulfill the potentialities of our being. To adapt words of St. Augustine, human existence makes sense if being grants what it commands, that is to say, if there are resources beyond our human resources to help us fulfill the claims that our very existence lays upon us.

The attitude described is what the religious man calls "faith." It is obvious that faith is not a mere belief but an existential attitude. We have already seen that this attitude includes acceptance and commitment, but what makes it a distinctively religious faith is its reference to what we have called so far only the "wider being" in the context of which man has his own being. It is then faith in being. Such faith obviously implies a belief, but this belief is clearly no speculative or academic world view but a belief arising out of an existential attitude, a self-understanding that is born in acceptance and commitment. The difference between the attitude of religious faith and the attitude of the man without it is also clear. Religious faith, as faith in being, looks to the wider being within which our existence is set for support; it discovers a meaning for existence that is already given with existence: the alternative attitude looks for no support from beyond man, who must rely on his own resources, and who must himself create for his life any meaning that it can have.

It has already been said however that human existence considered in isolation does not make sense and that the most acute atheistic philosophers are consciously philosophers of despair. This, I believe, is fundamentally true, but I do not wish to give the impression that it must be all or nothing. Life is not so simple as to present us with a plain choice of black or white. Even the philosopher who preaches despair does not usually shoot himself but finds some limited areas of "engagement," as he may call it. Many people without religious faith take a far more optimistic view of human existence than does Sartre, though it must frankly be said that probably many or most of them do not face the grimmer aspects of existence with the same candor as we find in Sartre. The man of faith, for his part, is not to be thought of as complacently anchored by his faith, for any faith worthy of the name will be subject to testing, and will not be a permanent possession but an attitude that has to be continually renewed.

Neither the man of faith nor the man of unfaith (if we may use the expression) has certitude. This is part of our finitude. We are thrown into a world and so we see it only from within. If we were to know with certitude the why and wherefore of our existence, whether we belong within some meaningful pattern or are absurd items flung up in a meaningless process, we would have to step outside of our world and see the whole range of being. But this is impossible, though people have tried to do it by constructing what they supposed to be rationally demonstrable and objectively valid metaphysical systems. But while we cannot know with certitude the answers to the enigma of human existence, we cannot help coming to some decision about how we are going to understand ourselves, for the very fact that we have to exist, to adopt policies of action, to pursue goals, and to choose standards of value means that implicitly we have already chosen to understand ourselves in one way or another. The limiting cases would seem to be what we have called religious faith at the one extreme and a Sartrean acceptance of absurdity at the other. Perhaps the majority of mankind find themselves somewhere between, drawn now toward the one pole, now toward the other.

But if there is no certitude, then is it just a toss-up, so to speak, which attitude one adopts? It is true that plenty has been said about a reasonable faith, but plenty has also been said about the ambiguity of our existence in the world. Is faith then just a leap in the dark?

Two replies may be made to this. The first is that at least it has been shown that the attitude of faith arises from the very structures of human existence itself. It is not a luxury but arises from our innate quest for selfhood and for a meaningful existence. No conclusive weight attaches to this point, but it is worth reminding ourselves that faith is not some strained perversion of our nature but an attitude that really does belong with the kind of existence that is ours.

Nowadays there are some who would challenge this assertion. They would say that even if it were once true that man had within himself the needs that predisposed him toward a religious faith, this is true no longer. Contemporary man has outgrown the need for what we have called "faith in being," and has placed his faith rather in his own skills and techniques. He has discovered that his problems are best solved through his own efforts, and he is content to confine his attention to the everyday world. There he constructs his own values, meanings, social structure, economic system, and so on, and concerns himself no longer with that wider being within which his own being is set.

There is, of course, a large measure of truth in this. In the course of what may be called the "education of the human race," childish beliefs in the supernatural have been left behind, and the kind of "faith" that really looked for a shortcut to problem-solving has been left behind too. But it does not follow—as Auguste Comte thought—that now we must turn to positivism, man must deem himself autonomous, and "faith in being" be replaced by faith in humanity. Actually, religious faith never was so puerile as its critics suggest, and certainly biblical faith was never like that. Faith in being, understood as commitment and acceptance, or as the submission of the human existent to the grace and judgment of being, has its own maturity, and we have claimed that some such faith is demanded by the structure of any finite human existence, ancient or modern, with its tensions, disorders, alienations, and yet with its questing for selfhood, wholeness, and meaning.

How do we settle the dispute between the claim that the quest for a religious faith arises out of the way our existence is constituted with the counterclaim that contemporary man has no such need? Is it just a case of opposing one generalization to another, or are different people differently constituted? Obviously, no proof can be offered. The only procedure seems to be the one that has been followed in this chapter: we describe the human existence known to us as carefully as we can, and we ask others to look at the description and see if they too recognize it as a true picture of the existence that is ours. We would perhaps draw attention especially to such critical matters as the disorder of human existence, and to that awareness of "lostness" which seems to alienate us from being. We might hope that this kind of procedure would show the inadequacy of taking man as self-sufficient, and would open up those dimensions of our being that lead us toward faith in a transhuman reality.

I think also that one would want to challenge more directly the belief that man "come of age" must be considered autonomous and independent. Insistence on one's autonomy is more typically the mark of adolescence than of maturity. Was Schleiermacher immature when he talked of "absolute dependence," or was he perhaps more sophisticated than the "cultured despisers of religion" to whom he addressed himself? Are Tillich, Bultmann, Niebuhr, and Barth to be classed as "immature" because, in various ways, they have all opposed the view that man is autonomous and have tried to interpret his life in terms of grace? I think one must concede that words like "dependence" may be too one-sided, and this book will talk rather in terms of man's cooperation with being, since this better recognizes our genuine responsibility. But it will be made clear enough that man's position is a decidedly subordinate one, and his effective co-working is made possible by grace. After all, as Karl Heim reminded us, if we were to think of the millions of years of the earth's history as compressed within twenty-four hours, then we would have to say that man had appeared on the scene at twenty-two seconds before midnight! [20] This surely makes him a somewhat junior partner in the enterprise.

This excursus on the autonomy of man arose in the course of a reply to the question whether faith is just a leap in the dark, and we had promised two replies. The second one is that so far we have been considering only the roots of the *quest* for a religious answer to the enigma of human existence, and we have been doing this in a very formal way. This is entirely in line with the procedure laid down for this style of philosophical theology. But now the time has come to pay more attention to the content of religious faith. We have spoken somewhat vaguely of "faith in being," and it is true that the words "grace" and "judgment" have been introduced to indicate the support and the demand which man's existence may have from the wider being in which it is set. But all this has had, of necessity, a somewhat artificial and *a priori* character about it. The religious man does indeed recognize the quest for grace that is rooted in his very being and that may lead him into the attitude of faith, but he certainly does not think of himself as groping his way along a dark road on which everything is shadowy and ambiguous, so that at the end he has either to leap into the dark or stay where he is, with the choice an arbitrary one. Moreover, there is a dialectic in this quest, which becomes sometimes a flight from being, in the face of the judgment and demand that are inseparable from grace. So the religious man, or the man of faith, speaks not so much of his quest as of the object of this quest meeting him; or, better still, that he becomes the object of a search directed toward him; that the initiative comes from beyond himself, and that faith, while indeed it has roots within himself, is established only when he is grasped, as it were, by that for which he was dimly and ignorantly seeking.

So now we have to push our inquiry further back, to the very sources of religious faith. We have to describe the experience in which man is touched or addressed by the gracious and judging presence, and in which he opts for faith rather than unfaith.

[20] *Christian Faith and Natural Science*, p. 11.

4 | Revelation

15. A GENERAL DESCRIPTION OF REVELATION

We have now to consider more carefully what can be meant by the claim of the religious man that his faith is made possible by the initiative of that toward which his faith is directed; or, to put the same point differently, that his *quest* for the sense of existence is met by the *gift* of a sense for existence. He experiences this initiative from beyond himself in various ways. In so far as it supports and strengthens his existence and helps to overcome its fragmentariness and impotence, he calls the gift that comes to him "grace." In so far as it lays claim on him and exposes the distortions of his existence, it may be called "judgment." In so far as it brings him a new understanding both of himself and of the wider being within which he has his being (for the understanding of these is correlative), then it may be called "revelation." The word "revelation" points therefore especially to the cognitive element in the experience.

Critics of religion and of theology have frequently attacked the notion of revelation. As Abraham Heschel has pointed out, resistance to the notion of revelation has had more than one motivation, and he mentions especially two conceptions that have militated against it: "One maintained that man was too great to be in need of divine guidance, and the other maintained that man was too small to be worthy of divine guidance. The first conception came from social science, and the second from natural science." [1] Confidence in man, born of the success of the scientific method, and the naturalistic view of man, resulting from the application of the same method, seem to constitute a paradox, but they certainly combine to make anything like revelation improbable.

It looks as if the religious man, having no rationally defensible grounds

[1] *God in Search of Man*, p. 169.

84

for his faith, appeals to some private source of knowledge; but since such private knowledge cannot be tested by established logical procedures, it must be dismissed as illusory. Critics of the idea of revelation can point to the stubborn way in which theologians have defended alleged truths of revelation, as, for instance, the assertion that the earth does not move, and they argue that this belief in revelation has been a hindrance to the advance of genuine knowledge, which is not given but has to be won by strenuous efforts of thought.

Recently some theologians too have become critical of the high place assigned to revelation. They suggest that the notion has been exaggerated, that there is little mention of it in the Bible, that it suggests a far clearer kind of knowing than the religious man actually has, and that it exalts the cognitive aspect of religion above the practical.[2]

There is some substance in all of these criticisms of revelation. Never again, we must hope, will theologians claim that revelation gives them a shortcut to the answers to problems which must properly be settled through the patient researches of the scientists. We must also hope that religion will not misunderstand itself through an excessive stress on the notions of right belief and correct dogma, as it has sometimes done, but will remain aware of its involvement in the practical issues of life. Faith is primarily an existential attitude, and the convictions that arise out of it defy precise formulation.

However, while these points may be conceded, this does not mean that revelation is to be thrown out or its significance minimized. If its role has sometimes been exaggerated and distorted, it nevertheless retains an important place. Religion is not just a practical matter, and theology, as the attempt to elucidate intellectually the content of faith, has its own special interest in those factors that belong to the cognitive side of religion. I have already asserted that revelation is "the primary source for theology" and "a basic category in theological thinking."[3] These assertions will be maintained and vindicated, but in order to do so, it will be necessary to offer a careful description of what is meant by revelation, the factors which it involves, the situation in which it takes place, the conditions that would have to be fulfilled for this kind of thing to happen, the kind of knowledge or understanding that might come by revelation, its scope, and limits.

Revelation suggests some kind of unveiling, whereby what has hitherto

[2] Cf. F. Gerald Downing, *Has Christianity a Revelation?*
[3] See above, p. 7.

been concealed from us is now opened up. This, however, would be true of all knowing. The Greeks thought of truth itself as ἀλήθεια, "unhidden-ness." We have attained truth when that which was concealed is made unhidden, brought out into the light. What is distinctive in the religious use of the word "revelation" is the thought that in this process, the initiative lies with that which is known. We do not bring it into the light or strip away what is concealing it, as we do in our researches into matters within the world, but rather that which is known comes into the light, or, better still, provides the light by which it is known and by which we in turn know ourselves. It is as if the familiar epistemological situation gets reversed.

Already we have explored the human side of the revelatory situation. We have taken note of the polarities and tensions of human existence, in which possibility and responsibility are conjoined with finitude and death. Out of this polarity is generated an anxiety (*Angst*) or fundamental malaise, a concern about existence itself with its potentialities and its precariousness. The quest for sense, coherence, a meaningful pattern, thus takes its rise from the very constitution of existence. The anxiety is heightened when, to the basic polarities of existence, there is added an awareness of its actual disorder and guilt. The quest for sense becomes also a quest for grace.

This anxiety is not a mere subjective emotion but a mode of awareness. But if we ask, Awareness of what? the answer must be a paradoxical one, Awareness of nothing! But here "awareness of nothing" does not mean just that there is no awareness at all. Perhaps one should say "awareness of nothingness" or "awareness of nullity." What is intended is the awareness of the precariousness of existence which at any time may lapse into nothing or is already lapsing into nothing. It may *cease* to be in death, and it *fails* to be in guilt. We become aware of a nullity that enters into the very way in which we are constituted. The mood of anxiety may bring more than this. The world too sinks to nothing, it gets stripped of the values and meanings that we normally assign to the things and events that belong within it, and it becomes indeterminate, characterized by the same kind of emptiness and nullity that we know in ourselves.

I do not believe that the kind of mood described is common. Indeed, we do our best to keep ourselves from falling into it, and we can learn as well from psychologists and anthropologists as from existentialist philosophers about the devices and illusions that we employ to tranquilize our fundamental anxiety in the face of our radical finitude and transience. Yet

I believe that the mood is universal in the sense that at one time or another it catches up with almost all of us.

This mood may be said to constitute our capacity for receiving revelation. It predisposes us to recognize the approach of holy being. In other words, I am asserting a continuity between the quest for sense and grace that arises out of man's existence, and the directionally opposite *quest for man* to which experiences of grace and revelation bear witness, a quest that is initiated outside of man and remains beyond his control. The continuity that leads from anxiety to the receiving of revealed truth was well seen by those Old Testament writers who declared the fear of the Lord to be the beginning of wisdom or knowledge.[4]

What is it then that confronts us and reveals itself when we have become aware of the nothingness of ourselves and our world? The answer is: Being. It is against the foil of nothing that for the first time our eyes are opened to the wonder of being, and this happens with the force of revelation. Being is all the time around us, but for the most part it does not get explicitly noticed. What we see are particular beings, the things and persons that are: only when these sink to nothing are we seized with the awareness of the being in virtue of which they are. This is not another being or a property of beings like their color or size or shape. It is different from any particular being or any property, yet we are aware of it as more beingful, so to speak, than anything else, for it is the condition that there may be anything whatsoever. It falls under none of our everyday categories, so that we do not grasp it conceptually. We may say, however, that we know it as presence and manifestation, and these notions will be developed later.

The religious experience of being, that is to say, the revelatory approach of being, is nowhere better described than in the classic analysis of Rudolf Otto.[5] In what he calls "creature-feeling" we can recognize what has been mentioned above as the mood of anxiety. This creature-feeling becomes awe in the presence of the holy. Otto's analysis is in terms of the *mysterium tremendum fascinans,* the mystery that is at once overwhelming and fascinating. The *mysterium* refers to the incomprehensible depth of the numinous presence, which does not fall under the ordinary categories of thought but is other than the familiar beings of the world. The *tremendum* stresses the otherness of holy being as over against the nullity and transience of our own limited being; it points to the transcendence

---

[4] Ps. 111:10; Prov. 1:7, 9:10.
[5] *The Idea of the Holy,* pp. 8–41.

of being. The *fascinans* points to what we have already called the "grace" of being which has unveiled itself so that we understand that it gives itself to us, that it is the source of our being and strengthens our being with its presence.

More will need to be said in due course about the meaning of this word "being" and how it is related to the key word of religious discourse, "God." Meanwhile, however, let it be said that the revelatory encounter with being, as it has been described here, is not, as has sometimes been claimed, "self-authenticating." It is indeed not too easy to know what this word means. In any case, it ought to be admitted that what we take to be this revelatory encounter or confrontation could be an illusion. Moreover, it should be noted also that some people have what has all the formal characters of a revelation of being, but experience being not as gracious but as alien and without any such content as the religious man ascribes to it.[6] The remarks that I have made on revelation, therefore, are simply intended as a description of what religious persons report. Because they experience being as gracious, they have faith in being, and thus such faith, as was pointed out before, is not just an arbitrary decision. But on the other hand, one cannot get behind the experience of the grace of being to know whether this is a valid experience or an illusory one. All that can be done is to offer a description of the experience, indeed, to trace it all the way from its sources in the way our human existence is constituted. We can only ask people to look at this situation as described, to compare it with what they know in themselves or their friends, to make some attempt at least to enter sympathetically into it, and then to decide. Actually, the scrutiny and analysis of this experience can be carried further, for instance, by comparing it with related types of experience, and this will be done in the later parts of the chapter. We need to test such an experience in every possible way, especially as its claims are so great. But in the long run, we shall still fall short of certitude. We cannot abolish faith to replace it by certitude, for our destiny as finite beings, seeing things from below up, so to speak, is that we have to commit ourselves in one way or another without conclusive proof. If there is an unclouded vision of being, it does not belong in our earthy existence.

Let me end this section by making three comments on the foregoing description of revelation.

1. It was called a "general" description, and its general and formal

---

[6] For an account of a non-religious revelation of being, see J.-P. Sartre, *La Nausée*.

character should be borne in mind. Any actual experience of revelation would be concrete, belonging to a particular person, at a particular place, in a particular situation, employing particular symbols. Karl Barth frequently insists on the particularity of God's self-revelation, telling us that the Bible does not permit us to set up the general thought of a being furnished with divine attributes but "concentrates our attention and thoughts upon one single point and what is to be known at that point." [7] This insistence on concreteness and particularity is acceptable, provided it is not arbitrarily restricted to the biblical revelation. The examples of revelation given in earlier parts of this book have been quite concrete—Moses at the burning bush, the theophanies of Poimandres and Krishna, the recognition of Jesus by the disciples as the Messiah. Let us remember then that one can hardly speak of a "general" revelation, though there is a universal possibility of revelation. But although revelation is always given in particular occasions of revelation, it is possible and indeed desirable to delineate the general structure of a revelatory happening, and this is what has been attempted here. Such a procedure may seem abstract and lifeless as compared with the concrete accounts of particular revelations, but it has to be done if philosophical theology is to grasp as clearly as possible what revelation is, and if the claims of revelation are to be evaluated. Our procedure, however, certainly does suppose that there may be many particular revelations, and is quite opposed to the notion of one exclusively particular revelation.

2. In the account of revelation given here, it is assumed that the person who receives the revelation sees and hears no more than any other person in the situation might see and hear. What is revealed is *not* another being, over and above those that can be perceived by anyone. Rather, one should say that the person who receives the revelation sees the same things *in a different way*. We might say that he sees them in depth, though this expression is in danger of becoming trivialized. Perhaps we should say then that he notices features of the situation that otherwise escape notice, as if he saw an extra dimension in it. In language which I hope to explain more fully later, we might say that he sees not only the particular beings (persons or things) that belong in the situation, but he becomes aware of the *being* that is *present* and *manifest* in, with, and through these particular beings.

3. In the description of revelation given above, I have talked in terms

---

[7] *Church Dogmatics*, vol. II/2, p. 52.

of a directly given revelation. This, however, is probably a relatively rare occurrence, and we must remember from an earlier discussion the distinction that was drawn between "classic" or "primordial" revelations on which communities of faith get founded, and the subsequent experience of the community in which the primordial revelation keeps coming alive, so to speak, in the ongoing life of the community so that the original disclosure of the holy is being continually renewed.[8] We may speak of "repetitive" revelation, and the sense of this adjective will be explained in the next section. For the moment, however, let us simply note that the general description of revelation given in this section is not meant to imply that every religious person has a direct revelation of being. For the great majority, it will be a case of reliving some classic revelation, but even such "repeating," if it is not just a conventional attachment to a religious community, will mean something like a first-hand participation in the pattern of awareness that we have tried to trace, from the sense of finitude to the sense of the presence of the holy.

16. REVELATION AND THE MODES OF THINKING AND KNOWING

Continuing our analysis of revelation, we must now turn to the task of trying to locate the revelatory experience in the area of man's general cognitive experience. It has been said that the revelatory experience is not self-authenticating and might be illusory. However, its trustworthiness would be supported if we found that it is not an experience utterly mysterious and isolated, and if we were able to find something like parallels and connections in our more mundane experience or in the accounts of knowing and thinking that we find in secular philosophers. It is true that there must be a uniqueness about revealed knowledge that sets a great difference between it and our everyday knowledge of relatively commonplace matters, and I do not wish to minimize this difference. Nevertheless, it would be a still greater error to think of revealed knowledge as completely unrelated to the more familiar modes of knowing. The philosophical theologian has a duty to try to show where this knowledge belongs within the entire field of knowledge. What is required is something like an epistemology of revelation, though the term "epistemology" is somewhat presumptuous for the limited treatment which the question receives here.

---

[8] See above, pp. 8–9.

I propose then to set out briefly a scheme or frame of reference in which we can locate the principal modes of thinking and knowing, and then ask whether we can find a place for revelation in this scheme. Readers will notice that the outlines of the scheme reflect the philosophy of Martin Heidegger, though there are considerable differences in detail and the scheme as here presented is much more explicit than one finds in Heidegger. Nevertheless, it is important to notice that this discussion of revelation can go on in terms drawn for the most part from secular philosophy, so that we are still adhering to the general procedures laid down earlier for philosophical theology.

The first level of thinking is the kind which Heidegger calls "calculative" thinking—sometimes, indeed, in his polemics against its dominance, he will hardly allow it to be called "thinking" at all. Nevertheless, this is probably the commonest mode of thinking and the one in which we are for the most part engaged in our everyday activities. Such thinking is in the subject-object pattern, for what we think about is an "object" to us, that is to say, it stands over against us and outside of us. Our thinking is directed toward handling, using, manipulating this object, and incorporating it within our instrumental "world." The most sophisticated development of such thinking is, of course, technology. In theoretical science, the elements of utility and concern are dimmed down so that the scientist approaches the attitude of the mere spectator; whether in fact one can ever reach the stage of pure beholding is doubtful, but in any case the objective character of that which we think about remains.

The knowledge corresponding to this kind of thinking is objective knowledge. In all such knowing, we transcend what is known. We *subject* it, in the sense of rising above it and, to some extent, mastering it. Even to have acquired some purely theoretical knowledge of natural phenomena is to have extended our control over the environment, if only in the sense that we are in a better position to predict the course of events. In the acquisition and extension of this kind of knowledge through calculative thinking, we are active and our objects are for the most part passive. Our activities are observing, experimenting, measuring, and also deducing, demonstrating, and showing connections.

This is not intended for a moment to be an exhaustive account of calculative thinking or all its possible ramifications, but it may be fairly claimed that enough has been said to mark out on our frame of reference a wide and easily recognizable style of knowing and thinking, and one possessing fairly definite characteristics.

SUBJECT/OBJECT (CALCULATIVE) OBJECTIVE KNOWLEDGE
SUBJECT / SUBJECT (PERSONAL) THINKING INTO.
PRIMORDIAL. (MEDITATE) KNOW SELF.
ESSENTIAL

A second level of thinking we may designate, in the most general way, as "existential" thinking. This kind of thinking is proper to existential or personal being. It does not aim, as calculative thinking does, at use or exploitation, though it may aim at well-being, either one's own or another's. This kind of thinking is also common in everyday existence. It does not take as its object what we think about, but rather recognizes what is thought about as another subject, having the same kind of being as the person who does the thinking. Most typically, then, this kind of thinking involves participation, a thinking into the existence of the other subject that is thought about, and this "thinking into" is possible because of the common kind of being on both sides. This kind of thinking can also become theoretical, where practical solicitude or interest has been dimmed down. Heidegger's own existential analytic is an illustration of this. It is a thinking about the constitution of human existence, yet it is not a calculative thinking that takes such existence as its object, but an existential thinking that proceeds on the basis of participation in existence. Whereas an objective account of fear is given in terms of physiological changes and overt behavior, Heidegger's existential analysis of fear is based on the existent's own first-hand participation in the experience of fear, and, prior to that, on his participation in a finite existence for which fear is a possibility.

A special case of existential thinking, and a very important one, is what is called "repetitive" thinking. The expression "repetition" is to be understood as meaning much more than a mere mechanical going over again. It implies rather going into some experience that has been handed down in such a way that it is, so to speak, brought into the present and its insights and possibilities made alive again. This can happen with an historical happening, or again with a document, say a poem or a saying, that has been handed down from the past. If we are to understand it, we must think *into* it, and so think *again* and *with* the agent or the author.

We can of course think of other persons in objective terms. This may sometimes be morally wrong, if we are considering the other person as simply an instrument, but in other cases there may be no moral question at all; a surgeon, for instance, surely has to take an objective view of his patient. The point however is that typically we are taking an abstract and reductionist view of persons if our thinking about them falls below the existential level.

Corresponding to this thinking is the mode of knowledge that we call "personal" knowledge. Martin Buber and others have familiarized us with the distinction between "I–it" and "I–thou," with the kind of knowing in which "I" have "it" for my object, and the kind in which "I" and "thou" meet and recognize each other as subjects. One obvious difference between this kind of knowing and the objective knowing that corresponds to calculative thinking is that whereas, as we have noted, the subject of calculative thinking is the active factor while its object is the passive target at which the process of discovery is aimed, there must be activity on both sides in the case of any personal knowing. We can know the other person only in so far as he makes himself known or lets himself be known; for we know him not only by his overt behavior but to the extent to which he opens himself to us and actively meets us in our approach to him. Hence in a truly personal knowledge we do not subject the other, or master, or transcend him, but meet him on a footing of mutuality and reciprocity.

It is often claimed by theologians that the kind of knowing that takes place in revelation is of this personal kind, and that revelation is an "I–thou" meeting between God and man. But there are many reasons for rejecting this as an unsatisfactory account. Let me mention three that seem conclusive. The first is that in any meeting between persons, there is an actual physical meeting, for a person is not a disembodied spirit. This physical aspect of the meeting is essential to it, for this is how words are spoken and heard, looks and gestures communicated and understood. It is very hard to suppose what a personal meeting or encounter could be like in the absence of the physical events which mediate it. Thus at the best the revelatory experience could be only analogous to an "I–thou" meeting, and remotely analogous at that. A second reason against the equation of revelation with an "I–thou" encounter is that in the latter, as we have seen, reciprocity and give-and-take are essential. There is no mastering or subjecting of one side by the other. In the revelatory experience, however, the person who receives the revelation is utterly transcended by the holy being that reveals itself; and this utter one-sidedness again implies that a personal encounter could be only a very remote analogue. A third reason is that an "I–thou" encounter is one in which two particular beings know each other. But it has already been said that in revelation we do not know another being, but simply being. This language has still to be clarified, but it should be clear to us even now that this constitutes another decisive objection against the description of the revelatory experience as an "I–thou" encounter.

Certainly personal knowledge and the related existential thinking bring us nearer to the revelatory experience than the objective knowledge that arises from calculative thinking, especially because personal knowledge is made possible only by the active self-disclosure of the person known, and so we get something like a parallel to the initiative of the holy in revealed knowledge. Thus the religious man has justification for using personal rather than impersonal language, though since both are inadequate, we shall still have to ask just how much justification there is for personal language, or indeed for any language at all that tries to express what seems to lie beyond all the categories of our ordinary speaking and thinking.

However, our consideration of the two modes of thinking and knowing, what we may call the "subject-object" mode and the "subject-subject" mode, raises the question whether we must not consider the possibility of a third mode, one in which I would be subjected to that which is known, one in which I am transcended, mastered, and, indeed, known myself. Here Heidegger's philosophy does point us to still another mode of thinking which may be what we are looking for. He calls this "primordial" or "essential" thinking. It has a meditative character which contrasts with the probing activity of calculative thinking. This primordial thinking rather waits and listens. Heidegger can even talk of it as an "occurrence of being" or as a thinking that "answers to the demands of being." [9] This primordial thinking is a philosophical thinking, but it is described as a thinking which responds to the address of being, and is explicitly compared both to the insights of religion and to those of poetry. This kind of philosophical thinking, then, provides a kind of paradigm for the understanding of what is meant by "revelation," and shows where revelation is to be located in the range of man's cognitive experience.

What would seem to happen both in the primordial thinking of the philosopher and in the revelatory experience of the religious man (if indeed these two can be definitely distinguished) is that the initiative passes to that which is known, so that we are seized by it and it impresses itself upon us. But what is known is not another being, but rather being itself, the being which communicates itself through all the particular beings by which it is present, by which it manifests itself, and not least through the depth of our own being, for we too are participants in being and indeed the only participants to which being opens itself, so that we not only are but we exist.

The knowledge that corresponds to primordial thinking has a gift-like character, and this is precisely what the religious man points to when he talks of "revealed" knowledge. We have seen, of course, that there must

---

[9] *Was ist Metaphysik?*, pp. 47, 49.

be a gift-like character even at the level of person-to-person knowing, but on the level of revelation, the gift-like character is enhanced and we have become almost passive recipients. Presumably, however, we are not *entirely* passive. All knowing involves an element of appropriation. For this reason, it was insisted earlier that there is a capacity for revelation. The response of appropriation constitutes, indeed, an essential element in the totality of the revelatory experience. It is much more true to say that being grasps us than that we grasp being, yet it grasps us in such a way that we are not simply overwhelmed by it. In the religious experience of revelation, the overwhelmingness of being is matched by its grace, the *tremendum* by the *fascinans*, for being gives itself and opens itself, so that we stand in the grace and openness of being. It reveals itself not only in otherness but also in kinship, so that even as we are grasped by it, we can to some extent grasp it in turn and hold to it.

At this point it is necessary to remind ourselves again that anxiety and joy, judgment and grace, the sense of otherness and the sense of kinship, the *tremendum* and the *fascinans*, man's sense of disorder and his transcending drive toward fulfillment, are always, so to speak, two sides of a single coin. Sometimes one may predominate, sometimes the other; they may be differently weighted in the experience of different individuals or generations; they may be variously evaluated by different interpreters; but finally they are inseparable and any attempt to seize on one side and to set it up in isolation can result only in superficiality.

In this section, we have been trying to locate the revelatory experience within the range of man's ways of knowing and thinking, and our argument could be strengthened by a brief consideration of some of the parallels between revelatory experience and esthetic experience. The latter seems to be another type of experience that touches upon the whole existence, strongly involving the feelings, yet certainly not without its cognitive aspect. Again, what is known in the esthetic experience is not some additional thing, beyond what is open to universal inspection, but rather the depth of what confronts us, a structure or a *Gestalt* that is noticed in the experience. This awareness, moreover, has a kind of gift-like character, for the "beautiful" or the "sublime," like the "holy" or the "numinous," seems to take possession of us. The artist sometimes testifies to his "inspiration" in terms not unlike the testimony of the recipient of a revelation. It is not surprising then that Heidegger sees in the perceptive thinking of the poet something very similar to that primordial thinking which is, in turn, close to what we call "revelation."

Also moral experience exhibits parallels with revelatory experience. Indeed, since the decline of the old natural theology, many people have believed that the argument from moral experience constitutes one of the strongest supports for theism. However that may be, one can at least acknowledge that in moral experience, one becomes aware of a claim, and this claim is characterized both by otherness and ultimacy. But can its otherness be explained by saying that this is the claim of society on the individual? Let us agree that the moral claim will usually be mediated through a society and will come to us in a form that is relative to that society. Nevertheless, this does not fully account for the otherness of the claim, and certainly not for its ultimacy. For a society too may have a claim laid upon it, and that claim will be characterized by otherness and ultimacy, just as much as any claim laid on an individual. When, for instance, we condemn a society as unjust, we are appealing to a criterion that transcends the society itself. We have already noted that conscience at its deepest is not just the deposit of conventions defining socially acceptable behavior but the drive toward an ideal of existence. We are confronted here again with the ambiguous relations between the social and the individual aspects of existence. Usually it is the sensitivity of individuals that leads to changes in social standards, and this at once places in question the belief that morality is just a product of society, reflecting its demands. The parallel between moral experience and revelatory experience is assuredly not decisive, but it is one more item in the cumulative argument for the validity of religious faith.

Here let it be said again that presumably a genuinely primordial thinking or a primordial experience of the revelation of being is rare. For most of us there can be only the repetitive thinking that follows in the course of some classic experience of the holy, as that experience has come down to us in a concrete symbolism, and as it has subsequently been lit up further by generations of thought and experience in the community of faith which it founded. Yet such repetitive thinking does bring us sufficiently close to the primordial experience to know what the approach of holy being is, so that our present existence too can move in the grace and openness of being and thereby, we may hope, find some healing for its disorder and a new possibility of bringing its potentialities to actualization.

17. REVELATION AND MOODS

Any attempted defense of the trustworthiness of revelation must face the question of the part played by affective states or moods in the revelatory experience, as it has been described in the foregoing pages. Stress has been laid on anxiety and the sense of finitude, and likewise on awe before the presence of the holy; allusion has been made to the teaching that the fear of the Lord constitutes the beginning of wisdom; and there has been an appeal to Otto's phenomenological analysis of the experience of the numinous. Does all this mean that the account given has approximated to Schleiermacher's view of religion, as essentially constituted by feeling? And does this in turn mean that I have conceded tacitly that religion is really a subjective affair, and that the statements arising out of religion, including the statements of theology, refer to nothing in the real world and have no cognitive status, but are simply "emotive utterances," as they have been called, sentences that simply evince our emotions?

If, however, there has been talk of anxiety, awe, and other feelings, there has also been talk of thinking and knowing, and clearly there has been no intention of making religion a phenomenon of emotional subjectivity. If by the "real world" we mean the world of particular beings, the things and persons actually existing in space and time, then perhaps it is the case that the statements of religion, or many of them, "refer to nothing in the real world." But what has been suggested above is that these statements refer to being, and while the word "being" has still to be clarified, it is already obvious that being cannot be considered as a particular being (and is therefore "nothing in the real world" if "real world" means the sum or system of particular beings), and yet is more truly beingful than any of the particular beings which *are* in virtue of their participation in being. We cannot think of being as something that is, because more basically still it is the condition that there may be anything of which we can say that it is.

Whereas our knowledge of particular beings comes through our perceiving them and through the intellectual appropriation of what is given in perception, our knowledge or awareness of being (if indeed we have any) is more broadly based. It arises out of the total range of our existence in the world, and not out of perception and intellection alone. It is only through our total experience of being in the world that we reach any understanding of being; and for us, being in the world means existing, that kind of being which is open to itself and which already has some understanding of its being implicit in it. Being, then, gets disclosed in existing. But existing is not just beholding or contemplating or perceiving, for it is also concern and involvement and participation. Feeling is always a constituent factor in existing. At any given time, feeling, understanding, and willing—or, if one prefers a more latinized terminology, affection, cognition, and volition—are all there together in existing. They are distinguishable aspects in the mental life of the existent, but they cannot be separated in the manner that was attempted in old-fashioned faculty psychologies. We are, however, disclosed to ourselves, and being is disclosed, in affection and volition as well as in cognition, or, perhaps better expressed, all affective and conative experience has its own understanding. In particular, feeling and understanding cannot be sharply separated, and consequently one cannot sharply separate so-called "emotive" and "informative" language.

Moreover, all affective states have "intentionality," as it is called, that is to say, they refer to some state of affairs beyond themselves. They are not purely subjective. The sentences in which they find expression when they are brought to words are not just "emotive" utterances, if by this is meant the expression of our own inner feelings. These sentences too point beyond the subject of the affective states. But to what do they refer? They do not seem to be objective assertions, like those based on the sense experience of things or persons perceived in the world. We must reply that affective states and the sentences in which they come to verbal expression refer not to objects but rather to situations, and furthermore, to situations in which the person who experiences the affective state is himself a participant. We are concerned here with something that is neither subjective nor objective, to an unbroken unity of subject and object within a situation or structure that is known from within. This unbroken unity is experienced on the level of feeling, while as yet there is no analytical breakdown of the situation in discursive or subject-object thinking. In feeling we intuit the situations in which we find ourselves, just as in sense perception we intuit objects in the environment. Both modes of intuition belong essentially to our openness as existents. Since the feelings that we have in mind are those that have been mentioned earlier in our discussions—anxiety, awe, and such like—perhaps we should speak of "moods" rather than of feelings in general. A mood is something like an attunement to the environment, an awareness and response to the total situation in which one finds oneself and in which one participates. No amount of objective perceiving could ever disclose that of which we become aware in the mood. Yet the mood does not show us anything that does not show up in perceiving. It simply lets us be aware of the situation as a whole and permits us to notice dimensions of that situation which are disclosed to a participant but may be veiled from a mere beholder.

Anxiety has played a key role in the foregoing discussions, and perhaps some justification should be offered for its prominence. It would seem that anxiety, as it has been described above, has a peculiar significance in so far as it tends to light up not just some particular situation but man's total situation in the world—man as the being in whom are conjoined possibility and facticity, responsibility and finitude. But even if this is conceded, perhaps the question will be asked whether the stress upon anxiety does not introduce an unhealthy, neurotic tendency into the description. In particular, one may remember Bonhoeffer's insistence that faith is not for the extremities of life but for its center, and his rightful criticisms of preachers and others who would frighten men into religiosity.[10] Perhaps much of our religion is indeed a neurotic clutching after security, yet anxiety is at the center of life because of the essential fragmentariness of our existence, and to recognize anxiety and attend to its disclosure is surely a mark of maturity. The man who thinks he has outgrown anxiety or that it is only a peripheral phenomenon may well be the immature person who has never been able to accept himself and who comforts himself with the illusion that all is in order. Let us remind ourselves again of the tensions between the polarities of existence, and of how easily we fall into imbalance, and move out to one extreme or the other. Aristotle's doctrine of the mean has some relevance here, for he applied it to feelings as well as to actions. The fact that anxiety can sometimes reach an extreme pitch where it becomes a pathological and disturbing factor should not disguise from us that there is a healthy anxiety or lead us to the opposite extreme of trying to suppress all anxiety or sweep it under the carpet. Anxiety belongs essentially to man's being and discloses him in the very center of that being as thrown possibility.

Let us remember too that (as Heidegger also asserts [11]) anxiety is near to awe. That is to say, it does not remain in the awareness of the nullity of existence, but opens our eyes to the wonder of being; and the religious experience of awe, as has already been pointed out, is an awareness of the grace of being as much as it is an awareness of the overwhelmingness of being. When these points are remembered, the objections to giving anxiety such an important role are lessened.

But perhaps a new objection will be raised here. It may be said that modern man does not feel awe. With the rise of science, the mystery has been taken out of things, so that they no longer excite awe but present a challenge to investigation. Whether this generalization can be accepted

[10] *Letters and Papers from Prison*, p. 165.
[11] *Was ist Metaphysik?*, p. 47.

and whether our apprehension of phenomena would not be greatly impoverished if it becomes dominated by calculative thinking are questions we need not answer. More fundamentally, the objection rests on a failure to understand what the religious man means by "awe." This has nothing to do with gaps in scientific knowledge, or with a superstitious dread in the face of ignorance as to *how* this or that phenomenon occurs. It is the far more basic wonder *that* there are phenomena at all, and this wonder would remain untouched, perhaps enhanced, even if science had answered all its questions. As Ludwig Wittgenstein rightly saw, "Not *how* the world is, is the mystical, but *that* it is." [12]

In this section a claim has been made on behalf of the trustworthiness of the awareness or insight that comes to us through certain moods or affective states, an awareness which is neither purely subjective nor purely objective, but which lights up the situation in which we find ourselves. This claim, I hope, has not been pressed in an exaggerated form, but it is nevertheless an important matter for what I have called the "epistemology" of revelation. If there is the kind of awareness of which I have spoken, then the claim of revelation is considerably strengthened; if there is no such awareness, then we seem to be driven toward positivism and toward the view that alleged revelations are in fact only illusions. But it has been my contention that a reasonable case for the validity of revelation can be made out. We can, I believe, trace something like a coherent pattern of experience that leads from man's questioning of his own existence to the religious confrontation with holy being; and this experience brings itself to expression in a way of thinking that has its own defensible and intelligible logic.

18. A FURTHER SCRUTINY OF REVELATION

The whole preceding part of this chapter has been a scrutiny of revelation, a description of the revelatory experience, and an examination of the conditions that would seem to be required for such an experience to be valid. But the matter is so important that we must scrutinize the claim of revelation in every way possible, and in this last section we shall consider what more, if anything, can be done to test revelation's credentials.

This brings us back to the question of revelation and reason. In discussing natural theology, we noted that a faith-conviction has always come

[12] *Tractatus Logico-Philosophicus*, p. 187.

prior to any attempt to prove the existence of God, and in the present chapter we have tried to push back the investigation beyond the rational arguments to the foundations of the prior faith-conviction. We have found these foundations in the revelatory experiences where man becomes aware of the presence and manifestation of holy being. It is now more than ever clear to us that the work of reason comes after the conviction that arises out of the revelatory experience, but reason's work is none the less important for being critical rather than speculative, subsequent to the religious conviction rather than foundational for it.

While the last section made claims for a cognitive aspect in some of our basic moods and feelings, the claim was not an exaggerated one, for these feelings are notoriously fallible. I may feel fear in a situation which does not in the least threaten me, and such false fears or phobias are very common. Perhaps then the whole revelatory experience, whether it has been known at first hand or, as is more likely, through "repetitive" thinking, is just an illusion, bolstered up by powerful feelings that have been misplaced. The feeling of a gracious presence may be just a kind of hallucination, brought on possibly by our desire or need for such a presence. Thus when the intensity of the feeling has passed, the religious man must try to let the situation be "recollected in tranquility," so that he can sift and question and test this experience from every point of view. He cannot indeed go behind it, but he can examine it and consider what grounds there are for trusting it and what for rejecting it.

The religious man may indeed experience some reluctance in raising the question of the trustworthiness of the revelation. H. H. Price remarks: "If you find yourself addressing someone and giving him your allegiance, it is a little late in the day to ask the question 'Does he exist?' "[13] Probably the question would not be raised unless faith had been challenged in some way. The person may have entered a period when his faith had grown weak and God seemed to be absent rather than present; or his faith may be under attack from persons who believe that it is erroneous. Or, again, if he is consciously theologizing, he may deem it necessary to question the grounds of faith. In any of these cases, his subsequent reflection can be an honest consideration of evidence and not just a rationalizing process.

These remarks bring us back to the traditional theistic proofs. Though they might never convince us starting from cold, as it were, they may have a confirmatory function. Especially in their modern formulations,

[13] In *Faith and the Philosophers*, ed. John Hick, p. 10.

they seek to bring together faith and reason by facing the question of whether the facts of the world, as known to us in science and everyday experience, are compatible with belief in the grace of being, as this is supposed to have been made known in revelation. We have already seen that the picture presented by our world is an ambiguous one, but it must at least be shown that the faith-conviction is compatible with what we learn about the world through our everyday experience.

Perhaps the religious man should be prepared to say what state of affairs he would acknowledge to be *incompatible* with his faith, and therefore one that falsifies it. Such a state of affairs, for instance, might be the presence in the world of massive, senseless, irremediable evil. But even to say this shows how difficult or impossible it would be to reach a conclusive demonstration. How could we definitely recognize such a state of affairs? However, the traditional preoccupation of theologians with the so-called "problem of evil" shows their sensitivity to such questions.

Certainly, it would not seem to be the case that at the beginning one could bring forward any clinching arguments on behalf of the validity of a religious faith, and indeed all one could ever hope to do would be to show its *reasonableness*, for it remains faith, and not demonstrable knowledge—just as the opposite point of view is not demonstrable either. But the reasonableness of a faith or of its corresponding revelation has to be weighed throughout the whole theological exposition of the revelation's content. In Christianity, for instance, the question of its reasonableness has to be judged in the light of all its teachings about creation, sin, providence, atonement, eschatology, and so on. In the end, the revelation must be judged as a whole, when all its implications have been unfolded. Does it make sense, and is it compatible with what we know of the world in everyday experience?

If revelation is to be scrutinized by reason, its claims must also be tested by conscience. It has already been pointed out that by "conscience" is not meant simply the social code as this has been built into an individual's existence.[14] Such a code, and the kind of conscience which does no more than reflect such a code, may indeed sometimes be opposed to some particular revelation or alleged revelation, but it might be a question whether the social code and the conscience formed by it were in a position to test the revelation or whether they might not find themselves judged and condemned by the revelation, as a higher insight. But we have

[14] See above, pp. 63–64.

seen that the foundational phenomenon of conscience is man's synoptic awareness of his being, in its authentic possibility and its actual disorder. Revelation is confirmed by conscience if, in ourselves or in the community, faith in the revelation overcomes the disorder, so that, in the well-known words of St. Thomas, we "perceive within ourselves the fruits of redemption." [15] Such language may seem presumptuous, but any talking about the holy can hardly fail to have some presumption in it. On the other hand, there have been alleged revelations that go against conscience, and these have been rejected because they have been judged disruptive rather than creative of selfhood and community.

Faith then takes its rise from the revelatory experience, though for the vast majority this will not be "primordial" revelation but a "repetitive" participation in such revelation, through the testimony of the community of faith. The revelatory experience can be located within the general range of disclosive experience, and some account given of its epistemological status. Revelation is then subjected to the scrutiny of reason and conscience, and presumably many reports of revelations or alleged revelations need to be profoundly modified or even rejected in the light of such scrutiny. But if we suppose that something has come through, and that the idea of revelation has stood up to the investigation, we may now go on to look more closely at the question of who or what does the revealing. So far I have confined myself to such expressions as "holy being," and have promised further clarification. The time has now come to offer it, and this will occupy us in the next chapter.

[15] From the Office for Corpus Christi.

5 | Being and God

19. THE CONTENT OF REVELATION

A popular misconception of revelation assumes that its content consists of a body of ready-made statements giving us information about matters inaccessible to our ordinary ways of knowing, so that without the revelation we would have remained in ignorance concerning them. This error has been very common in the Christian religion, where it has been encouraged by the Church's preoccupation with verbal formulations, whether the Bible itself, or the creeds, or particular dogmatic or confessional statements. Corresponding to this idea of revelation is an idea of faith as assent to the revealed statements.

It has already been made abundantly clear that faith is not primarily assent to propositions, but an existential attitude of acceptance and commitment; and that revelation is not primarily given in the form of statements, but it is rather the self-giving or self-communication of being. That which discloses itself in revelation seizes the whole being of man and cannot be adequately expressed within the limits of language. The verbal expression of faith is thus subsequent to an awareness that touches the whole existence and that escapes the attempt to formulate it completely in words. Not only are our verbal formulations inadequate, they may also be distorting, and this is what makes it so necessary to submit every report of a revelation to the most careful scrutiny. The content of the revelation itself, then, lies back of any verbal formulations of it.

But this fact should not be turned into an excuse for remaining utterly vague about what the content of revelation is. The prevalent error of supposing that the content of revelation consists of statements could not have arisen unless there were some justification for it. A revelation that could not be at all expressed in words would remain a purely private affair. It could not be communicated in an articulate fashion, though it might indeed show itself in an obscure and implicit way in the policies of action adopted by its recipient. But in the absence of articulate communication, there could hardly be a sharing of the revelation; and without a sharing, there could be no community of faith founded upon the revelation; and thus in turn there could be no transmission and no repetitive appropriation of the revelation.

Whatever its limits, language is our most precise and reliable way of communicating. More than that, it is doubtful whether there could be any knowing or thinking worthy of the name that did not need to embody itself in language. If revelation has a cognitive element, as is commonly supposed, then there must be some possibility of verbally expressing what is revealed. The whole theological endeavor on which we have embarked is sustained by the recognition of the importance of trying to bring to verbal expression our most fundamental existential convictions.

These remarks have been made as a *caveat* against some current tendencies to think of religion purely in practical terms, reducing its credal content to a minimum and shunning any definite formulation of belief. To go so far is to react much too violently against the intellectualist misconception of faith and to end up in a muddled anti-intellectualism which vaguely prizes faith for faith's sake, while faith is being all the time suppressed through the erosion of any definite content. The danger is that when one rightly denies that the content of revelation is a set of propositions to be received by faith, one leaves the real content of revelation so vague and indeterminate that there is reason to suspect whether anything has been revealed at all. The very use of the word "reveal" seems to entitle us to expect some clarity about what is revealed.

In terms of the language that has been used in the earlier parts of this book, the content of revelation is "being" or "holy being." Can we see what it is to which these words are seeking to point us?

Let us recall an earlier part of the argument in which there were distinguished three modes of thinking and knowing. It was pointed out there that we cannot study being objectively, as we can study particular beings in nature. Thus being cannot be transcribed into propositions or theories like those through which the sciences offer us a transcript of the phenomena of nature. If by "metaphysics" is understood the objective study of being, as an enterprise parallel to the scientific study of nature, then the content of revelation could never be transcribed in terms of a metaphysic.

It was also claimed, however, that the confrontation of man with being cannot be regarded as a personal subject-to-subject encounter either, though this is closer to the revelatory experience than a subject-to-object relation toward inanimate beings. So I must part company with the many theologians who in recent times have claimed that the content of revelation is a personal encounter, which subsequently gets transcribed into more or less inadequate statements. It has already been agreed that the notion of personal encounter has some merit as an analogue, but we have also seen that the analogy cannot be pressed too far.

We are driven to say that the confrontation with being is *sui generis*, and this "being" which is said to disclose itself to us in such a confrontation is like nothing else. But our ordinary language is adapted to talking about particular beings with which we have dealings in the world—the things that we handle and use, or the people with whom we have personal converse. Are we not then reduced to silence about "being"?

Certainly we can never talk of it as we do of persons or things. We can never talk of it in itself, so to speak, as if we could look at it from outside, or as if we could subsume it under some category of our thinking about particular beings. We ourselves *are*, and only through our participation in being can we think of it or name it, and only on the basis of its self-giving and self-disclosing to us can we know it. Thus if we say anything about being, we are also saying something about ourselves. Talk of being, however it may express itself grammatically, is neither subjective nor objective talking, but holds these two together. So it must be repeated that it is not metaphysical talk, since this tries to take being (or, more likely, the sum or totality of beings) for the *object* of a rational investigation.

But if the content of revelation is being, and if being cannot be conceived as either a thing or a person, what do we mean by "being"? Are we not perhaps just mystifying ourselves and other people by this talk? Is not "being" just an empty word, not a word that refers to anything, as do words like "cat" and "blue," but just a device used to indicate logical connections?

But if the word "being" does not refer to anything, has revelation any content at all? The skeptic who seems rightly to deny that revelation can open our eyes to *another being* (whether a person or a thing) seems also entitled to go on and say that there is nothing else that can reveal itself, and that talk about "being" is just the final confusion by which the religious man tries to hang on to the comforting belief that he has been granted a revelation. And if talk of "being" rather than of "God" has been intended as a device for keeping our philosophical theology within the orbit of a secular philosophical language and avoiding the religious vocabulary, then we may be told that the word "being," secular and everyday though it undoubtedly is (for we can hardly utter two sentences without employing the verb "to be"), is getting used here in just as mysterious and unintelligible a manner as was ever the word "God."

This would seem to be a crucial point in the development of our philosophical theology. How are we to determine the meaning of the word "being," how are we to show that it has an intelligible use in the contexts where we are employing it, and how precisely do we propose to relate it to the traditional religious word "God"?

20. THE MEANING OF BEING

What is the meaning of "being"? We must first recall the manner in which this question has arisen for us. It is not the metaphysical question of being—if there is such a question—that is to say, a detached, speculative question which one can take up or lay aside at pleasure. Our question is rather one that has arisen in an existential context. For we began by asking about ourselves, and it was the confrontation with the *nothingness* in our own existence that opened our eyes to the *being* which contrasts with nothing. So our question about being is not a theoretical question, in the sense of one that is asked by someone who merely beholds; it is an existential question in the sense that it is asked by someone who is involved in the question of being—someone for whom being, as Heidegger is so fond of saying, is an issue.[1] Man has to decide about his own being, in so far as he must choose among his possibilities. But he cannot properly understand his own being unless he has some understanding of being as such. Thus the existential question leads into the ontological question: this does not mean that it becomes a metaphysical or speculative question, but that the so-called "ontological" question is itself existentially oriented.

A useful first step in discussing what is meant by "being" is to say what being is *not*. It is true that we cannot expect to get very far by following a *via negationis*. Nevertheless, we shall at least guard ourselves against some errors, and as we rule out some of these, we shall thereby delimit more closely the area within which the meaning of "being" is to be sought.

1. Being cannot be regarded as itself a being, that is to say, as something that is. The point can be made more clearly in languages such as Greek,

---

[1] *Being and Time*, p. 8, etc.

Latin, German, where there are two distinct words for "being," one of which gets used when the reference is to being as such, the other when the reference is to some particular being. Other languages, such as English, have to get along with an ambiguity. If we reflect on the matter for a little, it is plain that "being," as the act or state or condition of being, is not the same as anything that is, and therefore not the same as anything which we can properly call a "being." In English, the two usages are ordinarily distinguishable by the fact that, in the first, "being" is used without the article or any pronominal adjective, whereas, in the second, the word "being" is normally preceded by "a" or "the" or "some" or "this" or some similar word. But this syntactical rule for distinguishing the usages is not invariable.

The difference can be brought out in another way by setting out to enumerate the beings to be found within the world, as stars, mountains, rivers, animals, trees and so on. Clearly, one would never add "being" to such a list; for this is not another being and does not belong in the same category or categories as the items listed. Yet in some way, being is common to all the beings.

Since being is not itself a being, then strictly speaking one should not say that "being is." Our grammar, however, is designed so that we can talk about beings. If we ever want to talk about being as such, then it would seem that ordinary grammar would need to be stretched. We have still to show that it makes some sense to talk about being, but meantime we may permit ourselves occasionally to use such expressions as "being is," if we are to say anything provisionally about being. This will do no harm if we remember that the language is being stretched beyond normal usage, and if we eventually offer some justification for this.

2. A few sentences back, it was stated that "in some way, being is common to all the beings." This might suggest that being is a property, but now it must be pointed out that being can no more be considered a property than it can be regarded as some particular being. Kant saw this in refuting the ontological argument. "By whatever and however many predicates we may think a thing—even if we completely determine it— we do not make the least addition to the thing when we further declare that this thing *is*." [2] We can satisfy ourselves about this much as we satisfied ourselves that being is not a being. For if we enumerate all the properties of a being, such as whiteness, hardness, roundness, and the like, we see that to add to the list "being," that is to say, to assert that the thing

[2] *Critique of Pure Reason*, B628.

is, would be to do something quite different than to add to the description, and that being is in a different category from the properties listed.

3. Following on the last point, we can go on to assert that being is not a class. This was already stated by Aristotle: "It is not possible that either unity or being should be a single genus of things." [3] He too was aware that being is not a property, for he says that there is no difference between a "man" and an "existent man." [4] Since we construct classes on the basis of common properties, then the point that being cannot be considered as a property means that it could not be used to constitute a class. In any case, the whole point of classification is to make distinctions within the total realm of the things that are (the beings), and thus it would be senseless to take the total realm itself as a class. In denying that being (and also unity) are classes, Aristotle seems to have indicated that these notions have some kind of universal applicability that raises them above the distinctions of the categories. In the Middle Ages, the number of such universally applicable characters was raised to six (or sometimes ten) and these constituted the *transcendentia*. This philosophical doctrine reappears in Heidegger's assertion that "being is the *transcendens* pure and simple." [5] What is meant by this linking of the ideas of "being" and "transcendence" we shall investigate later, but for the moment we simply note that being is no more the class of beings than it is a particular being or a property of beings.

4. It must also be denied that being can be equated with substance, the ὑποκείμενον or substratum sometimes supposed to underlie the phenomenal characteristics of beings. Leaving aside some of the other problems which the notion of "substance" raises, it cannot be equated with "being" because it is above all a static idea, having thinghood for its model. We have approached the idea of "being" through existence, rather than thinghood. This does not mean, however, that we are opposing a purely dynamic idea to the static notion of substance. Just as existence and selfhood imply both stability and dynamism, so the word "being" (we call it, significantly, a "verbal noun") has a double meaning, suggesting the act or energy of existing and also the existent entity in which this act expresses and manifests itself. The essence of being is precisely the dynamic "letting-be" (as we shall designate it) of the beings, and this is quite different from the traditional notion of substance, though perhaps it should replace that notion. Incidentally, we entirely avoid Tillich's notion of the "ground of

---

[3] *Metaphysics*, 998^b 21.
[4] Op. cit., 1003^b 27.
[5] *Being and Time*, p. 38.

being" which suffers not only from resembling too much the static idea of substance but is in addition, as I have shown elsewhere,[6] thoroughly ambiguous.

5. It may be added that being is not what philosophers have sometimes called the "absolute," whether this is conceived as the all-inclusive being or as the totality of beings or as the sum of beings; for it would be hard to see how such an absolute could be other than a being, even if we could hardly call it a "particular" being. But we have already seen that being is not *a* being, not even an all-inclusive being or a supreme being. If there were an inclusive or a supreme being, we would still have to inquire about the being of this being, the is-hood in virtue of which one could say that it is; and this *transcendens* would be more ultimate than our supposed absolute, for it would be the condition that there may be an absolute, or any being whatsoever.

Up till now, we have simply delimited the borders of the idea of being, and marked it off from what it is not. Can we now advance toward a more positive characterization? After all, St. Thomas claimed that "that which first falls under apprehension is *being,* the understanding of which is included in all things whatsoever a man apprehends." [7] If the understanding of being is so universal, why is it so difficult to give an account of it? We have already seen a partial answer to this question in the fact that the very universality of being leads to its getting overlooked, and that it is only against the background of nothing that an explicit awareness of being is awakened in us. We know too that often what lies closest to us is furthest from our explicit awareness. Can we hope then to move toward a fuller understanding of the meaning of "being" by trying to analyze and bring into the open the understanding of being which we already implicitly have—the understanding for which St. Thomas claims a priority, and which is attested by our continuous use of words expressive of being?

A first step toward the clarification of the meaning of "being" would be to consider the distinctions that are often made, either in ordinary speech or in the history of philosophy, between "being" and some other words. The very fact that these distinctions are made shows us that "being" is not just an empty word but that we have implicitly in mind some determinate meaning when we use it.[8] We shall say no more here about the distinction of being and nothing, the contrast which awakens us to

---

[6] *Twentieth-Century Religious Thought,* p. 367, n. 2.

[7] *Summa Theologiae,* Ia IIae, XCIV, 2.

[8] Cf. M. Heidegger, *An Introduction to Metaphysics,* p. 93ff.

awareness of being, but shall direct our attention to some other commonly recognized distinctions.

1. The first distinction to be considered is that between being and becoming. The distinction was already known to Greek philosophy. The contrast between being and becoming is less sharp than that between being and nothing, for becoming is supposed to lie somewhere between being and nothing. Whatever becomes must, in some sense, *already be;* yet the fact that it is becoming implies that it *is not yet* what it is on the way to becoming. Plato remarks: "If there be anything so constituted, as at the same time to be and not to be, must it not lie somewhere between pure being and pure nothing?" [9]

The fact that whatever becomes both is and is not shows that the distinction between being and becoming is of a peculiar kind. In so far as what becomes is, then becoming must be included in being as well as distinct from it. Two consequences seem to follow. The first is that being cannot be identified witih a static, changeless, undifferentiated ultimate; for as Hegel rightly pointed out, pure being, "simple and indeterminate," is just nothing.[10] In other words, the fundamental contrast between being and nothing would seem to be made possible only in so far as being includes becoming and gets differentiated, otherwise being and nothing would be indistinguishable. This would seem to be a sufficient answer to the complaints of those who say that a philosophy or theology which makes basic the idea of being results in a static, abstract system that cannot do justice to concrete dynamic experience. This complaint misunderstands what is meant by "being," for while being is indeed distinguished from becoming, we can talk about being and distinguish it from nothing only in so far as it includes becoming. The second consequence is that becoming is unintelligible apart from some conception of being, in which the becoming is included. A mere flux would be a chaos, and so would a sheer pluralism. While we have already seen that a static monism is to be rejected, we cannot go to the opposite extreme, for there could be no intelligibility without some unity and stability of being.

2. A second distinction is that between being and appearance. Again, this is a distinction that has long been recognized. It is the distinction between what *is* actually the case and what *appears* to be the case. For instance, the stick is actually straight, but it appears bent when partially immersed in water. But just as in the case of becoming, so with appearing,

---

[9] *Republic*, 477.
[10] *The Encyclopedia of the Philosophical Sciences*, Logic, Section 87.

that which appears *is* (for nothing can appear unless in some sense it is) and yet *may not be* what it purports to be. Appearing too belongs within being as well as being distinguished from being; and just as static undifferentiated being would be indistinguishable from nothing, so being which did not appear could not be distinguished from nothing. Being is nothing apart from its appearances. So by "being" we most decidedly do not mean some invisible, intangible realm that is supposed to lie back of the appearances, as a world of "things-in-themselves." Being gives itself in and through its appearances, and nowhere else. However, it can also be screened by its appearances, as in all the cases like the bent stick in water (a handy but trivial example) where the appearance misleads. Our aim must always be to see the appearances *in their being;* and this does not mean seeing *something else,* but rather seeing the appearances as they *are,* in depth as it were, as bearers of the presence and manifestation of being.

3. A distinction is often drawn between being and the ideal. This may take various forms. It may contrast something actual (the triangle drawn on the blackboard) with the concept of it; or, perhaps more frequently, there may be a moral valuation, as in the contrast between the condition of a society as it *is* and as it *ought to be.* Again there would seem to be no absolute disjunction between the two items that are distinguished. Rather, the distinction seems to call attention to different levels or, perhaps one should say, to different degrees of plenitude, not so much in being itself as in the manner in which being is present and manifest in the beings, or in the states of affairs which these beings constitute. It seems that the presence and manifestation of being can be impeded or distorted, and with such a state of affairs we contrast an "ideal" condition in which the fullness of being can manifest itself in and through some particular being or group of beings. Clearly this distinction is chiefly applicable in human affairs, and of course we have seen that it belongs to all human existence that it does not have a ready-made being but has to bring its potentialities for being to their fulfillment.

We have now considered the notion of "being" twice. The first time, our attention was directed to what being is *not;* the second time, we went through some traditional distinctions which reveal some of the determinate content that belongs to our idea of "being." We must now make a third attack on our problem and, in the light of what has already been said, try to fill out in the clearest and most affirmative terms that we can find, what we mean by "being."

1. First, it has become clear to us that there is a limit to what we can

say about being, for since being is not a being or a property or a class or even the sum of beings, it does not fall under any of our usual categories of thought, and so it must be regarded as strictly *incomparable*. That it does not fall under any of the usual categories may explain also why being can be so easily disregarded and forgotten, for, from the point of view that considers only beings and their properties, being itself is nothing. We have already seen ample reason to believe, however, that being is not just nothing nor is the word "being" an empty word. Being is rather a *transcendens* which, as above all categories, must remain mysterious, and yet is not just a blank incomprehensible. The very fact that it is the condition that there may be any beings or properties of beings is an indication that although we cannot say of being that it "is," and might even say it is "nothing that is," being "is" nevertheless more beingful than anything that is, for it is the prior condition that anything may be.

2. Would these paradoxes be sorted out somewhat if we thought of being as a kind of energy that permits beings to be? The word "energy" has too much the flavor of physical forces, and brings us back within the world of particular beings. Perhaps the word "act" would be better, for it suggests a more highly organized energy, a unified energy which recalls the peculiar relation of being and becoming sketched above. Of course, "energy" and "act" have been very closely associated ideas in the history of philosophy, even if the connotations of the words have diverged in modern times.

The expression which I prefer to use, however, to point to the characteristic of being as the condition that there may be any particular beings, is "letting-be." Being, strictly speaking, "is" not; but being "lets-be," and since letting-be is prior to particular instances of being, though other than these, we are justified in claiming that being is more beingful than any particular being that it lets-be, and we have justification too for using, with proper care and qualification, the expression "being is."

More must be said about the expression "letting-be," since I will be making a good deal of use of this idea in the chapters ahead. In ordinary English usage, to "let be" often means to leave alone, to refrain from interfering. This is not the sense that is intended here. By "letting-be" I mean something much more positive and active, as enabling to be, empowering to be, or bringing into being. The ultimate letting-be is part of the mystery of being, for we cannot answer the question why anything may be, rather than just nothing. But because we ourselves are and our being is open to us, we have some understanding of what it means to be let-be; and moreover, because we do have this peculiar mode of being as existents, we even have some idea in our experience of what it means for us to let-be, in a limited way.

The religious man experiences the letting-be of being as being's self-giving, the grace of being which pours itself out and confers being. But it has been conceded that there are also men, like the character in Sartre's novel,[11] who experience being as alien, so that its letting them be is like the imposition of a burden.

3. This brings us then to a third point. How do we read the character of this essentially mysterious letting-be, or how does it let itself be read? We come now to two other expressions which I have been using in connection with the exposition of the idea of being—the words "presence" and "manifestation." Being, we have seen, is nothing apart from its appearances in and through and with particular beings. What do we mean by talk of seeing the beings in a new way or seeing them in depth or in a further dimension, except that we become aware of the *presence* of being, that is to say, of what lets the beings be and mediates itself through them? Being, which is transcendent of every particular being and is thus "wholly other" and the furthest from us, is also the closest because it is present in every being, including our own being. One might also use the expression "participation": nothing can be unless it participates in being. This sentence is not, as it might appear at first sight, a tautology. It is meant to stress the presence and hence the openness and accessibility of being in the beings, as over against its distance and transcendence as the mysterious act or energy of letting-be. Being is, paradoxically, both the closest and the furthest.

The expression "manifestation" refers to being's opening itself in the beings. The manifestation of being is possible always and everywhere, for being is present in every particular being. But the manifestation may be most of the time latent, for we have seen how for the most part we do not *notice* being but concern ourselves only with the beings; and only in revelatory experiences, whether primordial or repetitive, does being itself take the initiative and communicate itself. Not only may being be hidden, it may be manifested in distorted ways. This can happen because, although being is present in every being and therefore at least potentially manifest in every being, some beings can manifest more fully than others the range and depth of being. This we have already learned from our earlier discussion of being and the ideal. An atom of hydrogen, for instance, and a

[11] See above, p. 88, n.6.

well-integrated human self are both beings that manifest being; but the self manifests being much more fully than the atom. Being cannot itself be a person, but it may well be most fully manifested in the intricate unity-in-diversity that constitutes personal being.

We may sum up then by saying that being "is" the incomparable that lets-be and that is present and manifests itself in and through the beings. But has this anything to do with what the religious man calls "God"?

21. GOD AND BEING

"God" is the key word of all religion and of all theology, and I have purposely been avoiding the use of the word until, in accordance with the policy that we have been following in our philosophical theology, we would be in a position to link the religious word with words employed in a secular philosophical discourse. This stage has now been reached, and my purpose in this section is to show the relation between God and being.

It should be said first of all that the words "God" and "being" are not synonyms. Few people, indeed, would suppose that they were. But the point is that some people experience being as indifferent or alien, as has already been pointed out more than once. Such people do not call being "God," for to use the word "God" means that one has taken up a certain attitude toward being, namely, the attitude of faith. It will be claimed that if we use the word "God," it does designate being; but we should be clear to begin with that "God" is not a neutral designation, as "being" is, but one that carries important existential connotations of valuation, commitment, worship, and so on. We could, however, say that "God" is synonymous with "holy being"; and the descriptions and analyses that have been put forward in the earlier pages of this book have been designed to show us that, in spite of admitted ambiguities, it makes sense to recognize the holiness of being, and to take up before it the faith-attitude of acceptance and commitment. Our final analysis of being as the *incomparable* that *lets-be* and is *present-and-manifest*, is strikingly parallel to the analysis of the numinous as *mysterium tremendum et fascinans*.

Much of our analysis has leaned upon the philosophy of Martin Heidegger, and although he talks of being in a religious or quasi-religious language, he has always made clear that being is not God. Are we not then about to make a false move when, having taken so much from Heidegger on which to base our philosophical or natural theology, we suddenly turn against him and do violence to his ideas by trying to turn his "being" into the "God" of religion?

I believe that a closer study of what Heidegger says will dispel any such suspicion. Perhaps rightly, he thinks that by "God" the theologian has traditionally meant not "being" but "some being" or "another being" in addition to the world; not, it may be, a "particular being," but still "*a* being," even if he is called the *ens realissimum* and regarded as the most beingful of all beings. Even an almighty being of this sort is still *toto coelo* different from being itself, and is transcended by being. One might say that the "forgetting of being" which Heidegger regards as characteristic of our Western culture has shown itself not only in the emergence of a technological and positivistic civilization that is concerned with particular beings and nothing else, but has shown itself too in the tendency of theology to think of God as *a* being rather than as being. In Heidegger's own philosophy, being tends to replace God and draws to itself the attributes traditionally assigned to God. The question posed for theology is whether the theologian too must not fight against the forgetting of being, and try to reconceive God not as *a* being, however exalted, but as being, which must in any case be more ultimate than any being.

Actually, our whole analysis up till now does point us to being as the focus of the religious man's faith, and therefore as what he means by "God." The idea of God has undergone many changes in the course of its history. At the *mythological* level, God was conceived anthropomorphically as a being much like ourselves, only more powerful, and he "dwelt" in a definite place, the top of a mountain, perhaps, or the sky. At the level of *traditional theism,* the earlier image had been considerably purged. Anthropomorphic elements were toned down in the interests of transcendence, though God was still thought of as a person, but a strange metaphysical kind of person without a body. He was no longer located in the sky, but he "dwelt" metaphorically beyond the world, though he kept it running and intervened in its affairs when necessary. He was another being in addition to the beings we know in the world. But science has shown us that the world can get along as a self-regulating entity and we do not need to posit some other being beyond it. In any case, such a being would not be an ultimate, because we could still ask about *his* being. Contemporary theology is beginning to move out of the phase in which "God" meant an exalted being beyond the world. The next phase would seem to be the identification of God with what I have called "holy being," and we may think of this as the phase of *existential-ontological theism.* So far is it from volatilizing or eliminating the idea of God that it makes it possible for this idea to have an ultimacy that it did not have in traditional theism.

The justification for identifying the God of religion with holy being can come only with the detailed working out of a theology based on such a conception. I hope to show that in Christian theology, the understanding of God as being rather than as *a* being will bring new intelligibility and relevance to many traditional doctrines.

However, the conception of God as being rather than as some being is sufficiently revolutionary as compared with popular ideas to demand some preliminary justification. We must remember, of course, that while in some regards the notion of God as being may seem revolutionary, it does in fact continue a long association of God with being in theological thought, an association that is found in the Greek Fathers, in St. Augustine and in St. Thomas, and which they in turn had taken over from the biblical tradition itself. But in the history of theological thought, the ambiguity of the word "being" has, for the most part, not been resolved. It is only in the contemporary era, with the challenge to the idea of God as *a* being, that theology is finding itself compelled to reexamine the traditional association of God with being, and to clarify whether God is to be understood as being or as the greatest among beings. At the same time, however, let it be said that if God is conceived as *immeasurably* the greatest being, so that he tends to be thought differently from particular beings altogether, then one is moving toward the thought of God as being; but this is happening only confusedly, for one has still been trying to think of God as a being and goes on trying to think of him in this way, even when the very use of a word like "immeasurably" indicates that one is trying to get away from the thought of *a* being altogether.

In addition to their other defects, the traditional theistic proofs seemed to be in error in trying to argue from the existence of some entities (particular beings) to the existence of another entity (an exalted being, admittedly, but one conceived in the same way as the particular beings). The subsequent amendments of the arguments, as, for instance, the insistence that a "first cause" must be of a different order from any subsequent or phenomenal causes, is basically an attempt to get away from the notion of *a* being to the notion of being. But again, this is happening only confusedly, and to recognize what is happening would demand giving the "proof" a new look altogether.

But does the equation of God with being and the denial that he is *a* being not amount to atheism? To this it may be replied that the word "atheism" must always be understood in relation to what it denies. Presumably most modern men deny the gods of mythology, and so from the point of view of a believer in these gods, they are atheists. Likewise, one may suppose, the denial that God is *a* being would seem to be atheism to one who believes that there is such a being. I have spoken of an "existential-ontological theism" as distinct from "traditional (or metaphysical) theism." This existential-ontological theism is opposed to its own corresponding atheism. This atheism is the denial of the holiness of being, and consequently the denial that man should have faith in being or take up the attitude of acceptance and commitment before being. The distinction between the believer and the atheist, or between faith and unfaith, is just as clear in existential-ontological theism as it was in metaphysical theism, and is perhaps more important, for here atheism, like faith itself, gets understood not so much in terms of accepting or denying a world view as in terms of taking up an existential attitude.

Can we, however, say that God "exists"? For the most part, we have been using the word "existence" in the restricted sense in which it is employed by the philosophers of existence, to mean exclusively the kind of being that belongs to man. If we use the word in this specialized sense, then we cannot say that God exists, just as we cannot say that a river exists, or a horse, or an angel. But this has nothing to do with the question of the "reality" of any of them. Traditionally, the word "existence" has been used in a much wider sense, to mean anything that has being. It is in this wider sense that one has been accustomed to argue for or against the "existence" of God. Strictly speaking, however, one cannot say that God "exists" in this way either, for if God is being and not *a* being, then one can no more say that God *is* than that being *is*. God (or being) *is* not, but rather *lets be*. But to let be is more primordial than to be, so that, as has already been said, being "is" more "beingful" than any possible being which it lets be; and this justifies us using such expressions as "being is," provided we remain aware of their logically "stretched" character—a character which will be clarified in the next chapter. So it can be asserted that, while to say "God exists" is strictly inaccurate and may be misleading if it makes us think of him as *some* being or other, yet it is more appropriate to say "God exists" than "God does not exist," since God's letting-be is prior to and the condition of the existence of any particular being. One is reminded of the rhetorical question of the psalmist: "He who planted the ear, does he not hear? He who formed the eye, does he not see?" [12] Just as it would be anthropomorphic to ascribe hearing or seeing literally to God, so it would be a reification of him to regard him as

---

[12] Ps. 93:9.

literally "existing," in the traditional sense. Yet since he is prior to seeing, hearing, and existing, and bestows being on whatever sees, hears, or exists, it is more appropriate to ascribe hearing, seeing, and existing to him, in an oblique sense, than to deny them; for the denial that he sees, hears, or exists would suggest that he falls below whatever sees, hears, and exists, whereas he so far transcends any such beings that their most positive characteristics fall short and fail to reach him.

The argument of the preceding paragraph can be put differently in a way that is perhaps nearer to the theological tradition by recalling the doctrine of *analogia entis.* According to this doctrine, the word "being" and likewise the words "is" and "exists" are not always used in the same sense, but sometimes analogically. If, for instance, I say that a particular chemical element "exists" in the sun, I am using the word "exists" in quite a passive sense; the chemical element is physically present in the sun, it can be discovered or detected there. If I say that man "exists" in the sense that Sartre and others say this, the word has a very active sense and indicates man separating himself from nature and choosing his own essence. But if I say that God "exists," then the dynamic, active sense of existing is raised to a new unimaginable level and the limitations of human existence are discarded. Provided that one is clear that the word "exists" (or "is") has an entire range of meanings, then it is appropriate to say "God exists."

Here perhaps something should be said about the meaning of the word "appropriate," which we use from time to time. Are we pleading the case for what is "appropriate" or "fitting," and failing to ask about what is true? In answer to this question, it must be replied that in the sense in which the word "appropriate" is used here, there is no opposition between what is appropriate and what is true, for appropriate language is precisely language that gives access to truth. The most fundamental meaning of "truth" is uncovering, or bringing to light. Truth is ἀλήθεια, unconcealment, so that we speak truly if what we say lights up what is talked about and shows it, as far as possible, without concealment or distortion. But to light up anything in this way is to let our minds "appropriate" it, in the sense of making it our own and incorporating it into our understanding. These points will become clearer in our discussion of the language of theology,[13] but it has seemed useful at this stage to point out the relation between "truth" and "appropriateness," lest it should be supposed that we are neglecting the former.

[13] See below, pp. 145–148.

But let us return to our main theme. The assertion "God exists" is not to be taken as meaning that there is to be found a being possessing such and such characteristics. "God exists" is a way of asserting what would perhaps be more exactly expressed as the holiness of being. But it is precisely the assertion of the holiness of being which is denied by atheism, so that our manner of interpreting the expression "God exists" in terms of God as being, makes not the slightest concession to atheism. It does, however, rule out obsolete and untenable mythological and metaphysical ways of thinking of God.

If it is allowed that the equation of God with being is not to be identified with atheism (for, rightly understood, it is the very opposite), what are we to say to the charge that our view is a kind of pantheism? Such a suggestion is equally wide of the mark, and rests on a gross misunderstanding. It has already been made clear that Being not only is not *a* being, but is not the sum of beings or the totality of beings or an all-inclusive being. Being "is" the *transcendens*, and this term indicates not only God's distinction from the world but his "wholly other" character as over against whatever is within the world. Yet at the same time, the acknowledgment that there "is" no being apart from beings, and that being "is" present-and-manifest in every being, guards against an exaggerated transcendence of God, such as has been common in recent theology, and seeks to do justice to his immanence.

Would then our identification of God with being constitute a variety of panentheism, understood as the doctrine which on the one hand opposes pantheism by holding that God's being is more and other than the universe, but which on the other differs from traditional theism in stressing the intimacy of God's relation to the world? Perhaps the view I have been putting forward can be described as panentheistic, but the word is not important, for panentheism is itself really a variety of theism, one which takes care to stress God's immanence equally with his transcendence.

At this point we must try to clarify the notions of transcendence and immanence as applied to God's relation to the world. In calling God "transcendent" we mean that he is other than the world, indeed, that there belongs to him a different order of being; and further that God's being is prior to the being of the world. It seems to me that both of these points are adequately recognized in the understanding of God as being. Being is of a different order from the beings, and the dynamic letting-be of being is prior to the derivative existence of the beings, whether persons or things. The concept of transcendence implies therefore that there is an element of asymmetry in God's relation to the world, and clearly this is essential to any truly theistic view, as opposed to a pantheistic one. But it does seem to me that in much traditional theism transcendence was stressed to the point at which any conception of immanence was almost lost. That traditional view worked with what might be called a "monarchical" model of God, that is to say, God was conceived as an exalted being bearing absolute rule over another being, the world—though admittedly this other being was of a different order. Still, both were beings, and the relation between the two was conceived as entirely asymmetrical: God affects the world, but the world does not affect God; God is entirely self-sufficient, so that the world adds nothing to him; the world is a product of the divine will, quite external to God and with the suggestion that God might have created or refrained from creating and it would have made no difference. It is at this point that the dialectic of theology demands that we take up the question of God's immanence. If we understand God as being, then his immanence in the world is just as fully recognized as his transcendence; the relation is that of being to the beings rather than that of one being to another, and we have seen that being is present and manifest in the beings. The traditional monarchical model is then qualified by what may be called an "organic" model of the God-world relation. This alternative model allows for some elements of symmetry and reciprocity in the relation of God and the world: God cannot be conceived apart from the world, for it is of his very essence (letting-be) to create; God is affected by the world as well as affecting it, for creation entails risk and vulnerability; God is in time and history, as well as above them.

All of these matters will receive fuller discussion later, but they are already implicit in the thought of God as being. This is not a confusion of God and the world, but it is a recognition of their intimate relatedness, and this accords in turn with a fully dialectical understanding of the transcendence and immanence of God.

The term "God" then is adequately indicated on the frame of reference by the expression "holy being." It follows that "God" has a twofold meaning: an ontological meaning, in so far as the word denotes being, and an existential meaning, in so far as it expresses an attitude of commitment to, or faith in, being. These two meanings belong together in the word "God" and are inseparable. The word is the key word of religion because it already expresses the basic religious conviction—that fact and value belong together, that being which gives being is also gracious being. The assertion "God exists" may be expressed in another way as meaning that being "is" not alien or neutral over against us, but that it both demands and sustains, so that through faith in being, we can ourselves advance into fullness of being and fulfill the potentialities of selfhood.

From now on, I shall use an initial capital for "Being" when the word is used as an alternative for "God." This will conform to traditional usage and will also distinguish this particular meaning from others. But we must be careful not to let this word "Being" betray us into a static notion of God. We have seen that Being always includes becoming, and that the essence of Being is the dynamic act of letting-be. So our thought of God is parallel to our way of thinking of the self or soul, expounded in an earlier chapter. In both cases, we have abandoned the traditional "substantial" (reified) conceptuality in favor of one that takes time and becoming seriously.

6 | The Language of Theology

The problem of religious language is an old one, for as soon as men began to reflect on religion and to discuss it, they became aware of the inadequacy of their language. Some of them recommended silence, on the ground that the content of religion is inexpressible in words, and that when we try to talk about it, we inevitably distort it. But very few have been satisfied with a rule of silence. Perhaps they have recognized that if religion has any worthwhile insights, these must be to some extent expressible in language, and they have sought to employ our language, sometimes in ways far removed from ordinary usage, to put into words that which they believe has been opened up to them in religion.

But while the problem of language has for long occupied those who have reflected on religion, it has received heightened attention in recent years. When I spoke briefly of theology's need to keep in touch with philosophy, I mentioned logical analysis as one of the current modes of philosophizing. Up till now, our philosophical theology has been influenced chiefly by existentialism, ontology, and phenomenology, the other modes of philosophizing that were mentioned in the same passage. But we cannot and should not ignore the analyst, whose critical function is to examine the discourse we use. He wants to know what it means, how it can claim truth, how, perhaps, it shelters confusion and is misleading both to those who use it and to this who hear it used. He wants to know how the words and sentence constructions used in theology are related to ordinary usages.

In the earlier phases of the interest in logical analysis, a strongly positivistic attitude prevailed in the school. Any sentence purporting to assert something about a real state of affairs, so it was held, must be capable of being verified, at least in principle, by some sense experience; for if a sentence is meaningful, then it must be capable of being true or false; there must in turn be some criterion for showing its truth or falsity, and the obvious criterion is sense experience. This works well enough with everyday statements like "The *Queen Elizabeth* is on the Atlantic" and can in various ways be extended to historical assertions and other special cases. But it is hard to see how it could ever be extended to religious assertions or seeming assertions, such as "Christ is at the right hand of the Father," for although grammatically this sentence is of the same pattern as the one about the ocean liner, there is in the case of the religious sentence no sense experience that would seem even remotely relevant to the question of its truth or falsity. So the positivists declared a sentence of this kind to be meaningless. Some of them would have added that it is an emotive utterance, evincing a feeling on the part of the person who uses the words, but not communicating to us any assertion that could be true or false.

This positivistic phase, however, involved too many questionable assumptions (including the verification principle itself) and was too much of an outrage on common sense to hold the field for long. It has been succeeded by a more open attitude on the part of the analyst, who no longer lays down in advance what are the conditions for a meaningful language but acknowledges that there may be many meaningful languages and proceeds to look for the various logics in terms of which these languages proceed. This, incidentally, would seem to be also a more genuinely empirical approach than was the case when the verification principle was enthroned as a kind of *a priori* criterion.

To the verification principle there succeeded the more flexible principle of *use*. The meaning of a language is to be looked for in the way it gets used. This, of course, still poses a major question for the theologian. Can he point to some coherent and intelligible way in which his language is used? Can he show that it does have a logic, so that we can see what it is trying to say? These questions may be difficult to answer, but at least they give the theologian a chance to justify his language, and do not rule it out from the start as nonsensical, in the style of the older positivism.

The recognition that there are (or may be) many meaningful languages and that the meaning is to be sought in the use brings an important consequence. It means that language, considered only as words and sentences, is an abstraction that has been torn away from the living context in which it gets used. The point is well made by Ludwig Wittgenstein, who himself pioneered the way from logical positivism to a much broader and more flexible conception of analysis. He writes: "Every sign *by itself* seems dead. *What* gives it life? In use it is alive. Is life breathed into it there? Or is the *use* its life?" [1] The point is that isolated elements of language "come alive" as they get used in wider contexts. The word becomes meaningful in the sentence. The sentence in turn may have to be placed in the context of the wider discussion to which it belonged. Eventually, however, this means that language itself has to be placed in the context of the life and experiences of the beings who use language; or, perhaps better, that language (words and sentences) has to be understood as the bearer of discourse (the conversing of intelligent, personal beings).

It is at this point that we see the convergence of logical analysis and existentialism. The stress laid by Wittgenstein and others on *living* use and on putting language into its human context affords a contact with the things that Heidegger has said about language as an existential phenomenon—indeed, as time has gone on, language has become in Heidegger's philosophy the existential phenomenon *par excellence* and the very key to Being.

But let us come back to the specific problem of theological language. If we accepted the verification principle, then there would be no point in going further, for on that basis one could never make out a case for theological language. It is doubtful also whether we could ever get anywhere by considering theological language merely syntactically, that is to say, as ordered words and sentences but apart from the existential context in which they are used. The justification of theological language is to be sought precisely by putting it in the context of the experiences which give rise to it and which are brought to expression in it. These are the experiences of the community of faith, in which men move from the questioning of their own being to the search for meaning and to the revelatory experience in which they are grasped by the grace of Being. The language in which they express this has its intelligible logic in the pattern of experience through which they move.

So far as a description of this pattern of experience has already been given in this book, the foundation has been laid for an explication of the basic logic of theological language. The experiences described and brought so far as possible into the open for scrutiny and examination provide the

[1] *Philosophical Investigations*, p. 128ᵉ.

frame of reference against which the meaning of theological language is to be seen. Already such words as "sin," "grace," "faith" and, finally, the word "God" itself have been assigned their meanings in the course of the existential analysis which must be coordinated with any logical analysis if indeed language is to be studied not as a dead precipitate but as living discourse in a community of human existents. Now, however, the structure and logic of theological language must be studied somewhat more closely.

23. LANGUAGE AND THE THEOLOGICAL SITUATION

What happens when something is said? It would seem that the typical act of saying belongs to a situation constituted by at least three factors: the person who does the saying, the person to whom something is said, and the matter about which something is said. The language (what is said, the words and sentences) becomes the link that brings together the three factors. Here we are going to think especially of what happens when what is said is a statement (rather than a command, question, or the like) and, above all, a theological statement. The analysis will take a threefold form, as we consider in turn each of the three factors and how it is related in the act of saying that brings them together.

First, then, we have to consider the person who does the saying. From his point of view, the language *expresses,* that is to say, brings out into the open and makes accessible what otherwise would have remained hidden in his private thought and experience. There are, however, different degrees to which our language can express our thought and experience. Some language expresses only what we observe as spectators, that is to say, it dims down everything that belongs to our feelings, valuations, interests, and striving in the situation, and expresses only what stands over against us as object. This language is as impersonal as possible, and ·the paradigmatic case is the language of science. Some modes of language, on the other hand, express a wider range of the existent's being in the world. They introduce precisely those personal elements which a strictly objective language dims down. Personal language is spoken by the whole self, not merely by the intelligent subject which is an abstraction from the self in its total range of experience. But it is utterly superficial to suppose that because a language introduces personal factors of valuation, feeling, and so on, it must be classed as "emotive" and denied any cognitive status or any claim to be thought true or fales. Such language need not be subjective. It may well light up a situation which we see through our participation, and I have already argued that affective states cannot be dismissed as mere subjective emotions.[2]

Considered, then, from the point of view of the person who does the saying, or in terms of what it expresses, the language of theology expresses total existence. Here the word "existence" is used for man's mode of being in the world, and the adjective "total" indicates the whole range of this being, as cognitive, affective, and conative. To put it in another way, theological language expresses faith, and we have seen that faith is not just an intellectual assent, but an existential attitude of the whole self —an attitude of acceptance and commitment in the face of being.

Thus theological language has a complex meaning. The dogmas of religion do not express the view of a neutral observer, as the pronouncements of science are supposed to do; on the other hand, they do not have (as some of the Catholic modernists were alleged to have held) only a practical sense, as expressing an intention to follow a policy of action, for although they do express something of the sort, this is inseparable from the conviction that such a policy is both demanded and supported by the structure of reality. Still less could theological statements be taken as expressing only subjective emotion, for again, although elements of feeling underlie them in a way which is not the case with scientific assertions, these affective elements are inseparable from what are believed to be insights into the way things are. This complexity of theological language was already made clear to us when we took note of the meaning of "God" as "holy being," an expression which points both to being and to our experience of and response to being as holy. Ian Ramsey has well described the complex mode of expression that belongs to religious and therefore to theological language, in terms of "commitment" and "discernment."[3] He rightly points out that if there were no discernment expressed in the language, then the commitment would be bigotry or fanaticism.

If then we are willing to agree that theological language, though admittedly impregnated with feeling and valuation, is nevertheless the vehicle for understanding and insight, so that it tells us something, we must now ask what it is that this language lights up for us. So we are considering now the relation between the language and that which it talks about. To what does this language *refer?* On what, so to speak, does it cast a spotlight, so that we can see what is talked about?

It must be replied, in view of all that has already been said, that theo-

---

[2] See above, pp. 64–65.
[3] *Religious Language,* p. 47.

logical language refers ultimately to Being. However, since it does not speak of Being as if this were an object that could be subjected to rational investigation, as in a metaphysical theory, but only of Being as known in the revelatory experience, then it talks always of Being as it relates itself to us. In theology, we talk of Being only as we ourselves are embraced by Being and have recognized its holiness. We can agree with Calvin's statement that "our mind cannot conceive of God without rendering some worship to him." [4]

But how can our language refer to Being? It would seem that our language is adapted to talking about beings, whether persons or things, and about the properties, relations, activities, and so on of these beings. Being is not itself a being, and it has already been described as an "incomparable," since it does not fall under any of the usual categories. Yet we have also seen that "being" is not an empty word or merely a logical operator. It is true that it refers to nothing in the world of particular beings, but this does not imply that it has no reference whatever, for the "nothing" to which it refers is more beingful than any particular being. We have traced the meaning of "being" from man's fundamental awareness of the "nothingness" of his own existence, and have tried to delimit more clearly what this word "being" signifies. But even if we have had some success in these matters, how can we say anything about being?

Already it has been indicated that this can be done only by a "stretching" of ordinary linguistic usage, and we have been using expressions like "being is" in the awareness that strictly speaking they are inappropriate or odd, but with the promise that such usages would be justified in due course.

It is clear that any assertions about Being cannot refer in the direct and straightforward way in which an assertion about an empirical fact refers, as when I say, "The cat is on the mat." But the fact that language does not refer in a straightforward manner but may refer in some rather odd way is no reason for despising such language. Indeed, as Ian Ramsey remarks, "we might even conclude in the end that the odder the language, the more it matters to us." [5] Certainly, if we can say anything about Being, it would matter much more to us than some trivial statement about where the cat happens to be sitting; but we would also expect that it would have a much more complex logic. One could argue that it is precisely by a stretching of ordinary usages that language develops and becomes capable

[4] *Institutes of Christian Religion*, I, ii, 1.
[5] *Religious Language*, p. 48.

of expressing and communicating in more and more sophisticated ways. It is not necessary to read very far in the literature of philosophy to learn how philosophers have done violence to the conventions of the language that they found in order to express their insights.

The language of religion and of theology abounds in modes of discourse in which language has been stretched beyond its normal usages. We would utterly misunderstand such language if we took it in its literal sense, as if it referred in a straightforward way; the reference of this language is rather to be understood as oblique, perhaps ostensibly pointing to some particular being, yet opening a way into an understanding of being. There are of course many purely secular examples of oblique language, in metaphor, allegory, and the like. Every language too is full of dead metaphors, and these show how its vocabulary has grown and become ever richer.

The odd character of religious and theological language is commonly recognized when we speak of it as "mythological," "symbolical," "analogical," "paradoxical," or whatever it may be. The necessity for this oddness is already plain to us: Being is not a being, but since our language is adapted to talking about beings, then we must talk of Being in the language appropriate to beings. The justification for such odd language lies in our doctrine that Being is present and manifest in the beings, and that indeed it is only in and through beings (including our own being) that we can have any understanding of Being. The presence and manifestation of Being in beings, or, alternatively expressed, the participation of beings in Being, justifies the logic of a language of beings that has been stretched to serve as a language of Being. This will have to be explicated in more detail for the different modes of religious and theological discourse, a task which will be undertaken in the next section.

Meantime, to complete our analysis, we have still to consider the act of saying from a third point of view, that of the person to whom something gets said. From his point of view, the language *communicates*, and this is to be understood primarily as a sharing. It is a sharing of the experience that is expressed in the language, and a sharing of that to which the language refers and which it seeks to light up. In the case of theological language, what is intended to be communicated is the understanding of Being that has been appropriated in the attitude of faith.

Such sharing, however, can take place only where the person who is addressed already has a common frame of reference with the person who addresses him. He has got to understand the language, and if he does not, then no communication takes place. He will not understand if, let us say, the language is a foreign one which he has never learned. But he will not understand either, if the language, though his own, is used in unfamiliar ways or implies a background of ideas that are unfamiliar. The contemporary man, for instance, may well find that a myth does not communicate, because he does not share the presuppositions of that particular myth; or again, that the language of the Church does not communicate because it alludes to experiences, stories, doctrines, practices, and the like that are shared by the members of the community of faith but are strange to him.

Failure to communicate raises the problem of translation and of interpretation. Can what is said be transposed into a language that will communicate to the person whom it is desired to address? It will be recalled that for interpretation there are needed two languages which can be used in parallel and each of which will illuminate the other.[6] This can happen in many different ways. The translation of, let us say, Greek into English is also an interpretation. The setting of one analogy alongside another is an interpretation in which both of them may be clarified. However, in seeking to interpret, we must look for the kind of language that will be as widely understood as possible, and this means a language with a universally accessible frame of reference. This is why so much stress has been laid in this book on the place of the language of existence and being. If communication is sharing, then we all share our human mode of existence; and if theological language is to be shown meaningful and is to communicate with the person who does not share the vocabulary of some particular community of faith, then it ought to be possible to offer an interpretation that will relate theological discourse to the frame of reference that we all share as human beings in the world. This has been a major aim of this philosophical theology, but our deliberate concentration on the somewhat austere language of existence and being should not blind us to the fact that most theological discourse takes place in more concrete modes. We must now look more closely at some of the commoner modes of theological discourse, and consider how they are related both among themselves and to the basic language of existence and being.

24. THE MODES OF THEOLOGICAL DISCOURSE

Theological discourse arises out of religious discourse, and its roots must be sought in the pre-theological language of religion. This is the language

---

[6] See above, pp. 37–38.

of *mythology*. One might say that mythology is a kind of primitive theology, in so far as the myths try to give verbal expression to the content of religious faith. But mythology falls short of theology properly so called, just as it falls short of philosophy, for, as compared with both of these studies, it lacks the ordered systematic approach that is characteristic of an intellectual discipline. Mythology may contain an implicit theology and perhaps an implicit philosophy too; but it is itself a matrix for theology, rather than a form of theology. On the other hand, elements of mythology may persist even in highly systematized theologies.

To characterize myth both briefly and adequately is not easy. Yet some attempt must be made to delimit the area of discourse that can properly be called "mythological," for some writers use the word "myth" far too loosely, to cover any kind of symbolical discourse; and since perhaps all our talking has a symbolic element in it, the frontiers of myth become so extended and so blurred that the word "myth" has no longer sufficient precision to be fit for use in a serious discussion of language.

The following remarks will perhaps serve as a minimal characterization of what we mean by "myth." The *form* of myth is narrative, and its language is therefore dramatic and concrete rather than scientific and generalizing. Yet this does not mean that the myth is tied to a particular occurrence, for the occurrence which it relates is taken to be in some sense a paradigm and significant for what goes on now. Moreover, ideas or images may get detached from the narrative and be used in other contexts, and these may be called "mythical" ideas, but their "home," so to speak, is in the mythical narrative; they presuppose this, and are ultimately to be understood in the light of it. Some students of mythology have seen in the concrete narrative form of the myth a consequence of the poverty of primitive language, which had relatively few words for abstract ideas. But on the other hand, the concrete narrative form has its own vivid power of communication—a power that is still exploited by novelists and dramatists in a post-mythical age. The *events* narrated in myth are, in one sense, of a piece with other events in the world, for they are accessible to the senses and can be seen, heard and, generally speaking, described in sensuous terms. This is to say that the language of myth is an objectifying language, and speaks of the mythical happenings in the same way as we would speak of any events in the world. But in another sense, these mythical events are different from ordinary events. They have frequently the character of miracles and wonders, and they are not subject to the ordinary considerations of space and time and causality. The mysteriousness of these events is heightened by the fact that they are put beyond the possibility of verification, for the action of the myth generally happens in some utterly remote region of space and time. The *persons* of the myth have the same twofold character as the events. In one sense they belong within the world, for they are seen and heard, or at least they manifest themselves through some sensible phenomena. Yet the principal actors in the myth are no ordinary persons, but gods or spirits or demons who come from "another world," a heaven or a hell, which again might be given an actual physical location in the sky or in the west or under the ground. Finally, we may notice the *evocative* character of mythical language. It is a language heavily laden with connotation. At the mythical level, the distinction of literal and figurative, of symbol and what is symbolized, has not yet been made. It could be made only when some alternative language became available, and an interpretation of the myth could be offered. While the objectifying language of myth seems to give it an inappropriate literalness, its extraordinary events and its supernatural *dramatis personae* make it suggestive of dimensions of experience beyond those of our everyday dealings with the world.

We ourselves live in a post-mythical age. Perhaps we have our own superstitions, but these are not "myths" within the meaning assigned to the word in the foregoing discussion. With the rise of science, the background of presuppositions on which mythical discourse proceeded has been gradually destroyed. Thus modern man finds that myth does not communicate to him, for the condition that language may communicate is precisely that one shares a frame of reference with the person who uses the language.

Yet perhaps the modern man can still catch something of the evocative and allusive character of the myth, and suspects that in spite of its apparent absurdities, it may contain insights that remain valid and are not to be dismissed as just primitive superstition. But if these insights are to be elicited, a new act of interpretation is called for, so that the insights of the myth can be expressed in a language that can communicate in a post-mythical world. It may be that in the end, after such an interpretation has been offered, one can go back to the myth with a new appreciation. Certainly, one's attitude will be different from that of the archaic mentality that lived in the as yet undifferentiated myth, for now one recognizes the myth as myth. Yet, if an interpretative key has been found, the dramatic form of the myth may be found to communicate its insights with a forcefulness that would not belong to an abstract language.

The most successful attempt to restate the meanings which the myths tried to express is the method of *demythologizing*, as developed by Rudolf Bultmann. "Its aim," he tells us, "is not to eliminate the mythological statements, but to interpret them; it is a method of hermeneutics." [7] In Bultmann's view, myth is primitive man's attempt to express in words an understanding of his own existence in the world. It is an attempt to answer the question, Who am I?—a question which is posed by existence itself, for we cannot exist responsibly without deciding to understand our existence in one way or another, even if such an understanding is not made explicit. Certainly one can see that this question comes before any speculative questions, and is much more likely to be the motivation of a creation-myth, let us say, than the relatively sophisticated and detached question, How did things begin?

Bultmann has been able to show how myths of the creation, the fall, the last things, can be existentially interpreted, and when this is done, the block in communication is at least to some extent overcome. The myths can be shown to conceal within themselves a self-understanding which is just as relevant today as ever—a self-understanding in which we are made aware of the finitude and disorder of a human existence that is always lived in the face of the end. The fact that Bultmann's method produces such a coherent and convincing picture is itself a remarkable testimony to the soundness of that method. He is surely right in stressing the existential orientation of religious language, and this needs to be stressed since the objectifying language of myth can easily obscure it from us.

The danger inherent in existential interpretation of myth is that it tends to subjectivize the whole content of the myth, so that all the ideas of the myth, including even the idea of "God," are taken to refer to elements of our own inner life. Bultmann himself would reject such an interpretation. He claims that existential interpretation is not a subjectivizing, for existence is encounter with what is other than the self, and in faith we encounter a transcendent reality that is independent of our existence and, indeed, prior to it. But to acknowledge this is to admit that the content of the myth cannot be exhaustively interpreted in statements that refer to human existence. The myth has also a transcendent reference, and while it does not speak of a transcendent reality apart from the way in which that reality relates to human existence, nevertheless it does not permit this reality to be absorbed into existence as a mere constitutive fac-

[7] *Jesus Christ and Mythology*, p. 18.

tor belonging to it. In his interpretation of myth, Bultmann finds it necessary to employ what he calls "analogical" language about "God's acts," "God's address" and so on, and whatever this may be, it is not straightforward talk about human existence.

It would seem then that an interpretation of myth, if it is not to shortchange the myth and leave out an essential element in its content, must take account of its ontological as well as its existential significance. The myth talks indeed of our human existence, but it talks of this existence in relation to Being, in so far as Being has disclosed itself. The myth seeks to express not only a self-understanding but an understanding of Being. This, however, brings us back to the question of how a language that can properly talk only of beings can be so stretched or modified that it can talk about Being. If this can be done at all, it can be done only in some such way as Bultmann suggests when he talks of "analogy," that is to say, by taking some phenomenon ("act," "address") that belongs properly within the existence of beings and then referring it indirectly to God or Being. But Bultmann never gets around to discussing this problem in any detail. His chief achievement has been to stress the existential character of myth.

If we are to pursue the interpretation of myth on the ontological level, then it would seem that we must find some way of dealing with the problem of *symbols*. In myth itself, the symbol and that which is symbolized have not yet been clearly distinguished. As soon as we recognize a symbol *as a symbol*, we have taken a step back from the myth and emerged from a purely mythological way of thinking and talking. Thus, although it is often said that myth is indispensable to the expression of religious truth, this statement is not accurate. What is meant is that religious or theological language cannot dispense with symbols, specifically, the symbols drawn from myth and perhaps even whole stories that belong to a particular context of mythology. But the fact that these symbols are now understood as symbols and that they can be discussed and illumined in an alternative interpretative language indicates that the person who can handle them in this way has transcended a purely mythical apprehension of the symbols. As I have said elsewhere,[8] the transition is like the one that lies between one's apprehension of a dream while the dream is going on, and one's apprehension of it after waking up, when perhaps one reflects on it and puzzles over what it might conceivably have "meant."

[8] *The Scope of Demythologizing*, p. 203.

In the widest sense of the word, a "symbol" is anything which is presented to the mind as standing for something else. In this broad sense, symbolism is all-pervasive of life, and there are almost innumerable kinds of symbols. A discussion of symbols in general would turn into an encyclopedic survey of human knowledge. So our first step must be to restrict within manageable dimensions the area which can profitably be discussed here, and even so our discussion will be all too brief. The restriction can be made by drawing some distinctions.

We notice first that words (and even the letters out of which written words are made up) are symbols, so that in the broad sense all language has a symbolic character. When, however, we speak of "symbolic language," we generally have a fairly definite kind of language in mind, a kind in which the words are not understood in their direct or proper reference but in which they, so to speak, bounce off that to which they properly refer so as to impinge at a distance on a more remote subject-matter, to which the speaker wishes to refer. We restrict ourselves then, in the first place, to symbolic language in the narrower sense, where it is distinguished from literal language.

We must also notice that while the language is symbolic, that which serves as the intermediary between the language and its ultimate referend can also be called a "symbol." For instance, when Christ is called the "light of the world," [9] the language is symbolic, for he is not being literally identified with physical illumination, and the reference bounces off the proper referend of the expression to some other referend. But not only the language is symbolic, for we can also say that light itself is a symbol, and that what enables light to function as a symbol are its actual properties, which become suggestive of that which it symbolizes.

This leads to a further distinction, that between a conventional symbol and an intrinsic one.[10] The conventional symbol has no connection with what it symbolizes other than the fact that some people have arbitrarily agreed to let it stand for this particular *symbolizandum*. The intrinsic symbol, on the other hand, has in itself a kinship with what it symbolizes. But the distinction between the two types is not so clear-cut as it is some-

---

[9] John 8:12.

[10] Tillich's distinction between "sign" (as arbitrary pointer) and "symbol" (as participating in what is symbolized) is to be avoided as at variance with good English usage. We say, "Clouds are a sign of rain," and there is obviously an intrinsic connection between the sign and what it signifies, nor could we substitute the word "symbol." On the other hand, we talk of "mathematical symbols," "symbolic logic" and the like, where the symbols are for the most part arbitrary.

times thought to be. This becomes apparent if we consider a slightly different statement of the distinction, given by Edwyn Bevan. He distinguishes between symbols which tell us nothing about what they symbolize and those which convey knowledge about what they symbolize.[11] It is interesting to notice that whereas Tillich thinks of a national flag as an intrinsic symbol because it "participates in the power and dignity of the nation for which it stands," [12] Bevan thinks of a flag as belonging to the first of the two classes of symbols which he distinguishes. It may *remind* us of everything that we have learned about a nation because we have been taught to associate it with that nation, but it does not open up for us any new understanding for it has no intrinsic connection with that for which it stands. But Bevan claims that there are other symbols which, by what they are in themselves, have a kinship with what they symbolize and can enable us to understand it. Among these he would put the most important religious symbols, such as light, which we have already mentioned.

In practice, it might be very difficult to distinguish sharply among symbols that were purely conventional, symbols which through historical association had come to "participate" in the qualities of their *symbolizanda*, and symbols possessing inherent characteristics having an affinity with the characteristics of what was symbolized. How blurred are these distinctions may be illustrated from the fact that the wheel has often been used as a symbol of industry in the West while in the East it symbolizes the cycle of existence. Both uses can claim to be based on intrinsic connections yet both obviously depend on historical associations and, one might say, on a whole world view. But while it is difficult to draw hard and fast lines, our discussion—and this is our second restriction—will be in the main confined to symbols which seem to have an intrinsic relation to their *symbolizanda* and can be illuminating for them.

Another point that emerges from these remarks deserves to be noticed. It is the fact that any particular symbol or group of symbols is operative within a more or less restricted group of people. There could hardly be a private symbol, for a symbol communicates only where there are the prerequisite shared presuppositions for communication. The national flag is a symbol for those who belong to the nation and have some idea of the history and ideals which the flag represents. But the flag would be meaningless to someone who knew nothing of this history. Religious symbols belong to a community of faith. The cross speaks to the Chris-

---

[11] *Symbolism and Belief*, pp. 11–12.
[12] *Dynamics of Faith*, p. 42.

tian, the crescent to the Muslim, but without a participation in the history of the community, no one could recognize what is conveyed by these symbols. But if there can be no private symbols, it may be doubted whether there could be any universal symbols either, symbols that would speak at all times and to all peoples. If there are any such symbols, they would be of the second kind mentioned by Bevan, and would have an intrinsic and illuminating connection with what they symbolized. But the illustration of the wheel, given above, makes us doubt whether there can be any intrinsic connections that would not be obscured or altered by historical circumstances. The symbol of light comes pretty near to being a universal symbol of God among the great religions of the world. Yet because light for the modern man has become just another physical phenomenon, it seems that even this symbol might cease to speak in some historical periods that lacked receptivity for it.

Perhaps in the interpretation of symbols we can never do more than illumine one set of symbols by another set—that is to say, it may be that we can never leave symbols entirely behind. But the fact that symbols communicate within smaller or larger groups indicates a direction in which interpretation should proceed. It must move from the less widely to the more widely received symbols, from those which operate in the small group to those which have a wider accessibility. It is for this reason that so much stress has been laid throughout this philosophical theology on the language of being and existence, for this is something like a universally communicable language, arising as it does out of existential structures and experiences common to all human beings. In so far as religious symbols can be related to this language, they are also related to the world of common experience and cannot be dismissed as just the illusions of some group or other. But while the process of interpretation is from the symbolism of the smaller group toward a more widely received language, this does not mean that the symbols are abandoned. Here, as always, interpretation has a reciprocal character and the two or more languages in which it proceeds throw light on one another. The particular symbols are illuminated by the language of existence and being, but these concrete symbols become in turn illuminating for relatively abstract statements of an existential or ontological character.

Our discussion so far has led us to restrict our consideration of symbolic language to the kind that is indirect in its reference and that employs symbols which can somehow be illuminating for the indirect referend, at which the symbolic statement is ultimately aimed. In the case of religious symbols, the language is finally anchored in the discourse of existence and being, a kind of discourse which we have already sought to justify by setting it in its living context and showing how it arises and what kind of logic guides it. But it still remains to show more clearly how religious symbols can be tied in with this language of being and existence, and, above all, how talk about particular beings or their properties can even indirectly refer to Being and be illuminating for it.

Our discussions have already prepared a way for answering these questions. But before any detailed answer is attempted, let it be said that the general ground for any possible symbolizing of Being by the beings must be some *analogia entis*. This analogy of being has been variously conceived in the history of philosophy. Perhaps too often it has been interpreted as meaning that God is a kind of super-being who differs from us chiefly in that he is the cause of his own being, but who nevertheless is as a distinct being. On the other hand Barth, in his eagerness to preserve the otherness of God and his distance from man, has denied that there is an analogy of being between them, though it seems to me that this denial raises difficulties over how we may talk about God, which Barth is able to resolve only in a completely arbitrary and unconvincing way in terms of the *analogia gratiae*. But surely the understanding of Being that has been set out in earlier sections of this theology enables us to interpret the *analogia entis* in a way that will neither assimilate God to man nor yet put an unbridgeable gulf between them. Being has been called an incomparable and a *transcendens*, and there could be no beings without the Being that lets them be; but Being is present and manifest in the beings, and apart from the beings, Being would become indistinguishable from nothing. Hence Being and the beings, though neither can be assimilated to the other, cannot be separated from each other either. This ontological doctrine corresponds to the religious experience of the holy as at once *tremendum* and *fascinosum*, as characterized by otherness and closeness.

We may now consider what kind of symbolism is made possible on the basis of this fundamental *analogia entis*. The symbols will be considered in two ways: from the side of the particular beings looking toward Being, and from the side of Being as it is present and manifest in the beings that it lets-be. The symbols have a corresponding twofold function (in accordance with the general function of interpretation) as they open up Being to the beings and yet at the same time open up the beings in the light of Being. This is why we can use the human relation of, let us say, fatherhood to illuminate God, and yet understand this human relation itself to be illuminated and judged by the ultimate relation to God.

1. Let us first then think of the symbols from the side of particular beings, looking toward Being. How is it possible for these symbols to illuminate Being?

The first answer is in terms of *existential response*. There are particular beings which can arouse in us the kind of response that is aroused by Being itself. My own teacher, C. A. Campbell, saw this similarity of response as a test of the appropriateness of symbols to stand for the incomparable (or, as he would say, "suprarational") being of God, as when he claims that "the recognition of the special affinity of the divine nature with goodness is implied in the recognition of the analogy between the emotion which the conception of *good* evokes in us and the emotion which the *mysterium fascinans* evokes." [13] In view of all that has been said already about the function of affective states in the disclosure of Being, and in view also of what Campbell and Otto believe about the experience of the *mysterium*, no one will suppose for a moment that Campbell is trying to justify symbols on the basis of our subjective feelings about them.[14] Rather, it is the case that there are things, persons, qualities, and so on that awaken in us such affective states as awe, reverence, loyalty; and it is in these states that Being discloses itself to us.

The existential response is an essential part of the symbol's status as a symbol, and if more attention were paid to it, then we would see that some criticisms of traditional symbols rather miss the point. The criticism of "height," for instance, as a symbol of God on the ground that we no longer think of God as "up there" misses the point that even at the mythological stage "height" was understood in terms of its existential connotations rather than in terms of spatial location so that it awakened (and still awakens) the response of humility and reverence before the power and majesty of the one who is elevated above the common level.[15] However, while we do well to attend to the element of existential response in symbolism and so bear in mind what we have already learned about the existential or evaluative character of all religious and theological discourse, an exclusive preoccupation with existential response would bring us back to Bultmann's position and would parallel his demythologizing with an existential desymbolizing. He does indeed call for this, and, within limits, rightly. But we must also consider how the symbol refers to Being.

[13] *On Selfhood and Godhood*, p. 356.
[14] F. Ferré comes near to making this criticism of Campbell. See *Language, Logic and God*, p. 101f.
[15] Cf. E. Bevan, *Symbolism and Belief*, pp. 28–81.

Still looking then from the beings toward Being, our second point about symbols is that they illuminate Being in terms of *similarity of relation*. If Being is incomparable with particular beings, it is hard to see how any property of a particular being could be like a property of Being, if indeed one could even talk about a property of Being. It is not, however, inconceivable that I might be related to a being or to a group of beings in a manner which in some regards might resemble my relation to Being. The similarity is not between a being and Being, for although there is affinity between Being and the beings, this affinity is not simple similarity. The similarity is between a relation of beings and a relation of Being to a being.

Since we are talking here of similarity as the basis for the symbolism, it might seem more appropriate to speak of "analogues" than of "symbols." The two are sometimes sharply contrasted, especially in some Catholic writers who, while defending analogy, attack symbolism. It seems to me, however, that the kind of symbolism attacked is supposed to empty theological language of any real content, and this is far from what is meant by "symbolism" in this book, as will become clear. However, as there are symbols which do not depend on similarity, it will be useful to use the expression "analogy" when we are discussing the illumination of Being that takes place by way of similarity of relation.

It is clear that what we call "similarity of relation" is an analogy of proportionality, and so an analogy in the original sense (ἄνα λόγον, "according to a ratio"). Of the four terms of the proportion, three denote beings, while the fourth term is Being. A good example comes from the Psalms: "As a father pities his children, so the Lord pities those who fear him." [16] Here the image of the father is applied to God, on the ground that those who "fear" him stand in a relation to him that is similar to the relation of the child to the father. Many familiar analogues are of the same kind—God as king, judge, shepherd, and so on. The illustration of height (God as "the most high") that was mentioned under the heading of "existential response" belongs also under "similarity of relation," just as fatherhood and the other examples quoted above could have been mentioned under "existential response." The point is, however, that when one talks of "similarity of relation," attention is directed to the actual structure or situation in which man relates to Being, rather than to his state of mind in this situation. The relation is, broadly speaking, one of dependence, as Schleiermacher saw, and the various analogues draw attention to this in

[16] Ps. 103:13.

its several aspects. These analogues do not indeed disclose to us Being "as it is in itself" (if one may so speak), but Being as related to us, and this of course is entirely in line with the view put forward above that theological language has always an existential-ontological character.

Some symbols (or perhaps we should still speak of "analogues"), such as "wisdom" or "goodness," or talk of God or Being as having certain attributes, may seem to demand a further consideration. To say that God is good can indeed be considered, as we have already seen, under the notion of existential response; and since we would be thinking of God's goodness toward us, we could likewise envisage it in terms of similarity of relation. But we may simply assert that God is wise or good, and we seem to suppose that we are attributing a property to God. Can we make any sense of this, if God is understood as Being, and hence neither a thing nor a person, and so apparently disqualified from having "properties" attributed to him?

The answer to this question about the validity of symbols is in terms of Being as *prior enabling condition*. We have seen that Being "is" neither a being nor a property, but since it is the condition that there may be any beings or properties at all, it is more "beingful" than any being or property. This point was already used to justify the language about God's "existence," for although God (or Being) "lets-be" rather than "is," so that strictly speaking one cannot say "God is," nevertheless since "letting-be" is the prior condition that anything is, it is less inappropriate to say "God is" than "God is not." God is more beingful, in the sense that "isness" is swallowed up in "letting-be."

Now, just as it is permissible to talk of the "existence" of God on the ground that he is the prior enabling condition of any existent entity, so it is less inappropriate to attribute to God the positive characteristics of existent beings than to deny them of him. But clearly they are not being literally attributed. Indeed, although we may say God is "wise" or "good," some such word as "infinitely" (a "qualifier," as Ian Ramsey calls it [17]) is understood in front of the adjective to show that it is being used in an "odd" way. We have no understanding of what the word "good" could literally mean when applied to God, for it must transcend any notions of goodness that we may have. Yet we are entitled to use it because it is more appropriate to say that God is good than that he is not good, for he is the prior enabling condition of all goodness whatsoever.

These remarks are reminiscent of the traditional doctrine of the *via*

[17] *Religious Language*, p. 62.

eminentiae, except that "Being" is probably understood in a different way. Our whole consideration of symbolism so far, however, has been close to the traditional doctrine of analogy, though we have laid more stress on the notion of existential response and have minimized the idea of likeness. But the problem that has always beset the traditional doctrine was that of showing that the analogues or symbols really do in some significant way bridge the gap between the beings of which we talk in our everyday language, and divine Being of which the religious man wishes to talk. So far, we do not seem to have achieved much in this direction. It will be remembered, however, that the question of symbolism is to be approached from two sides. Up till now, we have come at it from the side of the beings, looking toward transcendent Being as this may be opened to us by the beings. Now we must turn to the other side, and ask how Being might disclose itself symbolically in beings.

2. Let us begin by recalling that if Being is a *transcendens,* it is also immanent in the beings and is nothing apart from them; that if it is distinguishable from appearing, it yet includes appearing, and is not some supposed "thing-in-itself" behind the appearances. The word "Being" does not stand for some allegedly intangible, invisible, unverifiable being that exists in addition to the beings that we know in everyday experience, but stands for Being that gives itself in and with and through particular beings.

Hence religious symbolism gets its fundamental justification in terms of what I have called the "*presence and manifestation*" of Being in the beings. The expression "presence" gives the lie to any objection that a theory of symbolism voids religious assertions of "real" meaning. The symbol is not identified with what it symbolizes, but it makes it present. The expression "manifestation" is sufficiently flexible to cover the many possible ways in which Being communicates itself through the beings that it lets be. A being cannot be simply *like* Being, but every being is a clue to Being, indeed we might even say that beings are the language of Being, though this itself would be to use an analogy of proportionality, namely, that beings are to Being as language is to him who speaks. A fuller justification for this assertion will be given when we come to discuss the doctrine of creation. For the moment, it is enough to say that Being manifests itself in the beings not because they are like Being, any more than language is like a man, but because they express Being and participate in Being.

But are we not proving too much? For if everything that is participates in Being, and if Being is present-and-manifest in everything that is, then have we not got an embarrassing quantity of symbols on our hands, for everything that is affords a clue to Being and would seem to be a symbol of Being? It is indeed the case that everything that is can become a symbol of Being, for in some degree Being is present and manifest in it. Actually, in the history of religion an astonishing variety of entities has served for religious symbolism. But just as we noticed that while revelation may be a possibility at any time or place, there are nevertheless "classic" or "primordial" revelations that give rise to communities of faith, so we may say that while everything that is has the potentiality for becoming a symbol of Being, there are also classic symbols that establish themselves in a community of faith. These symbols are not arbitrarily adopted, but are associated with the classic revelation. They are not chosen by us, but rather are given by Being which has addressed us in and through them. The great symbols, analogues, and images of the Christian religion, for instance, the cross, the fatherhood of God, the suffering servant, have their depth of meaning only in the context of this particular revelation of God, and they cohere together in a constellation, as it were, each shedding light on the other.

But the fact that some entities function as symbols of Being while others do not is not just a matter of their association with some historical revelation. It is also the case that some entities are better suited to be symbols of Being than others. Here we must remind ourselves of the point made earlier, that although Being is present and therefore potentially manifest in every particular being, some manifest it more fully than others. The test of a symbol is its *adequacy* in lighting up Being, and one symbol or set of symbols may be preferred to another on the ground that it is more adequate.

This adequacy, in turn, may be considered in relation to the *range of participation* in Being which belongs to the entity that is to serve as a symbol. An inanimate object exhibits material being, while an animal exhibits not only material being but also organic being. In man, a material body and an animal organism are united with his distinctively personal being. This is the widest range of being that we know, and therefore symbols and images drawn from personal life have the highest degree of adequacy accessible to us. In many cases, even symbols that are themselves inanimate objects—the cross is a good illustration—derive their symbolic meaning from the part they play in personal existence. In the central Christian doctrine of the incarnation, it is a person who becomes the symbol of Being, the revelation of God. If anyone objects to Christ's being called a "symbol" on the ground that this detracts from the reality of incarnation, let it be remembered that God (Being) is present-and-manifest in the symbol, and it is hard to see how anything more can be meant by "incarnation." But this will be made clearer when we come to consider the person of Christ. For the present, it is enough to notice the primacy that belongs to personal symbols and images, as these are entities having the widest range of participation in Being and so best able to symbolize it.

A related but slightly different idea which must also be taken into account in evaluating the adequacy of symbols is the idea of the *hierarchy of beings*. This is, of course, a very widespread idea that has persisted from ancient times down to the theories of emergent evolution that get propounded by modern philosophers. Just as entities exhibit varying ranges of participation in Being, so, on this view, they can be arranged in an ascending series according as they show increasing range and complexity in their being. We could, for instance, imagine a series rising from the simplest kinds of physical entities up to the personal being of man, though the various grades and stages have been differently envisaged by different philosophers.

The relevance of this to symbolism will not become entirely apparent until we have studied the doctrine of creation.[18] But for the moment, let me suggest that as one surveys the rising grades of being, the character of Being is itself more clearly manifested. For whereas the lowest or simplest beings *are*, the higher ones not only *are* but *let-be*, and this becomes peculiarly true at the level of man's personal being, with its limited freedom and creativity. So again, the symbols that are drawn from the level of personal being have the highest adequacy, since they point to the letting-be of Being. Moreover, it will be shown that the essence of love is precisely letting-be; and for this reason love has become, not only in Christianity but in other religions besides, the supreme symbol of divine Being.

This completes our remarks on symbolism as viewed in terms of the immanence of Being in the beings. Taken in conjunction with the earlier account that looked from the beings toward transcendent Being, we have, I hope, good grounds for believing that religious symbols do give us insight into the mystery of the holy as it relates itself to man. To borrow a technological metaphor from G. S. Spinks,[19] symbols may be compared to the transformers on an electrical grid system, whereby "tremendous loads of power are broken down" and made accessible.

It was said that symbols are illuminating for each other, and this draws attention to a peculiarity of symbolic language. Different symbols may

---

18 See below, pp. 223–226.
19 *The Fundamentals of Religious Belief*, p. 75.

complement one another rather than stand in contradiction. Of course, there may also be irreconcilably different symbols. But we must avoid supposing that symbols are like theories, where, presumably, one is true and to be accepted, and the rest rejected as false. To exalt one symbol to exclusive status is to forget that even the most adequate symbol falls short of what it symbolizes. To absolutize a symbol is to identify it with its *symbolizandum,* and in the case of religious symbols, this means idolatry and all the distortions and errors that go with it.

These remarks bring us to another feature of theological language, and to another peculiarity of its logic—its *paradoxicality.* Just because symbols are symbols, that is to say, they both stand for what they symbolize and yet fall short of it, they must be at once affirmed and denied. St. Thomas remarks: "No name is predicated univocally of God and of creatures. Neither, on the other hand, are names applied to God and creatures in a purely equivocal sense." [20] If the names were applied univocally, then (in our terminology) we would be treating Being as *a* being, and one of the same order as the being from which the symbol or analogue was drawn; and if the names were applied quite equivocally, then the symbolism would be empty and would yield no insight into Being. So there must be a continual balancing of statements in theological language. This must not be allowed to become an excuse for unclear thinking or for laziness in seeking to resolve needless contradictions. But there will probably remain an indispensable element of paradox, and while a merely syntactical analysis might be tempted to dismiss this as illogicality, when we place it in its discourse-situation and see what it is trying to express in the indirect language of symbols, then we must accord it its right.

This all too summary treatment of the modes of theological language has, it is hoped, shown something of the logic that belongs to mythology, symbolism, analogy, and paradox, how these relate to each other, and how they relate to the basic language of being and existence. A fuller justification will come only with the detailed exposition of the various symbols in the second major division of this systematic theology, and to the extent to which we succeed in showing that these symbols can be expressive, illuminative, and communicative of that toward which religious faith is directed.

25. THE QUESTION OF TRUTH

Up to this point we have been concerned in the present chapter mainly with the question of the *meaning* of theological language, and it is correct

[20] *Summa Theologiae,* Ia, 13, 5.

that this question should come first in any discussion of language. But we have to go on to the question of the *truth* of theological language. This language claims to be true. Can we specify more clearly the nature of its truth claims and say what criteria are relevant for testing them?

We begin by assuming that truth is a polymorphous concept. This is surely a reasonable assumption; the truth, let us say, of a mathematical proposition, of a particular empirical matter of fact, of a general scientific hypothesis, of an assertion about the past, of a theological doctrine, is in each case different, and different considerations are relevant in judging the claim to truth. But this does not imply that any statement whatever could claim to be true and then have this claim supported by some highly esoteric concept of truth. There is something common to all the varieties of truth, and this would seem to be the claim that when a statement is true, it lets us see things as they really are, without distortion or concealment. This is a public claim, and so we have the right in each case to ask about criteria; but these would not be the same in each case.

What is the nature of the truth with which theology is concerned? We can answer in the first instance: existential truth. We recall that theology has its roots in man's quest for self-understanding and that this quest in turn is to be seen in the context of man as the existent, the unfinished being who is always in the process of self-transcendence, who is projecting his possibilities toward the ideal of an authentic humanity. We call this a "true" humanity, as distinguished from the distorted and obscured humanity of an inauthentic or sinful existence. The fundamental truth with which we have to do here then is an existential truth or a lived truth rather than a verbal truth; but it is none the less a truth, because it claims to bring to light what humanity truly is. As far as this kind of truth is concerned, Kierkegaard made the essential point when he said that it consists not in sentences, or concepts, or in the correspondence of thought with things, "not in knowing the truth but in being the truth." [21] This is what is intended here by the expression "existential truth," though something of the kind is already foreshadowed in the New Testament claim that Christ is the truth.[22] But since the human existent is never to be understood in isolation but only in the context of a society, a history, and eventually a cosmos, what we have called in the first instance existential truth tends to be developed into an existential-ontological truth.

It is important to hold fast the understanding that the fundamental truth

[21] *Training in Christianity*, p. 201.
[22] John 14:7.

with which theology deals is not the truth of propositions but the truth of the uncovering of man's being-in-the-world; and this is confirmed by what we have already considered in our discussion of revelation. On the other hand, man is a linguistic being. As was said at the beginning of this chapter, he is not content to contemplate the object of his religion in silence. Even to appropriate it, he must begin to use language and this use of language develops into the theological task, as we have understood it. The fact therefore that the fundamental truth of religion is an existential or lived truth does not relieve us of the theological task of trying to artic-ulate this truth in language and it does not relieve us either of specifying what criteria can be adduced for testing the truth of theological state-ments. However, one can see in a general way what is the broad criterion for the truth of theological statements: how far do they bring to light and faithfully testify to the fundamental revelation of man's being-in-the-world? But in saying this, one also sees the limitations of all theological language, for the reality to be described is richer than the language we bring to it and can never be fully expressed in words and sentences. Thus theological language can be only an approximation to truth. But this implies in turn that some theological formulations will be more adequate expressions of truth than others.

In the light of the foregoing discussion, we can set down a few criteria for judging the truth of theological statements.

1. The statements must be coherent among themselves. We have seen that theology is not just a collection of doctrines but has a unity. It seeks to express a unifying vision of man's life in its widest setting, of human existence in the presence of Being. Such a vision will be persuasive to the extent that it constitutes a harmonious whole and leaves out nothing of importance in the range of human experience.

2. Equally important is the test of coherence with our other well-founded beliefs, derived from the sciences, from history and other dis-ciplines. We cannot, for instance, formulate theological doctrines of crea-tion or providence that are at variance with what we believe about the physical world on scientific grounds. We cannot accept certain reports about the past if these conflict with well-tried findings of historical re-search. In such areas, it is clear that the criteria for establishing theological truth cannot be different from the criteria used in secular disciplines, and this is important in showing that in each case we are still concerned with *truth*.

3. From what we have learned about symbolism, dialectic, and develop-

ment in doctrine, we should also look for an openness of texture in theology. In a study where truth is, we hope, always being more fully appropriated but never totally grasped, finality and fixity are signs of error. There must be room for development, for the process of advancing into truth.

Can we say anything about the fundamental existential-ontological truth which theology is seeking to explicate? Or has this just got to be accepted, on the ground that any inquiry whatsoever must eventually come to some initial datum behind which it cannot inquire? Already in our discussion of revelation, the point was made that anything claiming to be revelation must be subjected to the sharpest scrutiny and cannot be arbitrarily accepted. Here again we might mention the phenomenon of conscience and the responsibility that arises in the face of its call. Human existence seems to have a built-in directedness, as it were, giving testimony about the direction in which a "true" humanity lies and making us aware also of our failure to attain it. We cannot go behind this fundamental self-awareness, which is our ultimate testimony to existential truth.

7 | Religion and Religions

26. SOME CHARACTERISTICS OF RELIGION

The words "religion" and "religious" have already been used quite freely in this book, but so far there has been no attempt to pin these words down in a precise way. This procedure has been permissible because only after the phenomena that we commonly call "religious" have been opened up can we see clearly what the basic characteristics of religion are.

Religion assumes such a variety of forms that attempts to give a succinct definition covering them all have usually turned out to be unsatisfactory. Moreover, definitions of religion often conceal an evaluation and already imply either that religion is illusory and an entirely subjective phenomenon or that it is indeed a valid experience of some transhuman reality. Some such evaluation is almost inevitable, but it should come after the phenomena have been studied, not before in some preliminary definition.

I do not propose to offer a definition of religion, but to list some of its basic characteristics. Also, since it has been shown in our descriptive philosophical theology that a reasonable case can be made out for the validity of religious faith, we shall take it that religion cannot be exhaustively characterized in subjective terms but is a commerce between man and the transhuman reality of God or Being.

1. Most basic of all the characteristics of religion is the impinging of God or holy Being upon man's existence. The initiative is from the side of God, who gives himself to man in revelation and grace. The divine initiative in revelation and grace would seem to be present in some form in all religion, and is certainly not peculiar to Christianity. As Gerardus van der Leeuw has expressed it, what is regarded as the "object" of reli-

gion is in fact the "subject," the "primary agent in the situation"; for "the religious man perceives that with which his religion deals as primal, as originative or causal," while God is the "agent in relation to man." [1] The universal initiative and primacy of the divine in religion should be borne in mind, as we shall see when we take notice of some tendentious accounts of religion—accounts which seek to identify it only with man's quest for God and, generally, with the human and subjective elements in religion.

2. Religion includes not only the impinging of holy Being upon man, but man's response. This is what we have already described as faith, in terms of commitment and acceptance. We have called faith an "existential attitude," an orientation of the whole man, and when we talk about the "religious man," we mean the man who is characterized by this attitude or orientation. In our account of faith, we tried to do justice to the initiative of the holy in awaking faith, but we felt it necessary also to show that man is so constituted that the quest for faith belongs to the very structure of his existence. This does not mean that man is "naturally religious," but it does recognize a continuity between man's quest for wholeness and self-hood, and the divine activity in grace and revelation. This is far from making religion a human activity, but it does recognize a root of religion in human existence.

3. The religious life finds concrete expression in various ways. Among these may be mentioned first the beliefs of the religious man. We have already noted that although belief is not to be confused with the much wider concept of faith, nevertheless every faith implies some beliefs and these can be made articulate. The earliest attempt to express in words the self-understanding of faith appears in the form of mythology. At a more sophisticated level, we come to the formulation of doctrines and creeds, and finally to the enterprise of systematic theology. Enough has been said already about the dangers of an intellectualizing of religion, when assent to creed and dogma takes the place of a more widely based faith. This is one of the commonest perversions of religion, but the fact that there is the danger of such perversion does not take away the need for trying to reach as far as possible a verbal expression of the content of faith, and every religion that has advanced beyond the stage of mythology does indeed have its creeds, doctrines, and theology. So long as these are not cut off from their roots in the existential attitude of faith in face of the revelation, they are necessary and wholesome elements in the whole structure of religion.

[1] *Religion in Essence and Manifestation*, vol. I, p. 23.

4. Side by side with the expression of faith in words goes its expression in action. We may indeed think of action as taking precedence over belief, and probably, on the level of primitive religions, ritual comes before myth, the acting out before the spelling out in words. There are, of course, many ways in which the religious man expresses his faith in action. Ritual, ceremonial, cultic acts—in a word, liturgy—form the core of this acting out of religious faith. From the earliest stages, however, liturgy tends to spill over from the specifically cultic act to color the whole way of life of those who engage in the cult. The ethical aspect becomes more and more stressed, and sometimes almost entirely replaces any cultic action. This happens especially when the cult has become divorced from the faith-attitude which it was meant to express, and has degenerated into a mere mechanical ritual. But again let us remember that the perversion of something provides no excuse for an all-out attack against it. There can be no religion without a cult, and even the most violent iconoclasts and puritans substitute some kind of cult for the one which they seek to abolish.

5. From the beginning, this book has stressed that faith belongs in a community of faith. Perhaps there are private faiths and private religions, but these are exceptional and, moreover, defective in so far as they lack the communal dimension that belongs to human existence in its very constitution. Every community, however, needs at least a minimal structure to preserve its identity and to maintain its cohesion as a group in which people really do belong together. The religious community therefore, with its greater or less degree of institutional structure, must be regarded as another basic characteristic of religion. Here again (and perhaps most of all at this point) there is danger of perversion, and the faults of a church are too well known to need any labored emphasis. In any case, these matters will all be treated more fully in due course. For the present, it is enough that we note community along with the other fundamental characteristics of religion.

By "religion," then, we understand the whole complex of structures that grows up around the giving and receiving of revelation. Through this complex, the attitude of faith finds expression in the world.

In any discussion of religion, however, we soon come to the distinction between a general abstract conception of religion and the concrete religions that are actually practiced. A few philosophers who have valued religion but who have stood apart from any concrete religion have occasionally advocated something like religion in the abstract. For the great majority of people, on the other hand, religion assumes a concrete form, and indeed even for the philosophers mentioned, it is bound to take on some definite shape. It originates in a particular occasion of revelation; this, in turn is received in a particular situation, and in a particular historical culture; the beliefs are formulated in symbols and language appropriate to the particular faith; likewise the practices are appropriate to this faith; while finally, it is within a particular community (though it may be an open rather than a closed community) that the revelation is transmitted and faith maintained.

The aim of a philosophical theology is to show, through description and interpretation, the conditions of the possibility of any religious faith whatsoever. This elucidation and, so far as is possible, vindication of general structures and concepts is necessary, if theology is to maintain its claim as an intellectual discipline. Thus, in the course of our philosophical theology, we have spoken in a general formal way of sin, revelation, grace, myth, symbols, God, Being, and these are, of course, ideas or phenomena common in one way or another to all or most religions.

But it cannot be pretended for a moment that these matters have been surveyed from some Olympian elevation, whence they could all be seen laid out in order. On the contrary, the notion of participation has been stressed from the very first; and this participation must always be participation in a particular religion. It is only from within a particular tradition of faith, in this case the Christian faith, that the theologian can venture to discuss the conditions of any faith whatsoever.

Does this particularity then invalidate the general inquiry that must start out from the particular point of view? It would seem clearly that it does not, and that many other inquiries have to proceed in a similar fashion. The philosopher of history, for instance, does not need to know all history equally well to construct his view of what history is; but the history from which his reflections take their rise has its particularity, and this particularity is sufficiently like that of the particularity of a religious tradition to make the philosophy of history an apposite comparison. Yet, on the other hand, the particular starting point does imply a perspective. In the philosophical theology that has been sketched out in the preceding chapters, it seems to me that the Christian perspective can be quite easily pointed out. This perspective converges on the notion of incarnation; the idea of incarnation, in turn, is conceivable only where there is both transcendence and immanence; and it is in terms of equiprimordial transcendence and immanence that we have presented the idea of holy Being (God).

Even to be aware of the perspective is a major step toward overcoming the possibility that it might be a distortion or a merely partisan point of view. Here we catch a glimpse of the impossible ideal of a universal philosophical theology, that is to say, one that would look along all perspectives and would gather up all revelation, all experiences, and all symbols of the holy. This is an impossible ideal for man as a being who is "there," that is to say, at a particular time and place in history. If the ideal is possible for anyone, then it could be only for a god or maybe an angel. With these remarks, we implicitly reject syncretism. We come back inevitably to the fact that we see from a perspective, though we can become aware of it. Our overcoming of the distorting possibility in a perspective (this distortion appears in religion most typically as fanaticism and intolerance) can come about only through exploring, as far as we can, the relation of religion to the religions, and of the religions to each other. This theme will engage us in the present chapter, before we turn from philosophical theology to the remaining divisions of the work in which our attention will be concentrated specifically on Christian theology.

But it seems that one further point must be cleared up before we can proceed to the discussion of the relation among the religions. We have talked of religion as the whole complex of structures that grows out of the revelation-faith situation, we have apparently equated the man of faith with the religious man and the community of faith with the religious community or church, and we seem to have given implicit approval to religion as a whole, though readily admitting that it is susceptible to various kinds of perversion. Before we go on to further discussion of religion, this would seem to be an appropriate place to pause and consider whether, in the light of our explorations of faith, revelation, and other phenomena, religion, as we have summed up its basic characteristics in this section, can be defended against its many detractors.

27. RELIGION AND ITS CRITICS

We might think that the critics of religion would be for the most part atheists, positivists, or skeptics of one kind or another, and that their criticism would be based on a rejection of some of the basic convictions that lie at the foundation of religion. At the present time, however, there is also a powerful theological critique of religion, especially among some Protestant thinkers. Thus a discussion of the critics of religion may begin by dividing them into two fairly well-defined groups: those who reject religion because they also reject such ideas as God, grace, revelation, and other matters supposed to be fundamental to religion; and those who reject religion, conceived as the whole structure (one might even say, machinery) that grows up around the life of faith, while holding strongly to God, faith, grace, and the like, and perhaps explicitly contrasting religion and faith, or religion and revelation.

We need not spend too much time over the first group, for we have perhaps already gone about as far as we can toward answering their criticisms. The philosophical theology that has been constructed is also an apologetic, insofar as it has succeeded in giving a clear and reasonable account of the foundations of faith and theology. It may be worthwhile however to remind ourselves in summary fashion of just how this philosophical theology has sought to counter objections to religious faith.

Much traditional criticism of religion was based on *metaphysics*, and appealed to some world view, such as materialism, which excluded the reality of God. With the general decline of metaphysics, this kind of criticism has become less common, and our reply to it has not been to try to demonstrate a rival metaphysic. Rather, we have accepted that the world is ambiguous and that faith, properly understood, implies risk. But we have also maintained that although one cannot demonstrate either a theistic or an atheistic metaphysic, faith that a holy presence makes itself known in our ambiguous world is a reasonable faith, and can point to its own patterns of evidence both in the world and in the quality of life which it builds up.

The contemporary philosopher is more likely to criticize religion on *analytical* grounds. If the religious man claims to have some insight into the way things are when he talks of God, can he show us what kind of logic underlies his language, or are we to dismiss it as mere confusion? In response to this criticism, we have tried to show that our talk of God does have an intelligible logic, and that we can see what this is and how the language makes sense when we set it in the context of the existential situation which gives rise to it and finds expression in it. This response is carried further when we recognize the symbolic character of religious language, and how its symbols function.

But the most widespread criticism of religion is on the grounds of the *positivism* that has become characteristic of our time. It rejects on the one hand any belief in a reality beyond the natural phenomena, and on the other hand it tries to explain religion in natural terms, whether psychologically, sociologically, or in some other way, but without thinking it necessary to invoke the idea of God or of any transhuman reality to account for religion. Our response to such positivistic criticism has been twofold. On one side, we have tried to think of God as Being in such a way that without diminishing the holiness or reality of God, we have nevertheless escaped the crude supernaturalism of supposing God to be a kind of *deus ex machina*. One does not need to be a positivist to find this crude supernaturalism inacceptable. On the other side, we have stressed participation as a necessary factor in knowing what religious faith is, and positivism, by its abstraction and its attempt to study religion only from the outside, gives by comparison a fragmented, partial, and distorted account of religion.

Since the positivist view of religion is so widely held, it deserves to be discussed a little further. Perhaps it gets its strongest support from modern psychology, and especially from the theories of Sigmund Freud, who shows how irrational many of our beliefs are and how we come to accept them not because of any intellectual conviction but because of deep unconscious drives that demand satisfaction. In his view, as in that of many other psychologists, religion is simply an illusion produced by our need for security. It has the structure of a neurosis or imbalance, and the idea of God is simply the projection of the image of the human father whom the religious man, in his failure to grow up, still needs to protect and shelter him from the real world.

I said earlier that one has to acknowledge that religion has indeed often been a haven for what is infantile and immature, and Freud's criticism is valid against this kind of religion.[2] But Freud does not allow for any progress in religion, otherwise he would have seen that as religion progresses, the elements of judgment, demand, and responsibility (no doubt present in some form from the beginning) become more pronounced, and religion becomes less and less an escape from life. Our own consideration of faith as "acceptance and commitment in the face of Being" cannot be fitted into the Freudian scheme—and of course Freud readily admitted that his account of religion did not cover all religion, but only the anthropomorphic sort, where the father-image is prominent. Yet even so, we cannot think of the father-image as just a projection. In our treatment of symbols, we tried to show that while indeed these have a subjective side in respect of their existential connotations, they are also in various ways akin to what they symbolize, and the appropriateness of the symbols depends on the adequacy of their kinship with the *symbolizanda*. Here again, of

2 See above, pp. 28, 55.

course, the risk of faith must be remembered, and it could be the case that the skeptical psychologist is right and God is no more than a figment of the human *psyche*. But our whole endeavor has been to show that it is reasonable to believe otherwise, and indeed *more reasonable*, because the understanding that comes through participation must, in these matters, reach far beyond what can be grasped in any external observation. Further, we have tried to show that a religious faith, so far from fragmenting personal existence, is actually a most powerful stabilizing and unifying factor. This would hardly be the case if it were merely an illusion, for then, as Freud claims, it would indeed be neurotic. But here we may notice that many students of man's mental life have at this point turned away from Freud's negative valuation of religion, and have gone rather along with Jung in acknowledging that religion can have a positive role in the integrating and strengthening of personal existence.

Another point calls for mention, and is very germane to what we are seeking to do in this chapter. What are we to say of Freud's genetic account of religious belief? Does the explanation of how a belief arises tell us about the truth or falsity of that belief? Perhaps it does, if it shows the belief to be the result of so-called "wishful" thinking, and therefore probably illusory, and this might be true of some kinds of "immature" or egocentric religion. But then would the belief of the atheist also be explicable in terms of his personal history, and in particular of his relation to his father? Perhaps this would also be true in some cases, but clearly we are in grave danger of lapsing into a kind of psychological skepticism in which we believe things because of our histories and not because the beliefs are true or false. Carried to extremes, this skepticism would make any kind of argument or discussion impossible. Each one would believe what his history had determined that he must believe. But the Freudian might reply that to have become aware of the genesis of one's beliefs is to be made free for the criticism of them. This would be something like what we said above about the awareness of a perspective bringing to some extent liberation from the narrowness of that perspective. But, as will be insisted later, a perspective is not a norm; and in any case, when the origins of conflicting beliefs have been traced, there remains the question of trying to decide which is true.

Some of these remarks would apply to other positivistic or naturalistic views of religion, such as the sociological positivism of Durkheim, who believed society to be the real object of religious devotion, and the theories of Marx and his successors who think of religion as a product of the socioeconomic process, and adduce to their criticism an admixture of materialist metaphysics as well. But it can be no part of our purpose to undertake to reply to all the criticisms of religion, for this would need a book in itself. It is sufficient if we have given a defensible account of religion, and one sufficiently flexible to respond to the various criticisms. I believe that such an account has been given, and have given here a few hints of how it could meet the critics.

But what are we to say to theologians who, while accepting revelation and faith, reject religion or are at least highly critical of it? Although there are many theologians who take such an attitude today, their position is not, of course, new. The Hebrew prophets were stern critics of religion. So were Jesus and many other spiritual leaders and reformers. To speak more accurately, they criticized some aspects of religion. Indeed, when we examine current theological criticisms of religion, the matter becomes to some extent a question of semantics—just what are we to mean by the word "religion"? But this does not exhaust the question. As with the Hebrew prophets and other reformers of the past, there is in the current criticism of religion a desire to maintain the integrity of faith and to prevent its being smothered in the religious structure that grows around it.

The most influential among the theological critics of religion has been Dietrich Bonhoeffer. In his earliest published work, he defined "religion" as "the touching of the human will by the divine, and the overcoming of the former by the latter, with resultant free action." [3] This is a fair definition. It preserves the divine initiative in religion, and is certainly not pejorative, as are some of the definitions placed at the beginning of hostile criticisms of religion. Yet even in this early work, Bonhoeffer's suspicion of religion is evident. He holds it to be a major misunderstanding of the Church when it is understood as a "religious community" in which people get together from "religious motives" and for "religious activities." [4] What Bonhoeffer is protesting against here is the tendency for religion to become a special department of life, and essentially this continues the classic critique of the Hebrew prophets. It remains, I believe, the leading theme in Bonhoeffer's latest fragmentary utterances about religion in his *Letters and Papers from Prison*, though here it has become expanded to a kind of theological counterpart to Freud's criticism of immature religion, for the special religious corner is needed only by those who have not become adult in their faith.

[3] *Sanctorum Communio*, p. 94.
[4] *Op. cit.*, pp. 87–88.

Understood in this way, Bonhoeffer's critique of religion is entirely acceptable. Surely, however, it is a misunderstanding of him to suppose that he had turned against that fundamental kind of religion defined in *Sanctorum Communio*, or against such religious practices of prayer, meditation, and the like, as seem to be necessary if anyone is to attain Christian maturity or to maintain himself in it. In a careful analysis of Bonhoeffer's remarks, Martin Thornton has persuasively argued that he was in fact looking for something like what has been traditionally called a "rule of life," and that this is a necessary bridge between faith and ethics, and an indispensable discipline for the attainment of Christian maturity.[5]

Bishop John Robinson's view, it seems to me, is essentially like that of Bonhoeffer. Robinson criticizes religion that has become departmentalized or has remained immature, but he acknowledges that religion is best understood in Tillich's sense as "the dimension of depth" in all the functions of life.[6] But the Bishop is far from consistent, and while we might well agree with his criticisms of religion that is immature and unrelated to life's daily concerns, he talks in other ways that make it very hard to see how there can be any "dimension of depth" in life at all. Sometimes he comes near to a Comtean positivism in which "God" has become just an exalted (and misleading) name for humanity; and sometimes he goes so far in stressing the self-sufficiency of contemporary secular man that he undercuts his own concern to present Christ as relevant to this contemporary man.

The Bishop draws back from following out these tendencies to their end, but the so-called "death of God" theologians in America have no such inhibitions.[7] They frankly accept a positivism which not only abolishes religion but also faith in God, and which reduces Christianity to an ethic centered in Jesus. I cannot call this "radical theology," for it seems to me that a truly radical theology lives in the tension of faith and doubt, whereas here the tension has been resolved by the abolition of God; and further, one would hesitate to give the name of "theology" to an enterprise which has rejected theology's key word, "God." The movement is to be seen rather as a parallel in the theological world to the iconoclasms that have appeared in our time in the worlds of music and the other arts. These iconoclasms may serve a useful purpose in stimulating fresh thought, and they may even themselves produce some interesting insights. But they

---

[5] Cf. *The Rock and the River*, pp. 49–64.

[6] *Honest to God*, p. 86, n. 2.

[7] Cf. Paul Van Buren, *The Secular Meaning of the Gospel;* William Hamilton, *New Essence of Christianity;* T. J. J. Altizer, *The Gospel of Christian Atheism.*

cannot in the long run be creative, and this remark certainly applies to the theological (or anti-theological) iconoclasts. The "death of God" must soon lead to the death of Christianity. If men are adult enough or self-sufficient enough to get along without God, surely they will soon be able to get along without Jesus too. The nostalgic longings of those who once had faith may keep a place for Jesus for a little longer, but soon he too will have to go. If the next generation needs any figure on which to focus its ethical aspirations, it will surely be able to find someone more up-to-date and appropriate than Jesus, for when we consider that his whole life was wrapped up in God, he is not really a very appropriate exemplar for the secular world.

Very different from these views is Karl Barth's criticism of religion. He explicitly contrasts religion with revelation, which is said to abolish religion; and for Barth, "revelation" is understood in a much narrower sense than the word has been used in this book, for he restricts it to the Christian revelation. Whereas the revelation is given by God to man, religion is said to be man's movement toward God. In religion, according to Barth, man "takes something for himself . . . he ventures to grasp at God." [8] Actually, this is a very tendentious way of talking about religion, and conflicts both with the definitions of Bonhoeffer and Tillich, mentioned above, and with our own list of basic characteristics, set out in the last section. One suspects that Barth here is influenced in his understanding of religion by his prejudice that the revelation of God in Christ is the one exclusive revelation, and that the ideas of God in the non-Christian religions are simply man-made projections. Such exclusivism will be strongly opposed in my own account of these matters. But the fact that Barth is able to hold that the Christian religion too comes under the judgment of the revelation indicates that once again we have to do with something more than just an arbitrary definition of religion. There is indeed a tendency for religion to become autonomous so that it subordinates and adapts to human use the God-given revelation, thus usurping the divine initiative. This happens in Christianity when the Christian faith is transformed into the Christian religion, but what Barth ought to recognize is that precisely the same thing happens in Islam, Buddhism, Hinduism, and elsewhere; these are not merely "religions," in his sense, and therefore to be contrasted with "revelation," for they too know revelation, grace, the divine initiative, even if they too level this down within the forms of re-

[8] *Church Dogmatics*, vol. I/2, p. 302.

ligion. Indeed, as anthropologists well know, the distinction goes right back to primitive experiences of the holy. There is the receptive experience of holy Being touching human life, and there is man's endeavor to grasp and utilize holy Being. The anthropologist, however, would normally call this latter phenomenon "magic," reserving the term "religion" for the experience in which the holy grasps man.

Slightly different again is the position of Emil Brunner. He claims that "the Christian faith is not one of the religions of the world." [9] He would indeed concede that Christianity may become a religion, but this is a kind of degeneration. On the other hand, he does not deny that non-Christian religions are based on revelation, but this is supposed to be a general, impersonal, timeless revelation, in sharp contrast to the revelation in Christ. It is hard to know where Brunner could have got his ideas about non-Christian religions, and it is pathetic to read his attempts to establish the *differentia* between them and the Christian faith. His view of religion and his attempt to exclude Christian faith from the general category of religion provide one more example of the parochial prejudice that God has granted one and only one revelation of himself.

These remarks on some of the more prominent theological critics of religion, while showing us that to some extent the criticism proceeds on the ground of loaded definitions of religion and may even sometimes be motivated by a desire to make an exclusive claim for the Christian revelation as the sole source of a genuine knowledge of God, nevertheless point to some substance in the complaint against religion. That religion can become a special area on its own, a luxury or a diversion or a place of refuge; that it can become a kind of machinery that robs God's revelation of its demand and otherness, familiarizing it and putting it at our disposal; that it can become immature in many ways—these are facts of which there can be no doubt, and we may be glad that the criticism of religion has not been left to skeptics and that there are still men in the prophetic tradition who criticize religion in the light of the revelation out of which it has arisen. While we cannot agree with Barth that religion is a human activity, it certainly has its human side as it includes the various ways in which man responds to the revelation. Even when these were sketched out in the last section on the basic characteristics of religion, mention was made of the possibilities of distortion and perversion. For every phenomenon in which man plays a part, even religion, has an ambiguous character and is liable

[9] *Revelation and Reason*, p. 258.

to the distortions and imbalances which so easily arise from the polarities of our existence.

But while it may freely be conceded that religion has an ambiguous character and often becomes perverted so that there has been and still is a good deal of bad religion (both Christian and non-Christian) in the world, it is quite absurd to fly to extremes as some people are doing nowadays, and to condemn wholesale all religion, and to imagine that we can have faith without the structure of religion. There is indeed a subtle pride in this point of view. Angels could presumably lead the life of faith without the apparatus of religion. Men, however, are not angels but embodied creatures of flesh and blood who live in a world and in a stream of history, in the midst of social and physical realities. Even man come of age cannot shrug off the facticity of his existence. On the contrary, the more adult he is, the more clearly and readily does he accept his finite embodied status. These matters will be fully discussed in the third major division of this work, dealing with applied theology. But let us clearly recognize that man being the embodied existent that he is, revelation and the response of faith must find concrete expression in what we call "religion," and that even those who in the name of faith or revelation rebel against religion do not escape from it. They produce their own version of religion, and this can turn out to be more distorted than the version they have rejected.

The criticism of religion, whether it comes from skeptics or from prophets, does not drive us to the abandonment of religion but keeps us aware of its ambiguous character, and of the need for ensuring that religion expresses rather than obscures the revelation and the life of faith which revelation engenders. But the manifold forms of religion and its manifold perversions demand continuous critical examination. Religion, after all, can permeate a whole culture, influencing its art, its institutions, its economics, its whole manner of life. So we find ourselves driven back with even more urgency to the task which presented itself at the end of the preceding section—the task of investigating religion further, and, in particular, of trying to see how the different forms of religion arise, and how they are related both to each other and to the basic structures of all religion.

28. TYPES OF RELIGION

The essence of religion, we have seen, is the self-manifestation of Being as this is received and appropriated in the life of faith. We have assumed (in agreement with catholic Christian teaching) that in all religion there is some genuine knowledge of God, genuine revelation, and genuine grace, and we have turned away from the view (held especially by such Protestant theologians as Calvin and Barth) that there is no genuine knowledge of God outside of the Christian revelation, and that what may be called "God" in non-Christian religions is simply an idea fabricated by the human mind. But to show why the first of these views is to be preferred to the second, it will be necessary to show why, if all religion flows from the self-giving of the one God, he has been so differently represented and worshipped in the multitudinous faiths of mankind.

Let me first name three possible factors which account for the diversity of form without losing sight of the underlying unity.

The first factor is *variation of symbolism.* We recall from an earlier discussion [10] that our talk about God or Being has an indirect symbolic character, and we have seen something of the structure and functioning of symbols. Symbols are not arbitrarily chosen. They grow up in the life of a people, and clearly those entities which are most significant for the existence of a particular people are most likely to establish themselves as symbols of Being. For instance, in ancient Egypt the sun-god Amon and the fertility-goddess Isis are two major symbols of numinous Being, probably because the whole life of the nation depended on the two great natural forces, the sun and the river. But the symbols need not come from nature. They may be taken from the history of the people, perhaps from some great moment of deliverance which had become for that people the focus of divine grace and revelation. Whatever the symbol or symbols might be, they would always fall short of the reality, though, as we have seen, they might have varying degrees of adequacy. They might also have varying potentialities for development; some might remain relatively fixed and perhaps eventually die, while others possess the capacity for expansion and renewal. This capacity for development would seem to belong to historical and personal symbols rather than to natural ones.

The variation of symbols goes a long way toward explaining not only the diversity of religions but also many of the distortions and perversions. All symbols, we have seen, have a paradoxical character and need to be both affirmed and denied. Where inadequate symbols are simply affirmed, distortion takes place, and the more inadequate the symbol, the greater the distortion. It must be remembered, however, that no symbol can be en-

[10] See above, pp. 134–145.

tirely adequate to the mystery of Being, and that every symbol or group of symbols belongs within a stream of history. A symbol may have become "classic" for a group sharing a given history, but if the group claims for this symbol a monopoly, so to speak, as the bearer of the divine revelation, then again we have distortion.

A second factor is the *psychology of the individual or group*. Allusion was made at an early stage of this work to the varieties of religious experience.[11] Persons brought up within the same religious community, nurtured on the same classic revelation and the symbols in which it has found expression, may nevertheless respond in diverse ways, though all of these may be responses of faith. Religion, and indeed faith too, include the human response, and since no two human beings are completely alike, the nature of the response varies. So we get mystics, prophets, ecstatics, revivalists, puritans and so on. These types cut across the divisions between the great historical faiths. A thoroughly Calvinistic Christian, believing in the absolute sovereignty of God and believing that this is expressed in a meticulously regulated providence and predestination, stands closer in many respects to a Muslim, who has fatalistically submitted to the power of God, than he stands to many of his fellow Christians; and a Sufi mystic in Islam may find more kinship with Christian mystics than with many of his coreligionists. Perhaps there is also a psychology of groups, whole nations or races tending to have certain mental or emotional characteristics, though of course this would be only in a general way and would not exclude many individual exceptions. Thus some peoples seem to be more emotional, others more phlegmatic; some outgoing, others relatively introspective; some given to colorful modes of expression, others to much more austere and reserved ways. So while the major historical faiths may contain all kinds of variations due to individual differences, there may nevertheless be a kind of normative position that is typical of the group as a whole. Thus, to return to our earlier examples, the thoroughgoing Calvinist represents an aberration within Christianity, while it is the Sufi mystic who is untypical within Islam.

That individual and group differences in psychological makeup account for many religious differences is undeniable. Religions ought to be sufficiently flexible to accommodate different types of persons, and indeed some groups are noted for their comprehensiveness. This may partly depend on the question, already noted, about the capacity of symbols for de-

---

[11] See above, p. 5.

velopment and communication. On the other hand, there can be no doubt that the absolutizing of what may be no more than psychological differences has been a frequent source of division in religion and has issued in some of the worst perversions.

With more diffidence, I mention as a possible third factor *variation in Being's own self-disclosure*. This is a much more speculative matter, and one can speak only in a very tentative manner of it. Nevertheless, when we consider that in the history of a culture there may be ages of faith when God's reality is, it would seem, overwhelmingly and convincingly present, but also ages of secularism when God seems silent or absent, it is at least a question whether such an alternation can be entirely accounted for in terms that are immanent to the development of the culture, or whether we must suppose that at different times God may draw near or withdraw himself. It is well known too that saintly individuals report periods of aridity in their lives when God seems to have removed to a distance. Furthermore, while we can to a large extent account for the varieties of religion in terms of differences of symbolism and differences of psychological response, there would seem to be more to it than this. While the symbols are partly determined by the circumstances of the culture within which they function as symbols of Being, they are surely in part also determined by the initiative of Being in the revelation, for it is in and through these particular symbols that Being declares and manifests itself. Thus we would have to suppose that the variation of symbols is in some degree linked with a variation of Being's self-disclosure, as it reveals itself now perhaps more in its transcendence, now more in its immanence.

Let me stress again that these remarks are very speculative and tentative. They raise the question whether, in a sense, Being has itself a history, over and above the history of our apprehension of Being. Perhaps indeed we must speak of a history of Being, if we are to allow for a genuine transcendence of Being and anything like an act of grace or revelation. But on the other hand, history belongs to Being, not Being to history. This in turns raises the question of Being in relation to time, and the further working out of this must be left to the contexts in which we shall discuss the doctrines of God, creation, and eschatology.

We now see what are the factors that bring about the diversity of religions, though we can also see that there is an underlying unity, in that all of the religions stem from Being's self-manifestation as this is received in faith. The next step is to try to discern some kind of structure in the family of religions and to arrange them in an intelligible order. There are obvious limits as to what can be done in this direction, for, as has already been pointed out, some of the variations cut across the borders of the historical religions, and again, there are all kinds of mixed and intermediate types. Nevertheless, we can discern a limited number of classic patterns of religion, and to see what these are is a major step toward understanding the relation of the religions to religion and to one another.

Two preliminary points need to be made before we proceed to the exposition of the types. The first is that we must hold fast to a logical basis of classification. There are many typologies of religion, but most of them suffer from the defect that they have very confused criteria, one religion being characterized by its conception of God, another by some psychological trait of its adherents, and so on. In accordance with the existential-ontological approach of this book, the criterion for differentiating and ordering the types will be the way in which holy Being is experienced in each. The second point is that we must recall that any survey of the types of religion must involve a perspective, for our human existence is such that we must see things from a limited point of view. The perspective need not be a norm (this matter will call for further discussion) but it is inescapable. In this book, the perspective is the Christian one. Being reveals itself as both transcendent and immanent, and this is implied in the central Christian idea of incarnation.

Now this perspective, taken in conjunction with the existential-ontological criterion already mentioned, leads to the construction of a typology in two convergent series. Moving out from the point of convergence, one series consists of those types of religion in which Being is experienced in increasing degrees of transcendence, until at the limit it is completely withdrawn, the stage where Being is "forgotten" and only the beings remain. The other series leads through those types of religion in which Being is experienced primarily as immanent, and here too at the limit Being disappears as holy Being, not by slipping over the horizon, so to speak, but by becoming fragmented and absorbed into the beings. The series are shown in the diagram on p. 167.

In a very general way, it may be said that the religions in the transcendence series share some other characteristics: they are interested in temporality and eschatology; their categories are personal, ethical, and rational; their worship tends to be austere and mainly verbal, and may be reduced to very meager propositions; their ideal is obedience to a demand. By contrast, the religions in the immanence series tend toward a timeless, unhistorical understanding; their categories are mystical, and either impersonal or suprapersonal; their worship tends toward elaborate ritual and may have high esthetic qualities, with an appreciation for symbol and gesture as well as for spoken word; their ideal is communion, or even absorption. Let me again say that there are many exceptions to these broad generalizations.

It should also be said that no succession, still less progression, of types in history is implied, though the more archaic types appear in one series and the more recent tend to be concentrated in the other. Also, the grouping has probably been too neatly balanced, but this is the almost inevitable result of having to take one's own perspective as the center of reference, and I hope that so far as this involves us in a certain artificiality, this will be redressed in the next section's discussion of the relation between the religions. For the present, however, let us characterize briefly the types in the two series, beginning with the transcendence series.

1. Closest to our starting point is a monotheism in which one God has created the world and transcends it, but is also active in it and reveals his will in the course of worldly events. What I have in mind is, of course, the religion of the Old Testament and Judaism, Christianity's nearest neighbors. The interest in time is apparent both in the Old Testament conception of history and in Jewish apocalyptic. God is conceived in personal ethical terms, and his most typical attribute is righteousness. He communicates by his word. Worship is relatively simple, and the prophets insist on the subordination of the cult to the demand for righteousness. The goal is the fulfilling of the law, not in any merely legalistic or external sense, but rather by letting it permeate the whole life of man.

2. There is a more severe kind of monotheism in which the transcendence of God over the world and over men is more sharply emphasized. The classic example is Islam. Stress is laid on the divine attribute of sovereignty, or power, though one should not forget the compensating attribute of mercy. Worship is again austere, and perhaps even more than in Hebrew religion is there an utter abhorrence of images or anything that might savor of idolatry. Moral duties are laid on the believer, but his attitude is better described as submission (the very meaning of the name "Islam") than obedience, while the utter power of God over man tends toward a fatalism.

3. The increased stress on the transcendence of God over the world can take a different form. He becomes so remote from the world that his power over it diminishes, and perhaps it is even believed that he did not create the world, and that it is the work of other powers, hostile to God. This type of religion recognizes the ambiguity of the world, and it does so in a dualistic world view, in which a transcendent God is opposed by one or more powers of evil. The classic example is Zoroastrianism, but the

TYPICAL CONTRASTS

Immanence	Transcendence
Timeless	*Eschatological*
Quietist	*Activist*
Impersonal	*Personal*
Mystical	*Rational*

Limiting case: *Fetishism* ⎮ Limiting case: *Atheism* ⎮

Immanence series ⎮ Transcendence series ⎮

TYPE 4—Animism
EXAMPLE: *Primitive Religions*

Type 4—Deism
EXAMPLE: *Confucianism*

Type 3—Polytheism
EXAMPLES: *Rig Veda,*
Egypt, Greece, etc.

Type 3—Dualism
EXAMPLES: *Zoroastrianism,*
Gnosticism

Type 2—Pantheism
EXAMPLE: *Hinduism*

Type 2—Sovereignty
EXAMPLE: *Islam*

Type 1—Cosmic Order
EXAMPLE: *Buddhism*

Type 1—Monotheism
EXAMPLE: *Judaism*

Existential-Ontological Theism
EXAMPLE: *Christianity*

DIAGRAM SHOWING RELIGIOUS TYPES
FROM A CHRISTIAN PERSPECTIVE

same kind of dualism is found in Gnosticism and Manichaeism. The interest in time is very obvious, for probably the Zoroastrians were the first to develop a cosmic eschatology and it may have been from them that the Jews and so eventually the Christians borrowed their eschatological ideas. Especially in Gnosticism, God is utterly remote, inaccessible, and unknowable. In the dualistic religions the believers are often confronted with an ethical demand, dramatized in terms of the war between the opposing powers, but in some of the Gnostic sects salvation could also be thought of in terms of a release to be gained through knowing the appropriate formulae of words.

4. Yet a further case is the one where God is made utterly remote but there is no consciousness of an opposing power. Thus God simply appears on the remote horizon and receives polite recognition, but for all practical purposes he might almost fade out. Perhaps he still lends some kind of aura to the moral code. Here the classic case would be Confucianism, though the deism of the seventeenth and eighteenth centuries would be rather similar. The outlook is essentially rationalistic and humanistic.

The limiting case is atheism, where God fades out of the picture altogether. It is one of the merits of van der Leeuw's study of religion that he has shown the place of atheism within the typology of religions.[12] Perhaps one could trace the lineage of the atheism of the West through the Protestant emphasis on divine transcendence leading into deism and finally to the vanishing of God. Contemporary atheism, having forgotten Being in its preoccupation with beings, relies on technology for the mastering of beings. In its belief in progress, it still retains the typical interest of this series in temporality and eschatology.

We turn now to the immanence series. Here too four major types may be distinguished. This time, however, we shall begin at the outermost limit and work inward to the center from which our perspective looks out. This order of exposition commends itself because in this series we can discern something like a course of historical development. The religion of India, for instance, would be able to provide illustrations of all four types, from primitive animism to the rise of Buddhism.

The limiting case at the end of this series is fetishism. Fetishism recognizes a vaguely diffused numinous power, like the *mana* of the Melanesians and its counterparts among other races, and tries to utilize by means of magic the objects in which *mana* is supposed to dwell. Fetishism is treated here as the limiting case because holy Being has disappeared into the beings. There is a parallel between fetishism at the limit of immanence and atheism at the limit of transcendence, though in atheism holy Being had disappeared beyond the beings. But both the fetishist and the atheist make man the measure of things, and set out to attain the domination of the

---

[12] *Religion in Essence and Manifestation*, vol. II, p. 600.

beings. Whereas, however, the contemporary atheist places his trust in technology, the fetishist places his in magic, the manipulation for his own ends of occult powers. We need not ask whether fetishism preceded religion or is a degeneration from religion (for any immature self-seeking religion is a kind of fetishism) or whether religion and magic originally coexisted in some undifferentiated matrix. The point is that in principle fetishism is distinct from what we have agreed to call "religion."

1. When we pass to what can properly be recognized as types of religion within the immanence series, we notice first the animism that is characteristic of most primitive peoples. The expression "animism" is used here in a wide sense to denote anything from belief in a vague numinous power supposed to be resident in some objects up to the more sophisticated belief in spirits as described in Tylor's classic study of primitive religion. In animism, holy Being is experienced as immanent in the beings, but it is experienced as fragmented and diffused. There is of course at this stage very little awareness of time. In spite of the seeming crudity of primitive ritual and belief, it has the seeds of more advanced insights.

2. The next type is polytheism. This presumably develops out of animism, and of course there are many well-known examples from Egypt, Mesopotamia, Greece, India and elsewhere. Being is still experienced as immanent and as fragmented, but is not so diffuse as in animism. It is focused now in great phenomena of nature, such as the sky, the sun, the sea; or the gods may assume a human form, as they did in Greece. There is a parallel between the experience of Being in polytheism and that in dualism, for in polytheism too the ambiguity of the world appears, as in stories of wars among the gods, the good against the bad. But polytheism differs sharply from dualism and remains true to the immanence series in having no sense of history or eschatology. Polytheism expresses itself in myth, and its myth is that of the eternal return.[13] Nature polytheism reflects the cycles of the seasons, but humanized polytheism also devalues time and history and conceives Being as timeless, as we see from the "immortals" of the Olympian religion.

3. At a more sophisticated level, we come to the thought of Being as the undifferentiated unity immanent in or, perhaps we should say, underlying the multiplicity of individual beings. Here we have a high pantheism, illustrated by some elements in Hinduism and also by some in Taoism. Change and multiplicity are only illusion. The reality is the "uncarved

---

[13] Cf. Mircea Eliade, *Cosmos and History*.

block," the one simple all-inclusive being. Even the gods are only appearances of the One. The goal of the religious life is communion with or rather union to the primal Being, and the typical form of the religious experience is mysticism.

4. It may seem, however, that a primal undifferentiated being is indistinguishable from nothing, and so Being is reduced from the One to simply the immanent cosmic order, in accordance with which the beings fulfill their various functions. An example of this experience of Being is the Hinayana Buddhism, as it emerges out of Hinduism. Other examples would be Taoism, in at least some of its aspects, and Stoicism. In all these examples, there is no personal God as symbol of Being, but an impersonal order (*dharma, tao, logos*) immanent in the world. Again, events move in cycles, symbolized by the Buddhist wheel of becoming, so that temporality and history are devalued. The ethic is quietist rather than activist, for it is one of non-attachment to finite things, and conformation and self-effacement in the order of the world.

The center from which these types have been described is itself a type, though it is scarcely necessary to characterize it here since its explication is our major concern in this whole work. It may suffice to remind ourselves that an effort has been made in this central type to maintain a proper balance between the transcendence and the immanence of holy Being, and that this especially characterizes Christianity, with its doctrine of an incarnation. However, let us also remind ourselves that there are many variations within Christianity itself, so that some forms of Christianity swing out on either side into other types; while on the other hand there are variations in non-Christian religions, particularly in Hinduism and Mahayana Buddhism, which swing in toward what (from our perspective) is taken as the central type.

The value of a typology such as has been worked out in this section is that it enables us to see both the unity and diversity of the religions, and affords a frame of reference for discussing their interrelations. To such a discussion we must now turn.

29. COMMITMENT AND OPENNESS IN RELIGION

It may be claimed first that the typology of religion worked out in the last section vindicates the attempt in our philosophical theology to talk of general structures of religion on the basis of participation in a particular religion. The attempt is vindicated because all religions can be seen as variations on a fundamental theme—the impinging of holy Being upon the being of man. When we become aware of the perspective from which we ourselves are looking, then this very awareness reduces the possibilities of distortion that arise from the inevitable particularity of one's own viewpoint.

Furthermore, it may be claimed that our typology also vindicates our preference for the catholic over the Calvinistic-Barthian view of the relation of our own particular faith, Christianity, to other faiths. The catholic view recognizes a genuine knowledge of God in the non-Christian religions, while the extreme Protestant view sees in them only error and idolatry. The two series of types make it clear that the Christian faith is continuous with non-Christian faiths, not discontinuous, as Barth claims, and that there is no one *exclusive* revelation of God. We therefore utterly reject the view that one religion is true and all the rest false; or (what we take to be a subtle restatement of the same error) that all religions are judged and rejected, including the Christian religion so far as it is a religion, by the one and only veridical revelation in Christ. Not only are such views intellectually indefensible but, because religious beliefs are never merely intellectual but are part of an existential attitude, they are also morally objectionable and are the root of fanaticism and pride.

I wish now, however, to appeal for an opening up of the catholic view itself, which, though it has recognized a genuine knowledge of God in the non-Christian religions, has too often been grudging in this recognition. I have purposely spoken in this chapter of a perspective, not of a norm, and I think the time has come for Christians to have a far more open and generous attitude toward other faiths.

Let me make it quite clear that I am not flying to the foolish extreme of saying that all religions are alike or of equal value, for our typology itself makes it abundantly evident that not only are there differences among the religions but that there are manifold possibilities for imbalance and perversion. Neither am I advocating a syncretism, for this would mean looking along all perspectives at once, and we have already noted that for a finite historical human being, this is an impossibility; or at least, those who try it usually end up with something intolerably superficial and sentimental. Least of all am I advocating an intellectualized abstract quintessence of common doctrine distilled from all the religions, for such a generalized faith would lack the concreteness that our embodied existence demands—and it will be remembered that our defense of "religion" against its critics turned partly on this need for the concrete and the this-worldly.

All I am saying is that one can commit oneself within one's own community of faith and in terms of the symbols established in that community, and yet believe that for a person in other circumstances, the same God reveals himself in another community and under different symbols, and that there may be nothing defective or inadequate about that person's commerce with God. Since we can see that other community only from the outside and cannot have intimate participation in it, we cannot say at first hand that there is revelation in that community, though *a fortiori* we could never deny it. But if we see in the persons of that community growth in selfhood and the workings of grace, can we doubt that God is indeed with them and is making himself known to them? And finally, should we not rejoice that the grace of holy Being is not narrowly confined to one community or one particular occasion and history of revelation?

The view advocated here is not contrary to catholic tradition but is rather an expansion of it and an updating in the light of present-day knowledge. The grudging attitude toward other faiths was occasioned by outmoded views about the world, and by lack of knowledge of and contacts with other cultures. Let me mention three reasons that impel us to abandon the old-time parochialism.

1. When Christianity was born in the first century, people supposed our earth to be at the center of things, so that terrestrial history was cosmic history. Moreover, this had been a short history, or at least short enough for people to know what had happened from "the beginning" down to their own day, and it was all going to end soon. Thus it was natural enough to suppose that there might be one exclusive or at any rate immeasurably superior revelation in the course of this very limited history. But along came Copernicus, and since his time our horizons keep on expanding. The overwhelming probability is that countless billions of "histories" have been enacted in the cosmos, and a space-age cosmology calls for a vastly enlarged understanding of divine grace and revelation. Now that man is reaching out into space, Alice Meynell's prediction is not so improbable:

> Doubtless we shall compare together, hear
> A million alien gospels, in what guise
> He trod the Pleiades, the Lyre, the Bear.

2. The antiquity and development of man himself and the achievements of alien cultures on our own planet were hardly known when the Bible was written or when classical theology was formulated. Indeed, they have been known with any precision only since the nineteenth century. Anthropologists investigated the religion of primitive man, and it became

clear that all religions, including biblical religion, have arisen out of primitive ideas and practices. This in no way devalues the religion of later stages, any more than science would be devalued in so far as it may have arisen out of magic. But anthropology does suggest a continuity among all religions. The study of comparative religion reinforces this view, and as the vast spiritual treasures of the Asian religions were opened up to the Western mind, it became clear that in spite of the alien conceptuality and symbolism, there are profound points of agreement. There becomes apparent a unity underlying all the diverse religions. We might well end this paragraph with a quotation to parallel the one that ended the preceding paragraph. This time we go to the blind Scottish hymn writer, George Matheson:

> Gather us in, thou Love that fillest all;
> Gather our rival faiths within thy fold.
> Rend each man's temple-veil and bid it fall,
> That we may know that thou hast been of old.

3. While in a theological exposition a merely practical consideration could have no weight, it is nevertheless excusable to adduce it as an additional point. The consideration is that religious pluralism will be with us for a long time if not forever, and it is desirable that the religions should not only find a *modus vivendi* but that they should actively seek closer understanding of each other and cooperate in common tasks. The spiritual predicament of mankind today cannot be thought of in terms of Christianity (or any other particular religion) against the rest, but rather in terms of the contrast between the knowledge of God and of the grace of holy Being on the one hand, and materialism and positivism on the other.

We therefore see the ideal relation between religions as one of tension or balance between commitment and openness; commitment to the particular tradition in which holy Being has addressed us, an existential commitment that cannot be replaced by some mixing of traditions or some vague "religion in general"; and at the same time, an open and positive attitude to other faiths, believing that in this area where distortion takes place so readily, each faith can both contribute to and learn from the others.

These remarks complete the first division of this work, the division that has dealt with philosophical theology. Bearing in mind its descriptions and analyses, we now go on to the explication of the particular religious faith and its concrete symbols which lies at the heart of our inquiry, to Christian theology proper.

PART TWO

SYMBOLIC
THEOLOGY

8 | The Tasks of Symbolic Theology

30. THE MATTER OF SYMBOLIC THEOLOGY

In the first division of this work, our concern was with general structures and concepts, such as faith, sin, grace, revelation, and so on. The treatment was to a large extent formal, and even when we talked of the content of revelation and of the faith in which revelation is received, we confined ourselves to such wide expressions as "holy Being." It was made clear throughout, however, that we were not defending the hypothesis of some abstract "general revelation," for all revelation is given on particular occasions and has its definite content. The last chapter explored the relation between the particular occasions and the general structures, and, it is hoped, both vindicated the generality of our earlier investigations and pointed to the need for a concrete working out of these in terms of a particular faith-content. As was made clear at the beginning, it is only on the basis of participation in a particular historical faith that one could sketch out even a general philosophical theology, as distinct from a detached study of religion. But in philosophical theology, the particular faith-commitment supplies only a perspective from which to approach the general questions. Now that these have been explored, we turn to the explication of the particular faith.

This means that we come now to specifically Christian theology, to the explication of that faith which centers in the revelation given in the person and work of Jesus Christ. This revelation has been transmitted in the Christian community, primarily in the scriptures of the community, but also in the community's tradition of life and thought, in which the revelation has already been developed and explicated in ways that have become part of the community's identity, so that they could scarcely be discarded without destroying the continuity of the community. The whole issue of tradition will demand fuller discussion when we come to talk about the nature of the community itself, but for the present it is simply being claimed that any explication of the Christian faith, while it must be rooted in the Bible as the primary testimony to the primordial revelation, cannot leap straight back across the centuries to the New Testament but must take account of the way in which the Church, in its creeds, in the decisions of its ecumenical councils (especially those of the early centuries), and, generally, in its collective wisdom and universal teaching, has understood and interpreted the faith which it holds and of which it is the guardian.

As already intimated, I propose to call this division of the work "symbolic theology." When this expression was first introduced and reasons given for preferring it over the more traditional expression, "dogmatic theology," it was stated that the reasons for the preference would become clearer after we had studied the logic of theological language. We have now done this, and I hope that one of the results of this study has indeed been to show us the appositeness of talking about "symbolic theology" to designate the explication of a faith that relates itself to a particular and concrete revelation of holy Being.

Our study showed us that all our talk of God must be indirect, because our language is primarily adapted for talking about beings, so that when we want to talk about Being, we have to stretch the everyday usages of language. We saw how, in various ways, beings and our talk about beings can open up for us insights into Being. The most general way of describing indirect language of this kind is to call it "symbolic," though we have seen that some parts of it might be more accurately called "analogical," some "paradoxical," and the undifferentiated language out of which these arise, "mythical."

There may, however, be some resistance to the expression "symbolic theology" on the ground that it may seem to take away reality from what is talked about, or again that it may seem to deny any genuine knowledge of whatever reality there may be. Our whole exposition of symbols should have made it clear that such fears are unfounded. It was shown that symbols, so far from being mere empty ciphers, have Being "present-and-manifest" in them, as was repeatedly said. They are not just ideas floating in our minds but are the concrete ways in which Being (God) accomplishes its self-giving and self-manifestation. Furthermore, it was shown that symbolic language is not just a poetic language of images, but does throw light on actual structures. The typical language of symbolic theology is a mixed one in which both images and concepts play their part. We should remember Paul Tillich's good advice: "One should never say, 'only a symbol,' but one should say, 'not less than a symbol'." [1] So we should be far from despising symbols for they have an indispensable part to play in our knowing, providing the only way in which we can attain insight into and talk about Being.

What then is the symbolic material in which the Christian revelation has found expression? It should be remembered that the theological interest lies primarily in verbal expression, that is to say, in articulating the faith in words, though the expression of faith in life and worship is at least equally important, perhaps more so, and has its own implied theology which we must not allow to slip out of sight. But we have already indicated where the verbal symbols of the Church's faith are to be found, namely, in the Bible and in the subsequent development of the Church's thought. These are the vehicles by which the content of the primordial revelation, so far as this could be put into words, has been passed on. An examination of this material will show us what the distinctively Christian symbols are, and what special marks, if any, may belong to these symbols as a whole.

While it would be impossible to attempt anything like a classification of this mass of material—the work of form-critics shows how complicated is the task of classifying even a small segment of the material—nevertheless some major categories may be recognized, and it is important that we should take note of them before embarking on the task of a theological explication of the material.

1. First among these categories may be mentioned *myth*, that is to say, material displaying all the characteristics which were earlier listed as belonging to the mythical mode of discourse.[2] There are in fact very few straightforward mythical narratives in the Bible, for the criticism of myth had already begun. The story of the creation of Adam and the subsequent fall comes within the category of myth, and there are allusions to older myths. But while intact myths are rare, mythological ideas are all-pervasive both in the Bible and in subsequent theology. Eschatological ideas derived from myths about the end color the whole of the gospel narrative, for instance.

[1] *Dynamics of Faith*, p. 45.
[2] See above, pp. 131–132.

2. Next may be mentioned a vast amount of imagery which may perhaps be broadly designated *analogical*. It differs from myth in that it is used with full consciousness of its symbolic character, and also in that it has much more of an *ad hoc* character and does not constitute in itself a cosmic story or series of stories. This miscellaneous material includes analogues, similes, metaphors, parables, allegories, and whatever other ways are employed of trying to point to God and to illuminate his meaning for human existence.

3. Very important and distinctive for the Christian revelation is *history*. In the Old Testament, God makes himself known in the history of Israel, which is interpreted as his deliverances and his judgments; while the New Testament message has as its center the history of Jesus Christ, and especially his death and resurrection. But while we rightly acknowledge the centrality of history in the biblical revelation, we must also acknowledge that it is history of a peculiar kind. It is not a scientific reconstruction of past events, as many modern scholars would understand history. Just as revelation, in order to be revelation, must include the reception and appropriation of the revelation by the person or community to whom it is directed, so history, considered as a vehicle of revelation, is already presented to us in an interpreted form, with the historical happenings represented as divine acts. Hence the historical material in Christianity tends to be incorporated into the mythical framework, and also to be embellished by legendary material illustrative of what is taken to be the "meaning" of the history. In many cases, it has become impossible to know what the facts of the matter were—just what would have been seen by a person present, or just what would have been heard. The question of history and its interpretation is one that is constantly arising in the context of Christian theology, and in various ways it will engage our attention. For the present, however, we simply note that Christianity differs from many religions in placing its revelation within the course of world history rather than in a timeless myth.

4. Yet another category of material is *dogma*—and it was indicated that although we propose to drop the adjective "dogmatic" and the expression "dogmatic theology," it might still be found useful to retain the noun "dogma." There is little dogma in the New Testament itself, but the formulation of dogmas, creeds, and definitions of belief became a major concern of the Church at quite an early stage in its existence. A dogma would seem to have at least three distinguishing marks: it has its basis in the revelation; it is proposed by the Church, as expressing the mind of the community on a particular issue; and it has a conceptual and

propositional form, being often expressed in a philosophical terminology. As is well known, dogmas were usually formulated when there was a threat that the Church's teaching in some area might be gravely distorted, and it had become necessary to state more precisely than had ever been done before just what the Church's teaching in this matter might be. Thus dogmas are interpretations. For historical reasons, some areas of the Church's teaching (such as the doctrine of the person of Christ) were interpreted rather precisely, while other areas (such as the doctrine of the work of Christ) were much less closely interpreted. In any case, however, what may have been an interpretation in the fourth century of our era will almost certainly stand in need of reinterpretation today, especially if it uses the language of an outmoded philosophy. So when it was said earlier in this section that the modern theologian cannot turn his back on credal symbols that have become elements in the community's identity, this certainly did not mean that he is simply to repeat these unaltered. This would be quite unintelligent deference to tradition. He is not to reject symbols that declare the Church's common mind, but he must, by what has earlier been described as "repetitive thinking," [3] penetrate behind the possibly quaint and even alien language of the dogma to the existential issues that agitated the Church at the time of the dogma's formulation, and appropriate for our own time and in our own language the essential insight which the dogma sought to express. Every interpretation, in course of time, demands a new act of interpretation. When it is remembered further that dogmas were usually formulated to exclude particular errors, so that they are frequently more explicit in what they rule out than in what they affirm, it will be understood that the formulation of a dogma does not mean that some final point has been reached and that future generations are excused from reflecting any more on the matter. The point has been well put by Karl Rahner, with special reference to christological dogma: "The clearest formulations, the most sanctified formulas, the classic condensations of the centuries-long work of the Church in prayer, reflection and struggle concerning God's mysteries; all these derive their life from the fact that they are not end but beginning, not goals but means, truths which open the way to the ever greater Truth." [4]

5. We must also notice the vast amount of what may be called *practical* material in the sources for symbolic theology. Under this category we include all the ethical material on the conduct of life, and also all the

[3] See above, p. 92.
[4] *Theological Investigations*, vol. I, p. 149.

directions and counsels on prayer, worship, the community, and so on. This is not to be dismissed as *merely* practical, as if it had nothing to do with theology. We have repeatedly observed that theology is *one* way in which faith expresses itself, but there are other and probably more important ways. Yet these ways are not to be separated, for ideally they are only aspects of the total expression of faith in the whole existence of man. What he does implies a theology, while theological convictions in turn have their influence on action. The practical side of Christian teaching is to be kept in view if the existential dimension of theology is to be maintained, and it is to be prevented from lapsing into an arid scholasticism.

This brief characterization of the major categories of material to which we must pay attention in any attempt at a theological explication of the specifically Christian revelation does not pretend to be exhaustive. Yet perhaps we are able to perceive from it something of the distinctive character of Christian symbolism as a whole. There is a preference, though not an exclusive preference, for the dynamic and dramatic, the temporal and historical, over generalized timeless truths. Even the traditional dogmas, with their abstract metaphysical terminology, were used to elucidate the person of Christ, or again the differentiated and fundamentally dynamic "life" of the triune God. This distinctive character of the Christian symbols will become more apparent as our symbolic theology is developed.

31. THE METHOD OF SYMBOLIC THEOLOGY

The transition from philosophical theology to symbolic theology involves also a shift in method, already hinted at in our general introductory remarks on method.[5] The shift is not, of course, a total one, but it may be expressed by saying that in this middle division of the work, interpretation will be our major concern, just as description played the principal role in the first division. But no sharp distinction can be made between them. Every description tends to become an interpretation, while any securely based interpretation must begin from a full and accurate description of what is to be interpreted—that is to say, from exposure to the matter itself, which is indeed the explicit aim of phenomenology.

It is worth noting that in the most recent discussions of hermeneutics, increasing stress seems to be laid just on this very business of letting our-

[5] See above, p. 38.

selves be exposed to the matter itself, rather than on concerning ourselves too much with our actual methods or with the prior understanding which in every case we undoubtedly bring to the tasks of interpretation. There is stress on the need to return to the sources, to listen and to let ourselves hear what is said in the classic expositions of the Christian revelation, rather than to allow these to be obscured for us by centuries of intervening and sometimes distorting transmission. As with so much else in contemporary theology, we can see here the influence of Heidegger (quite explicit in such students of hermeneutic method as Fuchs and Ebeling) and his doctrine of a repetitive thinking which reaches back and enters into the thinking of the text to be interpreted. In offering an interpretation of a passage from Sophocles, Heidegger prefaces it by saying: "We must attempt to hear only what is said. But . . . we are inexperienced at such hearing, and our ears are full of things that prevent us from hearing properly." [6]

Because of this need to hear what is said, the systematic theologian must continually pay attention to what can be learned from biblical theology and historical theology since these presumably do conduct us back to the sources and light them up for us. But now we must be on our guard against an exaggerated respect for these classic expositions of the Christian revelation, whether in the New Testament or in the thought of some great period of the Church's history, such as the Middle Ages or the Reformation. There is a tendency among scholars to retreat into one or other of these periods, and even if these scholars are hearing with perfect clarity what was being said, this does not make them in the slightest degree interpreters unless they can come back to our own time and speak the same matter in the language and categories of our day. Biblical and historical theology can have merely an antiquarian interest unless they subserve the task of a contemporary exposition of faith. Let us remember Rahner's remark that a classical formulation is not an end but a beginning.

I shall not repeat what was said back in the introduction about the principles of interpretation.[7] But since in the intervening part of the book we have constructed a philosophical theology, including a study of theological language, some points that were made only in a preliminary fashion in the earlier discussion can now be developed.

Thus it was claimed that an existential-ontological language would be an appropriate one for theological interpretation, though this had still to

---

[6] *An Introduction to Metaphysics*, p. 146.
[7] See above, pp. 36–38.

be shown. We are now in a position to evaluate the claim that was made then, for we have seen how a philosophical theology beginning from the analysis of human existence finds within that existence itself the question of being, and the development of this question leads in turn into a descriptive natural theology. Since we have seen that for an act of interpretation we require two parallel languages that can throw light on each other, we see how an existential-ontological language, describing universal structures and experiences of the human existent, can serve as the interpretative parallel for the symbolic language of a particular revelation.[8] Much of our symbolic theology will in fact be an interpretation of the Christian symbols in terms of the language of the philosophical theology developed in the first division. But we shall expect to find that as usual the process of interpretation involves a two-way traffic. If the existential-ontological language provides a frame of reference that will help us to locate and to understand the symbols, these concrete symbols will from their side enrich and vivify the relatively abstruse language of existence and being.

We are also in a position to understand better why the appropriate interpretative language should have been designated by the hyphenated expression "existential-ontological"—an expression which, it must be confessed, is clumsy enough. The excuse for this expression must be that it points to two aspects in the interpretation, both of which we take to be indispensable. The symbolic material to be interpreted must be related on the one hand to our existence, and on the other to Being, and we must firmly resist erroneous interpretations which swing out either on the one side or on the other.

Thus, we embrace not only the demythologizing method of Bultmann, and also the general method of existential interpretation which can be applied to material that would not strictly fall within the category of myth, but we reject any attempt at a purely existential theology.[9] Bultmann too rejects such an extreme development of his position, but there are and have been theologians and philosophers of religion who think of Christianity's symbolic material as setting forth nothing more than a manner of existence or a way of life for man. On this view, even statements about God are taken to be veiled statements about existence or possibly commands to act in a certain way. Religion becomes a purely practical matter, dogmas are interpreted as rules for the conduct of life, and the idea of God is taken to stand not for any independent or prior reality over against man but simply as a symbol of ideal existence. Our

8 See above, p. 137.
9 See my book, *The Scope of Demythologizing*, p. 152.

whole exposition of the revelatory situation in earlier parts of this book makes it clear that while indeed we acknowledge and indeed lay great stress on the existential dimension in theology, we have never thought of an existential interpretation as offering an exhaustive account of the content of faith. It has been consistently maintained that religion is more than a practical matter and yields insight into the transhuman and, indeed, primordial reality which we call God or Being. So existential interpretation (including interpretation in terms of an existentially conceived history) can never constitute a *complete* theological method, though it is certainly an indispensable element in any adequate theological method, and we may be glad that this is so clearly recognized at the present time.

So, on the other hand, our interpretation will be ontological in the sense that it will seek to elucidate from the symbolic material new and deeper understanding of Being. But here we must guard against the temptation of treating theology as if it were metaphysics and as if our aim were to provide just an intellectually satisfying account of God, the world, and man. With the rise of dogma in the early Church, concrete and existentially significant symbols tended to be edged out in favor of an abstract vocabulary of "substance," "nature," and the like. This kind of language does indeed serve to interpret and clarify the symbols, but then the dogmas come to be thought of as objective, neutrally descriptive truths. Then from time to time we get protests against the excessive intellectualizing of faith, and against the transforming of the God of religion into the God of the philosophers, the living God into a metaphysical construct. Luther, Pascal, Kierkegaard, Harnack, and a host of others have in the modern period recalled theology from metaphysical speculation to its existential dimensions. The peril today, however, is not that faith will be understood in intellectual terms but that this whole side of theology will be obscured and that the current antipathy to metaphysics will crush out the ontological aspect of theology. In Gogarten and his followers, for instance, history and metaphysics are set up in a dualistic opposition to each other, and it is implied that the theologian must choose between the historical and the metaphysical method. Here it is important, I think, to see that ontology and metaphysics, though they have often been identical enterprises, are not always so. Heidegger thinks of his own inquiry into Being as an "overcoming of metaphysics," and it is clear that there is certainly a major difference between what he is doing and the old style metaphysic. The latter was a rational inquiry, proceeding by strictly logical demonstration. Heidegger's inquiry, on the other hand, is existentially oriented throughout; it considers Being not objectively but by way of our own participation in Being; its appeal is not to deductive logic, but to the insights that we attain in such states of mind as anxiety. The objections to ontology in a theological·interpretation rest on a failure to distinguish contemporary ontology from old style metaphysics. There need be no sharp dualism between history and ontology, and indeed if there is, it is fatal to the theological enterprise. Our own discussion of Being in the earlier parts of this book was, following Heidegger, always existentially rooted and oriented. As such, it was in no danger of becoming an abstract speculative metaphysic. Provided that we continue to avoid this danger, the ontological aspect of theological interpretation must be as firmly maintained as the existential aspect.

Another way of pointing to the inseparability of the two aspects of existential-ontological interpretation is to remind ourselves of the meaning of the word "God," as this became clear to us in the earlier discussion.[10] The word "God," we have seen, is not just a synonym for "Being," for it is not a neutral designation. It never means less than "holy Being," that is to say, Being that impinges on our beings, demanding, judging, and sustaining, and Being to which in turn we give our allegiance. So any talk of God demands for its interpretation nothing less than an existential-ontological language.

32. THE ORDER OF SYMBOLIC THEOLOGY

Our philosophical theology set out from man, from the kind of existence and the range of experiences that are accessible to all of us, and from a phenomenological analysis of this starting point it advanced into the exploration of the self-disclosure of holy Being. There is no reason why symbolic theology should not also set out from man as he is portrayed in Christian teaching, and then follow a similar course of development into the exploration of other areas of doctrine. The Christian faith constitutes a whole. Its various doctrines and symbols are all interrelated, so that although we have to discuss them one at a time, no single one of them can properly be understood in isolation from all the others. In principle, therefore, one could begin with any single doctrine, and the exposition of it would lead into all the others and to the view of the whole which alone gives life and meaning to the particular doctrines.

It seems advisable, however, that we should choose another starting

[10] See above, p. 115.

point than man for our exposition of symbolic theology, for we are now in a different situation and faced with a different task from that which confronted us at the beginning of the book. At the beginning, an analysis of man seemed to be almost mandatory as the point of departure for a contemporary philosophical theology, for we saw that in a positivistic era one has to begin from the world of everyday experience, and cannot assume that talk of a transcendent reality would be even meaningful to one's hearers, to say nothing of its being accepted as true. This philosophical theology had also an apologetic function, for as it went along it developed, in terms of universally accessible experience, a frame of reference in relation to which the basic theological terms "sin," "grace," "faith," "revelation," and finally "God" could be seen to have clear and distinctive meanings. Assuming that the tasks of philosophical theology have been accomplished with such success as is possible in these fields, we now have much more freedom to choose our starting point for symbolic theology than we had in looking for a point of departure for philosophical theology. The basic theological ideas are there before us, and the basic structure of religious faith has been outlined. So the reasons that impelled us to select man as the starting point for our first general tour of the theological field are no longer operative now that we are ready to set out on a much more specific tour in terms of the concrete Christian revelation.

Our present starting point will in fact be the doctrine of God. This doctrine is chosen because in a very special way it has a central place and underlies all the other doctrines. In Christian theology, man, sin, creation, salvation, and whatever else may be talked about are all seen in the light of God. Furthermore, it will be remembered that when we offered a typology of religions, this was constructed on the basis of the way in which each religious type experienced and represented holy Being. This already implied that its symbols of Being (God) were what may be taken as most distinctive of the particular type.

When it is said that the doctrine of God will be the point of departure for our exposition of symbolic theology, this does not mean simply a general idea of holy Being, but the distinctively Christian idea of God. This in turn means the triune God, the God who is unity but is also the trinity of Father, Son, and Holy Spirit. This doctrine of the triune God already contains *in nuce* the whole Christian faith, so that reflection upon it will provide us with a center to which we can relate all the other doctrines as we pass through them. We shall not find ourselves discussing single doctrines in abstraction and then at the end trying to fit them together in a whole. The doctrine of the triune God, as the very heart of the Christian faith, will from the beginning ensure that this faith is expounded as a unitary whole.

It is of course true that the doctrine of the Holy Trinity, although certainly implied in the Bible, was relatively late in being explicitly formulated. In a sense, this is understandable, if it sums up the whole Christian experience of revelation as given over a period of time. One might think therefore that the doctrine of the triune God should also come at or near the end of a symbolic theology, as a summing up. This point of view, however, fails to consider how a systematic treatment differs from a chronological one, though this is a rather difficult question, to which we shall return in a moment. In a systematic treatment, it is not only permissible but desirable to take the most inclusive doctrine, even if it is the last to be formulated, and by unpacking it, so to speak, to show how the other doctrines tie in with it in a whole.

But there is still another point to be mentioned. Though this may seem surprising, it will be found that the doctrine of the triune God gathers up in a remarkable way the findings of our philosophical theology, and forms a close bond ɯetween the expositions of philosophical and symbolic theology. I have said this may seem surprising, for normally one would say that whereas some characteristics of God, such as his "existence," belong to the universal knowledge of God, his "three-in-oneness" belongs specifically to the Christian revelation. However, if one is to think at all of holy Being in dynamic rather than inert terms, as both transcendent and immanent and not just one or the other, as the *mysterium* that is both *tremendum* and *fascinans*, then if God had not revealed himself as triune, one would need to have invented the idea of his three-in-oneness, or at least something like it. Yet on further consideration, this is not really surprising; for it was conceded that even our philosophical theology had to be constructed from a given perspective, and this perspective was that of the particular Christian experience of God. It was argued that this did not invalidate the philosophical theology as a whole, but it did give to it the slant, so to speak, that goes with this particular perspective. It is in virtue of this slant that our philosophical theology links up with our exposition of symbolic theology through the spelling out of the idea of holy Being in terms of the Christian symbolism of the triune God.

When this basic doctrine has been expounded, the remaining Christian doctrines will follow in much their customary order—the doctrine of creation, including both man and the world; theodicy and the problem of evil; the incarnation; the work of Christ; the Holy Spirit and salvation; and the last things. This order, beginning with creation and ending with eschatology, brings us back to the question of the difference between a systematic and a chronological treatment. Actually, in the following exposition neither the doctrine of creation nor that of the last things will visualize events happening at the beginning or the end of time. Yet the narrative, dramatic form of Christian teaching (originally, the mythical form of all religious teaching) is still reflected in the systematic exposition.

One further point may be briefly mentioned. The Church, the word and sacraments, and the Christian ethic do not appear in this scheme. As was indicated earlier, they will be treated in a separate division dealing with applied theology. This is not meant for a moment to suggest that the approach to these themes is to be any less theological, or that they are any less integral to the Christian faith. It does recognize, however, that as having to do with the bodying forth of the Christian faith in the world, they have a much more pronounced practical character than most of the matters to be discussed in the present division, and for this reason it has seemed appropriate to reserve them for separate treatment.

9 | The Triune God

33. THE TRADITIONAL TRINITARIAN DOCTRINE

"The catholic faith is this: that we worship one God in trinity, and trinity in unity; neither confounding the persons nor dividing the substance. For there is one person of the Father, another of the Son, and another of the Holy Ghost; but the Godhead of the Father, of the Son and of the Holy Ghost is all one." So runs part of the *Quicunque vult* or so-called Athanasian Creed. The language will probably strike us nowadays as quaint, and we may be completely puzzled to know what is meant by the idea of a God who is one in three and three in one, one substance and three persons. It must be expected, however, that any language that tries to talk to us of the mystery of God will have some obscurities. We have already seen that it will have an oblique, symbolic character. Actually, the trinitarian language has a much more coherent logic than many of its critics have allowed.

This has been well brought out by Ian Ramsey. Applying the methods of logical analysis to the Athanasian Creed, he concludes that it "may be seen for the most part as a set of logical rules for constructing the trinitarian formula." Ramsey maintains that "the early christological and trinitarian controversies are wrongly seen if they are thought to be concerned with superscientific discoveries about God, as though the early Fathers had some special high-powered telescope with which to inspect the Godhead. What the early controversies settled were rather rules for our talking, and what came out of them at the end were new symbols for our use, and in particular the trinitarian formula. The Christian does not have the single word 'God' as his key word. He substitutes for that symbol another; and this other symbol is built out from that focus of our total commitment which is made up of elements of the Christian dispensation." [1]

[1] *Religious Language*, pp. 173–175.

I wish to draw particular attention to the last sentence quoted from Ramsey, for this emphasizes, and rightly so, the existential dimension of the trinitarian language. It is not an objective language, describing a fact laid out for our dispassionate inspection, whether with or without a high-powered telescope. It is a language rooted in existence, in the community's experience of the approach of God. At the same time, it is a language that tries to express an insight into the mystery of God. It has the mixed character that we have seen to belong to all theological language and which we express by the term "existential-ontological." Ramsey's terminology makes the same point in his talk of "commitment and discernment."

The first thing that we have to do is just to listen to this language of the one substance and three persons, to expose ourselves to it with its antiquated categories and its paradoxes, as far as possible without prejudice, to attempt that repetitive thinking in which we might hope to hear something of what the language was saying in the existential situation out of which it arose.

The Christian community believed that God, who had created heaven and earth, had become incarnate in a particular man and that furthermore he still dwelt with the community and guided it. This, we may say, was the narrative or mythological expression of their faith, and like us, they looked for an alternative interpretative language that would express the same faith in a different way. They came up with the trinitarian formula.

However puzzling its language may be to us, it was originally meant as an interpretation or elucidation. As Ian Ramsey acutely observes, the Christian could not get along with the single word "God" as his key word. A richer and fuller experience of deity demanded a more complex symbol for its expression. The Christian could not go along with a stark monotheism in which God is utterly transcendent and sovereign, and still less with a pantheism in which God is entirely and universally immanent; he could not embrace a monism in which all differences are swallowed up in the eternal unity of God, but still less a pluralism like that of the world of polytheism with its "many gods and many lords." The Christians confessed: "For us there is one God, the Father, from whom are all things and for whom we exist; and one Lord, Jesus Christ, through whom are all things and through whom we exist." [2] And in the course of further development this basic Christian conviction found expression in the doctrine of the Holy Trinity.

Thus we may say that the doctrine of the Trinity tries to elucidate the

[2] I Cor. 8:5–6.

picture of God as he appears in the biblical narrative and in the history of the Christian community. He is a God who embraces diversity in unity; who is both transcendent and immanent; who is dynamic and yet has stability. These insights the trinitarian formula is meant to safeguard, though let us again remember that the success of a formula of this kind is to be judged not only in terms of what it affirms—for this will always fall short of the mystery to which it points—but also in terms of the errors and distortions which it excludes.

But while these remarks may to some extent defend the traditional doctrine of the Trinity, it will be said that the formula of one substance and three persons constitutes an interpretation that has ceased to communicate, for it talks the language and moves in the universe of discourse of an obsolete philosophy. This does not mean, however, that the formula is to be rejected. Especially if it does indeed conceal within itself essential Christian insights, what is required is a new act of interpretation that will interpret in a contemporary language this ancient and hallowed formula of the Church, just as it in turn had interpreted the mythological and historical material that lies behind it.

Yet before we try to offer a contemporary interpretation, we need to listen further to some of the ancient words. The unity of God is expressed in his one "substance" or "essence" (*substantia,* οὐσία). No person of the Trinity is any less God than the others; in particular, the Son and the Holy Spirit are not demigods or intermediaries, subordinate to the Father. They are all one in respect of their Godhead. But what can be meant by talking of the "substance" or "essence" of God? St. Thomas gives us an answer to this, an answer which is very much in line with the positions that have been developed in the earlier parts of our own inquiry. He declares that in God, essence and being are identical, and that this is uniquely the case with God.[3] So if the three persons are of one substance, and this "substance" is Being, we are again directed to the understanding of God as Being, rather than *a* being, and likewise directed to understanding Father, Son, and Holy Spirit in terms of Being rather than as three beings. So our interpretation will be oriented back to the earlier analyses of Being.

If the unity of God is expressed in terms of substance, his trinity or diversity is conveyed by the talk of "persons." Everyone knows that the word "person" at that time when these formulations were being made

3 *Summa Theologiae,* 1a, 13, 11.

in the early Church did not bear the meaning that it has nowadays, of a conscious center of experience. It had in fact a much more shadowy meaning, and perhaps the wisest course is to leave the meaning shadowy. We may recall St. Augustine's words: "When the question is asked (concerning the Trinity) 'What three?' human language labors altogether under great poverty of speech. The answer, however, is given, 'Three persons,' not that it might be spoken but that it might not be left unspoken." [4] Our language is for talking about beings, and if we are right in saying that the persons of the Trinity are not beings, then we do strike on what St. Augustine calls "great poverty of speech," and have to turn to that stretching of language which brings us into symbolism and its resulting paradoxes. The word "persons" has become so misleading that perhaps we would do better to think of "movements" of Being, or "modes" of Being (provided it is not in the sense of temporary modes), but these too would be symbols. We might hope that one symbol would help to illuminate the other. Again, however, we are pointed to the analysis of Being for an interpretation.

The paradoxical character of the trinitarian formula and the need to maintain a balance between the thought of the one "substance" and the three "persons" was already apparent in the warning clause of the *Quicunque vult:* "neither confounding the persons nor dividing the substance."

Actually, it might seem that the danger of "dividing the substance" and ending up in a tritheism is the greater danger of the two. This is partly due to the modern connotations of the word "person," for while it would be true to say that a person in the fullest sense can only come into being in interaction with other persons, nevertheless a person always retains a separateness, for there would seem to be an inevitable privacy and impenetrability in personal being. Partly also we have to reckon with the Greek formulation of the doctrine, where the natural equivalent of the Latin *persona*, πρόσωπον, was dropped in favor of ὑπόστασις, an admittedly ambiguous word, but one that suggests an independent "substantial" being. It seems likely, however, that the word ὑπόστασις was preferred to πρόσωπον because the latter had been used for a temporary mode, while the former corrected this error by stressing permanence, rather than independence. The further terminology worked out for the expression of trinitarian doctrine reduces the danger of "dividing the substance" and seems to exclude

[4] *De Trinitate*, V, 9.

the possibility of taking "person" in the sense of a private self-contained entity or "hypostasis," understood as an independent being. A good example of the kind of terminology I have in mind is "circumincession" (also called περιχώρησις), referring to the supposed interpenetration of the three persons of the Trinity. However this notion may be interpreted, it clearly helps to safeguard the unity of the Godhead. But, as I hope to show, this can probably be better done in a contemporary language by expounding the doctrine of the Trinity in terms of Being.

One might also mention what theologians call "appropriation," language which ascribes to one "person" of the Trinity an activity or character that belongs to all three. For instance, we often speak of the Father as Creator, "maker of heaven and earth." But creation is not the work of the Father alone. Perhaps we concentrate too much on the Old Testament accounts of creation, but the New Testament speaks often of the work of the Son or Logos in creation: "All things were made through him"; "All things were created through him and for him." [5] The Spirit too has a part in creation, just as in turn the Father and the Spirit are joined with the Son in the work of reconciliation, or the new creation. Such "appropriations" are not mere conventions, for they may point to the special role of one or other of the persons, but they should not mislead us into wrongly separating the persons.

These considerations make it clear that the so-called "social analogy" for elucidating the Trinity is unsatisfactory. On that view, "person" is taken in something like its modern sense, and the Trinity is understood as like a society of persons. Even when we make every allowance for the fact that a person is constituted through his relation to other persons, such a model goes too far in the direction of "dividing the substance." Karl Barth is nearer the truth when he writes: "It is to the one single essence (substance) of God that there belongs what today we call the 'personality' of God." [6] But the social analogy has value in reminding us that because of the inescapable social dimension in man, any analogy between God and man must have in view man-in-community. When God says, "Let us (plural) make man in our image," [7] he creates not an individual human being but "male and female," and we must suppose that it is only in terms of this most primordial of human social relations that the divine image could be reflected. No doubt the divine life transcends the distinction known in human experience between the individual and the social poles,

[5] John 1:3; Col. 1:16.
[6] *Church Dogmatics*, I/1, p. 403.
[7] Gen. 1:26.

but it would be quite wrong to take the individual human being as in any way providing a satisfactory analogue.

On the other side, we find terminology that was used to maintain the distinctness of the persons and to prevent their being swallowed up in a monolithic Godhead. Such, for instance, is the language of "generation." The Son is "generated" (or "begotten") of the Father, and the word points to an asymmetrical relation between them. Yet the symbol of generation is such that it maintains the "unity of substance" as against any language like "making" or "creating." Also, as against Arius, it was maintained that the generation is from all time, so that there never was a time when the Son was not. This last point, as well as denying that the Son is a demigod, surely also means that the Father could not be who he is apart from the Son; that is to say, the distinctness of the persons is maintained, but any one of the persons is an abstraction from the fullness of God.

If the Son is generated by the Father, the Holy Spirit is said (in the Western Church) to "proceed" from the Father and the Son. Actually, in a more complex terminology, "procession" was used as a generic term with "generation" and "spiration" as the terms used for the specific modes of procession of the Son and the Holy Spirit respectively. Here we need not trouble ourselves with such niceties of terminology, but will confine ourselves to the expressions used in the Nicene Creed.

The use of such terms as "procession," "generation" and "spiration" suggests an understanding of God as dynamic in the highest degree. That trinitarian doctrine already implies that "God's being is being in motion, being in act" has been well argued by Eberhard Jüngel.[8] But our earlier consideration of God as Being also led us in the direction of a highly dynamic understanding of God. In the next section therefore we shall seek to express anew the insights of the trinitarian understanding of God, leaving aside the traditional language of "substance," "person," and the rest, and employing a language drawn from current philosophies of being and existence.

34. BEING AS UNITY AND TRINITY

We have noticed that the doctrine of the Trinity sums up a long history of revelatory experience, but one could make a similar claim for the doctrine of God as Being. Allusion was made in the last section to St. Thomas' teaching that God's essence is to be, and at an earlier stage mention was

---

[8] *Gottes Sein ist im Werden*, p. 14.

made also of the association of God and Being in the thought of St. Augustine and other early writers.[9] But the *locus classicus* to which the biblical and Christian revelation traces back its apprehension of God as Being (and this might be considered the point of convergence between philosophical theology and the specific theology that elucidates the biblical revelation) is that celebrated theophany of the Old Testament when God appears to Moses in the burning bush and reveals to him his name: I AM WHO I AM.[10]

Of course, I am well aware that this passage bristles with exegetical difficulties and that even the translation constitutes a problem.[11] Almost certainly, to begin with, the divine name Yahweh or Yah had nothing to do with the idea of being, and may, as has been claimed, have originated out of a cultic shout, or an exclamation of some sort. But this seems to be of no more than antiquarian interest. What is of theological interest is that even if it was the result of wrong etymology, the name of Yahweh became associated with the Hebrew verb *hyh* or *hwh*, meaning "to be." Presumably people were not interested in etymologies at all at that period and all that should be said is what Eichrodt says on the matter: "To Israelite ears the sound of the name suggested some affinity with the verb *hwh* or *hyh*." [12]

But even if we grant that at some time the Israelites did begin to think of a relation between Yahweh and being, it then becomes a very difficult problem to know how they visualized this relation. Many ingenious theories are put forward by modern scholars, but the only point generally agreed seems to be that whatever may have been meant at the time when the account of the theophany came to be written in its present form, the meaning would be much simpler and more straightforward than the subtle ontology which later theologians have based on the passage. It is often pointed out that the Hebrew verb *hyh* had a more dynamic sense than "to be," meaning something more like "to become," so that the expression I AM WHAT I AM is misleading if it suggests an immutable principle of being. We have already seen, of course, that any adequate notion of being includes becoming,[13] so that not only Hebrew thought but sound ontology demands a dynamic element in the interpretation, and thus the ex-

---

[9] See above, p. 117.
[10] Exod. 3:14.
[11] See Robert W. Gleason, S.J., *Yahweh, the God of the Old Testament*, pp. 116–120.
[12] *Theology of the Old Testament*, vol. I, p. 189.
[13] See above, p. 111.

pression I AM WHAT I AM would refer to the ongoing process of being, or to being in time and history rather than to a static being. A minority of scholars take the verb in a causal sense as "I cause to be . . ." or "I bring to pass . . . ," and although the majority reject this translation, it is one that would fit in remarkably well with the exposition of being given in the earlier part of this book, for in the language employed in the analyses of this book, we could translate: "I let be what I let be," and this is indeed precisely what we have understood by transcendent Being.

For we saw that when we say "God is" or "God exists," we have to understand the words "is" and "exists" in the most dynamic sense, that is to say, as God's letting-be. It is significant that the Bible does not begin by merely affirming God's existence but with his act of creation, which is the conferring of existence. His first utterance is: "Let there be light!" [14] and so begins the history of his letting-be.

Obviously, we can never know exactly what the Old Testament writer had in mind when he linked Yahweh with being, but he certainly initiated a line of thought that has proved most fruitful in its influence on subsequent reflection. In the New Testament, the notion of being becomes associated with Christ, especially in the Fourth Gospel, where so many of our Lord's utterances are introduced by the words, "I am." Most striking of all is the passage in which Jesus declares to the Jews: "Before Abraham was, I am." [15] It can hardly be doubted that the "I am" here is an allusion to the "I am" of the Old Testament. In any case, the saying is meant to assert the intimate relationship of Christ to the Father, and it expresses this in terms of being. Here then we see the doctrine of God as Being converging with the emerging doctrine of God as Trinity, for it is being ("I am") which expresses the unity of the first two persons of the Trinity.

But this merging of the God-as-Being conception with the nascent conception of God-as-Trinity had already been prepared over a long period. If, as was claimed in the last section, the doctrine of the Trinity safeguards a dynamic as opposed to a static understanding of God, and if in turn the Hebrew understanding of being was dynamic (that is to say, included becoming), then there is already an intrinsic connection between the thought of God as triune and the thought of God as Being. Already in the stories of Moses and God's dealings with him, we see something like an attempt to express an understanding of God as diversity in unity in the

[14] Gen. 1:3.
[15] John 8:58.

place assigned to the "angel of the name"; in some heterodox Jewish sects this angel became a divine hypostasis called "little Yahweh" (apparently standing for the outgoing aspect of God, as contrasted with his hiddenness and transcendence).[16] In the later literature we come to the well-known hypostatizations of the wisdom (σοφία) and the word (λόγος). These had not infringed on Jewish monotheism, but they recognized a richness and diversity in the Godhead which meant that the Christian doctrine of a second person of the Godhead found the ground already prepared, as it were. The Spirit is the last to be conceived as a distinct person, or hypostasis, of the Trinity, but here again the ancient conception of the Spirit of the Lord had made possible such a development.

These remarks have arisen in a discussion of the convergence of the doctrine of God as Being with the doctrine of God as Trinity. This, however, is the second convergence we have noted, for it will be remembered that earlier we saw that the thought of God as Being is itself the point of convergence between the understanding of God that belongs to philosophical theology and the understanding of him that belongs to the specific Christian revelation. These two convergences, taken together, indicate the continuous line from philosophical theology's conception of God as holy Being to the full Christian doctrine of God as triune. They help to explain further the point we made that any experience of holy Being as both dynamic and stable must conduce to a doctrine something like that of the Trinity, so that if God had not revealed himself as triune, we would have been compelled to think of him in some such way. This also helps us to see why in some non-Christian religions there is a definite tendency toward a trinitarian thought of God.

Holy Being, then, has let itself be known in the Christian community of faith under the trinitarian symbolism of Father, Son, and Holy Spirit, one God. These three "persons," however, are not just three stages in the community's experience, or three temporal phases in God's self-manifestation, but belong together in the "substance" of the Godhead, that is to say, in Being; for Being has let itself be understood not as monolithic but as, so to speak, the energy of letting-be, and the "persons" are—and again we must say "so to speak"—movements within this dynamic yet stable mystery that we call "Being." So now let us proceed to sketch out how this immensely complex structure can be, however dimly, conceived.

The Father may be called "primordial" Being. This expression is meant

---

[16] See G. Quispel in *The Jung Codex*, ed. F. L. Cross, pp. 67–68, 71.

to point to the ultimate act or energy of letting-be, the condition that there should be anything whatsoever, the source not only of whatever is but of all possibilities of being. If we tried to think the Father (primordial Being) in isolation, our thought would tend either toward the utterly remote and unknown transcendent God at an infinite distance from the beings, or toward God as undifferentiated Being, hardly distinguishable from the void or from nothing, something like a clear fathomless pool over which a ripple passes—the illusion of the finite world—before the stillness and limpidity are restored. We can find places for such ideas of God or Being in the typological scheme that was expounded earlier but they would not correspond to the Christian conception of God, or to the Old Testament one either, for we have seen that it was not to be understood in starkly monolithic terms but already allowed for distinctions foreshadowing those of Christian trinitarianism. We do not then think of primordial Being in isolation as an "uncarved block" or whatever, but as a source of outpouring which is inseparable from the whole structure of Being and which is something like a "movement" within it. To think triune Being, we must hold as fast to the unity as to the trinity. The Father, as primordial Being, is the depth of the mystery of God. We could not possibly know anything of him "in himself," we know him only in so far as he does pour himself out in the dynamics of Being and is revealed in and through the other persons who are joined with him in the unity of Being.

The second person of the Trinity, the Son, we shall call "expressive" Being. The energy of primordial Being is poured out through expressive Being and gives rise to the world of particular beings, having an intelligible structure and disposed in space and time. Being mediates itself to us through the beings. These beings, as we say, come into being and pass out of being, that is to say, they have a temporal character, so that Being (and certainly any dynamic Being) is understood by us in terms of time. In identifying the second person of the Trinity with expressive Being, we remember of course that the Son, in Christian theology, is also the Word, or Logos, the agent of the Father in the creation of the world as well as in its recreation. The Logos is expressive Being, that is to say, it is not to be identified with the beings through which it gains expression. Thus we say that the Logos, or second person, is "generated" by the Father or is "of one substance" (consubstantial) with the Father. In saying this, we assign the Logos to the side of Being, rather than to the side of the beings. However, the Logos expresses itself in the beings, or rather, the Logos expresses Being in the beings. The primordial Being of the Father, which would otherwise be entirely hidden, flows out through expressive Being to find its expression in the world of beings. Christians believe that the Father's Being finds expression above all in the finite being of Jesus, and in such a way that his being is caught up into Being itself. Why the being of a man should be the highest vehicle for the expression of Being, and how his particular being can somehow be thought of as at one with Being, are difficult questions which we must leave aside for the present, though we shall study them when we come to the theme of christology. For the moment, however, let us just remember that although the incarnate Logos in Jesus lived at a particular time, the second person of the Trinity, the Logos, or expressive Being, is co-eternal wiith the Father. This means that in Christian theology at least, we do not think of an original static un-differentiated Being, from which the movements of Being started up as something subsequent. Or to put it in another way, we do not think of a Father once dwelling in isolation (he would not be a Father in any case!) and then moving out into expressive Being. This would be something like the mistake of Arius. If the Son is eternally begotten, so that there never was a time when the Son was not, then Being has always been dynamic, and primordial Being has always been united with expressive Being. So again we are reminded of the unity and stability of Being through all its diversity and dynamism.

God's essence is Being, and Being, in turn, is letting-be. So it is of the essence of God to let be. He does not, as it were, hoard Being within himself, and if he did, could we speak at all of God? We only call him "God" and recognize him as holy Being, calling forth our worship, be-cause he pours out Being, moving out from primordial through expressive Being. Of this, more will be said when we come to the doctrine of crea-tion. For the present, however, we can already see that as Being moves out to manifest itself in the world of beings, it involves itself in what can only be called "risk." What constitutes Being as God, as holy Being that gives itself and demands our allegiance, is precisely that it does not gather itself together as pure immutable Being but that it goes out into the open-ness of a world of beings, a world of change and multiplicity and possibil-ity. We talk of "risk" because in this process Being could become split, fragmented, and torn within itself. The risk becomes acute when the uni-verse brings forth beings, such as man, who have responsibility and a limited freedom that empowers them up to a point to manage their own lives and even to manipulate nature. Their destiny is to be guardians of Being, and they give us, even at this stage of the exposition, an idea of the astonishing reach of divine creation. But it belongs to a guardian that he can be faithful or unfaithful with regard to whatever has been committed to him. Man (and any other beings of limited freedom and responsibility like man) can forget Being and their guardianship of Being, and can choose to be for themselves, gathering up their being and ceasing to manifest that letting-be which is the essence of the Being of which they were constituted the guardians. Or to put it in another way, they can become alienated from Being, although they have received their being from the letting-be of Being; and having become alienated from Being, they themselves slip back from fuller being to less being, and toward nothing. This in turn frustrates the letting-be of Being, for the beings that Being has let be fail to fulfill their potentialities for being, and slip back from them.

This situation, which can be more fully grasped only after we have considered the doctrines of creation and creaturely being, and also the problem of evil, has been outlined so that we can see more clearly the place and function of the third person of the Trinity. We may designate him "unitive" Being, for it is in the "unity of the Holy Ghost" that the Church in her liturgy ascribes glory to the Father and the Son, and, more generally, it is the function of the Spirit to maintain, strengthen and, where need be, restore the unity of Being with the beings, a unity which is constantly threatened. But the unity which the Spirit builds up is a higher unity than would have been possible had Being never moved out of primordial Being through expressive Being, for the new unity which the Spirit builds is a unity of freedom, a unity comprehending a diversity of free responsible beings. Presumably the Spirit, as unitive Being, maintains the unity of creation on the lower levels of beings—we may recall that according to the creation story, "in the beginning" and while "the earth was without form and void; and darkness was upon the face of the deep," even then, to speak mythologically, "the Spirit of God was moving over the face of the waters." [17] But what the operation of the Spirit may be on the lower or natural levels of beings, we need not speculate, and it is in accordance with our existential-ontological method that we should look rather to the levels that we know by direct existential participation. These are the levels at which we typically think of the Spirit's action, an action on those free existents who are also called "spirits"; we can perhaps form some notion of the Spirit's operation upon man, but hardly on an ocean. In calling man "spiritual," attention is being drawn to his openness to Be-

---

[17] Gen. 1:1–2.

ing, that is to say, to his existence, in the full sense of this word. Being is present and manifests itself in every particular being, but most of the time we may miss it altogether. We have already described the revelatory situation in which, so to speak, our eyes are opened to Being, and this happens because Being has itself grasped us and communicated itself to us. It is in some such way as this that we must understand the operation of the Holy Spirit, and this is a unifying operation because it relates the beings to Being, so that the beings that belong in the world are seen not as self-subsistent entities but as beings in which Being is itself present-and-manifest; while correspondingly we know ourselves not as autonomous beings, but as guardians of Being.

What has been attempted here is a statement in existential-ontological terms that would be interpretative or reinterpretative both for the traditional trinitarian symbols of Father, Son, and Holy Spirit and for the classic interpretation of these in the nowadays archaic language of "substance," "persons," and the like. The interpretation offered here has the further advantage that it firmly links this key doctrine of Christian symbolic theology with the conceptual scheme worked out in our philosophical theology. But it will be remembered that this kind of interpretation always moves in two ways, one language illuminating the other and then being illuminated by it in turn. Now that we have moved into the area of the Christian symbols, we must hope that in their concreteness they will increasingly illuminate and bring to life the formal existential-ontological language. With this hope in mind, we turn now to the next stage in this exposition of the Christian understanding of God—the stage of filling out our thought of the triune God in terms of his basic characteristics and attributes.

35. THE ATTRIBUTES OF GOD

The attributes of God have been variously enumerated, and they have also been classified in different ways. Here we shall not adhere too strictly to any of the traditional lists or ways of dividing the attributes, but shall simply try to relate some of the more important traditional adjectives that have been applied to God (for instance, "immutable," "omnipotent," "just") to the conception of God that has been developed in our exposition, where necessary reinterpreting the traditional descriptions.

We conceived God as holy Being. We conceived Being, in turn, as both transcendent and immanent—transcendent because it is not itself a being or a property of beings but the prior condition that there may be any beings or properties, and immanent because it is present-and-manifest in every particular being. We conceived it further as both dynamic and stable, and formulated this in terms of primordial Being, expressive Being, and unitive Being. These conceptions supply our basic frame of reference for an interpretation of the attributes. Among them, a special elucidatory role will be found to belong to the notions of transcendence and immanence. These can hardly be themselves considered attributes of God, but only if we have a right grasp of the balance between them can we hope to make much sense of the attributes. One of the rather obvious and unfortunate features of the history of theology, especially in the modern period, has been the tendency to go to extremes in stressing either the immanence of God at the expense of his transcendence, or *vice versa*. If the nineteenth century was an age of theological immanentism, the first half of the twentieth century so stressed God's sovereign transcendence that any sense of his presence in the world was almost lost.[18] It seems to me that one of the most valuable consequences of trying to think of God as Being rather than as *a* being, or *the* supreme being, is that we are then compelled to think of him as both transcendent and immanent. However, I have sufficiently dwelt on this conjunction of transcendence and immanence in Being to be excused from developing the theme further here.[19] So we simply remind ourselves of the importance of this conjunction in all our analyses up till now, and we can make further use of it in our discussion of the attributes. It will be convenient to take these under four heads.

1. First of all, we may consider some of the divine attributes in relation to the *mystery* of God. Being we have called the "incomparable," for it falls under none of the familiar categories. God is represented in the Bible as incomparable: "To whom then will you liken God, or what likeness compare with him?"[20] But the more usual theological expression is "incomprehensible." So in the Athanasian Creed: "The Father incomprehensible, the Son incomprehensible and the Holy Ghost incomprehensible." God or Being is suprarational, and escapes the grasp of our intellect. But on the other hand, the adjectives "incomparable," "incomprehensible," "suprarational," do not imply that God or Being is just a cipher, an empty name. We have already sufficiently talked of revelation and of symbolism. As both transcendent and immanent, God is at once beyond every possible

[18] A notable exception is the work of the Scottish theologian, John Baillie, who, while acknowledging the need for the new stress on transcendence, contended that this should not blind us to the truth in the notion of immanence. See *Our Knowledge of God*, p. 228ff.

[19] See above, pp. 120–121.

[20] Isa. 40:18.

being, yet present and manifest in every one of these beings. We may recall that Being includes appearing, though it is distinct from it.[21] Without the beings in and through which it appears and in which it is present, Being would be indistinguishable from nothing. Hence, as we have seen, we can symbolize God in terms of particular beings, and we can do so the more adequately, the greater the range of being that any particular being displays. This is the justification for talking of God in personal language, and for regarding him as personal. But this adjective "personal" is predicated of God symbolically, not literally. This fact seems to distress some people, but it need not. We can certainly assert that God is not less than personal, and that the dynamic diversity-in-unity of personal life affords our best symbol of the mystery of God. But it cannot exhaustively comprehend this mystery. In general, the discussion of the attributes in relation to the mystery of God points us to the paradoxical, or dialectical, character that belongs to every adjective applied to the incomparable, which nonetheless draws near in revelation and presence. God is both hidden and manifest, our highest attributes fall short, yet in so far as they make God unhidden, they are true.

2. We now turn to consider a group of attributes that may be centered in the notion of his *overwhelmingness*. The attributes already discussed in connection with mystery pointed us not only to a dialectical symbolism but also to the theology of the *via negativa*, and most of the attributes to be considered now arise from the contrast between God and man, and deny that God is limited in the ways that man is limited. However, every negative expression of this kind tends to acquire a positive significance, and we have to be critical of what is admitted into this significance. Again we have got to bear in mind the basically existential approach which we have adopted, so that we admit into the meanings of these expressions what can be securely rooted in an existential relation to God, and exclude whatever may be merely abstract speculation. The choice of the word "overwhelmingness" for the focus of our discussion helps us to preserve the existential dimension in our interpretation, for this word describes God as he relates to man, God as the *tremendum*.

Among the traditional attributes to be considered here, a useful beginning can be made with "infinity," which illustrates more clearly than some of the others the basic existential reference of these negative words. To say that God is "infinite" means primarily not that he is very big, or ex-

[21] See above, pp. 111–112.

tended through all space, but that man cannot measure him. The word points to the deeply felt contrast between man's own limited, fragile existence and what has in the revelatory moment touched his life—overwhelming Being; or again, to the contrast between those objects in the world which man can exploit and manipulate (and in this scientific age we recognize that measurement is the way to such mastery) and the presence of Being, which we can never have at our disposal and which masters us. To take some abstract notion of infinity from metaphysics or mathematics and to apply it to God seems to me a thoroughly mistaken procedure; though to say this is not to deny that such notions might have some illustrative or interpretative value as analogues. But their defect is that they miss the existential dimension that is basic. The word "infinite," when spoken of God, points to the contrast between our particular beings as "beings-there" (*Dasein*) and Being itself as that which makes any being-there possible. Arguments as to whether God is finite or infinite in a metaphysical sense, and whether one can find a clear metaphysical sense for the word "infinite," are matters which the theologian can leave aside. He has no means of answering them, for to settle such questions would demand a godlike knowledge of all time and all existence, far removed from the kind of knowledge that belongs to faith. Something rather similar can be said about the word "eternal." Many theologies, it seems to me, suffer from a confused and unexamined use of this word. As the question of God and time will be raised in the next few paragraphs and further discussed later in the book, it will be enough to say here that the adjective "eternal," as applied to God, is not to be understood speculatively as "timelessness" or "unending duration" or anything of the sort, but that the clue to such understanding of the word as may be had must be sought by beginning from the temporality of our own existence and developing the contrast between this and Being.

A few other words may be considered here. The notion of God's "omnipotence" has caused a lot of trouble, and philosophers have often shown the kind of contradictions that arise if "omnipotence" is taken to mean an arbitrary power to do anything. It is true that some theologians have so emphasized divine sovereignty as to make God look something like a capricious despot. But most have taken the view that in talking of God's will and freedom, "we ought" (as St. Anselm expresses it) "so reasonably to understand these as that we may not seem to impugn his dignity." [22] St.

---

[22] *Cur Deus Homo*, I, xvii.

Anselm's point is that when we talk of the omnipotence of God, we do not mean an irrational force that might break out in any direction, but a power that is ordered and which cannot therefore do some things without disrupting itself. When we talked earlier of the risk involved in Being's going forth, it was clear that we must visualize this as constituting a self-imposed limitation on God's power, especially if we take seriously his creation of beings who, within limits, have themselves freedom and responsibility. So omnipotence could never mean a sheer power to do anything, and anyhow such a power in itself would hardly call forth our worship. But if we think of the contrast between the very limited possibilities open to any man in a particular situation and what must be the possibilities for Being as such, we get a clue to a more intelligible and more religiously defensible meaning. God's omnipotence means that he himself, not any factical situation, is the source and also the horizon of all possibilities, and only those are excluded that are inconsistent with the structure and dynamics of God himself. "Omniscience" similarly implies freedom from a single perspective, such as is characteristic of our human knowing, for God (Being) both transcends every perspective and occupies every perspective at once. "Omnipresence" is not to be taken objectively to mean that God is diffused through space like some all-pervasive ether, but again that he is not tied to the factical situation that is a basic characteristic of our human "being-there."

These attributes associated with overwhelmingness are, like the others, to be taken dialectically. They have been interpreted here as pointing up the otherness of God, his utter contrastingness with man. Yet it will be remembered that this otherness is not absolute. There is also a kinship, an *analogia entis*, for transcendent Being is also immanent in every being. If this were not so, we would not even be able to grasp or express the contrast. The "overwhelming" attributes tend to become quite unintelligible and even nonsensical when absolutized and considered in abstraction. They get their meaning and justification only in terms of the paradoxical relation of contrast and affinity between Being and the beings.

3. The next group of attributes to be considered are those which center on the *dynamism* of God. The dynamic character of God has been very much before us in the earlier discussions, both as the fundamental act or energy of letting-be and as the meaning of the trinitarian symbols. But again, it has to be emphasized that we have to understand this in a dialectical way, as has indeed been made clear in our discussion of how being is both distinct from and yet includes becoming, in our conjunction of

dynamism with stability, and in our interpretation of the traditional language of "three persons" and "one substance."

The traditional attribute which seems most obviously to call for discussion here is the one expressed in the adjective "immutable." This declares God to be incapable of change. It is abundantly clear from our previous analyses and discussions that we cannot accept this to mean that God remains in a static condition, and we have even said that it is hard to see how Being that was supposed to be utterly monolithic and inert could deserve the name of "God." Certainly, the God of the biblical revelation is not like this. Yet it is this very God that Christian theologians have called "immutable," and this can hardly be explained away just by saying that they superimposed on the biblical revelation the inapposite ideas of Greek philosophy. The ascription of immutability arises out of the paradox or dialectic of dynamism and stability, and even asserts a priority for stability. This can be vindicated, for becoming is included in being, not the other way round. Yet becoming is distinct from being, and without becoming we could not know about any being, nor could there be anything like holy Being. On the other hand, if all were dynamism and change, this would be chaos. The immutability of God points to his consistency, which was already mentioned in a similar fashion in connection with his omnipotence. Perhaps a better and more biblical term than either "immutable" or "consistent" would be "faithful." It stands for God's unchangingness through change, so to speak. Although the Christian and biblical revelation refers, as we have seen, to a narrative or a "salvation-history" this is not meant to suggest that God himself undergoes fundamental changes, for instance, that a God of wrath becomes mollified at a certain time to a God of grace. Let us remember that the unity of the human self was elucidated at an early stage of our argument in terms of an overarching commitment that pulls together the manifold concerns of life.[23] Once more, what is known in a fragmentary way in us mutable human existents becomes the contrasting ground for an assertion about God's immutability or faithfulness. But this is not meant for a moment to rule out his dynamism, for it is only in terms of a history of action that it makes any sense to talk about this kind of immutability, that is to say, faithfulness.

These considerations raise acutely a question at which we have several times taken a glance, without coming to grips with it—the question of Being in relation to time. The question first arose when, in view of the

---

[23] See above, pp. 76–78.

many ways in which Being has been understood and symbolized, we found ourselves asking whether Being has itself a history.[24] In asserting the faithfulness of God or consistency of Being, we seem now to have implied that Being has no history. This would also be in line with the contention that Being includes becoming. If Being is, as Heidegger expresses it, "the *transcendens* pure and simple," [25] then it is more appropriate to say that history (and also time) are "in" Being rather than that Being is in time or history. Yet in so far as Being includes becoming, it has taken time into itself, and manifests itself in time and history; more than this, it expands and realizes itself in history, more and more unfolding its resources. Just as the trinitarian symbols, while indeed reflecting the community's temporal or historical experience of God, nevertheless point to something in God himself, so time and history are not just forms under which we perceive a timeless and non-historical Being. They really belong to Being, and without them Being could not be dynamic, it could not manifest itself, it could not be God or holy Being: it could be only an inert static Being, and about this we would know nothing for we ourselves would not *be*. But Being is not *in* time and history, as if these were more ultimate than Being. Rather, the expansion and expression of Being creates time and history. This language is again to be explained with regard to our own human experience. We are not "in" time, as a thing or an animal that hops along from instant to instant; we are rather temporal as taking in past, present, and future, in the manner described when we talked about the meaning of selfhood. This gives us some clue to the relation of Being and time, and also reinforces the claim of selfhood (personal being) to serve as our most adequate symbol for Being.

These matters will be further discussed in connection with the themes of creation and eschatology, the beginning and the end. But for the meantime, we may relate them to yet another divine attribute, that of "perfection." Does the dynamic character of God and his self-expression in time and history conflict with his perfection? Or does it conflict even with his "goodness," for what is goodness but positive fulfillment? We must, I think, reply that the attributes of goodness and perfection are not canceled, but that we have to translate these too into more dynamic terms. Goodness cannot be just a state of rest, or perfection a static end-state. Both of these are again seen from the human viewpoint, and at any moment they represent fulfillment and attainment. But this does not rule out

[24] See above, p. 164.
[25] *Being and Time*, p. 62.

the idea of ever higher grades of perfection and goodness as the context is widened. "Higher grades" of perfection may sound nonsense, for is not that which is perfect complete and finished? We shall come back to this problem in the chapter on eschatology, but let me plead for an interim acceptance of the possibility of the idea by citing a supporting illustration —that what can be properly called "goodness" or "perfection" in a child gets replaced by new ideals of goodness and perfection in the wider context of adult life.

4. Let me finally say something about the divine attributes that relate to *holiness*. Some of those already considered might seem to belong here, for holiness, if we follow Otto's analysis, itself includes mystery, overwhelmingness, and dynamism. This serves to remind us that all the attributes belong together, and are indeed only our oblique and inadequate attempt to point, one at a time, to aspects of God that go beyond what we can grasp. But of all the adjectives applicable to God, "holy" is the most characteristic and the one that is most existentially rooted. It is no accident that in this book the expressions "God" and "holy Being" have been treated as equivalent.

The adjective "holy," as well as pointing to the mystery (*mysterium*) of God, also points to our existential response when the mystery impinges upon us. The response is twofold—the experience of the holy as demanding, judging, overpowering (*tremendum*), and the experience of the holy as granting, saving, empowering (*fascinans*). In more traditional language, it is the experience of the *wrath* of God and his *grace*. We express the former in terms of such attributes as God's "righteousness" and his "justice." These expressions do not mean that God conforms to a code of laws any more than his "wrath" indicates anger. They are simply expressions of what we have already called his "faithfulness" to himself, the stability of the divine order which does indeed judge and condemn the disorder of sin. God's grace, on the other hand, we express in the attributes of "love" and "mercy." These are not really different from his righteousness and justice, for ultimately they are all rooted in his "letting-be." This is his fundamental act or energy which gets fragmentarily symbolized in the several attributes. But of all the attributes, love has a supreme place, for self-giving love is what comes nearest to expressing the mystery of the divine letting-be.

The attributes of God are finally all one. They are aspects of his being, for the one fundamental thing we can say about God is that he *is* in the strong sense that he *lets be*. Already this identification of God with the fundamental act of Being ascribes to him in an eminent way every affirmative attribute. Hence, as St. Augustine says, "it is the same to God to be and to be great." [26] Likewise, it is the same for him to be and to be righteous, to be and to be loving and so on. Being is not a vacuous abstraction, but a *plenum*. Neither is it a magician's hat from which one could draw out any attribute one pleased. Rather, Being is the dynamic reality that draws near in revelation, grace and judgment. But when we look back in the light of this self-communication of Being to us, then, as E. L. Mascall has said, "we are able to see that *ipsum esse subsistens* is pregnant with all the fullness of Christian truth." [27]

This stress on the ultimate unity of all the attributes comes appropriately at the end of our discussion, for it warns us against one of the commonest mistakes or misunderstandings in the way we talk about God. We tend to play off the attributes one against the other, or to oppose the persons of the Trinity and associate each of them with some particular attribute, or to think that at a given time God is characterized by one attribute and at another time by a different one. Thus it gets suggested that God is involved in a kind of inner conflict between his justice and his love, or that the Father is just and the Son merciful, or that in the Old Testament God is wrathful but becomes gracious in the New Testament. It might seem unnecessary to mention such errors, were they not so prevalent and did they not assume such subtle forms. Let us therefore bear in mind that our language about the Trinity and our talk of the attributes, while indeed it points to the immensely rich diversity-in-unity of God, falls far short of the reality. Our symbols reflect the fragmentary sequential thinking of our own finite intelligences and should never distract us from the unity of God in whom all this is gathered up.

[26] *De Trinitate*, V, 10.
[27] *He Who Is*, p. 82.

10 | Creation and Creaturely Beings

36. AN APPROACH TO THE DOCTRINE OF CREATION

In the last chapter our thought was directed to the triune God, for here we have the cardinal doctrine of Christian theology, the one which leads into all the other doctrines and holds them together in a unitary structure. Already in expounding the Christian understanding of God we had to speak of God's relation to the world. The God of the Christian faith is not a God who is undifferentiated self-enclosed Being—indeed, it is doubtful if such Being could be called "God," and certainly we could never know anything about it. The God of the Christian faith is a dynamic God who goes out into a world of beings. We expressed this in terms of God's letting-be, which moves out from primordial Being through expressive Being to bring into being a world of particular beings. We now turn to consider the beings in their relation to God, and the obvious starting point for this inquiry is the traditional doctrine of creation.

It has more than once been suggested in the course of this book that since pure Being would be indistinguishable from nothing, Being is inseparable from beings. Yet at the same time there was recognized a priority of Being over beings; Being is the *transcendens*, it is already thought with every being, it is the condition that there may be any beings whatsoever. A being is a being in virtue of the fact that it is, but Being is not something that is but rather the letting-be that is prior to any is-ness. So while Being may be inseparable from beings, it is nevertheless the *fons et origo* of all beings. The beings are subordinate to and dependent on Being, which lets them be. This letting-be is the creativity of Being, and the dependence of the beings is their creatureliness.

Here we must notice that the account of creation to be given here, as outlined in the preceding paragraph, will differ from many of the traditional accounts. These thought of creation as a relation between one being or many beings (the world or the constituents of the world) on the one hand, and another being (God) on the other; that is to say, the beings were traced back to another being which was supposed to have produced them. This in turn reflected the way of conceiving creation in the ancient myths of the beginning, current in every culture. These myths, as we shall see, still have a symbolic value and contain their own insights, but they seriously mislead us if we carry over uncritically into our doctrine of creation the formal structure of the myth, and visualize creation as a relation between one set of beings (all that belongs to the world) and another being or set of beings (God or the gods). To trace back one being to the productive activity of another being or set of beings is a perfectly valid procedure when we are dealing with beings that are all within the world, but it breaks down if we try to trace the provenance of the world as a whole or the "ultimate" provenance of beings that are within the world. This is what Kant saw when he criticized the cosmological argument for God's existence. We must then get away from the idea that a doctrine of creation is intended to tell us about the production of beings that belong in the world by a being who is outside of the world.

When we think of God as Being, not another being, then the question about creation becomes the question about the status of particular beings. The question is not, How did the world begin? or, Who made it? but rather, What does it mean to be a creature? or, How does it affect our understanding of ourselves and our world to believe that we and it are creations of God?

This suggests that our first step toward an interpretation of the doctrine of creation is to take man himself rather than nature as the paradigm of creaturely beings. There are many reasons for this. In the past, the theologian's speculations about nature have so often led him into conflict with the scientist that we must be very careful in what we assert about nature, though this certainly does not mean that we have to be silent about it. But more importantly, our existential approach to theology in general would suggest that this particular question of creation is also to be considered existentially, that is to say, as a question relevant to understanding our own existence in the world rather than as a speculative question about how things began. We get rather striking confirmation of the predominantly existential motivation behind the interest in creation if we consider the two creation stories at the beginning of the Old Testament. The second of these, which is much the older, begins with the creation of man, and then an environment is built up around him. The motive of the story is to find an identity, a self-understanding, and the world of nature comes into the picture almost incidentally. In the first and later story, a much more sophisticated kind of thinking is reflected, one that is moving out of the mythological into something like a speculative level of discourse. Now a good deal is said about the ordered creation of nature, yet the existential interest is still strong, for man is represented as the culmination of God's work, and the earth is there that he may "subdue it, and have dominion over the fish of the sea and over the birds of the air and over every living thing that moves upon the earth." [1]

In any case, it is in man alone, that is to say, in ourselves, that we have any first-hand knowledge of creaturely being. Animals, plants, things—however much we may open them up through the natural sciences, their being remains in a sense alien to us, for we can see it only from without, we cannot experience it from within. Only human existence do we know from within, for this is the existence that is ours and that is open to us. So we are in profound agreement with Karl Rahner's assertion that "it is at men above all that we must look in order to learn what the Creator-creature relationship is." [2] Actually, our earlier analyses have already supplied the groundwork for an understanding of creatureliness. When man reflects upon the understanding of himself that is already implicit in his existence, he perceives the fragmentary, incomplete character of his being. This is indeed not yet a perception of his creatureliness, but only of the problematic character of his existence. As we have seen, he might conclude that this fragmentary existence of his is an absurdity. It is when he goes on to understand this existence as the gift of Being, as a responsibility laid upon him and yet a responsibility in which he is sustained and supported by Being, that he begins to understand his creaturely status. This takes place when the quest for meaning that is inherent in human existence is met by Being's self-revelation. So the basic meaning of creatureliness is dependence. To know oneself as creature is to see oneself in the light of Being, that is to say, not as an autonomous being, but as a being who is at once answerable for his being and empowered to fuller being, at once the subject of a demand and the recipient of grace.

It is by reduction or abstraction from our first-hand understanding of creatureliness that we understand nature as creation. In spite of all the marvels of nature, we recognize that it is constituted by lower grades of

[1] Gen. 1.28.
[2] *Theological Investigations*, vol. I, p. 164, n. 1.

beings, that is to say, beings that have a narrower range of participation in Being than has man. Even those animals with which we may feel some kinship are not, like ourselves, answerable for their being. Thus in nature we see a form of creatureliness in which answerability for the being that has been conferred is absent and there is sheer dependence and contingency. Scientists such as Carl von Weizsäcker have rightly seen that the Christian doctrine of creation has been a major factor in secularizing nature and making possible the rise of science, in accordance with the command to subdue the earth.[3] For the recognition that nature is creation, and indeed a lower level of creation than man, destroys animism and the worship of the creation in the so-called "gods" of nature, thus opening the way to the scientific exploration of nature.

However, this thesis should not be exaggerated, for the Hebrews, in spite of their doctrine of creation, made no progress in science and had a lower level of technical civilization than most of their "pagan" neighbors. The Greeks, whose outlook is frequently contrasted by biblical scholars with the Hebrew way of thinking, were in fact the pioneers of science, both on its theoretical side (logic and mathematics) and in the matter-of-fact observation of nature (for instance, Aristotle's descriptions of animals). Moreover, to believe that nature is God's creation also guards against a completely autonomous and anthropocentric exploitation of nature. Man is steward rather than lord of the world; and although the gods are driven out of nature, matter is accorded a value, as God's creation, which we shall see more fully unfolded in the doctrines of the incarnation and the sacraments.

For the present, however, we come back to the basic conception of creatureliness as dependence, to which, in the case of man, is conjoined answerability. This conception may be used to illuminate two points that have been traditionally associated with the Christian doctrine of creation.

The first is the notion of *creatio ex nihilo*. Presumably this doctrine was framed to stress the utter difference between an act of creation which gives rise to the world, and the familiar act of producing *within the world* one thing from another thing—a difference to which we have already drawn attention.[4] The difference needed to be stressed because the act of producing something out of something else is the most obvious analogy for creation, and like all analogies it has to be taken dialectically or paradoxically, and its inappropriate features denied; and further, the difference

---

[3] *The Relevance of Science*, p. 178.
[4] See above, p. 212.

was stressed in order to differentiate the Christian doctrine of creation from Plato's teaching, according to which the world is made out of a pre-existent matter. But we should notice that this distinction is not very clear. A matter (ὕλη) that is formless and completely without any determinate characteristics would be indistinguishable from nothing, and so too (as we have had occasion to mention more than once) would be pure undifferentiated being.

The importance of a doctrine of *creatio ex nihilo* would seem to be that it draws attention to the fact that any particular being stands, so to speak, between nothing and Being. It *is*, in so far as it participates in Being, but at any time it may cease to be. It both is and is not, for in order for anything to be something particular and determinate, and recognizable as such, it is necessary that we should be able to say not only what it is, but what it is not. This means in effect that negativity enters into the very way in which any particular being is constituted, or that nullity (nothingness) is an essential constituent of creaturehood. Again, man is the paradigmatic case, for we have seen that he actually experiences the "nothing" that enters into his existence.[5] But this negativity, which in man can get raised to the level of explicit consciousness, is a universal characteristic of creaturely beings.

Recognition of this illuminates, in turn, what was said about the "risk" accepted when primordial Being moves out through expressive Being into the openness of creation. The risk is that beings may get lost in nothing. What this implies will be seen when we come to the problem of evil. But it lies at the root of the ambiguity of the world, and is the world characteristic that has been seized and stressed by dualistic religions which see the world as a battleground. Yet something of the dualistic view is found in all religion, and certainly in Christianity. Dualism genuinely reflects the twofold possibility of all creaturely being—to advance into fuller being, or to slip back into the nothing whence it has come. We can express this in another way by saying that creation does not produce a ready-made world. Just as we have seen that selfhood is not ready-made but has to be attained, so a world in which responsible selves are to have a place is a world that must be attained. This is recognized in both the Old Testament accounts of creation, with their talk of man subduing the earth and naming the animals—activities in which he helps to shape the world and to advance it into fuller being. But this cooperative venture in which respon-

---

[5] See above, p. 86.

sible creatures have their part must be attended by the possibility of failure, by the risk that the potentialities for worldhood may not be attained. The religious man, however, believes that creation has a direction. His faith is that Being can go out into nothing, can become finite and expose itself to the threat of nothing, can overcome nullity and attain its end.

The second point to be discussed here is once more the problem of time in relation to Being. The exposition of creatureliness in terms of dependence puts to the side the question about creation as a beginning in time. It may be remembered that when we talked about the relations of theology and science, the question of whether the world had a beginning in time was mentioned as an illustration of the kind of problem that nowadays must be turned over to scientific cosmology. It presents us with the kind of question which, in principle, is capable of being settled by empirical observation, and which probably will be settled as, by radio-telescopes or other means, science probes further into the remote history of the universe. We shall then learn whether there was a time when the cosmic process began, or whether it has always been going on much as we see it now. Theology can have nothing to say on this matter, and, on the other hand, whatever answer science may produce, this would not affect the doctrine of creation, as it is expounded here. For this doctrine is not an assertion that things began at a given time in the past, but is an attempt to describe the characteristics of creaturely beings. If this is the true purpose of a doctrine of creation, then we see once more the value of an existential approach, and the corresponding danger of an approach through nature, since the latter can so easily become the question of how things began and can trespass into an area that properly belongs to science.

This discussion of a beginning in time can hardly fail to remind us of St. Augustine's well-known treatment of the problem. When asked about what God was doing or what was going on before the creation, his remark about those who ask the question is: "Let them see that there could be no time without a created being, and let them cease to speak that vanity." [6] We cannot imagine creation without time, for the creature is precisely transient, with the possibility of ceasing to be. But on the other hand, we cannot imagine time without the coming into being and passing out of being of the creatures. Here, however, we must remember what has already been said about time in relation to the dynamic character of God. An inert, static Being could hardly be called "God." Holy Being is already the self-giving, self-outpouring God symbolized in the doctrine of

[6] *Confessions*, xi, 30.

the Trinity. But while God implies this dynamic ongoing life, it was said that it is more appropriate to say that time is in Being than that Being is in time.[7] What this in effect means is that the true "beginning" of creation is not some moment of past time but simply God or Being. He is the ἀρχή or *principium* that lets be whatever is, but he is this at any time and at all times.

Our existential approach to the question of creation, taking man himself as the paradigm of creaturely being, has shown that the basic characteristic of creatureliness is dependence, which in man can take the form of a conscious receptive response to divine grace; that further, all creatures stand as it were between nothing and being, threatened by nullity, so that all creation involves risk; and finally, that time is needed both for the being of the creature and for the dynamism of Being itself, though a doctrine of creation does not require us to suppose that this time ever had a beginning, in the sense of a first moment. Creation, the Bible asserts, is good, or rather, "very good." [8] In spite of the risk involved, the risk of a split in Being, of disorder among the beings and their dissolution into nothing, creation is claimed to be good. It is so because by bringing about an almost infinite diversity of beings, it makes possible an almost infinitely richer and fuller unity than would have been possible had Being (to speak figuratively) remained enclosed in itself in a pure undifferentiated unity. Being lets-be, but it does so only at risk to itself, only by giving itself and going out into openness. To see this is to see that the creativity of Being or God is basically the same as the love of God.

Now however we shall consider some of the traditional Christian imagery and symbolism of creation, in order to seek a better understanding.

37. MODELS OF CREATION

Christian theology has employed two models or analogues to elucidate the mystery of creation, and a consideration of these will help to clarify and expand our thinking about this theme. These models are "making" and "emanation." The first of these is the fundamental one, taken from the Bible and developed through centuries of theological thought. The second has little foundation in the scriptures, but it entered into Christian theology at an early stage and has, as will be shown, its own value in correcting and supplementing the other model.

The image associated with the notion of "making" is that of a craftsman

[7] See above, pp. 207–208.
[8] Gen. 1:31.

producing an article for use. We have already noted that, like all analogues, this one is defective at certain points—it represents the relation between Being and the beings as a relation between beings, and it fails to express the notion of *creatio ex nihilo*. It is, however, the usual biblical analogy: "God made the firmament"; "God made the two great lights"; "God made the beasts of the earth"; "The Lord God made the earth and the heavens"; "The Lord God formed man of dust from the ground"; "The rib which the Lord God had taken from the man he made into a woman"; and so on.[9] This analogy stresses the transcendence of God, who *makes* the world, whether directly as in the older creation myth or indirectly through his spoken word, as in the more sophisticated story. Thus the analogy also stresses the distance and the difference of being between God and the creatures. Furthermore, it represents the creation as a free act on the part of God.

The image usually associated with the notion of emanation is that of the sun sending forth its rays. As already said, this idea of creation is not very biblical, and often enough the ideas of emanation and creation are opposed to each other, though here we have chosen to oppose rather the ideas of emanation and making, subsuming both of them under the inclusive notion of creation. This procedure can be vindicated on the grounds that early Christian theologians such as Origen began to introduce the idea of emanation as interpretative of creation, and in one way or another the idea has continued to influence interpretation right down to our own time. It should not be regarded as a rival idea to the biblical one, or dismissed as extraneous because of its neo-Platonist provenance. It should indeed be regarded as secondary to the biblical idea, but as such it provides certain correctives and gives expression to insights that are not clearly presented in the image of making. Thus emanation suggests the immanence of God in the creation. It also stresses affinity and even closeness between the source and that which has sprung from it, though it certainly does not suggest for a moment that the creatures (the rays in the analogy) have anything like the same "substantial" being as the Creator (the sun). Finally, it avoids the impression that creation could be considered like an arbitrary act, but it does this by moving too far in another direction and suggesting that creation is like a natural process.

I have outlined these two models of creation because I believe that their insights have to be combined. After all, whatever image we use will be

---

[9] Gen. 1:7, 1:16, 1:25, 2:4, 2:7, 2:22.

inadequate, and there is a good case for correcting one image by another. If it is objected that in this case only one image seems to have a firm basis in the Bible, I think it can be replied that the other image too, though it must be subordinate to the first, does conserve insights that are scripturally based and has moreover been sanctioned by a long tradition of theological use from the Fathers to modern times.

Our teaching has been that Being combines its transcendence as the mysterious act of letting-be with its immanence as present-and-manifest in all particular beings. The image of making presents us with the idea of transcendent letting-be, but, unless it is suitably modified, it may entirely miss the idea of an immanent presence. The image of emanation insists on the other hand that God does really put himself into the creation, so that the risk of creation really matters to him, and he is really involved in it and concerned with it. Now, an image of pure emanation probably goes too far in this direction and leads us toward a pantheism in which all things are part of God, the human soul is a divine spark, and so on. This is certainly not Christian teaching yet the rejection of this extreme should not be allowed to blind us to the genuine truth for which a doctrine of emanation contends. Many writers have tried to find a middle position in thinking of the creation as analogous to a work of art, the point being that the artist really does put something of himself into such a work, while remaining external to it. But it may be doubted whether this does full justice to the immanence of God in the creation, or whether it expresses that degree of concern with and involvement in the creation that in the Christian religion finds its eventual expression in a doctrine of incarnation. It is all a question of maintaining a right balance of transcendence and immanence, and perhaps this is best done by holding side by side in their tension with one another the models of making and emanation.

These questions can be further opened up by considering creation in relation to the persons of the triune God. This matter has already come glancingly to our notice,[10] and now we must pay some further attention to it.

Since the Father is primordial Being, the ultimate letting-be, it is natural that we should especially associate him with creation, and in the creeds he is specifically designated "maker of heaven and earth." The tendency to think of the Father as Creator to the point almost of equating the two is perhaps reinforced by our habit of thinking of creation so much in terms

[10] See above, p. 194.

of the Old Testament narratives, to the neglect of what the New Testament says on the subject. This predominance of the Father in our thought of creation tends in turn to stress the divine transcendence and to lay a very heavy emphasis on the model of making. But the work of creation belongs to the triune God, and when we attend to the Son and the Holy Spirit in creation, this helps to redress the balance.

The New Testament speaks frequently of the Son or Logos as the agent through whom creation is effected. "All things were made through him, and without him was not anything made that was made." "In him all things were created, in heaven and on earth, visible and invisible, whether thrones or dominions or principalities or authorities—all things were created through him and for him." God "has spoken to us by a Son, whom he appointed the heir of all things, through whom also he created the world." [11] Many more quotations could be added, but these are enough to show that the teaching is clear and that it is common to several of the New Testament writers.

Now, we talked of the Son (Logos) as expressive Being, and it was pointed out that the traditional language which speaks of the Son in relation to the Father as "generated" or "begotten" preserves the unity of substance (Being) as between Father and Son, and is to be contrasted with the language of "creating" which sets a difference between God and the creature. Expressive Being is not the creation, but the agent through which the creation comes into being. In other words, expressive Being is God in one of his ways of being; expressive Being is not the world, nor anything less than God. Yet it is precisely here that we have to find ways of expressing more adequately the immanence of God in the creation, for expressive Being, the outgoing life of God, is not only agent in creation but does really enter into creation. The combination in the Son of transcendence and immanence is well expressed by St. Paul: "He is before all things, and in him all things hold together." [12] In the same passage, St. Paul has spoken of the Son as "the first-born of all creation." [13] These questions belong to christology, and will be discussed there, but already—and not surprisingly—the christological center of the Christian faith is foreshadowed in our discussion of creation. God, we may say, is so intimately involved with his creation that in a remarkable way Creator and creature become one in the incarnation. But this can only be because the possibility (we might even be permitted to say, the purpose) is already there

[11] John 1:3; Col. 1:16; Heb. 1:2.
[12] Col. 1:17.
[13] Col. 1:15.

in creation, and in the transcendent-immanent relation between expressive Being and the beings.

We can also consider this briefly from the side of man. He belongs to the creation and is not God. Yet, as we have already seen and as we shall see more clearly very soon, man, as existent, has a special place in creation and an openness to Being, the possibility of a special relation to God. While there has been stressed above the difference between the "generation" of the Son and the "creation" of man (with all other creatures), just as the Son involves himself in creaturely being, so there is the possibility for man to become one with the Son and to participate in the life of God. It is true that he is quoting a pagan poem—though he quotes him with approval—when St. Paul is represented as saying, concerning the relation of all men to God, "For we are indeed his offspring." [14] This might seem to contradict the distinction between generation and creation, or between expressive Being and creaturely beings. But rightly understood, such an expression as "we are his offspring" has the same justification as has the model of emanation alongside the model of making, and it contends for a truth which will shortly become clearer to us.

It remains to say something of the work of the Holy Spirit in creation. Typically, we think of the Spirit as operating at the level of "spiritual" beings, bringing men by their conscious and willing response into a higher unity with each other and with God. Thus we are probably inclined to associate the work of the Spirit with consummation rather than with creation. But we already noted that at the creation the Spirit is said to have been moving over the waters, and allusion was made to the mystery of his operation at levels of creaturely being lower than that of man's existent or "spiritual" being.[15] We get a remarkable statement about the work of the Spirit in all creation from St. Paul. He says that "the creation waits with eager longing for the revealing of the sons of God," and he enlarges on this by declaring that "the whole creation has been groaning in travail together until now; and not only the creation, but we ourselves, who have the first fruits of the Spirit, groan inwardly as we wait for adoption as sons." [16] Here we have the picture of the Spirit, as unitive Being, lifting the whole creation toward God, bringing the beings into a reconciling unity with Being, yet without destroying their diversity, so that this is a higher and fuller unity than would have been possible had Being remained in itself and not gone out into the risk of creation. The culmination of

[14] Acts 17:28.
[15] See above, p. 201.
[16] Rom. 8:19 and 22–23.

this unity that the Spirit builds is the free conscious communion of spiritual (existent) beings with Being, which is in effect their "adoption as sons," that is to say, their participation in the life of God, so that the creatures will indeed have fulfilled their potentiality to become "offspring." But although this is the culmination, it is clear that the operation of the Spirit is represented as taking place at all levels, through the "whole creation." The "groaning" of the creation is the inarticulate response of creaturely beings to the unitive movement of the Spirit, a response that is below the level of that free, explicit, and conscious response that takes place on the level of man's existence. Nowadays we might call the inarticulate, unconscious "travail" of the lower levels of creation a *nisus*, or striving toward a goal, which these creaturely beings, below the level of conscious thought, certainly do not see, yet toward which they seem to move. But these remarks have brought us to the point where we must try to sketch out a theology of nature.

38. NATURE

It is sometimes objected that an existential approach to theology does not allow for a theology of nature. This objection is valid in some extreme cases, where existence (or perhaps history) and nature are so sharply separated that a kind of dualism has been set up, and a theology founded in the first of these two kinds of being has no way of coming to grips with the other and utterly alien kind of being. There is something like a Gnostic element in this way of thinking. Our own method, however, has been consistently called "existential-ontological." For very good reasons, it begins from man's existential being rather than from the being of nature, but it has no intention of being shut up in some narrow kind of existentialism. I have already said that it is from awareness of and reflection on our own creaturely being that, by a process of abstraction, we can form an idea of the creatureliness of nature. But this first approach to an understanding of the creatureliness of nature can be filled out in various ways.

We may begin by reflecting for a moment on the meaning of this word "nature." It has to do with being born, arising, and etymologically it comes from the same root as "genesis." Heidegger thinks that the Latin word *natura* was a poor translation of the Greek φύσις, and that in general the Romans obscured the Greek philosophical vocabulary when they translated it. The Greek φύσις is, in turn, the noun corresponding to the verb φύειν, which is one of the words that serves to express the idea of "being"—it is indeed cognate with "being." Φύειν, however, expresses "being" in a special way. According to Heidegger (and this is very much in line with some of our earlier remarks) φύειν expresses "being" in such a way as to include "becoming" as well as "being" in what he calls "the restricted sense of inert duration." Hence, φύσις, or "nature," is said to be "the process of arising, of emerging from the hidden." [17] Nature then is the emergence of the beings, and this can be visualized, as has been already suggested, in terms of primordial Being's going out through expressive Being into the risk of creation, that is to say, into the threat of dissolution into nothing, for every created being both is and is not, and it is by standing between nothing and Being that any particular being can be the determinate being that it is.

So all the beings that go to constitute nature share in the basic creatureliness of man, whom we took as the paradigm of creaturely beings. But it becomes clear that the various beings that occur in nature form a kind of series. If the creatureliness that belongs to them is to be understood by abstraction from our first-hand understanding of man's creatureliness, then all of them appear to lack that answerability which belongs to man's peculiar existential constitution as a responsible being, but it is also clear that some of the creatures stand closer to man than others, and that the kind of being that belongs to them requires less abstraction to grasp it than the kind of being that belongs to some of the others.

What we notice, in fact, is the hierarchy of beings. In one form or another, this has always been known to man at least since he began to emerge from an animistic understanding of the world. A hierarchy of beings is recognized in the more sophisticated of the two creation stories in Genesis, where the creation of the world is exhibited as an ordered sequence, beginning with the elemental energies and the physical framework of nature, and rising through the varied forms of living organisms to man. The recognition of several levels of natural being has persisted in the history of philosophy down to modern times, when it has found more precise expression in connection with the ideas of evolution and emergence. Different philosophers have worked out the scheme in different ways, some recognizing more, some fewer levels of being, some going right back to space-time itself as the lowest level and ultimate matrix of nature, others beginning with matter. Basic levels that appear in all schemes are matter, life, and mind (or spirit or existence).

---

[17] *An Introduction to Metaphysics*, pp. 13–15, and p. 17.

The philosophers whom we have in mind (examples are C. Lloyd Morgan, Samuel Alexander, Pierre Teilhard de Chardin) speak of "emergence" in nature to indicate that each new level brings forth an element of novelty, a new kind of being that could not be explained just in terms of the factors operating on the level below, though it arises out of this level. This thought of emergence fits in very well with the notion of φύσις as emergence, already mentioned, though this fundamental emergence is that of determinate, finite, created beings from the hiddenness of Being itself. Furthermore, each emergent level in the various schemes gathers up the lower levels into a new unity. Thus, a living organism is also a material thing, but not a *mere* material thing; while in turn man, as existing, is also a living organism and also a material thing, but he is not *merely* any of these—and perhaps we should not say either that he is *also* any of them, for they have all been gathered up and transformed in the new unity of personal being. The very fact that these emergent unities are not to be explained in terms of the factors operative on the lower levels alone, and that something like critical moments of emergence seem to be posited, reinforces our claim that the true starting point for an investigation of these matters is existence, from which we then proceed by abstraction down the scale. On the whole, the philosophers mentioned at the beginning of this paragraph work from nature rather than from existence, and have been mentioned here because, in spite of their starting point, their theory of emergent levels converges with an account of nature that begins from human existence and proceeds downward. It is likely that the creation narrative of Genesis also worked downward from human existence in formulating its account of the levels of creation. We have already noted that the earlier creation story centers on the creation of man, and moreover, the later account came after the Hebrew prophets had formulated a belief in God's control of history, and many theologians have seen in the creation story an extension to nature of the providential control which the people had existentially experienced in their history.

Let us suppose then that we admit something like a hierarchy of beings, an ordered series of kinds of being that are exhibited in nature. We seem to be justified in speaking of "levels" and in distinguishing "higher" and "lower" levels because, as we have seen, some kinds of being include others, and thus display a wider range of being and a higher unity that embraces a more multiple diversity. Philosophers of emergence have often claimed that complexity is the factor that distinguishes the different levels, and that increasing complexity on a particular level eventually reaches a critical point at which there occurs a leap to the next level, where the complexity is gathered up in a new and more comprehensive unity. This account has a considerable measure of probability, but we must see if we can express this understanding of nature in more definitely theological terms, since our problem here is a theology of nature rather than a philosophy of nature.

It is in line with what has just been said to recognize that the higher levels in the hierarchy of beings exhibit a wider range of Being, or at least have the potentiality for doing so. For Being is present and manifest in the beings; and those beings which are able to display in their kind of being the widest diversity in unity are the most adequate symbols of Being, that is to say, are best able to be the vehicles of Being's self-communication.[18]

These points may now be linked in turn with the teaching of St. Thomas. He maintains that all things tend to be like God, or to imitate God—though we may suppose that this cannot be any external imitation (which would be impossible) but rather a participation. Presumably even the atom of hydrogen has a minimal participation in Being and a tendency, if we may so speak, to "imitate" Being, in so far as it plays its part in building up the fabric of the world. But what is most typical of God (Being) is, in the language we have used, his "letting-be," his conferring of being, his self-giving to the beings. This letting-be is both his creativity and his love. In St. Thomas' language, "It is out of his goodness that God bestows being on others." [19] Thus the fullest imitation of or participation in God comes about when the creature in turn "lets be": "all things seek to be like God by being causes of others." [20] Now it is clear that this gives us another way—and a more theological one—for distinguishing the levels or hierarchy of beings. Living beings which reproduce themselves participate in "letting-be" more than do inanimate things; but on a far higher level is man who, with his capacity—however limited—for creativity and love brings the "imitation" of God on to an altogether new level, that of free cooperation in letting-be. This will call for fuller discussion when we speak of man himself, but here we see both his continuity with and his distinctness from nature. Perhaps the chief merit and certainly the most existential element in Teilhard de Chardin's book *The Phenomenon of Man* is the way in which he shows how tendencies that work blindly in

18 See above, p. 143.
19 *Summa contra Gentiles*, III, 21.
20 *Ibid.*

nature come to self-consciousness and take over responsible self-direction in man.

But our theme for the present is nature. If all things do indeed "imitate" God, and if there is continuity as well as distinctness between nature and man, then we see good reason for the Church's rejection of the ancient Gnostic heresies that regarded matter as evil, and we ourselves must be on our guard against modern errors of the same sort—views which set up an unbridgeable dualism between existence (or history) and nature, or which take an impossibly "spiritualized" view of man by devaluing the physical dimensions of his existence, for instance, in some of the attacks made on the material and institutional aspects of religion. As a sacramental religion, Christianity explicitly recognizes the value of material being. We have already noted how in some mysterious way we can suppose that the Holy Spirit operates even in material being. St. Thomas points out that if all things tend to be like God, then they must tend to be like him in his goodness. God himself in the creation story is said to have pronounced his work to be "very good." [21] We might add that his goodness, like his creativity and his love, is founded in his "letting-be," the basic characteristic of Being.

It would be difficult to find a better statement of the Christian understanding of the created world than we find in the words of a pre-Christian philosopher, Plato: "Let me tell you then why the creator made this world of generation. He was good, and the good can never have any jealousy of anything. And being free from jealousy, he desired that all things should be as like himself as they could be. This is in the truest sense the origin of creation and of the world: God desired that all things should be good and nothing bad, so far as this was attainable." [22]

39. MAN

Our discussion of the theology of nature has brought us to man, the culminating point of that hierarchy of beings that can be seen on this earth. On the one hand, I have wanted to stress man's continuity with nature, and thus his essential creatureliness; but on the other hand, such a leap is made with the emergence in man of rational, responsible being, that we cannot treat him as just a part of nature. One of the meanings intended when we say that man "exists" is just that he stands out from the back-

[21] Gen. 1:31.
[22] *Timaeus*, 30–31.

ground of nature. He has indeed been shaped by nature, yet in turn he proceeds to shape nature and to extend his control over it.

We have already spent a considerable amount of space in the discussion of man. An entire chapter was devoted to the analysis of human existence, and this served as the starting point for our philosophical theology.[23] This philosophical theology (or new style natural theology, if anyone prefers to call it such) was oriented throughout to the description of the structures of human existence, and to the exploration of human experience in some of its dimensions. In the course of all this, enough has been said about man and his existence in the world to excuse us from attempting a further detailed account, now that we are considering man in the light of the Christian doctrine of creation. However, some of the main points can be recapitulated here and brought into relation to the doctrine of creation, and to some of the distinctively Christian and biblical ideas that have been used to present the understanding of man as he is seen from the viewpoint of the Christian revelation. Let us recall once more that in such interpretation, there is always reciprocal illumination. If it is the understanding of ourselves already given with existence that makes possible a philosophical theology and, indeed, makes possible our response to any revelation or our recognition of any revelation, the revelation will in turn shed new light on that "natural" understanding of ourselves from which we set out. Perhaps it is even the case that one can only properly understand who man is when one has seen who Christ is, for it is in the light of Christ and his cross that both the actual sinfulness of man is revealed, and also his potential destiny of sonship. Yet on the other hand, Christ could mean nothing to us if we had not started off from the awareness of our own existence and of the questions implied in it.

So we can raise again the question of man at this point, hoping to get a clearer view of human existence in the light of the doctrine of creation, but recognizing that more still may be learned as the Christian faith unfolds itself, especially in the doctrines of Christ's person and work. Yet our exploration of all of these must remain oriented by that "natural" understanding of existence which is given to us with our existence.

We need not linger too long over the finitude of man, which is constantly stressed in the Bible. It is effectively symbolized as "dust" in the ancient creation myth.[24] As made out of dust, man is firmly located among creaturely beings. We would misunderstand the symbol if we thought that

[23] See above, pp. 59–83.
[24] Gen. 2:7.

the dust refers to man's body, and that this is contrasted with his soul (or "breath of life"). The biblical writers treat man, at least in the main, as a unity. Dust symbolizes not so much the body, in the sense of the visible, material constituent of man's being, but rather all the factors in man's existence that belong to his facticity, as a being brought forth by nature and never freed from nature, however much he may transcend in certain respects a merely natural kind of being.

The factical or finite pole of man's existence is perhaps chiefly represented by the biblical writers in terms of his transience. This is a common theme both in the Old Testament and in the New: "Thou dost sweep men away; they are like a dream, like grass which is renewed in the morning: in the morning it flourishes and is renewed; in the evening it fades and withers"; or "What is your life? For you are a mist that appears for a little time and then vanishes." [25] But as well as his transience, man's irrationality and his impotence are noted. The fact that death appears in the myth of the fall as the penalty for sin tends to obscure the distinction between finitude (which belongs intrinsically to human existence) and sin (which is an imbalance or perversion affecting existence). Of this, more will have to be said when we consider the doctrine of sin. For the moment, however, it is enough to notice that the Christian and biblical doctrine of man fully recognizes his creatureliness and his continuity with all other creaturely beings.

Must we not say, however, that modern science compels us to break off the consideration of man when we have understood him to be dust of the ground, that is to say, entirely a part of nature, though admittedly a very complicated part? Biology has shown man's continuity with the animal kingdom, and such sciences as sociology and psychology make it clear that overt human behavior can be a proper subject matter for scientific study. It can be replied—and validly, I believe—that all of these sciences abstract from the full concreteness of human existence, and miss out on precisely what is "existential" in man. But are we not now coming to the point where the researches of cybernetics will penetrate the last stronghold, man's mind and consciousness, and show that these too belong with nature?

Electronic machines excel man in various kinds of calculative thinking. Admittedly, this is the lowest kind of thinking, and it is good that we can shift the drudgery of it to machines, just as so much heavy manual labor has long since been transferred to machines. But let us suppose that better

[25] Ps. 90:5–6; James 4:14.

machines are built, to take over higher mental operations; let us suppose even that a machine gets built that becomes conscious and capable of spontaneous acts. What would this say about man? I do not think it would tell us anything new about man. It would simply confirm what we pretty well know already, that our mental life needs a highly complex material substratum. Our supposed invention would tell us more about machines than about men, namely, that when an electronic machine achieves a certain degree of complexity, it ceases to be a machine and becomes a rudimentary existent, as a new level of being has emerged, comparable to the emergence of the living from the non-living at a lower stage of evolution.

Carl von Weizsäcker has made some sensible remarks on these topics. He acknowledges that in theory it might not be impossible to build a creature with distinctly human traits, and yet in another sense it might be impossible: and "the reason might be just that what you need to make a man is history; perhaps it cannot be done in less than four thousand million years." [26]

Certainly the Bible claims for man a distinctive place in the creation. This distinctiveness (which philosophy calls "existence") finds theological expression in the doctrine of an *imago Dei*, or image of God, in which man is made. If man is formed of the dust of the ground, he is also said to have had breathed into him by God the breath of life; in the other version of the creation story, "God said, 'Let us make man in our image, after our likeness' . . . so God created man in his own image, in the image of God created he him." [27] Perhaps at one time the notion of man made to the image of God was taken in a mythological way, so that man would be supposed to bear an actual physical resemblance to God. As mythological ways of thinking were transcended, the affinity between God and man was seen rather in their both having a "spiritual" mode of being. Early Christian writers account for the fact that man is rational (λόγικος) by supposing that he has somehow a share or reflection of the divine Word (Λόγος), that factor in God which is directed outward upon the world and through which creation takes place. But while this stress on the *Logos* as the point of affinity between God and man conforms to the Greek view that what makes man distinctive is precisely his rationality—he is ζῷον λόγον ἔχον—yet this is not to be understood, in the context of Christian theology, in a narrowly intellectual sense. The full meaning of the claim that man is made to the image of God can be better conveyed in the con-

[26] *The Relevance of Science*, p. 140.
[27] Gen. 2:7, 1:26–27.

temporary language of "existence." What distinguishes man from other creatures is that he "exists," and to exist is to have an openness, which is perhaps the best clue to the mysterious affinity of God and man. Just as God opens himself into the creation and pours out being, and therefore has "letting-be" as his essence, so man is most truly himself and realizes his essence in the openness of an existence in which he too can let be, in responsibility, in creativity, and in love.

The doctrine of an *imago Dei* has to be sharply distinguished from pantheistic theories in which man (or, more often, the rational element in man) is regarded as a fragment of God. Christian teaching clearly puts man among creaturely beings; the fact that he is made to the image of God does not annul or contradict his creatureliness. But if one has to interpret the notion of the divine image in such a way as to avoid any suggestion of pantheism, it is equally necessary to avoid the error of some theologians who minimize the doctrine of the divine image in man, and who stress the gulf between the otherness and transcendence of God on the one hand, and the creaturely finitude of man on the other. No doubt the motive of these theologians is to glorify God, but sometimes by depreciating man too far, they drag down God with him, for they lessen the wonder of God's creation as a creation in which free beings have been brought forth, and they make God's sovereignty a mere external control rather than a claim to inward, voluntary allegiance. Of course, we have still to ask how far this image of God in man might be defaced or even obliterated by sin. There is no intention of maintaining that man as he actually is, always and everywhere, manifests the divine image in an unmistakable and undistorted way. But there is a tendency among theologians who excessively stress the divine sovereignty to demean man even apart from his sinfulness and to set an infinite distance between God and man. This prevents us from attaching any significance to man's peculiar place in creation and, as has already been pointed out, undervalues God's work in creation and drags him down to lower modes of operation. Furthermore, as William Adams Brown has rightly said, "the doctrine of a kinship between God and man gives the standard for measuring the significance of sin." [28] If one minimizes the kinship, then what we call the "fall" of man must be correspondingly minimized, for he has less far to fall. But curiously enough, those who are accustomed to exaggerate the distance between God and man are the very people who tend to make most of the

---

[28] *Christian Theology in Outline*, p. 239.

doctrine of a fall and run to another exaggeration in teaching a doctrine of total depravity. To these questions we shall come back in due course.

We must think of the *imago Dei* more in terms of a potentiality for being that is given to man with his very being, than in terms of a fixed "endowment" or "nature." Man is a creature, but as the creature that "exists," he has an openness into which he can move outward and upward. Indeed, the whole hierarchy of beings can be seen as an open series in which at each stage the tendency to be like God emerges more strongly. At the level of human existence we have passed beyond the levels of beings having fixed essences to existent being, and we have already seen that while man is a creature of God, he has the potentiality for becoming the "offspring" of God or for being "adopted" into sonship and so of somehow participating in God's life. It is when we consider this openness whereby creaturely being may be taken up into holy Being that we get, so to speak, a breathtaking view of creation in all its unimaginable possibilities. This view reminds us once again that all our models must be inadequate, though they do indeed point to something of the splendor that holy Being brings forth in creation.

The consideration of man in the light of the biblical teaching on creation brings home to us more sharply the tension or polarity inherent in human existing. He is a creature, brought forth by nature and remaining subject in many respects to nature's laws. Yet he is also made to the image of God, and stands before possibilities that seem endless. As the early Christian writer Theophilus of Antioch expressed it, "God gave man an opportunity for progress, so that by growing and becoming mature and furthermore having been declared a god, he might also ascend into heaven." [29] But this means that man is creative as well as creaturely and that he is given a share with God in shaping that still unfinished creation in which his life is set. The activities of tending the garden and naming the animals in the creation story are only the beginnings of a long process by which man more and more converts mere nature into a humanized world. That world is organized in terms of human needs and activities, and of human science. In it, things no longer confront us in their sheer givenness and strangeness; they have been assigned a place and a meaning in an environment that is seen from the human point of view.

But it is just at this point that the tension is most acutely experienced, and we have become especially aware of it in an age of high technology.

[29] *Ad Autolycum*, II, 24.

Man is tempted to move from being guardian of the world to becoming its exploiter, from use to reckless abuse. He forgets that he is also a creature and must have respect for nature's laws. Abraham Heschel has well expressed the dilemma: "There are two primary ways in which man relates himself to the world that surrounds him: *manipulation* and *appreciation.* In the first way he sees in what surrounds him things to be handled, forces to be managed, objects to be put to use. In the second way he sees in what surrounds him things to be acknowledged, understood, valued or admired." [30] Both ways of seeing the world are necessary to man, but it is not easy to hold them together. In an activistic time, theologians have too much stressed dominion as the meaning of the divine image in man, but contemplation and acceptance are just as much needed for the ordering of human life.

It will be understood that in all that has been said here, man is understood not just as individual but in the inescapable social dimensions of his being. This is very clear in both of the biblical creation stories. In the first, both man and woman are needed in their community to reflect the image of God; and in the second, Adam is incomplete until Eve is created as his companion.

What we have already seen of the open, self-transcending nature of man leads us to the question of his destiny. Creature though he is, he does not find completion or satisfaction in creaturely goods. Because he is constituted as an existent with potentiality for becoming the "offspring" of God, man has the sense and taste for the infinite (Schleiermacher), his heart is restless until it finds rest in God (St. Augustine). This was indeed the basis for our whole philosophical or natural theology, as worked out in the first division of this book; but now we can look back and see it in a new perspective from the viewpoint of the doctrine of creation.

That man does not find satisfaction in the beings but is driven on to the quest of Being itself means either that he is doomed to frustration and to the pursuit of an illusion or that he does indeed have a destiny that lies beyond the horizon of what is possible for any other creature that we know. Whether this destiny would be an immortal destiny, or what precisely we might mean by "immortality," are questions that must be deferred for the present. Let us say simply that his destiny is to participate in the fullest and most conscious way possible in God. All things indeed participate in God (Being) but man's destiny is to participate freely, re-

[30] *Who Is Man?*, p. 82.

sponsibly, gladly, with love, to become a coworker with God in creation, a guardian of Being to whom has been entrusted the capacity to let-be. Man's participation in God could never be interpreted as an absorption into God, as in pantheism. Such absorption would be the nullifying of the whole process of creation, so that this would have been just a waste. For creation, as we have considered it here, is precisely the coming out or emergence of particular beings, so that instead of a (purely hypothetical) undifferentiated primordial Being, there is the wealth of differentiated beings, and these are built up into an ever wider diversity-in-unity. The more multiple the created beings, the richer is the unity, or at least the potential unity, and all this richness would be shattered and destroyed by the collapse of everything into the stillness of an inert monolithic Being. The idea of such Being is not for a moment to be compared with that of Being that goes out into what we have already been constrained to call the "breathtaking" splendor of a creation where Being confers itself, gives itself, entrusts itself to the beings that have been called out of nothing to participation in and cooperation with Being itself.

Yet commensurate with the grandeur of this creation is its risk. This risk becomes specially apparent with the appearance of man, for with the gift of responsibility and the capacity for letting-be, there inevitably goes the possibility of rebellion rather than cooperation, of being for himself rather than letting-be. We have been talking of man in his basic constitution and his ideal possibilities, but we have still to consider sin, which even at the level of philosophical theology was apparent as the disorder and imbalance of existence.

40. THE HOLY ANGELS

We have seen that creation can be considered as a hierarchy of beings. All of them participate in Being and tend to move toward "likeness" to God, but they manifest Being in many different ways and over many different ranges. Some manifest Being over a wider range than others, and so we can think of them as constituting an order, and this in turn corresponds roughly to the ordered levels of entities described in philosophies of emergence. Hitherto we have thought of man as heading the series, and he does indeed stand at the apex of that hierarchy of beings that can be observed on our planet, for he is the one who gathers up into the new unity of personal, responsible being the several levels of being that are stretched out below him and that constitute nature. There is, however, no reason why we should suppose that the series must terminate with man, and this is recognized both by contemporary philosophies which visualize levels of being beyond man's being and by ancient mythologies which introduced the idea of beings intermediate between man and God. More than ever nowadays, as we learn more and more of the inconceivable vastness of space and time and of the infinite proliferation of worlds, it becomes a probability of the highest order that there are or have been or will be beings that surpass man in the hierarchy of beings.

How such higher beings might be constituted or what kind of experience they might have, we cannot know and it would be idle to speculate. As has been mentioned, we can penetrate into the mystery of those levels of beings below man, such as animal life, by a procedure of abstraction. We might perhaps try to penetrate into the mystery of possible levels of beings above man by a procedure of extrapolation. But such a procedure is always very risky and in any case, if in these higher beings there is some really novel form of experience beyond the range of our own, we would be unable to form any idea of it, just as a cat would be unable to know what our human experience is like.

It might seem then that there would be little profit in attempting any discussion of the angels, those higher beings that have been traditionally recognized in Christian faith and theology. As they have usually been represented, they belong to the mythology and poetry of religion rather than to theology. In the Bible itself, it would in many cases be hard to know whether the mention of angels should be understood as implying the activity of some higher order of beings or whether it is simply a pictorial way of representing the action of God or his self-communication in the world. In the early parts of the Old Testament, the "angel of the Lord" is hardly to be distinguished from God himself, who was supposed to appear sensibly upon the earth. For instance, in the story of the theophany to Moses, it is the "angel of the Lord" who appears to him in the burning bush, but it is "God" or the "Lord" who speaks to him out of the bush.[31] In the New Testament also, it would seem that mention of angels is sometimes simply a device for expressing a revelatory experience. For instance, it is interesting to compare the nativity stories in St. Matthew and St. Luke. In the latter, the angels seem to be represented as actual personal beings who come and go as bearers of divine messages; but in the former they appear in dreams, and it is the dream that is the vehicle for the communi-

[31] Exod. 3:2, 3:4.

cation.[32] But whatever problems there may be in deciding about the usage in particular passages or authors, there is no doubt that the biblical writers did believe in a higher order of beings whom they called "angels" and who are well described as "ministering spirits sent forth to serve." [33]

When we turn from the mythological and poetic references to angels to attempts to conceptualize them and to describe their constitution, we may think that we are entering a realm of pure speculation. St. Thomas spends a considerable amount of space in discussing the angels, but many of the questions which he raises may seem to us remote and unreal, as, for instance, "whether the movement of an angel is instantaneous." [34] But we should not be too impatient with St. Thomas' discussion, which is in fact an interesting example of extrapolation, in so far as it seeks to analyze the idea of a purely spiritual creature.[35] Such an analysis may become purely speculative, but it also has an existential and theological interest when it is oriented to the problem of man's own existence and is not considered as just a disinterested metaphysical hypothesis.

The concept of angelic being, or the being of a purely spiritual creature, can be seen as a limiting case of creaturely being. We can form an idea of it by eliminating from the concept of human existence much of what is symbolized by the "dust of the ground," such as sensuous desires and whatever else ties us to an earthly existence; and correspondingly we might imagine a vast increase in spiritual and intellectual capacity.

Apart altogether from the question of whether such purely spiritual creatures may exist, there is theological significance in this idea of the angelic, just as there is also theological significance in the idea of the demonic, aside from the question of whether there are any actual demons. The theological significance of the angelic may be considered both negatively and positively.

Negatively, the concept of angelic being sets a boundary to some aspirations of human existence. The angels are thought of as constituting a *different* order of beings, and so they are never in the Bible set up as examples for man, nor could an angel be a mediator between God and man. The limiting case of angelic or purely spiritual creaturehood is set over against the polar being ("existence") that belongs to man, not as a judgment of it or as a kind of being after which man should strive, but rather

[32] Matt. 1:20, 2:13, 2:19, 2:22; Luke 1:11, 1:26, 2:9.
[33] Heb. 1:14.
[34] *Summa Theologiae*, Ia, 53, 3.
[35] *Op. cit.*, Ia, 50.

as a foil in which we understand our human existence better and learn not to despise the material but to integrate it into man's own kind of creaturely being, that is to say, an embodied and factical existence. Indeed, the word "angelism" has been coined to denote a false spirituality in man, a proud attempt to live as a purely spiritual and intellectual being or to place excessive reliance on his spiritual and intellectual capacities. This is imbalance and distortion of human existence, and therefore sin.

As if to emphasize the perils of angelism, the traditional material concerning the angels contains the myth of the primeval rebellion of some of the angels against God and their consequent fall. The point of the story is simply that angelic or purely spiritual being is no guarantee against sin, and does not result in the elimination of sin. On the contrary, it suggests that spiritual sin is graver than any sensuous sin. This spiritual sin is pride, and ultimate idolatry.

Hence we may think of the angel as setting a limit to man's being. Like the cherubim who are said to have kept guard outside the garden of Eden,[36] the concept of the angelic marks the boundary beyond which man cannot trespass. We have our own constitution as creatures, the particular constitution that we call "existence," and we have to *be* as existents. We have indeed seen that existence is itself open, not fixed, and that its possibilities can unfold from creaturehood to sonship, and to participation in God. How far they go, we do not know, as the creature presses on in likeness to God. "We are God's children now; it does not yet appear what we shall be, but we know that when he appears we shall be like him." [37] But this mystery of ultimate human destiny has nothing to do with a kind of lane-jumping in which we do not accept the kind of being that is ours in creation, and try to exchange it for another kind. The Christian faith holds before us the God-man, not the angel, as the fullest expression of a truly human destiny.

It may be that I have spent too long over the negative significance of the angels. While indeed they do appear in the Bible as agents of God's judgment and restraint, they are more often represented as helpful, "sent forth to serve for the sake of those who are to obtain salvation." [38]

Positively, the concept of the angelic stands for the unity and order of the whole creation in the service of Being; not merely at the level of cosmic process, but at the level of conscious and free cooperation. God has

---

[36] Gen. 3:24.
[37] I John 3:2.
[38] Heb. 1:14.

"ordained and constituted the services of angels and men in a wonderful order." [39] Man is sometimes afflicted with a sense of loneliness on his little planet, the only "existent" upon earth, perhaps just an accident in the cosmos. But if the Christian doctrine of creation is true, then man is no accident, and presumably he is not alone. He must be one of countless races of beings on which the Creator has conferred being, and some of these races must, like man himself, have risen to consciousness and freedom whereby they can gladly cooperate with God. Some must have moved further in the hierarchy of beings, so that they constitute higher orders of creaturely beings. The doctrine of the angels opens our eyes to this vast, unimaginable cooperative striving and service, as all things seek to be like God and to attain fullness of being in him. One may recall here the story of Elisha's servant whose courage was renewed by a vision of supporting angels.[40]

This incident is particularly relevant for understanding the significance of the angels in a contemporary formulation of the doctrine of creation. The doctrine of the angels directs our minds to the vastness and richness of the creation, and every advance of science opens up still more distant horizons. Any merely humanistic creed that makes man the measure of all things or regards him as the sole author of values is narrow and parochial. The panorama of creation must be far more breathtaking than we can guess in our corner of the cosmos, for there must be many higher orders of beings whose service is joined with ours under God.

41. DEMONS OR EVIL SPIRITS

In common with other religions, Christianity has recognized still another class of creaturely beings—the demons or evil spirits. Belief in the existence of such spirits has now largely declined, but throughout most of Christian history it was virtually universal, and it is prominent in the New Testament. In the developed form of the belief, there was visualized a whole host of evil spirits under the rule of Satan or Lucifer and constituting a kind of "kingdom of darkness" opposed to the rule of God.

In Christian theology, these demonic powers were always considered creatures, even if creatures of superior force and cunning. They were never considered to constitute an independent reality equiprimordial with God, as in some eastern dualistic religions. But if these are evil creatures,

[39] *Book of Common Prayer*, Collect for St. Michael and All Angels.
[40] II Kings 6:15-17.

they could not have been created evil by a God who made everything very good. Thus their existence was explained by a myth of a fall of angels who had revolted against God before man was created.

If our speculation in the last section that there may be in the universe races of creatures superior to man in their intellectual and spiritual powers and therefore comparable to the angels of tradition is a reasonable one, then it is quite possible that some of these superior beings are "fallen angels" and thus comparable to the demons of tradition. We have noted repeatedly the risk of creation, and the more powerful the creatures brought forth, the greater is the risk and the greater the vulnerability of God's enterprise in creation.

But even if there are corrupted beings of superhuman power, they would seem to have little to do with the demons and evil spirits of traditional belief. For the latter have been eliminated through the secularization of our understanding of nature and the consequent decline of animism. The evils once attributed to demons—sickness of body or mind, failure of crops, infertility of herds, and so on—are now understood in different ways. The once extensive empire of the demons has shrunk away. As Frazer wrote, "For ages the army of spirits, once so near, has been receding further and further from us, banished by the magic wand of science from hearth and home, from ruined cell and ivied tower, from haunted glade and lonely mere. . . . Only in poets' dreams is it given to catch a glimpse of the last flutter of the standards of the retreating host, to hear the beat of their invisible wings, the sound of their mocking laughter." [41] Few will regret the disappearance of the demons, for life must have been unimaginably oppressive when dark spirits were supposed to be lurking all around.

We should not lose sight of the fact, however, that the demons did represent in a mythological way some truths about evil which can easily be overlooked if we take too superficial a view of the subject. Among these truths are: the depth and mystery of evil; the superhuman dimensions of evil; its sometimes apparently systemic character; and the fact that a spiritual nature is no safeguard against evil and may indeed issue in the worst forms of evil. These matters will come up for discussion in the next chapter, when we explicitly consider the threat of evil to the creation.

---

[41] *The Golden Bough*, pp. 546–547.

11 | God, the World, and Evil

42. PROVIDENCE

In the exposition of Christian doctrine, the doctrine of creation is usually followed by a doctrine of providence, which asserts that the same God who gave being to the world continues to govern its affairs. In this book, however, it is clear that no sharp distinction can be made between creation and providence, for we did not tie creation to a moment of time at the beginning, but rather interpreted the doctrine of creation as meaning the dependence of the beings at all times on Being that lets them be. Only if creation is thought of as an event in the past is it necessary to bring forward a distinct doctrine of providence to establish God's continuing interest in his world and to indicate that he is not a kind of absentee landlord who set things going long ago and now leaves the world to its own devices. In the present system, the assertion of God's providence is just another way of asserting his constant creating and sustaining energy.

But it is another way to which we have to pay some attention, for it draws attention to a special aspect of divine creativity. Faith in providence asserts that creativity has a positive character, of which purposefulness in human activities might provide an analogy. Creativity is not just a random creativity, or one that might be overcome by dissolution and annihilation, or even halted and held steady by these. Rather it is an ordered movement into ever fuller and richer kinds of being. Faith in providence asserts this definite movement in the creation, an overcoming of deficiencies and distortions and a fuller realizing of potentialities.

Of course, it is not being denied that there are elements of randomness in the processes of nature. Perhaps it is only through random collocations and combinations that all the potentialities latent in the fundamental particles of the physical universe can be explored and realized. In theology too we need not suppose that every event that happens and every development that takes place is serving some serious purpose of God. In the profusion of living forms, the psalmist sees a kind of playfulness of the divine creativity: "Yonder is the sea, great and wide, which teems with things innumerable, living things both small and great. There go the ships, and Leviathan which thou didst form to sport in it." [1] But all is not randomness and play, or we could make no sense of it. Randomness and play occur in a context of order.

When we consider the course of events in nature, we can distinguish three kinds of happening. First, there is, as we have said, an element of randomness; some things seem to happen by sheer chance, and this tychastic type of happening is, we are told by modern physicists, typical of the tiny particles out of which matter is constituted. Second, there is an element of necessity; at the level of those macroscopic events which we perceive going on around us, there is a reliable regularity. Third, however much we may have moved away from an animistic way of looking at the world, there are some features of the process which seem analogous to what we know as free purposive behavior in our own experience, and these may lead us to suppose that the universe has some goal or some general direction. If theologians have been too ready to stress what seemed to them like purpose—and it is generally admitted that they have been too ready—then some scientists and philosophers have been too ready to attribute everything to chance. Actually one might argue that it is more reasonable to appeal to the higher principle (purpose) than to the lower (chance) as a clue to the character of the universe, seeing that the universe has brought forth purposive beings; and one could argue further that if creation is the open, unfinished process which we described in the last chapter, then one would expect to find evidences of untidiness and loose ends, of chance and necessity, alongside whatever one might claim to discern of purpose. But it is impossible to prove conclusively either that the universe is moving to some goal or that its present and future states depend only on chance.

Belief in providence is not a speculative hypothesis founded on large-scale observation of nature and history. As far as nature is concerned, although one can observe evolution, there is also devolution, and—as has been conceded in our discussion of natural theology—the picture that the

[1] Ps. 104:24-25.

world presents is an ambiguous one. What were once taken to be evidences of teleology and perhaps even of a divine beneficence are now for the most part satisfyingly explained by science in other ways, and nature hardly offers convincing evidence for even a general providence, to say nothing of one that might be supposed to concern itself with particular existences. History is just as ambiguous as nature. Here also we have already forsworn any ambition to construct a metaphysic of history in the style of St. Augustine or Hegel.[2] Our knowledge of history is far too fragmentary to permit anything of the sort. About most of man's long sojourn on earth (so-called prehistory) we know practically nothing, and even about the very recent period of the past five thousand years or so that have emerged into the light of recorded history, we know only a fraction. On this basis, it would be impossible to pretend to trace some grand scheme in history. The "sacred" history recorded in the Bible is itself only a tiny fragment, and cannot be used to construct a metaphysic of history, although it may be illuminative and interpretative in other ways. Moreover, the fragments that we do see are as ambiguous as the events of nature, and he would be indeed a bold optimist who would claim that he could see in them the working out of a providential scheme.

Belief in providence, like belief in creation itself, is founded existentially. It is through happenings that increase and strengthen our being—that do so not because of our own efforts primarily, but sometimes even in spite of our own efforts—that we come to believe in providence; and we do so because in these happenings we have become aware of the presence of Being, acting on us and in us, and giving itself to us. Historically, it has been through classic happenings of this kind, such as Israel's exodus from Egypt and the cross of Christ, that communities of faith have come to believe in God's providential dealing. In the case of most individuals, they have probably learned the doctrine first in the community of faith and then confirmed it in their own experience. This existential or personal basis of the belief in providence prevents us from regarding it as a mere mechanical process.

Let us consider the foundations of the belief in greater detail. We can see how such a belief, originating existentially, may become extended into a conviction of God's government of the universe, though not as a metaphysical speculation but rather as an act of faith. In the Bible, perhaps the clearest and earliest statement of a belief in providence occurs in the story of Joseph. As so often occurs in such cases, Joseph's story

---

[2] See above, p. 25.

points to events which *in spite of* the intention of the human agents have turned out for good. His brothers had sold him into slavery, but as a result he had been able to save his whole clan; and Joseph concludes, "So it was not you who sent me here, but God." [3] Joseph's claim that there is a divine overruling of events may seem too naïvely individualistic, since he appeals to his own personal history as the ground for this belief. But presumably Joseph—or the writer who tells his story—set the personal history within the wider history of the community, and this too was interpreted in providential terms. The Hebrews understood their history as the working out of a destiny to which God had called Abraham and his descendants. God was supposed to have made a covenant with his people, and their history is interpreted in terms of the covenant relationship, God remaining faithful, renewing the covenant and guiding the people toward their destiny even when they have fallen away from it. Then the prophets extend the idea of God's providential guidance outside of the covenanted community. The Persian king Cyrus, for instance, is actually called the Lord's "anointed one," and the "shepherd" who will "fulfill the purpose" of God.[4] Yet a further step is taken, as we have already seen,[5] when in the later and more sophisticated creation story of Genesis, God's providential control is regarded as extending to nature, for many Old Testament scholars hold that this particular account of creation was made possible by the prophetic belief in God's rule in history. Thus we can see how there is a continuity all the way from an individual conviction that God's grace has been experienced in the events of a personal life to the belief in God's providential rule over both history and nature. The belief is existentially based throughout, and never becomes a speculative hypothesis grounded on a theory of history or of nature. However, a time might come when the belief would be brought into confrontation with the evidences of nature and history, and perhaps an attempt made to find confirmation for it in these evidences, or—because the evidences are so ambiguous—an attempt made to justify the belief in the face of facts that appear to conflict with it (the so-called "problem of evil").

But leaving aside these questions for the moment, let us consider again the belief that emerges from the existential awareness of God's presence and activity in life stories, in histories, or even in nature. The content of this

---

[3] Gen. 45:8.
[4] Isa. 45:1, 44:28.
[5] See above, p. 224.

belief, as has been said already, is that Being overcomes the nothing into which it has gone in creation; that although creation implies risk, nevertheless the movement is toward realization of potentialities-of-being, and the overcoming of dissolution, frustration, annihilation. Since the actual picture is always, it would seem, an ambiguous one, the belief in providence has to be held often in the face of facts that appear to contradict it. It is by no means obvious that "in everything God works for good," [6] but then this was not obvious to St. Paul who wrote these words. It has to be insisted again that this doctrine begins as an act of faith and hope, an attitude to life; it does not begin as a speculation about the world, and certainly not a speculation that can be thought up in the study away from the actual conflicts and decisions of life.

But is this equivalent to an admission that a belief in providence is just an emotional attitude, a kind of whistling to keep our courage up? Two replies can be made to this objection. The first is to remind ourselves of all that has been said in the earlier part of this book on the relation of feeling and understanding; an existential attitude is not just some subjective emotional frame of mind, but is also a way of understanding the world and one's existence in it, even if this understanding has not, in many cases, been made explicit in words. The second point is to acknowledge frankly that when this understanding has been brought to explicit expression, then it must be subjected to every test we can devise; and again we may refer back to the early parts of the book, where it was insisted that although a faith must be existentially founded, it must also be a *reasonable* faith—not one that could be rationally demonstrated (for this would be no faith) but one that can be reasonably defended. Actually, even from Old Testament times, those who have believed in providence have been well aware of the evidences that count against such a belief, or seem to count against it, and have tried to come to grips with the problem these evidences present.

It should also be said that the belief in providence that is developed in the Bible is a mature and adult belief. It is very far from a groundless optimism (this is more characteristic of humanism) or any infantile belief that the universe ought to be ordered to fit in with one's own ego-centered desires and ambitions. The Hebrew prophets' belief in providence was not just a belief in divine favors, or a belief that everything must turn out well for Israel in the end. It was belief in an ordering of history by a God

[6] Rom. 8:28.

who is holy and righteous as well as merciful, so that his providence might be experienced as a discipline, and indeed the prophets have as much to say about God's judgment of Israel as about his favor. A mature belief in providence must hold together all the "attributes" that we have seen to belong to God,[7] so that there is always more than one side to the experience of God's providence. The same act discloses both his favor and his judgment, both his "wrath" and his grace. Yet this is not to say that providence is a vague blanket idea that could cover anything that might happen. Such an idea would be so thin in content as to be valueless. The belief in providence does assert a direction in events, a direction which we can sometimes know as grace as we move with it, sometimes as judgment when we go against it; and this direction is toward ever fuller being.

If one did not think of the idea of providence in this dialectical way, but thought of it purely as divine favor, then not only would this be an infantile belief and one that for most people might seem to have little evidential support, it could also be a morally dangerous belief. An individual or a nation that has become seized of the idea of enjoying a special divine favor and of being appointed to a divine destiny can become utterly overwhelming and tyrannous toward others. The biblical and Christian conception of providence keeps well clear of such error, though some who have claimed to be in the biblical and Christian tradition have fallen into it and turned out to be mere fanatics. Here again it is important to remind ourselves that individual religious experience—in this case, experiences of God's providence—needs to be checked in the light of the experience of the whole community of faith, and that even the community's experience at any given time needs to be viewed in the light of the whole history of the community and of the revelation on which it was founded. Since the Christian community is bound to acclaim the crucifixion of Christ as the supreme manifestation of the divine providence, then this is also to assert the dialectical character of God's providential action, and so far as the community and its constituent members abide by this, they are safeguarded against a distorted understanding of providence.

It is clear from the way in which we have developed the notion of providence that it is to be distinguished from what is usually called "fate." A belief in fate accepts that whatever happens has been determined in advance by some sovereign power, perhaps God, or even some agency more ultimate than God. A true fatalism therefore excludes free will, and

[7] See above, p. 210.

thus human responsibility. The existential approach to the doctrine of providence has already been asserted to keep us from understanding providence as merely a mechanical process. It may now be asserted further that it keeps us from understanding providence in fatalistic terms. Our thought has rather been that in its highest manifestations providence enlists free cooperation of responsible creaturely beings.

The danger of confusing providence with fate arises when a belief that begins as an existential conviction is projected into the world of objects as a metaphysical system, and then it must be understood as a system in which all happenings are rigidly determined in advance. The danger may be seen very clearly in Calvin's doctrine of providence, and this is a further warning of so stressing the difference between God and man in an attempt to uphold God's glory and sovereignty, that in fact the relation between them is debased to the subpersonal level where man is little more than a puppet and God too has been degraded to the one who pulls the strings.

Calvin rightly maintains that providence is not a mere foreknowledge or prevision; the doctrine of providence is important only if God actively has a part in bringing events about, and "his providence extends not less to the hand than to the eye." [8] But Calvin goes on to make it clear that he does not think of this as only a general control or direction over events. It is a direct act of governing which regulates every single happening. "It is certain," he maintains, "that not a drop of rain falls without the express command of God." More seriously still, he asserts that even human actions (including bad actions) merely carry out what God has previously determined. According to Calvin, "men do nothing save at the secret instigation of God, and do not discuss or deliberate on anything but what he has previously decreed with himself, and brings to pass by his secret directions." [9] If this were indeed the case, it would make utter nonsense of any belief in human responsibility.

In spite of the protestations of some of his admirers, Calvin's view must be rejected as unworthy not only of man but of God as Christians understand him, for God is not exalted but debased by being turned into the author of fate. We shall have to criticize Calvin's tendency toward fatalism again in connection with the doctrine of election. But meantime we may notice that he is not entirely consistent in expounding the doctrine of providence, and in answering some objections, he makes a remark

[8] *Institutes of the Christian Religion*, I, xvi, 4.
[9] *Op. cit.*, I, xviii, 1.

which moves toward a more existential way of taking the doctrine and eases the rigor of some of his statements. He argues that the divine government does not rule out "second" causes, nor yet does it deprive men of freedom to choose, for "he who has fixed the boundaries of our life has at the same time entrusted us with the care of it, provided us with the means of preserving it, forewarned us of the dangers to which we are exposed, and supplied cautions and remedies that we may not be overwhelmed unawares." [10]

It is along such lines that one would have to answer the charge that a belief in providence contradicts belief in our own freedom and responsibility. An existential-ontological interpretation of the doctrine thinks of providence as much more flexible than a deterministic scheme, and it would find more truth in Calvin's modification of his teaching than in the core of the teaching itself. Man does have freedom and responsibility, but this is always factical and limited; or to come nearer to Calvin's actual words, we are "entrusted" with the responsibility for existence, yet Being (or God) who has entrusted us with our being has also "fixed the boundaries of our life." Whatever man does, he can never break through these boundaries or reverse the trend of creation, which goes from nothing toward fuller being. Whatever analogies one might use here would be inadequate in some respect or other. One could think of a kind of self-righting mechanism, but this would be to make providence precisely into the mechanical process which, on an existential interpretation, we have tried to avoid making it. The analogy of a strong chess player who, whatever move his opponent will make, can still bring the game around to the way he intends it to go, is perhaps slightly better. But then, someone may ask, what about this risk of which so much has been said at various points in the exposition? Is the risk of creation not a genuine risk at all, because Being is bound to triumph over the nullity into which it goes in the work of creation?

These questions already point us to what is a more serious challenge to belief in providence and indeed to the entire faith in God as holy Being than the objection already considered, for they open up the problem of evil. But before we turn to this problem, we must pay attention to another matter which may be considered as a special case of providence—the matter of miracles.

[10] Op. cit., I, xvii, 4.

43. MIRACLES

In a minimal sense, a miracle is an event that excites wonder. Certainly every event that might be called a "miracle" would do this, and there must be many such events, but it is evident that in a religious context the word "miracle" carries more than just this minimal sense. It is believed that God is in the event in some special way, that he is the author of it, and intends to achieve some special end by it.

In theology therefore a miracle is understood not just as a happening that excites wonder but as an "act" of God. Such an act may be a vehicle for revelation or for grace or for judgment or for all of these together. Thus we could say that a miracle is a providential act, in line with what has already been said about providence. While presumably all happenings can be somehow related to the divine providence, since God is present and active in the whole world-process, it is clear that some happenings count for more than others, or are more important or significant than others. Even if all events belong within a continuous series, some stand out within the series as critical moments in its unfolding. So it is not very helpful to say, as did some nineteenth-century idealist philosophers and theologians, that everything is miracle. They said this because they wanted to get away from the idea of sporadic interventions by a God standing outside of the world; but since they also wished to stress God's presence in every event of the world because of his immanence in the universal process, they preferred to say that everything is miracle rather than that nothing is. However, if *everything* can be called "miracle," the word has been generalized to the point where it has been virtually devoided of content. We have to see whether we can find a satisfactory way of describing what it is that makes a miracle stand out as some distinctive event.

Here we come up against the traditional view that a miracle has its distinctiveness because it is an event which breaks into the order of nature. By this it is meant that the so-called "laws" or regular procedures of nature are on some occasions suspended, so that miraculous events take place without "natural" causes and as the consequence of "supernatural" agency; or, in some accounts of the matter, there is added to the natural causes operating in a given situation a supernatural cause, and the result produced is other than it would have been, had only the natural causes been at work.

It is this traditional account of the distinctiveness of miracle that makes the conception very difficult for modern minds, and might even suggest to the theologian that "miracle" is a discredited and outmoded word that ought to be banished from his vocabulary. The way of understanding miracle that appeals to breaks in the natural order and to supernatural interventions belongs to the mythological outlook [11] and cannot commend itself in a post-mythological climate of thought.

The traditional conception of miracle is irreconcilable with our modern understanding of both science and history. Science proceeds on the assumption that whatever events occur in the world can be accounted for in terms of other events that also belong within the world; and if on some occasions we are unable to give a complete account of some happening —and presumably all our accounts fall short of completeness—the scientific conviction is that further research will bring to light further factors in the situation, but factors that will turn out to be just as immanent and this-worldly as those already known. The historian likewise explicates events in terms of other events that belong to the same series. Ernst Troeltsch spoke of "analogy" and "correlation" as two basic principles of historical method. By the first, he meant that the historian can recognize as historical events only happenings analogous to those that occur in our own experience; and by the second, that all events belong within the context of an immanent process.

Sometimes indeed one hears protests against these attitudes. We are told that science does not imply rigid determinism, and perhaps an appeal is made to the "uncertainty" principle of modern quantum dynamics. But this has nothing whatever to do with the question of supernatural intervention, or of miracle as such an intervention. We may be told also that Troeltsch's view of history was too much dominated by scientific models and was too little existential. But actually Troeltsch was perfectly aware of the difference between natural science and historical science, and between what he called the "causality" of natural and of historical events. Whether or not they get explicitly formulated, the scientific and historical attitudes that look for explications in terms of immanent factors are in fact part of the modern outlook that molds our thinking for most of our waking life, and there is no reason why we should put it aside from time to time so that we can give recognition to miracles, understood as supernatural irruptions into the natural order.

It is true of course that there may be problematic events the factual occurrence of which is well attested, yet which have not been accounted for in terms of immanent causal factors. As an illustration, one may mention stories of miraculous healings. That healings of the kind recorded

---

[11] See above, pp. 231–232.

in the New Testament have in fact occurred seems probable—much more probable, one must say, than that so-called "nature" miracles took place. The reason for our assigning the healing miracles this higher degree of probability is that the same kind of events are reported today from Lourdes and elsewhere, so that our judgment rests on an implicit acceptance of Troeltsch's principle of analogy. But we should note that we cannot affirm any more than that these events are problematical. We cannot, in our present state of knowledge concerning nature or man, explain how these events come about. This does not for a moment entitle us to say that there must have been the irruption of a supernatural agency. Rather, we have a duty to struggle against any mythological explanation and try harder to find an explanation in terms of this-worldly factors. The event may still be regarded as a miracle in the sense of an event that excites wonder and in which God's presence and activity become known; but this is quite independent of any attempt to represent the event as a supernatural intervention—an attempt which in any case would probably be eventually superseded by a "natural" explanation as our knowledge of man and nature got extended.

If miracle in the sense of supernatural intervention is irreconcilable with science and history, it is also objectionable theologically. It is objectionable because it goes back to a mythological outlook and expects God to manifest himself and prove himself in some extraordinary sensible phenomena. While the early Christian writers used many arguments to establish the claims of their faith, and some of these arguments seem strange to us, most of these writers wisely avoided putting too much weight on any appeal to miracles reportedly done by Jesus. In this, they were following his own teaching and example. One of his temptations is said to have been to throw himself down from the pinnacle of the temple and so, presumably, convince the people by a spectacular display in which he would be saved from harm by angelic intervention.[12] He firmly rejects any approach to his ministry that would involve this kind of marvel and magic. He condemns the kind of mentality that looks for such "signs."[13] Moreover, he points out that such signs will not convince anyone in whom more sober approaches have failed to awaken faith: "If they do not hear Moses and the prophets, neither will they be convinced if someone should rise from the dead."[14] They would not be convinced because the true meaning of a miracle does not lie in some extraordinary publicly observ-

[12] Luke 4:9–12.
[13] Matt. 12:39.
[14] Luke 16:31.

able event, but in God's presence and self-manifestation in the event. This is not something publicly observable, nor is it something that requires some prodigy, or breach in nature, for its occurrence. What is distinctive about miracle is God's presence and self-manifestation in the event. The mythological way of thinking tried to express this distinctiveness by making the event itself something magical or supernatural, divorced from the natural sequence of events; but in doing this, it shifted attention away from the essence of miracle (the divine presence and self-manifestation) to the discredited and mistaken idea of miracle as a magic sign. Actually, if we look at stories of miracles and see how these stories have developed, we can sometimes see how some natural event which was indeed a miracle, a vehicle for God's action, gets transformed into a supernatural event as the story is embroidered by legends. The inflation of the natural event into the spectacular sign is the way by which the mythological mentality seeks to express the distinctiveness and significance of the event for religious faith. But God's acting or his presence cannot be proved by publicly observable events, and the attempt to transform the miracle into a public prodigy ends up by obscuring and discrediting the genuine miracle, understood as revelatory event.

Miracle, like providence and revelation, has the character of ambiguity. From one point of view, the event is seen as a perfectly ordinary event; from another point of view, it is an event that opens up Being and becomes a vehicle for Being's revelation or grace or judgment or address. There is no public, universally observable character that attests a miracle as such. But does this mean then that the event is a miracle only in someone's subjective apprehension of it? And is the designation of the event as "miracle" just an arbitrary label stuck upon it by someone who happens to have been deeply impressed by it? The same kind of questions arise here as arose earlier in our discussion of revelation. We shall try to answer them by examining an actual miracle.

The example chosen is the crossing of the Red Sea by the people of Israel, a miracle that impressed itself so deeply upon the mind of the people that they always looked back to it as God's great providential act on their behalf and indeed as the very foundation of their existence as a community. As is well known, the account [15] as we now have it is put together from various sources. Scholars differ over the details of how these sources are to be disentangled, but the broad outlines are clear enough. According

---

[15] Exod. 14:5-31.

to the older version, we can visualize an incident which can be understood as perfectly "natural" in the sense that it does not involve any happenings that would contradict our ordinary experience of natural phenomena. In this account, the Israelites were already encamped by the shore, and the Egyptians were in pursuit. The combination of a strong wind with a low tide enabled the Israelites to get across. The Egyptians tried to follow, but their chariots got stuck in the sand and they were caught by the incoming tide. The later version transforms the story into a "supernatural" event by introducing magical elements. Moses stretches his rod over the sea, the waters divide and stand like walls on both sides. The Israelites go through, and the Egyptians foolishly attempt to follow and are overwhelmed by the water as it falls back down upon them.

The first version of the story, as has been said, describes what can be regarded as an ordinary natural event, and anyone who is determined to regard it as this and nothing more would say that the whole thing was just a lucky coincidence for the Israelites and that only their superstitious outlook led them to see it as God's act of deliverance. The second version may be regarded as the mythological way of trying to express the wonder which Israel had experienced in face of the event, and the meaning which they attached to it as an act of God. By representing the event as supernatural or magical—Moses waves his wand and the waters divide and stand up like walls—this version certainly succeeds in pointing to the distinctiveness of the event, but like all mythology it obscures the real significance of the event by objectifying the divine act in terms of sensible phenomena, whereas this significance is really God's grace and judgment experienced by the people in an event which, though dramatic and memorable, was nevertheless (as we may suppose) perfectly natural.

For the understanding of a miracle such as the crossing of the Red Sea, we must recall all that was said in connection with such matters as revelation and symbols. Just as every event could be potentially a revelatory event, and yet there is, properly speaking, no "general revelation" but particular concrete occasions when events take on a revelatory dimension; and just as everything that is could be a symbol of Being because it *is* in virtue of the presence of Being, and yet in fact some entities function as symbols and others do not, while among those that function in this way, some do so more adequately than others; so every event, in so far as it is embraced within the divine providence, can be understood as potentially an event manifesting God's action, yet some particular concrete events stand out in a special way in the experiences of individuals or communities as vehicles of the divine action, and such events are miracles. Equally with all other events, these can be seen as natural happenings; yet to the person or community addressed in and through them, they are vehicles of God's grace or revelation or judgment.

Let me here introduce the notion of "focusing" as a useful idea for explicating miracles, and an idea of which we shall have occasion to make further use later. God's presence and activity are everywhere and always; yet we experience these intensely in particular concrete happenings, in which, as it were, they have been focused. As was said before, there is little point in talking of everything as miracle. We need not however try to detach any event from the natural series within which it belongs in order for that event to be experienced as a focus of divine action, that is to say, as a miracle.

But we must come back to the question whether this account of miracle has not entirely subjectivized the matter and made the designation of any event as a miracle a quite arbitrary matter. Let us remind ourselves again that even if one were to claim some publicly observable characteristics in a miracle (such as a suspension of the regular operation of natural process), this would not establish a divine act, for this could not be detected by any empirical test. But even when we reject some publicly observable anomaly, or magical phenomenon, this does not mean that miracle is being understood subjectively. In analogy with the earlier treatment of revelation and symbolism, miracle too has to be understood in existential-ontological terms, that is to say, as belonging both to our human existence and to holy Being that transcends our existence. It is clear that miracle has its existential pole. Often, as in the crossing of the Red Sea, miracle occurs in what Jaspers has called the "limit-situation." This is the situation where all superficial supports and interpretations have been stripped away, so that existence is disclosed to itself in a fundamental way. This makes us ready to notice in events dimensions that normally escape us. But these dimensions really belong to the events, and are not just projected on them by us in our need. As revelation is a movement of Being in us, and as symbols are genuinely kin to what they illuminate, so miracle is the approach and self-disclosure of Being to us in and with and through the focusing event, bringing grace or revelation or judgment as the case may be.

This can no more be proved (or for that matter disproved) than revelation itself, but in both cases one can only ask whether the claim that holy Being has drawn near is a reasonable claim or more likely to be an illusion. It seems to me to get strong support from the fact that the miracle is also an interpretative event, in the light of which experience as a whole receives a coherent meaning. The miracle focuses the presence and action that underlies the whole and makes sense of the whole. The miracle is, moreover, not an isolated occasion, for the same presence and the same grace (or judgment) announce themselves in other events. The crossing of the Red Sea was a major focus in the experience of Israel, but around this focus their continuing history was understood in terms of the same divine acting, and their faith was confirmed because at all kinds of lesser foci in the national experience God's presence was known again in grace or judgment, and a total experience was built up that made sense and strengthened existence and selfhood and community.

In the Christian faith, the supreme miracle is the incarnation. From one point of view, Jesus represented simply another human life, the life of a turbulent innovator in the eyes of most who saw him. But to the disciples, this life was the focusing of the presence and action of God. Faith perceived the dimension which is not publicly observable, and could not be. Was this leap of faith just an arbitrary leap, or could it be reasonably defended? Certainly, it could neither be proved nor disproved by any observation or argument. But it is confirmed in the community's subsequent life of faith, where the miracle of incarnation interprets the community's existence, lends meaning to it, strengthens its being. And again, the miracle does not remain isolated but is confirmed in a whole series of "miracles," foci of the divine presence and acting. These happen in the life and experiences of the community of faith, continually leading it into fuller being, thereby showing that they have no illusory character. The sacraments, for instance, are such foci. Talk of the "miracle of the mass" is not just superstitious talk but points to the focusing of the divine presence in the eucharist. Another example is afforded by the lives of the saints. Men have attributed "miracles" to them, and this may often have been in the mythological way of ascribing public marvels to them. But this need not obscure the genuine sense in which sainthood is the focusing in a human life of the divine presence. Miracle is not magic, but the focusing of holy Being's presence and action amid the events, things, and persons of the world, and this has the highest reality.

44. NATURAL EVIL

We must now return to the problem that was raised at the end of the section on providence—the problem of evil. Can one really believe in providence in a universe that seems to include so much that is evil? Can one really find the focus of illumination in events taken to be miracles, or are not these events just lucky accidents? Even if we acknowledge God, are we really allowing for the "risk" of creation if we hold to a doctrine of providence and claim that God is good and that his goodness will eventually triumph? Is the truth of the matter perhaps that we are determined to believe in God and his goodness and providence, and that, whatever happens, we will go on believing? Thus we allow nothing to falsify such a belief, and whatever happens that seems to count against it is explained away as not "really" contradicting our faith. Contemporary philosophers are not slow to point out that a belief that can be held no matter what happens, and that is compatible with any state of affairs, is a pretty jejune belief, and would seem to assert nothing of importance.

With such questions in mind, we must face the problem of evil, and first we are going to consider "natural" evil. Whether indeed any kind of evil should be called "natural" is doubtful, but the expression is commonly used and is useful as a way of designating that kind of evil which is not attributable to human agency but arises from natural factors. Examples would be earthquakes, storms, famine, disease, and the like. Nevertheless, it would seem that in judging these to be evil, there is reference to some human suffering as a consequence of them. For this reason, it seemed doubtful if it is proper to speak of a purely "natural" evil. It is true of course that there is also a vast amount of animal suffering, to say nothing of all the waste and frustration that seems to have gone on in the evolution of the world, and this might be called "evil" apart from any human involvement in it.

But are we not departing from our usual existential-ontological method in raising the question of natural evil before coming to the evil which man himself causes? In the themes with which we have dealt up till now, we have begun from the existential level, and then proceeded reductively to consider those levels which we can know only from the outside. Are we justified in taking a different approach here?

We are, and the reason is that evil is not a positive phenomenon which could be considered in its "higher" manifestations before we turned to its "lower" forms. We have reversed our procedure precisely because evil is a reversal of the positive, affirmative tendency toward being, a reversal of the very creative act of letting-be. Thus evil has no place in the hierarchy of beings, and there is no "higher" evil that manifests more being as distinct from a "lower" evil that manifests less. Evil is essentially negative and destructive, and thus the enemy of beings. But there are indeed evils that are more terrible than others because they bring greater destruction, not only quantitatively but also qualitatively. Thus we can talk about the greater or the lesser of two evils, but this does not mean that one of them is any more positive or has more being than the other, for the so-called "greater" evil is simply the one that devastates more beings or beings that stand higher in the hierarchy of beings.

In denying to evil any kind of positive being of its own, we likewise turn away from any ultimate dualism. There is a dualism of sorts between Being and nothing, but not an ultimate dualism, since we do not have two positive principles opposed to each other. Since the Christian faith rejects an ultimate dualism, as we have seen in sketching the typology of religions, then it would seem that a Christian view of evil must represent it as negation, as *privatio boni*. This is the view to which St. Augustine came after having passed through a Manichaean phase in which he had accepted that evil expresses a distinct will in the universe, contrary to that of God; but the negative character of evil had already been succinctly expressed by Christian writers, notably by St. Athanasius, who wrote: "What is evil is not, but what is good is." [16] To understand this statement, however, we have to set it in the context of St. Athanasius' view of creation. Evil is not simply to be identified with nothing or what is not, for presumably this nothing is neutral and without any characteristics at all, either good or evil. As St. Athanasius understands the matter, evil is rather "lapsing into nothing" or "ceasing to be" (both of these expressions translate his word φθόρα) which is a standing threat to all created beings. These beings have been created out of nothing, and it is possible for them to slip back into nothing or to advance into the potentialities for being which belong to them. Evil is this slipping back toward nothing, a reversal and defeat of the creative process.

I have earlier maintained that creation involves risk, and the time has come to look at this more closely. In creation, God gives being, and he gives it to the plurality of particular beings. But what constitutes a particular or finite being is just that it is determinate; and whatever is determinate is what it is just in so far as it is *not* anything else. To have any determinate character is to be without some other characters. Hence creation may be considered as the going out of Being into nothing and the acceptance by Being of the limitations of determinate characteristics. All this makes possible the expression of Being in a richly diversified community

[16] *De Incarnatione*, iv, 5.

of beings that would utterly transcend in value and interest what we can only visualize as a hypothetical limiting case, namely, a purely undifferentiated primal Being. But this creative process inevitably involves risk. There is a genuine self-giving of Being. We have already seen that this imposes a self-limitation on God, when we discussed the problem of his omnipotence.[17] But more than this, it means that God risks himself, so to speak, with the nothing; he opens himself and pours himself out into nothing. His very essence is to let be, to confer being. He lets be by giving himself, for he is Being; and in giving himself in this way, he places himself in jeopardy, for he takes the risk that Being may be dissolved in nothing. Did Bonhoeffer have something like this in mind when he talked about the "weakness" of God, the God who manifests himself in the crucified Christ as placing himself at the mercy of the world?[18] One would have to say, however, that this weakness of God is his strength. We have seen that a God who securely hoarded his being would be no God, and perhaps nothing at all. Only the God who does confer being and so goes out from himself into creation and into the risks of finite being that is bounded by nothing—only this God is *holy* Being and lays claim to our worship and allegiance. Only this God is a God of love, for love is precisely his self-giving and letting-be.

The more love (letting-be) exposes itself in risk, the more it accomplishes in conferring being and, indeed, in calling the beings out of nothing. So we may believe that even where God appears in weakness—or better, precisely there—he also manifests his invincible power. We may believe that God is good, and that his providence works to advance the conquest of nothing by Being. But such a belief does not deny that the risk is a real one, or, above all, that the whole activity of God, in creation, reconciliation, and consummation, is a costly activity. We have seen that the simile of the sun and its rays, as used by exponents of theories of emanation, has only a very limited application within a Christian context. Yet perhaps one aspect of this application is this, that just as the sun warms and enlivens the earth by burning up its own substance, so it must be at real cost to himself that God creates, reconciles, consummates. Such, at any rate, would seem to be implied in any understanding of God that looks to the cross of Christ for the center of revelation. The simile must not be pushed too far; the sun will eventually burn out, we suppose, but we believe that God's resources are not limited, and that he will go on

---

[17] See above, pp. 205–206.
[18] *Letters and Papers from Prison*, p. 164.

spending himself in love as he builds up his unimaginably rich commonwealth of beings.

Yet this faith in providence and in the steady overcoming of negativity by positive beingness, as implied in the belief in providence, has to be held along with a belief in God's self-spending. If the risk is real and the cost is real, there must be a tragic element in the whole creative process. That there is such a tragic element is surely obvious from the ambiguous character of the world. If anyone sees phenomena which he takes to be evidences for teleology, someone else can point to clear evidences for dysteleology. There are few more ingeniously contrived life cycles (if one may so speak) than that of the parasitic organism that causes malaria; but if this is "design," it is evil design—evil in the sense defined above, for a low form of being, a mere unthinking speck of living matter, causes distress and destruction in qualitatively higher beings. Again, the process of evolution on the earth's surface looks more like a groping procedure of trial and error, with fantastic waste, than like the carrying through of a preconceived plan. Actually, no amount of empirical generalization could ever conclusively establish either the theistic (providential) or the atheistic (tychastic) view of the world. The evidence is too conflicting. Belief in providence, as we have seen, is existentially rooted in the experiences of God's acting in specific individual or communal histories, in miracle and revelatory act, and from such experiences grows the wider belief in the divine government of natural process and the tendency for good (what is) to overcome evil (what is not). This is not a hypothetical belief to be attained by weighing empirical evidences, but an act of faith based on what are accepted as valid experiences of God's acting.

But this faith, if it is to be consistently held in the face of the conflicting evidences, must be shown to be a reasonable faith. The account already given of Being's self-giving and of its going out into the nothing in the risk of creation is meant to show the reasonableness of the belief. Though the final outcome of the process may be assured, there must be many a reverse and many a detour along the way. This tragic element, as we called it, would seem to be inseparable from the creation of particular beings which, being determinate, are bounded by negativity. Hence some kind of "cosmic fall" seems to be inherent in the very notion of creation, and some kind of natural evil seems to be necessary. Yet since the creation is "very good," in the sense that it must utterly transcend in worth and interest any undifferentiated being, the risk has to be taken, and there could be no "God" (holy Being) without it.

When the expression "tragic" is used, or when it is asserted that "some kind of natural evil seems to be necessary," this is not meant to say that there is some kind of fate, perhaps more ultimate than God, which decrees that the world should have a tragic character and that evil should afflict it. Such a supposition would be utterly impossible for us, because God has been identified with Being, and there can "be" nothing more ultimate than Being. The talk of tragedy and of the necessity of natural evil is to be differently interpreted. It sees this natural evil as an inevitable accompaniment in the creation of a universe of particular beings. It is not a fate imposed but a risk taken, and justified by the incomparable worth of the end.

This may look something like traditional "instrumental" views of evil, and indeed it has something in common with them, though not coinciding with them. Needless to say, we reject the view that natural evil is to be understood as an instrument of God's justice, whereby he punishes the wicked. This ancient and tenacious belief is already shown to be inadequate in the Old Testament drama of Job, and it is explicitly rejected by Jesus, as when he states that the eighteen people killed by the falling of a tower were not struck down because they were worse than other people.[19] There is more to be said for the view that natural evil can be understood as an instrument of God's education of the human race, for it surely is true that in a universe where no one could suffer or get hurt, there would not be possible any development in depth of character or of personal relations; or, to put the matter in another way, without the threat of nullity and frustration, there could be little development of selfhood. Yet even when one allows for this educative instrumentality of natural evil, much that seems excessive, wasteful, and just senseless remains. Here I think we have simply to acknowledge that these are loose ends that are not integrated into the main creative process or into God's providential act, side effects, as it were, which arise inevitably and which have to be risked. This may seem complacent, or even callous, to the victim of such a loose end, but here I think one has got to say also that a final judgment on whether something is just senselessly evil or not could hardly be made except in the light of the end. It may be that God is not content to leave loose ends as loose ends, but somehow proceeds to gather them up too. Creation passes into reconciliation, and reconciliation into consummation, though in a sense these three are simply aspects or phases of a single great movement of Being. We shall come back to this in eschatology.

[19] Luke 13:4-5.

But if there is a problem of natural evil, so that we have to acknowledge what I have called "loose ends" and "side effects" on the level of natural processes, surely the problem becomes more acute still when we come to the level of existents, beings which have freedom and responsibility. With this, we come to the question of sin.

45. SIN

The basic existential and ontological structures of man's being and how these can fall into disorder, imbalance, and alienation were discussed at an early stage of our argument.[20] Already at that stage the word "sin" was introduced to denote this disorder and imbalance, especially in its aspect of alienation from Being, though this fundamental alienation cannot be isolated from other kinds—alienation from other people, from the world, from one's own selfhood. Furthermore, in the earlier discussion we agreed that sin is universal or, in St. Paul's words, "all have sinned and fall short of the glory of God";[21] and that the consequences of sin are grievously disabling in human life, though we stopped short of a doctrine of total depravity, for if indeed "the heavenly image in man was effaced,"[22] then he would surely have ceased to be man.

There is no need for us to go over again the ground covered in the earlier discussion and what we learned there about the fundamental characteristics of sin. What we must do now is to deepen and enlarge our understanding of sin by bringing it into the light of the biblical revelation, as that has been expounded so far. We can now see more clearly what sin means, when it is set against the doctrines of God, creation, and providence, and indeed, as was already mentioned, the full seriousness of sin can only become apparent when we have understood the full potentialities of human existence as created in the image of God. But this last point reminds us that even the present account of sin must still be an interim one, and that its final seriousness can be seen only when it is set against the full revelation in the person and work of Christ.

Our earlier discussion of the disorder and imbalance of human existence made contact with the theological conception of sin when it was shown that this disorder and imbalance can be understood as alienation from Being. But in traditional theological language, this *aversio a Deo* is understood as at the same time a *conversio ad creaturam*. This means that

[20] See above, pp. 68–73.
[21] Rom. 3:23.
[22] Calvin, *Institutes*, II, i, 5.

in his quest for meaning and strengthening of his existence—a quest which we have seen to arise out of the very constitution of existence itself—man turns away from Being to the beings (from God to the creatures). Ontologically expressed, this is the "forgetting of Being," of which Heidegger speaks; theologically expressed, it is idolatry. The basic sin is indeed idolatry, the effort to found life upon the beings, perhaps on man himself, to understand life and give it meaning in terms of finite entities alone, to the exclusion of Being. We call this forgetting of Being "idolatry," because the beings have supplanted Being, the creatures have taken over God's place. The only possible result must be a terrible distortion of existence. St. Paul, speaking of the perversion of man's life through sin, climaxes his argument by pointing to idolatry as the source of the trouble: "They exchanged the truth about God for a lie and worshiped and served the creature rather than the Creator." [23] It was surely no accident but a very profound truth about the human condition that caused to be placed first among the Ten Commandments the injunction: "You shall have no other gods before me!" [24]

Needless to say, idolatry is not just a kind of mistaken belief, a failure to understand "how things are." Like faith, it is an attitude of commitment, and indeed idolatry is a kind of perversion of faith. It has the same motivation—the inherent quest for meaning and selfhood. But idolatry can lead only to the stunting and distorting of the self, as was indeed seen very clearly in the Old Testament.[25] The claim that idolatry is the basic sin is confirmed when we consider the various manners in which the idolatrous self is distorted or inhibited from growth, and compare them with the kinds of imbalance among the polarities of human existence, described earlier. Man's idolizing of himself and his powers leads to the sins of pride, which are in the end presumably the most destructive and the most terrible in perverting relations between man and man. Again with astonishing insight, the Old Testament plainly saw that the aspiration to be gods operates very widely with men; so it was both in the story of the fall and in that of the tower of Babel.[26] But this temptation for man to idolize himself and become his own God has reached overwhelming proportions in the current technological age when the forgetting of Being has come to a pitch. One regrets to say that some advocates of a "religionless" Chris-

---

tianity appear to have fallen victims to the same kind of anthropolatry. In all such cases, self-idolatry leads into those sins of pride, and so of division, which constitute one form of existential imbalance. On the other side, idolizing of things leads into the sins of indulgence and greed. Again, this is typical of the technological era, when the multiplication of devices has in turn multiplied artificial needs and appetites. These may be less gross than the appetites of a less sophisticated time (though this is doubtful) but they are no less dehumanizing. We already noted that both kinds of imbalance, sins of pride and sins of indulgence, can and usually do go together, and this is easily intelligible in the light of their common origin in idolatry.

We have been speaking of sin as an attitude, and indeed we even suggested that idolatry could be regarded as a kind of perverted faith, a misplaced commitment. The sinful attitude expresses itself in sinful acts, and of course in popular usage "sin" usually means some actual sin or deed of wrongdoing. Theologically, however, the interest lies rather in the attitude than in the particular deeds which flow from it, for it is the attitude that is the fundamental evil. This attitude, we have maintained, is fundamentally idolatry, an *aversio a Deo et conversio ad creaturam*. But now it must be pointed out that just as particular sinful deeds are referred to the sinful attitude of the agent, this in turn is not to be understood in an individualistic way but is to be seen in all its seriousness as the massive and wrongful orientation of human society. New Testament writers talk of the "world," or κόσμος, and when they do so, they rarely mean the physical world, but rather human society as a whole. Their way of talking about the world is paradoxical, or dialectical. Thus, if we take the Fourth Gospel as an illustration, God has made the world through his word, so that it is his creation and is good; and therefore God loves the world and seeks its good.[27] But on the other hand, the world is hostile to God, and the disciples are warned against it.[28] A comment may be made here on the current fashion in some circles for a "worldly" or "secular" Christianity. It is noticeable that this particular demand has arisen for the most part among those who come from those Protestant traditions that have in the past utterly rejected the world through doctrines of total depravity and the like. A reaction has set in that seeks to make up for this negative attitude to the world by hastening to the opposite half-truth of uncritical acceptance of the world. The biblical and also the catholic view has

[27] John 1:10, 3:16, etc.
[28] John 17:14, 12:25, etc.

avoided both of these extreme errors. It has accepted what remains good in the world (as in the catholic recognition of natural theology, natural law, and the like) and yet it has dialectically judged the world to be in its actual condition fallen, sinful, and in rebellion against God. The world, like the individual, is fallen, but this should not be interpreted as a total deprivation of whatever stamp of divine Being was given in creation.

When we think of sin as not merely a particular action, and not merely even the attitude of an individual, but a massive disorientation and perversion of human society as a whole, we begin to perceive the really terrifying character of sin. For the "world," or κόσμος, the collective mass of mankind in its solidarity, is answerable to no one, and has a hardness and irresponsibility that one rarely finds in individuals. These individuals are, as it were, sucked into the world and carried along with it, being deprived of their own responsibility and swept along by forces beyond their control. The notion of the dehumanized irresponsible mass has been well described by Heidegger as the phenomenon of *"das Man,"* the impersonal "they" whom we never identify but who dictate to us our standards and our policies.[29] The individual, or again the small group, may be utterly helpless and impotent within this anonymous mass, and there can take place a kind of "escalation" of evil as collective standards and patterns of behavior establish themselves and irresistibly carry everyone along. A parallel kind of escalation can arise from our relation to the world of things. Increasingly, things are brought within the system of human instruments, and this is in principle good, since man is the responsible creature who has, so to speak, been made the steward of creation. But if he idolizes this world of things, he becomes himself caught up in it, and may find himself dragged along as part of the machinery in a direction in which he does not wish to go. In the present age of urban societies and technological culture, these dangers are ever present. It is futile to think of turning the clock back—we could not, even if we wanted to, for we are "caught" in the escalatory process that we cannot even slow down— but we are far from knowing where we are going or what we are doing to ourselves.

The sense of helplessness in the face of some movements or situations for which no one seems directly responsible and which no one seems able to control has led to the thought of sin as somehow superhuman. This is what is meant when we speak of sin as "demonic." The expression need

---

[29] *Being and Time,* p. 126ff.

not be taken to mean that there are at work quasi-personal beings of superhuman power who direct that power to evil ends. There may indeed be demons in this sense, and our earlier discussion of angels might lend plausibility to the idea that there are "fallen angels." However, even if there are such, they provide no explanation of sin, but simply push the problem one stage further back. If there were demons quite independent of God, as dualistic views have maintained, this would be an explanation of evil; but such a dualistic view is rejected by Christianity, for the demons of the Bible are fallen angels, and even if one were to accept that they had corrupted man, one would still need to ask about who had corrupted them. The answer could only be that they had corrupted themselves; and this indeed is the tradition, for Lucifer fell through pride, that is to say, through idolizing his own creaturely being. There is no need for us then to suppose that man fell by any other agency than his own, and St. Paul, though he can speak of demons, nevertheless explicitly states that it was through human agency that "sin came into the world." [30]

The context of corporate sin in which every human life has to be lived was well described by Schleiermacher as "the sinfulness which is prior to all action" and which is "not something which pertains severally to each individual and exists in relation to him by himself, but in each the work of all, and in all the work of each." [31] Some theologians have gone so far as to talk of a "kingdom of sin." The expression can be criticized as suggesting a demonic realm opposed in dualistic fashion to the kingdom of God, and perhaps also as suggesting that sin, which we have seen to be essentially lack and distortion, has a positive character parallel to that of goodness. Nevertheless, the expression does convey that social and systemic character of sin that tends to be overlooked in individualistic accounts. Ritschl has some sober remarks on the kingdom of sin. Under its domination, he says, "We become accustomed to standing forms of sin and acquiesce in them as the ordinary expression of human nature." [32] But all this has its origin in man.

Certainly, the tracing back of the origin of sin to man himself safeguards the notion of our responsibility, even if in particular situations we find sin overpowering and inescapable. How we can think of man as still responsible can perhaps best be seen if we consider the doctrine of original sin. Back of actual sins and of individual and even social orientations to-

[30] Rom. 5:12.
[31] *The Christian Faith*, pp. 287–288.
[32] *Justification and Reconciliation*, p. 338.

ward sin, this notion of original sin points to some basic tendency toward sin. The idea is that we do not start from innocence and then fall into sin, but that we are already in sin. But this can hardly be interpreted as just a fate laid upon man. Surely existence as such is not sinful. If so, sin may be deplored, but it can hardly be laid to anyone's blame.

We did indeed agree that there is a tragic element in the creative process, and presumably man, as creature, shares in this. There is this much truth in the view of Origen and others who have thought of creation as itself a kind of fall. But can the apparently inevitable evil which the risk of creation brings for man as for every creaturely being (where "evil" means descent into negativity, as outlined in the last section) be properly called sin? Whatever the shortcomings of F. R. Tennant's view of sin, he was surely justified in stressing accountability as an essential element in any satisfactory account of the matter.[33] The mere fact that we are not God, or some unitary Being, but a multiplicity of beings each with his own center of consciousness and interest, and his own perspective on the world, does not seem in itself to constitute sinfulness. It is presumably the condition that makes sin possible, for the pull or tendency that operates from the beginning is to set up each one's center as the center of everything, and so to fall into self-idolatry. Yet we have to remember that our existence is polar, and so ambiguous. Already in our first survey of the meaning of human existence, we noted the polarity of individuality and community.[34] If human existence is from the first ego-centered, it is also true, as we noted even from the phenomenon of sexuality, that existence is from the first self-transcending and communal. In the biblical narrative, Adam is represented as incomplete until the creation of Eve.[35] His existence is basically an existence in community, just as much as it is an individually centered existence.

Such considerations lead us to the question whether Christian theologians have, in general, sufficiently distinguished between sin and finitude; or whether finitude, which certainly is a basic characteristic of human existence, has been given due weight. As an illustration of the confusion, one has only to mention the traditional doctrine, drawn from Genesis, that death is the punishment for sin.[36] Apart altogether from sin, death belongs to finitude. As was already mentioned, death itself has an ambiguous character; it can be regarded as an evil, and so a fitting punishment for sin, and

---

[33] *The Concepts of Sin*, p. 245.
[34] See above, pp. 66–68.
[35] Gen. 2:18.
[36] Gen. 3:3.

yet death, as an end to life, would seem to be essential to any realization of selfhood, as has been argued in pointing to death as the *eschaton* of existence.[37] An existence that went on endlessly in time would seem to be senseless and pointless—much more so than, *pace* Sartre, an existence terminated by death.

When we try to make a clear distinction between sin and finitude, the problem of original sin and responsibility becomes eased. We cannot blame man for being finite, nor call him "sinful" because each man has his own center from which he looks out on the world. This is indeed the condition that makes sin possible, it belongs to the tragic and inevitable risk of creation, and it may even imply some sort of basic "guiltiness," as Heidegger argues.[38] Yet on the other hand it has been argued in our exposition of the doctrine of creation that it is precisely this same finitude, this gift of being to the innumerable particular beings, that makes possible that commonwealth of beings which, as a diversity in unity, would be higher than any monolithic unbroken Being. So the very creation of individual centers of being that makes sin possible also makes possible a community of love and fellowship, and to make the one possible, the other has to be made possible also.

It is not the mere fact of finitude, the fact that there are innumerable particular beings with their own centers, that constitutes sin, but the fact that already the particular being has decided for particular being and has forgotten Being. Even if in individual cases there is no deliberate conscious decision of this kind, this does not take away responsibility. We are inclined to view these matters far too individualistically. If we find ourselves born into a human society—the "world"—that is disordered so that inevitably each individual existence shares its disorder, and if we find ourselves caught up in a kind of escalation of sin so that each individual existence is carried away and is impotent to halt the process, this does not mean that we are the hapless victims of an overpowering fate, so that we deserve pity rather than blame. Both sin and responsibility are communal as well as individual; and does not each individual confirm and reinforce the wrong orientation of the society into which he has been born?

Let us return to the subject of sin in relation to death. While we have rightly criticized the view that links death exclusively to sin and fails to see that death is also implicit in finitude, nevertheless there is a profound truth in the thought of death as the consequence of sin. It is not to be thought of as an arbitrary punishment awarded for sin, but rather as the

---

[37] See above, p. 78.
[38] *Being and Time*, p. 280ff.

working out of sin in existence, for just as an existence that commits itself to Being attains to selfhood and its own fullest being, so an existence that idolatrously commits itself to some particular being (or beings) is already on the way to the disruption of selfhood, and to its lowest level of being. The doctrine of original sin warns that in a fallen humanity, every individual must be caught in this declination. Death, too, has to be seen as wider than an individual phenomenon. As St. Athanasius has expressed it, "death having gained upon men, and corruption abiding upon them, the race of men was being destroyed; the rational man made in God's image was disappearing, and the handiwork of God was in process of dissolution." [39]

Man is unable of himself to reverse this process. This was already clear to us in our early analysis of human existence when, among its polarities, we contrasted those of responsibility and impotence.[40] Now we see this more clearly in the light of the Christian doctrine of creation, and of man, the creature who has been made in the divine image. Sin is a slavery for the race and for the individual, yet a slavery that has arisen through voluntary decision. It is as if there is a critical moment at which the action initiated by man becomes a kind of runaway escalation that drags its initiator along, whether he wills it or not. The point is clearly made by Buber: "Sin is not an undertaking which man can break off when the situation becomes critical, but a process started by him, the control of which is withdrawn from him at a fixed moment." [41]

At the same time, however, we must not subscribe to a doctrine of total depravity. St. Athanasius wisely uses the imperfect tense when he describes the fall of the race into dissolution. Man does not cease to be human, but he loses the power to fulfill the potentialities of a fully human existence, and this, as we have seen, sends him in quest of the grace which could alone solve his predicament.

But the very fact that the quest for grace is aroused in man is itself a powerful testimony against any doctrine of total depravity. Even if it is true that the full seriousness of sin becomes apparent only in the light of the doctrines of creation and reconciliation, yet the so-called "natural" man, as we have seen, is already aware of the disorder and imbalance of his existence, individual and communal. To be aware of this disorder is to be dissatisfied with it, and this is not sin, but the first step away from sin.

[39] *De Incarnatione*, VI, 1.
[40] See above, pp. 63–64.
[41] *Two Types of Faith*, p. 84.

As Hegel pointed out, the "feeling of a life disrupted" must become the "longing" for what has been missed. "The deficiency is recognized (by the trespasser) as *a part of himself*, as what was to have been in him, and is not." [42]

If there is original sin, there is also original righteousness, if only in the form of longing for release and for fullness of existence. Whether one wishes to call this "natural," or whether one wishes to speak of a "grace" that is universal and not tied to any special occasion of revelation, seems to me to be a matter of indifference.

If there were no residuum of original righteousness even in fallen man, no continuing tendency to transcend toward the fulfilling of the image of God and no common grace in creation, then it would be hard to see how salvation could be possible. It would be hard also to see how our ordinary relative moral judgments would be possible, how we could say that one action is better than another, or one evil less than another, if everything that proceeds from man is damnable. The moral theologians' traditional distinction between grave sins and venial sins may often appear artificial, but it does try to come to grips with the complexities and ambiguities of man's spiritual life. To recognize that not everything human is equally sinful and even that there are flashes of goodness in fallen humanity is not in any way to underrate the seriousness of sin.

Just as natural evil is the dissolution of beings into nothing, so sin is the still more terrible dissolution of the highest earthly creature into nothing, through his own wrong decisions. Whether the sin of man aggravates disorder in the rest of creation and heightens what we called the "cosmic fall" is an open question, and very possibly it does. But natural evil and human sin are alike unavoidable possibilities in a creation the end of which is good. We have already seen how God's creating activity, which accepts the risk, is continued into his providential activity, in which the beings are sustained and strengthened in face of the threat of disintegration. This providential activity widens into the whole conception of God's reconciling activity, whereby the threat of evil and sin is met and overcome. To this theme we now turn.

[42] *On Christianity: Early Theological Writings*, pp. 230–231 (italics mine).

12 | The Person of Jesus Christ

46. RECONCILIATION AND HISTORICAL REVELATION

Creation involves risk, and this risk in turn issues in sin and evil which threaten the creatures with dissolution and distortion. We quoted St. Athanasius' remark that "the race of man was being destroyed . . . and the handiwork of God was in process of dissolution." The same writer goes on to say: "So, as the rational creatures were wasting and such works in course of ruin, what was God in his goodness to do? Suffer corruption to prevail against them, and death to hold them fast? And where then would be the benefit of their having been made in the first place?" [1] This is indeed a crucial question. What justification is there for a creation so ambiguous as the one we know, a creation in which sin and evil make such inroads? If this is the fate of the creatures, then, as St. Athanasius bluntly adds, "better were they not made than, once made, left to neglect and ruin."

Actually, we have already seen the beginning of an answer to such questions. It was made clear that by "creation" is not meant simply that God set things going in the beginning. Creation, involving risk, passes without interruption into providence, whereby the threat of dissolution is continually being overcome. Providence, in turn, is continuous with reconciliation; or, to express it in another way, reconciliation is the highest providential activity of God. By "reconciliation" is meant the activity whereby the disorders of existence are healed, its imbalances redressed, its alienations bridged over. Reconciliation in turn is continuous with consumma-

[1] *De Incarnatione*, VI, 7.

tion, the bringing of creation to its perfection. Creation, reconciliation, and consummation are not three successive activities of God, still less could we think that he has to engage in reconciliation because creation was unsuccessful. The three indeed are represented successively in the narrative presentation of the Christian faith, but theologically they must be seen as three moments in God's great unitary action. Creation, reconciliation, and consummation are not separate acts but only distinguishable aspects of one awe-inspiring movement of God—his love or letting-be, whereby he confers, sustains, and perfects the being of the creatures.

Not only St. Athanasius but St. Irenaeus and many other early Christian writers rightly connected the doctrines of reconciliation and creation. Both of these activities were ascribed to the Logos, eventually conceived as the second person of the triune God—"expressive Being," in the terminology of this book—and it was believed that what the Logos does in reconciliation is continuous with what he does in creation. It is true that at a given time in history the Logos had been made flesh in Jesus of Nazareth, but this was not the beginning of his work. St. Justin explicitly deals with the objection made by opponents who pointed out that, according to Christian teaching, the Logos had been incarnate in Jesus only one hundred and fifty years before his time, and who demanded to know whether all who lived before that were irresponsible. St. Justin replies that the Logos had always been in the world, that the providential acts described in the Old Testament are to be ascribed to the agency of the Logos and furthermore that in this same Logos "every race of men were partakers." [2] It is not that at a given moment God adds the activity of reconciliation to his previous activities, or that we can set a time when his reconciling activity began. Rather, it is the case that at a given time there was a new and decisive revelation of an activity that had always been going on, an activity that is equiprimordial with creation itself. This is made abundantly clear in many passages of the New Testament, especially by St. Paul. He talks of "the mystery hidden for ages and generations but now made manifest to his saints"; or again, of "the revelation of the mystery which was kept secret for long ages but is now disclosed and through the prophetic writings is made known to all nations." [3] Many other examples could be given, not only from St. Paul. God's reconciling activity has been from the beginning, and is inseparable from his creating activity. This means not only that the two are coextensive in time, but also they are coextensive in

[2] *Apology I*, xlvi.
[3] Col. 1:26; Rom. 16:25–26.

extent, so that, as we have already claimed in discussing the relation of Christianity to other faiths, God's saving activity is universal. It is as wide as creation because creating and reconciling are not separate activities but moments of the same activity.

These remarks, of course, are not intended in the slightest degree to detract from the importance of historical revelation. No event of history initiated God's reconciling work, which goes on always. But the Christian gospel is no less a gospel, or a proclamation of good news, because it points to a new and decisive revelation of the mystery of the divine activity—an activity which, as has often been said in these pages, cannot be read off as something obvious in a world which presents itself as ambiguous.

Man needs some concrete manifestation of God's activity, some manifestation that can seize him and bring him to the attitude of faith. No doubt there have been many revelations, and these have come through many kinds of vehicles. We can recognize with St. Justin the operation of the same Logos, that is to say, of the same God in all of them. In some cases, the Logos has grasped men through ideas or timeless symbols. In biblical religion, however, history has been the vehicle for revelation. In the Old Testament, God's reconciling and saving work is seen in his historical providential dealings with Israel, and especially in the succession of covenants which he makes with them, from the covenant with Abraham onward. The people may break a covenant and slip back into idolatry, but God is represented as continually seeking to restore and renew the relationship with himself; and this is at the same time a restoration and renewal of the people in their very being. Already out of these many revelatory experiences of God's reconciling work there was being born the hope of some decisive event in which God would come to his people, in which the grace of Being would be openly shown and poured out. The New Testament claims that this climax of God's reconciling work did come with the historical revelation in Jesus Christ. "When the time had fully come, God sent forth his son." [4] This, for Christianity, is the classic, or primordial, revelation on which the community of faith is founded and which determines its way of understanding Being (God) and of comporting itself toward Being. The earlier historical revelations of the Old Testament, taken over by the Christian community as part of its heritage, are regarded as summed up and brought to their completion in the new, decisive historical revelation in Christ, who is "sent forth" in the "fullness" of

[4] Gal. 4:4.

the time. The fullness of time is seen as a critical moment of history when God's reconciling work moves out into the open and takes a new and decisive leap forward toward building up that commonwealth of beings which would realize the potentialities of the creation.

Jesus Christ then is for Christian faith the decisive or paradigmatic revelation of God. In the language of this book, we can also call him the "symbol" of Being. It should hardly be necessary at this stage to insist again that in using this word "symbol," no diminution or unreality in Christ's relation to Being is intended. On the contrary, it will be recalled that on many occasions we have insisted that Being is present-and-manifest in any being that symbolizes it, that is to say, there is a real inward relation between the two. The expression "present-and-manifest" is peculiarly appropriate when we think of Christ as the revelation, or the revelatory symbol, of God; for "presence" in Greek is παρουσία, and "manifestation" is ἐπιφάνεια, and these are precisely the words that have been traditionally used for the revelation of God in Christ: "advent" and "epiphany." In Christ takes place the "advent" of God, his coming to be present, or his dwelling among us; and there likewise takes place the "epiphany" of God, the manifestation or showing forth of his grace and truth. "And the Logos became flesh and dwelt among us, full of grace and truth; we have beheld his glory, glory as of the only Son from the Father." [5]

Still another expression with which we have become familiar in the foregoing pages has an appropriate application here. This is the expression "focusing," which was introduced in connection with the notion of miracle or providential act. Not all events, we have seen, are equally significant, though indeed all constitute a continuous series. Some events stand out as events of God's acting, for these events have power to address men at the deepest level of their existence, to seize them, as it were, and bring them into the attitude of faith. These we can call "revelatory events" or "providential acts" or "miracles." The event of Jesus Christ is, for Christian faith, the supreme miracle, the high tide of God's providential activity. As such, it focuses the presence and activity which are indeed everywhere, but of which we remain unaware until such a focusing occurs, and the "mystery hidden for ages" is made "manifest." Jesus Christ then is the focus where the mystery of Being is disclosed.

These remarks already indicate how we shall try to elucidate the doctrine of the incarnation, that is to say, of God's coming in the flesh. We

[5] John 1:14.

shall try to think of this in terms of the presence and manifestation (advent and epiphany) of Being in the particular historical being of Jesus Christ, in whom for us the revelation of the mystery of Being has been focused.

Mention was made of timeless symbols through which the Logos has made itself known to men, and these were contrasted with the historical symbols of biblical and Christian faith. Here a few words may be said about the appropriateness of historical symbols. This appropriateness consists in their combination of the existential and ontological dimensions of revelation—a combination which perhaps they achieve in a uniquely effective way.

The historical symbol has an existential dimension in so far as it lights up for us our own being and our hitherto undisclosed possibilities of existence. It is our initial understanding of existence, which we get with our own existence, that enables us to enter into the understanding of history and into the experiences of the great historical agents; but to do this is to stretch the frontiers of that initial understanding of existence, so that we come back from the historical instance with a renewed and expanded self-understanding. In Christ, as the paradigmatic existence, we receive a renewed understanding of ourselves that amounts to a new possibility of existence, as we shall see in due course.

But the historical symbol has also an ontological import. If history is through and through existential, that is to say, if it has to do not with mere happening but with existence in its acting, becoming, and being, then the theme of history is personal being. The historical symbol is a personal symbol, and, in the particular case with which we are concerned, Christ is seen as the fulfillment of selfhood, of that potentiality for a truly personal being which is the potentiality given with existence. But then we have already seen that personal being is the most appropriate symbol for Being itself; for personal being stands highest in that hierarchy of beings which all seek to be like God, and personal being, as showing the richest diversity in unity and the highest possibilities for creativity and love, gives to our minds the fullest disclosure of the mystery of Being that we can receive.

Thus the historical symbol is an existential-ontological one, presenting in a remarkable combination the revelation of both existence and Being. This, incidentally, affords a further confirmation of the virtue of our existential-ontological method in theology, for it indicates that this method has not been arbitrarily selected but has an inner affinity with the peculiar character of the biblical and Christian revelation, as one given in historical terms.

47. THE HISTORICAL JESUS

It will be remembered that when we talked of providence and miracle, it was said that any providential act or miracle would, from one point of view, appear as just an ordinary event, indistinguishable from any other. It has no "magical" character, no publicly demonstrable properties that would isolate it from the series of events in which it has its place. This was said to guard against superstitious beliefs about miracles. Yet on the other hand, to those for whom the event is a miracle, it does have an extraordinary character, for they have perceived this event in the depth of its significance, or rather the event has seized them and brought to them a disclosure of Being.

Now, if Jesus Christ is, from the point of view of Christian faith, the supreme miracle, the culmination of God's providential and revealing activity, then he must present the same double aspect as any other miracle or providential act. To the first Christian disciples and to their successors, Jesus of Nazareth appeared as the revelation of the Father; he was, so to speak, seen in depth as the particular being in whom the presence and manifestation of Being itself has been focused. Yet this same Jesus could be seen also as just another member of the human race, as indeed he was, and if one were to think specially about him at all, he would not be considered a revelation of God but possibly as a dangerous innovator or a disturber of the peace, or maybe as an outstanding moral teacher, according to one's point of view. Most of his contemporaries, whether Jews or Romans, presumably saw him (if they took any notice of him at all) as just a rabbi or a revolutionary or whatever; and many people since have thought of him as simply a figure of history, perhaps interesting, instructive, and even deserving of respect and reverence, but not as the incarnation of God or the focus of God's acting. Those who are prepared to assert that "God was in Christ reconciling the world to himself" [6] go far beyond the publicly observable historical phenomenon and give expression to a faith into which they have been brought because what they have seen in Christ has worked upon them in some manner and led them to believe that in Christ God has become present to them in his reconciling work.

Christian theology speaks from the standpoint of faith, and so the datum

[6] II Cor. 5:19.

from which it sets out is Jesus Christ as the revelation of God. But theology is also a reflective and interpretative discipline, and in trying to work out the meaning of faith in the revelation given in Christ, it must consider how this revelation is related to the historical phenomenon which was the vehicle for it. It must, in short, ask about the Jesus of history, the publicly observable facts that were seen by disciples and non-disciples alike. After all, it was from these publicly observable facts that the disciples themselves had to begin; and we shall see that there is much to be said on behalf of the type of christology that begins, as it were, from below up, from the human career that is received as the manifestation of God rather than from the notion of the pre-existent Logos that has then to be conceived as taking a body and appearing as a particular existent.

But the question of the historical Jesus, as everyone knows, bristles with difficulties. What were these publicly observable phenomena? Nineteenth-century scholars spent a great deal of time and effort in trying to isolate the "facts" about the historical Jesus, and to disentangle him from what they regarded as the "accretions," mythological, theological, and metaphysical, that had gathered around him. Adolf Harnack may be taken as one of the most erudite of these researchers, and one of the clearest exponents of the point of view which so many of them shared. His aim was to return to the actual Jesus and to the pristine faith which he taught and practiced before it had become overlaid and distorted by the development of ecclesiastical dogma.

Presumably the new positivistic spirit that had begun to arise after Immanuel Kant's discrediting of metaphysics motivated much of the nineteenth-century research into the historical Jesus. In any case, the story of this chapter in New Testament scholarship and the eventual failure to lay bare the historical Jesus is well known from Albert Schweitzer's account in *The Quest of the Historical Jesus*. Nowadays it is universally recognized that the simple historical "facts" about Jesus cannot be isolated. The gospels, which are virtually our only sources of information about him, are precisely *gospels*—proclamations of Jesus as the one in whom God has come, not accounts of his life. This is true not only of the Fourth Gospel, the most obviously theological of all, but also of the Synoptic Gospels. The oldest of these, St. Mark's Gospel, is so far from taking us back to the historical, human Jesus of Nazareth that Bultmann is constrained to say that Jesus in this gospel "is the very Son of God walking the earth." [7] The researches of form-criticism have made it clear that the Jesus of history has, to a much greater extent than hitherto recognized,

[7] *The History of the Synoptic Tradition*, p. 241.

slipped beyond the horizon of what we can know, and that the figure presented in the gospels, and the incidents concerning him are, to say the least, strongly colored by the faith and teaching of the early Church. The historical, human Jesus has, in the thought of the Church, been transformed into the supernatural Christ whose setting is not historical but mythical, for he is the pre-existent redeemer who came down from heaven, sojourned on earth, and atoned by his death for sin, then rose from the dead and ascended into the heaven whence he had first come; and the expectation was that soon he would return on the clouds to consummate his redeeming work. The story of Jesus in the gospels is told in the light of this conception of the supernatural Christ, and the beliefs of the Church about Jesus as the Christ have been read back into the story of his life. For instance, Bultmann and others would claim that Jesus did not think of himself as Messiah, and that the application to him or the acceptance by him of this title in his lifetime is not an accurate reporting of the historical facts but a projection of the Church's belief onto Jesus. And similarly they would claim that many other things in the gospels do not represent events that actually took place but are put there to show that Jesus really was Messiah—as, for instance, that he fulfilled what were taken to be messianic predictions in the Old Testament, as D. F. Strauss had already argued a hundred years before Bultmann.

The current skepticism about the historical Jesus raises some problems for the systematic theologian. Clearly, he does not want to have his theology dependent on the notoriously changeable views of New Testament scholars. At the same time, of course, he has to recognize that theology, since it speaks out of faith, must share something of the risk of faith; and that it cannot expect to base itself on invulnerable certitudes, but must in many cases be content with reasonable probabilities, and perhaps in some cases even with leaps of faith which, though not unreasonable, have nevertheless to be taken in the face of ambiguous evidence. One would hope that in questions of historical fact, it will often be possible to reach reasonable probability, and sometimes even overwhelming probability. But how important is this for theology in the matter of the historical Jesus?

It seems to me that we cannot just dismiss the question of the historical Jesus and say that it does not matter for faith or theology whether we have any knowledge of him or not. The full reason for saying this will be made clear before we come to the end of this section, though I have already argued the point elsewhere.[8] But for the moment, let us simply

[8] *The Scope of Demythologizing*, pp. 90–101; *Studies in Christian Existentialism*, pp. 138–150.

recall that we have stressed the historical character of the Christian revelation, and pointed to some characteristics of historical revelation that might seem to give it an advantage over timeless revelatory symbols. If Christ is simply a timeless, mythical figure, then our talk about historical revelation has been idle. If there is no significance at all to be attached to the historical existence of Jesus, then Christ is on the same plane as other timeless mythical figures who appeared as redeemers in the myths of the mystery cults, Mithras, Attis, Osiris, and the rest. Surely we must hesitate to go along with some of the more radical disciples of Bultmann who are prepared to cut the link with the historical Jesus altogether (if indeed we still have a link!). We must hesitate because we remember that the catholic creeds place the event of Jesus Christ firmly in the framework of world history, and because the Church has throughout its history uncompromisingly opposed any docetic view that would take away from Jesus his full humanity as an historical person who, in St. Ignatius' words, "was truly born, and did eat and drink; he was truly persecuted under Pontius Pilate; he was truly crucified, and died, in the sight of beings in heaven and on earth, and under the earth." [9]

However, let us notice that New Testament scholarship by no means pushes us into an utter skepticism concerning the historical Jesus. It has indeed placed in doubt many matters that were once perhaps taken for granted, and it would be foolish not to recognize this; but it has been equally decisive in rejecting the so-called "Christ-myth" theories, which considered the figure of Jesus to be a purely mythical production of the early Christian communities. Bultmann assures us that "form-critics do not dispute the view that the Church had its origin in the works of Jesus, and has preserved many of his sayings in its literary creations." [10] While some of Bultmann's disciples have gone to the extreme of indifference concerning the historical Jesus, others have tried to reopen the question in ways that might avoid the errors of the nineteenth-century quest.[11]

While Bultmann has always differentiated the story of Jesus from the myths of the mystery cults, he has not been enthusiastic about the efforts of some of his disciples to renew the quest of the historical Jesus. Sometimes he talks as if we could know little more than that Jesus actually lived, and that he was crucified under Pontius Pilate; and even then, Bultmann feels constrained to add that we cannot know with certainty what

[9] Trall., ix.
[10] *The History of the Synoptic Tradition*, p. 40.
[11] See J. M. Robinson, *The New Quest of the Historical Jesus*.

Jesus' attitude to his death may have been.[12] He seems willing, "with a bit of caution," to fill out these bare facts with a kind of minimal portrait of Jesus, for "a few of his personal characteristics" may be inferred from the Synoptic Gospels. So we are told: "Characteristic for him are exorcisms, the breach of the Sabbath commandment, the abandonment of ritual purifications, polemic against Jewish legalism, fellowship with outcasts such as publicans and harlots, sympathy for women and children; it can also be seen that Jesus was not an ascetic like St. John the Baptist, but gladly ate, and drank a glass of wine. Perhaps we may add that he called disciples and assembled about himself a small company of followers—men and women." [13] This is not all, for Bultmann also thinks that Jesus had the consciousness of a prophetic vocation, though he does not think that it was the consciousness of being Messiah. Moreover, as we have already noted, Bultmann believes that much of this prophetic teaching has been preserved, and he summarizes it as the eschatological proclamation of the imminence of the reign of God and, in unity with this, the ethical demand for an inward, radical obedience in love, as opposed to any outward legalistic conformity.[14]

All of this certainly falls far short of even the barest biography of Jesus, but what is more important is that it tells us what kind of man he was. Bultmann acknowledges this in another place where, agreeing that particular incidents in the gospels may not be accurate historical reports, he nevertheless affirms that "the general character of Jesus' life is rightly portrayed in them, on the basis of historical recollection." [15] But is this not all that we need to know about the historical Jesus? To know that he was one who taught that in the face of the end men are called to radical self-giving love, and that he himself lived this way even to the point where he gave himself up to death—this is the essence of the historical Jesus, and it still remains accessible to us. We cannot indeed say that there is certainty here, but there is a high degree of probability, and even the most skeptical researchers have hardly shaken it. Neither Jesus nor his message would have been remembered unless he was indeed the kind of person portrayed in the gospels.

It is now time for me to return to the question of the theological signifi-

---

[12] See his essay, "The Primitive Christian Kerygma and the Historical Jesus" in *The Historical Jesus and the Kerygmatic Christ*, ed. C. E. Braaten and R. A. Harrisville, pp. 23–24.
[13] *Ibid.*, pp. 22–23.
[14] *Theology of the New Testament*, vol. I, pp. 3–32.
[15] *The History of the Synoptic Tradition*, p. 50.

cance of the historical Jesus, and to say what is the importance, from a theological point of view, of affirming at least this minimal truth, that there was indeed a historic person who suffered under Pontius Pilate and whose manner of life was of the kind portrayed in the gospels. The importance is that we thereby affirm also that the way of life which lies at the heart of the Christian proclamation is not something utopian or belonging to a wish-world, but something that has been realized in history, under the conditions of being-in-the-world. Ernst Käsemann has expressed this point well by saying that with the question of the historical reality of Jesus, there stands or falls the claim that "earthly corporeality" is the sphere of revelation.[16] In different words, we could say that upon the minimal assertion about the historical Jesus (stated above as "that there was indeed a historic person who suffered under Pontius Pilate and whose manner of life was of the kind portrayed in the gospels"), there depends the question of whether the Christian way of life is factical possibility and therefore to be taken seriously, or is merely an idealized possibility and perhaps just a fanciful escape from the harsh realities of historical existence.

But while this minimum of historical factuality is important for Christian faith, the publicly observable events themselves—as in the case of all miracles or providential acts—become the vehicle for God's address or God's acting. For those for whom the events are "revelation," they are seen in depth. The first Christians had been aware of the approach and presence of God in the events of Jesus' life and death, and they tried to express this by transposing the history of Jesus into a mythological framework whereby he was seen as a supernatural pre-existent being who had "come down" from heaven, had done his appointed work on earth, and then returned to the heavenly places. I may quote Käsemann again: "The significance of Jesus for faith was so profound that even in the very earliest days it almost entirely swallowed up his earthly history." [17] Something of this kind seems to happen, of course, to many of the really outstanding figures in the history of the human race. Even in their lifetime, or very soon thereafter, they begin to be surrounded by legend. This makes it hard or impossible to write anything like a biography of them, yet the very legends preserve the memory of the kind of men that these were, and as they impressed themselves on those who knew them. So it is to the full picture of Jesus in the gospels that we must now turn—Jesus pre-

[16] *Essays on New Testament Themes,* p. 32.
[17] *Op. cit.,* p. 23.

sented as the Christ, set in the mythological framework of supernatural action, and interpreted in myth and legends that are meant to light up and draw attention to the significance of Jesus "in depth," that is to say, the revelation of Being that is given in and through this particular being, Jesus of Nazareth.

48. THE CHRIST OF FAITH IN THE GOSPELS

In the preceding section, we have talked about the historical Jesus, and although this actual human figure who lived at a particular time is indispensable to a full statement of Christian faith and theology, nevertheless the historical Jesus is an abstraction from the picture given in the gospels. In all four gospels, we see Jesus already understood as the Christ of faith. We are not presented with the neutral, publicly observable historical phenomenon, for this has already been incorporated into a very complex structure of religious and mythological ideas—such as the idea of a three-decker universe of heaven, earth, and underworld; of an eschatological time scale that runs through definite ages from the beginning to the end; of messianic predictions given by Old Testament prophets and now being fulfilled; of an open texture of events in the world whereby they can be caused not by other events in the world but by supernatural agencies, whether divine or demonic; and of many other notions that belonged to the mentality of New Testament times. In many cases, some historical happening undoubtedly underlies the story, but it may have been so elaborated by legendary accretions that it is impossible to know what the historical happening was; and in other cases, especially those where some prophecy or alleged prophecy is said to get fulfilled, there must be a strong suspicion that details of the story have been invented to fit in with what was supposed to be messianic prophecy.

We must take the story as it stands and try to understand what it intends to assert about the meaning of Jesus, recognized as the Christ of faith. In this historical person, Jesus of Nazareth, some people had seen nothing extraordinary, but the disciples had seen the presence of God among them, and the evangelists are trying to express this experience. In our own day we might have to express this differently, but we shall get nowhere unless we can sympathetically listen to what the evangelists say and try to see what they claimed to see in him whom they recognized as the Christ. The best procedure will be to consider a series of incidents described in the gospels, incidents that are sometimes called the "mysteries of Christ," and are presented as critical moments in the revelation given in Christ. These incidents may be more or less historical, more or less legendary, but we need not be too eager to try to separate the historical and the legendary, even if this were possible, for the story is now a unity that seeks to present the Christ of faith.

1. First among these special "moments" in the career of Jesus comes the *nativity*. There can be little doubt that the stories that have come down to us are legendary rather than historical. The birth of Jesus would be an obscure affair, and only when something like a novelistic interest had begun to arise would stories of his birth be told. St. Mark's Gospel has nothing on the subject, but the Gospels of St. Matthew and St. Luke have detailed narratives of the birth, and even more elaborate stories are to be found in later apocryphal gospels. Yet, the very fact that such stories are legendary makes it easier to detect their theological import. However different the two traditions of the nativity in the canonical gospels may be, they are agreed in teaching the doctrine of a virgin birth,[18] and this is their main interest as far as the question of christology is concerned.

It is very surprising that the doctrine of the virgin birth should arouse so much controversy. No one, indeed, should be deterred from the Christian faith through inability to accept this doctrine, which, as has often been pointed out, is not explicitly mentioned by either St. Paul or St. John or St. Mark, although presumably all of these writers give us perfectly adequate accounts of the essentials of the faith. Yet probably the doubts and difficulties occasioned by this doctrine usually arise from misunderstanding. It has to be judged above all from a theological point of view. Since the conception of a child is not a publicly observable event open to historical investigation, there is little point in talking about the historicity of the virgin birth. The question to be considered is whether this doctrine helps to explicate the person of Christ, whether it enables us better to see Jesus as the incarnate Word.

Some scholars deny that the doctrine of the virgin birth can help toward a true understanding of the person of Christ. They point to myths of virgin births in pagan and non-Christian religions, and argue that the admission of such ideas into Christianity encourages us to think of Christ as a kind of demigod, like Achilles, say, or Herakles. However, the same objection could be brought against the use of the expression "Son of God," which many New Testament scholars believe to be of Hellenistic origin.

---

[18] Matt. 1:18–24; Luke 1:26–38.

The fact that an idea or an expression may come from some pagan source or at least might have pagan connotations is no decisive objection against it, for such interpretative ideas are themselves capable of being "stretched" or developed (in this case, christianized); and, so far as they are symbols that fall short of what they symbolize, they must always be used dialectically (that is to say, at once affirmed and denied), and illuminated by alternative symbols.

Another objection to the doctrine of the virgin birth is that it takes away from the true humanity of Christ. If he was truly man, so it is said, we must think of him as having a fully normal human conception. But the trouble about this objection is that it takes the whole matter far too literally, as if it were a question of biology rather than of theology. This mistake is very obvious in Emil Brunner's discussion of the doctrine.[19] He thinks it is an attempt to explain God's acting in terms of a biological anomaly. But the expression "birth"—precisely like "death"—does not, in the New Testament, have the matter-of-fact biological connotation that it has today. Both "birth" and "death" were mysteries, with an almost numinous character; and certainly there was no knowledge of conception in terms of later biology. The doctrine of the virgin birth is meant to point to Christ's origin in God. This man, Jesus, "born of the virgin Mary," as the creed asserts in opposition to all docetism, is nevertheless the one who has come from God and in whom God's advent and epiphany (presence and manifestation) have taken place.

In all such revelatory happening, God has the initiative, and Karl Barth has rightly maintained that the doctrine of the virgin birth upholds the divine initiative in the incarnation.[20] One could expand Barth's insight to make the point that this doctrine holds that the appearance of the Christ is not just the evolution or unfolding of "natural" human tendencies, but is God's work; and this is entirely in line with the whole argument of this book, where it has been held that human existence only comes to the realization of its potentialities through the divine action. In the case of Christ, this divine action is so integral to his being that we think of him as bringing together in one person divinity and humanity. It is interesting, moreover, to note that in both gospels which mention the virgin birth, specific reference is made to the action of the Holy Spirit.[21] This is what we might expect, and it is entirely in line with the doctrine of the Holy Spirit

---

[19] *The Mediator*, pp. 324–327.
[20] *Church Dogmatics*, I/2, p. 177.
[21] Matt. 1:20; Luke 1:35.

adumbrated in an earlier part of this book,[22] where it was said that the Spirit is to be understood as "unitive Being," and that his function is to bring into unity and to maintain in unity the beings with Being. Since an incarnation is to be understood precisely as the union of a being with Being in the fullest and most intimate way possible—we shall consider later how this could be—then such an incarnation would be preeminently a work of the Holy Spirit. Such a union is conceivable only as one in which the initiative is from the side of Being, so that a doctrine of the virgin birth, in ascribing the initiative in incarnation to unitive Being (the Holy Spirit) is an appropriate symbol.

The action of the Holy Spirit, however, is—at least on the personal level—not imposed *nolens volens,* but calls for the free response of the existent (spiritual) being to whom it is addressed. This is in fact given in the Blessed Virgin's "Let it be to me according to your word." [23] In this era of ecumenical exchange, no theology can fail to say something on the subject of mariology. The place and function of Mary, like the question of the virgin birth, are extensions of christological doctrine. But I propose to defer the mariological question until we come to the doctrine of the Church; for ecclesiology too, as the doctrine of the Body of Christ, stands in the closest relation to questions of christology and the incarnation.

2. Next among the "moments" in the career of Jesus, the *baptism* calls for attention. There can be no doubt that Jesus was in fact baptized by St. John the Baptist; the very fact that this was "a baptism of repentance for the forgiveness of sins" [24] made it embarrassing for the disciples of a later time to explain why Jesus should have been baptized, as we see from St. Matthew's Gospel,[25] and the story of the baptism would not have been told unless it had in fact happened and was well known. But the simple fact, whatever its original significance may have been, has been transposed into a mythico-theological framework, and the incident is used to light up Jesus in depth as the Christ of God. The Holy Spirit descends upon him, and a voice from heaven attests his divine Sonship. While in St. Mark, these details are most naturally read as belonging to the inner experience of Jesus (perhaps as inward vision and audition), in St. Luke the legend-making tendency has asserted itself and the events are publicly observable, for the dove appears "in bodily form" and the voice is apparently heard

22 See above, pp. 201–202.
23 Luke 1:38.
24 Luke 3:3.
25 Matt. 3:14–15.

by all (as it is in St. Matthew, where the second person of the verb is changed to third person).[26]

The search for the "facts" behind the story of the baptism has been described by Charles Guignebert as "one of those questions of gospel history which discourage and baffle investigation." [27] It may well be the case that, as a matter of historical fact, Jesus had responded to the teaching of the Baptist, had been baptized by him, and had perhaps even become a disciple, or an adherent of whatever community the Baptist may have had around him. But if these were the "facts," they certainly do not appear in the stories we have, and they would not have been palatable facts to the evangelists. Whatever the "facts" may have been, they have dropped out of sight, and the incident is narrated with a theological motive. It is now this theological meaning that is paramount, and it is this meaning which is of interest to us.

The story has become one of vocation, and this is surely very relevant to the task of trying to explicate the person of Christ. A vocation makes sense only in the context of a process of growth and commitment. The incarnation, understood as the advent and epiphany (presence and manifestation) of Being in Jesus Christ, is not to be understood magically as something that happened "automatically" in a moment, say at the moment of conception, or the moment of birth, or even at this moment of baptism. Just as we have argued that the self and selfhood are not things or properties conferred on the existent at the beginning, but are to be understood existentially as ways of being that are to be attained (or not attained) in the course of existence, it must now be asserted that the same is true of christhood. The full implications of this assertion will become clear in the working out of our christology, but for the present it is enough to say that we see it already implied in the gospel presentation of the baptism as vocation.

A moment of vocation implies that there has been a growing sense of vocation; but, furthermore, the decisive moment of commitment does not rule out (rather, it entails) a continued development of the sense of vocation, and an unfolding *ambulando* of a content which may not have been explicit in the moment of commitment itself. Let us suppose, for the sake of argument, that the "factual" history behind the baptism story is simply Jesus' joining himself to the community of the Baptist, and that no further intention was explicit in his mind at the time. Nevertheless, the evangelists

[26] Mark 1:9–11; Matt. 3:13–17; Luke 3:21–22.
[27] *Jesus*, p. 146.

are not wrong in taking this decisive moment of his career as a pivotal moment and projecting upon it thoughts and intentions that Jesus may have explicitly entertained only at a later time, or even thoughts that may have first come to the primitive Christian community after Jesus' lifetime. The vexing question of whether in his lifetime Jesus thought of himself as Messiah, for instance, is one that can be left open without affecting our understanding of the baptism story. Jesus must have had his moment of vocation, that is to say, of decisive commitment to his career, and this moment must have been both preceded and followed by a developing understanding of all that his vocation implied. Being a disciple of the Baptist, being a messianic prophet, being the Messiah himself, understanding the messianic office in terms of the suffering servant of deutero-Isaiah—some or all of these may have been successive elements in our Lord's understanding of his vocation, or some of these points may have become explicit only in the subsequent reflection of the disciples. Yet they all belong in a unitary career and are implicit in it, no matter when any particular item got unpacked. Thus the story of the baptism, while it is meant to point to Jesus as the Christ, implies his full humanity as one who responded to a call and commitment that would only fully unfold as he went along. This story justifies an existential rather than supernatural approach to the question of the meaning of christhood. It will be understood that the word "supernatural" is used here in the bad sense of magical. It need hardly be said that it is not being denied that christhood is a work that God or Being, not man or any particular being, initiates and brings to perfection. Just as we made this assertion in connection with the nativity, and pointed to the agency of the Holy Spirit in that event, so now we must again note the part played by the Spirit in the baptism. "He saw the heavens opened and the Spirit descending upon him like a dove." [28] The vocation of the man Jesus to christhood is attributed to the action of unitive Being, for, as has already been said, anything like an incarnation would be preeminently a work of unitive Being or the Holy Spirit.

3. We pass now to the *temptations* of Jesus. Here there is no publicly observable event behind the story, so the question of what the historical "fact" may have been scarcely arises. The account as we have it is legendary and symbolical, but it is nonetheless theologically perceptive, and again it is the theological significance that matters. One can say, however, that there must have been such moments of temptation in the career of

---

[28] Mark 1:10.

Jesus, if he was indeed a human being. The temptation story is an implicate of the vocation story, and it is not surprising that we find comparable stories told about such men as the Buddha and Zoroaster.

The content of the three specific temptations is interesting in view of what we have seen earlier concerning the understanding of man, sin, and the saving activity of God. The first and second temptations (following the order in St. Matthew [29]) are introduced by the expression, "If you are the Son of God . . . ," and this would seem to suggest that they are being presented as messianic temptations, so that implicitly the ideas of messiahship which they represent are being rejected. The first temptation, to make stones bread, suggests what in modern parlance we might call a "social gospel," aimed at the amelioration of the material conditions of life; but this is set aside as inadequate, because of the simple truth that man *exists*. To say that "man shall not live by bread alone" is to recognize that his need cannot be met below the level of existentiality. Not the quantitative proliferation of biological life but the authentic and genuinely human existence that lets be is the aim of the Christian gospel. The second temptation, to leap from the pinnacle of the temple, is surely, in spite of what Bultmann says about it,[30] the rejection of thaumaturgy as a way of creating belief in a messianic mission. It is indeed true that Jesus' healings and exorcisms are presented as signs of his authority, but in some way they are also dependent on faith, and are quite different from the sensational kind of magic envisaged in the second temptation. About this temptation, T. W. Manson rightly says: "To thrust oneself into peril, merely to provide God with the occasion for a miracle, is not faith but presumption." [31] By contrast with these false paths, the path to be followed by Jesus is one that would appeal to men in the full range of their existence, and the action of God in Jesus would be at a deeper level than that of publicly observable marvels.

Possibly these remarks get strengthened when we consider the third temptation, which is not peculiarly messianic and which can be understood as affirming Jesus' humanity and his solidarity with the rest of mankind. For this third temptation is to worship Satan for the sake of world dominion, and this of course is idolatry, the prizing of the creation above the Creator, and we have seen that this is the root form of sin.[32] Not only

---

[29] Matt. 4:1–11; cf. Luke 4:1–13.
[30] *The History of the Synoptic Tradition*, p. 255.
[31] *The Mission and Message of Jesus*, p. 337.
[32] See above, pp. 260–261.

was Jesus not immune from this universal temptation, but like all other persons with more than ordinary talents, he would be peculiarly affected by it. The narrative here shows him decisively rejecting the temptation, and this introduces still another christological theme—the sinlessness of Jesus. Precisely how we are to understand the meaning of this idea will be considered later.

4. Another "moment" in the gospel narrative having considerable christological significance is the story of the *transfiguration*. Nowadays most commentators seem to believe that this story tells of a post-resurrection experience of the disciples, and they may well be correct. But the interest of the story is theological, not historical (it is called a "vision," ὅραμα, in St. Matthew [33]), and we have to ask what it contributes to our understanding of Jesus as the Christ. Let us notice that in all three Synoptic Gospels [34] the story comes after the disclosure that Christ is to suffer, just as the stories of the resurrection appearances come after the actual sufferings of Christ. Whether the transfiguration and the antecedent disclosure of suffering took place in Jesus' lifetime, or whether both of these incidents have been placed in his lifetime by the early Church in the light of its postresurrection faith, this story seems to me to express in a remarkable way the transition that must have taken place from the disciples' acquaintance with the human Jesus to their faith in the same Jesus as the Christ—a transition that has rightly earned the name of "transfiguration."

For the story begins with the human Jesus—the Jesus who has recently disclosed that he is going to suffer (or who has in fact suffered, if we think of the transfiguration as post-resurrection). Christ's humanity seems to be further stressed by his association with Moses and Elijah, which indicates his continuity with the prophets. But then he is said to shine with a light like that of the sun, the divine presence is experienced in the overshadowing cloud, and a heavenly voice attests his Sonship. What does this symbolical language mean, except it is trying to bring to expression that perceiving in depth which we have taken to be characteristic of the recognition of miracle? In pictorial language, the story is telling how in the man Jesus the disciples found the focus of Being, where it became present-and-manifest in its advent and epiphany. Jesus is on the one hand a human being, even one in all the weakness of humanity as caught in suffering, whether anticipated or already realized; yet in this wholly human and suf-

---

[33] Matt. 17:9.
[34] Mark 9:2–8; Matt. 17:1–8; Luke 9:28–36.

fering figure, the revelation of God and the drawing near of Being take place for the disciples.

5. This leads us to the *passion*, the central incident in the whole story and the one to which the evangelists devote most attention. So central is it that we must consider it by itself in a separate chapter devoted to the work of Christ. But some aspects of it need to be considered here, because of their importance for an understanding of the person of Christ. Four points call for notice.

The first is the need to maintain the closest connection between the doctrine of Christ's person and that of his work. Christology becomes artificial when it becomes immersed in metaphysical distinctions about how Christ is constituted and neglects to consider what he does. Since Christ's cross and passion are seen as the culminating point of his saving work, they must be kept continually in view if we are to avoid the dangers of a merely academic christology, and ensure that the doctrine has a genuine existential dimension. We need not go so far as to let christology be altogether swallowed up in soteriology, or as to claim that the meaning of Christ's person can be exhaustively stated in terms of his existential significance for us, but no adequate christology can be lacking in an existential dimension. Due attention to the passion and death of Jesus, corresponding to the prominence accorded to these events in the gospel narrative, will ensure that our christology will have a strong existential character.

The second point is that recognition of the death of Jesus in its christological significance is also the strongest affirmation of the historical dimension in christology. In our discussion of the historical Jesus, we saw the theological importance of claiming that he is a historical rather than a mythical figure. We noted also that the most fully attested historical "fact" in the life of Jesus was his crucifixion under Pontius Pilate—the fact that is affirmed in the creeds, and the one that St. Ignatius recognizes as publicly observable, when he says that Christ "died in the sight of beings in heaven and on earth and under the earth." Of course, the passion narrative in the gospels is heavily laden with theological interpretation, just like the other "moments" or "mysteries" that we are considering in this section, but it stands out as the moment in which theological interpretation and historical factuality converge.

The third point is that the story of the passion is the strongest possible affirmation of the humanity of Christ. Even in our preliminary analysis of human existence, we saw the paramount importance of death in the constitution of such an existence. To be human is to be given over to death.

So we find that in every docetic or Gnostic attempt to speak of the person of Christ, his death gets explained away—he only seemed to suffer and die, St. Simon of Cyrene died in his place, or whatever the explanation may have been in any particular heresy. If then we hold fast to the centrality of the passion in our christology, we shall be recognizing the full humanity of Christ and keeping away from any docetic error.

The fourth and last point is that, in a way still to be analyzed but already hinted at when we spoke of the transfiguration, the passion and death of Jesus become the events whereby the human Jesus is revealed as the Christ of faith, or whereby the presence of God manifests itself in this man. Again, the way has been prepared for such an explication by our earlier studies of the being of man, where it was shown that death has a twofold character and can assume a positive, even an absolute, role in human existence, as well as being the mark of finitude.

6. It is obvious that the *resurrection* is not an historical event in the same way that the cross is, that is to say, not a publicly observable event. It is meant to affirm that God acted in Jesus, and the earliest mentions of the resurrection speak of it as God's act, not Christ's. In the preaching of St. Peter, God raised him up, and in the earliest written discussion of the resurrection, St. Paul uses the passive voice.[35] We have already seen plainly enough that an act of God is not a publicly observable event or a phenomenon open to sense perception, though it manifests itself in and through such occasions. Stories of the empty tomb and of accompanying marvels look like examples of the usual mythologizing tendency, which seeks to express the faith that God has acted in terms of objectifiable and empirically verifiable phenomena. Even if such stories could be proved to be veridical accounts of observed events, they would not in the least establish that God had acted in these events, for no such evidence is relevant to such a question.

Not the discovery of an empty tomb but the "appearances" of the risen Lord to his disciples seem to be the origin of belief in the resurrection of Jesus. The oldest account of the matter, that of St. Paul writing to the Corinthians, mentions only the appearances. Though he says nothing about St. Mary Magdalene, she was probably the first to whom an appearance was made, followed by St. Peter and others. St. Paul clearly counts his own vision of Jesus experienced on the way to Damascus to have been of the same order as the appearances experienced by the others.[36]

[35] Acts 2:32; I Cor. 15:4, etc.
[36] I Cor. 15:8.

There would be no profit in speculating about the nature of these appearances, any more than trying to establish that the tomb was empty. As with other miracles, the miracle of the resurrection is ambiguous. The skeptic will see in it nothing but a subjective vision or even a hallucination; but from the point of view of faith, it is the perception of the self-giving Christ in depth, so that this Christ is seen as the one in whom God is. Faith is born that God is indeed self-giving love and that life is truly attained through death, and this is the Easter faith. In the light of the whole Christian revelation, it is a reasonable faith, but it certainly cannot be proved or even made to look reasonable by irrelevant arguments about whether the tomb was empty. The only "proof" is that in the living Christian community, then and today, the person of Christ still lives and the living God still acts through him to reconcile and make whole.

Although the understanding of the resurrection just stated avoids the more speculative elaborations of the doctrine, it is far from being a reductionist account, and it is emphatically not saying simply that Jesus lives on as the Christian community. There are three assertions underlying the account, and these would seem to be essential to any adequate doctrine of the resurrection. First, Christ lives on. As the one who has fulfilled the potentialities of human existence and has indeed raised that existence to a new level, he has revealed its potentiality for an eternal life in God; he has "abolished death and brought life and immortality to light." [37] Second, (and this second point is dependent on the first one), the disciples experienced a new life in themselves. They had experienced a transformation from the life of sin and self-centeredness to a life open toward God in Christ, and they came to call this "eternal life" for they believed that even death could not terminate this relation to God. They were sharers in Christ's resurrection, and it is the Christian experience of new life in Christ that allows us to have an analogy whereby we can assign a meaning to the concept of resurrection beyond the crude meaning (clearly rejected by St. Paul [38]) of the resuscitation of a corpse. Third, all this tells us something about God. The resurrection means that he can bring forth the new. His working never comes to a dead end, for he can always open up a new possibility. This is what we meant by the providence of God, discussed in an earlier chapter. The cross speaks of God standing with his creatures in the flux of events; the resurrection speaks of his always being ahead of events. Both symbols seem essential to the idea of God.

[37] II Tim. 1:10.
[38] I Cor. 15:35ff.

7. The *ascension* is a purely mythical event and reflects a cosmology that has long since been abandoned. Yet as a symbol intended to express the significance of Christ, it has both appropriateness and truth as the culmination of the story. Christ's being "lifted up" into a cloud [39] (symbolizing the divine presence) suggests both that he has become the exalted Lord in the minds of the disciples, the Christ of faith and one with the Father; and, less subjectively, that the offering of his life is received by God (as the smoke of the ancient sacrifices had gone up into the sky).

The ascension is not a separate event—indeed, we shall see that in an important sense it is one and the same as the humiliation of Christ; or rather, these two are opposite sides of the same event. The ascension is the final symbol in the series of "mysteries" by which the evangelists seek to portray the man Jesus of Nazareth in depth, so that he becomes the transparent revealer of God and so that we see him as the Christ of faith.

We have concentrated attention on the most critical events in the career of Jesus as narrated in the gospels, but these moments simply highlight the understanding of Jesus that is presented by the whole gospel narrative. The accounts of his teaching show him as one having a unique kind of authority, while the stories of his healings and exorcisms see these events as signs of the inbreaking kingdom of God. The total effect then, both in the "mysteries" and in the remainder of the gospel material, is to present us with one who is unquestionably human and yet one in whom, as the evangelists were convinced, God has become present and manifest.

49. LORD AND WORD

We now have before us, in outline, the tradition concerning Jesus Christ, as this has been preserved and transmitted in the Christian community. We have seen that the core of this tradition is an actual historical figure, though we have only very meager factual information about him; we have seen also how this historical figure was transformed into the Christ of faith, the Christ who is presented to us in the gospels in scenes that are partly historical, partly legendary, partly mythical. This was the manner and the language in which these early disciples tried to express their conviction that the very presence of God had come among them in a new and signal way in Jesus. Obviously, however, we in the twentieth century would not use the same concepts and language as people used in the first

[39] Acts 1:9.

century, and their way of trying to express the significance of Jesus Christ is largely foreign to us, for we do not share the background of mythological ideas that are indispensable if talk about pre-existence, voices from heaven, exorcisms, ascension, and the like are to communicate. The fact that the mythological ideas of the New Testament have become so familiar during the centuries in which Christianity has been an all-pervading factor in Western culture now obscures from us the recognition of how far we have moved from the presuppositions of all mythology. If we are to understand Jesus as the Christ of faith, we must look for a new interpretation.

There was, of course, considerable diversity of interpretation among the early disciples themselves, and a consideration of some other ways in which they sought to express the meaning of Christ's person may help us on the way to a contemporary interpretation. So next after the dramatic, narrative mode of expression in myth and legend, we turn to the titles given to Jesus. These too are in part culled from the religious and mythological ideas of the first century, from sources both Jewish and Hellenistic, but they tend to focus in more definite images the understanding of Jesus as the Christ.

It is not our intention here to attempt any detailed consideration of the titles given to Jesus in the New Testament. This task belongs to biblical rather than systematic theology, and in any case the importance of the titles has probably been overestimated in recent christological discussion, and too little attention given to some of the less easily classifiable but none the less significant New Testament data, such as that "authority" of Jesus, about which G. Bornkamm has written.[40]

However, some brief discussion of the titles is demanded, and it will provide a useful pointer toward the form which any adequate christology must assume. The multiplicity of titles shows us that from the beginning there were a number of ways in which the person of Christ might be interpreted. Each title already contains the seeds of a type of christology, and although these different types of christology do not contradict one another, they cannot easily be combined. Each draws attention to some aspect of the many-sided reality of Jesus Christ.

The earliest of the titles, "Messiah," naturally came from the background of Judaism and the Old Testament. It means literally "the anointed one," and could stand for the king of Israel or for the nation itself. The Messiah

---

[40] *Jesus of Nazareth*, pp. 60–61.

came to be understood as a promised ideal king who would deliver the nation and rule in righteousness. From this idea arises the possibility of a politico-ethical christology, a this-worldly interpretation of Christ as the Lord of man's social, moral, and political life. The political aspect has, from the beginning, been muted, and in isolation it would be a very impoverished understanding of the Christ. As John Knox remarks, "The gospel tradition does not permit us to miss the political bearings of Jesus' career, but they are certainly obscured." [41] But even though it has been obscured, this is a valid aspect of christhood and is revived from time to time, most recently in the black theology of the United States and the liberation theology of South America.

The title "Son of Man" comes also from the Jewish background. Scholars disagree sharply among themselves about its meaning—indeed, it probably bears several meanings in the gospels. One influential strain of interpretation sees the Son of Man as an otherworldly figure of Jewish apocalyptic, who would be sent by God to judge the world and inaugurate the new age. It is most unlikely that Jesus ever thought of himself in such a way, but certainly such ideas came to be applied to him and he was understood as the inaugurator of the new age.

It was suggested earlier that the title "Son of God" may have come from the Hellenistic background, though it must be noted too that sometimes the kings of the Old Testament were addressed as "sons" of God. Whatever the origin of the title, it suggests neither the man who is exalted by God to messianic office, nor the heavenly man who comes down to execute a mission on earth, but one who combines deity and humanity, a "God-man." It may have been to avoid the danger of thinking of Jesus Christ as like the demigods of pagan mythology that he came to be called the "only begotten Son." Nevertheless, it was this idea of the "God-man" which was at the center of the classical christology of the early centuries and which, not surprisingly, turned to Greek metaphysics for the solution of the problem.

There were however two titles applied to Jesus that from the beginning had a greater universality and which form the foundation for any adequate christology. These titles were "Lord" and "Word." They may be said to have had a greater universality from the beginning because each of them has its history and connotations in both Jewish and Greek sources. "Lord" (κύριος) is regularly used in the Septuagint for God, while in the

---

[41] *The Death of Christ*, p. 29.

Greek mystery religions it was used for the deity of the particular cult. "Word" (λόγος) is an important term in the Hebrew tradition, for it was through his word that God acted and communicated himself, while in the Greek tradition the word or Logos had come to be recognized as the organizing and governing principle of the world; and of course Philo of Alexandria had already firmly welded together the two traditions by New Testament times. Some biblical theologians try to trace the titles given to Jesus exclusively or primarily to Hebrew sources, and tend to regard the introduction of Hellenistic connotations as a post-biblical and regrettable development. This seems to be a very shortsighted point of view. Paul Tillich rightly says about the so-called "Hellenization of the gospel" that "it was inescapable not only because of the necessity of introducing the gospel into the Hellenistic world but also because the discovery of the ontological question by the Greek mind is universally relevant." [42]

The two titles "Lord" and "Word" have universality not merely because they transcend the limits of a purely Hebrew or purely Hellenistic reference, but because together they constitute an existential-ontological interpretation of Christ's person; and of course we have seen that an adequate theological language has always this twofold character.

The title "Lord" provides the existential element. This is never a disinterested word or a neutral description. To call someone "Lord" is to assign a rank to him, and thus to express an attitude toward him. The history of the word "Lord" in Jewish and Greek usage would indeed indicate that when used in a religious context, the word assigned a supreme rank, and therefore expressed an attitude of absolute commitment. So the title "Lord" initiates an existential type of christology, and this way of thinking has been strongly represented in modern times, from Ritschl's characterization of christological assertions as "value-judgments" down to Bultmann's insistence that soteriology takes precedence over christology. The recognition of the need for an existential dimension in christology is to be welcomed, and is entirely in line with all that has been said above about theological language and the kind of assertions that are made in symbolic theology. The demand for an existential dimension is the more necessary, because the traditional christological formulas have frequently been understood (or misunderstood) as merely metaphysical descriptions. Yet we have made it abundantly clear that any attempt to work out a purely existential theology (whether in the field of christology or elsewhere) is

[42] *Biblical Religion and the Search for Ultimate Reality*, p. 60.

a distortion. There is at least a considerable danger that in some quarters the rediscovery of an existential dimension in christology and the stress being laid upon it may obscure the appreciation that an ontological dimension is equally needed.

The ontological side of christology is initiated and safeguarded by the recognition of Jesus as the "Word" or Logos. We have already used the term "Logos" for the second person of the triune God, that is to say, for expressive Being. It is through expressive Being that Being goes out in creation into a world of beings. To claim that in Jesus "the Word became flesh" [43] is to assert that in and through this particular being, Being has found signal expression. We have seen that Being is present and potentially manifest in all beings, but that since these constitute a hierarchy, some are capable of manifesting Being in a greater range than others. The highest place in this hierarchy was claimed for personal beings. Now among these personal beings a special claim is being made for Jesus Christ, as the person in whom Being has been signally present and manifest, that is to say, has achieved its advent and epiphany. The fuller explication of the basis of this claim has still to be made. But in the meantime, let the ontological claim be registered alongside the existential claim as two equally primordial and equally necessary sides to any adequate christology. Jesus is both Lord and Word, existentially the one who commands absolute allegiance, and ontologically the one who renders present-and-manifest holy Being.

The titles "Lord" and "Word" set before us two indispensable elements in any adequate understanding of the person of Christ. We shall endeavor to do justice to both in constructing an existential-ontological statement of the doctrine. But now we must consider how the twofold assertion that Jesus is Lord and Word is related to another twofold assertion that is vital to any christology—that Jesus is both God and man.

50. TRUE GOD AND TRUE MAN

Both in the narrative presentation of Jesus Christ in the Synoptic Gospels and in the implicit christology of the titles applied to Jesus throughout the New Testament there is the clear assertion that in some mysterious and paradoxical way, this Jesus combines in himself Godhood and manhood. This is asserted too in those more reflective and theological parts of the New Testament, such as the Johannine and Pauline writings, and the

---

[43] John 1:14.

Epistle to the Hebrews. Again, it is not the business of this book to attempt a detailed study of New Testament theology, and there are available many studies of the material by New Testament scholars.[44] Although there are many differences of emphases, and although both St. Paul and St. John have sometimes been accused of stressing the divinity of Christ at the expense of his humanity, the New Testament is agreed that both his divinity and his humanity need to be asserted. One of the most balanced statements is found in the Epistle to the Hebrews. It begins with a strong assertion of Christ's close relation to the Father: "He reflects the glory of God and bears the very stamp of his nature, upholding the universe by his word of power"; but soon this document is pointing to the necessity for a true humanity in anyone who could be a genuine mediator between God and man: "He had to be made like his brethren in every respect, so that he might become a merciful and faithful high priest in the service of God, to make expiation for the sins of the people. For because he himself has suffered and been tempted, he is able to help those who are tempted." [45] The Christ is not a mere intermediary between God and man, a kind of demigod or angel or something of the sort, but a genuine mediator, and hence one who has his being on both sides of the divide, and is thus both God and man; or, to express it in another way, christhood implies incarnation, and incarnation means the bringing together in one person of Godhood and manhood.

How is the assertion that Jesus is both man and God related to the assertion that he is both Lord and Word? These two do not coincide, yet they are related in various ways. The assertion of Christ's manhood is intrinsic to any existential christology, and indeed such a christology will usually be of the kind that begins "from below up," that is to say, begins with the humanity of Jesus and goes on to show his divinity, as against the kind of christology that begins in more speculative fashion with the second person of the Trinity and considers how this second person can become man. The relation between the manhood of Christ and the existential dimension of christology is to be seen both in the recognition that Christ is the goal or limit toward which human existence tends (he is "Lord"), and also, as has already been contended, in the fact of his historicity, which makes this limiting case a "factical" one and therefore one that can seriously engage our existential interest, as a merely ideal or imaginary figure could not do. On the other hand, the ontological dimension of christology relates pri-

[44] See, e.g., Oscar Cullmann, *The Christology of the New Testament.*
[45] Heb. 1:3, 2:17–18.

marily to Christ's manifestation of Being, that is to say, to his Godhood, and thus a purely ontological christology tends to become an academic exercise. However, it was said that there is not an exact coincidence between the assertion that Christ is Lord and Word, and the assertion that he is man and God. It is precisely as these two indispensable assertions, each of them itself twofold, are allowed to interact on each other that an adequate christology can be brought forth. The assertion of Christ's Lordship and the according to him of the ultimate allegiance that such an assertion implies carries him beyond the limits of human existence, so that we recognize him as God; for if we gave such allegiance to anyone less than God, we would be idolaters—and this, as has often been pointed out, was the basic objection to Arianism. On the other hand, the recognition of Christ as God, if this is not to be disinterested metaphysical speculation, must go on to assert that the Word was made flesh and to recognize that this Word has met us and addressed us on the level of human existence; for only so would there be the slightest religious interest in Christ.

What these remarks imply is that the doctrine of the God-man must be interpreted in an existential-ontological way; and we must at all costs avoid the dichotomy between an existential christology based on the recognition of Christ as Lord and an ontological christology based on the recognition of him as the Word. The various strands—Lord and Word, humanity and deity, the existential and the ontological, have all to be woven together.

Clearly, however, they are interwoven in a very complex way. It seems that we must assert that at the limit of human existence (in the sense, that is to say, of the goal of human fulfillment) Christ manifests divine Being, so that in him humanity and deity come together. Thinking of this from the other side, it would presumably be conceivable if, in this particular being of Jesus Christ, expressive Being had perfectly expressed itself. If indeed Jesus Christ is true God and true man, we seem driven to posit a kind of open place, as it were, where divine Being and human existence come together; or again, where creaturely being, which seeks to be like God, has actually attained to the level of deity. For the paradox of the God-man, Jesus Christ, is that not only does he belong to God, as the second person of the Trinity, but he also belongs to the creation as "the firstborn of all creation." [46]

As in our earlier discussion of the triune God, it will be profitable to call to mind the traditional language of christology. This language was it-

[46] Col. 1:15.

self originally explicative and interpretative, though to modern ears it sounds archaic and needs reinterpretation. So far as it is still understood, it is usually taken to mean some metaphysical analysis of the person of Christ, and so to be defective in that existential dimension which is requisite to any adequate christology. But there can be little doubt that if we could think ourselves sympathetically into the great christological controversies of the early Church, we would discover that behind the seemingly abstruse language, issues of vital existential concern were at stake.

The core of the traditional christology is, of course, the two-nature doctrine of the Chalcedonian definition, which speaks of "one and the same Christ, Son, Lord, Only-begotten, recognized in two natures (φύσεσιν), without confusion, without change, without division, without separation; the distinction of natures being in no way annulled by the union, but rather the characteristics of each nature being preserved and coming together to form one person (πρόσωπον) and subsistence (ὑπόστασιν), not as parted or separated into two persons, but one and the same Son and Only-begotten God the Word, Lord Jesus Christ."

It seems to me that the key word for interpreting this statement is "nature" (φύσις). If we take "nature" to mean a fixed stock of characteristics which constitutes anything as the kind of thing that it is, then we are up against grave difficulties. Admittedly, this is the traditional way of taking the word "nature," and it would lead into the traditional metaphysical interpretation of the Chalcedonian christology. But what sense can we make of the idea of one "subsistence," that is to say, one particular being, that nevertheless has two "natures" in the sense mentioned? Again, we have learned that man, as an existent, does not have a "nature" in the sense that, let us say, some kind of mineral has a nature, some basic stock of characteristics that constitutes it that kind of mineral. As existent, man is always incomplete and on his way, so that if it is proper to talk of him having a "nature," this must be conceived as open-ended. And furthermore, what could we mean by the "nature" of God? If it is erroneous to talk of man's "nature," at least in the sense of a fixed stock of basic characteristics, it is presumptuous to talk of God's "nature" in a similar sense. It is true that we can recognize in God some basic attributes,[47] but to claim to know his "nature" (always in the sense explained above) would be to claim to grasp God in a way that is incompatible with his transcendence and mystery.

---

[47] See above, pp. 202–210.

But let us suppose that we can interpret "nature" in another way. Such a way has already been outlined, when we considered the meaning of "nature" (φύσις) in connection with the doctrine of creation.[48] There it was said that "nature" is to be understood as emerging, coming into the light. This we took to be the ontological significance of the word (for the root φυ is one of the Indo-European roots used to express Being) which is prior to any relatively artificial and sophisticated metaphysical usage, and the basis for it. It is true that in our earlier discussion we were talking about "nature" in the sense of the material world and the forces at work in it, while now we are talking of "nature" as we use the expression in such phrases as "the nature of man" or "the nature of God." But this second usage, like the first, goes back to the fundamental ontological sense of emerging or coming to the light. If we take "nature" in this basic sense, then the christological talk about the two natures not only makes sense, but makes very good sense indeed.

For then human nature is to be understood as an "emerging." Can we define this more precisely? Actually, we have already seen something of what it means. We have seen that man is called out of nothing into creaturely being; then, as St. Paul says, we "receive adoption as sons"[49]; and finally, as St. John has it, "we are God's children now; it does not yet appear what we shall be, but we know that when he appears we shall be like him."[50] We recognize in this the doctrine with which we are already familiar, that all created things tend toward likeness to God, and that in the case of man, as existing and not having a fixed essence, there is no end in sight along the road he can travel—"it does not yet appear what we shall be." Man's "nature" is this emerging or coming to the light. So we can understand how it is that Christ has a complete human "nature," and what was meant by saying that at the limit of existence, that is to say, at the furthest point along the road toward fulfilling or unfolding this "nature" (existence), he manifests divine Being. Karl Rahner, in a plea for a more existential and dynamic understanding of the traditional two-nature language, though he does not explicitly talk of φύσις as "emerging," makes some points that are very similar to the argument of this paragraph. He declares that "Christ has always been involved in the whole of history as its prospective entelechy"; and he also asserts that "human being is a reality absolutely open upwards; a reality which reaches its highest (though

[48] See above, pp. 222–223.
[49] Gal. 4:5.
[50] I John 3:2.

indeed 'unexacted') perfection, the realization of the highest possibility of man's being, when in it the Logos himself becomes existent in the world." [51]

However, the christology which begins from below up, and which traces the human "nature" of Christ in terms of an existence that emerges onto ever higher levels, is not by any means meant to be a kind of evolutionary christology, as if the emergence of christhood were a kind of automatic product of the world-process. We already registered a protest against such a view in upholding the symbol of the virgin birth as safeguarding the divine initiative in the incarnation. This can now be stated more clearly, when we consider the divine "nature," also to be understood as "emerging." This idea too is familiar to us, for the second person of the Trinity we saw to be "expressive Being." It is through expressive Being that God emerges from his hiddenness and comes to light. But clearly this self-manifestation of Being can take place most fully in a particular being that has no fixed "nature" but whose very "nature" is an existence, an emerging, so that it can express more and more Being. If we can think of expressive Being (the Logos) finding perfect expression in a particular being (and such a being could only be a personal or existent being), then in this particular being the two natures would come together in a unity. Only in the next section shall we see how we could conceive of expressive Being fully expressing itself in a particular being. But even this thought is not entirely foreign to our earlier discussions, for we saw that in creation, God really does in a manner put himself into what he creates, in varying degrees.

The two natures are said to come together in "one person and subsistence." Here the word "subsistence" (ὑπόστασις) means what we usually call "particular being," and the particular being is, of course, Jesus Christ, and a person in the modern sense of the word, for it is only personal being (or existence) that has the openness that would permit it to come into union with holy Being. But we can now say more plainly what this unity is, the unity that permits us to say both that humanity and divinity come together in Jesus Christ, and that this Christ in turn is "of the same essence" (ὁμοούσιος) with the Father. For the principle of unity here (as also in the doctrine of the Trinity) is Being; and the essence of Being, in turn, is letting-be. Personal being is superior to lower forms of creaturely being, and so more "like to God," because of its capacity for letting-be.

[51] *Theological Investigations*, vol. I, pp. 167, 183.

It is where this capacity for letting-be is raised to an absolute level that a particular personal being could manifest holy Being, and so unite in one person the two natures, and at the same time be of one essence (substance) with the Father, the primordial letting-be. To show how this comes about will be the endeavor of the next section of the present chapter.

51. CHRIST AS THE FOCUS OF BEING

In our discussions of the phrases "Lord and Word" and "True God and True Man," we have talked for the most part in a formal way about the ontological and existential conditions that are implied in any adequate conception of christhood. We now have to come back and consider the whole matter more concretely in relation to Jesus Christ, as we saw him to be in the earlier sections on "The Historical Jesus" and "The Christ of Faith in the Gospels." It is this particular being, Jesus Christ, whom the Christian religion proclaims to be the incarnate Word, the God-man.

If we hold fast to the existential dimension in the understanding of christhood, as already expounded, so that we see christology as a kind of transcendent anthropology (as Rahner also has done), with christhood as the goal toward which created existence moves, then the first point to be made is that we must be prepared to acknowledge a dynamic character in the incarnation, and this means some kind of development. We cannot think (this would be indeed mythological!) of the Logos being "implanted" in Jesus at his conception, or, for that matter, at his birth, or his baptism. In seeing a parallel between anthropology and christology, we have also to see a parallel between selfhood and christhood. We have already seen that the self is not some kind of substance that gets put into the body at the beginning of the individual's life, but is rather the "form" or "entelechy" of an embodied existence in the world, and as such is something that has to be brought into being in the deeds and decisions of life. In the same way, we may suppose that the incarnation is to be understood not as an instantaneous happening but as a process of coming together, and that Jesus progressively realized his christhood. Such growth is, indeed, attested in the gospels [52] and, in discussing the "mystery" of the baptism, we saw that this kind of growth is an implicate of a vocation such as we may suppose Jesus to have had, whether or not this vocation was explicitly to the messianic office.[53]

[52] Luke 2:52.
[53] See above, pp. 282–284.

Just as christhood (which may indeed be equated with the selfhood of Christ) is to be understood as coming about through a process of growth, so the attributes of christhood would not suddenly appear from nowhere, as it were, but would develop with christhood itself. This applies to the important attribute of sinlessness. Several contemporary theologians, who are rightly concerned to stress the humanity of Jesus as against what they consider to be the docetic tendency of traditional christology, have questioned the validity of this doctrine of the sinlessness of Christ; for, they say, we cannot suppose him to have been fully man, and yet to have avoided the universal taint of sin. They argue that even if Jesus in his individual life refrained from sinful acts, nevertheless, since sin is more than such individual acts and has a social character, he could not have escaped being caught up in the disorder of society as a whole, if indeed he was in solidarity with the human race.

Perhaps the first comment to be made here is that we should remember that sin is not implied in human existence, but is rather a disorder of humanity; and it is worthwhile to remind ourselves of the frequent confusion in theology between sin and finitude, to which our attention was earlier called.[54] Yet even so, it would seem that any individual human life, if truly human, could not be insulated from the attitudes of the society in the context of which it was placed; or again, could not be entirely exempt from that almost tragic guilt which seems to be inseparable from the relative and finite character of human action. But then, if we anchor Christ so firmly in the fallen race of Adam, how can we think of him as a Savior? Or what sense does it make to claim that he can reverse that drift toward sin and dissolution which mankind of itself cannot reverse?

The way out of these difficulties, as it seems to me, must consider sinlessness as the end of a process of development, and when we consider it in this way, then we need not separate Christ from the human race in a manner that would compromise his true humanity. But first of all, we must fix the meaning of "sinlessness." This is a confusing expression, for it is a double negative. Sin itself is a negative—a disorder and a separation from God; sinlessness is in turn the negation of the negativity of sin. Thus "sinlessness" means that the disorder is overcome, and that the separation from God is replaced by a coming together of God and man. In other words, sinlessness describes an aspect of christhood, and like christhood, it is gained in the deeds and decisions of life, and is certainly not a merely

[54] See above, pp. 264–265.

negative "dreaming innocence." Such sinlessness, when attained, may indeed separate from the ordinary mass of humanity, but just in the same way as christhood separates from the ordinary mass of humanity—in both cases, humanity is brought to a higher level. It does not cease to be true manhood, but it becomes God-manhood, true manhood united with true Godhood.

But how do we see this movement toward a perfect or sinless selfhood, which is also christhood and incarnation, taking place? If we reject the idea that the Logos gets implanted in a human body at conception, where do we see the coming together of man and God? The answer to this must be that we see it in the death of Christ. Already in our preliminary analysis of human existence, we noted that death, as well as being the mark of human finitude, also provides the perspective in relation to which a unified self can come into being.[55] A parallel statement can be made about christhood. The death of Christ is taken up into his life as its climax and fulfillment, and it is in the moment of death that christhood fully emerges.

In an earlier mention of the passion and death of Christ, it was said that they have a fourfold importance for the understanding of his person: they relate his person to his work, they establish his place in world history, they affirm his complete humanity, and they point the way to understanding how that humanity is taken up into deity. It was promised that there would be a fuller explication of this last point, and the time has now come to offer it.

God is absolute letting-be, and letting-be is the ontological foundation of love. Letting-be is also self-giving or self-spending, so that God's creative work is a work of love and self-giving, into which he has put himself. In so far as created beings themselves manifest creativity, love, self-giving, they tend to be like God. This self-giving is supremely manifest in the particular being, Jesus Christ. Just as there is a self-emptying, or *kenosis*, of God as he pours out Being, so Christ empties himself in the life that is portrayed in the gospels. But how could this relative self-emptying in a finite particular being manifest the absolute letting-be of God? To this, it must be replied that death is the one absolute in human life. By this is meant not just the moment of physical death, but the taking up of death into life, so that existence itself becomes a being-toward-death. Christ's self-giving, his love or letting-be, becomes complete and absolute in the accepting of the cross. Selfhood passes into christhood, the human Jesus

[55] See above, pp. 78–79.

becomes the Christ of faith, there is the convergence of the human and divine "natures" in the one person. Likewise there is the attainment of "sinlessness," understood affirmatively as the overcoming of the separation of God and man, and with this, Christ breaks out of the sin-bound human situation, and opens up the new life, symbolized by the resurrection. In the words of Cardinal Newman's great hymn, we have here "God's presence, and his very self, and essence all-divine." [56] Christ's most utter self-abasement is also his ascension, when we recognize that God is in Christ. This is the transfiguration, when the light of Being shines forth in this particular being. Again, let it be stressed that although this treatment of the problem of Christ's person begins "from below up," it implies no naturalistic evolutionism, or any so-called "adoptianism." From first to last, this is the work of Being in its great threefold action of creation, reconciliation, and consummation. The incarnation is the supreme providential act or miracle of history. It will be remembered that the characteristic of such an event is that it focuses Being in its presence and manifestation, its advent and epiphany. Jesus Christ may be properly understood as the focus of Being, the particular being in whom the advent and epiphany take place, so that he is taken up into Being itself and we see in him the coming into one of deity and humanity, of creative Being and creaturely being.[57] And what we see in Christ is the destiny that God has set before humanity; Christ is the first fruits, but the Christian hope is that "in Christ" God will bring all men to God-manhood. This we shall consider when we come to eschatology.

52. THE DEFINITIVENESS OF JESUS CHRIST

Christian faith claims that Jesus Christ is the focus of Being, the center of its presence-and-manifestation among the beings; or, in the more traditional language of St. Paul, that "in him the whole fullness of deity dwells bodily." [58] How is such a claim possible?

The whole of this chapter has been devoted to explicating the claim and to showing the grounds on which it rests.. But now we must come to grips more closely with the question of what is often called the "unique-

[56] *The English Hymnal*, No. 471.
[57] Although we proceed by different routes, this conclusion is not very different, even in its language, from Norman Pittenger's understanding of Jesus as "the unique focus for a universal presence and operation"—*The Word Incarnate*, p. 192.
[58] Col. 2:9.

ness" of Jesus Christ. Why is it in him rather than elsewhere that we claim to see the focus of Being?

Partly, one can answer this question only by saying that this has in fact been the way things have turned out. The unique place of Jesus Christ is part of the givenness of history. Skeptics will say that this is just an accident, but those who believe that history has a meaning and a goal will see the place of Jesus Christ as providential. And here again we have to remind ourselves that when we speak of Jesus Christ—or of any other person—we cannot mean simply the individual, Jesus of Nazareth, in isolation, for no individual exists apart from social relations. Each must be seen in a social and historical setting. The Christ-event which is said to be the focus of Being certainly has its center and origin in this particular person, Jesus Christ, but he is unintelligible apart from the whole complex of relationships which bind him to Israel, to the Church, to the entire human race, and it is this vast ongoing movement of spiritual transformation and renewal that has to be borne in mind when we consider the claim made for Christ.

But could not similar claims be made for the founders of Buddhism and Islam? Here we must recall our earlier discussion of the religions and particularly the recommendation of an attitude of "commitment and openness" on the part of the Christian toward other faiths.[59] Is it possible to make the tremendous claims for Jesus Christ that Christian faith and theology do make, and still be open to other faiths? Or if one does try to be open to the truth in other faiths, has not one secretly qualified the unique place that Christian faith ascribes to Jesus Christ?

First of all, I would have to say that the word "unique" is not helpful in discussing this question. Not only Jesus Christ, but every person is unique, and therefore so is Mohammed and so is Gautama. The words "absolute" and "final" are equally unhelpful. Such words imply, as Troeltsch pointed out, "a knowledge of God that exhausts its essence and idea, that is withdrawn from all change and enrichment, that overleaps the bounds of history."[60] Clearly, this runs counter to the stress laid throughout this book on man's finite and unfinished condition and to his involvement in history, so that he can never stand outside of the historical process and see things from an absolute or godlike point of view. In place of the words rejected, I shall use the expression "definitive" for Jesus Christ as under-

[59] See above, pp. 170–173.
[60] *The Absoluteness of Christianity*, p. 119.

stood in Christian faith. He is definitive in the sense that for Christians he defines in normative fashion both the nature of man (which he has brought to a new level) and the nature of God (for the divine Logos, expressive Being, has found its fullest expression in him). This is an affirmation of faith, made from within history, and not an attempt to pronounce from some vantage point above history. As such, it is content to make an affirmation about Christ and to refrain from negative judgments concerning the truth in other faiths. It recognizes too that while Christ possesses fullness and a definitive status, our apprehension of that fullness is always imperfect.

It was said above that what we are calling the definitiveness of Jesus Christ is to be accepted as a given of history. However, more has to be said. Christ has been accepted as definitive because he has addressed men at the deepest level of conscience, where conscience is understood as man's fundamental self-awareness as one summoned to an authentic personal and communal existence. Or, to put the matter in another and more theological way, Christ is recognized as the definitive fulfillment of that image of God of which all men are at least dimly aware as a given potentiality toward which they are called to transcend. In the words of one New Testament writer, Christ is "the express image of God." [61]

Attempts are sometimes made to specify Christ's definitiveness more closely. Is it his self-giving love that causes men to confess that here is the express image of God? Or his freedom? Or his utter obedience to the Father in fulfilling his vocation? Or his spiritual creativity, his capacity for letting others be? Or, as Pannenberg has claimed, is it the fact of his resurrection that constitutes "the ground of his unity with God?" [62]

I do not think that one can point to some single characteristic and place all the weight on it by itself. Rather, one may say that in Jesus Christ there is an entire constellation, so to speak, of qualities which we recognize as constituting the essence of authentic personal being. In this sense, Pannenberg's stress on the resurrection is well taken, for resurrection includes the other qualities. We have seen that the concept of resurrection has, as an important part of its meaning, precisely the emergence of a new level of human and personal existence.

---

[61] Heb. 1:3.
[62] *Jesus—God and Man*, p. 53.

53. CHRISTOLOGY AND PARADOX

From the very beginning of this study of theology we have been aware of the inescapable element of paradox that enters into all theological language, and so of the need for a dialectical method which allows for the possibility that every statement made may need to be corrected by a statement of apparently opposite tendency. Even in discussing the nature of man, we were very much aware of the tensions and oppositions. But the element of paradox reaches its highest pitch now that we have come to the doctrine of the God-man. "That God has existed in human form," wrote Kierkegaard, "has been born, grown up and so forth, is surely the paradox *sensu strictissimo*, the absolute paradox." [63]

The paradox cannot be dissolved; it is inherent in the attempt by finite minds to reflect on ultimate issues. But even so we have a duty to reflect as deeply as possible and to show, so far as we can, that the paradox is a dialectical conjunction of opposites and not sheer nonsense or irreconcilable contradiction. So before we leave the subject of the person of Christ, we shall take up three aspects of the God-man paradox where the tensions seem most acute: particularity versus universality, historicity versus pre-existence, adoptionism versus incarnationism.

We begin with the problem of particularity—or, as some might say, the scandal of particularity. Is it conceivable that if God had wished to grant a universal knowledge of himself, the bearer of the revelation could have been a particular man living at a particular time in a particular locality, with all the limitations that such particularity implies? To press the point further, could it have been *this* particular man, this Jesus of Nazareth, about whom we do not even have much in the way of clear historical information? Many who have felt the scandal of particularity in this way have tried to resolve the problem in the same way as Kant and many other idealist philosophers. Acknowledging that a truth must first appear in a concrete instance, they have held that this is accidental, and that we can go on to grasp the truth in its universality, without further regard to the contingent circumstances of its first appearance. Thus the story of the historical incarnation of the Logos in Jesus Christ becomes the general truth of the unity of God and man, and the story itself is regarded as simply an illustration of the general truth, in the same way, let us say, as the story of Adam's fall may be considered a useful myth illustrating the universal fallen condition of mankind.

[63] *Concluding Unscientific Postscript*, pp. 194–195.

But the inadequacy of such a solution has already become apparent to us in our earlier discussion of the historical Jesus. Christianity proclaims not an idealized possibility of existence but the appearance of the ideal in history, not just a Logos but the Logos made flesh. Furthermore, the particular is not narrowly enclosed in its own particularity. We remind ourselves again that Jesus Christ is not understood in isolation but as the center of a whole nexus of events, and such a nexus has an inexhaustibility about it, so that it can become a paradigm for many other situations; but it does so precisely in its concreteness, and not by being turned into a general free-floating truth. The Christ-event has perhaps more claim than any other event or reality of any kind to be considered the "concrete universal" of philosophers. Moreover, it is not clear why the particular happenings inaugurating the Christian vision of the world should be considered merely accidental or contingent. At least, this would be to ignore such New Testament statements as "when the time had fully come, God sent forth his Son." [64] The implication of such a statement is that the Christ-event coincided with a tide in human affairs that gave to that event a universal dimension not evident to the casual observer.

Of course, it might be replied that just this is the trouble—that the particular intellectual climate prevailing at that time, including messianic expectations, ideas of incarnation, mystery religions and so on, gave birth to an interpretation of the life and death of Jesus Christ such as we would never dream of applying to him today. Perhaps there is some epistemological confusion behind such statements, as if it were supposed that somehow there are "plain facts" about Jesus Christ that could be disengaged from the tradition so that we could consider them directly, or that there are universal norms of interpretation (presumably our own!) that are free from the tendentious slants that have conditioned the understanding belonging to other particular historical eras. But leaving aside such confusions, one can agree that first-century categories do not provide an interpretative framework for the twentieth century. But is this not what theology and christology are about? We are trying to interpret today in categories of our own time the Christ who meets us only in the tradition, including the developments that have taken place since New Testament times. Also, we are trying to reach a contemporary interpretation in responsible continuity with the tradition. Although the structuralist interpretation of myth developed by Levi-Strauss and his followers appears

---

[64] Gal. 4:4.

to me to have many questionable features, I believe it has established that among all the relativities of particular tribes and circumstances, there are at work some stable universal structures of the human mind which persist through the many particular stories, and I think this fact is relevant when we consider the changes that have taken place in the Christian understanding of Jesus Christ.

These paragraphs do not pretend to solve the paradox of particularity and universality, but they will serve their purpose if they have shown the need to keep both sides of the paradox in dialectical interplay.

We turn next to another aspect of the christological paradox—the seeming contradiction between pre-existence and historicity. Is it only a seeming contradiction, or are the two ideas quite irreconcilable?

The present desire among theologians to affirm beyond any doubt the true humanity of Jesus Christ and to be rid of the last traces of docetism has led some of them to reject any doctrine of pre-existence. But that is a pretty drastic step to take, for, as John Robinson has pointed out, belief in Christ's pre-existence is "deeply embedded in the New Testament presentation of Christ." [65] All the major christological documents of the New Testament express the belief that Christ is the eternal Son who dwelt "in heaven" with the Father before he came to earth. Yet equally important for the New Testament is a belief in Christ's true humanity; he was born, lived, and died at a definite period, and as against the docetics, the Church firmly held that this historicity of Jesus Christ was no mere appearance or illusion but a genuine segment of events on earth. But does not a belief in pre-existence make nonsense of these claims, so that one would have to say that Christ only *seemed* to be born, he only *looked* like a man, but was really an alien being, having no relevance to the human condition?

It seems hardly adequate to say that Christ pre-existed as the divine Logos, while in his humanity, as Jesus of Nazareth, he was a being of time and history. The inadequacy of such an interpretation of the paradox lies in its separation of the divine and human in Christ, whereas the tradition is that in some sense the whole Christ pre-existed. On the other hand, there is little attraction in the elaborate speculation of Origen that the soul of Jesus (like all rational souls in Platonist philosophy) had existed from the beginning and was joined to the Logos.[66] But would it make sense to say that from the beginning of creation, the Logos has been coming to

65 *The Human Face of God*, p. 144.
66 *De Principiis*, II, 6.

expression in Jesus Christ, so that Christ has been present in creation from the beginning as its aim? He has been prefigured at every stage. This is to take the view that the universe is not only a "vale of soul-making" but has christhood as its goal. Or, alternatively, this is the extension of the idea of sacred history to the whole cosmic process.

These considerations bring us at once to a closely related aspect of the paradox—the opposition between adoptionism and incarnationism as two fundamental types of christology. The terminology is not very satisfactory and there is bound to be a measure of anachronism in the usage, but it is convenient to use the term "adoptionism" for the type of christology which interprets the person of Christ as the raising of a human being to the level of deity, while "incarnationism" means the "descent" of God into a truly human existence.

As John Knox has shown, the New Testament itself witnesses to a progression from adoptionism to incarnationism.[67] But the early preaching about the raising of the crucified Jesus to be Lord and Christ became more and more overshadowed by the fully incarnational theology, so that throughout most of the Church's history incarnationism has had a completely dominant place in the Church's teaching, and adoptionism has been suspect as heresy. It can hardly be denied that the result was a loss of the sense of the true humanity of Christ and the rise of something like an unconscious docetism.

In modern times, there has been a sharp reaction and an attempt to recover the full humanity of Christ. From the teaching of Schleiermacher that Christ is "the one in whom the creation of human nature, which up to this point had existed only in a provisional state, was perfected," [68] down to the present, there has been a steady stream of christological teaching that begins from the human Jesus rather than from the eternal Logos. But now the danger is that the truths of incarnationism may be lost or obscured, and in the last resort it is incarnationism rather than adoptionism that offers the profounder interpretation.

The two views are not finally opposed. Each requires and corrects the other, and either of them in isolation produces distortion. My own approach in this chapter has been frankly the approach from below, from the human Jesus, and it could not be otherwise in a theology which seeks to apply the existential method seriously and consistently. Yet that ap-

[67] *The Humanity and Divinity of Christ*, p. 5ff.
[68] *The Christian Faith*, p. 374.

proach has been made with the understanding that adoptionism, when considered in depth, cannot fail to complete itself in incarnationism, precisely as happened in the New Testament. For how could a man be raised to deity unless God had already descended in humility into him? This is what was meant when it was said above that "from first to last, this is the work of Being"; and these words in turn echo St. Paul: "All this is from God, who through Christ reconciled us to himself." [69]

But although we end with a full doctrine of incarnation, the paradox remains, and the path to that doctrine is an existential and anthropological one. As Pannenberg has remarked, "All christological considerations tend toward the side of the incarnation. It can, however, only constitute the conclusion of christology. If it is put instead at the beginning, all christological concepts are given a mythological tone." [70]

Any study of the person of Christ must remain to some extent artificial until we have gone on to consider his work. Although the incarnation is from first to last a work of God, it implies also the full coworking of this truly human person, Jesus of Nazareth, tempted like other men, yet "obedient unto death, even death on a cross." [71] We must now study more closely this obedient work, by which Christ has opened up for all men a new potentiality for being.

[69] II Cor. 5:18.
[70] *Jesus—God and Man*, p. 279.
[71] Phil. 2:8.

13 | The Work of Christ

54. PRELIMINARY REMARKS ON THE WORK OF CHRIST

Throughout our discussion of the doctrine of the person of Christ, stress was laid on the need to relate this to his work, and at the end of the last chapter we were pointed to a fuller inquiry into the work of Christ. The doctrines of the person of Christ and of the work of Christ are really inseparable, and are simply aspects of the Church's single confession of Christ as Lord and Word. Existentialist theologians like Bultmann and Gogarten who make the confession of Christ's deity a consequence of the experience of his saving work are right in so far as they are protesting against any abstract speculation about the person of Christ; but they are wrong if they permit the question of christology to be entirely swallowed up in that of soteriology. Thus, while we have acknowledged the existential dimension in the doctrine of the person of Christ, we have tried not to evade the ontological question, and it is only after our exploration of this question that we now turn specifically to the doctrine of the work of Christ.

Just as we cannot separate the two doctrines of the person and the work, so, when we turn to the doctrine of Christ's work, we may not separate his life and his death. Already in introducing the theme of the incarnation, we spoke of this in connection with God's reconciling work. Frequently, however, when one speaks of "reconciliation," or still more of "atonement," in Christian theology, there is a tendency to think almost exclusively of Christ's death. The cross does, of course, occupy the central place in the doctrine of the atonement, but the cross cannot be understood apart from the life which it ended. Already in the New Testament we can see the difference of emphasis betwen St. John, with his stress on the incarnation, and St. Paul, with his stress on the atoning death. St. John sets before us the presence of God in the incarnate Word, who can say: "The words that I have spoken to you are spirit and life." [1] St. Paul, on the other hand, preaches Christ as crucified and risen, and as having changed the human situation by his death and resurrection. Some of the early Greek fathers virtually equate incarnation and atonement. In Western theology, however, it is the death that atones, and in St. Anselm's famous theory, it is the death alone that constitutes the "satisfaction." We must try to avoid any separation of the life and death. Our attention will indeed be focused on the death of the cross, but only because this is the finish and culmination of Christ's work. It has its significance only in the context of Christ's life as its climax and summation.

In an earlier section, we outlined some of the outstanding "moments" or "mysteries" in the career of Jesus, as depicted in the gospels. Among these was his passion, but the passion narrative is of such importance in the gospels and is told in such detail that it could be subdivided itself into a series of "moments" or "mysteries" that seemed specially significant to the evangelists. I shall not attempt to analyze these moments of the passion story in even the brief fashion that was attempted in the case of the major moments in the whole story of Christ's life, but I shall mention the more important, and make just a few comments. It will be understood that these "moments" in the passion story are like the others we have considered. Some of them undoubtedly have an historical basis, but they have all been theologically colored and some of them have been elaborated in legendary or mythological directions, or have been adapted to fulfilling supposed messianic prophecies in the Old Testament.

Confining ourselves to the last few hours of Christ's life, we may say that the principal "moments" in the drama of the passion were: the agony in the garden; the betrayal and arrest; the trial and scourging; the crucifixion; the burial; and (although it does not appear in the canonical gospels) there may be added the descent into hell.

For the most part, these incidents in the passion story and the sayings which they contain (such as the "Seven Words from the Cross") present in an intensified form the same aspects of Christ as we found presented in the earlier series of incidents taken from his whole career. Again we are presented with a human figure seen in depth, so that the divine presence and action in him may become perceptible. Perhaps two *motifs* are especially prominent. One is obedience; this comes out strongly in the incident

[1] John 6:63.

of the agony in the garden, which stands at the beginning of the passion drama much as the story of the temptations stands at the beginning of Jesus' public ministry, and these two "moments" have much in common. But of course the note of obedience continues to be struck throughout the remaining scenes of the passion, so that at every point one has the impression that although this is a human drama with human actors, it is also a divine drama in which God is the sole actor. Jesus obediently fulfills the divine will, and is "delivered up according to the definite plan and foreknowledge of God." [2] The other prominent *motif* is that of absolute self-giving, and this, as we have already seen, is how Jesus manifests the essential activity of God on the human level. This second *motif* too runs through all the moments of the passion, and perhaps culminates in that mythical thought of the descent into hell, which is paradoxically also the ascent to God.

Thus, in a manner, the death and passion present us in concentrated and heightened form with the same traits as are exhibited in the whole career of Jesus Christ, as he is depicted in the gospels, and so the death, though the center of his work, is continuous with his life. But how can we think of it as somehow affecting a reconciliation or atonement? For us in the twentieth century, it seems to be just an event of long ago, perhaps interesting and inspiring, but not specifically affecting us. How could we possibly think of it as vitally altering our situation in the world? Did it even make any great difference to the people who were living at the time of the crucifixion? Even if we were disposed to acknowledge that this life can be understood as something like an incarnation or coming together of the divine and the human, is this not just an isolated instance, a sport that history has thrown up and that becomes less and less important as it recedes into the past? At any rate, it is very hard to see how it could be a "saving" event for people today.

It must be said that one is not much helped in answering such questions by the insistence (especially common among Protestant theologians) on the "once-for-all" character of Christ's saving work, and above all of his death on the cross. There is, of course, a "once-for-all" character in any event of history. It happens on a particular datable occasion, and we have agreed that it is important to maintain this link with factual world history when discussing the theological significance of Jesus Christ. But it is not the datable occurrence, the bare "fact" that could have been observed

[2] Acts 2:23.

by anyone there at the time, that is of interest to faith and theology. It is rather this fact as seen in depth, as revelatory and providential event, as the vehicle for God's acting. When the event is understood in this way, it acquires a new dimension that does not indeed take it out of the series of datable happenings but that relates it also to the activity of God, who is at once stable and dynamic. We must recall our earlier discussion about reconciliation and historical revelation, in which we saw that reconciliation is not a separate or later activity of God but is present in all his activity.[3] Lest we be tempted to construct too elaborate a theory of atonement, or to suppose that some particularly complex historical happening was necessary for God to be able to accept men, we should call to mind Christ's own parable of the prodigal who finds the father willing to receive him, though there is no special machinery to make possible a reconciliation, and still less is there any demand that the son should give his assent to a doctrine of atonement.[4] The first step toward salvation is taken when the son becomes aware of the disorder of his own existence, so that, as was indicated earlier, wherever there is awareness of sin, there is no total depravity, for such awareness is not itself sin but a turning from it.[5] But the father, in turn, does not need to be placated; before the son "came to himself," the father was already awaiting and desiring his return; he sees him at a distance, and is already on his way to meet him and bring him home. This parable stresses the unchanging character of God's attitude and work, which is always one of reconciliation. It is necessary indeed that some particular historical event should bring to light in a signal way "the mystery hidden for ages and generations," [6] but no historical event changes God's attitude, or makes him from a wrathful God into a gracious God, or allows his reconciling work to get started—such thoughts are utterly to be rejected.

But how then are we to think of this signal event of Christ's saving work so that we can fully recognize it as the high-water mark of God's providential activity, and yet at the same time acknowledge that this activity has never been wanting and that God's reconciliation is equiprimordial with his creation? The Church has never formulated a doctrine of the atonement with the same precision with which it has tried to define the person of Christ. Instead, we find several explanatory models that

---

[3] See above, p. 269.
[4] Luke 15:11–32.
[5] See above, p. 266.
[6] Col. 1:26.

have developed side by side. Even in the New Testament, a considerable variety of ways of understanding the atoning work of Christ is to be found.[7] Sometimes these have been developed into rival theories, and the history of theology has not been without instances of bitter debate over the "correct" doctrine. But models, after all, are not theories; that is to say, they are not intended to be precise conceptual accounts. Perhaps some models would turn out to be incompatible with one another, but we have also to be open to the possibility that one model may be needed to complement another, and that this complementing may take place in a paradoxical way, since any model has to be both affirmed and denied. I have always admired Cranmer's wisdom when he talks inclusively of the "sacrifice, oblation and satisfaction." [8]

These remarks are not to be taken as implying that we must find room for all the models of the atonement that have been used in Christian theology, or even for all that are found in the New Testament. Here, as elsewhere, some symbols are more adequate than others, while a few symbols that have been used are so inadequate and can be so easily perverted and made misleading that they had better be rejected altogether. One model that, as it seems to me, has usually been developed in such a way that it becomes sub-Christian in its thought of God and its idea of reconciliation, is the notion of substitutionary punishment, the thought that Christ was punished by the Father for the sins of men and in the place of men. It is true that some passages in St. Paul might seem to support such an interpretation of Christ's work, but they can be taken in a different sense, and Taylor, for instance, maintains that "St. Paul does not hold a theory of vicarious punishment." [9] Other scattered passages in the New Testament might lend stronger support, and, of course, the idea of vicarious punishment has had considerable importance in the history of the doctrine of the atonement, especially in Calvinism and fundamentalist evangelicalism. But this view of the atonement, as it has usually been expressed, is an example of the kind of doctrine which, even if it could claim support from the Bible or the history of theology, would still have to be rejected because of the affront which it offers to reason and conscience. I do not wish to deny that there are some points in this particular interpretation of the atonement that have value—for instance, its stress on the costliness of atoning work. Yet I should think that its more valuable insights are con-

[7] Cf. Vincent Taylor, *The Atonement in New Testament Teaching.*
[8] *Book of Common Prayer*, The Order for Holy Communion.
[9] *Op. cit.*, p. 127.

served in related but more adequate models of the atonement, such as the model of sacrifice, of which we shall have more to say.

Many of the traditional models are so deeply involved in the mythology or religious practices of another age that they cannot be accepted as they stand. But they should not be rejected without further consideration, for it is possible that when demythologized they can yield important insights.

The traditional division of views of the atonement into "objective" and "subjective" is unsatisfactory. The objective views were supposed to recognize an atonement outside of man and independent of him. The model might be that of a "sacrifice," or possibly a "satisfaction," offered to the Father by the Son, and winning for the human race forgiveness and a new life. Over against such views, the subjective interpretations concentrated rather on the impression and influence that the life and death of Jesus had exercised upon men, who responded to this manifestation of love by becoming loving themselves. But we have already seen in our consideration of theological language that the assertions of faith are neither objective nor subjective, but combine elements of both objectivity and subjectivity, or, better expressed, transcend the subject-object distinction. What is true of the assertions of faith is true *a fortiori* of the assertions of theology. Thus there could be no satisfactory view of the atonement that was purely objective, any more than there could be an acceptable subjective view.

Objective views of the atonement do not sufficiently stress the existential dimension. Man cannot be saved as, let us say, a burning building can be saved, by an action that is entirely external to him. This would be to make the whole matter subpersonal. Man is saved only in so far as he responds to and appropriates into his existence the saving activity that is directed toward him. So we must criticize any attempt to represent the atonement as a "transaction" that goes on outside of those who are at stake in the matter. This does not mean that the extent of atonement is measurable in terms of explicit and conscious awareness of it. It may be that the atonement is already potentially accomplished for men who have never given the matter a thought, but it is only fulfilled and becomes "atonement" in the full sense as it is consciously appropriated. Still another fault of the objective view is that it tends to be backward-looking—this is connected with undue emphasis on the "once-for-all." So we get the stress laid on what John McLeod Campbell called the "retrospective aspect" of atonement (the mainly negative aspect of a deliverance from sin and punishment) and neglect of what Campbell himself wished to stress—the "prospective aspect" of atonement as a continuing work that has a primarily future and affirmative direction, "referring to the good it bestows." [10]

On the other hand, the subjective view is also open to serious criticism. Even though it is insisted that love is awakened in man only in response to God's love as exhibited in Christ, one has the impression that the "subjective" theories never really get beyond the notion of an *imitatio Christi*. A supreme example of love is given in Christ, and we are to follow it. This takes no account of what we know as the impotence of the human will, nor does it sufficiently recognize the "escalation" of sin in human society and the problem of trying to reverse the prevailing trends. The subjective view, while right in seeing that atonement must be understood in personal terms and so as influencing man's way of life as a result of his own acceptance of reconciliation, misses the dimension of grace that takes the initiative and works in the very being of man, not indeed to take away his responsibility but to enable him to fulfill the demands which he accepts.

So while there are elements of truth in both the objective and subjective views of atonement, we must look for a model that will transcend the distinction, and unite the truth in the apparently conflicting points of view. If we recall the traditional threefold office of Christ as prophet, priest, and king, and if we think of the prophetic office as finding expression chiefly in the subjective view of his work (his moral influence) and the priestly office as finding expression in the objective view (and especially in the sacrificial model), then perhaps it is to his kingly office that we must look for an understanding of his work that will embrace the other two and overcome the division between subjective and objective views on the matter. Christ's kingly office has found expression chiefly in the so-called "classic" view of atonement. This view was in fact the prevailing interpretation of the doctrine of Christ's work for a thousand years, before the split between "objective" and "subjective" views appeared with the divergent theories of St. Anselm and Pierre Abelard. In recent years, this classic view of atonement has been rescued from oblivion and its merits brilliantly vindicated by Gustaf Aulén.[11] It seems to me to offer the most promising basis for a contemporary statement of the work of Christ, and to the consideration of this classic view we shall now turn.

---

[10] *The Nature of the Atonement*, p. 4.
[11] Cf. *Christus Victor*.

55. THE CLASSIC VIEW OF ATONEMENT

To express the matter briefly, the classic view of the atonement sees the work of Christ, finished on the cross, as a victory over all the powers that enslave man, and so a deliverance from them. And perhaps it should be added that this victory is always to be understood as God's victory.

The expression "the work of Christ finished on the cross" has been taken from Aulén, and it is worth quoting his own statement of why this expression is used. "It is intended to indicate the central place which the cross has in Christian faith, and also to emphasize that the cross must be seen in connection with the whole life of Christ. The cross summarizes the totality of his life and work." [12] This statement of Aulén is entirely in agreement with our own remarks in the opening paragraphs of this chapter.

The classic view of atonement is already clearly expressed in the New Testament. There we see the work of Jesus portrayed as a battle against the demons that afflict the life of man. His finished work on the cross is his complete triumph over these demonic, enslaving powers. St. Paul tells us that God "has delivered us from the kingdom of darkness and transferred us to the kingdom of his beloved Son." [13] He has abolished the claim of these dark powers over us: "this he set aside, nailing it to the cross." [14] And he has thus utterly discomfited them, and taken away their power over man: "He disarmed the principalities and powers and made a public example of them, triumphing over them in him." [15] The model of struggle, victory, and triumph comes through clearly, and this model is developed (sometimes by way of fantastic elaborations) in patristic theology. The main outline, however, remains constant. Man has fallen into the grip of dark powers; Christ comes into this situation, and battles against these powers; with his cross comes the overwhelming victory, bringing deliverance and new life to man.

One defect in Aulén's rehabilitation of the classic view of atonement was his failure to come to grips with the mythological background of the principalities and powers. However, our own earlier remarks on sin provide us with a way of demythologizing the classic view of atonement. We agreed that the root sin is idolatry. This is what enslaves man, and estranges him from his true being, from his neighbor, and from God. But we saw also that to worship an idol (or to make an ultimate concern

[12] *The Faith of the Christian Church*, p. 224.
[13] Col. 1:13.
[14] Col. 2:14.
[15] Col. 2:15.

of something that is not ultimate, in the terminology of Paul Tillich) is precisely to give to it a demonic power. A profound truth lies behind the belief of ancient Christians that an idol is not just nothing, but a demon; for the idol, in so far as it has become the focus of a distorted existential concern, reacts by further distorting, enslaving, and finally destroying the being of the person who has given it allegiance. The identification of idols and demons had already taken place back in Old Testament times: "They sacrificed to demons which were no gods, to gods they had never known, to new gods that had come in of late, whom your fathers had never dreaded. You were unmindful of the Rock that begot you, and you forgot the God who gave you birth." [16] This is precisely the forgetting of Being, the exaltation of the beings above Being; an idolatrous worship of the beings which in turn have enslaved us and react upon us with demonic effect. It is surely not being overpessimistic to see this state of affairs as specially characteristic of the technological era, when indeed "new gods have come in of late."

How then does Christ obtain his victory? Here we may recall his temptations, especially the third one, when he rejects making worldly power his ultimate concern, and this is equated with worshipping Satan. The rejection of this temptation runs through his career. He will not enslave himself to any idol, but acknowledges only the Father's authority. This is the *motif* of obedience, which we saw to be central to the passion. But to refuse to idolize any being (whether worldly beings or one's own being or even humanity) is to deprive that being of any possibility of acquiring demonic power. It is to break the dominion of the demons, and to put them to flight. This Christ finally does in giving himself utterly in the passion and death. Here we come to the other *motif* of self-giving, which we also affirmed to be central in the story of the passion. One's own self is the last idol, and to give even oneself unreservedly is indeed to have become like God and to have vanquished the last demon. The death of Christ on the cross is continuous with his life and mission, but it is the signal climax by which his work completes itself. This work is the overcoming of the enslavements, distortions, and alienations to which man falls victim through idolatry—evils so great that he rightly calls them demonic, for they have escalated beyond his control. At the same time, this work is the opening up of a new possibility of existence, an existence oriented toward Being, sustained by the grace of Being, and made capable

---

[16] Deut. 32:17–18.

of self-giving love. In other words, the affirming activity of Being, operative in the whole providential work of God and especially in this culminating providential work of the cross, sustains and establishes the beings in face of the threat of their dissolution into nothing.

The classic view of atonement gathers up in itself the most important elements in both the subjective and objective views, thus transcending them. Although subjective and objective accounts are by themselves inadequate and misleading, they both make useful contributions toward understanding the atonement when they are brought into relation to the classic view and treated as supplementary models.

In so far as the classic view shows us a life of perfect obedience, overcoming every temptation to idolatry and remaining faithful even to the cross, it includes the subjective view. It holds up to us this life as the paradigm of human existence and appeals for the response of a like obedience. It might even be said in some sense to move men to obedience, and perhaps as they meditate on this life, its image gains a hold upon them and influences the character of their existence. But perhaps any great example can do this, and by and large, the subjective side can be only part of the doctrine of atonement. It hardly gets beyond the notion of an *imitatio Christi,* and while this is true so far as it goes, it does not go far enough to meet man's trapped and impotent condition in his fallen society.

But surely the classic view also includes an objective side. The self-giving of Christ is continuous with the self-giving of God, and the whole work of atonement is God's. The model of sacrifice is particularly relevant here. The priestly type of religion in the Old Testament differs from the prophetic type precisely in asserting that something needs to be done *for* man, something that he is powerless to do for himself in response to the demands of God upon him. Even if priestly religion often fell into superstition and deserved the strictures of the prophets, it nevertheless held to a truth which the prophets overlooked. Thus the Epistle to the Hebrews rightly sees the work of Christ as continuous with the old sacrificial worship of Israel. We need not try to work out the details of the analogy or its elements of appropriateness and inappropriateness. Let it be simply said that the self-giving of Christ, understood as the new sacrifice in which priest and victim are one and the same, brings God's constant self-giving for his creation right into the creation. Here that absolute self-giving, which is of the essence of God, has appeared in history in the work of Jesus Christ, and this is a work *on behalf of* man, a work of grace. It not only makes a demand (as an example does) but it lays hold on the human race, empowers a change of direction, brings the dynamic activity of God into the midst of human society. But this objective element is completely safeguarded in the classic view of atonement.

Christ the king, who wins his victory over the enslaving forces, is also Christ the prophet who gives us the "example" [17] of obedience, but still more he is the priest who utterly gives himself as sacrificial victim and thereby brings right into human history the reconciling activity of God in a new and decisive manner.

But even if we allow that a demythologized version of the classic view of atonement can provide us with a way of representing the work of Christ that seems both adequate and intelligible, some stubborn questions still remain. After two thousand years, are the results of this victory particularly apparent? We talked of a "finished work," but in many ways it would seem far from finished, for men are apparently just as much enslaved as ever. Again, while we have talked of Christ's victory as being also both an example and a sacrifice, and have tried in this way to relate it to the life of mankind in general, all this still remains obscure. The notion of a mere example is quite unsatisfactory, but have we really got beyond this by introducing the model of sacrifice? Clearly, we had no intention of thinking of the sacrifice as a kind of propitiation of the Father—this would take us back into the already rejected ideas of an "objective transaction" between Father and Son. The notion of sacrifice, however, was needed to stress the costliness of atonement, and that this cost is paid by God who holds the initiative throughout. But although this allows us to talk of something being done on behalf of man, it is still not clear how this happens. We must look for answers to some of these questions.

56. THE ATONEMENT AS TURNING-POINT

Mention was made above of John McLeod Campbell's stress on the prospective view of the atonement as an event still going on and still moving toward a fulfillment, rather than as merely a "once-for-all" event of the past. This was only part of his attempt to break out the impersonal legalistic categories of so much traditional teaching about the atonement toward a more personal or existential understanding of the whole matter.

At the heart of his teaching was his attempt to give "depth of meaning to the expression 'a sacrifice for sin' " or to interpret the sacrifice as "a

---

[17] Cf. *Book of Common Prayer*, Collect for Palm Sunday.

moral and spiritual expiation." Attention is shifted from the actual physical death and suffering of Jesus to their inward significance. Campbell found this significance in "a perfect repentance for all the sin of man, a perfect sorrow, a perfect contrition." [18]

Such a perfect repentance and sorrow can be understood as a turning— a turning in and for mankind away from sin and alienation into unity with God. This, of course, is continuous with the whole career of Jesus, but it reaches its climax in the passion, which brings a new and painful awareness of the depth of sin in human life but brings also that ultimate self-giving of Jesus, and we have seen that this can be understood as the consummation of his unity with the Father.

When we think in this way, then we direct our attention not so much to the death on the cross as to the agony in the garden as the clue to the meaning of the passion. For this is the moment of fundamental decision, like the temptations at the beginning of Jesus' career. It is also the moment of extreme anguish, when he was "greatly distressed and troubled" and told his disciples, "My soul is very sorrowful, even to death." [19] Whatever might happen after this time of agony, as the drama moved toward the moment of death, would depend increasingly on factors like physical stamina. But in this moment of inward anguish lies the "moral and spiritual expiation," when, in the context of sin and against the pull of sin, Jesus makes his act of submission and self-giving. Christians think of the cross and passion of Christ as the great turning-point of history, and this is justified because in Christ there was this decisive turning to the Father. There had emerged a new righteousness that had proved stronger than sin, and this leads us back for a moment to the classic view of the atonement as struggle and victory, and links that way of understanding it with the idea of costly and painful sacrifice.

In these paragraphs we have seen how the understanding of atonement as victory over the powers of evil can be deepened and filled out by attending to the sacrifice model, with its emphasis on the price paid for the victory. But we have tried to do this in a way that is thoroughly personal and avoids any quasi-legal or quasi-magical understandings of sacrifice, propitiation, satisfaction, and the like. We have, I think, remained true to the parable of the prodigal son who repents and is received by the father without the need for any elaborate machinery of reconciliation. Further,

---

[18] *The Nature of the Atonement*, p. 137.
[19] Mark 14:33-34.

by seeing the atonement as a turning-point rather than an event complete and finished in itself, we are allowing for its continuing significance.

Of course, neither Campbell's teaching on the atonement nor the way I have developed it is free from problems. How can one man sorrow or repent for the sins of others? How can he represent them in a matter of deep personal responsibility? These questions will call for further study, but we can remind ourselves here that sin has its corporate dimension and that everyone should repent of those corporate sins, even if he is not himself directly and personally responsible for them. So it is not fanciful to think of Christ sorrowing and repenting over the sins of the race. On the other side, as we have said so often, Christ himself is to be understood not just as the individual Jesus of Nazareth but already as the beginning of a new community into which individuals are constantly being "incorporated."

A more serious objection, perhaps, comes from New Testament critics who would challenge any attempt to speak of the personal or inner life of Jesus and who would tell us that we cannot know how he understood his own passion and death. It is interesting to recall that the first great skeptical critic of modern times, Samuel Reimarus, made precisely the point that the New Testament interpretation of the death of Jesus is false. According to him, Jesus went up to Jerusalem not to die, but to launch an armed revolt against the Romans. When this failed, he died a disappointed and disillusioned man, as witness the cry of dereliction from the cross.[20]

Reimarus' thesis cannot stand, nor any of the variations on it by more recent writers. It contradicts everything we know of Jesus' teaching, and is contradicted in turn by the behavior of Jesus' first disciples who were not revolutionaries or nationalists but, on the contrary, renounced violence and sought to break down ethnic barriers. Nevertheless, Reimarus' exaggerated thesis points to a more moderate criticism of the traditional belief concerning Jesus' understanding of his death. That traditional belief, found already in the gospels, shows him as foreseeing in detail his passion, crucifixion, and resurrection. There can be little doubt that the evangelists have read back into the events their later understanding of them as all happening according to the plan of God. But what was all clear in retrospect would not be at all clear in prospect. There would be something unreal about Jesus if we thought of him acting out, as it were,

[20] *Fragments*, p. 145ff.

a part according to a script already written. This would contradict what we have learned already about his vocation—indeed, it would contradict his genuine humanity. It may be that Jesus went up to Jerusalem hoping that things would turn out very differently from the way they did. But there must have come that moment when he finally realized that faithfulness to his vocation meant death, and when he accepted that, and it is that moment that is represented to us in the mystery of the agony in the garden. Like the other mysteries, this one is partly recollection, partly interpretation, and both of these strands constitute its theological significance and truth.

But now we must pursue further the questions of how Christ's atoning work and victory over evil can be appropriated today and how they can extend to the multitudes of human beings.

57. THE ATONEMENT AND ITS APPLICATION

There is a sense in which one could say that the remainder of this book will be devoted to answering the questions raised at the end of the preceding section, for in our discussion of the Christian life, of the last things, and of the working out of Christian faith in the ordered life of the Church, we shall be trying to set forth in all these areas the significance and relevance of God's presence and work in Christ. But for the present, we shall indicate briefly how one might answer the two major points posed in the questions—how the victory and the reconciliation which it is said to have accomplished are relevant two thousand years after the event; and how the work of Christ is extended to the wider life of mankind in general.

The first question, the one about the extension of Christ's work in time, is answered by pointing to the paradoxical character that belongs to any great creative event in history. In one sense, it is an event that happened at a given time in the past (it is, in this sense, "once-for-all"). Yet in another sense, the more the event is genuinely creative, the more it is an event that is continually being made present again, so that it happens, not literally or factually, but none the less truly over and over again in the experiences of those who have made it part of their history. Some events in history open up new possibilities of existence; but these possibilities remain open only so long as these events are genuinely appropriated by those who come after, and the primordial expansion of the existential horizons takes place again. Such events are called by Nietzsche "monumental," by Heidegger "authentic repeatable possibilities," by Bultmann, with an eye especially to the work of Christ, "eschatological." They are events in which some signal disclosure of existence or Being has taken place, and which continue to be re-presented in such a way that the disclosure still takes place, and likewise the commitment associated with it. To believe in the cross of Christ, that is to say, to accept it as a saving or atoning work, is well described by Bultmann as "to make the cross of Christ our own." [21] This means to relive the cross in our own experience in the sense of following Christ in his rejection of idolatry and his obedience to the demand for self-giving. Incidentally, it may be noted that Bultmann's usual ways of talking about the work of Christ place him very much in the tradition of the classic view of atonement, mediated, no doubt, through Luther.

The thought of the cross as eschatological event, at once past and present and capable of becoming present again and again, helps us to understand how the work of Christ is not tied to the moment of its occurrence in world history, but is as continuous as that reconciling work of God which it expresses. Our earlier remarks on history had, of course, prepared the way for this. But we must not exaggerate the extent to which this idea of the eschatological or authentic, repeatable event can help. We still seem to be left with something like an *imitatio Christi*.

Here I think we must say that the eschatological event, in so far as it is a disclosure of Being, has a revelatory and gracious character, in the sense that it is an event in which Being itself acts. The difficult problem of how to reconcile the initiative of God (Being) in salvation with the responsibility of man will occupy us further in the next chapter. But for the present, let us recognize in the work of Christ (both the "once-for-all" event and its "representations") the work also of the Holy Spirit as unitive Being, so that the event is an event of grace, working in those whom it addresses and making possible their response of faith.

The way in which the event gets extended in time shows also the way in which we must look for the victory and liberation in our time. We must not be misled by the mythological language of a triumph over the principalities and powers, as if some objectively existing demons had been destroyed by Christ two thousand years ago, so that they would never trouble man again. If the demonic is simply the escalated evil that springs from idolatry, then man is continually threatened by the demonic,

[21] *Kerygma and Myth*, p. 36.

and the victory must be won over and over again, precisely by "making Christ's cross our own." Jesus himself is reported to have talked of the need for the disciple to take up the cross.[22] Empowered by the unitive Being of the Holy Spirit operating through the revelatory event of the cross, the disciple commits himself in faith, that is to say, rejects the temptations of idolatry and gives himself in love.

We have still to deal with the other main question—how the work of Christ is extended to the mass of mankind. It is perhaps fair to claim that this question has been partly answered in the answering of the question about extension in time, for we have shown how the victory of Christ is repeated in the lives of the disciples. But in our answer to the first question, we followed Bultmann pretty closely, and it can hardly be denied that his account suffers from being too individualistic. We have seen in an earlier discussion of sin that this is more than individual disobedience or disorientation, and has a social character; in the same way, reconciliation must aim at the human race as a whole, and at the overcoming of sin in its communal dimensions. When we talked of the sinlessness of Christ, we agreed that this must not be interpreted in a way that would separate him from the rest of mankind, for this would destroy the possibility of his being a true mediator. But interpreting sinlessness in an affirmative way, we claimed that it could be understood as an overcoming and reversing of the tendency toward sin that operates in human society. While this victory was won by the single person, Jesus Christ, his final obedience was precisely the utter giving up of himself. This was the founding of the Christian community, though just as we have thought of the incarnation and the work of Christ as a process rather than an instantaneous happening, so we may think of the coming into being of the community as also a process, and even as a simultaneous process. This new community which itself began with the incarnation and with Christ's victory over the powers of sin and evil is the ever-expanding center in which Christ's reconciling work continues.

We have said that reconciliation aims at the human race as a whole. It is as wide as creation, and potentially all men are embraced within its outreach. This may not mean that all men must explicitly accept the particular symbols of the Christian revelation. We have already made clear our conviction that other faiths too have a revelation that comes from the one God, and that can be therefore only a revelation that likewise leads to

---

[22] Mark 8:34.

reconciliation. "In the early Christian centuries," writes R. C. Zaehner, "the catholic Church rejoiced to build into herself whatever in paganism she found compatible with and adaptable to the revelation of which she deemed herself to be the depository." [23] Perhaps it is even more necessary that we should be prepared to do this in the contemporary world. Without in any way taking away from the historical and eschatological work of Christ, we can recognize its continuity and kinship with that universal reconciling work of God in all creation, a work that has as its goal the gathering of all creaturely beings into a commonwealth of love.

Thus the work of Christ, finished on the cross, while in one sense a "once-for-all" event of history, is at the same time an event for all times, an eschatological event that continues in the community of faith. It focuses and spearheads the universal reconciling work of God, a work that is inseparable from his creating on the one hand, and from his consummating on the other.

---

[23] *Christianity and Other Religions,* p. 8.

14 | The Holy Spirit and Salvation

58. THE PERSON OF THE HOLY SPIRIT

We must now turn our thoughts to the Holy Spirit, the third person of the triune God. In the account of the descent of the Spirit on the nascent Church, we read of the sound "like the rush of a mighty wind" and of "tongues as of fire" resting on each of the disciples.[1] The images of wind and fire are evocative of the nature of the Spirit. In the ancient world wind and fire were two of the most subtle and elusive elements—free, spontaneous, unpredictable, yet powerful and universal in their effects. For a beginning, then, we can say that the Spirit is God present and active in the midst of the creation. This is a dynamic presence of God, who has come forth into the creation and is at work in it.

The use of the words "come forth" is significant. At a much earlier stage in this book, we took note of the presence of "spirit" in man and suggested that this means much the same as "existence" in the distinctive sense in which that word is used of man, to denote his capacity to go out from himself in freedom, creativity, love and so on.[2] The word that we use about the relation of the Holy Spirit to the triune God is that he "proceeds." The Spirit is God coming forth into the creation to indwell it and to build it up. In discussing creation, we did note the activity of the Spirit, both his brooding upon the primordial waters and his incessant striving and sighing in the movement of creation toward its consummation. The Spirit's role seems to be not so much *creatio ex nihilo* as the

---

[1] Acts 2:2–3.
[2] See above, p. 62.

328

drawing out of the potentialities of creation at all levels. For this reason therefore we have called the Spirit "unitive Being," for the Spirit that has proceeded into the creation labors there to build it up into a harmonious whole, at one in itself and with God.

How does the Spirit differ from the Logos? Some theologians have argued that there is no difference, and that we need distinguish only two aspects of the divine Being: the outgoing aspect (Spirit or Logos) and the inner being of God (the Father). But apart from the fact that this view could lead to a dangerous dualism, it does not take sufficient cognizance of the distinction between Logos and Spirit. The Logos is "logical" in the sense that it brings understanding, clarity, definition. The Spirit is more of a striving than a Logos, proceeding from the numinous depths of God and working on the will and emotions of man. To some extent, we can agree with John V. Taylor's remark: "There is more of Dionysus than Apollo in the Holy Spirit." [3]

But at this point we have to be very much on guard against dividing the substance of the Trinity. The Spirit is not God without the Logos, nor the Logos without the Spirit, nor both without the Father. As will be shown later, the Holy Spirit, though distinct from the Logos, has to be understood in the closest association with Jesus Christ. Likewise the highest workings of the Spirit in human life are to be seen not in bizarre forms of ecstasy but in personal and ethical qualities which can be considered truly "ecstatic" in so far as they draw human beings out of themselves and their narrow self-interest.

One further point may be made here about the person of the Holy Spirit. It is the Spirit that most clearly introduces a feminine element into the Christian understanding of God. It is often said that this understanding of God is too exclusively masculine, and there may be some substance in the charge since the Old Testament understanding of God was forged in the midst of the struggle against the Canaanite fertility cults. But if the image of God needed both man and woman for its representation,[4] this implies that already in divine Being there must be, though in an eminent way beyond what we can conceive, whatever is affirmative in sexuality and sociality, in masculinity and femininity. The Spirit, brooding on the

---

[3] *The Go-Between God*, p. 50.
[4] This point is not invalidated by the fact that God became incarnate in a male person, for every person has both masculine and feminine characteristics, and furthermore Jesus of Nazareth is intelligible as the Christ only as the source and center of a new *social* reality.

waters, travailing in the creation, building unity and wholeness, most clearly suggests the feminine principle, though in other respects, the Spirit is masculine. God transcends the distinction of sex, but he does this not by sheer exclusion, but by prefiguring whatever is of value in sexuality on an altogether higher level.

59. THE PROCESSION OF THE HOLY SPIRIT

We have noted the intimate connection between the Holy Spirit and the idea of procession. The connection is already established in the New Testament, where Jesus is represented as saying: "But when the Counselor comes, whom I shall send to you from the Father, even the Spirit of truth, who proceeds from the Father, he will bear witness to me." [5] In this verse, the Spirit is said to proceed from the Father, though he is also said to be sent by the Son. The interpretation of his procession in relation to the other persons of the divine Triunity has led to one of the most stubborn doctrinal divisions in the history of the Christian Church. The Eastern Church, following the original version of the Niceno-Constantinopolitan Creed, believes in the procession of the Holy Spirit from the Father alone. In the Western Church, first in Spain in the sixth century and not at Rome itself until the eleventh century, the words "and from the Son" (*Filioque*) were inserted into the creed, and most Western theologians have argued that the Holy Spirit proceeds from the Father and the Son.

Is this one of those disputes that collapses into a mere quibbling over words when it is analyzed? It is not so simple as that. There are real and important issues at stake. But it is certainly one of those theological disputes in which there seems to be an element of truth on both sides, and each side in some ways corrects the other. Historically, of course, it was doubtless wrong for the West to act unilaterally in making an addition to a universally accepted creed composed by an ecumenical council. Belief that the Holy Spirit proceeds from the Father and the Son is not an article that should be made *de fide* in the Church. It is, however, a theological opinion which there are good reasons for holding.

The great merit of the Western view is that it compels us always to think of the Spirit in the closest relation to the Son; and it could be argued that in several passages of the New Testament there seems to be no clear

[5] John 15:26.

distinction between the Holy Spirit and the Spirit of Jesus or even the risen Christ.

The advantage of refusing to think of the Spirit apart from the Son is fourfold.

1. It gives definite content to our understanding of the Spirit. The idea of the Holy Spirit can easily become very vague, so that people then give to it whatever content they please. But Christians think of Jesus Christ as the one on whom the Spirit descended in fullness, so that the life of the Spirit is manifested in Christ.

2. This in turn ensures that the Spirit is understood primarily in a personal way. Sometimes the Spirit, symbolized as wind or fire, has been represented as an impersonal force invading human lives. But if the Spirit is most fully manifested in Jesus Christ, then we look for his action in the realm of the personal and ethical.

3. Next, we are provided with a criterion for discerning or testing the spirits—something that it has been necessary to do since New Testament times. Not everyone who claims to be inspired or spirit-filled has the Holy Spirit. Some forms of spiritual enthusiasm have an almost demonic character. In the church at Corinth, according to St. Paul, there were members who in their spiritual frenzy shouted, "Jesus be accursed!" [6] and in that church generally there seemed to be a preference for lower spiritual gifts over higher ones, and this is already a form of idolatry and therefore a slide toward the demonic. The test must be whether any alleged spiritual gifts build up the kind of life manifested in Jesus Christ as the bearer of the Spirit.

4. Finally, the Western view guards against any separation of Spirit and Logos. If one is determined to think of the Spirit and Jesus together, then at the human level there should be less danger of a merely emotional or ecstatic spiritualism, cut off from the guidance of the understanding, though equally there should be no arid intellectualism without emotional color or the commitment of the will.

But when all this has been said, one must also recognize that there are arguments on the other side. Here are some points that may be brought forward in favor of the view that the Holy Spirit proceeds from the Father alone.

1. The Eastern view makes it clear that the activity of the Spirit is as wide as the creation. Just as the Holy Spirit was active in the ages before

[6] I Cor. 12:3.

the incarnation, so today he may be active outside of the specifically Christian community and tradition, and we have to be open to perceive his activity anywhere and at any time. This is part of the Spirit's freedom and spontaneity.

2. It is sometimes argued that if one confesses that the Spirit proceeds from both the Father and the Son, then one is introducing two ultimate principles of reality and so falling into a dualism.

3. It is argued too that the Western view subordinates the Spirit to the Son, and that in practice this has led to a general neglect of the Spirit in the West.

I believe that the West has the stronger case, and in particular I find the second and third arguments for the Eastern view unconvincing. Perhaps a compromise expression, such as "from the Father through the Son," would resolve the difficulties; or perhaps it is better just to let the two views stand in a dialectical relation. The relevance of this ancient controversy will become more apparent in the next section on the work of the Spirit.

60. THE WORK OF THE HOLY SPIRIT

In describing the triune God of Christian faith, we spoke of the Holy Spirit as unitive Being. This already indicates how the work of the Spirit is to be conceived. It is the work of maintaining unity and, where need be, renewing it, throughout the whole extent of Being and beings. Thus the work of the Spirit is simply another aspect of the reconciling work of God, and so another aspect of the work of Christ. This work of Christ, as we have seen, has both an objective and a subjective side. Objectively, it is an event in world history, but more than that, it is an event of God's providential and revelatory acting. It is only fully able to effect its reconciling intention, however, when it has been seen "in depth" as an event of God's providence, and been subjectively accepted as such. It is this perceiving in depth, this apprehension of the divine presence and activity in the observable happenings, that we attribute to the work of the Holy Spirit. To most people in the first century, Jesus, if they had heard of him, was just an innovator or revolutionary who had paid the appropriate penalty. To the disciples, he was the Christ of God. But this was not something observable like the color of his eyes. So when St. Peter confesses him to be the Christ, Jesus says to him that "flesh and blood has not revealed this to you." [7] This is a revelatory experience, and if we recall what

[7] Matt. 16:17.

was said about revelation in an earlier part of this work,[8] it is a way of knowing in which, so to speak, that which is known seizes hold of us and makes itself known to us, or, in the language that Heidegger uses in connection with primordial thinking, this is the occurrence of Being in us.

It is true that revelation involves God in all his aspects, primordial, expressive, and unitive, but our apprehension of the revelation we rightly associate in a special way with the work of the Holy Spirit (unitive Being). Perhaps most people think of the Holy Spirit as the most shadowy member of the divine Trinity, but this should not be so. If we remember that the Spirit *is* God, in one of the modes or movements of holy Being, and not some mysterious entity other than God, then we also understand that he is God at his closest to us. He is Being as immanent in our creaturely being, and it is through him that we can hear the voice of Being addressed to us from beyond ourselves, whether it comes to us through the particular being of Jesus Christ, or through some other particular being.

The Spirit is associated especially with truth. He is the "Spirit of truth" who "will guide you into all the truth." [9] Such truth is not, of course, merely an intellectual comprehension. It is the unhiddenness (ἀλήθεια) of existence and Being, their laying bare through the very communication of Being in us and to us. In the Christian revelation, this means the perceiving of Christ in the depth of his being, as the very focus of holy Being.

The Holy Spirit then is God's coming to man in an inward way to enlighten and strengthen him; it is the awakening in man of the realization of his kinship with Being, an awakening brought about by Being itself that is already immanent in man. When we say that the work of the Spirit is "to enlighten and strengthen," we have in mind his typical activities of revelation and grace. Of revelation, the opening of our eyes to Being in and through the beings, we have already said a good deal. Of grace also, much has been said already, but the time has come to ask more fully about it. If we do think of the grace of Being as somehow inwardly sustaining us, does this not take away our freedom and responsibility? If so, does it not destroy the whole conception of existence from which our theological exposition set out at the beginning?

It is true that the action of the Holy Spirit has sometimes been conceived in ways that would almost reduce men to the level of puppets and that would be totally incompatible with any theology that tried to work with existential and personal categories—perhaps totally incompatible with

8 See above, pp. 84–103.
9 John 16:13.

the Christian faith itself, if this presupposes that man exists responsibly. In the Old Testament, the Holy Spirit, or Spirit of God, gave special powers to men, such as the ability to interpret dreams [10] or to prophesy.[11] Even in the New Testament, the Spirit might be supposed to "possess" a man and cause him, let us say, to speak ecstatically "with tongues." This is a sub-personal mode of operation, in which man is simply manipulated. We did indeed take note of the possibility that the Spirit may somehow operate upon lower levels of creaturely being.[12] But this could not be enlightening for the manner in which the Spirit might operate upon man, who is himself "spirit," that is to say, an existent who stands in the openness of possibility and responsibility.

However, although the New Testament retains vestiges of the idea that the Spirit is some quasi-magical force that operates subpersonally and irresistibly, the new conception of the Spirit arising out of the new revelation in Christ departs from the idea that his work is chiefly to be seen in occult happenings like interpreting dreams, predicting the future, or speaking with tongues, and looks for that work instead in the highest qualities of personal being. When St. Paul discusses "spiritual gifts," he does indeed still recognize the more ecstatic *charismata*, but the "higher gifts" are personal, and the most excellent is love.[13] These higher gifts, moreover, are not restricted to exceptional individuals, but are characteristic of the whole community of faith. Elsewhere he contrasts with "the works of the flesh" (immorality, impurity, licentiousness, idolatry, sorcery, enmity, strife, jealousy, anger, selfishness, dissension, party spirit, envy, drunkenness, carousing, and the like), "the fruit of the Spirit," and this fruit is summed up in the entirely personal qualities of love, joy, peace, patience, kindness, goodness, faithfulness, gentleness, self-control.[14]

Now, it is beyond dispute that the qualities mentioned above have value only in so far as there is some measure of freedom and spontaneity in their exercise. A robot cannot love. It might indeed be so constructed as to go through the motions of virtuous conduct, but this would be a mere caricature of what we mean by the words "kindness," "goodness," "gentleness," and the like. It would be harder to judge the case of a person who had been conditioned by, let us say, drugs, or psychological techniques, into al-

---

[10] Gen. 41:38.
[11] Num. 24:2.
[12] See above, pp. 201, 221.
[13] I Cor. 12:31.
[14] Gal. 5:19–23.

ways behaving with gentleness. Even so, we would perhaps think of him as scarcely a person, if his behavior was entirely determined by external factors. We must then try to conceive of the action of the Holy Spirit in such a way that while indeed we recognize his initiative, we do not destroy that measure of freedom and responsibility that is indispensable to the conception of personal existence in man. If we fail to do this, then Christianity offers not the salvation (making whole) of human existence, but really an escape from existence, whereby we shed its responsibility and become marionettes, to be arbitrarily and externally operated by this mysterious Spirit of God.

These remarks bring us to consider the traditional opposition between Augustinianism and Pelagianism. The Augustinian view tends to lay the entire stress on the grace of the Holy Spirit, operating in man, as the sole source of the Christian life and whatever good qualities it may exhibit. Undoubtedly St. Augustine was right in upholding against Pelagius the divine initiative in salvation and the need for our wills to be assisted. This whole matter of the divine initiative is something that has been stressed throughout this book, beginning from our consideration of the nature of revelation. But St. Augustine went too far in elevating a datum of Christian experience into rigid views about predestination, irresistible grace, indefectible perseverance, and the like. Such views are incompatible with a genuinely personal being in man, and Pelagianism had at least this grain of truth, that it insisted on an element of freedom and responsibility in man, for without these man would no longer exist, but would have declined to the level of being of an animal, or a thing.

The openness of man's being, as existence, is such that the paradox of grace is possible and conceivable. On the one hand, Being is immanent in man, so that he lives in the light of Being, and his very thought and action can be the occurrence of Being in him. We have seen that revelation, like the "essential" or "primordial" thinking of which Heidegger speaks, can be regarded in this way; and the saints speak of the love for God as not just their response to God's love for them, but somehow as the very movement of God's Spirit within them, God being on both sides. On the other hand, Being has entrusted itself to man and made him its guardian. We have talked of the "risk" of creation, and also of the wonder of a creation that would be not just a mechanism but a commonwealth of free spirits united in love. This makes sense only if man has a measure of freedom and is not overwhelmed by compulsive forces, whether "total depravity" on one side, or "irresistible grace" on the other. Creation would lose its value if there were not free decision or commitment on the part of man, even if it is God that makes this decision possible for him by putting it within his grasp; and creation would likewise lose its value unless we could attach genuine meaning to the notion of the "risk" of creation and to the "co-operation" of the creatures with God.

So we must try to steer a middle way between an extreme Augustinianism (or Calvinism) and Pelagianism, though without necessarily embracing any of the historical forms of so-called "semi-Pelagianism," or "synergism." On the one hand, we must firmly hold to the divine initiative in the work of man's salvation, and to the active operation of the Holy Spirit in this. Yet we have also to safeguard the freedom with which man makes the gift of salvation his own, or, to put it otherwise, makes a commitment of faith. The concept of "existence" together with the notion of Being at once transcendent of and immanent in all particular beings enables us to have some understanding of how man can live by a grace that he recognizes as coming from God, and yet in this experience can be most fully himself. It is the paradox of which St. Paul speaks when he bids us: "Work out your own salvation with fear and trembling; for God is at work in you, both to will and to work for his good pleasure." [15]

Salvation, or the making whole, of man involves the polarity of the individual and communal aspects of all existing. Too much stress on decision and commitment tends to overemphasize individual salvation, and to lose sight of the fact that there can be no genuine salvation for an individual apart from the community of faith. The very notion of a self-giving implies going out from the individual existence. In the New Testament we hear of the "fellowship" of the Spirit, or "participation" in the Spirit (κοινωνία πνεύματος).[16] So the community of faith is also a community of the Spirit, who works in and through it and gives to it its unity. The community becomes the agency by which the Spirit works in the world and by which it continues the work of reconciliation begun by Christ, or rather, raised to a new level in Christ. Thus, just as the Spirit descended upon Christ at his baptism, so also the Spirit is represented as descending upon the Church on the feast of Pentecost. As the Spirit was active, as unitive Being, in the incarnation, or coming together, of God and man in the person of Christ, so it continues this same work of unification in the community of faith.

A fuller exposition of the nature of this community and the work of

---

[15] Phil. 2:12–13.
[16] II Cor. 13:14; Phil. 2:1.

the Spirit in it can come only when we have considered the doctrines of the Church and of the last things (God's consummating work). However, it is perhaps unnecessary to say that we do not think of the work of the Spirit or of grace as confined to the Church. Just as we have insisted all along that revelation is not confined to the particular occasion of revelation on which the Christian faith is founded, and that reconciliation is as wide as creation, so it must now be insisted that "the Spirit blows where it wills" [17] and is not confined to any group of mankind, or to any particular "channels of grace." This is not in any way to depreciate the particular community of faith in which the Christian finds the work of the Spirit centered, or the particular ways, such as the sacraments, in which its work is realized, and full value will be given to these in due course. But it would be foolish not to recognize a wider operation of the Spirit, which is indeed evidenced by the appearance of the "fruit of the Spirit" outside of the official community of faith. Sometimes, indeed, this working of the Spirit outside of the community is like a judgment upon the community itself, just as we remember that the Israelites saw God's providential activity outside of their own community, and experienced it as his judgment. For judgment and grace are like the obverse and reverse sides of the same act.

But here we are concerned with the work of the Holy Spirit within the community of Christian faith, and with the manner in which the reconciling work of Christ is applied by the Spirit within this community. We shall try to see this as both a gift and a task—a gift in so far as it is a work of grace and the initiative remains with God; a task in so far as man must cooperate with the Spirit of God and appropriate the gifts offered to him.

61. ENTRY INTO THE CHRISTIAN LIFE

We have now to consider how the work of Christ effects wholeness or salvation in human life. Salvation is a process that goes on in time, both a process in the human race as a whole, and in the individual life. In the present section, we shall be thinking especially of the beginning of this process, that is to say, of entry into the Christian life. This entry may be itself an extended process, and probably it is so with most individuals who grow up in the Christian community and gradually become more and more identified with it. For others, it may be almost an instantaneous con-

[17] John 3:8.

version experience, a sudden passage from one way of life to another. Yet even in such cases it is probably true that more gradual processes of change have been going on, perhaps at subconscious levels.

The process of entry is, on the one hand, experienced as being drawn into the life of faith, or perhaps even being seized by it. The work of Christ acts upon the person concerned, and this is what we have already recognized as the element of grace, the divine initiative of God in Christ and of God in his Spirit, opening our eyes to the significance of Christ. On the other hand, the process of entry is also experienced as something that the believer himself does, as an act of commitment performed by his whole being. In the following analysis, we shall try to see how both of these elements, the divine initiative and man's cooperation, work together, though sometimes this may come through more clearly than at other times. We are leaving aside for the present the consideration of such outward and visible acts as baptism, and considering simply the experience of the Christian as he appropriates the work of Christ. We shall describe four stages in the process of entry, though it may well be that these four are not successive but are distinguishable aspects in a unitary experience.

1. The first stage, or moment, is *conviction* of sin, which has long been recognized as a work of the Holy Spirit. This is the third time in the course of this book that we have mentioned the awareness of sin.[18] On the first occasion, we took note of what might be called the "natural" awareness of sin, a variable but almost universal awareness of the disorder of human existence, and we have seen that this very awareness, which is not itself sin, is a sufficient refutation of any doctrine of total depravity. Next, in connection with the doctrine of creation, we had occasion to consider sin again, and in the light of this doctrine and what it shows us of the potentialities of our human existence, a deeper understanding of sin and of its threat was attained. But now sin is to be seen in its full dimension, when the Spirit convicts us of sin in the light of what is revealed in the person and work of Christ.

A. C. Garnett makes the claim that the death of Christ, understood together with his life, is not just an example for imitation: "its real dynamic in the spiritual life of the world comes from its power to *convict the world of sin.*"[19] The point should not be exaggerated, but there is a genuine insight here. An act of grace, we have seen, is at the same time an act of judgment. The work of Christ is a saving work that lights up and

---

[18] See above, pp. 68–73, 259–267.
[19] *A Realistic Philosophy of Religion*, p. 317.

indeed brings to us Being, christhood, and selfhood; but inevitably at the same time it reveals how far away we are from these, and indeed how we reject them, as Christ was rejected. In making unhidden the disclosure of existence and Being in Christ, the Holy Spirit makes unhidden the extent and depth of human sinfulness in a way that goes beyond any previous awareness that we may have had of it. What began as an uneasiness in face of the disorder of human existence has been deepened and intensified to the point where, in the presence of Christ, the sinner must say of his sins that "the burden of them is intolerable." [20]

This analysis of what we mean by "conviction of sin" affords a useful illustration of how the work of the Spirit does not violate but cooperates with the tendencies that belong to human existence. Man's natural awareness of sin is heightened and intensified by the Spirit so that it is "noticed" in a new way and understood in greater depth; but it is certainly not imposed upon man from outside. Or again, man's conscience, his critical self-awareness, is sharpened and made more perceptive, so that he becomes aware in a new way of the distance that separates his actual existence from the fulfilling of his potentialities in true selfhood; but this is no violation of his being, but the raising of it to a higher level. Grace does not abolish our freedom and the basic constitution of our being, for that would really be to abolish us as men; rather, in the famous teaching of St. Thomas, grace perfects nature. There are other elements of the Christian life in which it will not be so easy to show the coming together of the work of the Spirit and the tendencies that already belong to our existence, as it has been in the case of conviction of sin, but in principle these two sides are always there, and the divine initiative does not abolish the human side.

2. Next among the "moments" of entry into the Christian life we consider *repentance*. The call to repentance appears at the beginning of every phase of the biblical message. According to Martin Buber, who points out that the Hebrew word corresponding to "repentance" meant concretely a "turning of the whole person," the call to turn is "the primary word of the prophets of Israel." [21] According to St. Matthew's Gospel, "Repent, for the kingdom of heaven is at hand," was the message of St. John the Baptist, and precisely the same words are attributed to Jesus at the beginning of his ministry.[22] The first preaching of the apostles is said to have been: "Repent, and be baptized." [23]

[20] *Book of Common Prayer*, Order of Holy Communion.
[21] *Two Types of Faith*, pp. 26–27.
[22] Matt. 3:2; 4:17.
[23] Acts 2:38.

Repentance is already implied in conviction of sin, for to be aware of sin is to be dissatisfied with oneself, and so to be already seeking to turn away from where one actually is. But let it again be said that it is only for convenience of exposition that one can distinguish "stages" of entry into the Christian life, and that these are really all so intertwined as to be inseparable. Conviction of sin by itself might lead to despair rather than to repentance, were it not that the very revelation that convinces of sin also offers promise of reconciliation—that grace and judgment belong equiprimordially to the same event. Likewise the "turning away" of repentance, which is a turning away from sin and thus from idols, is at the same time a "turning toward," a turning toward God, or Being, who had been forgotten in preoccupation with the beings. On the side of human existence, this means a turning from egocentricity, which tries to hoard up and make secure one's own individual being, in the direction of an existence that is more "like to God," that is to say, an existence that becomes creative by pouring out and conferring its own being and so achieving the highest kind of selfhood.

Two further points may be briefly made about repentance. The first is that it keeps happening throughout the Christian life, reminding us that this life cannot itself be turned into a secure possession—if this happens, it has been distorted into a new idolatry—but that it must continually be renewed, and never achieves completion so long as we live under the conditions of earthly life. The second point is that in repentance, it might seem that what man does is primary, and indeed there could be no true repentance, or turning, unless this were one's very own act. But here once more we must not try to isolate this "moment" from the whole experience in which it is involved. Repentance relates on the one hand to conviction of sin, and in this, as already noted, the Spirit has quickened our perception both of sin and of the possibility of reconciliation; while on the other hand, the man who turns in repentance believes that even this, though his own act, is made possible for him by God's initiative, as we shall see when we consider the next moment.

3. This next moment is *election*, though perhaps this technical theological term has had its day, and we would be better advised to speak simply of "choosing," for the doctrine of election simply tries to express what is implied in Jesus' words to his disciples: "You did not choose me, but I chose you." [24] The doctrine of election is one of the strongest expressions of the divine initiative in the process of salvation.

[24] John 15:16.

Unfortunately, this doctrine more than any other has been perverted in such a way as to deprive man of any responsibility or, for that matter, of any genuine humanity. This happens when the experience of being called or chosen, the experience of being seized by the reconciling work of Christ through the Spirit, gets objectified into a theory of predestination, such as we find in Calvin. There the fact that many men may hear the Christian message of reconciliation but only some of them respond, or that of those who do respond only some remain constant, or that in some sense "many are called but few are chosen," [25] is interpreted in terms of a double activity of God: he chooses some and rejects others, and already in advance he has predestined each individual to one or other of the two groups—to the elect who have been marked out for salvation, or to the reprobate whose destiny is damnation. This fantastic exaggeration of the divine initiative into a fatalism is repugnant not merely because it dehumanizes man but also because it presents us with a God who is not worthy to be worshipped, and certainly a very different God from the one about whom we have been thinking. This is not the God whose essence is to let-be, to confer being; and not the God who reveals himself in the person and work of Christ.

The distortion that occurs in predestinationism shows us what happens when the existential dimension of theology becomes obscured. But if we hold fast to this existential dimension, then the doctrine of election has its proper place. Through the revelation in Christ, man knows himself to be chosen, and chosen to be. He is called out of nothing into existence, out of disordered existence into a reconciled existence, eventually called to have his being in God. God's calling and choosing, we shall maintain, are for all men. The notion of reprobation or rejection does not refer to anything that God does, but is simply a hypothetical idea which provides, as it were, the foil to the experience of election and heightens the sense of being chosen. For only one who believes himself chosen to be, so that his being has been conferred upon him, can think of the possibility that it might have been otherwise, that our world might have been different, that Being might not have been holy and worshipful, that chaos and nullity might prevail instead of the creating, reconciling, and consummating activity of a God who lets-be and establishes the beings in ever fuller being. Reprobation is simply the imagined possibility of the opposite experience to that which men actually have. If the idea has any value at all, it can only be that it heightens man's gratitude to God for choosing him to be,

[25] Matt. 22:14.

and encourages his resolve to make his full response from the human side to the divine election and so give his necessary cooperation toward the building up of that free commonwealth of love which is being unfolded in creation.

4. Next we come to *justification*. The terminology here is even more archaic than the talk about election, but some mention of justification has to be made if only because of the important role which the idea has played in the history of Christian theology and especially because it was the major theological issue in Luther's controversy with the Catholic teaching of his time. Even so, the whole notion of justification has been vastly exaggerated in the attention that has been paid to it. It is one element in the Christian experience of reconciliation, but this particular explanatory model of justification, borrowed originally from the lawcourts, is neither indispensable nor specially illuminating. Particularly when the doctrine is taken too literally and attempts are made to work it out in detail as "imputed righteousness" and the like, it becomes merely confusing and misleading, and also involves us in untenable theories about the atonement.

What is trying to find expression in the doctrine of justification is the experience of being accepted by Being, of emerging from lostness and alienation into a right relation with Being. Thus another model used to describe what happens is that of forgiveness, which takes place when a cause of estrangement between two persons is overcome through the initiative of one of them, and a good relation restored. Justification, in the sense of acceptance by Being and coming into a right relation to Being, is already implied in election. Whatever terminology we employ, something like justification is a matter of concern to every human existent. With some, there may be a feeling of guilt and sinfulness that looks for forgiveness and a new beginning; with others, there may be the sense of frustration and what is called "meaninglessness," with the accompanying need to have a place in the scheme of things—a place that may be very small, but is nevertheless one's own and that somehow matters. To be "chosen" or "called" and also "justified" by Being is to have the assurance that one counts for something in the world.

The Protestant insistence on justification by grace through faith alone is meant to stress that this is entirely a work of God. We are "justified freely by his grace," or "justified by faith apart from works of law," and our "righteousness" (worth) is not our own but the "righteousness of God" which he has conferred on us through the work of Christ.[26] So far

---

[26] Rom. 8:30; 3:24-25, 28.

as the Protestant insistence on "justification by faith alone" is meant to acknowledge that man cannot of himself escape from sin and set his existence in order, and that this can come about only through the initiative of divine grace, and so far even as the doctrine was a protest against certain abuses in the medieval penitential system, then we can go along with it. But unfortunately the "*sola fide*" has often been exaggerated, and we have to guard against some of the errors to which it has led.

The principal danger is that justification gets separated from actual growth in righteousness or in the Christian virtues, the process traditionally known by another archaic term, "sanctification." Justification gets thought of as something external, a so-called "forensic" justification, a kind of acquittal or "declaring just" that takes no account of the actual condition of the person so acquitted. When the doctrine of justification by faith is taken to such extremes, it needs to be corrected. It must happen *in* man as well as *for* him, and to this extent it is also a "making just," since in restoring a right relationship with God, it sets man on the way to a right ordering of his own existence. It must be not only backward-looking, having regard to what God has done, but even more forward-looking as opening up the new life of grace that has been made possible. In brief, if justification is to take place on a level not lower than that of personal existence, it must, like all the other moments we have considered, have in it an element of free human cooperation which, while indeed subordinate to the divine action, is nevertheless indispensable. If we bear this in mind and avoid extreme formulations, then we may well find, as Hans Küng has sought to show, that the gulf between Catholic and Protestant views of justification is not unbridgeable. He remarks: "Protestants speak of a declaration of justice and Catholics of a making just. But Protestants speak of a declaring just which includes a making just; and Catholics of a making just which supposes a declaring just. Is it not time to stop arguing about imaginary differences?" [27]

62. GROWTH IN THE CHRISTIAN LIFE

From the question of entry into the Christian life, we proceed to that of growth and progress in it; or, in the traditional language, from justification to sanctification. Again, however, we are not to think of a sharp separation, but rather only of distinguishable aspects of a unitary process. Also, we are still to think in terms of a work that is initiated and carried through

[27] *Justification*, p. 221.

by God working in human lives, and yet a work which needs man's response, cooperation, and highest effort if it is to go forward. It is a life in the Spirit, dependent on the gifts of the Spirit, and so on the divine grace. It is also called a life "in Christ," and this expression too points to the divine grace, for it is as if the pattern of existence manifested in Christ has seized the disciple and is molding his existence; this is not an external "imitation" of Christ but rather, in Bonhoeffer's language, a "conformation" of the Christian to Christ. Yet while the giftlike character of this life must always be stressed, it is also a life that makes demands and requires a genuine "synergism," or coworking, between the supporting grace of God and the free human commitments which that grace can perfect and bring to achievement.

When talking of entry into the Christian life, it was said that this is not to be thought of as something that is done once for all, and specifically it was mentioned that repentance will be a recurring phenomenon of the Christian life. If this is so, can we properly speak of a growth or progress in this life? Surely we can, for although it would be presumptuous (as well as being contrary to what we know of human existence) to suppose that the Christian life could ever be a secure possession, and although the commitment of faith needs to be renewed continually in new situations, nevertheless this is accompanied by a deepening understanding of what faith involves and a fuller commitment to it. This in turn means growth in unified selfhood. While indeed faith can never be "proved" without ceasing to be faith, it nevertheless provides its own confirmation in so far as the life of faith, as it goes along, becomes steadily more unified and effective, and the faith on which it is based is found illuminating for the grappling with and overcoming of an ever wider range of problems. There is always the possibility that faith may break down under an intolerable strain, or that a man may come to a situation which so utterly contradicts his faith that he has to abandon it—for again faith would cease to be faith if it were not in some sense "falsifiable." But there was this much truth in the traditional doctrine of a "perseverance of the saints" that if indeed divine grace is working in the Christian life, so that this life is supported and carried forward by the whole universal action of God in creation, reconciliation, and consummation, then typically there will be progress in this life. It will never, under the conditions of our historical existence, attain its goal or be fully conformed to Christ; but it should approach this asymptotically, as it were.

The structure of the Christian life can be expounded in various ways.

As a life in the Spirit, it could be set forth in terms of the gifts of the Spirit or the fruits of the Spirit as described by St. Paul, or in terms of the traditional "seven gifts" of the Church's teaching.[28] As a life in Christ, it is being conformed to the pattern which we have already considered in some detail, in the chapters on the person and work of Christ.

The present exposition, however, will be in terms of the three characteristics which St. Paul, after his discussion of the gifts of the Spirit, names as central to the Christian life—faith, hope, and love.[29] These are sometimes called the "theological virtues" as distinct from the natural virtues of classical moral philosophy. They are not "virtues" in the ordinary sense, but rather the opening up of a new dimension in man's "natural" quest for virtue and the "good life," whereby the aspirations that belong to him in the very potentialities of his being are caught up and perfected by divine grace.

Concerning the first of the three characteristics, *faith*, a good deal has already been said in the course of this book. We have seen that it can be described in terms of commitment and acceptance, and that while on the one hand we can think of it—and must think of it—as man's responsible decision, it is made possible, and so granted, by the gracious approach and self-disclosure of Being.[30] But our descriptions up till now have been formal; they have attempted to describe the structure of any attitude of faith whatsoever, or at least, of any attitude of religious faith. Just as our conception of sin was heightened and made concrete when we reconsidered it in the light of the specific revelation in Jesus Christ, so our conception of faith must be brought into a more definite relation to the content of the Christian revelation. To make faith specific in this way is not to make an exclusive claim for Christianity as the sole guardian of faith, for we have already insisted on many occasions that there is continuity between Christian faith and the other great religious faiths of mankind. But it has been made clear that this does not imply that the various faiths are to be diluted down to what is common to each of them. If an arrogant exclusiveness is to be deplored, just as bad, or even worse, is the vague kind of "faith for faith's sake" that has no definite content because it tries to embrace everything. This is a particular danger in pluralistic societies and in some forms of the ecumenical movement, where

---

[28] See the present author's "The Seven Gifts of the Holy Ghost" in *Studies in Christian Existentialism*, p. 247ff.

[29] I Cor. 13:13.

[30] See above, p. 80.

every distinct content of faith gets leveled down and religious faith itself is threatened with being swallowed up in a creeping humanism.

The central content of Christian faith is the event of Jesus Christ—the incarnation, cross, and resurrection. The life of faith is constantly oriented to these happenings, which faith brings into the present as possibilities for our existence here and now. These events empower faith, since they are the way by which the divine grace reaches us; but faith in turn appropriates the events by the decision to live in accordance with them and to conform the existence of the believer to the pattern of dying and rising made present and manifested in Christ. It is in virtue of its content that Christian faith may be seen either to have affinity with some other particular faith, or perhaps be seen in opposition to it. If, for instance, one could call the devotion of a fanatical Nazi a "faith," then this would be a faith incompatible with Christian faith, and also, we may add, both with man's "natural" aspirations toward faith and with the faiths of the great historical world religions. As has been suggested earlier, the sorting out of "true faith" from its counterfeits would seem to be a pragmatic one. True faith does in fact lead to selfhood, to community, to making more and more sense of life in the world; while an inadequate or illusory faith eventually proves itself—if not in the individual, then in the community—to be sterile and even self-destructive.

Faith in Jesus Christ has, in the preceding paragraph, been paradoxically described in terms of both grace and decision, and this is the familiar paradox of the divine and human action meeting together in the personal dimensions of the Christian life. This life is on the one hand obedience, which is an essential constituent of faith. It conforms the believer to Christ's own obedience. His own will is offered to God, so that the divine grace may work in and through him. Yet on the other hand this very obedience is freedom. It is freedom from the tyranny of things, if these have been idolized, and it is freedom likewise from the frustration and meaninglessness of a life impotent in the face of guilt. The strange paradox is that the man who asserts his freedom and autonomy loses it through his self-idolatry; while the man who lives in obedience and dependence toward God is set free from the very things that are most oppressive and distorting, and becomes most responsibly his true self. God's service is found to be perfect freedom. "Whoever would save his life shall lose it; and whoever loses his life for my sake and the gospel's will save it." [31]

---

[31] Mark 8:35.

In these remarks about Christian faith, I have stressed the point that was made in the earlier and more general discussion of faith—that it is always something much wider than belief, for it belongs to the whole range of existence. Thus we have spoken of it in terms of commitment, acceptance, decision, obedience, grace, freedom. Yet we should not lose sight of the fact that faith does have its cognitive aspect, and includes belief. A reasonable faith is not a blind leap, but a step taken in the light of all the thought and consideration that we can bring to bear on it. Here again we meet the paradox of the gift that is at the same time a task. The knowledge of God in Christ is the gift of his revelation; but we have to think out what is involved in this as best we can. Every disciple has a duty to clarify and work out the content of his faith as best he can. The community as a whole has a duty to do this, and this work of the community of faith, as we have seen, is theology. All the ramifications of belief will not be clear at the moment of commitment to the life of faith. This is true not only of the individual but of the community of faith which, throughout its history, is always advancing into deeper understanding of the content of its faith (though admittedly it may sometimes be falling back). Such advance is, on the other hand, the work of the Holy Spirit leading into truth; but on the other hand, it demands an unfaltering effort of thought as the community seeks to express and interpret, and, more than that, to grasp more adequately its classic faith in changing historical and cultural contexts.

Next after faith, St. Paul mentions *hope*. The Christian hope is not to be confused with the optimism that characterizes some eras of history, when human power and knowledge are expanding and it seems that man can build for himself a secure and prosperous future. Christianity ought to welcome the progress of the sciences, though it has sometimes through fear impeded them. It ought to strive also for the channeling of new knowledge and powers into ways that can benefit mankind as a whole. But Christianity is too realistic to be carried away by a facile optimism that sees in the expansion of knowledge and technological development the salvation of the human race and the solution of its problems. Human fallibility and sinfulness are not so easily overcome.

Thus the Christian hope is in God's activity and presence in the world. Again this hope, as Christian, is specific—it is based on the presence and activity of God in Christ, seen as the focus and culmination of a presence and activity that extend throughout the created world. The God who confers, sustains, and perfects the being of the creatures, and who has signally demonstrated his work in Christ and his cross, is the ground of Christian hope. He is the ground even for any optimism in human achievement, for only as such achievement is guided and promoted by divine grace can it in the long run be brought to good effect. Hence Christian hope is a dynamic.

The Christian hope is eschatological, in the sense that it looks forward to the consummation of the divine work in creation and reconciliation. But this does not mean that it is otherworldly, still less that it is escapist. What may reasonably be hoped for will become clearer in the next chapter, when we shall consider the last things. But even at this stage let us clearly understand that the Christian hope has to do with where we are now, in the midst of this world; and that its eschatological consummation really does depend on how we cooperate now with God's work, for this cooperation is not a matter of indifference but something on which God counts, so to speak, in taking the risk of creation and in laying the being that he pours out open to the threat of dissolution into nothing. So while we rightly emphasize God and his work as the ground of Christian hope, we have to recognize here as everywhere else in the Christian life the need for man's obedient response.

Greatest among the theological "virtues" is *love*. This is most excellent of the Spirit's gifts and the culminating quality of the Christian life. It is indeed the culminating quality of human existence, for we have seen in our consideration of the person of Jesus Christ that it was his manifestation of absolute love that constitutes his God-manhood; for one in whom love has become absolute is carried to the very uppermost limits of the unfolding of human potentialities, so that he becomes one with God and the miracle of incarnation takes place.

This is so because love, in its ontological sense, is letting-be. Love usually gets defined in terms of union, or the drive toward union, but such a definition is too egocentric. Love does indeed lead to community, but to aim primarily at uniting the other person to oneself, or oneself to him, is not the secret of love and may even be destructive of genuine community.[32] Love is letting-be, not of course in the sense of standing off from someone or something, but in the positive and active sense of enabling-to-be. When we talk of "letting-be," we are to understand both parts of this hyphenated expression in a strong sense—"letting" as "empowering," and

---

[32] Cf. Bonhoeffer's criticism of Schleiermacher's definition of love, *Sanctorum Communio*, p. 123.

"be" as enjoying the maximal range of being that is open to the particular being concerned. Most typically, "letting-be" means helping a person into the full realization of his potentialities for being; and the greatest love will be costly, since it will be accomplished by the spending of one's own being.

Love is letting-be even where this may demand the loosening of the bonds that bind the beloved person to oneself; this might well be the most costly of demands, and it is in the light of this kind of love that a drive toward union may seem egocentric. The parent, for instance, really loves the child by letting the child come into his potentialities for independent being, not by keeping him close. It may well be that the more adult relationship establishes a deeper community of being between the two, but it is not impossible to visualize a case where really to love a person might mean that one has to renounce the treasured contact and association with that person, if only so that person can realize what there is in him to be.

The Christian religion affirms that "God is love" [33] and this is so because love is letting-be, and we have seen that the very essence of God as Being is to let-be, to confer, sustain, and perfect the being of the creatures. Christ is the God-man because he is the human existent who manifests an absolute love and so is the one in whom creaturely being converges with Being that creates. The Christian, so far as his life is being conformed to Christ, manifests the letting-be of love, and so is adopted into sonship and brought into a closer relation to God.

We have been talking of an agapastic love rather than of the kind which is called *eros*. This ἀγάπη which we designate "letting-be" and which consists in a self-spending is, above all, the love of God toward his creation, and so the love of Christ and derivatively the love of Christians— though again let it be understood that no exclusive claim is being made here. This agapastic love is usually contrasted with ἔρως, and in so far as ἔρως retains any self-centeredness, the contrast is justified. But according to the account that has been given in this book, we can assert that these two apparently contrasted forms of love are not ultimately opposed, for the one passes into the other, and again we have an instance of the so-called "natural" becoming perfected, or perhaps transformed, by grace. For "erotic" love (the adjective has, in modern use, been all too arbitrarily narrowed to the sexual passion) manifests itself at its highest in the quest of the creature for God. We have seen, in studying the doctrine of crea-

[33] I John 4:8.

tion, that all created beings have a tendency to be like God, and that as we ascend the scale of beings, we come to those which, in a certain degree, are like God in being creative and in their power to let-be. So the longing to be like God (ἔρως) contains in itself the seed of ἀγάπη, for in so far as the longing is fulfilled (not indeed by our effort, but by divine grace) the love that longs is transformed into the love that lets-be. As this happens, we understand that it is the same love on both sides—the love of God toward us that lets us be, and the love of God operating in us by the Holy Spirit and directing us to God, who in turn empowers us to share in his own letting-be. As this divine love works in men, every natural affection and relationship is worked upon and transformed by it. As Kierkegaard saw, God "becomes the third party in every relationship of love." [34] This implies that we see the beloved person "in depth," that is to say, in relation to Being or God, and not just as another being. There is not, as Nicolai Hartmann thought, a kind of competition between our love for God and our love for some fellow human being. On the contrary, it is when God too is loved in and through the other human person that love is purged from self-centeredness and becomes the love that "seeks not her own." [35]

So the life that begins with conviction of sin, repentance, election, justification, passes into the progressive work of sanctification, in which the Holy Spirit more and more conforms this life to Christ, deepening and extending it in faith, hope, and love. What then is to be the end of this life, and indeed of the whole creation in which such a manner of life has been brought forth? With this question, we pass to the theme of eschatology.

[34] *Works of Love*, p. 124.
[35] I Cor. 13:5.

15 | The Last Things

63. THE ESCHATOLOGICAL PERSPECTIVE

Since around 1900, and especially as the result of the researches of such New Testament scholars as Johannes Weiss and Albert Schweitzer, it has come to be accepted that the teaching of the New Testament is to be understood against the background of eschatology. In Bultmann's words, "it has become more and more clear that the eschatological expectation and hope are the core of the New Testament preaching throughout." [1] Thus whereas nineteenth-century liberals thought of the kingdom of God as a moral ideal after which men must aspire and which will be progressively realized, twentieth-century scholars tell us that for Jesus and the first disciples, the kingdom of God was to break in suddenly, not as a result of moral advance but by the supernatural intervention of God.

Of course, the expression "eschatology" can be understood in many different ways. Some scholars see the beginnings of biblical eschatology in the expectation of an ideal ruler of Israel. Some of the early prophets entertained such an expectation, for instance, Isaiah, who visualized a descendant of the house of David on whom "the Spirit of the Lord shall rest." [2] Whether such expectations should properly be called "eschatological" is a matter of definition. They do not seem to visualize any sharp break with the existing order, but speak of an ideal state of affairs within history, when there will be justice, peace, good government, and prosperity. On the other hand, this ideal is not just a secular one. The ideal is to be realized not through human achievements (as in modern humanism) or through an immanent principle of history (as in the Marxist dialectic) but through the "Spirit of the Lord."

[1] *Jesus Christ and Mythology*, p. 13.
[2] Isa. 11:2.

In later Judaism, as is well known, these expectations took a different turn. In the apocalyptic literature, the hope is not for an ideal within history, but rather for one that lies beyond history and is discontinuous with the present world order. Its inaugurator would be no human descendant of the house of David but the supernatural "Son of Man," and what he would inaugurate would be nothing less than a new age, or a new world, to replace the existing order.

It is this second and more strongly supernaturalistic type of eschatology that was dominant when the New Testament was written and which gets taken over in its pages. Admittedly most of the New Testament writers avoid the more lurid details of Jewish apocalyptic, but the basic ideas are all represented. There is to be a sudden end to the age by a supernatural intervention, expected by some of these writers in their own lifetime;[3] the Son of Man will come in glory; there will be a judgment at which all must give account; the faithful will pass to their reward in heaven; and the wicked will receive their punishment in hell.

These ideas are so thoroughly mythological and so foreign to our modern ways of thinking that we can understand something of the fright that seized the old liberal theologians when Weiss and Schweitzer discredited their subjective interpretations of the New Testament and told them that we must come to terms with eschatology. Obviously, if the eschatological ideas are so deeply pervasive of the New Testament, there can be no adequate interpretation that fails to take due note of them. But how can we make sense of such ideas today? We cannot take them as they stand, for they are tied up with a mythological mentality that we do not and indeed cannot share. We might perhaps visualize an end to the world, but this would be a "natural" end in accordance with our understanding of the world as a self-regulating entity, and would have nothing to do with the traditional eschatological notion of a supernatural irruption.

Actually, eschatology became a problem requiring interpretation at a very early stage of the Christian community's history. The world did not come to an end as expected. Already in a late New Testament writing we hear the kind of questions that were being asked: "Where is the promise of his coming? For ever since the fathers fell asleep, all things have continued as they were from the beginning of creation."[4] The New Testament itself, and particularly the Fourth Gospel, also a relatively late

[3] Cf. Mark 9:1; I Thess. 4:15.
[4] II Pet. 3:4.

document, begins to reinterpret eschatology in the light of the primitive community's disappointed expectations.[5]

But before we look at this question of interpretation, let us note a further distinction that has to be made in understanding the expression "eschatology." We can think of it in terms of the *individual*. For him, the "last things" relate to death and whatever may come after death. From prehistoric times, it would seem, the final destiny of the individual has been a matter of religious concern, and certainly it has had an important place in the great historical religions. This question of man's final destiny is, of course, a part of the whole question of human existence, and this, as we have seen, is the question from which the search for religious illumination takes its rise. As against this narrow concern with individual destiny, the expression "eschatology" may—and usually does—have a wider concern in view. But here it seems that a further distinction has to be made. The wider concern may be about the final destiny of a *community*, and presumably the early biblical eschatology was primarily concerned about the destiny of Israel. Or the wider concern may have in view nothing less than the whole *cosmos*. What is to be the final destiny of our world and of its inhabitants? When expressed in this way, the eschatological question appears as the counterpart to the question of creation.

The distinctions drawn here between individual, communal, and cosmic eschatologies have to be borne in mind as well as the earlier distinctions between historical and suprahistorical eschatologies. So we have a very complicated frame of reference to keep before us as we return to the question of the interpretation of the New Testament teaching about the last things.

One possible interpretation would be to push the expected eschatological happenings to a *remote and indefinite future*. The coming of the Son of Man in glory, the judgment, the establishment of the kingdom—these things did not happen at once, as the first disciples had expected, so the first move toward a reappraisal might well be to suppose that it was all going to take longer. St. Paul himself seems to have moved from the expectation of an almost imminent end to the belief that the end would be delayed until Israel too had been saved.[5] The traditional eschatology of the Church has been of the deferred futuristic type. Some time in the indefinite future, the promised events will take place. This doctrine has been

---

[5] Cf. the teaching of I Thessalonians with that of Romans.

eked out by the belief that a kind of interim judgment is passed on each individual soul at death.

But this whole attempt at interpretation is unsatisfactory. It still moves in the mythological ideas of the original eschatology, and the whole notion of a divine intervention and the false kind of supernaturalism which it implies is not made any the less inconceivable by being quietly deferred to the never-never of the distant future. Furthermore, such a procedure robs eschatology of its existential significance, which was precisely the sense of urgency and responsibility that it brought into an existence conceived as existence in the face of the end. Eschatology has been existentially neutralized when the end gets removed to the distant future. Still a further objection is that the whole matter has been made quite otherworldly. It is perhaps a fair question whether Jewish apocalyptic and also some forms of belief in immortality were not simply escape-mechanisms by which one could flee into fantasy from an actual situation that had become too depressing to bear. Certainly, much of the traditional Christian eschatology, whether conceived as the cosmic drama of the indefinite future or as the future bliss of the individual after death, has rightly deserved the censures of Marxists and Freudians who have seen in it the flight from the realities of present existence.

An alternative interpretation is in terms of a *realized* eschatology. The promised events have already happened. Appeal is made especially to St. John's Gospel, where the believer already "has eternal life" and has "passed from death to life"; where the "judgment of this world" is now; and where, according to some scholars, the coming of the Holy Spirit, or the "other Counselor," is to be understood as the return of Christ.[6] This realized eschatology certainly restores the existential dimension of the belief, and this happens above all when, as in Bultmann, the New Testament eschatology is understood as not only realized but individualized. For every individual does live eschatologically when he knows himself to be living in the face of his own death; he works out his judgment by his daily deeds and decisions; and so far as he attains an authentic existence, he is laying hold of "eternal life."

This kind of interpretation is certainly an advance on the futuristic type, and it has good support in some parts of the New Testament. But it is defective precisely because it gains most plausibility from being individualized, thus leaving out the whole cosmic and communal dimensions of

---

[6] John 5:24, 12:31, 14:16.

New Testament teaching. As far as the cosmos as a whole is concerned, or even the human race, the eschatological expectations are far from being realized. There can be no doubt that the New Testament writers themselves intended much more than what is left when demythologizing has treated their eschatology as realized and individualized. Thus, while St. John's Gospel does indeed abandon a purely future eschatology and brings the eschatological ideas into the here and now of our existence, commentators are generally agreed that the future reference has not been entirely relinquished.[7] In the Synoptic Gospels one likewise meets the paradox of the kingdom that is about to come, and yet has already been inaugurated and so is present.

As with so many other theological questions, this one about the meaning of the last things is not to be answered by a simple decision between the competing theories, in this case of a futuristic and a realized eschatology. A satisfactory answer—that is to say, an answer that can meet the problem of eschatology in all the various dimensions and on all the various levels brought out in the earlier part of this discussion—must somehow combine the insights of both the realized and the futuristic interpretations. This is simply to urge that we must once again seek an existential-ontological interpretation; for it is realized eschatology that best expresses the existential significance of the last things, but it is in the more difficult mythological images of futuristic eschatology that we are to seek out the ontological significance.

The outlines of an interpretation of the last things have already appeared in some of the earlier chapters of this systematic theology. It has been insisted that we are not to think of creating, reconciling, and consummating as three successive actions of God, but rather as three distinguishable but inseparable aspects of the one great action of holy Being, which is at once dynamic and stable. We have seen that the doctrine of creation need not be taken to imply that the world had a beginning in time.[8] Similarly, an eschatological doctrine does not necessarily imply an end of the world in time. Theologically, the doctrine of creation was understood as meaning that man and the world are dependent upon holy Being, and this creaturely status is compatible with the possibility that there always has been a world. In a parallel way, the doctrine of eschatology means theologically that man and the world are destined for holy

---

[7] Cf., e.g., C. K. Barrett, *The Gospel according to St. John*, p. 179.
[8] See above, p. 216.

Being and will find their completion and fulfillment in God, but this is quite compatible with the possibility that the world may continue to endure forever. Indeed, if we are to think of Being as not only stable but dynamic (and we must think of it in this way if it is to be taken as holy Being and thus as God), then it is hard to see how there ever could be an end to the world; for then God (Being) would have retired into undifferentiated Being as a kind of motionless uncarved block, and it is only Being that pours itself out through expressive Being that can claim adoration and allegiance, and that can rightly be named "God." An end in time, in the sense of a stopping, would be a kind of death, even if something like a perfection had been achieved. So just as we have thought of creation and reconciliation as continuous ongoing activities of holy Being, so we must try to conceive consummation as likewise continuous.

It may be asked, however, whether science permits us to do so. The principle of entropy, which points to the running down of energy systems, has sometimes been taken to mean that the whole cosmos will eventually grind to a standstill. There has always been doubt as to whether one may legitimately apply the principle to the universe as a whole, and with recent theories of "continuous creation," the idea of a "death of the universe" seems to have become less probable. The theological implications of such a view have been variously interpreted. Let me say frankly, however, that if it were shown that the universe is indeed headed for an all-enveloping death, then this might seem to constitute a state of affairs so wasteful and negative that it might be held to falsify Christian faith and abolish Christian hope.

Still, it is always very difficult to specify just what would finally falsify a whole belief system, such as the Christian faith. While I do think that the loss and waste involved in a "death of the universe" would raise a major question mark, it may be that at this point I am not sufficiently recognizing the transcendence of God in relation to the creation or that I am not sufficiently reckoning with the possibilities of transformation, for these, after all, must go far beyond what we can understand. So we must note that an alternative view is possible, and it has been well stated by John Knox: "If the worst should come, God's being does not depend on man's fate on this planet. We know that, either late or soon, eventually this fate is death, as surely as death is the earthly fate of every man. But our faith and hope in God are not confined within this 'bourne of time and place.' Not merely from generation to generation, but from everlasting to everlasting, he is God; and in ways beyond our understanding and in worlds beyond our imagining, he will fulfill the loving purpose of his creative work." [9] These words are certainly speculative, but in a universe of such mystery as ours, they are not empty and are a reasonable corollary of the central doctrines of the Christian faith.

In thinking of a continuous consummation, Christian hope seeks a way of remaining consistent with the thought of God's continuous work in creation and reconciliation, and also of combining the insight of both futuristic and realized accounts of the last things. Only a consummating work that is coextensive with the work of creation and reconciliation can interpret the paradox of an eschatology that has already happened and that nevertheless, as it points to what has happened and is happening, holds before us the hope of what is yet to happen.

Perhaps we could say that eschatology is the element that introduces perspective into the Christian theological picture. We have already seen that death supplies the perspective in an individual existence, and makes possible something like a unified selfhood. In the same manner, it is the doctrine of an end that organizes the Christian understanding of the world, and which, together with the doctrines of creation and reconciliation, brings hope and meaning into the picture. The God who creates (holy Being that lets-be) is also the destiny toward which all created things are drawn—a destiny not of death, but of new creativity and letting-be. Just as, if we pursued the converging lines of a perspective toward their vanishing point on the horizon, we would find that they did not meet but that new vistas had opened out, so it may well be that we would never find any final point in time, and that the end would always be greater and more comprehensive than we had imagined. But this whole question of the end, whether for the individual, the community, or the cosmos, must be further elucidated as we try to see them in the eschatological perspective of the Christian faith.

64. COSMIC AND INDIVIDUAL DESTINIES

As the title of this section announces, we are about to embark on a more metaphysical and speculative flight than we have so far permitted ourselves in this book. Strictly speaking, we cannot *know* the ultimate destinies of the world or of man, and indeed we have stressed that this very lack of prevision is an essential element in man's finitude. The Bible itself

[9] *Never Far from Home*, p. 170.

encourages a measure of agnosticism in these matters. St. Paul declares that what God has prepared "no eye has seen, nor ear heard, nor the heart of man conceived" [10]; and St. John declares that "it does not yet appear what we shall be." [11] Of course, both of them are thinking of the God who has revealed his love in Christ, so that their words represent, as I have said, only a measure of agnosticism. They serve as a warning against any too detailed speculation, but both St. Paul and St. John believed that this ultimate destiny would be entirely in accordance with what they had learned of God in Christ. We have already spoken of the Christian *hope*, which is to be set over against the fact that our finitude precludes our knowing. Surely, however, it is permissible within limits to try to spell out this hope, if only to show that it is, like other items in the Christian faith, reasonable, in the sense that we can conceive its possibility without having to contradict other well-established beliefs that we may have about our world or about human existence.

Actually, while I said that we are going to embark on a more speculative flight, this will be closely related to the ideas of Being and existence that have been developed in the earlier part of this book. The speculation consists mainly in drawing an analogy between Being and the particular kind of being that belongs to man. We have seen that although Being is incomparable, since it is not some other being, it nevertheless has affinity to the beings in so far as it is present and manifest in the beings and lets them be. Moreover, in the hierarchy of beings, man stands highest as having most affinity to God. The analogy that we have in mind is indeed nothing other than the traditional *analogia entis*. But can we expound this more fully?

We have seen that what constitutes existence is temporality, the stretching of existence through the dimensions of past, present, and future; and moreover, what constitutes selfhood is the bringing into a unity of these three dimensions of temporality, as the existent draws them into one through acceptance of the remembered past, commitment to an overarching possibility of the future, and openness in the present to both of these. Is it possible then to suppose some analogous structure in Being? It has been repeatedly said that we cannot think of holy Being apart from a dynamism, and we cannot in turn think of a dynamic of Being apart from time.[12] Being needs time in which to expand and express itself, just as the

---

[10] I Cor. 2:9.
[11] I John 3:2.
[12] See above, p. 111.

human existent needs temporality to realize selfhood. Yet Being is not only dynamic but stable, just as a self is not a mere series of "nows" but a unity which gathers up the flow of instants and embraces them in a whole. In the language that we used in expounding the doctrine of the triune God, let us recall that we have to reckon with unitive Being as well as expressive Being. Let us recall too that time is in Being rather than Being in time.

So we can visualize (and our language can be only very approximate, seeming to describe as something that happened once what is more likely to be a never-ending and never-beginning activity) the emergence of primordial Being through expressive Being into time and history, yet in such a way that through its self-outpouring from its original unbroken unity, a new and richer unity is being all the time built up through unitive Being, a unity that with every creative outpouring becomes richer and fuller still. The end would be all things gathered up in God, all things brought to the fulfillment of their potentialities for being, at one among themselves and at one with Being from which they have come and for which they are destined. But this end too could not be thought of as a point that will eventually be reached, for at every point new vistas will open up. Being must remain at once stable and dynamic. A static perfection, achieved once for all, would be frozenness. We have to visualize rather what, already long ago in the idealist tradition, Sir Henry Jones described as a "moving from perfection to perfection." [13] As the context widens through the constant expansion of the horizons of time and history, so the ideal of perfection becomes richer. That a movement toward this perfection is taking place cannot be proved, but we have seen how we can regard this as a reasonable faith in an ambiguous world. The present speculations are certainly not meant to be proof, but perhaps they reinforce the claim that the Christian hope is a reasonable one, for they give some inkling of how we might conceive the kind of stability-in-dynamism that seems to be demanded.

But have we perhaps been so concerned with the question of the destiny of the cosmos that we have lost sight altogether of the individual human existence? Or are we to suppose that individual existents are entirely subordinated to the cosmic process, and are simply swallowed up in the grander destiny of the whole? Perhaps our reference to idealism has made it appear as if Being is going to turn out to be just a new version of the all-devouring Absolute of nineteenth-century Hegelianism.

[13] *A Faith that Enquires*, p. 359.

Certainly, it ought to be said that any worthy conception of the ultimate destiny of the individual must be purged from every trace of egocentricity. Often one has the impression that arguments for immortality or for the continued existence of the individual are infected by a wrong kind of self-regard. If the fulfillment of individual existence is to be somehow like God, then this means learning the love that loses itself by pouring itself out; and this might mean that the individual existent must be prepared to vanish utterly into the whole, and for the sake of the whole.

Yet, on the other hand, such absorption would seem to defeat the very meaning of that complex divine activity which we have described as creation-reconciliation-consummation. If everything is to return to an undifferentiated unity, then creation would have been pointless in the first place, and all the risk of creation, and its suffering and striving, would have been sheer waste. Rather, our belief is that the whole process only makes sense in so far as, in the risk and struggle of creation, that which *is* is advancing into fuller potentialities of being and is overcoming the forces that tend toward dissolution; and that continually a richer and more fully diversified unity is being built up. This unity is far more valuable than any merely undifferentiated unity, and furthermore, each new stage in this unity is more valuable than the more restricted one that went before it. The end, we have seen reason to believe, would be a commonwealth of free responsible beings united in love; and this great end is possible only if finite existents are preserved in some kind of individual identity. Here again, we may emphasize that the highest love is not the drive toward union, but rather letting-be.

The individual, so far as he lays hold on the potentialities of existence and becomes a unified self, transcends the mere succession of "nows" and unifies his past, present, and future. But we have seen that he does this through "grace," through the very movement of Being in him. Can we then suppose that as the individual achieves his own being and so transcends a mere successiveness (so that temporality is in him, rather than he in time), he is also taken up into that wider unifying action of Being, on which we speculated earlier? We can only dimly imagine what it might be like for *all time* to be gathered up in a vast unity, analogous to that in which an integrated self gathers up the past, present, and future of a limited existence. The Bible hints at the contrast between the unification of time in Being and the unification of temporality in existence in the words: "A thousand years in thy sight are but as yesterday when it is past, or as a watch in the night." [14] But we can visualize this gathering up

14 Ps. 90:4.

of all time and all beings in God, and in such a way that their distinctness would be preserved. Certainly, they would be utterly transformed, and we could not guess what their mode of experience might be—and here we may recall the measure of agnosticism that we noted in the New Testament.

These remarks might seem to favor the doctrine usually known as "conditional immortality," for we seem to be saying that if the individual achieves selfhood and so is caught up into the constructive movement of Being, then he has his place in that structure of Being that transcends the passage of time; and the implication seems to be that if the individual fails to achieve selfhood, then he slips back into the nothing out of which he had come. A doctrine of conditional immortality is at least preferable to the barbarous doctrine of an eternal hell, and of this more will be said later. But perhaps the Christian hope can carry us further even than a belief in conditional immortality. If God is indeed absolute letting-be, and if his letting-be has power to overcome the risks of dissolution, then perhaps in the end (so we must speak) no individual existence that has been called out of nothing will utterly return to nothing, but will move nearer to the fulfillment of its potentialities, as the horizons of time and history continually expand, and it is set in an ever wider reconciling context. In other words, we prefer a doctrine of "universalism" to one of "conditional immortality," and this seems more in line with the eschatological hope that all things will indeed find their fullness in God.

These remarks imply that, after all, achievement of selfhood and fullness of being is a matter of degree, and a sharp dividing line cannot be drawn between the "righteous" and the "wicked." Just as we may suppose that on the one side, no individual human existence is irretrievably lost, it seems that we must likewise suppose on the other side that no individual existence comes to complete perfection. Just as we saw that the "end" of the cosmos is not some static perfection, but a movement from perfection to perfection, we must even more strongly assert that the goal of a human existence cannot be static, but, even if we call it a "perfection," must be an expanding perfection within the continually expanding perfections of Being. Since to exist is to be temporal, the attainment of a static perfection would mean the end of existence. It is perhaps significant that prayers for the departed seem to have moved from the thought of the attainment of static rest to that of increasing perfection. In 1549 the *Book of Common Prayer* besought for them "thy mercy and everlasting peace"; the current American edition prays for their "continual growth in thy love and service." What this implies for our understanding of the ideas of heaven, hell, and the intermediate state (for clearly we must visualize such an intermediate state) will need to be considered in the next section.

Meantime, let us remind ourselves of what the present section is supposed to have done for our inquiry. It has been based on the one hand on the Christian hope, and this in turn arises from the whole fabric of Christian faith and theology; it is this hope that allows us to believe in a destiny of fulfillment for both the cosmos and the individual. Our remarks have been based on the other hand on the deployment of those ontological and existential notions which have underlain our whole theological exposition, and the purpose of bringing them into this particular discussion has been to show that the Christian hope is not mere fantasy but can, within the limits that are imposed on us, be expounded within an intelligible and reasonable framework of thought. In the light of this exposition, we can now press forward to a fuller interpretation of the last things.

65. THE PRINCIPAL ESCHATOLOGICAL IDEAS INTERPRETED

1. The first eschatological idea to be considered, and perhaps the most fundamental, is *eternal life*. This expression is preferable to "immortality," which is a word with at least two defects. One of these is that it implies some kind of substantial soul, and that the substance of this soul is imperishable and so endures forever. At an early stage of our theological inquiry, we rejected the idea of a ready-made substantial soul, and also the idea that a unitary self needs some substratum that persists in a thinglike way.[15] Instead, we saw that the self or soul is a potentiality of existence to be realized (or lost) in the deeds and decisions of life; and that its relation to time is quite different from that of a thing that persists through successive instants. The other defect in the expression "immortality" is that it suggests a soul that carries on apart from the body. When we try to think of it, the notion of a disembodied existence is very hard to conceive, and should probably not be called "existence" at all. For one only exists as one is in relation to other persons and things, and such relations are possible only through the body. The New Testament speaks of "resurrection" rather than of "immortality," and thereby ensures that a full existence is meant, even if, as St. Paul seems to have done, one is asked to

---

[15] See above, pp. 74-76.

imagine a "spiritual body" as distinct from the "natural body." [16] Whatever else this may mean, it recognizes that to exist is to be in a world, and it is only by having a body of some sort that one can be in a world. Thus immortality, in the sense of the persistence forever of an imperishable disembodied soul-substance, would seem to be only a shadowy kind of sub-existence, like the kind visualized in Hades or Sheol, and it might well turn out to be intolerably boring and frustrating.

But if we rule out these possibilities, what are we to understand by "eternal life"? We must take our clue from the way in which the self transcends the succession of "nows." As selfhood develops, one becomes less and less the creature of the instant, subject to its passing circumstances or desires, and one attains more and more a unified existence that transcends mere successiveness and integrates past, present, and future. This is already to have, so to speak, a "taste" of eternal life; and since presumably every human being will at some time attain enough of selfhood to have such a taste, then, as has often been argued, man already has in him the quest for an "eternal" destiny and cannot be satisfied with merely transient goods. Moreover, if we take this approach to the meaning of "eternal life," it is easily understandable how, as in the Fourth Gospel, such life can be thought of as accessible to us here and now.

Obviously, however, the full meaning of "eternal life" must go far beyond what is, after all, the universal human experience of transcending mere successiveness. "Eternal life" is the limit toward which this transcending of the instant points. But since it is such transcending of the instant that makes possible selfhood, then "eternal life" lies at the limit of selfhood. From our previous discussions, however, we have seen that the limit of selfhood is christhood, for the Christ is the one who brought to fulfillment all the possibilities of selfhood.[17] But Christ is the one who, by his utter self-giving, is taken up into Godhood; or, alternatively expressed he is the incarnate one in whom manhood and Godhood converge. To attain "eternal life" is to be adopted as sons with Christ into the life of God. Christ is rightly called "the first fruits of those who have fallen asleep" but who will "in Christ . . . be made alive." [18] We have already speculated on how the individual existence may be taken up into the vaster movement of Being, and, eschatologically speaking, this would seem to be the universal human destiny, of which we see the prototype in Christ.

[16] I Cor. 15:44.
[17] See above, p. 300.
[18] I Cor. 15:20, 22.

And while we have talked here of Christ's being "taken up" into God-hood, it was made clear in our christological discussion that this is not to be understood in any evolutionist or adoptionist sense, but is at the same time God's coming down to us. Hence we are not suggesting that eternal life is man's automatic progress toward deity, but rather that this is the movement of Being in him, the movement of the grace of which Christ was the bearer and revealer. What is visualized is not an arrogant human attempt to become divine, but rather the kind of deification which the Fathers envisaged, whereby all human life would be permeated by grace and fulfilled in the divine consummation. What took place in the Christ who, by utterly giving himself, "ascended" to be with God, is destined to take place in all mankind, following in the way of his cross and resurrection. In St. Athanasius' famous words, "he was made man that we might be made God." [19] If this statement seems too strong, we may prefer St. Irenaeus' remark that the Spirit "purifies man and raises him up to the life of God." [20] Such will be the completion of that "eternal life" into which in varying degrees men enter now, and for which, by the very constitution of his existence, man is impelled to seek.

2. Next something may be said briefly about *judgment*. As a present, continuous activity, judgment is hardly to be distinguished from providence, to which we devoted an earlier discussion.[21] It will be remembered that providence was understood as God's activity in establishing and advancing the being of the creatures in the face of the risk of dissolution. Judgment is an aspect of this activity. As has been already stated, it is the reverse side of grace, the two together constituting God's providential work. Judgment can be thought of as a kind of sifting, whereby the distortions of evil are brought to defeat and dissolution and the tendencies toward authentic being are advanced.

In an ambiguous world where good and evil seem to be about equally matched, this belief in judgment remains on the level of faith. We have already discussed, in connection with the problems of providence and evil, the grounds on which a belief in judgment may be held. Belief in a final judgment is the hope that what is now ambiguous will resolve itself, and the advance of good over evil will decisively prevail. This ambiguous world is, in the imagery of the gospel parable, like a field in which wheat and weeds are growing together. Belief in a last judgment is the hope that

19 *De Incarnatione*, liv, 3.
20 *Adv. Haer.*, IV, ix, 2.
21 See above, pp. 239–246.

weeds will be eliminated and the good wheat brought to maturity.[22] This need not mean a destruction or dissolution of the beings that have become distorted. Judgment and grace, let us remember, are two sides of a single activity, and we have already seen reason to prefer "universalism" to a doctrine of "conditional immortality" and *a fortiori* to any doctrine of everlasting punishment.

Belief in a judgment which is not merely ongoing but is also final, in the sense that it is a transforming of evil into good, a healing of injuries, a restoring of what had been destroyed or blighted, is an inevitable consequence of the belief that there is a righteous God, or that Being is gracious. It is worth noting that, in a world where there is so much manifest injustice and waste, it has been the demand for justice rather than any self-centered so-called "wishful thinking" that has been a major force in the rise of eschatological beliefs. A modern theologian who has made much of eschatology and especially of the idea of the resurrection of the dead, Jürgen Moltmann, claims that this idea is "a way toward expressing belief in the righteousness of God. As the righteousness of God, it cannot be limited, even by death. So God will summon both dead and living before his judgment seat." [23] Admittedly, the language here is mythological, but the demand for righteousness remains with us today and still calls for the transformation and renewal of history, represented by the idea of judgment.

3. *Heaven* is one of the most difficult of the eschatological ideas, partly because it has become entangled in so much mythological imagery, but perhaps more importantly because it so easily becomes associated with egocentric longings. This arises from our way of talking about heaven as a "reward." It certainly is not a reward in the sense of being some kind of external compensation for the life of faith, and least of all a compensation that might be supposed to make up for the renunciations of faith. Such a view of heaven is indeed despicable.

Heaven is not a reward that gets added on to the life of faith, hope, and love, but it is simply the end of that life, that is to say, the working out of the life that is oriented by these principles. Understood in this way, there is nothing either mythological or egocentric about heaven. The symbol stands for fullness of being; it is the fruition toward which the existent advances as he is brought into "eternal life." Since this fruition is an in-

---

[22] Matt. 13:30.
[23] *The Crucified God*, p. 174.

creasing closeness to Being, so that the individual being converges upon Being and is taken up into Being, heaven is rightly identified with the "beatific vision," that direct indubitable awareness of the immediate presence of God which may be contrasted with the attitude of faith where, in this ambiguous world, we "see in a mirror dimly." [24] But this closeness to God is the furthest thing imaginable from the satisfaction of an egocentric craving. We have seen that to be "like to God" is to have the capacity for letting-be, for conferring being. This likeness to God, which we see at its highest in Christ, means the outpouring of one's own being. It was a sound insight which led the early Church to believe that only the martyrs might immediately enter heaven and that other Christians would need purification; for the martyrs are those who have utterly transcended selfish being, and attained a likeness to Christ, and so to God. If this can be talked about at all as a "reward," it is the reward of having been delivered from any seeking for rewards. This is nothing but the perfecting of self-giving love. The only reward of such love is an increased capacity for it.

Rightly interpreted, then, heaven is neither mythological nor egocentric, but is simply the goal of human existence. We may think of it as the upper limit, but presumably, in line with our earlier discussion, every attainment of this limit would disclose further possibilities beyond it.

4. If heaven is fullness of being and the upper limit of human existence, *hell* may be taken as loss of being and the lower limit. Loss of being need not mean annihilation, but includes every declination from a genuinely personal existence and every divergence from the fulfillment of authentic potentialities for being. Thus hell, like the other eschatological ideas, can stand for a present phenomenon and can in varying degrees be experienced here and now. To talk of hell as a "punishment" is just as unsatisfactory as to talk of heaven as a "reward." Hell is not some external or arbitrary punishment that gets assigned for sin, but is simply the working out of sin itself, as it destroys the distinctively personal being of the sinner.

Whether in fact anyone ever comes to the point of utterly losing his personal being, or of falling away altogether from the potentialities of such being, may be doubted. If this should happen, then we would be committed to a doctrine of "conditional immortality," as we have already mentioned. This utter limit of hell would be annihilation, or at least the annihilation of the possibility for personal being. Since salvation is itself personal, and must therefore be freely accepted, God cannot impose it

---

[24] I Cor. 13:12.

upon anyone, so we must at least leave open the possibility that this kind of annihilation might be the final destiny for some. Yet since we have refused to draw a sharp line between the "righteous" and the "wicked," and since we have suggested that even for the man made righteous, heaven is not finally attained, but each heaven opens up new possibilities of perfection, so on the other side we seem compelled to say that the sinner never gets to the point of complete loss and so never gets beyond the reconciling activity of God. Needless to say, we utterly reject the idea of a hell where God everlastingly punishes the wicked, without hope of deliverance. Even earthly penologists are more enlightened nowadays. Rather we must believe that God will never cease from his quest for universal reconciliation, and we can firmly hope for his victory in this quest, though recognizing that this victory can only come when at last there is the free cooperation of every responsible creature.

5. Our discussion of heaven and hell has made it clear that we must also take cognizance of the state of *purgatory*, or, as some nineteenth-century Anglican theologians preferred to call it, the "intermediate state." It is hard to understand why Protestant theologians have such a violent prejudice against this conception, for it seems to me to be indispensable to any reasonable understanding of Christian eschatology. If, as in the present work, we think of heaven and hell as limits to be approached rather than final conditions in which to remain; if we try to visualize eschatology in dynamic rather than in static terms; if we refuse to draw any hard and fast line between the "righteous" and the "wicked," or between the "elect" and the "reprobate"; if we reject the idea that God's reconciling work is restricted to the people living at this particular moment, and believe that his reconciliation can reach anywhere, so that it makes sense to pray for the departed; above all, if we entertain any universalist hopes of salvation for the whole creation, then we are committed to the belief in an intermediate state, whether or not we call it "purgatory."

The name "purgatory" is, however, entirely appropriate, for it points to the process by which we are fitted for that union with God which is our ultimate destiny. Heaven, purgatory, and hell are not sharply separated, but form a kind of continuum through which the soul may move, perhaps from the near-annihilation of sin to the closest union with God. Indeed, the concept of purgatory served the valuable purpose of introducing the dynamic, moving element into the traditional scheme, where heaven and hell could easily be mistaken for fixed immutable states.

Just as heaven and hell, in varying degrees, can be experienced in the present, so purgatory belongs to present experience. It is one aspect of that process of sanctification, whereby we are conformed to Christ. But as with the other ideas, the meaning of "purgatory" extends beyond the here and now. If the ultimate destiny of the individual is somehow to be taken up into the vaster movement of Being, then purgatory is the process by which he becomes fitted for this. He is called out of nothing into existence, from existence to selfhood, from selfhood to christhood and incorporation into God. This whole movement is a process of purification. Let us recall again St. Irenaeus' words about the Spirit who "purifies man and raises him up to the life of God."

The prejudice against the idea of purgatory is perhaps in part due to some of the traditional imagery, and to the stress that has been laid on the sufferings of purgatory. Thus Tillich complains that "in Catholic doctrine, mere suffering does the purging" and he argues that "it is a theological mistake to derive transformation from pain alone instead of from grace which gives blessedness within pain." [25] But this is to misunderstand the association of suffering with purgatory. This is to be understood analogously with the association of heaven with reward and hell with punishment, that is to say, as an intrinsic, existential relation. The kind of "suffering" envisaged in purgatory is not an external penalty that has to be paid, but is our suffering with Christ, our being crucified with him as we are conformed to him, the painful surrender of the ego-centered self that the God-centered self of love may take its place. This is precisely that "blessedness within pain," of which Tillich speaks. We have insisted throughout that grace and judgment are two sides of one activity. Even to recognize God in Christ, we have seen, is also to know the pain of conviction of sin.[26] But this kind of pain is not "mere suffering." It is not an externally inflicted pain, but the intrinsic pain inseparable from transfiguration, from sharing in the death and resurrection of Christ. Purgatory itself is nothing but this dying and rising. In the splendid words of Romano Guardini, "death upon death has to be endured so that new life may arise." [27]

6. The crowning eschatological idea is that of the *kingdom of God*. This recalls us from our discussions of the destiny of the individual to that of the ἔσχατον of holy Being itself, and of course only within this immeasurably vaster frame can the individual have his destiny.

[25] *Systematic Theology*, vol. III, p. 417.
[26] See above, pp. 338–339.
[27] *The Last Things*, p. 46.

We have already sufficiently indicated how the kingdom of God is to be conceived. It would be a commonwealth of free beings, united in Being and with each other through love, yet since this is the love that lets-be, preserving a diversity that heightens the value of the unity far above that of any undifferentiated unity.

The kingdom of God would be the full manifestation of the holiness of Being, which at present is seen only by faith in a world that presents an ambiguous face. Here we can understand too what is meant by the thought of Christ's coming again "with glory" to inaugurate the fullness of the kingdom. For while we have claimed that Christ is the "focus" of holy Being, and that this has made its advent and epiphany in him, we acknowledged too that the human life of Jesus of Nazareth was, like everything else in this world, an ambiguous phenomenon. Christian faith sees that life "in depth" and hails it as the incarnation of God; but it can be seen also as just another human existence, more or less important according to one's point of view. To speak of his coming "with glory" is to point to that feature of the kingdom of God which means the resolution of the ambiguities of the world and the unmistakable manifestation of the holiness of Being.

Like the other eschatological phenomena, the kingdom of God is already present. It is not to be identified with the Church (we shall speak of this later) though one might hope that the Church, together with any other communities of the Spirit, might be, so to speak, the spearhead of the kingdom in the world. But the Church itself shares too much of the world's ambiguity to be regarded as the kingdom, which still lies ahead.

Here we may recall the contrast between the nineteenth-century ethical-progressive view of the kingdom, and the twentieth-century stress on its supra-historical and cataclysmic nature. Probably the pendulum has swung too violently, and a theology of the kingdom needs to combine the two insights. The older liberal view was surely right in recognizing that some measure of human cooperation is needed for the realizing of the kingdom, and surely right also in acknowledging a growth of the kingdom in the world. In spite of what New Testament scholars of the opposite persuasion may say, this would seem to be the natural interpretation of those parables of the kingdom that compare it to a seed that grows into a mighty tree, or to the leaven that works in the bread.[28] But the eschatological interpretation rightly rules out any evolutionary humanism

---

[28] Matt. 13:31–33.

in these conceptions. It is God who is the author of the kingdom, and it is his grace that is realizing it, albeit with the free cooperation of human beings. And while the eschatological interpretation may seem to become otherworldly in placing the kingdom beyond history, it is only being realistic. It is utopian and foolish to suppose that the kingdom could be realized on earth, though on the other hand it is not foolish to strive toward its increasing realization, for the Christian hope encourages us to believe that it really is the "entelechy" of the cosmos. But its realization (and we have already seen that this can never be final) can only be in that vaster synthesis of Being, gathering up past, present, and future, and perfecting all things in an ever-widening context. This we can comprehend only in a very dim fashion, but the revelation of God's grace on the one hand and reflection on existence and Being on the other combine to assure us that this is a reasonable hope and worthy of our highest allegiance and endeavors.

PART THREE

APPLIED THEOLOGY

16 | The Tasks of Applied Theology

66. FAITH AND EMBODIED EXISTENCE

In this third division of our work, we are not abandoning theology or even becoming less theological, but we shall have to deal more directly with the relation of theology to the ordering of our lives in the world. The datum for theology is faith, and faith, as we have seen, is not merely belief but an existential attitude. Theology tries to bring faith to coherent verbal expression, and so claims to be an intellectual enterprise. But faith expresses itself in many other ways than in words, and it would be something less than faith if it did not issue in a quality of life. Theology does not usurp these other ways, but it has a duty to serve and to guide them. The better we understand our faith and the revelation on which it is based, the more understandingly shall we be able to express that faith over the whole range of existence. It is not being claimed that theology precedes action, for we have said from the beginning that theology arises out of the commitment of faith; but on the other hand, action that is not guided by reflection becomes blind and impulsive. Theological understanding only grows in the course of involvement in the concrete situation of faith, yet the life of faith itself is lit up and strengthened by the kind of understanding that theology brings. In the first and second divisions of this work, while we have always striven to keep open an existential dimension in our theologizing, we have been chiefly concerned with the exposition of ideas and symbols within the structure of philosophical and symbolic theology. Now we have to consider what theological guidelines can be provided for the concrete expression of Christian faith in the world.

Already we touched on the relation of faith to religion,[1] and religion

[1] See above, pp. 157–161.

was defended against its detractors because, as the whole complex of structures that grow out of the faith-revelation situation, religion is required by existents whose very being is a being-in-the-world. To exist is to exist as an embodied person, involved whether we like it or not in institutions, laws, customs, and the like. Perhaps a purely private religious faith might keep itself uncontaminated from these earthly vehicles, but we are concerned not with private faith but with the faith of the Christian community, and it is hard to see how this could subsist at all without some institutional structures.

It seems to me a strange contradiction that some of those who are most forward in advocating a "worldly" or "secular" Christianity think that they can best do this by attacking "religion" and its structures and institutions. No doubt, as we shall see, many of their criticisms are valid. But a faith that is secular and worldly is precisely the kind of faith that must express itself in the institutionalized fabric of human existence. Only individualism, or worse still a false spirituality, tries to escape from historical embodied institutions which are inseparable from a worldly existence. Baron Von Hügel wrote again and again of the need of institutional structures as part of what it means to be embodied human beings in history, and as an implicate too of the incarnation. In one place he writes: "Complete humility imperatively demands my continuous recognition of my own multiform need of my fellow-creatures, especially of those wiser and better than myself, and of my lifelong need of training, discipline, incorporation; full humility requires filial obedience and docility towards men and institutions." [2] Likewise St. Paul, in the most spontaneous days of Christianity's unfolding, never forgot that "we have this treasure in earthen vessels." [3]

Man's possibility is always inseparable from his facticity, and this means that he needs earthly structures—institutional, ritual, legal, customary, and of many other kinds—in which his spiritual activities can be channeled and stabilized. Everyone knows that this immediately brings the danger that these activities will be conventionalized and deprived of worth. To institutionalize them may mean simply to domesticate them and render them harmless. Their spontaneity is killed, and perhaps we secretly wish it so, for we have found these new possibilities disturbing. We want to tame them and bring them under control, and so far as the institutions of

---

[2] *Essays and Addresses on the Philosophy of Religion*, First Series, p. 264.
[3] II Cor. 4:7.

religion do this with man's experience of holy Being, then criticism of religion is a task that needs to be continually undertaken. But the fact that these institutional forms can be abused does not mean that they should be abandoned. We may see a parallel between the institutions, rituals, and regulations of religion and the symbols which we saw to be inseparable from any thinking about God. These symbols were compared to transformers that break down what in itself would be overwhelming, so that it becomes accessible. In the same way, the "earthen vessels" of religion bring grace and revelation to bear on the life of a society within the world. It is absurd to see in them an attempt to "manage" or "manipulate" God (even if this is to be acknowledged as a danger) for without such worldly means faith would remain vaporized and disembodied, and certainly no communal faith could long survive in such a manner, and still less could it be effective.

The earthly structures which constitute the religious apparatus through which faith expresses itself and functions in the world are of various kinds. A faith that is more than individual will embody itself in an *association,* using the word "association" in the sense defined by R. M. MacIver for an "organization established within society for the achievement of conscious and therefore limited purposes." [4] Just how suitable this definition is for a specifically religious association, we shall consider later. But for the present, let us recognize that what hitherto we have for the most part called the "community of faith" will, in the concrete, take the form of an association, usually a "church," but always an association of some sort, even in the case of sectarian groups, or groups that have become disaffected with the regular church. Associations, in turn, can hardly operate apart from *institutions,* which we understand (again following MacIver) as "recognized modes in accordance with which communities and associations regulate their activities." [5] Among the structures of institutionalized religion one would mention the *ritual acts* in which the cult embodies itself; the *sacred books* which are the repository of revelation, though not identical with revelation; the *creeds* and *dogmas* in which the common faith has expressed itself, so that they have become as it were badges or identifying marks of those who belong to this community. There are also *offices,* for every religion, including those that set out to be egalitarian, has its leadership and its special functions. Finally, there

---

[4] *The Modern State,* p. 5.
[5] *Ibid.,* p. 6.

must be at least a minimum of commonly accepted *laws*, or *rules*, to ensure the coherence and proper functioning of the apparatus.

It is understandable that many people who might be willing to follow us through the unfolding of philosophical theology and even of symbolic theology should hesitate to accompany us further into this region that we have called "applied theology." Cannot we do without all this cumbrous mechanism? Even if reduced to its simplest elements, must not the whole institutional side of religion impose upon us the burden of a complex and rigid apparatus? And must it not (like similar secular organizations) have a tendency always to proliferate itself and to develop new complexities? And must not this in turn result in a killing of the spontaneity of faith, a false schematizing of revelation, and a hardening of the whole experience of the holy into a legalism—precisely the kind of legalism against which the great protagonists of faith have protested through the ages—from the Hebrew prophets through Jesus and St. Paul to the Reformers and even to the modern existentialists, from whose insights we have drawn so much in these studies? Is not the only application of Christian theology that we can accept as valid simply the life of love?

All of this has a large measure of truth, and can find much support in the actual history of Christianity, where again and again the apparatus has come to count for more than that which it was supposed to serve, and the faith that was meant to liberate and to lead to selfhood has been transformed into a legalistic encumbrance. Yet while we must always be alert to protect the fragile plant of spontaneous, personal being, we must also recognize that institutional structures were intended precisely to protect this plant, even if they sometimes smother it. Man is possibility, and from this comes his freedom, his creativity, his power to love, and everything else that falls under the inexact but useful word, "spiritual"; but he is also facticity, tied to the world and to earthly modes of existence. To recognize the necessity of earthly forms in religion is simply to accept who we are and where we are, and this is more properly called "worldly" Christianity than the kind of religion that aims at bypassing all institutional forms in hope of expressing itself in a purely "spiritual" manner.

Presumably the eschatological ideal (the kingdom of God) would not need the apparatus that man needs while he is still *in via*. In his vision of heaven, the writer of Revelation says, "I saw no temple in the city, for its temple is the Lord God the Almighty, and the Lamb." [6] Voltaire's hero in

[6] Rev. 21:22.

the land of Eldorado saw no temples and wondered if the people had any faith in God; he was told that they had indeed, but that their worship was constituted by their daily work.[7] But what might be true "at the end," or true for man if he were, as Voltaire and many of his contemporaries supposed, capable of leading a purely "rational" existence, is not true of man as he actually lives in world history, and to pretend that it is would be a strange kind of angelism. To try to escape or bypass historical institutions is impossible for two reasons—man's embodiment, and also his sin.

It may be remembered that Voltaire's hero did not find any lawcourts, legislature, or prison in Eldorado, for the inhabitants had no need of these things in their spontaneous rationality. Calvin had a more realistic and less utopian view of the matter when he recognized that civil government is necessary to man's historical condition, and apparently believed that even a bad government is far preferable to anarchy.[8] But the principle illustrated here by the case of civil government has much wider application. An instructive example is the institution of marriage. Nothing could be more spontaneous and less amenable to regulation than the love between the sexes. Yet in a world where promiscuity, seduction, prostitution, and many other cheapenings and perversions of such love take place all the time, it is necessary that there should be some institution to protect this love. Ideally, perhaps, it should be independent of any institutional regulation; but in a sinful world, this would be too great a threat to the very survival of such love. The institution may in some isolated cases stifle or pervert the very love that it is meant to protect. But any institutional apparatus is bound to have its defects, and on the whole, the institution protects far more than it damages. "The institution of marriage," it has been finely said, "is ordained to guard, to hallow and to perfect the sacred gift of love." [9]

The purpose of these illustrations is to point to like necessities in the field of Christian faith and religion. The faith of the community can continue and can make itself felt in the world only if it is willing to embody itself in worldly institutions. This is indeed part of the risk of faith. The risk here is that faith can become depersonalized, collectivized, conventionalized. It can become a meaningless custom, as Kierkegaard thought it had become in the state religion of his country. But while recognizing

---

[7] *Candide*, chap. xviii.
[8] *Institutes of the Christian Religion*, IV, xx.
[9] *The Book of Common Order* (Church of Scotland), Order for the Solemnization of Marriage.

this, we must try, in this part of our work as in the earlier parts, to follow a *via media*, and not allow ourselves to be driven from one unsatisfactory extreme to another that would turn out to be as unsatisfactory as the first. The extremes in this case are, on the one hand, an institutional rigidity that stifles authentic faith; and on the other, an extravagant spontaneity that falsely spiritualizes our human condition and insufficiently recognizes our embodied and sinful situation in the world.

Part of the greatness of Christian faith is precisely its ability to take up the earthly and to make it the vehicle for holy Being's self-expression. As the religion of the incarnation, it is also the great sacramental religion, in the widest sense of the expression. In the well-known words of William Temple, Christianity "is the most avowedly materialist of all the great religions. . . . By the very nature of its central doctrine, Christianity is committed to a belief in the ultimate significance of the historical process, and in the reality of matter and its place in the divine scheme." [10]

67. CRITERIA FOR APPLIED THEOLOGY

In entering the field of what we have called "applied theology," we are of course entering the most controversial area of theology. It is over such questions as the nature of the Church and its ministry, the meaning of the sacraments (and even their number!), the forms of Christian worship, the norms of Christian conduct in matters of marriage and divorce and the like, that the most violent and divisive disputes among Christians have arisen. If we are to adhere to our intention of following a *via media* and of avoiding extreme and partisan positions, we must allow for reasonable flexibility and inclusiveness. Indeed, the very fact that we have chosen to set up a third division of this systematic theology and to consider in it some matters that traditionally belong to dogmatic theology and so might have been expected to find their place in our second division, indicates that we do not consider these questions of "applied" theology to have the same centrality as, let us say, the doctrines of creation or of the work of Christ. Local conditions and particular histories may well exercise a legitimate influence in deciding how, in some particular country or region, the Christian community shall be organized, or what, in a particular culture or subculture, shall be the institutional forms of its worship or the rules governing the conduct of its members. A rich diversity is undoubtedly a source of great strength to the Christian community as a whole.

10 *Nature, Man and God*, p. 478.

Yet it is clear that everything cannot be left to the particular situation or its context. A community requires an identity. The stronger a community is, the richer diversity it can contain, yet there is a critical point somewhere when the diversity begins to subvert the identity of the community and begins its dissolution. There have to be some basic identifying characteristics of the community, running through all its diversity. These characteristics have to be recognizable in more than one way. We have got to be able to recognize the community as the same community in its geographical spread at any particular time; we have likewise to be able to recognize it as the same community in its historical extension, as it stretches through time. So over against that freedom that belongs to particular situations and histories, we have to set the basic minimum of structural characteristics that give to the community its cohesiveness and its identity.

Actually, from the very beginning, as we can see clearly from the New Testament, the Church has contained considerable diversity. Yet from the beginning also it has had to strive to maintain its identity and has exercised discipline over individuals or groups who had departed too far from its norms, in some cases even expelling them. This in turn raises the question of authority. How does one judge the norms within which diversity is permissible and acceptable, but beyond which the individual or the group may not go without subverting the identity of the Christian community as a whole and so perhaps risking expulsion from that community?

It might seem that this question could be simply answered by saying that since the revelation in Christ is the classic or primordial revelation on which the Christian community of faith has been founded, then this revelation constitutes the authority in accordance with which the community is to order its structure and functions. But unfortunately this answer is much too simple. As we have seen already, the primordial revelation has been transmitted to us both in the scriptures and in the teaching of the Church, so that immediately one runs into the conflict between those who appeal to the authority of the written word and those who locate the authority in the tradition of the living community. But furthermore, as soon as one recognizes that a human, fallible element is involved in both scripture and traditional teaching, then reason demands to judge. On top of all this, there will be innumerable claims to give the "correct" interpretation of the original revelation. The position becomes even more complicated when the question is one on which there may seem to be conflicting views in scripture, or the scriptural teaching is unclear, or it is hard to see how the Christian revelation has anything whatever to do with the matter in dispute.

The position described here may remind us of the one which we confronted at the beginning of this study of theology, when we asked about the sources or formative factors in theology.[11] We decided then that an exclusive preoccupation with any one source led to an unbalanced theology, and now it will be maintained that the same is true in the field of applied theology. As we look around on the various churches, denominations, and groups all professing the Christian faith, we can roughly classify them according to the particular norm or authority which each recognizes and on which its organization and practices are based. The Roman Catholic Church has chiefly stressed tradition. The original deposit of faith, entrusted to the Church, has been passed on and unfolded through the successors of the apostles; and above all, through the successors of St. Peter, the popes, who are regarded as the infallible exponents of the faith. By and large, this makes for a fairly rigid and conservative structure. Yet from time to time there have been returns to the sources of faith, and recently there has been the astonishing renewal of the Roman communion, giving the lie to the suspicion that the Roman position is one of rigid unchanging traditionalism. Among Protestants, the stress has been on the supremacy of the Bible. In an extreme form, this becomes the belief that nothing is to be taught or practiced unless it is explicitly authorized in the Bible. In practice, however, Protestants have always left some place for tradition, and recently they are becoming more explicitly aware of the claims of tradition. One has also to distinguish between what may be called the "main-line" Protestants whose interpretation of scripture was always governed by the consensus of the Church, and the groups of enthusiasts or pentecostalists or whatever they might be called whose interpretations of the scriptures have been subordinated to their own particular experiences of spiritual illumination. On the whole, however, all of those groups, both on the main line and on the fringes, have thought of themselves as approximating to a "pure" New Testament Christianity, and have probably, at least until recently, left too little room for the growth and unfolding of Christian belief and practice in the developing life of the community. Anglicans and Orthodox we may locate somewhere between the "main-line" Protestants and the Roman Catholics. But there is still another group for whom authority has resided chiefly in rational specula-

---

[11] See above, pp. 4–18.

tion and criticism. Of course, Roman Catholic and Anglican theology give a place to reason. Here, however, we are thinking of liberal Protestant groups, such as Unitarians, among whom the authority of revelation, however transmitted, is minimized, perhaps to the level of a "general revelation," and for whom authority belongs to reason and conscience.

So just as we decided that it is necessary to hold in balance the various formative factors in theology, and not to allow any one of them an overriding dominance, so in our working out of the problems of applied theology, we shall try to hold a balance among the various criteria to the authority of which appeal is made in these matters. The great historical exemplar of a multiform authority in applied theology is Richard Hooker. On the one hand he opposed the claims of papal authority, but on the other hand he was equally resistant to the Puritan demand that everything should be based on a more or less literalistic interpretation of scripture. In Hooker's synthesis, scripture, tradition, and reason all had their place.

We shall try to work with the same three factors in what follows. A useful analogy, though admittedly it is a fairly remote one, can be seen in the constitution of the United States. There, as is well known, there is a "division of powers," as among the executive, the legislative, and the judiciary organs of the state. I do not wish to press the analogy in detail, for what is important in it is simply this notion of checks and counterchecks that balance each other and ensure both stability and the possibility of ordered change and progress. The same kind of division of powers or authority seems to be desirable too in those questions which lie within the province of applied theology. There is indeed one supreme authority here, God as he is revealed in Christ. But as we understand the revelation only imperfectly and only through the various ways in which it is given to us, we are least likely to stray from its essential content if we approach it in various ways and allow the various accounts and interpretations of God's Word to correct each other.

The Bible may be taken perhaps as the basic authority, for it has a fixity and objectivity that give the kind of stability that is needed if the community of faith is to preserve an identity. Yet this community of faith is not the community of a book, but a living community. Its faith came before the book, and indeed it was the community which determined the canon of scripture. Thus the scripture must be interpreted in accordance with the mind of the whole community, both as extended in space and as stretched through time, as St. Vincent of Lerins recognized. This makes clear the place of the tradition of the Church—not a body of esoteric, unwritten teaching, but a consensus as to what the teaching means. More than this, tradition is important in deciding about those matters, such as the ministry, about which there may not be sufficiently clear guidance in the scriptures. The fact that the Church for most of its time and in most of its provinces has had a particular form of the ministry, or has recognized certain creeds or confessional symbols, has built these into its identity in such a way that they must be recognized as so closely belonging to it that they cannot be denied or discarded without threatening the identity of the community. But finally, reason and conscience (practical or moral reason) must also have their critical authority alongside scripture and tradition, for only so can the ancient teaching be renewed and reinterpreted and made relevant to new conditions. In this way, development is made possible. Sometimes this development may take the form of radical change, and then there is the danger of dissolution. At such times, the checks of scripture and tradition must come into play if the identity of the community is not to be lost. However, history has shown that the Christian community can undergo very far-reaching change without becoming dissolved. This is perhaps what one would expect in a faith which proclaims that man can find himself only through losing himself.

The threefold type of authority envisaged here, and constituted by scripture, by the consensus of the community, and by reason, guards against a petrified "fundamentalism" on the one hand, and against runaway change on the other. It allows for a community that can be at once stable and dynamic.

68. THEMES OF AN APPLIED THEOLOGY

The general theme of applied theology is the working out of faith in the world, and we have seen that this leads us into the area of associations, institutions, rules, and so on. So all the matters of which we have to speak have a double aspect. On the one hand, they are phenomena within the world, and thus they may be proper objects of study for the sociologist, the psychologist, the student of esthetics, and many others. Yet on the other hand, we believe that these phenomena, something like the revelatory events, providential acts and miracles discussed earlier, have another side to them, and can be seen "in depth" as embodiments of faith and vehicles of grace. In other words, no merely sociological account of the Church and no merely psychological or esthetic appraisal of worship can be deemed adequate. These can be understood properly only when full account is taken of their theological dimension. Moreover, this dimension is primary, for it is faith that has brought these phenomena into being as vehicles for its expression in the world. Yet this does not mean that theology can set up a monopoly of wisdom in those matters. As the explication of faith, theology can help to make clear which embodiments most truly give expression to the content of faith. But since these embodiments through which faith finds its expression are phenomena that belong within the contexts of society, of history, of nature, of economic structures and all the rest, then non-theological factors have also to be studied, and certainly, if one is not to become merely utopian, one must learn to deal with what is possible in these various contexts. This, in turn, can be learned only from the secular sciences which study these fields. Thus, to give an obvious example, we have to be prepared to learn about the Church from the sociologist as well as from the theologian.

Actually, applied theology tends to merge into a number of specialized disciplines which have a mixed character, in so far as they draw not only on theology but on other subjects besides. A good illustration of this is furnished by liturgics. As its foundation, it undoubtedly requires a sound theology of worship, and this might even be called its primary requisite. But it also demands a knowledge of psychology, of esthetics, of the history of the cult, and other matters besides. Applied theology, as we understand it here, is not trying to supplant the special work of such disciplines. What it will seek to do is to provide the theological foundations for the various areas, laying down these foundations in terms of our earlier studies of philosophical and symbolic theology. But the detailed applications will be left to the specialized disciplines, such as liturgics, homiletics, moral theology, ecclesiastical polity and the like—disciplines which bring their own particular knowledge and interests into relation with theological principles. We can scarcely avoid becoming involved in some questions that may properly belong to one or other of these specialized disciplines, or of taking into account some non-theological factors, but in the main we shall try to confine ourselves to setting out the broad guidelines which theology might be expected to provide, and we shall endeavor not to trespass upon the detailed questions.

The first major theme to be considered is the Church itself. What, from a theological point of view, is to be said about the essence, structure, functions, and aims of the Church? Does this question, in turn, imply that a relatively stable pattern should be discernible in the Church at all times and in all places, recognizable through all the variation and diversity that may be found on account of local or historical or cultural factors? How is the Church, as an earthly association, related to the eschatological entity of the kingdom of heaven? In these discussions, we must take care not to get caught in the false disjunction between structure and function. These cannot be separated, and neither of them can be absolutized at the expense of the other. They may have to be differently weighted in different historical situations, but each must receive some weight if the Church is to have both the stability and the dynamism necessary to her health.

A closely related theme is that of the ministry. The same dialectical tensions emerge, for the ministry can be understood as a structure within the Church, while more broadly, it is the service of the Church, its diaconic function, and so scarcely distinguishable from its mission. How do we think of these questions? Is the distinction of clergy and laity, or of different orders within the clergy, simply a matter of preference, to be settled in accordance with functional needs or local conditions? Or does it have some theological justification—or does it lack all theological justification? How does it stand with the mission of the Church, in the light of what has been already said about the relation of Christianity to other faiths?

A further theme is provided by the various organs through which the Church operates, and chiefly the word and sacraments. What is involved in proclaiming the word? What are we to say of the tension between word and sacraments? Is there a rivalry between them, involving some genuine theological issue, or are they complementary? What in turn are the sacraments, assuming that they are not social ceremonies to mark the various stages of life, or psychological exercises by which people refurnish themselves with enough energy to be able to face up to the demands of daily living?

Still another area to be explored is that of worship and prayer. Every faith, if it is not just private but is held by a community, seems to issue in cultic acts. It has already been argued that a cult is justified, and even necessary. But if so, how are we to think of it? Is its importance all "subjective," so to speak, or is there some "objective" validity in worship—if indeed this language of "objective" and "subjective" is permissible here at all? The question of a theology of prayer is just about as difficult as any we might consider. But only a facing of such questions can provide the kind of theological guidance that would be foundational to any study of liturgy, though in such a study admittedly there would need to be brought to bear upon the problems considerations drawn from secular disciplines.

Finally, there is the vast question of the application of the Christian faith to the multitudinous problems of the modern world. The Church, as an association, finds itself involved with other associations, notably with the state. The individual Christian is daily involved in questions of economics, sex, social relations. All of these questions are multidimensional, so that the study of any one of them involves knowledge drawn from many areas of special study. Yet the Christian believes that his faith is relevant to all of them, and this amounts to saying that all of them have a theological dimension, for theology is the clarification of faith. Theology has got to provide some kind of guidance for the approach to such questions, while at the same time freely acknowledging that it offers no shortcuts or panaceas, and that many other disciplines have indispensable contributions to make if practical solutions are to be found.

Into these complicated areas we must now venture. However, the present chapter has already provided us with a line of approach—we have seen the need to follow a *via media* between the spontaneity of faith and the fixity of institutions, and we have learned the value of a flexible, composite norm that will take account of scripture, tradition, and common sense.

17 | The Church

69. PRELIMINARY REMARKS ON THE CHURCH

Probably more gets written on the Church nowadays than an any other single theological theme. Most of this writing has a practical orientation. We hear about the Church in relation to rapid social change, the Church in a secular society, the Church and reunion, the Church in mission. But however valuable some of the insights gained in these various fields may be, they need to be guided and correlated by a theological understanding of the Church. In this chapter, therefore, we shall first try to elucidate the understanding of the Church already implicit in those theological doctrines that we have been studying, and then we shall move from the theological understanding of the Church in the direction of its concrete, practical problems in the modern world—though, of course, the detailed working out of these problems lies outside of the scope of this book.

When we were discussing the doctrine of the person of Christ, it was stated that ecclesiology, or the doctrine of the Church, is closely related to christology. But we saw that christology, in turn, is closely related to the doctrine of creation, and that we may think of christhood as the limit of manhood, or the point where it passes into God-manhood. On the other hand, the doctrine of the Church is closely related also to eschatology, for there we saw that the dominant idea is the kingdom of heaven, and there is implied some kind of relation between the kingdom and the Church. So our first step toward reaching a theological understanding of the Church will be to view it in the light of these three major areas of doctrine that have already been explored in earlier parts of our study—creation, christology, eschatology.

Let us begin by asserting that the Church is already implicit in creation. We have seen that creation is the self-outpouring of Being, whereby there is getting built up a commonwealth of beings freely united in love. The Church is a necessary stage in this great action of Being, so that to believe in creation is already to believe in the Church, and there is a sense in which the Church was there "in the beginning" and is coeval with the world.

To make such a claim is to set aside as of little interest to theology the questions sometimes asked about the "origin" of the Church—questions as to whether Jesus himself founded a Church, or as to when the Church came into being, say at the calling of the apostles, or at the Feast of Pentecost. As far back as we can go, there always has been a community of faith. Thus St. Paul and other early Christians saw the Church as the successor of Israel, the "Israel of God." [1] The Church (ἐκκλησία) was the assembly that God had summoned, just as Israel was the nation that he had chosen. The Epistle to the Hebrews is more universalistic, for it traces the history of faith back beyond Abraham, the founder of the Hebrew nation, to such mythical figures as Abel, Enoch, and Noah, who belong to the whole human race.[2] This, of course, is very much in line with what we have said above, both about the relation of Christianity to other faiths and about the operation of the Holy Spirit outside of the regular churchly channels. It also accords with the assertions made in earlier parts of this book that reconciliation is not subsequent to, but synchronous with creation, or rather that these two are distinguishable aspects of a single activity; and that grace is as wide as creation itself. What in the earlier parts of the book was called the "community of faith" is wider than the Church, if this is understood to mean the visible, historical Christian community. There always has been a community of faith in the world, continuous with the Church, and its prototype; and there still is in the world a community of faith that stretches beyond the frontiers of the Church, in the narrow sense. For this reason too, one cannot draw a hard and fast line between the Church and the "world."

These basic ideas about the Church can be clarified and deepened if we reflect for a moment on the meaning of the expression "people of God." The Church is said to be "a chosen race, a royal priesthood, a holy nation, God's own people." [3] In calling the Church "people," there is recognition of its essentially human character and of its ties with the whole human race; but in adding the qualification "of God," there is the assertion that to this people there belongs a depth and significance that differ-

[1] Gal. 6:16.
[2] Heb. 11:4–7.
[3] I Pet. 2:9.

entiate them from people in general. A dialectic of identity and difference is at work here.

Various aspects of this dialectic come to expression in the stories that are told about the beginning, under Abraham, of the Hebrew nation, represented as a people called and chosen by God.[4] Significantly, Abraham himself can be understood both as individual and as community. He can be seen as foreshadowing the Christian Church, yet his going out in search of an authentic life and community can be seen also as a parable of the universal human condition which we have called "existence" or "transcendence." The new people is constituted by an act of separation, when Abraham turns his back on the cities of Mesopotamia and goes out into the desert; but eventually we find him interceding for the cities of the plain, thereby acknowledging his continuing solidarity with people other than his own. Very much later in the history of Israel, the universalist spirit becomes more explicit, and it is increasingly understood that, ideally, all mankind constitutes the people of God; but this does not take away the need for a special people, whose destiny and service it is to realize and to represent an authentic existence for all. Finally the Christian Church breaks out altogether from the national mold to become a new kind of people of God; yet, in spite of its novelty, it remains in continuity both with the old Israel and, beyond that, with the wider aspirations of the race.

However, while the Church is continuous with the wider community of faith that extends indefinitely both in time and space, the Church itself, as the consciously Christian Church, the community of those holding the Christian faith, becomes more clearly understood when we shift our attention from the doctrine of creation to the doctrine of the incarnation. The incarnation was explicated in terms of the coming together of the human and the divine, of a creaturely being with Being, or again, in terms of the raising of manhood to God-manhood. The Church is to be understood as the community in which this raising of manhood to God-manhood, which we see in Christ, continues. The Church therefore is rightly called the "body of Christ," which is its most distinctive title.[5] Within the Church, humanity is being conformed to christhood, a transfiguration, resurrection, ascension is going on as the believers participate in the life of Christ,[6] or in a couple of words, there is a "new creation." [7]

---

[4] Gen. 12ff.

[5] I Cor. 12:27; Eph. 1:23; Col. 1:18.

[6] Cf. the collects and office hymns for the Feasts of the Transfiguration, Easter, and Ascension.

[7] II Cor. 5:17.

This new creation takes place "in Christ," to use St. Paul's expression. While this expression undoubtedly has a mystical and devotional connotation and expresses union with the living Christ, as Adolf Deissmann has well shown,[8] it also means, in quite concrete terms, "in the Church," which is Christ's body as a visible, tangible entity in the world. John Knox remarks: "To be in Christ is to belong to a new corporate reality. . . . The 'new creation' has taken place, and the Church is the historical embodiment of the new humanity." [9]

In view of these remarks, we see also that it is correct to talk of the Church as an "extension" of the incarnation. However, this expression has to be used with great care. It will be remembered from our discussion of christology that we conceived incarnation as a process, rather than something that happens all at once. Even in Christ, there was growth (this is demanded by his humanity), and we saw the consummation of the incarnation at the point when Jesus utterly gave himself in the death of the cross and so manifested in the flesh the utter self-giving love of God. Now the Church has not achieved this consummation of the incarnation—if it had, then it would have utterly given itself up, and would have disappeared as this earthly entity which we know. This remark will be clarified shortly. At the moment, it is enough to say that the Church is an ongoing incarnation. It has not yet attained "to the measure of the stature of the fullness of Christ." [10] Christ is the "first fruits" [11] of the new creation, the resurrected humanity, and we may think of the saints as having also attained to full stature, though, as was suggested in the chapter on eschatology, we should think in terms of a movement from perfection to perfection rather than of some static end-condition. However, the point that I wish to make here is that while the Church may properly be called the extension of the incarnation, this must not be understood to put it on the same level as Christ or to attribute to it an exaggerated status and authority. The Church is Christ's body, but he is the head of the body. The incarnation which reached its completion in him is in process in the Church. Our hope is indeed that it is moving toward completion in the Church too, but at any given time, the Church is a mixed body. It is not free from sin, and there may even be times when it slips back. The notion of the Church as a process of sanctification and incarnation is well brought out in the traditional ways of talking about the "Church militant," the "Church ex-

---

[8] *Paul: a Study in Social and Religious History*, p. 138.
[9] *The Church and the Reality of Christ*, p. 104.
[10] Eph. 4:13.
[11] I Cor. 15:23.

pectant," and the "Church triumphant," which set out the whole panorama of the movement from sinful existence through purification to oneness with God.

Already there have been eschatological allusions in what we have been saying about the Church, so this brings us to the last of the three doctrines to which we have been trying to relate the idea of the Church—the doctrine of the last things. The point to be made here is that the Church is much less than the kingdom of God, and it would once more be an exaggerated idea of the Church to identify it with the kingdom. For the kingdom is an eschatological conception, and the Church is rather to be thought of as a stage on the way from actual sinful humanity to the kingdom; alternatively, if we think of the Church as extending from its militant aspect to its triumphant aspect, we may regard it as a kind of bridge between the place where humanity actually is and its destiny as the kingdom of God.

While the Church is not to be identified with the eschatological notion of the kingdom, the kind of relation that subsists between them means that the Church has its eschatological aspect too. We may think of the kingdom as the entelechy of the Church, the perfect unfolding of the potentialities that are already manifesting themselves in the Church. Then, if we also accept the Christian hope and believe that the tendencies toward fullness of being will prove stronger than tendencies toward dissolution, we may acknowledge that the Church has its own indefectibility. "The powers of death shall not prevail against it." [12] But this is not to claim infallibility for the Church. It is indeed to assert a measure of authority for it and to declare its normal superiority over individual judgment. But since the Church is at any given time something less than the kingdom, its authority is not absolute and, as has been shown already, must be counterbalanced by the authority of scripture and also by that of reason. If the statement that General Councils "may err, and sometimes have erred" [13] seems to be somewhat negative, it is not to be taken as implying in the slightest degree any disrespect for the Church, but is simply an acknowledgment that the Church, understood as process rather than fulfillment, and so as less than Christ and less than the kingdom, does not have absolute authority "even in the things pertaining to God."

The Church could become the kingdom and so fulfill itself only by

---

[12] Matt. 16:18.
[13] *Book of Common Prayer*, Articles of Religion, xxi.

losing itself as the separately existing Church. This is the price which the kind of transfiguration demanded by incarnation requires. Just so the human Jesus had to give himself utterly to be transfigured into the eternal Christ. If the Church were to realize itself in the kingdom, then we would have reached that state of affairs to which we alluded earlier,[14] when there would be no temple, no distinctive Church set over against the world, for the Church and the world would have become identified in the inclusive kingdom. The kingdom is the entelechy of the world as well as of the Church, so its realization would mean the disappearance of the Church as a distinctive entity.

So far we have been thinking of the Church in theological terms and setting it in the whole context of Christian doctrine, but this theological entity has an embodied, concrete, historical being in the world. At an earlier stage, we took note that, from a sociological point of view, the Church could be considered as an association, that is to say, an organized group within society, having a conscious and limited purpose.[15] We promised to come back and consider the appositeness of this description, and now that we have sketched in the theological background of the Church, the time has come to fulfill our promise.

Up to a point, it is correct to describe the Church as an "association," since at any given time it is a group within society, less than, let us say, the nation, or humanity as a whole. Yet there seems to be at least two ways in which the Church bursts through this concept of "association." On the one hand, it does not seem to have a "limited" purpose, since its end is the all-inclusive kingdom—"all-inclusive" not only in the sense of taking all men into itself, but also of comprehending the whole of life, in all its aspects. Thus the Church, in respect of its purpose, would be an association of a very peculiar kind. It is the association that aims at finally losing itself in the kingdom. On the other hand, so far as it is an association, the Church shares the ambiguity that belongs to other religious phenomena we have considered. To the positivistic sociologist, the Church will appear as simply a social phenomenon, and he may think that he can give an exhaustive account of it. But to those within the Church as "the household of faith," [16] this social phenomenon is seen "in depth" as the extension of the incarnation, the anticipation of the kingdom, the community of the Spirit, the spearhead of God's presence and acting in the world. It

[14] See above, pp. 376–377.
[15] See above, p. 375.
[16] Gal. 6:10.

is in and through the Church (as well as in the wider community of faith) that the beings are coming together with Being and the great action of Being, in creation, reconciliation, and consummation, is going forward. It is in and through the Church that Being addresses, judges, heals, and sustains particular beings.

These remarks help us to understand better the warning given at the beginning of this section when we pointed to the limitations that attend any merely pragmatic or sociological considerations of the Church. In Ian Ramsey's words, "social, even scientific, language about the Church is not only possible but necessary, and may well be illuminating; but it must be set alongside other language which talks of the Church as the distinctive Christian institution which it claims to be." [17] Such language Ramsey sees as pointing to the "mystery" of the Church, and he rightly gives it a directing role over other language about the Church. In our own terminology, seeing "in depth" corresponds to what is meant here by "mystery." There may have been times when the mystery of the Church has been overstressed, and its all too earthly characteristics ignored. But the opposite danger seems to threaten today, and so we make no excuse for giving theological considerations priority over any others in our study of the Church.

70. *THE BLESSED VIRGIN MARY*

The title of this section will, I suppose, stir varied reactions among my readers. Some who are of strong Protestant background and who fear anything that savors of what is wrongly called "mariolatry" may be rather alarmed. However, I can assure them that everything that will be said in this section will, so far as I can judge, have a sound scriptural basis. Other readers who may not react so strongly may nevertheless think that this section is a superfluous interlude, a concession perhaps to piety, but something that could be left out without making any serious difference to the whole body of Christian theology set forth in this book. Let me at once acknowledge that mariology is a more peripheral theme in Christian theology than the doctrines that were discussed in the second division of this work, and perhaps for this reason a consideration of Mary has been deferred to this point, though when the matter was first mentioned,[18] it was

---

[17] *Models and Mystery*, p. 44.
[18] See above, p. 282.

pointed out that mariology could be discussed either in relation to christology or in relation to ecclesiology—and of course christology and ecclesiology are themselves closely related. However, even if mariology is not central, there is no reason for omitting it. While we are trying to expound the Christian faith with reasonable economy and without getting lost in a morass of detail, we also want to expound the faith in its fullness, and it seems to me that a study of the Blessed Virgin does make a definite contribution toward understanding the Church and its relation to Christ. Finally, there may be some who think that here I am introducing a needlessly controversial and divisive topic. They forget that when, at an earlier stage of this book, a brief discussion of mariology was promised, the reason given was that no ecumenical theology could afford to ignore it. If the divisions of Christendom are to be overcome, it can only be through frank discussion of such issues, not by evasion. A distinguished Protestant theologian, Max Thurian, who has recently written a book on this theme of mariology, says: "Instead of being a cause of division amongst us, Christian reflection on the role of the Virgin Mary should be a cause for rejoicing and a source of prayer. . . . It is both theologically essential and spiritually profitable to consider the vocation of Mary with some freedom." [19]

If it is difficult, as we have seen, to say much about the "historical" Jesus, it would be even more difficult to say much about the "historical" Mary. We can observe the same tendencies at work in the stories of the Virgin as we saw in the stories about Christ. The oldest gospel tells hardly anything about her beyond her name. The three later canonical gospels narrate a number of incidents in which she plays a leading part. The apocryphal gospels go on to supply something like a biography, from the beginning of her life to the end. We must come to the same conclusions here as we did in the case of the stories about Christ. Even if we confine ourselves to the stories about the Virgin in the canonical gospels—the annunciation, the visitation, the purification, the station at the cross, to mention the more important—we are bound to say that these are partly historical and partly legendary, and that, like the stories of Christ's temptation, transfiguration, and the like, they are stories which aim not at giving historical information but at conveying truths of faith. This is implied in the traditional designation of such stories as "mysteries."

How then is the Blessed Virgin presented to us in these incidents or mysteries that are related in the gospels? It seems to me that the best clue

[19] *Mary, Mother of the Lord, Figure of the Church*, p. 7.

to the interpretation of her place in the New Testament teaching is afforded by the title "Mother of the Church." It was partly for this reason that we deferred a consideration of Mary's place in theology until we came to the doctrine of the Church. "Mother of the Church" is the title which Pope Paul VI proclaimed as appropriate to the Blessed Virgin when he adjourned the Vatican Council in 1964, and I believe that this particular title, more than any other provides an interpretation of Mary's place on which Roman Catholics, Orthodox, Anglicans, and Protestants could agree.

The title has a firm scriptural basis. St. John's Gospel tells that the dying Jesus commended his mother to the care of the beloved disciple with the words, "Woman, behold your son . . . Behold your mother!" [20] In this gospel, which is above all theological and in which incidents are narrated only for their theological interest, it is surely highly probable that the words, "Behold your mother!" are addressed to the whole Christian community.

As religious imagery rather than matter-of-fact description, the title "Mother of the Church" is not to be taken in a literal way. It does not mean, for instance, that Mary *originated* the Church. We have already seen that there is a sense in which there has always been a Church, and that there is little point in looking for some definite moment when it began, though certainly there were critical moments in its emergence and development.

We may say that the title "Mother of the Church" would seem to have two closely related but nonetheless distinguishable meanings. The first accords to the Blessed Virgin a certain priority in the Church, as one who played an indispensable part in the Christian drama of incarnation and salvation. This has long been recognized by the Church, which counts Mary chief among the saints, and has paid her the tribute of what John Keble, in his well-known hymn, called "all but adoring love." [21] The fact that such reverence and devotion has sometimes been unfortunately exaggerated explains the equally unfortunate reaction against Mary among many Protestants. The second and related meaning of the title sees Mary as the prototype of the Church. Just as we have seen that Israel could be considered as a prototype of the Church, so could Mary who, in some respects, sums up the vocation of Israel in her own vocation. In this second meaning, we are thinking not so much of Mary's priority in the Church as of the

[20] John 19:26.
[21] *The English Hymnal*, No. 216.

parallels between her and the Church. What we see in Mary, we ought to see in the Church. Her free cooperative obedience in the incarnation is demanded also of the Church, if God is to be present and active in our world today. The Church too, as St. Paul says, is a mother.[22] Yet the fact that the Church is also set forth as a bride [23] reminds us again that such images and analogies are not to be pushed too far.

In what follows, we shall briefly consider three of the incidents or mysteries associated with Mary in the canonical gospels, and see what they tell us both about herself, as first among the saints, and about the Church of which she is the prototype.

1. Little need be said about the *annunciation* beyond what was said about this incident earlier in connection with the doctrine of the virgin birth.[24] Principally, as was insisted then, the incident stresses the initiative of God. Incarnation takes place through the action of the Holy Spirit, or unitive Being. This is as true in the Church as it was in the case of Mary, for just as she was the bearer of the Christ, so the Church, his body, brings christhood into the world. But this takes place through the action of the Spirit in the Church, which again is the community of the Spirit. Here we must remember that we are dealing with images, not concepts, so that they are used with a freedom that would not be appropriate if one were working with strictly ordered logical notions. The Church is at once the body of Christ, the mother of the faithful, the community of the Spirit. But the point to be stressed is that in the Church as in Mary, God is at work. She is called "full of grace" (even if this is not a very good translation of the angelic greeting) [25] and the Church is likewise the community of grace. If the Church is merely an association of people united for some purpose (even if it is a good purpose), then there is no theology of the Church, and we can hand the matter over entirely to the sociologist. What is distinctive about the Church is that it is the locus of God's acting, the agent by which he incarnates himself in the world, and because of this, the theology of the Church takes precedence over any sociological study of its nature and function. Moreover, it is the presence of God in his Church that gives the Church whatever authority it has, just as it is God's presence in Mary and in the saints generally that entitles them to the reverence of the Church.

Yet we are reminded again that all God's action is personal, and that the

---

[22] Gal. 4:26.
[23] See below, pp. 513–514.
[24] See above, pp. 280–282.
[25] Luke 1:28.

unitive activity of the Spirit is not an automatic cosmic process. Mary's words, "Let it be to me according to your word," [26] are a great confession of dependence and obedience, freely accepted. Here again she is the prototype of the Church, for it is only through this free and complete submission and cooperation that incarnation can take place and God can work toward the kingdom. Here we are reminded again of the humanity of Christ, the humanity which the references to his being born of Mary are supposed to safeguard in the creeds. This humanity was essential to his mediatorial office, and it is essential if there is to be any "extension" of the incarnation as a stage toward its consummation in the kingdom of God. In the "mystery" of the annunciation, Mary freely gives up her humanity to the working of God's grace, and in so doing pioneers the role of the Church, as working with God.

2. Some fruitful suggestions on the character of the Church are also to be gathered from the incident of the *visitation*. Here, both in Elizabeth's greeting and in the great hymn of the *Magnificat*, we meet the key word "blessed" which is peculiarly associated with the Virgin.[27] She is "blessed among women," and she says of herself that "from henceforth all generations shall call me blessed." To discover the meaning of the word "blessed" (μακαρίος or εὐλογημένος) in the usage of the gospels, it is surely reasonable to look at the Beatitudes, these utterances of Jesus in which he tells us who are the blessed.[28] The qualities set forth there are those which we see also in the Blessed Virgin. St. Augustine thought of the Beatitudes as representing the process of sanctification in the Christian life, from the recognition of our poverty, or humility, before God to our perfecting as peacemakers, regarded by him as the highest beatitude; for, says St. Augustine, "to the peacemakers the likeness of God is given." [29] So the blessedness of the Virgin adumbrates the blessedness of the Church—no earthly happiness, but a "likeness to God" which means a participation in God's self-giving love, or, to put it in other words, the ministry of reconciliation. This, as we shall see again, is the high vocation of the Church.

3. Something must also be said about Mary's *station* at the cross.[30] Again, when we remember the theological character of the Fourth Gospel, we shall not suppose that this incident, moving though it is, has been in-

---

[26] Luke 1:38.
[27] Luke 1:42, 48.
[28] Luke 6:20-22; Matt. 5:2-12.
[29] *Our Lord's Sermon on the Mount*, V, 12.
[30] John 19:25-27.

cluded in the narrative just to heighten the dramatic effect. Rather, it is the parable of perfect unity and conformity with Christ, of the most complete identification and participation with him in his passion. We have already seen that through such participation or "dying with" Christ, the cross becomes intelligible as a saving act that brings wholeness. What closer participation is imaginable than that portrayed in the Fourth Gospel's picture of Mary at the cross? Kierkegaard has some very perceptive remarks about Mary's relation to Christ's suffering. He claims that Mary's own suffering is not to be understood as only a natural grief at the sight of Jesus' death, but as a sharing in his self-emptying, as if Mary were experiencing something of what Christ expressed in his cry of dereliction; and Mary's suffering is experienced in turn by every disciple who knows "the complete emptying of the human element in the face of God." [31] So here again Mary appears as the prototype of the life of the Church, which must share in the suffering of Christ and must indeed finally give up itself altogether as a distinct association if it is to be resurrected and transfigured into the kingdom of God.

Perhaps it is in a similar way that we may understand some of the puzzling harsh sayings of Jesus to his mother.[32] Is the point that natural affection has to be subjected to the higher love than lets-be, and the desire for union and association sacrificed to the vocation of the other? [33] Both Jesus and Mary were required, by their respective vocations, to bring their love for each other to the highest possible level.

All that has been said about Mary so far has fairly clear scriptural support, as was claimed at the beginning of the section. But there are two doctrines about Mary, both of them *de fide* in the Roman Catholic Church, which do not seem to have any direct support in the New Testament. I mean the dogmas of her immaculate conception and her assumption into heaven. We can scarcely ignore them, but are we then to dismiss them as accretions, springing from the exaggerated cult of Mary? I believe that these two dogmas, when purged of mythological elements, can be interpreted as implications of more central Christian teaching. Theologically, of course, their significance does not lie in anything they say about the private biography of Mary but as pointing to moments in the life of the community of faith, for here again there is an intimate parallel between Mary and the Church.

[31] *The Last Years*, pp. 38–40, 111.
[32] Mark 3:31–35; etc.
[33] See above, p. 349.

Immaculate conception, in spite of the negative adjective, is, like the sinlessness of Jesus, a thoroughly affirmative idea. It is to be understood in connection with that "original righteousness," which, we claimed, was never totally obliterated by original sin; and with that "common grace," given in creation itself and never totally quenched. That righteousness and grace were nurtured and strengthened in the people of God, the nation of Israel, until the people had come to the point of receptivity when the Logos could become flesh among them—the point represented by Mary's response to the annunciation.

Assumption, which implies the same mythological background as the ascension of Jesus, looks to the consummation of the Church. Mary, the perfect type of the Church, is taken up by Christ to share in his risen and ascended existence.

One could develop in many other ways the comparison between Mary and the Church, and of course this has been done for centuries. However, the kind of typology in which such an enterprise becomes involved is foreign to the method of our own work. We content ourselves with the points made above, for these show clearly enough that among all the "types" of the Church, Mary is preeminent, and signally elucidates the Church's character.

It will be noted that we have said nothing about the supposed relation between reverence for the Blessed Virgin and the need for a feminine element in religion. It may well be true, as a matter of historical fact, that the veneration of the Virgin is related to ancient Near Eastern and Mediterranean worship of the Mother Goddess, just as many other features of Christian worship have pagan precursors. It may also be true that reverence for the Virgin satisfies a psychological need, missed by a too masculine conception of God; and that such reverence encourages a kind of piety that is warmer and more personal than the austere and not very attractive virtues of the Puritans. But these considerations have no direct bearing on the theological question about Mary, and can be used neither to support nor to detract from the place traditionally given to her in the Church. Berdyaev is completely correct when he affirms that reverence for the Blessed Virgin "is essentially distinct from pagan worship of the female principle." [34] The practical benefits or, as has sometimes happened, abuses, which reverence for Mary has brought, cannot be determinative of her place in Christian thought and devotion. This has to be considered

---

[34] *The Beginning and the End*, p. 246.

in theological terms, that is to say, in the light of christology, ecclesiology, and the transformed anthropology that goes with them, as we have tried to show. If we have consistently held throughout this book that theological thinking must be rooted in the existential dimension of faith, we have maintained equally that practical attitudes have to be correlated with theological reflection and, where necessary, corrected by it. It seems to me, however, that it is precisely a renewed theological consideration of the issues involved that will increasingly lead Protestants (as it has led some of them already) to abandon their negative attitudes toward Mary, and to join with their Catholic brethren (and with the New Testament) in a glad *Ave Maria!*

71. THE SAINTS

This is a suitable place in which to say something about the saints generally, for although Mary is reckoned first among the saints of the Church, she is first of "a great multitude which no man could number, from every nation, from all tribes and peoples and tongues." [35] If we learn something of the Church's character from Mary, we would expect this understanding to be broadened and deepened when we consider the diversity and catholicity of the saints. Neither the Church nor the Christian life which goes on within it exemplifies some narrow pattern, but, as we saw to be implicit even in the notion of creation, brings to maturity the greatest possible diversity in unity. The extraordinary variety of those whom the Church calls "saints" is sufficient warning against any rigidly narrow idea of the Church, which must rather be comprehensive enough to contain and encourage within itself the manifold potentialities of existence.

The expression "saints" has been used in the Church in two principal ways. In the New Testament it was applied to any Christians. They formed in each city the community of the Holy Spirit, and so they were thought of as the "saints at Jerusalem," or wherever it might be. But in the later and more common usage, the expression stands for those whom the Church recognizes as having signally manifested the Holy Spirit and as having been conformed to Christ. Perhaps both meanings are implied in the designation of the Church as the "communion of saints," a phrase which occurs in the Apostles' Creed. All Christians belong to this communion or fellowship, in which the work of sanctification is going on;

---

[35] Rev. 7:9.

but the meaning and character of the fellowship is specially evident in those who have attained such a degree of sanctification as to be recognized as "saints" by the Christian community as a whole. Thus the saints in general stand to the Church in the same kind of twofold relation as we saw in the case of Mary—they have a priority within the Church, as those who have attained and who are therefore called the "Church triumphant"; yet they have also an affinity with the whole Church, in so far as the characteristics which they manifest should be seen to be emerging in the whole body of Christians.

Once again, the central characteristic held up before us is self-giving love. This is what is most typical of sainthood, however diverse its manifestations. In our discussion of eschatology, we saw how it used to be supposed in the Church that the martyrs had no need of purgation because by utterly giving themselves they had attained to the fullest potentialities of their existence.[36] The martyr is perhaps the most obvious kind of saint (and traditionally, of course, all the twelve apostles, except St. John, were martyrs). But as time went on, the Church recognized that there are modes of self-denial and self-renunciation other than giving oneself to physical death that may be to no less a degree the expression of the love of Christ. Hence the range of sainthood comes to embrace an extraordinary diversity of human gifts and callings.

But the martyr remains the norm of sainthood, both because he exemplifies the most obvious kind of self-giving and also because the name of "martyr" points to his function as "witness." The lives of the saints testify to the reality of God's sanctifying work in the world. The saints are the "cloud of witnesses" [37] which surrounds the Church militant and show, as it were, what is going on in the Church and to what quality of existence it is leading.

In remembering and honoring its saints by yearly commemorations or in other ways, the Church is not showing a sentimental nostalgia for its past. Rather, this is a real communion of saints. We may compare the communion of saints to that taking up of the past into a unity of past, present, and future which we saw to be basic for selfhood and which, we speculated, may be characteristic also of Being. In the communion of saints, the Church accepts its heritage and confesses its identity; but paradoxically this very heritage is the self-giving love of the martyrs and con-

36 See above, p. 366.
37 Heb. 12:1.

fessors—a love which they in turn learned from Christ. Thus in accepting this heritage, the Church *ipso facto* commits itself to a future in which it must lose itself in order to transcend itself and become the kingdom of God.

It may be the case that as far as general theological principles are concerned, our consideration of the saints has added little or nothing that we had not already met in other connections. But the space devoted to a discussion of them is justified on the same ground as was mentioned in our similar discussion of the Blessed Virgin—it lights up for us the fullness of Christian faith and theology by bringing before us something of the vast range of concrete manifestations that all lead back to the few central truths that are basic to our religion. And if our contentions about the demands of an embodied existence are correct, then these concrete manifestations are needed, if the basic truths are to come to life and be operative in actual historical existence.

72. THE NOTES OF THE CHURCH AND THEIR EMBODIMENT

In the preceding sections of this chapter, we have tried to set forth some basic characteristics of the Church. The time has now come to gather these together in a more coherent scheme, and also to bring them down to earth, as it were, by considering the actual visible structures in which they find expression. For up till now, we have (quite justifiably) been looking for the essence of the Church in terms of its highest manifestations and in relation to those theological doctrines which determine its direction and destiny. But if we lay too much stress on these ways of conceiving the Church, we can come out with that mistaken understanding of the Church which gives to it a premature glory and confuses it with the eschatological kingdom of God. If indeed we believe that the Church is a theological entity as well as a sociological one, then we should expect to see even in the dustiest epochs of "the Church militant here on earth" some glimmerings of the glory which, as we hope, shall yet be revealed in it. But the treasure is very much in earthen vessels, and the Church is a mixed phenomenon. It unfolds creation and ministers reconciliation, but it falls short of consummation.

Our discussion may be conveniently organized around the four traditional notes of the Church, as the one, holy, catholic and apostolic Church. Unity, holiness, catholicity, and apostolicity will be found to sum up those essential characteristics of the Church which have emerged in the earlier discussions. We shall see how in the actual historical Church these notes may be more or less visible, according as the essence of the Church is emerging more or less purely.[38] The Christian hope is that these notes will come through more and more clearly as the, Church moves toward its consummation. But at any given time, we see them only "more or less." Moreover, each of them needs some visible or institutional structure for its embodiment and protection, but, as with all "earthen vessels," while these are quite indispensable, they are never perfect.

We have first to say something about the *unity* of the Church, though this is such an inclusive concept that it can hardly be separated from the other three marks of the Church. In its fullest sense, the unity of the Church implies its holiness, catholicity, and apostolicity. However, there is a basic unity which can be discussed at the outset.

The basic unity has as its center Jesus Christ himself. The Christian community of faith is at one in confessing that Jesus Christ is Lord, and the unity which he establishes extends through and holds together the many Christian groups. We have seen already that the most appropriate of all the titles of the Church is the "body of Christ." [39] Christ is the head of the body, and therefore the source of its unity. It is he who makes it a body, a unitary coordinated organism, rather than a collection of individual entities. Yet this very metaphor of the body also stresses the diversity in unity. St. Paul declares: "The body does not consist of one member, but of many," [40] and he is at pains to show the diversity of gifts and functions that are necessary to the life of the body. We see that the richer is the diversity, the stronger is the unity and interdependence. We are reminded also by this picture that the Church is a microcosm, for this diversity in unity we recognize as the end of creation itself; and while the Church is the fellowship of the Holy Spirit, the same Spirit is "unitive Being," that movement in Being which builds up ever larger and richer unities. So we see too that the Church has indefinite edges—it merges into the wider community of faith, and eventually into the whole divine work of creation-reconciliation-consummation. But the Christian sees it as the spearhead of this work, though its ultimate destiny may be to lose itself and transcend itself in the still wider unity of the consummated kingdom.

The problem of the Church's unity—as of the wider unity of mankind,

---

[38] Cf. *The Westminster Confession of Faith*, xxv, 4.
[39] See above, p. 388.
[40] I Cor. 12:14.

to which it is closely related—is rightly to balance the unity against the diversity. A unity that flattens out all diversity falls far below that free kind of unity which we saw to be at once the glory and the risk of creation. The first is the unity of a machine, the second a unity of persons. Cardinal Bea has well said: "A unity that does not respect the principle of freedom may eventually create a certain form of unity, but not a human one; it is not a unity of free and responsible men, but of slaves." [41] But if there is a unity that swallows up freedom, there is also a diversity that breaks up unity rather than contributing to it. The member lives to itself in a false autonomy, eventually destroying itself and perhaps the whole body with it.

It is important to remember that in his great prayer for his disciples, Christ asked "that they may be one," and immediately went on to indicate that this unity should be like the unity of the Father and the Son.[42] The ultimate model for the Church's unity is therefore the unity of the triune God, a unity embracing the richest diversity and thus one in which there is neither stifling absorption nor damaging division.

The historical Church has sometimes more, sometimes less manifested something like a genuine unity in Christ. Even in New Testament times, there was destructive divisiveness and factionalism, and no period of the Church's history has been without its schisms, heresies, and dissensions. But although we hear a lot about "our unhappy divisions," we ought to remember that just as offensive to true unity has been the false unity that has characterized other phases of the Church's history—the outward uniformity that has suppressed legitimate differences and has been imposed by force. The genuine diversity-in-unity of the body of Christ needs to be defended against uniformity just as much as against divisiveness.

After many centuries of oscillating between enforced uniformity and an almost wanton divisiveness, the Church has in modern times set its face toward a genuine Christian unity, and probably ecumenism has become the most important movement in the Church's development in the twentieth century. Already it has banished many of the ancient prejudices and rivalries, and created an altogether better feeling of solidarity among Christians.

Yet there are many dangers in ecumenism, and these are enhanced by the indiscriminate enthusiasm which it seems to engender. On the one hand, there is the danger of submerging legitimate differences, and thereby

[41] *Unity in Freedom*, pp. 6–7.
[42] John 17:11.

impoverishing the body which is enriched and strengthened by these differences. In spite of protestations to the contrary, most schemes of union put forward seem to aim (perhaps inevitably) at the greatest measure of uniformity and compromise, based on the lowest common denominator of the various groups involved, or sometimes on the attempt to lump together in an incongruous mass different traditions of belief and practice. A nondescript church of this kind would probably turn out to be weaker than a group of churches expressing the Christian faith in its authentic diversity. Perhaps the best schemes of union worked out so far have been those between the Roman Catholic Church and the Uniat Orthodox Churches. Here the various liturgies, customs, and languages have been preserved in their integrity, and these unions could well be taken as models for the future. On the other hand, there has also been a danger that the conception of unity has not been global enough. Most schemes of union are confined to one country and concern the denominations operating within the national borders. The unity of the Church, however, utterly transcends national considerations, and it is most unfortunate—especially in the modern world—that the churches should duplicate and reinforce national frontiers. The unity represented by a body like the Anglican communion, provided it is a genuine union of concern and mutual responsibility, is, as international and interracial, a far more effective witness to unity in Christ than would be a national "merger" of denominations. A national church can hardly avoid identifying itself too closely with the interests of the nation to which it belongs and is bound to be limited by the characteristics, some good and some bad, of its group.

The most obvious visible sign of the Church's unity is the Bible. If indeed the center of the Church's unity is Jesus Christ, as the head of the body, then the Bible is the embodiment of that unity because it is the written word, testifying to the manifestation of the living Word in the flesh. The Bible is also the most widespread visible sign of the unity of faith that belongs to the whole body of Christians, for some groups that do not even have the sacraments (Quakers, Salvation Army) and yet which are undeniably Christians, have the Bible. The Bible therefore stretches out as far as what we have called the "indefinite" borders of the Church. More than this, however, the Bible links the Church with the wider community of faith, for the Bible contains not only the distinctively Christian New Testament but also the Hebrew scriptures; and although to the Christian theologian this is the "Old Testament" and is read in a Christian perspective, no reasonable person would deny that in and by themselves, the Hebrew scriptures have been produced out of the experiences of faith and revelation, and still function as vehicles of revelation in Judaism. Hence the Bible links Christianity with Judaism and so eventually with the faith adventure of the world's religions.

Because of its universal acceptance among Christians, the Bible already constitutes a remarkable foundation for unity, and any ecumenical theology must be firmly rooted in the Bible. But this is certainly not meant to imply that such an ecumenical theology must be narrowly biblicist. The kind of theology that has been produced in Protestant ecumenical circles has up till now been too much dominated by the somewhat narrow idea of a "biblical" theology, free from external cultural influences, such as was fashionable in the earlier days of the Barthian movement. Far more allowance has to be made—as the later Barth seems to recognize—for subsequent development in the Church, that is to say, for tradition. The canon of the Bible itself, after all, was fixed by the Church. In doing this, the Church set up a visible embodiment to protect the unity of its faith. At the same time, however, it erected a standard to which it submits itself. So we come back to the idea of a division of authority. This reminds us too that the note of unity in the Church has an inclusiveness that spills over into the other notes, and the full conception of unity and its visible embodiment cannot be reached until we have talked also of the remaining three notes.

Next among the notes comes *holiness*. Here it is very much a case of "more or less," and to many it will seem that the Church has often been less rather than more holy. We have to be clear, however, about what the "holiness" of the Church means. It cannot mean an otherworldly holiness that keeps its hands clean, so to speak, by avoiding contamination with earthly things. In our discussion of the saints, stress was laid on the variety of gifts and vocations. The "holiness" of the saints is not an escape from the world (though there will always be some whose vocation is to protest against materialistic preoccupations by a life of withdrawal), but obedience in a particular situation. "Let it be to me according to your word." [43] In again quoting these words of the Virgin, I am trying to make the point that holiness means being an agent of the incarnation, letting Christ be formed in the Church and in the world. Or in the more ontological language that we have used from time to time, holiness is cooperation with the letting-be of Being, it is the strengthening and promoting

[43] Luke 1:38.

of the beings as against the threat of dissolution. But normally this can be done only by the maximal participation and involvement in the life of the world.

The Church is the communion of saints, and the achievements of the saints remain as a constant testimony and encouragement to the reality of grace in the Church. But here again we must be careful not to form an exaggerated idea of the Church as it is *in via*. It has innumerable blind spots and lapses. We may believe in its ultimate indefectibility and that holiness, in the sense explained, is making headway, so that the Church and indeed all mankind is being sanctified by God's reconciling work. But we have already distinguished indefectibility from infallibility. In many particular instances, the Church utterly falls short of holiness, and may even, through its support of wrong causes or a reactionary politico-social *status quo*, or sometimes through the idolizing of its own structure, work against sanctification. Yet one would hope—and legitimately, since this is simply part of the eschatological Christian hope—that these lapses would be episodes which would be eventually overcome in the total life of the Church.

The visible embodiment of the Church's holiness is its sacramental life. Since the sacraments will be discussed in detail in a later chapter,[44] only some brief remarks need to be made here; but in any case, the whole basic philosophy of this book, with its stress on how Being becomes present and manifest in and through the beings, lends itself readily to the sacramental and incarnational principle. The sacraments may be understood as the growing points, as it were, at which the divine grace sanctifies the Church and conforms its life to Christ. They are also the ways by which the existence of the individual is incorporated into the body of Christ. Yet once again, as in the case of the Bible, we must avoid rigidity. In both cases, one can develop a "fundamentalism" that mistakes the earthen vessel for the treasure that it contains. We have seen that there are some Christian groups that have discarded the commonly accepted sacraments. It is not to be denied that grace operates in them too, for the operation of the divine Spirit is not confined to the recognized sacraments, any more than it is confined to the Christian religion. It may even be that these groups constitute a warning against the overprizing of sacramental forms. Yet even such groups have sacraments of a sort, whatever they may call them, for the grace of Being cannot reach us save through the beings in which it is present and manifest. We must not idolize particular sacramental forms,

44 See below, pp. 447–486.

yet on the other hand the forms which are rooted in the Bible and which have been developed in the Church's tradition and proved of value in her devotional life are bound to command a very special respect and reverence. These are the institutional forms, suited to our embodied existence, that protect and foster the growth of holiness, first in the Church and then in all humanity.

We pass to the third note of the Church—*catholicity*. There are two distinct but related ideas implied in this third note. "Catholicity" means, first of all, universality. The Church is for all men, for what goes on in the Church, as we have seen, is simply the spearhead of what is going on in the creation as a whole. The end of the Church and the end of creation converge upon the kingdom of God. The Church cannot be complete until the whole creation is complete, and then of course the distinction between the Church and the rest of creation will have disappeared. This means that the Church must be an open rather than a closed society. In its catholic outreach, it abolishes the divisive demarcations that set one segment of society against another, though it does not obliterate the variety of human beings but enriches the unity of the whole by giving scope to many kinds of gifts and vocations. St. Paul affirms that "in Christ" there is "neither Jew nor Greek, there is neither slave nor free, there is neither male nor female" [45]; but he is equally clear that "there are varieties of gifts . . . varieties of service . . . varieties of working." [46] It is this inclusive unity-with-diversity that constitutes the catholicity of the Church as universality. But "catholicity" also means authenticity, that is to say, authenticity of belief and practice in the Church. This second meaning is related to the first, for it has in view the consensus of the Church. The authentic faith is to be learned by considering the universal faith. So from New Testament times onward, we find that when some weighty matter is to be decided, this is done by summoning a council and ascertaining the consensus of the Church.

The structures in which the catholicity of the Church gets embodied are primarily the catholic creeds, especially the Apostles' and Nicene; and also the pronouncements of the universally recognized councils of the Church, such as those of Nicaea and Chalcedon. They give considered expression to the mind of the universal Church, speaking, as it believes, under the guidance of the Spirit.

---

[45] Gal. 3:28.
[46] I Cor. 12:4–6.

The creeds are catholic in both senses of the word. They set forth the authentic faith, but they are not to be thought of as sets of propositions to be intellectually received. We have insisted from the beginning of this study that faith is more than belief; it is an existential attitude. This comes out clearly in the reciting of the creeds by the Christian community. The creeds express the identity of the community. The only qualification required for joining the community is to share its faith, and to join with the members of the community in the creed is to identify with them, to participate in their attitude toward Christ, toward existence, toward Being.

Perhaps relatively few Christians understand fully on the intellectual level the contents of the ancient creeds. In any case, the creeds and the pronouncements of the ancient councils were aimed at excluding errors, and were certainly not intended to exclude further study. They leave plenty of room for freedom and development in theological discussion. The attempt to define too many doctrines too precisely is an error, for it overestimates the importance of the visible structure and forgets that this structure has not been produced for its own sake but in order to protect and foster a living faith, which cannot be completely transcribed into words.

If we remember the double meaning of catholicity, we shall not be in danger of confusing it with correct doctrine. There may be churches which stick to the letter of correct doctrine and which yet offend against catholicity because they deny the universality of the Church. We do in fact hear from time to time about churches which exclude from their membership and even from their worship persons of a different race from the members; and often enough, such churches pride themselves on their orthodoxy and their conservative (not to say reactionary) theology. No matter how orthodox these congregations may be, they have cut themselves off from true catholicity by denying the universal character of the Church. They can no longer have any part in that ever-widening fellowship which cannot stop short of all creation, and which will be transformed into the kingdom when it coincides with creation—and only then. Such so-called churches are moving in the opposite direction into isolation and disintegration, like branches that have been severed from the vine. This is true even if (as one must charitably hope) their attitude springs from ignorance rather than from malice against their human brethren.

Thus the case with catholicity is like those we have already met in connection with unity and holiness. There is a structural form within the world that both expresses and protects the truly catholic being of the

Church, but we must again hold the balance between inner and outer, between spontaneity and the fixity of forms. The creeds and the ancient christological formulae are so built into the Church that they express its very identity and let its members experience their solidarity in this universal community; but they are meaningless if they do not protect and enhance a faith that reaches into all the dimensions of existence.

The last note that we have to consider is *apostolicity*, and this one perhaps gives rise to the greatest controversy. Apostolicity is not too sharply distinguished from catholicity, especially in the second of the two senses of "catholicity." The apostolic Church is the authentic Church, continuing the teaching and practice of the apostles, who had been "eyewitnesses" of the events proclaimed in the Church's message (κήρυγμα), and who had been commissioned by Christ himself. Faithfulness to the apostles appears as a mark of the New Testament Church in its earliest period: "they devoted themselves to the apostles' teaching." [47] Before long, many heretical sects were springing up, as the Christian teaching coalesced with Gnostic and other religious ideas of the time. The authentic Christian community had to distinguish itself and its message from the heterodox groups, and it sought to do this by establishing its continuity with the apostles. The respect in which the apostles were held is attested by the well-known fact that there are several books in the New Testament written by anonymous authors but ascribed to leading apostles, so as to gain for them an authority that they could not otherwise have. But of course, the heretics played the same game, and we have many apocryphal writings that also bear the names of apostles. Eventually the Church, as we have already noted, decided which books were to be regarded as authoritative, and the canon was formed. But since there were, both inside and outside the canon as it was eventually formed, books claiming to be written by apostles, the matter was not settled just by the question of authorship, but by the Church's own living continuity with the apostles. Even in ancient times, there were doubts as to the authorship of some of the New Testament documents, and in modern times these doubts have crystallized in some cases into virtual certainty. But this does not in the slightest degree alter the Church's attitude toward these documents, for whether or not their actual authors were apostles, their teaching is in accordance with the apostolic tradition, as this was received and continued among the first generations of Christians.

Whereas "catholicity" indicates the authenticity of the Church's practice

[47] Acts 2:42.

and teaching by pointing to the consensus of Christians throughout the world, "apostolicity" has to do rather with the extension of the Church through time, its continuity and identity through the ages. Though it must indeed change in many ways, it can claim to be the Church of Jesus Christ only if it has retained at least a minimal degree of continuity with Christ, first through his apostles and then through the generations of their successors. Again, we can make a comparison between the Church and a self. As the commitment of faith plays an important part in unifying a self, so that we can recognize it as the same self as it moves through time, so too the community of faith is united by the same faith that has spanned the centuries. The formulations of that faith have changed and will change, but the existential attitude which constitutes the core of the faith has remained constant. So the inner meaning, if we may so speak, of the apostolicity of the Church is its constancy in the faith of the apostles.

As with the other notes of the Church, the note of apostolicity has its own embodiment or institutional form to protect it. This form is the episcopate. This office, publicly transmitted by the apostles to their successors and then on through the generations, is the overt, institutional vehicle for ensuring the continuity of that heritage of faith and practice which was likewise transmitted by the apostles.

There will be a discussion of the ministry of the Church and its various orders and functions in the next chapter, so I do not propose to embark here on any lengthy remarks about the office of a bishop. Let me simply draw attention to the parallel between the episcopate and the other "embodiments" (the canon of Scripture, the sacraments, the creeds) which we met when considering the first three notes of the Church. The episcopate, like the others, protects by an outward institution the inner life of the Church. In all the threats of heresy and perversion to which it has been exposed, not only in the early centuries but later, the Church has held to its apostolic heritage and this has been in no small measure due to the specific office of the bishop, as the guardian of that heritage, and also, let it be said, to the qualities of most of those who have held this office. The episcopate cannot be treated as if it were on a different footing from the other embodied forms associated with the fundamental notes of the Church.

The case has been put so well and clearly by John Knox that I can do no better than summarize his argument. He shows how the various features of the early Catholic Church were intended to establish its unity and integrity, and were not only *ad hoc* responses to the Gnostic threat but developments of the New Testament understanding of the Church. In

particular, he draws an analogy among the canon, the creeds, and the episcopate. All came to be regarded as "apostolic," which means "that the
early Catholic Church, which in reality established these forms (or in
whose experience they were first established), thought of itself as doing
no more than recognizing what had been established by the apostles themselves." It is not a question of whether, as a matter of historical fact, the
apostles wrote the books ascribed to them in the New Testament; or
whether the Apostles' Creed was actually composed by the apostles; or
whether the apostolic ministry in the form of the historic episcopate was
plainly and universally present from the beginning. We are to think of
these rather in the context of the Church as "a visible, historical community," possessing an identity and yet developing in response to new
demands and opportunities. The point about the various forms is that although they required time before they developed to the point where they
clearly emerge in history, they express the mind and character of the
Church as it had been since the apostles.[48]

The argument summarized here is entirely compatible with the views
developed in this book of embodied existence in the world, of community
as extending through time in a manner analogous to selfhood, and of the
Church as a community of faith which must express and protect its being
through specific institutional forms that have now become part of its identity. For these reasons, we have to agree with John Knox when he says:
"I for one have no hesitancy in ascribing the same status to episcopacy as
to canon and creed." [49]

It is time for us to draw together the findings of this section on the
notes of the Church. As an actual historical association, the Church exhibits "more or less" the unity, holiness, catholicity, and apostolicity which
will fully belong to it only when it gives itself up in order to become the
kingdom of God. It exhibits unity the more it is obedient to Christ as its
head; holiness, the more the divine Spirit is immanent and active within it;
catholicity and apostolicity, the more it manifests the authentic Christian
faith that brings men into community across the barriers of geography,
race, culture, or even time. Because it is embodied in an earthly existence,
the Church has its treasures in earthen vessels that are not to be despised,
and we have listed as the four most vital to it: the Holy Scriptures, the
sacraments, the catholic creeds, and the historic episcopate.

The reader will have noticed that the four institutional forms or em-

---

[48] Cf. *The Early Church and the Coming Great Church*, pp. 142–155.
[49] *Op. cit.*, p. 152.

bodiments mentioned as expressing and supporting the four fundamental notes of the Church are identical with the four points put forward in the nineteenth century as the *sine qua non* for a reunion of the Church, in the so-called "Chicago-Lambeth Quadrilateral." This still remains the basic minimum required for any possible reunion. Within this basic framework, one would certainly hope that there would be the maximal degree of freedom and variety, and I have already suggested that Rome's relation to the Uniat churches provides the best model for union without drab uniformity. It must be remembered too that no claim is made that only churches which have this fourfold structure are "true" churches. It was already conceded that even Christian groups that do not have the sacraments are not to be thought of as "excluded," and it has also been maintained that the Church merges at its borders into the wider community of faith and eventually into the world. God's Spirit is not confined to particular institutional channels. On the other hand, the Church cannot live without an institutional structure, and the four forms that have been described may be said to constitute the normative shape of the Church, a shape that has proved its value in most of its provinces throughout most of its history. Yet I would again agree with John Knox that one would not wish to see these structures accepted for merely pragmatic reasons, not "even to promote church union." [50] They are to be accepted in the end because they have been built into the identity of the Church, and body forth in the world the being of the Church as the body of Christ, one, holy, catholic and apostolic.

While I have been quite emphatic in upholding the four notes of the Church and the traditional forms in which they have been embodied, this does not mean that all the institutional accretions that have gathered along the way must also be preserved. Within the framework of the "quadrilateral," there is endless scope for variety and experiment, though stability and continuing identity are likewise assured. We should indeed expect that in our changing world, new forms of church life must be developed. What, in detail, these might be, is not our business to say, but we can well envisage that house-churches, industrial missions, vocational groups, *ad hoc* actions in critical situations and the like may all be required and in some cases may prove much more effective than some of the cumbrous machinery that has come down to us. Actually, the demands are very different in different areas of the Church. For instance, they are one thing

[50] *Op. cit.*, p. 144.

where the Church suffers from the danger of popularity, but quite another where the danger is persecution. It is always worth remembering that in the most glorious period of all in its history, the first three centuries, the Church had hardly any of the "apparatus" or "plant," still less of the appalling bureaucracy, that now seems to be taken for granted. Yet it must also be remembered that it was precisely in that early period that the Church protected and stabilized her life and mission by firmly basing herself on that fourfold foundation which bodied itself forth in the canon, the sacraments, the creeds, and the apostolic ministry.

73. THE PAPACY

In the last section it was argued that the episcopate serves as the sign of one of the Church's fundamental notes and has therefore an assured place in the classic form or embodied structure of the Church. But would not a very similar kind of argument make out an equally good case for the papacy? Certainly the papacy is an institution so ancient and so important in the Church that we cannot fail to give due consideration to its place, in spite of all the controversy that has raged around it.

If the New Testament makes clear the special status of the apostles, surely it also makes it clear that St. Peter had a certain primacy among them. He was obviously the leader, and is reported as the first to have recognized Jesus as the Messiah, and the first of the apostles to have seen the risen Christ.[51] More specifically, Christ declares him to be the rock on which he will build the Church[52]; and it is to St. Peter that the risen Lord commends the care of the Church in the postlude to the Fourth Gospel.[53] After we leave the New Testament, there are many obscurities. Did St. Peter go to Rome? Did he become leader or bishop of the church there? Did any special prerogatives which he may have had pass to his successors in the see of Rome? These questions cannot be answered with confidence, yet perhaps there is just as much obscurity over the question of the rise of the New Testament canon or the development of the sacraments or the emergence of a definitely structured ministry. If we are prepared to call the latter three "apostolic," should we deny the title to the papacy? If we accept St. John's Gospel as canonical and "apostolic" in the sense which John Knox intends, although we do not accept that it

[51] Mark 8:29; I Cor. 15:5; etc.
[52] Matt. 16:18.
[53] John 21:15–19.

was written by St. John, can we not also say that the papacy expresses the mind and intention of the apostles and is indeed foreshadowed in the New Testament, though it required time for its explicit emergence into history? (Actually, the papacy emerged earlier and more definitely than many Protestant historians have been willing to acknowledge). And finally, can one not say (and surely one can!) that the papacy too was invaluable in nurturing the Church and in preserving its unity and integrity through the early centuries, just as much as the other embodiments we have considered?

These arguments seem persuasive, yet there is one point at which we must take issue. We were able to go along with John Knox's case for the episcopacy because it was already completely supported by everything that had been said earlier about existence in the world, selfhood, historical being, the nature of community, and so on. If the office of the bishop were not already there, something like it would have been demanded by the theological structure already built up. But it is different in the case of the papacy. We have set our face all along against individualism, and it would be entirely contrary to the whole trend of our theology, whether philosophical or symbolic, to allow that the apostolic character of the Church could depend on a succession of individuals. We begin with the college of apostles, and we must suppose that their successors too constitute a college. This too is in accordance with our view of the division of authority among several organs, a view which once again would be incompatible with the excessive concentration of authority in a single individual.

This mention of authority brings up the question of the "infallibility" which came to be attributed to the Pope. Even when we allow that papal infallibility is a much more limited affair than Protestants commonly understand it to be, we have already rejected the notion of any infallibility in the Church. We have seen indeed that the Christian faith seems to imply that the Church has a measure of indefectibility,[54] but this does not mean that it is infallible on every or any particular occasion, and still less that this infallibility could belong to an individual rather than to a conciliar or collegiate group.

It is possible, however, that the issue is obscured by the use of the term "infallibility." Like some other terms we have encountered in this book, this one, though negative in form, really expresses a deeply affirmative

---

[54] See above, p. 390.

idea. For what is freedom from error if it is not penetration into truth? Could we say that just as a compass needle, when distracting influences have been removed, turns unfailingly toward the north, so the mind of the Church, when fully open to the Holy Spirit, turns unfailingly toward the truth? This would be the fulfillment of Christ's promise to the disciples, "When the Spirit of truth comes, he will guide you into all the truth." [55] This certainly does not mean that on any particular occasion there can be a verbal formulation that is totally free from error or that is delivered from the cultural and historical relativity that affects all verbalizations. Also, the relation to truth belongs to the whole Church, though clearly its leadership bears a special responsibility in this matter. On the other hand, this affirmative idea that underlies infallibility is not just the same as indefectibility. Whereas indefectibility is a deduction from the doctrine of the last things and teaches that in the end the Church will come to that consummation which God has destined for it, what we are talking about here is the belief that on its way to the end the Church may on particular occasions seek so to open its mind to the divine Spirit that it is led into truth. This is surely an implicate of the doctrine of the Church and is the kernel of truth in the idea of infallibility. But again let it be said that this particular term is a misleading one.

Cardinal Bea has made the further point that papal infallibility can be understood as a check on the particularism of national churches.[56] We have much sympathy with this point of view, as is clear from the fact that several times in this book we warn against the attempts to form united national churches, as envisaged by so many Protestant ecumenists. But the best safeguard against this particularism is surely an international college of bishops rather than the Pope alone, especially since the papacy for so long has itself been closely associated with a single nation.

Our argument is that the papacy is not an *additional* structure required by the one holy catholic and apostolic Church alongside those of scripture, sacraments, creeds, and episcopate. The alleged parallel between the considerations that establish the place of the episcopate and those that are advanced on behalf of the papacy breaks down. But this is not to say for a moment that the institution of the papacy is to be rejected. We can think of it as included within the structure of the episcopate, and as having within the episcopate a primacy which many persons outside of the

---

55 John 16:13.
56 *Unity in Freedom*, p. 89.

Roman communion would be willing to acknowledge. Frederick C. Grant has written that "the papacy is one of the most priceless elements in the Christian heritage. Reformed and restored to a pristine state in which, among the Church's leaders, it should once more be first among equals, *primus inter pares*, rather than a monarchical sovereignty, the papacy might very well become the acknowledged leader, guide and chief of the whole Christian Church, and the greatest influence for good in the whole world." [57]

The papacy is not, as we have already said, a structure or embodiment *additional* to the episcopate, but it has its place within the episcopate, and belongs to the fullness of the Church. Of course, the whole question of the relation of the papacy to the episcopate, and of the so-called "collegiality" of the bishops, is under consideration within the Roman communion.[58] The First Vatican Council in 1870 pronounced on papal infallibility, but was adjourned before it got around to making a compensating statement about the episcopate. At the Second Vatican Council, the influence of the episcopate was greatly enhanced, and Pope Paul VI indicated in 1965 that the college of bishops would henceforth have a permanent and more significant role in the government of the Church. There is at least the possibility of developments that could make the papacy a center of unity for all Christians. Recent pontiffs, and especially Pope John XXIII, have demonstrated in a remarkable manner how much vitality and influence can still belong to the successors of St. Peter after nineteen centuries.

At the very least, we have to affirm that any vision of a reunited Church, one, holy, catholic and apostolic, must envisage it in communion with the most illustrious of the apostolic sees. Anything short of this can be regarded as only an interim step; and anything that might make this ultimate consummation more difficult should be scrupulously avoided.

74. THE AUTHORITY OF THE CHURCH

At several points in our discussion there has loomed the difficult question of authority. When we introduced the theme of an applied theology in general, we took note that in this area there operates a kind of composite authority, constituted by the Bible, the Church, and the judgments of

---

[57] *Rome and Reunion*, p. 144.
[58] Cf. Karl Rahner, *Inquiries*, pp. 303–400.

reason and conscience.[59] In our discussion of the Church, the question of authority has come up again—both with regard to the authority of the Church in general and with regard to the authority of organs within the Church, especially the papacy. These questions call for further discussion. The reason for putting this discussion within the chapter on the Church is not because we are saying that the Church has an authority more ultimate than that of the Bible or common sense, but because it is actually within the community that authority has to be exercised and decisions made. Who is to define what Christian faith is except the believing Christian community itself? It is the community to which Christ has given the command, "Go and teach all nations!" [60] It is therefore a community having a teaching office or *magisterium*, and since this was conferred by Christ, it must carry great weight, and would normally prevail over the opinions of individual Christians or groups of Christians.

However, this authority of the Church, whether in matters of doctrine, order, or practice, is limited in several ways.

1. It is, as we have seen, a *derived* authority. It stems from Jesus Christ and must be subject ultimately to him. Since it is the Bible, especially the New Testament, that contains the apostolic witness to Christ, this means in practice that the authority of the Bible qualifies that of the Church. It would be hard to say, however, that one is more ultimate than the other. The Church produced the New Testament and settled its canon. Yet, having done so, it also in a sense made itself subject to the New Testament. In a similar fashion, a nation decides its constitution, but having done so, it remains governed by that constitution; at the same time, the constitution is not, as it were, a dead hand on the nation, but is a living and creative instrument as it is continually reinterpreted by the nation in the light of fresh needs and new understandings. The corresponding reciprocity between Church and New Testament is well expressed by Robert Terwilliger: "It is the book which the Church created, and the book which creates the Church." [61]

2. The authority of the Church requires *consensus*. Admittedly, in the Church as in every community, there must be leadership. In the earliest days, the twelve had a special responsibility, and it was to them that the commission to teach was entrusted. Their apostolic office passed in due course to the episcopate, including the pope, and a special degree of au-

---

[59] See above, pp. 379–382.
[60] Matt. 28:19.
[61] *Christian Believing*, p. 55.

thority within the Church belongs to them. But this could never be absolute or exercised in isolation from the whole body of the faithful. "There was not first an apostolate which gathered a body of believers about itself; nor was there a completely structureless collection of believers which gave authority to the apostles to speak and act on its behalf. From the first, there was the fellowship of believers finding its unity in the twelve." [62] So this brings to light a further reciprocity, and a consequent qualification of authority in the Church. An interesting illustration of the point is that there were gatherings in the early Church with all the external marks of general councils, but the pronouncements of these gatherings never gained authority because they failed to win a consensus in the whole Church. It need hardly be added that our talk here of consensus does not in the slightest deny the need for debate and controversy on the way to any such consensus.

3. The authority of the Church is *relativized* by historical and cultural factors. We have seen that the notes of the Church are eschatological and belong in their fullness to her consummation. While on the way, the Church only more or less attains to unity, holiness, catholicity, and apostolicity. Even in those moments when the mind of the Church is open to the Holy Spirit, the only kind of "infallibility" that can be claimed is a directedness toward the truth, not the possession of truth in its entirety or in absolute form. Furthermore, even the consensus of the faithful is a consensus at a given time in relation to a given problem encountered under given circumstances.

4. Every authoritative utterance of the Church has to be tested for *intellectual integrity*. Here we meet once again the role of the theologian in the community of faith. The theologian is not just an independent student of religion but a responsible spokesman for the believing community. Where this is forgotten, there is the danger of a "papacy of scholars," just as oppressive and even more elitist than the tyranny of ecclesiastics or uncritical biblicism. But the authority of the Church will be enhanced if theologians and biblical scholars are taken seriously by ecclesiastical leaders, and care is taken to ensure that the Church's pronouncements can find support in the best available scholarship.

Two other points of a different kind may be made about the authority of the Church. The first is that such authority must maintain its independence of outside pressures, especially that of the state. The tendency of

---

[62] *Doctrine in the Church of England*, p. 115.

the Church in history to become a department of the state and so to have its authority made subservient to that of the state has been disastrous. The other point is that, unlike the authority of the state, that of the Church can never be harsh or oppressive. It is an authority inspired by and exercised in love, directed only to building up the body of Christ.

18 | Ministry and Mission

75. *THE GENERAL MINISTRY OF THE PEOPLE OF GOD*

The words "ministry" and "mission" point to the same phenomenon, though they draw attention to different aspects of it. Both words designate the activity or function that belongs to the Church as a necessary stage in the movement from creation to the consummation of the kingdom of God. The ministry of the Church is its work in helping to let-be the new community of beings; and, in a secondary sense, the ministry is the structure of the Church (necessary to it) by which it performs this work. The mission of the Church is the same work, but considered in its outgoing and expanding aspect.

The ministry of the Church is its service. Christ himself was identified with the "servant of the Lord" of whom we read in deutero-Isaiah. The Church, as continuing the work of Christ in the world, has also the role of a servant, and we can think of the image of the "servant of the Lord" as one that elucidates the character of the Church alongside the other images, of which something has been said already, such as "body of Christ" and "Israel of God."

This linking of the ministry of the Church with the ministry of Christ is fundamental. All Christian ministry, whether we are thinking of the ministry of the whole people or of the ministry of those ordained to special offices, is a participation in the ministry of Christ. The many-sided character of Christian ministry is already foreshadowed in the many dimensions of Christ's ministry. He is the Servant, the Good Shepherd, the High Priest, the Prophet, and thus service, shepherding, priesthood, proclaiming are all constitutive elements in Christian ministry, though clearly the importance of each of these will vary in different forms of the ministry.

The ministry of the Church is quite simply and adequately described by St. Paul as "the ministry of reconciliation." [1] This ministry of reconciliation, he declares, is given by God to those who themselves have been reconciled to him through Christ. This implies that the ministry of reconciliation belongs to the whole Church. All Christians are, in a sense, ministers; and indeed, if Christ himself is the servant of the Lord and the agent of God's reconciling work, and if to be a Christian means to be conformed to Christ, then clearly every Christian shares in Christ's own ministry or service. Because for a long time the Church has had a professional ministry, the universal and quite fundamental ministry of all Christians tends to drop out of sight. Luther reemphasized it at the Reformation in his insistence on the priesthood that belongs to every Christian, but he was simply recalling St. Peter's teaching that the Church, as "God's own people," is "a royal priesthood" or "a holy priesthood to offer spiritual sacrifices acceptable to God through Jesus Christ." [2] More recently, the liturgical movement has also stressed the ministry of the whole Church by seeking to make more real and meaningful the participation (which has always belonged to them) of the laity in the eucharist.

This universal ministry, which belongs to all Christians, is quite fundamental. We shall see that it by no means rules out various special ministries, but it can be said that without this basic ministry of reconciliation, no other ministry can have any value. The common distinction between clergy and laity is a distinction within the all-embracing ministry of reconciliation. This distinction has indeed its proper significance, which is not to be overlooked, but it must not be thought of as a sharp dividing line in the Church. The expression "laity" stands for the whole people (λαός) of God, and the whole people of God includes the clergy. The clergy are themselves baptized into the universal ministry of the Church, and are laymen before they become clergymen. They do not cease to belong to the universal ministry given to them in baptism, but add to this an additional ministry. The layman, on his part, is not just the passive recipient of the Church's ministry. As a baptized person, he shares in the apostolate of the whole Church. In Karl Rahner's words, "by the very nature of

[1] II Cor. 5:18.
[2] I Pet. 2:5, 9.

being a member of the mystical body of Christ, he is also an active co-operator in the fulfillment of her mission and mandate." [3]

The current interest in what is called the "apostolate" of the laity points to renewed attempts to explore and utilize the vast potentialities of the universal Christian ministry that is entrusted to all members of the Church. Of course, we should recognize that this ministry always has been exercised. In our present secular civilization, however, it may well be that new and important roles are opening up for the layman. The Churches as "holy" places and the clergy as persons in "holy" orders touch only a segment of the great masses in modern industrialized and urbanized societies. While we have been critical of some features of the demand for a "religionless" Christianity, we have conceded that there are other features that have to be taken seriously, if Christianity is to make an impact in the contemporary world. One thing that seems clearly demanded by the secularized situation of today is a fuller recognition and a higher valuation of the lay apostolate.

It is not the business of this book—nor does it lie within our competence—to say how this is to be done in detail, but it is our business to indicate the theological basis, and this we are seeking to do in drawing attention to the fundamental ministry of the whole Church and in urging the active cooperation of the layman in it. This may mean that we shall have to be more prepared to recognize the Spirit's working outside of the usual ecclesiastical channels, and that we shall also need to be willing to give to the laity more initiative and responsibility than they have usually enjoyed. Both of these points can be illustrated by another mention of the Salvation Army. We already pointed out that although it has no sacraments, we could not for a moment deny that it receives and transmits divine grace. Its founder, William Booth, could be regarded as a pioneer of "secular" Christianity in the best sense, and one who long ago saw the need for the laity to assume a much more active role in the industrialized modern world. In the somewhat ironical words of his biographer, "Booth was not aiming for settled communities of virtuous folk sitting under a favorite preacher." [4]

We should stress, however, that we visualize the ministry of the laity chiefly in terms of practical service, having nothing ostensibly "churchy" or "religious" about it—and again, the Salvation Army provides a good

---

[3] *Theological Investigations,* vol. II, p. 326.
[4] Richard Collier, *The General Next to God,* p. 56.

example. The ministry of reconciliation is the ministry of responding to those in need, and without this, any other kind of ministry is empty. This fundamental ministry is our cooperation in God's great work of letting-be. There are innumerable opportunities here for laymen to exercise a full and effective ministry. In our complex modern society, there are many areas where only laymen with specialized training in these areas really know what is going on there, and where only they have the possibility of trying to ensure that what is done in these areas will be directed to the fuller being of the people affected or (if this sounds too utopian) will not deprive people of their potentialities for fuller being. But we shall say more on this later.[5]

We do not, on the other hand, visualize the ministry of the laity as a pale imitation of the ministry of the clergy. The layman's ministry has too much dignity and importance to be reduced to these terms. The clergy share in the universal ministry that belongs to the whole people of God, but they have their own special ministries in addition. The most effective laymen are likely to be those whose own ministry is backed up by the nurture of the word and sacraments, which they receive in turn at the hands of the ordained ministers of the Church.

76. THE SPECIAL MINISTRIES: DIACONATE, PRESBYTERATE, EPISCOPATE

Our stress upon the universal and fundamental ministry of reconciliation is not meant to rule out or in any way detract from the importance of the specific ministries of the Church, reserved to those who have been duly ordained to them. Once more we have to hold a proper balance between, on the one hand, freedom and spontaneity, and, on the other, the need for form and order. The Church, at times when the normal channels of its working have become constricted and conventionalized, should, we may presume, be neither surprised nor scandalized if the workings of the Spirit show themselves outside of these channels. Yet it would soon be necessary to channel these new workings of the Spirit in definite forms, if they were not to be scattered and lost. It is clear from the New Testament that even in the earliest days there were definite ministries, and the importance and necessity of these increased as the threat from Gnostic and other heresies grew. The distinctive Christian message would soon have disappeared if

[5] See below, pp. 518–519.

every free-lance preacher and self-appointed minister had had equal standing. There had to be duly appointed guardians of the authentic faith. By the end of the first century we find St. Clement writing: "The apostles for our sakes received the gospel from the Lord Jesus Christ; Jesus Christ was sent from God. Christ then is from God, and the apostles from Christ. Both therefore came in due order from the will of God. Having therefore received his instructions, they went forth . . . and, as they preached in the country and in the towns, they appointed their first fruits (having proved them by the Spirit) to be bishops and deacons of them that should believe." [6] St. Ignatius writes: "Wherever the bishop appears, there let the people be, just as, wheresoever Christ Jesus is, there is the catholic Church. It is not permitted either to baptize or hold a love-feast apart from the bishop. But whatever he may approve, that is well-pleasing to God, that everything which you do may be sound and valid." [7] We are not for the moment concerned about the precise meaning of the word "bishop" here (if indeed it had a precise meaning) but only about the recognition from the earliest days of the necessity of a duly ordained ministry.

The stress on the necessity and dignity of the ordained ministry is not by any means only a "catholic" view. One could hardly find a stronger or more persuasive statement than the one given by Calvin. Christ is the head of the Church, but he uses a human ministry. Such ministers Calvin does not hesitate to call Christ's "substitutes." He declares that "the Church cannot be kept safe, unless supported by those guards to which the Lord has been pleased to commit its safety." Not merely to seek to abolish the ministry but even "to disparage it as of minor importance" is to plot "the ruin and destruction of the Church." "For neither are the light and heat of the sun, nor meat and drink, so necessary to sustain and cherish that present life, as is the apostolical and pastoral office to preserve a church in the earth." [8]

The expression "in the earth" which closes the quotation from Calvin is a reminder that we are dealing with the Church as an association that operates in history, not as the ideal or eschatological kingdom. Every kind of association, if it is not to fall apart, needs some kind of leadership or government or authority, and indeed we find something of the sort even in those Christian groups that think of themselves as most "free" from eccle-

[6] Cor. xliii.
[7] Smyrn. viii.
[8] *Institutes of the Christian Religion*, IV, iii.

siastical forms. We may be told that Jesus Christ is the sole head of the Church, and of course all Christians recognize him as such. But clearly (as Calvin also says) Jesus Christ does not in person decide about the day-to-day questions that confront the community of faith. To some extent, the whole community must decide about these questions, yet the community needs guidance, and it must have leaders who will interpret to it the mind of Christ on the matters in question. The Church is certainly not an egalitarian institution. John Krumm rightly remarks: "There are limits to democracy in any Church which can claim the name of Christian. The authentic Christian gospel is not established by a majority vote; it comes down from two thousand years of Christian experience and testimony, which has overwhelming weight and authority." [9]

If we accept that the Church is a *theological* as well as a *sociological* entity (and if not, we may as well forsake it), then we are recognizing that it is an association that has been brought into being *from above downward*, so to speak. It is the community of grace, of incarnation, of the Spirit. But this in turn implies the recognition of a relatively independent status belonging to the ordained ministry within the Church. Actually, this is recognized among the great majority of Christians, Roman, Orthodox, Anglican, Calvinist, and Lutheran, for the ministers of these churches are ordained *only* by those who have themselves already been ordained to the ministry and who alone have the authority to confer this ministry. We should be clear about the fundamental difference between this understanding of the ministry and that which prevails in those Protestant groups whose ministers are ordained by the congregation, or general body of Christians. Strictly speaking, this is not ordination but a "setting apart," in which the special ministry is regarded not as an "order" but simply as a specialized function within the general ministry, and thus a function for which those responsible for the general ministry can set apart suitable persons from their own number. While we have ourselves stressed the continuity of the general and special ministries of the Church, it seems to me that this *assimilation* of the special into the general ministry among those who entrust ordination, in whole or in part, to the congregation, must be rejected, for while it rightly sees the continuity of all Christian ministry with the fundamental ministry of reconciliation, it fails to see the distinctive character of the special ministries.

Of course, the congregation or people does have its distinctive litur-

[9] *Why I am an Episcopalian*, p. 101.

gical role in ordination. The people present from among themselves those who are to be ordained and to whose ordination they assent. But the actual ordaining is done by those who are themselves ordained, for this is a sacramental act and is therefore performed by those who are ministers of the sacraments. In calling the act "sacramental," we are recognizing that it is not just the authorizing of certain persons to perform distinctive functions in the Church, but is a conferring of grace on these persons themselves. The special ministries are not to be understood exhaustively in functional terms; they have also an ontological dimension, they are *ways of being* in the Church. The call of a person to the ministry and his response, and then his solemn ordination, affect him in the depth of his being. As R. C. Moberly expressed it in a classic work on the ministry, "There are not only priestly functions or priestly prerogatives; there is also a priestly spirit and a priestly heart—more vital to the true reality of priesthood than any mere performance of priestly functions." [10]

The word that has been traditionally used by theologians to designate this ontological dimension of ministry is "character." There is nothing magical about such character, nor does it fall ready-made from heaven at ordination. Ministerial character, in the theological sense of the term, is very much like moral character, in the ethical sense of the term; that is to say, it is a formation of the person, the building up of a distinctive pattern of personal being, the shape of which is determined by certain dominant interests. The functional and ontological understandings of ministry are complementary, not competitive. It is through the doing of acts that character is formed, then character in turn informs the acts. Ministerial functions without the depth of ministerial character would be only an outward appearance. We stress again that there is nothing magic about such character; and just as the calling to the ordained ministry can be understood as an extension of the election that belongs to all Christian experience, so ministerial character can be understood as a special development of the character which baptism opens to all Christians.

We have already claimed that the ordained ministry is nothing less than the embodiment of a fundamental note of the Church. We have seen how Christ entrusted the leadership of the community to his apostles, and how they bequeathed it in turn to their successors. I am not saying for a moment that the Church was generated by the ministry, but neither should one fall into the opposite mistake of thinking that the ministry can be gen-

[10] *Ministerial Priesthood*, p. 261.

erated *from below upward* by the Church. The Church and its ministry are equally primordial, the ministry belonging to the very structure of the Church.

It is indeed necessary to the health of the whole Church that the ordained ministry should have a certain independence of status. Only so can it exercise one of its most important ministries—the prophetic ministry, in which not only the world but the people of God too have be set continually in the light of God's demands and judgments, as these are understood in the Christian revelation.

Perhaps enough has been said to make the case for a distinct ordered ministry within the Church, differentiated from the general ministry of the people of God. We must now try to establish more clearly what is the difference between the general ministry, shared by all Christians, and the specific ministry or ministries by which a part of the Church exercises care and leadership for the whole. We have already said that there is no sharp cleavage between clergy and laity, and this must be reaffirmed. The fundamental ministry is the ministry of reconciliation, and this is given to every Christian who is by baptism incorporated into the body of Christ. Thus it is a ministry which belongs to the clergy as well as the laity, though in any actual situation it may be exercised in different ways, and in some situations the layman, in others the clergyman, may be better able to minister. The specific ministry of the clergy then must be thought of as additional to the general ministry. So we come to the thought of grades of fullness in the ministry. It is not the case that the clergy have a ministry and the laity have none, but that the clergy have a fuller ministry. As well as the general ministry, they have the ministry of the word and sacraments. Even this the laity share to some extent, but there are some acts that have been reserved exclusively to the ordained minister. He is constituted the guardian of the word and sacraments, and these in turn are the vehicles for the continuance and propagation of the Christian faith.

Those within the people of God who have the fullness of the ministry come to it in a double way, which shows us again the by now familiar correspondence of inward and outward, of personal experience and of the institutional form which is designed to express and protect the experience. The experience is God's calling or vocation. Already in the Old Testament, prophets like Isaiah and Jeremiah vividly attest that their prophetic ministry was laid upon them by God and that the initiative lay with him. The same is true in the New Testament and in the subsequent Christian ministry, as everyone knows from the testimony of the great spiritual leaders of the Church. We may think of this inward call from God as simply an extension of the election which, as we have seen, is a moment in the normal Christian experience, however it may vary from one person to another.[11] All who are elected are elected to the general ministry of the Church; and since all Christians are elected (for the initiative is with God), then all Christians are called to the ministry of reconciliation. But for some, the call is to the fuller and more specific ministries, and we can understand such an experience of vocation as of a piece with election in general Christian experience. But such calling is not in itself enough to constitute anyone a minister of the Church. Just as election in general Christian experience has its corresponding outward form in baptism, so the calling to a specific ministry must have its outward form in ordination. In ordination, those who have themselves the ministerial office and have been constituted the guardians of the Church's faith, test the calling of the ordinand and, if satisfied, admit him to office in the Church.

This outward form must be considered just as essential to the ministry as inward calling, otherwise the door is opened to chaos and the disintegration of the Church. To think otherwise is really to deny the earthly and historical character of our existence. Once again, the point is very well made by Calvin. He shrewdly points out that if anyone in the history of the Church could claim to be a valid minister on the grounds of inward calling alone, that one would be St. Paul, who is represented as having been directly called and addressed by Christ. But in fact, St. Paul not only received baptism but, with Barnabas, was set apart by the Church and had hands laid on him before he was dispatched on his mission.[12] "Why this setting apart and laying on of hands," asks Calvin, "after the Holy Spirit had attested their election, except that ecclesiastical discipline might be preserved in appointing ministers by men?" [13] Of course, we have to keep a sane balance. Again let it be affirmed that if the Church has become somnolent or corrupt, the Spirit will carry on its unitive action outside of the usual forms and structures, or perhaps outside of the Church altogether. But such cases are exceptional, and it is soon necessary to come back to forms and structures of some kind. Only in very grave circumstances should anyone take upon himself the responsibility of rejecting the established forms; and even in such cases, when one considers the schisms that have in the past weakened the Church, it is a question whether such persons would not have done better to exercise patience.

[11] See above, pp. 340–342.
[12] Acts 13:2–3.
[13] *Institutes of the Christian Religion*, IV, iii.

In any case, ordination by laying on of hands on the part of those who are already ordained ministers is, and since New Testament times has been, the regular way of admitting men to the specific ministries of the Church. Ordination is parallel to baptism, which admits to the membership and therefore to the general ministry of the Church. The Holy Spirit, we may suppose, is not restricted to either of these vehicles, but they have an indispensable function in the economy of the Church on earth, and a willingness to recognize their value and to submit to their regular operation is itself an evidence of the unitive action of the Spirit. These outward, visible, public acts which the Church performs in the name of God are a necessary protection for the gifts of the Spirit, as well as being our safeguard against subjectivism and fanaticism. They give a certain objective character to the ministry. They stress the office, rather than the man or his personality. What he does is not done by his own power or his own virtue. He acts by authority of the Church and in the name of God. It is, of course, the business of the Church to judge of the inward calling of those offering themselves for its ministry, before they are ordained to it. But (as has been clearly recognized by, among others, St. Augustine and Calvin) no man's personal qualities can sustain the weight of the ministry, and the effectiveness of the office does not stand or fall with the man himself.

Now we must take a further step. We have seen that the ordained ministry is distinct from, though continuous with, the general ministry of reconciliation. It is not nobler or better than that ministry (for nothing could be) but it is a fuller ministry, with special responsibilities in the Church. The further step is to recognize that within this ordained ministry itself, there are several orders of ministry, representing degrees of fullness. Here we strike on the most controversial question concerning the ministry, yet the answers seem clear enough. There can be no question that in the New Testament, several kinds of ministry are recognized. More than this, however, it is surely quite clear that the difference between these kinds of ministries is not merely one of function. They are orders of ministry, some more authoritative than others. The apostles have not only a different function from, let us say, prophets and evangelists—actually, they include in themselves the other ministries—but themselves have an additional ministry which gives them their special authority. When they appoint the seven to a particular ministry,[14] this is part of their own ministry that they depute to them, in order that they may themselves be free to devote more time "to prayer and the ministry of the word." When Philip

---

[14] Acts 6:34.

the evangelist baptizes converts in Samaria, the apostles come down to complete his work and set their seal on it.[15] These are almost arbitrarily chosen incidents, for the whole tenor of the New Testament makes plain the authority of the apostles. Even St. Paul recognizes not just difference of function but difference in order and authority. Ernst Käsemann remarks: "Equality is not for Paul a principle of church order." [16]

What the New Testament—with Christ himself—undoubtedly does condemn is the seeking for power and preeminence among Christians, and the exercise of authority in a self-regarding way. It must be confessed that there has been plenty of this in the Church, and that the experience of it has kindled in some the distrust of what they call "prelacy." The Church, after all, is only on its way to holiness, and so sin remains, and even the offices of the Church can be used (or rather, abused) by careerists in search of notoriety and power. Spiritual authority gets confounded with worldly position, and as a result the whole conception of spiritual authority and the offices to which it attaches are brought into disrepute. But once again, *abusus non tollit usum.* The sin of pride which leads to these perversions of the ministerial offices is so universal that in any case the abolition of the offices will not prevent this sin from making its inroads. Even in Christian groups which abhor "prelacy" and pride themselves on the "parity" of their ministers, there is no lack of power politics. Indeed, the game is played even more dangerously, because it depends on invisible pressures, the cult of personalities, and many other hidden factors through which power and authority can be exercised behind the scenes; if there always is the risk of power, surely it is better that it be openly attached to public offices. But the true Christian authority is not this kind of power at all, nor does it feed anyone's ego. It is an authority that is conferred by Christ. It is not "earned" by the holder of the office nor can it be to him a cause of pride. It is a responsibility laid upon him to be an "ambassador" of Christ and to speak "on behalf of Christ." [17] The authority belongs to the office, to the Church, ultimately to Christ from whom the office has come. The higher the ministerial office, the more it is to be recognized as a gift conferred, and the more humility does it require from its holder, as he exercises the daunting responsibilities entrusted to him.

We have claimed that there are not only diverse functions in the or-

[15] Acts 8:14.
[16] "Ministry and Community in the New Testament" in *Essays on New Testament Themes*, p. 76.
[17] II Cor. 5:20.

dained ministry but diverse orders, and that this has been the case from New Testament times onward. But everyone knows that the picture of the ministry that can be gathered from the New Testament is a very complicated one, and its interpretation is uncertain. When we read, for instance, that "his gifts were that some should be apostles, some prophets, some evangelists, some pastors and teachers, for the equipment of the saints, for the work of the ministry, for building up the body of Christ," [18] we readily understand that while this list does indeed show us the diversity of ministries in the primitive Church, it cannot be taken as normative, for we find other ministries mentioned elsewhere in the New Testament, and probably there were local variations, though all seem to have acknowledged the authority of the apostles. The "quest for the historical ministry," if one may coin the phrase, is as hopeless as the quest for the historical Jesus. We can say that from the beginning, there was diversity, and there was also an authoritative order of ministers, the apostles. But to try to go much beyond this and to seek to establish a definite ministerial structure as typical of the whole of the primitive Church is wasted labor.

Even if there had been an "original" pattern of the ministry and one could discover what it was, this would not be specially important. It is clear that there must have been a formative period in which changes in the institutional forms would be required as the Church moved out from being a revolutionary movement in Judaism to becoming a settled, worldwide community. The "evangelists," who presumably went from town to town, would be replaced by settled pastors. Apparently, the ecstatic "prophets" soon died out, as a distinct kind of ministers. Here, as elsewhere, we have to consider not only the beginning (which we can know only very imperfectly), but also the way in which it was developed in the actual life of the Church. What we do find is that in the first few centuries, throughout the whole Church, the various kinds of ministry of which we read in the New Testament had become consolidated into the familiar three orders of bishops, priests, and deacons. The bishops were thought of as the successors of the apostles, who were supposed to have founded, as a result of their ministerial labors, the principal sees of the ancient Church; the priests (or presbyters) corresponded to the pastors indifferently called "bishops" or "presbyters" in the New Testament; while the deacons represented those inferior orders of ministry which we can also see in the New Testament. Alongside the New Testament, we have to

[18] Eph. 4:11-12.

recognize the living development within the Church. It is impossible to avoid the conclusion that from an early time the regular and universal pattern of the Christian ministry was the threefold one of bishops, priests, and deacons, and that this is a natural development from the New Testament picture itself.

The threefold ministry, like other structures in the Church, has a measure of flexibility and even of healthy untidiness, and this allows for possibilities of development and adaptation within the overall pattern. Thus the variable and indefinite kinds of ministry mentioned in the New Testament are reflected by the continuation in both the Eastern and Western Churches of so-called "minor" orders—lectors, acolytes, subdeacons, and the like. Actually, in the Western Church subdeacons came to be counted as a fourth "major" order alongside bishops, priests, and deacons; and it has sometimes been suggested that deaconesses should have a similar status. These matters are mentioned not because they are of any special importance in themselves, but because the existence of these "intermediate" ministries helps to prevent a rigid distinction between clergy and laity. It is worth considering also whether some of these orders could not be used in new and creative ways to employ the energies of laymen. In the modern world, the ministries of clergy and laymen sometimes cross over, so to speak. The worker-priest, though ordained to the ministry of word and sacraments, may function for a large part of his time in a secular occupation. On the other hand, perhaps an increasing number of persons who want to serve the Church will opt to do so in a lay, or part-time capacity, and for them some of the "minor" orders or, as I shall shortly recommend, a revived diaconate, may be the means of giving them their definite place and dignity in the Church. This is much more than just a question of conferring on people high-sounding names and offices, for it would be a way of redressing the Church's structure in the direction of increased lay participation. So the threefold ministry has, and should have, ragged edges that prevent a clean-cut distinction from the laity.

Since we began with the general ministry of the whole Church, the ministry of reconciliation, and moved on from there to consider the specific ministries to which Christians might be additionally called and ordained, it is convenient to retain the same ascending order in our discussion, and to take the three traditional orders of the ministry in increasing degrees of fullness. So we shall begin by saying something of the diaconate, and then pass on to the priesthood and the episcopate.

The order of deacons is the least clearly defined of the three orders of the ministry. Its prototype is usually seen in the ministry of St. Stephen and his companions, though they were not actually called "deacons." [19] They were, however, ordained to a specific ministry by prayer and laying on of hands. Their duties were to assist the apostles, particularly by caring for persons in need and distributing alms. But it seems that St. Stephen also conducted a notable preaching ministry, and the very fact that he is the Church's protomartyr should prevent us from supposing that the "diaconate" that he and his companions exercised was just some minor administrative office. The duties of deacons varied in the early Church, and perhaps the only way in which one could define these duties is to say that the work of the deacon was to assist the priest or bishop, both in the liturgy and in the pastoral care and administration of the congregation. On the other hand, the deacon did not have power to do these things by himself.

The very flexibility and even vagueness that has attended the historical role of the deacon may well have the advantage of making it easier to rehabilitate this particular ministry and to make it more effective in the modern situation. At present, among Anglicans and Roman Catholics, the diaconate is simply a stage to the priesthood. Among Protestants, "deacons," where the term is used at all, are lay officers of the Church, and, in the case of Presbyterian churches which have deacons, they are specifically charged with "secular" duties (such as the upkeep of church buildings) while "spiritual" functions are reserved to elders. No doubt it is desirable to continue a measure of flexibility, but out of the present confusion there might be reborn a more definite role for the deacon. This could be an office held in perpetuity by persons who earn their living in "secular" occupations (as it can already be in some churches); but it would be an office with definitely "spiritual," that is to say, pastoral and liturgical functions, supportive to but, of course, not usurping the functions of the priest; and it would be an office having an unequivocal status and dignity within the apostolic ministry, so that suitable candidates would be ordained to it by the bishop, as the original "seven" were ordained by the apostles. Such a revival of the diaconate would be quite compatible with the continuation of the office as a kind of apprenticeship for candidates for the priesthood. The practical advantage of a greatly expanded diaconate having a new dignity and status is that it would serve to reduce the gap between clergy and laity, for, as already indicated, we are thinking of these deacons as persons whose daily work will be in "secular" employment.

[19] Acts 6: 1–6.

I have deliberately used the word "persons" in the last paragraph so as not to exclude the possibility that women might be ordained as deacons. We have seen already that sex is one of the "worldly" disqualifications specifically abolished, along with race and social status, in the Christian community.[20] I can find no valid theological objections to the ordination of women, and even the tradition of the Church in this matter is probably just a continuation of Old Testament attitudes, in so far as the Christian ministry may have been originally modeled on offices in Judaism. At the same time, however, one must wait for a development of a consensus on this matter within the Church as a whole, in all its major branches. It would be a divisive step for one diocese, one regional church, or even one communion, to act unilaterally in this matter. It is to be hoped that such a consensus may some time be reached. If it is, then the next step would surely be to open the possibility of admitting suitable women to the higher offices of the ministry. For while it is true that the fact of there having been "deaconesses" in both the earlier and more recent periods of Church history makes it easier to visualize the admission of women to the diaconate, this order is continuous with those above it, and in principle there would be no barrier to advancement on the ground of sex alone.

It must be acknowledged, however, that this argument rests on the supposition of a continuity between the diaconate and the "superior" orders of the presbyterate and the episcopate, and while in fact the diaconate has long been regarded as a stepping stone to the presbyterate, our own argument has been in favor of recognizing the intrinsic worth of the diaconate as a permanent order in its own right. This accords with the early understanding of the deacon as assistant to the bishop, and with the fact that there is a discontinuity between the diaconate and the higher orders, because the diaconate has never been regarded as sharing in that special priestly office (*sacerdotium*) which belongs to bishops and presbyters. For many people, therefore, the question of women in the ministry does not turn on their admission to the diaconate, but on the question of whether sex is a relevant issue in the exercise of *sacerdotium*. I would say myself that it is not, but again I would urge the need for a very large measure of consensus as a condition for so fundamental a change in practice.

We pass on to the office of priest, or presbyter. Here again there is a tangled and uncertain background of development. How the Christian presbyter was related to the officer of the same name in Judaism; whether

---

[20] See above, p. 407.

"presbyter" and "bishop" were, to begin with, names for the same office in the Church, and whether in course of time the presbyter had his office delegated to him by the bishop, as the latter began to be considered as something like the "apostle" of an older terminology; how the term "presbyter" or "priest" came to be identified with the traditional sacerdotal office and the offering of sacrifice, and especially with the priestly office of Christ [21]—these are historical questions on which, as we have said at an earlier stage, no final certainty can be reached, but which, in any case, cannot be decisive for the theological understanding of the ministry that grew up in the living body of Christ, the Church itself. Actually, a much clearer picture of the ministerial functions of the presbyterate emerged, and has remained, than has been the case with the diaconate. This, of course, may be due to the fact that the presbyterate became, as it were, the backbone of the Christian ministry, the most numerous and widespread of the three offices, performing the day-to-day functions of the ministry in every Christian church and parish.

It is true of course that there has been great variation of emphasis in the ways of conceiving the presbyter's duties. In the Middle Ages, there was too much stress on the sacerdotal aspect, and especially the offering of the eucharistic sacrifice. In Protestantism, the pendulum swung too much the other way, and the stress was all on preaching and instruction. But fundamentally, there has been agreement in regarding the priest or presbyter as the one who has the twofold duty of proclaiming the word and administering the sacraments. The office of a priest must be conceived widely enough to allow for a proper balance of the two sides of his duty; and in turn we must have a sufficiently wide and balanced view of what we mean by "word" and "sacraments."

Since there will be a full discussion of the word and sacraments later in this book,[22] we shall simply say here that the function of both of them is to make God and his saving work in Christ *present*. The priest, to whom is committed the proclaiming of the word and the ministration of the sacraments, is thus the one who makes-present the saving work of God in these particular ways, and in this sense represents God. (I need hardly remind the reader that God and his saving work may be "made-present" in other ways than through word and sacraments, so I am not granting to the priest here a monopoly of spiritual power.) The proclaiming of the

---

[21] Heb. 5:10.
[22] See below, pp. 447–486.

word and the ministration of the sacraments may be understood as the two poles of the priest's making-present. God-in-Christ is present in the proclaiming of the word, God, as St. Paul says, "entrusting to us the ministry of reconciliation" and "making his appeal through us." [23] God-in-Christ is also present in the celebration of the sacraments, especially the eucharist in which we speak particularly of the "real presence"; and although this expression is not from the New Testament, Käsemann has rightly pointed out that "it expresses exactly what St. Paul wants to say." [24]

I have spoken of the word and sacraments as the two "poles" of the priest's making-present because there is a certain tension between them, and stress upon one or the other leads to a distinctive (and, I believe, unbalanced) view of the presbyter's office.

Protestants, by and large, have stressed the proclaiming of the word. The minister is, above all, preacher and teacher, and the very word "priest" is disliked. Now, this is valuable in so far as it demands high qualities in the minister. Not everyone who asks to be admitted to this office is to be lightly received. There must be rigorous training, education in the biblical and theological disciplines, and an acquaintance too with the culture of one's time, so that the minister can be a true and effective interpreter of the word. All this is very good, and is an understandable reaction against the medieval image of the priest whose preoccupation with the sacraments made him seem like a kind of magician, especially if he was lacking in general education and personal integrity. This conception of the ministry is valuable also in so far as it helps to build up an educated laity with a good understanding of the faith. Just as the Protestant minister in his seminary receives the kind of education that fits him for the proclaiming and interpreting of the word, so he himself in his parish trains and educates his people. Clearly, if we are looking for a more effective ministry of the laity, then the Church has got to give the laity better training and instruction; and this is to be found in churches where the ministry of the word is prized, and where preaching and teaching are of a high standard.

But the weakness of this conception of the presbyter's office is that it puts too much weight on personal qualities. Certainly, we must expect high personal qualities in the Christian minister, and the New Testament is quite clear about this. But we have already seen that the office itself is the most important thing, and that the minister, however excellent, cannot

[23] II Cor. 5:19–20.
[24] "The Pauline Doctrine of the Lord's Supper" in *Essays on New Testament Themes*, p. 128.

in himself bear the weight of his office. The effectiveness of the Church's ministry should not depend, as so often it does in Protestant churches, on the minister's power as a preacher or on any other personal qualities belonging to him.

This brings us to the second pole, the sacraments, and like other institutional forms, these sacraments provide a protection and a mode of operation that is not dependent on the personality of the priest. They remind us too that his ministry is nothing of his own, but is conferred by God through his Church. On this side, there is no doubt the danger that the ministry may become mechanical, and that superstitious attitudes may grow up; or again, it may be thought that the personal qualities of the minister are of no importance at all. But it is remarkable how the Christian sacraments rise above these dangers. If the Protestant ministry of preaching is, on the whole, more successful in building up an educated people of God, the priestly ministration of the sacraments has been more successful in the whole area of pastoral care and guidance, for, as we shall see, the Christian sacraments provide for the care and strengthening of life all the way from the cradle to the grave. Within this sacramental framework, the priest makes-present the divine grace at every stage and in every need.

Outside of the pulpit, the Protestant minister is nowadays often puzzled about his role. What can he do that is not better done by the trained psychiatric worker or the social welfare worker? At least some of this puzzlement is due to the neglect in Protestantism of the sacramental system. Some of the traditional sacraments have been dropped altogether, and even the eucharist, though it is honored, is hardly ever the center of worship. The priest who operates through the sacramental system finds that although it may need some updating and modification to meet the modern situation, it nevertheless is still extraordinarily effective in meeting human need and in building up the body of Christ.

The fullest conception of the priestly office, then, while it certainly demands the highest qualities, both moral and intellectual, in those who offer themselves for it, remembers that ultimately this office is a gift and depends on God's working through it. The office is more than the man, God's grace is more than any individual charisma. It is to protect this basic and absolutely necessary truth that the sacramental system has been built up as the vehicle for the priest's functioning, and his office itself can be regarded as a sacrament.

Throughout most of the Church's history, the priest has operated in the local congregation, serving a particular parish or neighborhood. It is often said nowadays that in our modern society, the parochial organization of the ministry has become obsolete. Modern society is characterized by urbanization and mobility, whereas the parish ministry visualized a predominantly rural society in which people rarely left their neighborhoods. Certainly, the old pattern of one priest to one church is on the way out, for the concentration of population in the cities and also the ease of transportation in the countryside have made possible team ministries, and these are probably more effective, as they allow for greater specialization and are less wasteful of manpower. But even beyond the repatterning of the parochial ministry, there is a place and a need for new experimental kinds of ministries not tied to the parish church at all, such as ministries in industry, or to special social and occupational groups that are held together by other than residential factors.

At the same time, we must be careful about the danger of too lightly depreciating the parish ministry. While there are all kinds of new nonresidential social groupings that offer the possibility of new kinds of ministry, this does not mean the end of the parish ministry, though it means that it cannot have a monopoly any more. It is interesting to note that Harvey Cox, in his study of the Church in urban society, while he calls for flexibility in experimenting with new forms of church life, visualizes these *alongside* the parish church rather than as supplanting it.[25] It seems to me that while there must indeed be differentiated and specialized ministries, a special importance belongs to the ministry that reaches people where they *live;* for this touches them at the level of the *family,* and although the family too is changing, it remains a basic social unit, and we shall see later that it has a very special place in the Christian dispensation.[26]

We have also to remember that, apart from the relatively small number of Christians who have explicitly adopted a "congregationalist" polity, the unit of the Christian community is *not* the local church, but a wider grouping, the diocese, conference, or whatever it may be called. In the secular world nowadays, planning and strategy are increasingly being carried out on the regional level. The same kind of thing will have to be done in the Church, and within the regional grouping, taken as a whole, there should be scope for flexible differentiated ministries which are nevertheless coordinated within the grouping. Our individualism tends to make us all "congregationalists" in practice, but it is time for us to get away

[25] *The Secular City,* pp. 157–158.
[26] See below, pp. 512–516.

from our overprizing of the local congregation to a renewed appreciation for the wider body of Christ, first in our own region and then beyond it.

Whatever new structures may emerge, it is likely that the brunt of the ministry will still be borne by the presbyterate. But one last point should be made. The office of a priest should always be a pastoral office, however it may become specialized. One of the alarming features of the contemporary Church is the increasing number of ministers who are being assigned to posts (in administration and the like) that have no obvious pastoral responsibilities. Such posts might be appropriate to lay members of the Church, or to an expanded order of deacons, as visualized above. But the presbyterate should never be without some pastoral responsibility, even if it is of a specialized kind.

Our mention of the diocese or regional grouping leads on to the office of a bishop. The bishop has the fullness of the ministry. He has in himself all the other ministries, but in a unique way, he represents the Church as a whole. Thus he has the special ministry of conferring ministries in ordination, and this is what is most typical and distinctive of him, as the bearer of the apostolic ministry. Enough was said about this function of the episcopate when we discussed the notes of the Church to make it unnecessary to add anything here. The bishop is also specially associated with the rite of confirmation. This makes it clear that the candidate is being admitted not just to some local group but to the whole Church, and makes it clear also that the bishop is not some remote prince or governor, but himself a chief pastor of the flock. His ministry is fundamentally the same as that which belongs to every Christian—the ministry of reconciliation—but it is the fullness of the ministry, charged with a special responsibility for the safeguarding and advancing of the apostolic faith and order.

No more than other kinds of ministers is the bishop a law unto himself, for he is bound to regard his fellow bishops. His office is characterized far more by responsibility than by power, for his is "the care of all the churches." [27] But as the faithful discharger of this responsibility, he deserves from the Church the same honor that it accorded first to the apostles and then to their successors.

No doubt there is a sense in which the original apostles were unique. They were the founders of the new Christian community and stood in a special relation to Christ. But there is equally no doubt that the New Testament envisages the transmission of the essential apostolic office to suc-

[27] II Cor. 11:28.

cessors in the ministry. The fathers of Vatican II were admittedly schematizing what was in fact a tangled and only partially known history, yet
we can recognize the general truth of their claim that "Christ sent the
apostles, just as he himself had been sent by the Father; through these
same apostles he made their successors, the bishops, sharers in his consecration and mission." [28] By "apostolic succession" is meant the succession
of new generation of Christians to the apostolic faith and the apostolic
mission, and wherever that faith and that mission are to be found, there
is a measure of apostolic succession. The normal sign of continuity with
the apostles is the orderly transmission of the episcopal office. The bishops
or chief pastors of the Church are the visible, personal embodiment of its
continuity with the Church of the apostles.

77. MINISTERIAL COLLEGIALITY

We have already met the term "collegiality" in our discussion of the
papacy,[29] but it is an idea with broader implications and the word has
come to be used in a general way for the shared responsibility and mutual
concern that ought to exist in the Church among all its ministers and, indeed, among all the faithful, for all have some share in ministry. The principle of collegiality safeguards both the unity of all Christian ministry and
its diversity. It safeguards the unity, because it implies that ministerial acts
take place in the context of the Church. Thus, for instance, it makes very
questionable the act of some individual *episcopus vagans* who performs
an ordination out of the setting of the Church—and one would have to
add that the very notion of an individual having some inherent sacramental power implies a magical idea of ministry quite foreign to the doctrine expounded above. Collegiality likewise safeguards the diversity of
ministry. If it rules out individualism, it also rules out the false egalitarianism which would permit any Christian to perform any ministerial act
whatever. Collegiality is simply the recognition that the Church is truly
a people or a body, that is to say, a differentiated unity.

Collegiality affects every area of the Church's life. Three such areas call
for brief mention.

The first is the government of the Church. Though the Church is not
a democracy, it is not an autocracy either. At every level, there should be
consultation in its decision-making—the pope with the bishops, the bish-

---

[28] *The Documents of Vatican II*, p. 534.
[29] See above, p. 416.

ops with the presbyters, the presbyters with the people in the parishes. This first application of the collegial principle we may call *conciliarity*.

Similar remarks apply in the area of liturgy. At the end of the first century, St. Clement of Rome was writing, "Let each of you, brethren, in his own order give thanks to God with a good conscience, not transgressing the appointed rule of his service, in reverence." [30] It would seem that in the early Church, worship was a truly corporate act, using the ministries of all though not confusing the distinctive ministries of bishop, deacon, layman, or whoever it might be. But for many centuries this corporate celebration of the liturgy was to a large extent lost, and instead of being president of a worshipping people, the bishop or presbyter became rather a solo performer before an audience. One of the greatest achievements of the modern liturgical movement has been its progress toward restoring a truly corporate worship. This may be called *concelebration*, in the broadest sense of that term.

The third area is theology itself, and this is where much remains to be done. While the bishops have a special responsibility for doctrine, the modern bishop is often too busy with the affairs of his diocese to have time for theological reflection in depth. Theologians, on their part, can easily become absorbed in academic questions only marginally related to the current problems of the Church. Parish clergy and lay people will probably be better acquainted than bishops or theologians with the actualities of contemporary society, but they may be lacking in theological knowledge. There seems to be a clear case for a ministry of theological teamwork, a thinking out together by bishops, theologians, clergy, and people of the meaning of Christian faith in the current situation. Such a cooperative venture I have elsewhere called *co-theologizing*.[31]

If in the preceding section stress was laid on the different orders of ministry and their distinctive contributions, this discussion of collegiality has made it clear that the diverse ministries best yield their fruits when they work together in mission and worship.

78. THE MISSION OF THE CHURCH

Mission is inherent in the very notion of the Church. We have seen that the Church is a stage in the process that leads from creation through reconciliation to consummation. The end of this movement is the kingdom of

---

[30] Cor. xli.
[31] *The Faith of the People of God*, p. 18.

God, an all-embracing commonwealth of love and freedom, in which all humanity—and indeed all creation—will be renovated and transformed. Since the Church is moving toward this kingdom as its limit and goal, the Church is an expanding community. We have already stressed that it is an open community, reaching out beyond itself across borders that are not sharply defined.

The gospels represent Jesus himself as having entrusted the Church's mission to the apostles. According to the short ending of St. Mark, "Jesus himself sent out by means of them, from east to west, the sacred and imperishable proclamation of eternal salvation." St. Matthew and St. Luke likewise report that the risen Christ sent out his disciples to carry the gospel to all nations.[32] The New Testament shows us the beginning of this missionary work, especially the labors of St. Paul. Tradition tells of the missionary journeys of the other apostles, and however legendary some of this material may be, the spread of Christianity in the first few generations attests indubitably to intense missionary activity on the part of the earliest Christians. In the subsequent centuries, the Church has been sometimes more, sometimes less, engaged in mission, but probably there has always been some missionary activity going on. We must remember too that behind each of the long-established churches that we find today in what we call "Christian countries," there is a story of missionary origins.

But how does this acknowledgment that mission is inherent in the being of the Church fit in with what has been said at an earlier stage concerning the relation of Christianity to other faiths? [33] There, it will be remembered, we pleaded for a much more generous and open attitude on the part of Christians toward other faiths, and for the recognition that God has not confined his revelation to a single channel. Does this not take away the motivation that lies behind mission? And furthermore, when we came to deal with eschatology and declared ourselves persuaded of the truth of universalism,[34] did this not further weaken any motivation to mission, such as stirred those who undertook their missionary labors in the conviction that apart from an explicit faith in Christ, a man must be condemned to everlasting punishment?

I think we must frankly say that some of the motives that impelled men to mission are no longer operative if we reject the notion of an exclusive divine revelation in the Christian faith (or even of an immeasurably su-

---

[32] Matt. 28:19-20; Luke 24:47.
[33] See above, pp. 170-173.
[34] See above, p. 361.

perior one) and if we reject too the notion that all who do not explicitly accept the Christian faith (let us say, by baptism) are destined to eternal punishment. On the other hand, I think there are still important motives remaining. The Church still has a missionary task, but this will in some respects be differently conceived, as compared with earlier periods. In fact, everyone knows that the whole conception of mission has been changing rapidly in the past few decades, and in particular there has been a revulsion against the association of Christianity with exclusively Western formulations, and a new respect on the part of missionaries for indigenous cultures. So far, this is a development in the right direction, but it must be carried further.

But what is meant by saying that respect for indigenous cultures and so for non-Christian religions must be carried further? Does it mean that there should be no endeavor to persuade the non-Christian to embrace the Christian faith? Would this not be a total reversal of past attitudes? And would it not be carrying openness to such lengths that we would in fact have abandoned the commitment which was claimed to be equally important, and would also have resiled from our earlier position that for the Christian Jesus Christ is definitive?

I do not think there is a contradiction here, but the problem is delicate and complex. The Christian does indeed acknowledge Christ to be the definitive revelation of God, the fully incarnate Logos, and this is a belief to be shared with others and communicated to them. But if the Christian also believes that these others have received a revelation of the same Logos in their own faiths, then he is acknowledging that in some sense the form of Christ is hidden in these faiths. He is not bringing Christ to the non-Christian for the first time (as if he were not already there!) but he might very well think of himself as awakening the non-Christian to a more explicit awareness of the Christ who is already hidden in his faith.

At an earlier stage in this book, there was set forth a typology of religions, but it was pointed out that the typology is not only a typology of faiths, but tends to repeat itself within each faith. To put it differently, we could say that each faith, as a distinctive mode of participation in the truth of the Logos, has the potentiality for growing into the whole truth of the Logos. This suggests that the Christian communication of Christ to the non-Christian would take the form of helping him to recognize Christ in his own tradition and encouraging that tradition to grow into Christ. But clearly such communication would be reciprocal or dialogical. For even if Jesus Christ is the fullness of the divine truth, at any given time Christians are not fully possessed of that truth. Hence the reverence for life in Buddhism, the transcending of racial differences in Islam, the adherence to non-violence in Hinduism, may all be ways in which the pressure of the non-Christian religions causes the Christian to recognize hitherto neglected elements in his own tradition. Thus when Christianity affects a non-Christian religion—or even a secular ideology—there may well be a helpful reaction upon Christianity. As Heinz R. Schlette has put it, "The religious mind and culture in question brings its characteristic spirituality into Christianity and not merely as an external and extrinsic addition, but as an enrichment and extension of a catholicity which is never absolute and perfect." [35] The same writer does not visualize the replacement of the non-Christian religions by Christianity, but sees them continuing side by side for an indefinite time and in mutually helpful dialogue. Apparently sharing the universalism which we have ourselves embraced, he reverses the traditional terminology and says that for the majority of mankind the religions are "the ordinary way of salvation" while Christianity is the "extraordinary way."

This last expression, the "extraordinary way," conceals in itself a difficult question about the Christian Church. We have said that the Church is a stage on the way from the world to the kingdom of heaven. Is it necessary for all men to be gathered into the Church before the kingdom can come? Or is the Church a representative community—both representing the kingdom in the midst of the world, and representing the world toward God in its serving, witnessing, and praying among and for all men? On this second view, the Church is not the lump itself but the leaven in the lump, working toward that moment of transfiguration when "the kingdoms of this world have become the kingdom of our Lord and of his Christ." [36] It would seem to be this second view toward which the reflections of this book have directed us.

The abiding motive of mission is love, and we have seen that Christian love is the self-giving that lets-be. This always has been the fundamental motive for Christian mission, the history of which abounds in examples of sacrifice and martyrdom. But perhaps this fundamental motive has too often been combined with other motives which need to be looked at very carefully. There has been too much thought of *gaining* converts, of *winning* the world, of *expanding* the Church. The Church, like the individual

---

[35] *Towards a Theology of Religions*, p. 101.
[36] Rev. 11:15.

Christian and like Christ himself, is called to give itself. The end set before it is the kingdom, in which it will lose itself. The aim of the Church is not to *win* the world, but rather to identify itself with the world, even to lose itself in the world, in such a way as to bring nearer the kingdom in which the distinction of Church and world will be lost. What is important is the manifesting and propagating of Christ's self-giving love, and the awakening of this in ever wider areas of human society. But this may well happen without these areas becoming incorporated into the Christian Church or explicitly confessing the Christian faith. Here we have to remember that the Christian Church is continuous with a wider community of faith,[37] and that wherever the love that springs from reverence for Being is active, there God has drawn near and revealed himself, and there christhood (by whatever name it may be called) is laying hold of human life and filling it with the grace of Being.

There can never be an end to the Christian mission that goes forth in loving service, so long as the kingdom is still unrealized. But perhaps in the modern world the time has come for an end to the kind of mission that proselytizes, especially from sister faiths which, though under different symbols, are responding to the same God and realizing the same quality of life.

I do not mean by this that Christian missions are to restrict themselves to the humanitarian fields of health, education and the like, in which they have been engaged for a long time. They have both a right and a duty to confess that these things are done in the name of Christ. It may well be the case too that sometimes they will operate in regions where the indigenous religions have yielded to the demonic perversions that can appear in any religion, and in such cases it may be right now, as it was in the past, to aim at conversion. But even in such cases, there must be proper respect for the other person and for his traditions. I may quote some words of Martin Buber: "The desire to influence the other does not mean the effort to change the other, to inject one's own 'rightness' into him; but it means the effort to let that which is recognized as right, as just, as true . . . through one's influence take seed and grow in the form suited to individuation." [38]

But even if such procedures are legitimate in dealing with adherents of animistic cults, I do not think that the Christian missionary should aim at converting adherents of the so-called "higher" religions in which, as I be-

[37] See above, pp. 387, 402.
[38] *The Knowledge of Man*, p. 69.

lieve, God's saving grace is already recognizably at work. Let us take a practical question, which will serve as a kind of test case. Do we really think it a good thing, or a Christian duty, to aim at the conversion of the Jews? Would Martin Buber, for instance, have been any better or any nearer to God if he had become a Christian? Would his conversion have been of any benefit to Christians or Jews or mankind? I, for one, have no hesitation in answering these questions in the negative. I think it better that this man should have realized God's grace and brought us God's message (as I believe he did) within the context of his own culture and religion. There he was authentic. But if we concede the case with the Jews, then, in principle, we have conceded it with all the non-Christian faiths. There is indeed a special affinity between Christianity and Judaism, but I have little patience with the view, sometimes heard, that Christians and Jews together share a specially privileged position as over against other faiths. There is little point in breaking down one barrier in order to erect a new one. We must learn a breadth and generosity that goes far beyond the Judeo-Christian tradition. For example, what I have just written about Buber could equally well be applied to Mahatma Gandhi.

A colossal missionary task still lies ahead if the kingdom is to be brought nearer. But, as we all know, this task nowadays is as challenging among the "secularized" Christian nations of the west, engulfed in a grasping materialism, as it is among peoples that have never been Christian. As I suggested earlier in this book, the time has come for Christianity and the other great world religions to think in terms of sharing a mission to the loveless and unloved masses of humanity, rather than in sending missions to convert each other. This would be a global ecumenism, with a sharing of wisdom and resources that might lead to great steps forward. I have made it clear that ecumenism, both on the Christian and the extra-Christian levels, should not mean a leveling down to uniformity or some sickly syncretism, but a loyal pursuit of the vision of the kingdom as given to each of us, with the recognition that others are advancing to the same goal by different routes.

19 | The Word and Sacraments

79. RE-PRESENTING CHRIST

The Church is the community of Christian faith. As such, it represents Christ in the world. This representing can be understood in a double sense, though both sides of the representing are closely connected. On the one hand, the Church represents Christ vicariously. We have already seen that, in the Pauline metaphor, the Church is "ambassador" for Christ in the world. It continues to proclaim his message in his name, and to do his work in his name. It represents Christ in its ministry, first in its general ministry of reconciliation belonging to all its members, and then in its specific ministries to which some of its members have been duly ordained. On the other hand, the Church re-presents Christ in the sense of making him present in the world. It does so in virtue of the fact that it is his body, or an "extension of the incarnation." We have seen that this latter expression needs to be used with care, but it rightly points to the continuing living presence of Christ in the earthly and embodied fellowship of the Spirit, which is the Church.

In recognizing the Church as the community of faith which re-presents Christ in the world, our attention is directed once more to a phenomenon which we have already encountered on several occasions. We met it right at the beginning of our study [1] when we noted that among the formative factors in theology, one has to reckon both with present experience in the community of faith and with the primordial revelation on which the community had been founded. We saw that these are intimately related, for

[1] See above, p. 8.

on the one hand, we could hardly believe at all in a primordial revelation unless we had ourselves some present first-hand experience of the holy, while on the other hand, the present experience of the community is controlled and given its form by the primordial revelation. The expression, "primordial" here means not only *original*, but *orginative*, for the revelations on which the great communities of faith have been founded have proved themselves to have a capacity for precisely this kind of renewal and fruitfulness in the subsequent experience of the community. We met the same phenomenon very strikingly again when we considered the work of Christ,[2] and had to ask how an event which, from one point of view, occurred long ago in world history, could be considered also as a saving event in the present. It is this same phenomenon of the interrelatedness of past and present in the revelatory event to which we have to return in our consideration of how the Church represents Christ.

We have recognized that the Church itself is a double-sided phenomenon. As the community of faith, it is founded upon the divine action in the world, that is to say, on grace and revelation; but it has these treasures in earthen vessels, for this community of faith appears in the world as a social phenomenon, more precisely, as an association having of necessity specific structures to maintain its identity and to protect its life. We have seen in outline the four basic structures of scripture, sacraments, creed, and ministry, corresponding to and protecting the four basic notes of unity, holiness, catholicity, and apostolicity. We have considered in more detail one of these structures, the ministry, which gives a distinctive continuity and identity to the Christian community. In so far as the creeds are summary statements of Christian faith, we need say no more about them, since this whole book is an exposition of this faith. But the time has come for a further consideration of the word and sacraments, since these are the particular vehicles or structures which the Church employs in its re-presenting of Christ, or in bringing the primordial revelation into the present experience of the community.

At the risk of being wearisome after all that has already been said on this theme, we must nevertheless assert once more that there is no question of a manipulation of the divine presence here. Such manipulation belongs to magic, not to religion. But religion does require definite forms under which the divine presence is to be known, and these are forms that have grown out of the religion's own history and symbolism. To say that reli-

2 See above, pp. 324–327.

gion needs them is to say that man needs them, because of his finite embodied condition. The employment of such definite forms in the Church does not in the slightest degree detract from the divine initiative. While indeed we talk of the Church as re-presenting Christ in the word and sacraments, this cannot be understood in any other sense than that Christ makes himself present in his Church through its word and sacraments. The Church, the community of Christian faith, was itself brought into being in the first place by God's transcendent act, that is to say, by the self-manifestation of expressive Being in the particular being of Jesus Christ. This incarnation, we insisted, is to be understood in terms of the grace of Being, not as the "natural" evolution of the beings. What is true of the very coming into being of the Church, as founded on and originating in this incarnation, is true of the subsequent acts by which the Church renews its being by realizing once more the divine presence. These acts have a definite, earthly form (human words, or the human actions of the sacraments), but they are nevertheless vehicles for the divine action, coming to man just as freely as it came in the event that founded the Church. The word and sacraments have the same kind of ambiguity that runs through so many of the phenomena of faith considered in these pages—the Church itself, the death of Christ, his person, miracles, providence; from one point of view, they are phenomena within the world, but seen in depth, they become the places where Being makes itself present-and-manifest in and through particular beings, and in granting this advent and epiphany, grants also grace and wholeness.

Of the word and sacraments we may use the same expression which we have used above in other contexts for the same kind of phenomenon—the expression "focusing." In the word and sacraments, the divine presence is focused so as to communicate itself to us with a directness and intensity like that of the incarnation itself, which indeed is re-presented in the proclaiming of the word and in the celebration of the sacraments.

We have spoken so far of the word and sacraments together, and they do share this basic function of making-present. It is utterly absurd to suppose that there is any rivalry between the ways of making-present, and it is sad indeed that in the history of Christianity there has sometimes been an exaggerated respect for the word at the expense of the sacraments, or the other way round. Both of them have an indispensable part to play in mediating the divine presence. There is an interesting illustration of this in the traditional ceremonial of the eucharist. At the reading of the gospel, the book is elevated, for at that moment it has become the focus of the divine presence and action; whereas after the consecration, the host is elevated as the focus of Christ's presence.

But while it has been necessary to stress the basic affinity of word and sacraments because of the unfortunate tendency to set them in opposition, this must not obscure the fact that there is a difference between these modes of making-present. Generally speaking, the word, whether written or read or preached, has, because of its verbal form, a conceptual character, or at any rate, a more definitely conceptual character that belongs to the sacraments. The word is to be *heard;* and to be heard is to be *understood.* We are not to think of such understanding in a narrowly intellectualist sense, for it will be an existential understanding that touches on the whole of existence; and while verbal communication operates on a conceptual level, this does not rule out the symbols, images, and connotations which, as we have seen, are characteristic of the language of faith. But even when we make all these allowances, we must nevertheless recognize that the word, however presented, communicates the divine action in a way that is primarily directed to the *minds* of those who are addressed. The sacraments (and again we are speaking in a general way) communicate on a much broader front. They too make use of words, but they also employ ritual acts which impinge upon the sight and other senses. When we consider the priority that sight enjoys among the senses, and especially the importance of sight in recognizing presence, we can readily understand that the sense of the divine presence may be more intensely conveyed in sacramental action than in the verbal communication of the word. Moreover, we have learned that just as important as the explicit verbal communications which we consciously hear with our ears and comprehend with our minds are the unconscious impressions which we absorb through all the senses; and there can be no doubt that the impressions of the divine presence in the sacraments do enter into the being of the Christian at levels other than those of explicit verbal communication.

In assigning to the sacraments a wider range of communicative power than belongs to the word, we may seem to be giving to them a measure of precedence over the word. It probably is true that the sacraments can realize the divine presence in an effectual manner for many persons who might find it difficult to understand either the word of scripture or the preaching of this word. But, rightly understood, the very difference between word and sacraments makes each of them necessary to the other. The word needs the concreteness and breadth of the sacraments; while the sacraments need the conceptual and intelligible structure afforded by the word. Where one too much overshadows the other, the results have always been unfortunate.

Calvin set out with the intention of holding word and sacraments in a proper balance, but in fact he subordinated the sacraments to the word by making them *verbum visibile*.[3] So in spite of his intention, in the Calvinist tradition (as in Protestantism generally) preaching has quite overshadowed the sacraments, and the type of Christian faith that has developed has been intellectual, ethical, dependent on the hearer's faith and comprehension, and thus inevitably a somewhat middle-class business. The opposite danger was exhibited in medieval Catholicism, where the word was submerged in the sacraments, and preaching, as the proclaiming and interpreting of the word, was largely neglected. For then the sacraments came to be regarded superstitiously as magic rites, and there was an absence of that understanding which the proclaiming and hearing of the word provides. If neglect of the sacraments lays too much stress on the subjective faith of the believer, neglect of the word makes the sacraments into automatically effective rites which are scarcely to be distinguished from magic. Since the whole existential-ontological approach of this book has aimed at transcending the disjunction of subjective and objective, it is clear that we can go along neither with a receptionism which would make the effectiveness of the sacraments depend on the subjective frame of mind of the recipient nor with an *ex opere operato* theory which would make this effectiveness quite objectively independent of the persons receiving the sacraments. However, the best way to guard against these opposite distortions is to hold together as indispensable to each other the word and sacraments.

We should make it clear therefore that the following discussion of the word and sacraments will hold on the one hand to the belief that in these vehicles or modes of the Church's action there is a genuine *ontological* presence of God, which is not to be explained away in psychological terms or made dependent upon the believer's subjective states of mind. Yet on the other hand it will be held that the word and sacraments are effectual only in so far as the person to whom they are directed relates to them in an *existential* manner, though this is obviously going to vary considerably from one sacrament to another.

By the "word," we mean the Bible and its proclamation in the preaching of the Church. We have already seen that in a remarkable way this

---

[3] *Institutes of the Christian Religion*, IV, xiv.

symbolizes the unity of the Church, both because it bears witness to the living Word, Jesus Christ, the head of the Church, and because it is accepted by practically all who call themselves Christians. The proclaiming and interpreting of the biblical message is a major task and duty laid upon the ordained ministry, and yet just because this task makes heavy demands on personal qualities and abilities, we see once more the necessity for maintaining the place of the sacraments alongside the word, for they provide an "objective" structure which does not depend on the abilities of the minister nor, for that matter, on the insight or powers of understanding of the hearer, at least, to the same extent as is the case in preaching.

But what we mean by the "sacraments" is more debatable. Typically, they have an "objective" form, visible and dramatic, conjoined with a form of words. We have said that, like the word, they focus the divine presence in the community of faith. But it might be thought that this is too broad a description of the sacraments. Would this not imply that many of the symbols of which we spoke at an earlier stage could be called "sacraments"? or that Christ, the incarnate Word, is a sacrament? or that the Church is a sacrament? or that one's neighbor is a sacrament? In a sense, we can indeed say that all of these can be called "sacraments" and have been so called by theological writers. Our fundamental conviction that Being is present-and-manifest in the beings implies that this is a sacramental world, so that the range of possible "sacraments" is very great, and we have been consistent in recognizing that the divine action is not confined to the ecclesiastically recognized channels.

However, if we use a word in too wide and general a sense, it becomes too imprecise. When we talk of the "sacraments," we mean those particular vehicles which have become established in the practice of the Christian Church. Two of these, baptism and the eucharist, have a special position because they are represented in the New Testament as having been directly instituted by Christ. Modern biblical scholarship, however, would hesitate to pronounce with certainty just what Christ had instituted and what had arisen in the development of the Church. It thus tends to leave indefinite the distinction between the so-called "dominical" sacraments and the five other vehicles which, along with baptism and the eucharist, have constituted the traditional seven sacraments of the Church. Of these other five, confirmation is clearly so closely associated with baptism that it can be claimed to share the same sacramental character; ordination, as we have seen, is also parallel in many ways to baptism [4]; it is harder to see how marriage, as a universal human institution, should be considered

4 See above, pp. 421, 426.

as a Christian sacrament, though it is entirely appropriate that this fundamental area of human life should be brought within the sphere of the sacraments; on the other hand, it can be argued that the sacrament of penance has as much claim to be of dominical institution as have baptism and
the eucharist [5]; while unction is a sacramental act that has a history going
back to the earliest days of the Church, and is well attested in the New
Testament. So we can find no objection to using the expression "sacraments" to cover all seven of the vehicles that have been so called for many
centuries, though recognizing that some of these are more important than
others, and that a special significance belongs to baptism and the eucharist.

The sacraments (and this is true whether we think of two or seven)
are so diverse that it is hard to see what they have in common other than
the general points made above that would extend beyond the sacraments
properly so called—namely, that they have an "objective" form, visible
and dramatic; that this is conjoined with a form of words; and that they
focus the divine presence in the community of faith. Beyond that, there
are great differences. In some sacraments, the outward and visible elements
are much more striking than in others; again, in some the participation and
involvement in an active way of the recipients is much more obvious than
in others where the recipients are relatively passive, just as they are in the
hearing of the word; some of the sacraments (such as baptism and ordination) are given once only to each individual, while others are given and
received repeatedly, especially the Holy Communion.

The differences among the sacraments will be discussed as we take them
in turn, but these differences become explicable when we try to see the
sacraments as a whole, especially the traditional seven as constituting a
unity which grew up in the Church's experience. For this range of the
sacraments corresponds to the range of human life itself, and provides a
vehicle for realizing the divine presence and the reconciliation which it
brings for every condition of life and for every stage of life. In a very
remarkable way, the Church's sacramental system spans the whole of life
and provides in different and appropriate ways for life's different needs.
There are sacraments for the beginning of life, for its middle, and for its
end; there are sacraments for health and for sickness; there are sacraments
for those who live "in the world" and for those whose vocation is to a
specific ministry. The sacraments provide the institutional structure for
that sanctification of human life and its conformation to Christ, of which
the outlines have already been sketched.

But we have already made it clear that the sacraments, whether taken

[5] John 20:19–23, etc.

singly or together, must be accompanied by the word if their work of reconciliation and sanctification is to be effective. So before we say anything further about them, it will be necessary for us to speak at greater length of the word and of its function of making-present.

80. THE WORD

As a convenient starting point for our discussion of the word, we may remind ourselves of Barth's teaching that this word of God meets us in a threefold form: there is the living Word, Jesus Christ himself, the bearer and the fullness of the Christian revelation; then there is the written word, the Bible, which witnesses to the living Word; and finally there is the proclaimed word, the living voice of the Church as, in its preaching and teaching, it too witnesses to the living Word by interpreting and applying the written word. The living Word, or incarnate Lord, has priority and gives birth to the other two forms of the word; but it is only through the mediation of the written word and the proclaimed word that we have access to Christ, the revealed Word.[6]

Any discussion of the word must keep in mind this threefold form that Barth has indicated, and must also remember that the three forms constitute a unity. This is very much in line with what has been said earlier in this book about the word, and especially about the written word of scripture and its relation to Christ on the one hand and to the living tradition and teaching of the Church on the other. It is unnecessary to repeat here points that have already been plainly established.[7] But we may remind ourselves that the scripture in itself is not revelation, but testifies to the revelation in Christ; and that it is in the living context of the Church, as the community of the Spirit, that scripture comes alive, as it were, so that in the human words of the scripture, as read or preached, the word of God addresses us. It is in this sense that we can think of the scripture as "inspired." It is the vehicle for the divine word, and through it Christ is made present.

The interrelation of Christ, as incarnate Word, and of scripture, as written word, and of preaching, as proclaimed word, can be more fully elucidated if we pay closer attention to what we mean by "word." In the analysis of language that was given in the first or philosophical division of

[6] *Church Dogmatics*, I/1, p. 98ff.
[7] See above, pp. 9-13, 381-382.

our theology, it was claimed that discourse has a threefold function: it expresses, it refers, and it communicates.[8] This threefold function is typical of any word or *logos*, and it is something like this that we see reflected in the threefold form of the word of God. As we learned in our discussion of christology, it is expressive Being, as the second person of the triune God, that perfectly *expresses* itself in the particular being of Jesus Christ. Scripture, in turn, *refers* to Christ, and through Christ to Being; for the scriptures of the Old and New Testaments have for their theme the story of Being's self-revelation as this has been given in the community for which these writings constitute, as we have seen, a kind of "memory," whereby the classic revelation remains accessible. Finally, the proclaiming of the word in and by the community *communicates* the revelation; and since communication implies a shared world of ideas, such communication also implies interpretation, so that the preaching and teaching of the Church must always be seeking to interpret the classic revelation to the people of each time and country in the medium of a shared language and a shared conceptuality.

But while Barth's view of the threefold form of the word fits in very well with our own theory of the threefold function of language, we must remember that in both cases the three factors that have been distinguished for the sake of a clarifying analysis are not sharply separable, and in fact constitute a unity. This follows too from our earlier insistence that language cannot properly be understood in abstraction from the concrete living situation where it is *in use*, in this case, from the existential context of the community of faith.

In the case of the word of God, we can understand this unity that embraces the three factors as due to the unitive action of the Holy Spirit, acting in the community of the Spirit. It is this unitive action of the Spirit that brings into one the spoken word of the Church's proclamation, the written word of her scriptures, and the incarnate Word in and through whom Being has made itself known. Thus the making-present that is accomplished by the word is, like all making-present of God, not something that man accomplishes by his agency but God's making himself present, through the action in finite beings of that unitive Being in which they live and move and have their individual beings. Whenever a human word is heard as a divine word, something takes place that is analogous to what has been described in the analyses of revelation, of miracle, of the incar-

[8] See above, pp. 126–130.

nation itself. There is, moreover, the same ambiguity, for what is actually heard or is open to public inspection is a human utterance in the world. But this can also be heard "in depth" as the voice of Being, and we can so hear it because we already belong to Being and the grace of Being operates in us.

But if we thus unreservedly assert that the word of God is heard *as* the word of God because God himself lets himself be made-present in it, how does this square with our earlier statement that the preaching and teaching of the Church makes a particularly heavy demand on the personal qualities of her ministers, as compared with the sacraments which have a more "objective" structure and are therefore much less likely than preaching to depend on the ability of the performer?

There is, however, no contradiction in asserting both that the proclaiming of the word makes a particularly heavy demand on the minister of the word, and that it can make God present only because God makes himself present in the word. This is just one more example of that co-working that belongs to the very nature of the Church and that is already implied in the creation of beings who are at once free and finite. The proclaiming of the word is a task and a responsibility for the Church. Its ministers who are charged with this task must have the highest qualities and be subjected to the most stringent training so that they have the fullest possible understanding both of the content of the classic revelation and of the minds of their contemporaries to whom they must interpret this revelation. On the other hand, they could never hope that their human words could be the bearers of the divine word unless these words were governed first by the words of the scriptures, which the Church has accepted as the normative record of the revelation, and then were further caught up, through the unitive action of the Spirit, together with the words of scriptures into a unity with the living Word to whom these human words alike testify; and even then, if the word is to strike home, it is necessary that the same unitive Being that is in the word should move also in the being of the hearer, so that the word is recognized as God's word. Thus, whenever the word is proclaimed and heard, something akin to revelation takes place; but it is not primordial revelation, but the making-present of the primordial revelation on which the community of faith was founded.

Thus, on the one hand, the proclaiming of the word demands from those who are charged with it the greatest efforts in the theological disciplines that are required for the interpretation and presentation of the content of the faith. Yet such interpretation can never be a manipulation, for the word has a life of its own, and the task of the teacher or preacher is to let it be heard. Words are not just dead things. They belong in the existential context of interpersonal communication, and indeed, more than this, they belong in the very context of Being. As Heidegger is fond of saying, the word is the "dwelling-place of Being" (*das Haus des Seins*). The word has a kind of life of its own, so that even when someone says something, he may well be saying more than he consciously intends. This is surely true of great poets and literary men, whose words continue to yield almost inexhaustible interpretations. Yet such interpretation has to be guarded and limited by the text and by a sound hermeneutical science. In the case of the word of God, the written text in isolation is deprived of life; taken just as "letters," it is dead. But the Spirit makes it alive [9] in the community of faith, so that God again speaks through it and makes himself present, as he did in the primordial revelation.

This discussion of the word as having its life in the context of the community raises again the question of the distribution of authority, though this time we are viewing the question from the side of the Bible. It is true that the Bible was produced by the community of faith, has its life in that community and is interpreted by it. Yet just because the Bible contains the word *of God* in its written form, it also retains an independence over against the community. For the Church has never wholly taken the word into possession and has never exhaustively interpreted the word. We have to reckon with what Karl Barth calls "the Bible not yet interpreted, the free Bible which remains free in face of all interpretation." [10] This is the power of the Bible to yield from its inexhaustible depth new truths—truths which may place the community itself under judgment and summon it to the renewal of its life.

The proclaiming of the word and instruction in the word is of first-class importance if the community of faith is to be an understanding community, firmly grasping the content of its faith, and safeguarded against error and superstition. It will be seen therefore that the tasks of preaching and teaching are closely related to the task of theology. They share with theology the task of unfolding and communicating an understanding of the faith, and so they must be theologically grounded; but to their theological basis they bring other skills also, educational, psychological, homiletical, and the like, and they have a more *ad hoc* character as they are addressed to different groups whose special needs demand different approaches.

[9] II Cor. 3:6.
[10] *Church Dogmatics*, vol. I/1, p. 297.

Not only is the word important for the understanding of the community, it is equally important for its moral level. The Christian faith, like all the higher religions, has its ethical character. The word combines grace and judgment, so that it is a prophetic word. Thus its steady proclamation and its application to the problems of human behavior and human relations stir the conviction of sin and the need for repentance and renewal, without which the community of faith can itself sink back into moral torpor and self-complacency.

But while we must stress the importance and centrality of the word as the vehicle committed to the Church for the re-presenting of the primordial revelation and for seeing the present situation in the light of this revelation, we have also to remember that the revelation is more than a message, that Christ and then the Church are more than the bearers of a message. Faith, in turn, is not exhausted in terms of understanding and moral commitment. There is also the whole depth of religion that finds expression in such words as "communion" and "incorporation." If those varieties of Christianity that concentrate almost exclusively on the ministry of the word strike us as sometimes rather cold, abstract, and moralistic in their expression of Christian faith, this is because the word lacks its necessary complement in the sacraments, and to these we now turn.

81. BAPTISM AND CONFIRMATION

The ritual use of water for purificatory purposes is found in many religions, and it is entirely understandable that the important part which water plays in human life should have caused to gather around it a wealth of existential connotations that fit it for use as a religious symbol. Although Christian baptism presumably had its origins chiefly from Jewish antecedents, and especially from the baptism of St. John the Baptist, there are obvious parallels with rites in other religions and this points us again to the similarity of structure underlying the multiplicity of faiths. The various communities of faith have their ritual forms by which they admit their members, and it is rather a striking fact to find how much these rites resemble one another, even in the symbolism which they employ.

Baptism by water in the threefold name (perhaps sometimes to begin with in the name of Jesus alone) seems to have been the rite of initiation into the Christian community from the earliest time.[11] We have seen that

---

[11] Matt. 28:19; Acts 2:38.

Jesus himself was baptized by St. John the Baptist, and although this may have originally been understood as his joining himself to the community of the Baptist, it came to be understood as marking the beginning of his ministry in the fullness of the Spirit.[12] Jesus in turn is represented as having commanded his disciples to baptize those who would accept the gospel and join themselves to the community of faith.

As the sacrament of initiation, baptism is to be understood as the outward, visible form which serves as a vehicle and a protection for what we earlier described as the process of "entry into the Christian life." [13] We can discern in baptism the same major elements or moments as were indicated in the earlier analysis, though we shall treat them here in a slightly different order. Just as we saw entry into the Christian life to be a work of the Holy Spirit, to which man responds in faith, so baptism is also a work of the Spirit, through the agency of the Church as the community of the Spirit, and to this work of the Spirit in baptism (including infant baptism) there corresponds an answering faith of which we shall say more later. This structure of baptism, as a work of the Spirit with a response of faith, holds also for the other sacraments, and constitutes a parallel to the structure which we have already seen to belong to the proclaiming of the word. This structure rules out any merely subjective account of the sacraments, though it also denies any magical or automatic sacramental efficacy. It demands the same kind of existential-ontological account that we have consistently used in this theology.

1. Baptism includes the moments described in our remarks on entry into the Christian life as *conviction of sin and repentance*. These moments, as we should remind ourselves, are not to be separated from each other, or from the other moments which analysis can discern within the full and unitary experience of entry into the Christian life. To seek baptism is to acknowledge that human existence is not in order and needs to be reoriented. In this regard, Christian baptism, as is clear from the early chapters of Acts, resembles the baptism given by St. John the Baptist in being "a baptism of repentance for the remission of sins." [14] Baptism is an acknowledgment of sin, but we have seen that such acknowledgment is not itself sin but rather the first step to renewal, for it implies a "turning away" from sin which, in the full Christian experience from which these moments of conviction and repentance are inseparable, is also a "turning to-

[12] See above, pp. 282–284.
[13] See above, pp. 337–343.
[14] Mark 1:4.

ward" the life of grace and reconciliation. However, these moments of conviction and repentance, as well as being essential elements in the entry into the Christian life, continue the ancient purificatory significance of those prototypes and parallels to Christian baptism, and retain the universal symbolism of water as a cleansing agent.

2. Baptism also includes the moment of *justification*, and we have seen that this somewhat archaic term implies being accepted, finding an identity, counting as someone. It is appropriate that the child receives his name at baptism, for this is his being accepted and given an identity. Moreover, it is appropriate that we speak of his *Christian* name. He is accepted by *Being*, but in the concrete rite of baptism, this means his being accepted in the *Christian community*. St. Paul tells us we are "all baptized into one body," the body of Christ.[15] Through baptism we are accepted, incorporated, delivered from the isolation of meaninglessness and set in the living context of the community of faith, as members that count in it. Perhaps then it is most properly under this aspect, the aspect of acceptance or justification, that we can think of baptism as the sacrament of initiation whereby the individual is taken into and made a lively but still distinct member of the one body.

3. Baptism is also the form under which there begins the work of *sanctification*. In the earlier discussion, we found it necessary to stress that sanctification should not be separated from justification, and that the misunderstanding of the latter arises from ways of talking which seem to regard it as a mere "declaring righteous" apart from any actual "making righteous" by the Spirit. This point needs to be stressed further here, and indeed it now receives strong support when we consider the New Testament teaching about baptism. For although baptism is the beginning of the Christian life, the New Testament does not think of this as just some new formal or forensic status, but as an actual receiving of the Holy Spirit. It is true that there is some variation in the relation between baptism and the receiving of the Holy Spirit, and this is what we should expect in view of the flexibility not only of the sacraments but of all outward forms—a flexibility of which we have spoken already and will have more to say in due course. But to be baptized means normally to receive the Holy Spirit.[16] This follows also from the character of the Church as the community of the Spirit, so that to be incorporated into the Church

15 I Cor. 12:13.
16 Acts 2:38.

is to be received into the community of the Spirit. Furthermore, it is a fulfillment of the christianizing of the ancient rite of baptism. St. John the Baptist had baptized with water, but Christian baptism, it was promised, would be by the Spirit.[17] The descent of the Spirit upon him was a major feature of Christ's own baptism.[18] It need hardly be said that in claiming that baptism implies a receiving of the Spirit, we are not suggesting for a moment that some marvelous transformation instantaneously takes place or that some extraordinary charismatic manifestations are to be looked for. But we are quite definitely saying that Christian baptism means nothing less than that sanctification *has begun*, and that within the community of the Spirit, the baptized person is already caught up in the movement of unitive Being.

4. Baptism is also inclusive of the moment of election, which we saw to be also part of the process of entry into the Christian life; but in the present discussion, we prefer to designate this election as *vocation*. We have already drawn attention to the resemblances between baptism and ordination.[19] In calling baptism a rite of vocation, we are developing this point further. Baptism is the vocation, or even the ordination, to that general ministry of the Church which all its members share, the ministry of reconciliation. Here we may remind ourselves again of the baptism of Christ and of how this event, whatever its original character may have been, is represented in the gospels as his commitment to his ministry. The baptism of the Christian is likewise the rite that commits him to the general ministry of the Church. But just as has been said in the case of some of the other aspects of baptism, and as was made very clear when we talked about the vocation of Christ himself, we do not think of these things as happening in an instant. They take time to unfold, and this is indeed recognized by the adding of confirmation to baptism. But vocation and sanctification are just as surely aspects of the sacrament of baptism, and really present in it, as are repentance and justification.

We have still not mentioned what is perhaps the most distinctive characterization of Christian baptism, given by St. Paul when he sees it as a dramatic and visible representation of being buried and rising again with Christ,[20] of participating in his death and resurrection. We are "baptized into his death" and raised into "newness of life." This characterization of

---

[17] Mark 1:8.
[18] Mark 1:10.
[19] See above, pp. 421, 426.
[20] Rom. 6:4.

baptism does not so much add to the ways of describing it that we have already considered, as rather it gathers them up to show us the unity of the sacrament. Baptism is at the beginning of the Christian life, yet in a sense it contains already *in nuce* (as the Holy Eucharist also does) the whole of the Christian life as a conformation to the life of Christ.

Many of the remarks made about baptism in the foregoing paragraphs are parallel to what has already been said about the proclaiming and hearing of the word, and confirm that word and sacraments go together as ways of making-present the divine grace. Nevertheless, we can now begin to see some differences between these two modes of making-present. There is the obvious difference that in the proclaiming of the word, the evangelical mode, the vehicle is verbal, while in baptism, the sacramental mode, there is also the visible element of water and the visible act of baptism. But there is more to the difference than this, and the sacrament cannot be adequately characterized as *verbum visibile*. In baptism, the recipient participates in the action of the sacrament. It is a *doing*, as well as a speaking, hearing, seeing. The man of Ethiopia to whom St. Philip preached the gospel made the response of faith to the proclamation, but then in addition he submitted to baptism,[21] and this dramatic kind of participation shows, along with the visible element, the broader existential range of the sacrament as compared with the word.

In mentioning the man of Ethiopia, we have alluded to a case of adult baptism, and presumably in the primitive Church this would be the normal pattern. Nowadays however the normal pattern is infant baptism, for the Church believes—rightly, as we shall show—that the beginning of the Christian life can and should coincide with the beginning of the individual's life. But infant baptism raises further questions about the difference between the word and sacraments. In the evangelical mode of making-present, there is the conscious and explicit response of faith on the part of the person addressed; and clearly, in the case of adult baptism, one can point to the same kind of response in the sacramental mode. But what are we to say in the case of infant baptism? Here let us remind ourselves that we already pointed to the capacity of the sacraments, with their broader existential basis in action and in the senses as well as in words, to affect us not only through the conscious understanding but on the all-important subconscious levels as well. This is true even of adult baptism, where the sense of incorporation and also the reality of incorporation go beyond what is explicitly understood at the time. But it is specifically exemplified

21 Acts 8:26–40.

in the case of infant baptism. Here the child is totally unaware of the significance of the sacrament. Yet in and through this sacrament, he is already in a perfectly real way incorporated into the body of Christ. In being brought into the community, the center of his life is shifted from his isolated individual being to the body of which he is now a member, and this is the cancelation of original sin, the "turning away" and the "turning toward" which constitute repentance. From this very moment of baptism, the child is unconsciously incorporated into the community, the recipient of its love and interest, and therefore the recipient of grace. We must not think of this purely in existential or sociological terms. There is a real ontological basis also, for already in this child who has been brought into the community of the Spirit, the action of unitive Being is going on. The initiative in grace and reconciliation belongs always with God, and certainly does not need to wait until the child becomes explicitly conscious of such possibilities. Moreover, as the child's life is molded by divine grace mediated through the community of faith, he enters into the vocation of the Christian and, even without his being aware of it, begins to exercise the ministry of reconciliation. All these things, of course, are not tied to a moment of time. They are present already in baptism, but their unfolding is, like the attainment of selfhood, a matter of time.

These considerations, as well as expanding our view of the way in which the sacraments in general can re-present or make-present Christ and his work, also allow us to reply to critics of the practice of infant baptism. These critics take the line that the New Testament envisages only adult baptisms, and that the kind of experience which baptism embodies— acknowledgment of sin, repentance, receiving of the Holy Ghost, and so on—can be conceived only in the context of an adult life.

It may indeed be true that there is no clear New Testament sanction for infant baptism. Calvin and others who have thought it necessary to produce a biblical warrant for everything that is done or believed in the Church have tried hard to show that infant baptism has such a warrant, but although the practice is undoubtedly very early, the New Testament evidence is inconclusive. Of course, from the point of view of this book and of others who accept that scripture is to be supplemented by the tradition of the Church, the almost universal practice of infant baptism in the Church throughout its history is an entirely sufficient and satisfactory warrant and authority. But our discussion of the nature of sacramental action permits us to adduce very sound theological reasons in support of infant baptism.

The rejection of infant baptism is due to an exaggerated individualism which is a common fault in evangelical Protestantism. Fundamentally, the error is a mistaken idea of human existence itself. There is no isolated existence, but only existence with others. When this is understood, then it is also understood that explicit verbal communication and conscious individual decisions, important though they are, do not by any means constitute the whole of life. If we make them paramount in Christianity, then we have arbitrarily narrowed the existential range of God's approach to man through Christ and his Church. The rejection of infant baptism is the result of such a narrowing, and goes even beyond Calvinism in entirely assimilating the operation of the sacraments to that of the word.

Some things about baptism may be a matter of indifference, as, for instance, whether it should be performed by dipping the person into the water or by pouring water over him. With sound common sense, Calvin remarks that this kind of thing might well depend on local climatic conditions! [22] But the question of whether baptism is to be administered in infancy or delayed until adolescence cannot be treated as one of indifference, and well-intentioned persons who think that opposing views on the matter could be accommodated by making infant baptism optional are deeply in error and have not understood the nature of a sacrament, and above all, have not understood the meaning of "incorporation." The question of whether baptism is to be given to a child is not one that can be left to the subjective preference of the parent or of the local minister, for to deny the sacrament to the child is to deprive him of his right to be incorporated into the household of faith and to grow up within that sacramental structure which the Church, through long wisdom and experience and under the guidance of the Spirit, has so designed that the whole of our human life, from beginning to end, may be supported by the divine grace.

At the same time, we have made it clear that sacramental efficacy is not a matter of magic, and even if the sacraments do, as we have contended, work upon the recipient in ways that go beyond his explicit awareness, nevertheless the fullest efficacy of the sacraments requires the response of faith and the cooperation of the recipient, though this would seem to be more obviously demanded in some sacraments than in others. In the case of baptism, while the child to begin with is unconscious of the influences that are working upon him in the context of the body of Christ, such influences will come increasingly to his conscious notice and will

[22] *Institutes of the Christian Religion*, IV, xvi.

elicit his response; for we are not to suppose that everything happens in an instant, but rather that there is initiated a process which accomplishes itself in that temporality whereby our finite existence is constituted.

Let us remember again that while the sacramental structure is essential to the Church, as a community that exists in the world and has an embodied being, the operation of the Spirit is never tied to the structure. It is possible on the one hand for the sacrament of baptism to be given, and yet for its normal course of unfolding to be frustrated and not brought to maturity; and it is possible on the other hand for the Spirit to move in those who have not received the sacrament but who are nevertheless brought within the community of the Spirit. We have illustrations of both cases in the New Testament. The converts made by St. Philip in Samaria were baptized, but did not receive the Holy Spirit at that time.[23] However, Cornelius and his companions at Caesarea received the Holy Spirit although unbaptized.[24] While the second of these cases shows us that the operation of the Spirit is not confined to the sacramental channels, nevertheless the continuation of the story shows us the respect in which baptism was held, for those men who had already received the Holy Spirit were subsequently baptized [25]—just as we noted earlier that although St. Paul might claim, if anyone could, to have an immediate call from God to the ministry, this was none the less regularized by his being ordained by the Church, through prayer and laying on of hands. Thus the fact that the Spirit is not confined to the sacramental channels is certainly not understood in the New Testament as implying that these channels are to be ignored or lightly esteemed. But we have still to say something about the other case cited above—that of the disciples at Samaria who were baptized without receiving the Holy Spirit, and this case seems to raise more serious problems.

Presumably the converts at Samaria had a very imperfect understanding of what they had been converted to or of what baptism meant—and this seems to be implied in the story, which indicates that they were a superstitious people, easily impressed by miracle and magic.[26] They provide an extreme illustration of the danger that arises when there is lacking an adequate faith-response and understanding on the part of the recipient of the sacrament. The same kind of thing might happen today in mis-

[23] Acts 8:16.
[24] Acts 10:44.
[25] Acts 10:48.
[26] Acts 8:6, 9–11.

sionary areas where whole communities sometimes move into the Church in a body; but a commoner parallel is what happens in settled Christian communities, where children are baptized as a matter of course, and the ceremony may be regarded as little more than a social convention. Many clergy are rightly worried by this devaluation of the sacrament of baptism, though perhaps the fault has lain chiefly with the Church itself, in its failure to interest itself sufficiently in the children baptized into its membership and so in its failure to fulfill its role as the community of the Spirit through which the Spirit will normally act upon the child.

But just as the danger of indiscriminate (or perhaps we should say, undiscriminated) baptism has been there almost from the beginning of the Church, so also from the beginning the Church has sought to provide a remedy and corrective within the sacramental structure itself, in the sacrament of confirmation. The very name of this sacrament indicates that it does not stand as something complete in itself, but is to be regarded as a complement to and a strengthening of what has been done in baptism. The sequel of the story about the converts in Samaria shows us very clearly the prototype of confirmation—indeed, we may say the first confirmation of which we have record. Two of the apostles, the chief ministers or bishops of the primitive Church, came down from Jerusalem. Although we are not explicitly informed about what took place, we must suppose that there was some examination of the faith of the converts and perhaps further instruction. We must suppose this unless we are prepared to accept that what followed was quite magical. For the apostles then laid their hands on the baptized converts, with prayer, and then the gift of the Holy Spirit was given.[27]

The sacrament of confirmation has been variously administered in different parts of the Church, and there is always the danger that confirmation too can be reduced to a convention, just as may happen with baptism. It seems to me, for instance, that the practice in the Eastern Church of administering confirmation to an infant immediately after baptism, and of reducing the connection of confirmation with the chief minister, has deprived it of the two principal features in which its value has mainly consisted. If confirmation is to have its full place in the sacramental structure of the Church, it should provide for a conscious, understanding act of faith on the part of the confirmand, and it should be administered by the bishop himself. These two points call for brief comment.

[27] Acts 8:17.

Without in the very least detracting from the value of baptism in itself or depreciating that growth in grace, at first unconscious, then increasingly conscious, which we have seen to belong to infant baptism, we must nevertheless acknowledge the desirability of coming to a point where the response of faith is deliberate and explicit. Thus it is desirable that confirmation should take place when the baptized person has attained in himself the capacity for at least a measure of the faith and understanding which, at the moment of baptism, belonged primarily to the community into which he was incorporated but which he has learned to share consciously with the other members of the community. It is impossible to lay down any age for confirmation, since the development of one individual differs from that of another. On the whole, however, one should think of this sacrament as belonging to the stage of life at which a measure of responsibility is attained, just as baptism belongs to that first stage of life when the child is still entirely dependent on the family and community. But if confirmation is to be a genuinely important complement to baptism, and if merely conventional baptism that seems to go no further than the ceremony itself is to be discouraged and reduced, then it would seem that the links between baptism and confirmation need to be strengthened. This might be done in two ways. One is by stressing the communal aspect of baptism and the responsibility of the community toward the child received into its fellowship; the other is by strengthening the instruction of the children in the community, which is simply the recognition once more that sacraments and word must go together.

The second point we made about confirmation was that its character as an episcopal act must be maintained and stressed. Not only does this follow the New Testament precedent, according to which confirmation was administered by the apostles, it also helps to make clear the seriousness of confirmation and to prevent its becoming also a formality that a person observes at a certain age of life. Confirmation by the bishop shows that the confirmand is not just joining some local club, but is being admitted to the membership of the whole Church of Christ, with all the duties and privileges which pertain to such membership. It is appropriate that the Church should act through its chief minister on such an occasion, for it is not, after all, the baptized person who confirms his baptism by making his response of faith, but the Church which confirms it by binding the baptized person more closely to itself and by admitting him to the fullness of her mysteries. This is his justification or acceptance in the fullest sense, when he becomes a responsible member of the body, and it is right that this act of grace should be performed by the chief pastor who represents the whole Church and who exercises the fullness of its ministry.

It is important to notice that in the foregoing discussion of baptism and confirmation, no attempt has been made to divide up the significance of the rite of Christian initiation, assigning some "moments" to baptism, others to confirmation. Occasionally theologians—perhaps making too much of the story of the Samaritan converts mentioned above—have claimed that it is in confirmation that the gift of the Spirit is given. Our own view, however, has been that baptism itself is a baptism into the Spirit—a sharing in the "baptism" of the Church by the Spirit at Pentecost, just as it is a sharing in the death and resurrection of Christ. Confirmation does not add anything that was absent in baptism, but is rather a deepening and ratification of what has already taken place. This does not mean, of course, that there may not be a difference of emphasis, which is in fact brought out by the different ritual acts. Baptism with water is obviously more suggestive of the washing away of sins and of dying and rising with Christ; while the laying on of hands (or, alternatively, anointing with oil) is more suggestive of empowering, that part of Christian initiation which we have likened to ordination. But a difference of emphasis cannot be invoked in order to break up the unity of baptism-confirmation as the total sacramental embodiment of entry into the Christian life.

But if baptism and confirmation constitute a unity, how do we reconcile this with the preference expressed above for the normal Western practice of baptizing in infancy and confirming several years later in late childhood or early adolescence—a practice which, though it has been established for many centuries, cannot claim to be primitive? I think that good reasons have already been given for the preference—the affirmative reason that entry into the Christian life is not the work of a moment but takes time, and the negative reasons that the alternative practices either lay too much stress on the conscious response of the individual believer (in the case where baptism is deferred to adulthood) or else virtually eliminate this response (in the case where everything is already completed in infancy). But although the practice I have commended has strong theological and pastoral considerations in its favor, it has no exclusive claim, and in fact different practices will no doubt continue within the Christian Church.

82. THE HOLY EUCHARIST

We come now to the most venerated of all the Christian sacraments, the Holy Eucharist. The eucharist has such a richness of content and enfolds in itself such a wealth of meaning and a breadth of symbolism that it is hard indeed to speak adequately of it. This richness is reflected in the diversity of ways in which this sacrament has been named. It is the eucharist, or thanksgiving; it is the mass, and whatever this may have meant originally, it has come to suggest sacrifice; it is the Holy Communion, in which the worshipper is united with God through Christ, and also with his fellow-worshippers in the body of Christ; it is the Lord's Supper, and this title reminds us of the dominical connection of the sacrament, and that in it we receive from Christ the grace that sustains and nourishes the Christian life. This very richness of the eucharist shows us the need for studying each sacrament by itself and not trying to subsume them all in too facile a manner under a few general characteristics.

Of course, the eucharist does exhibit the characteristics which we associate with the sacraments in general, and this particular sacrament, because of its preeminence, might even be taken as the paradigm of all Christian sacraments. It makes use of outward, visible elements, in this case, bread and wine. It enshrines as its core and inner meaning a making-present of Christ and his grace. It incorporates the recipient into the body of Christ and conforms his existence to the pattern of Christ. All this and more is included in the eucharist, and exemplifies the character of the sacraments generally.

In the course of its long history, the eucharist has shown many variations, for there is a legitimate flexibility in sacramental forms. Yet through all the variations a basic pattern has persisted, and certain words and actions have been almost universal. The following remarks about the eucharist are not founded on any one particular version of the liturgy, and would be applicable to the sacrament as it is celebrated in most of the major communions of the Christian Church.

Our interpretation of this sacrament, as of the other matters treated in this book, will be in existential-ontological terms. As usual, this means ruling out from the beginning some extreme positions, and endeavoring to follow a *via media*. As existential, our interpretation rules out any automatic or magical view of the sacrament. The sacramental action cannot be something that happens entirely *extra nos*, any more than the original work of Christ, re-presented in the sacrament, could be understood in purely objective terms. The action of the sacrament cannot be regarded as operating on lower than personal levels, and this means that our own existential participation in the sacrament is an essential element in the action, so that this action is not just something that operates on us in a purely objective way. It is true, as has already been said in connection with sacraments generally, that the action need not be entirely on the level of what is consciously and explicitly understood. The eucharist has indeed such wealth of meaning that probably no one is ever fully aware of its action upon him. But there must be some existential dimension in this as in all sacramental action. On the other hand, as ontological, our interpretation rules out any merely subjective account of the sacrament, such as one finds among some Protestant groups. The eucharist is decidedly not a mere memorial, or a way of helping us to remember what Christ did a long time ago. It is a genuine re-presenting of Christ's work. In this sacrament, as in the others, the initiative is with God; it is he who acts in the sacrament and makes himself present. So we reject any accounts of the sacrament that lay the stress on how we feel or on the state of our faith—theories of receptionism and the like which visualize the sacramental action as going on primarily in the mind of the recipient. Just as we have firmly resisted any purely existential views of revelation, of the person of Christ and of many other matters in theology, and have in each case maintained an ontological dimension, we make the same point in the theology of the eucharist.

Such an existential-ontological interpretation, I believe, is in any case the most faithful way of expressing the understanding of the eucharist to be found in the New Testament. If we take St. Paul's teaching, we have already had occasion to notice Käsemann's assertion that the notion of a "real presence" is a central element in that teaching. There is certainly no support in St. Paul for the thought that the sacrament is a mere memorial, or that it is only in some metaphorical sense that Christ is present and his body given and received. Indeed, St. Paul's ideas still move to such an extent on the mythological level that we might think that he had a magical understanding of the sacrament, were it not that just when he seems to be getting most involved in myth and magic, he clearly states the existential dimension of the sacrament. We refer to the extraordinary passage in which he says that some of the Corinthians had become sick and others had died through unworthy participation in the eucharist.[28] This almost looks like a magical interpretation of the sacrament, until we

[28] I Cor. 11:30.

remember that if St. Paul had thought of the sacrament and its efficacy in *purely* objective and automatic terms, then it would have been, in St. Ignatius' phrase, the "medicine of immortality" [29] to all who received it, irrespective of *how* they received it. But what St. Paul is saying is that an unworthy receiving makes all the difference. Obviously, he is as far as possible from any subjective theory of the sacrament. But he does recognize—as has been stressed on many occasions in the course of this book—that every act of grace can be seen also as an act of judgment, and that God's ontological action is inseparable from man's existential relation to it.

We shall now make a few general observations on the eucharist, relating it to and distinguishing it from the other sacraments and the word. Then we shall treat in more detail of two central characteristics of the eucharist.

The first general observation has to do with the fact that the eucharist is received usually many times in the life of the Christian, whereas some other sacraments, such as baptism and confirmation, are administered once only. Although other ways of explaining this difference are possible, we prefer to see it as having to do with the relation of baptism and confirmation to entry into the Christian life, as was already explained when we analyzed the inner meaning of baptism in terms of acknowledgment of sin, repentance, justification, and vocation; whereas the eucharist is the sacrament which provides the structure and support for the growth of the Christian life in the process of sanctification.

Of course, the distinction between the sacrament given once and the sacrament given repeatedly is not to be made too rigid. We insisted in our discussion of entry into the Christian life that this entry is not to be thought of as something that takes place once for all, but rather as an act of commitment that has to be renewed in each situation as it arises; and we insisted also that justification is not to be separated from sanctification. Thus we could not be very happy about language which accounted for baptism's being given only once in terms of the conferring of a "status." This would seem to detract from the living, existential character of faith-commitment. In actual fact, the Easter ceremonies in many churches provide an opportunity for the renewing of baptismal vows, and in some of them there is a symbolic sprinkling of the people with the newly blessed waters of baptism. This is a recognition that the Christian life is an ongoing process, and the eucharist, given repeatedly as the outward vehicle

---

[29] Eph. 20.

of continuing sanctifying grace, is more typical of sacramental action than the kind of sacrament given once for all.

When this principle of growth and development is admitted, there can also be some flexibility in the order in which the sacraments are administered. It may be, for instance, that in some cases there are considerations that favor admission to first communion before confirmation. It is sometimes argued that admission to communion should take place at a relatively early age, and confirmation be deferred until the confirmand appreciates the full seriousness of the step. It seems to me, however, that even if this may sometimes be done with advantage, there is more to be said in favor of the order in which confirmation, or at least being "ready and desirous" for confirmation, should come first, and obviously a first communion following almost immediately after confirmation helps to point up the meaning and importance of that rite. Surely a capacity to appreciate the meaning of the eucharist implies a capacity to appreciate the seriousness of confirmation. It would be a mistaken policy to try to upgrade the value of confirmation by taking steps that might cheapen the eucharist. As the very center of Christian life and worship, the mystery of the eucharist needs to be safeguarded, and anything like indiscriminate admission to it is not only injurious to the Church but a disservice to those so admitted, since they are not taught to appreciate the full privilege and significance of admission to communion. Thus, while there will undoubtedly be exceptions, admission to communion should normally follow upon that solemn act of episcopal confirmation which admits to full membership in the body of Christ, with all its rights and obligations.

Another general point to be made about the eucharist, and one which again makes clear its paradigmatic role among the sacraments, is its evidently communal character. It is *par excellence* the sacrament of *corpus Christi*, the body of Christ. There is no such thing as a "solitary mass." In recent times, the corporate character of the eucharist has been emphasized by encouraging the full participation of the people in their parts of the liturgy, for instance, in presenting the offering of bread and wine. But there always have been parts of the liturgy that belonged to the various orders of ministry, including the general ministry that belongs to all; and although certain parts of the liturgy are reserved to the priest, the total action is one in which he acts together with the whole congregation of the faithful. Moreover, the communion in which all receive the same bread and drink of the same cup realizes in a very impressive way the oneness of the members of the community with each other, as well as their communion with God. "We who are many are one body, for we all partake of the same loaf."[30] The eucharist is the holy banquet, *sacrum convivium*, and this Latin word well expresses the notion of a common life. We have often spoken on earlier pages of the Church as the spearhead of the kingdom, as if in the Church the realization of the perfect community was already taking place. We may think of this as specially the case in the fellowship of the eucharist, where God may be said to be granting a foretaste of the consummation of his work in creation and reconciliation.

As we have mentioned, recent liturgical reforms have tended to stress the social aspect of the eucharist. This has been especially the case in the Roman Catholic Church, where formerly the communal dimension of the eucharist had been obscured by such practices as non-communicating masses. But the trouble is that the recovery of a forgotten or obscured dimension may lead to its exaggeration, and so to the obscuring of other dimensions that are equally important. There has been a danger of this in the recent heavy emphasis on the eucharist as a holy banquet. We have to remember that the eucharist has other dimensions besides, and that it was always more than, and distinct from, a mere *agape* or love-feast.[31] Roman liturgical reforms therefore should not be followed too slavishly by other Christian communions, for it is very likely that in these other communions, any imbalance in eucharistic doctrine or practice will be different from the Roman one, and will need to be compensated for in quite a different manner. Moreover, it would seem that in the Roman Catholic Church itself, there is now the recognition that the recent social emphasis can be carried too far, and that it can then threaten other equally valid dimensions of the eucharist, as well as forms of eucharistic devotion that depend upon them. Thus, even if one may be unhappy about the apparent absolutizing of the traditional "substance" language in the encyclical *Mysterium fidei* of 1965, one must nevertheless acknowledge that in this document Pope Paul VI is trying to maintain a proper balance in the understanding of the eucharist, so that the genuine gains of the liturgical revival shall not be lost through exaggerations that might lead to new distortions in place of the old ones.

This discussion shows us again that the eucharist is the paradigm among the sacraments. When we spoke of baptism, we noted that since it is

---

[30] I Cor. 10:17.
[31] Cf. Gregory Dix, *The Shape of the Liturgy*, p. 19ff.

often given to a single individual, the action of the whole Church in this sacrament tends to get obscured, and we had to plead for the recognition of its communal character by asking that the community of faith be made aware of its responsibility toward the baptized person, perhaps, when possible, by having the baptism in the presence of the whole community. As will be mentioned later, the communal character of some other sacraments can also be obscured and needs to be brought out. The eucharistic paradigm clearly shows that sacramental action takes place within the community, the body of Christ and the fellowship of the Spirit, and that in the sacramental life as common life (*convivium*), each is supported by all the others with whom he is united in the body.

A further point about the eucharist is the very clear way in which it exhibits the unity of word and sacraments. Indeed, the celebration of the eucharist through all its variations shows two distinct parts—the ministry of the word, and the ministry of the sacrament proper. The first part has its climax in the reading of the gospel, and we have already noted the recognition of God's presence in this proclaiming of his word as parallel to the recognition in the second part of the eucharist of the divine presence in the consecrated elements.[32] And just as the congregation responds to the sacramental presence by receiving together the holy communion, so they respond to the presence of God in his proclaimed word by affirming together the creed which expresses their faith. (The Eastern form, "We believe . . . ," expresses this communal response better than the Western "I believe . . .") However, the point is that once more the eucharist proves itself to be the norm. In a way that goes beyond what we find in any of the other sacraments, or in the ministry of the word apart from the sacraments, the eucharist combines word and sacrament in a unique manner. It shows us the inseparability of the two, and thus the inseparability of understanding and incorporation, of spirit and sense, of existential and ontological, over the whole range of Christian life and experience.

Still another paradigmatic character of the eucharist is the way in which it gathers into a unity the dimensions of past, present, and future. It reaches into the past, for it is done in remembrance of Christ and his work. It has its eschatological dimension, for it is done until his coming, and prefigures the heavenly banquet. But it is above all a making-present, in which both the past and the future events are, in a sense, realized in the moment. Since we shall discuss these matters at greater length in the

[32] See above, pp. 449–450.

chapter on worship,[33] and since we are turning at once to the question of Christ's presence in the eucharist, we shall not expand the point meantime.

So far we have been talking about the eucharist in fairly general terms, and showing how in a preeminent way it exhibits the character of that sacramental structure which protects and nourishes the Christian life, from its first awakening all through its growth and maturing. We have still to pay attention to the specific character of the eucharist as a particular way of re-presenting Christ and making-present his work and grace. In these matters too the eucharist has a preeminence. There are two topics that call for discussion here—the eucharistic sacrifice and the real presence.

Obviously the eucharist is not a literal repetition of Christ's sacrifice, considered as an event that took place once for all at a definite time in world history. On the other hand, the eucharist would seem to share the character of that "repetitive" historical thinking, of which we have spoken earlier and in which an historical event is somehow reenacted in present existence. We have seen that God's reconciling work is not tied to a moment of time but is present at all times. The word "repetition" can be misleading, but we must affirm that in a genuine sense the eucharist is a re-presenting of Christ's work. The symbolism is so rich and varies from one form of the rite to another in so many points of detail that the attempt to present its meaning in a concise theological statement must seem schematic and abstract.

We may begin by recalling what was said about the use of the image of sacrifice when we sought to interpret the meaning of the work of Christ. We rejected any idea of a transaction entirely *extra nos*, such as a satisfaction offered to God or a mere shedding of blood. The important point, as we saw it, was Christ's self-giving, and this became a work of salvation for us as we in turn got caught up in it. In the words used in the earlier passage, "the self-giving of Christ, understood as the new sacrifice in which priest and victim are one and the same, brings God's constant self-giving for his creation right into the creation." [34] What we have to show now is how the eucharist provides the forms and structure by which Christ's sacrifice is re-presented in the Christian community today, so that the self-giving which he manifested, and which is the very essence of God himself, realizes itself now in the Christian community, so that this community—and eventually all humanity—is conformed to Christ and made "like to God," which is indeed the destiny of the created being.

---

[33] See below, pp. 491–492.
[34] See above, p. 320.

Amid the many variations of the eucharistic rite, there are especially two points that touch on the idea of sacrifice. These have to be distinguished, and usually it is easy enough to do so. There is the offering of bread and wine *before* the consecration—we shall refer to this as the "offertory"; and there is the offering of these elements *after* the consecration, when they have been made the vehicles that re-present the body and blood of Christ—we shall call this the "oblation."

The offering of the bread and wine before consecration is something that is done by all, and, as already mentioned, recent liturgical reform has tended to stress the people's part in the offertory. The bread and wine which are brought to the altar, the products of human labor and the means of human sustenance, stand for the people themselves. They offer themselves in this act, so that their lives may be submitted to God and transformed by his grace. Here we note that element of cooperation from the human side that is required by the kind of creation in which we live, and to which we have frequently drawn attention. Yet, so that even this offertory should not be understood as something that man does of his own, altogether apart from God, it comes after the ministry of the word and may be regarded as part of our response to the word. God needs our free self-offering, yet whatever we do, he is always ahead of us in what he has done.

The oblation as distinct from the offertory is done by the priest alone, for in this he is acting in Christ's place, and this means that it is Christ who makes the oblation. In the eucharist too he is still priest and victim, and he offers himself in that complete self-giving that in his earthly historical existence marked the culmination of the incarnation. But, as has been already pointed out, this cannot be understood as a literal repetition of the sacrifice of Calvary. It is indeed a making-present, but in a different way, and a way which brings out the character of the sacrifice as a saving happening. For the breaking and outpouring of the consecrated elements and their reception by the communicants mean that Christ is offering in union with himself the congregation and indeed, ideally, all humanity. The lives brought to the altar in the offertory are incorporated into Christ, so that they share in his sacrifice, are conformed to his image, are sanctified by his Spirit, and so brought to their fulfillment in God.

The many-sided significance of the eucharistic sacrifice may become clearer to us if we consider the plurality of meanings that belong to the expression "body of Christ." In its literal sense, Christ's body was his actual personal being-in-the-world nineteen centuries ago, the incarnation of the

Word in the once-for-all events of the career of Jesus of Nazareth. This body is no longer with us or accessible in a direct way. We may say with Cranmer, if we wish, that it is "in heaven," though we would certainly not wish to understand this, as Cranmer seems to have done, as a local designation. The body of Christ is also the sacramental host that now re-presents him in the eucharist, that is offered to God, broken, and distributed to the worshippers. Finally, the body of Christ is the worshipping community itself, incorporated in Christ in their baptism, bound more closely to him in confirmation, and now being steadily conformed to him through their participation in the eucharist.

An interesting, though not an exact, parallel can be drawn between the threefold form of the body sketched out in the preceding paragraph, and the threefold form of the word to which reference was earlier made.[35] In each of the two cases, it is the first of the three forms—the incarnate Word and the actual historical body respectively—that generates and gives being to the other two. Yet in each case also it is through the mediation of the derivative forms that we have access to the primordial form—through scripture and proclamation to the incarnate Word, through consecrated elements and worshipping community to the historical person. And finally, in each case it is in their living unity that the three forms teach us the fullness of what is intended by the "word of God" and the "body of Christ."

But already this mention of the body of Christ has brought us from the discussion of eucharistic sacrifice to the closely related question of the real presence in the eucharist. We have already seen that the body of Christ, in the sense of the Church, can be rightly called an "extension of the incarnation." The same can be said about the body of Christ as the eucharistic host, though with such differences of meaning as are appropriate to the two usages of the expression "body of Christ." We have made such constant use of the idea of presence throughout this whole exposition of Christian theology that the outlines of our view of the real presence in the eucharist must be already apparent to the reader. Nevertheless, this particular mode of the divine presence is so important and has, unfortunately, been the subject for so much controversy in the Church, that we may be excused for spending some time upon it.

Perhaps something should first be said about the doctrine of transubstantiation, as set forth by St. Thomas and his successors. Contrary to

---

[35] See above, pp. 454–455.

the view of many Protestant polemicists, this doctrine is so far from embracing a magical understanding of the eucharist that it is in fact one of the strongest possible safeguards against such magical views. What St. Thomas is saying is that there is no change in the sensible accidents of the bread and wine, that is to say, precisely that there is no magic. His description of the real presence in the eucharist points to the same kind of ambiguity as appeared in our own analyses of miracles, providence, and even the incarnation itself. From one point of view, nothing can be seen in any of these events but just the natural phenomena, and there is no breach of the natural order that could be discerned by the senses. But the eye of faith may see the event "in depth," as we have usually expressed ourselves, and be aware of God's presence and action in the event. Likewise St. Thomas tells us that it is "faith, our outward sense befriending" [36] that perceives the divine presence in the eucharist.

But we have to part company with St. Thomas when he claims that, although there is no change in the accidents or sensible phenomena, there is a change in the metaphysical "substance" which is supposed to underlie the phenomena. It is not that we object to the belief in an ontological change. Indeed, the Church had believed in such a change for many centuries before the language of transubstantiation was introduced. If, as some modern Roman Catholic theologians tell us, the term "transubstantiation" is now understood as simply affirming a real conversion of the eucharistic elements, then it might seem an unexceptionable term. But in fact the term implies the whole philosophical background of Aristotelian and Thomistic categories. Here again we have to say that we do not object to the deployment of philosophical categories as such in the attempt to work out a eucharistic theology. It is the duty of the theologian to make the mysteries of faith as intelligible as possible, and he does this without infringing the ultimate mystery. Lateran IV, the council which introduced transubstantiation terminology into the official dogmatic language of the Church, clearly stated that the ultimate agency of the change is *potestas divina*, the divine power, the mystery whereby Being makes itself present in and through the beings.

The reason for our parting company with St. Thomas is his use of these particular categories, "substance" and "accident," for the philosophical context from which they come and in which they have meaning is not the one that we have been consistently employing. In our existential-

[36] In the hymn, *Tantum ergo, English Hymnal*, No. 326.

ontological view, the world is not seen as an aggregate of substances, but as a structure of meaning. We have seen how man has been constantly incorporating the merely natural world into a humanized world as he assigns significance to an ever widening range of phenomena. A thing is what it is in virtue of its place in an intelligible world. This, by the way, is not a subjective understanding of worldhood, though it is not a purely objective one either. The world is constructed partly by the human existent in terms of his interest and his modes of understanding, but its shape is determined also by the given phenomena. Though the question of "presence" in the eucharist should not be too narrowly tied to the consecrated elements. it should be remembered right away that neither bread nor wine is a simple or natural substance; both of them are the results of human labor, and in both of them the merely natural has already been incorporated into the human world. Bread and wine are already understood in their significance for human existence, as food and drink, as basic supports of life. Furthermore, their place in human existence is so basic that round both of them a great wealth of symbolic connotations had already grown up long before bread and wine were associated with the Christian eucharist.

We see the eucharistic presence as a special case of what we have often spoken of in these pages as the "presence-and-manifestation" of Being in the beings. This presence is, of course, everywhere, but we have also seen how it becomes "focused" in particular beings and particular events. This is how we accounted for miracles, providential acts, and for the incarnation itself, and we now see the eucharist as an extension of this series.

In all of these cases in which Being becomes present-and-manifest, one cannot speak of either a subjective or an objective happening, for since we ourselves participate in this very Being, the subject-object pattern is transcended. As far as the eucharistic presence is concerned, it is certainly ontological, and depends on the initiative and approach of Being in and through the particular beings, the elements of bread and wine, in which the focusing takes place. But the presence is just as certainly existential, for such focusing of Being and the event of Being's presence-and-manifestation take place only in the living context of the body of Christ, understood in its fullest sense, as explained above.

The presence of Christ in the eucharist is a personal presence, and, like all personal presence, it is multidimensional. He is present in the community which is his body, he is present in the bishop or presiding minister whom he has sent, he is present in the word which re-presents him, as well as being present in the consecrated bread and wine. But all personal presence is embodied presence, not merely spiritual presence; and in this embodiment, the bread and wine play a central role. What does it mean to claim that in the eucharist the bread and wine become for the worshipping community the body and blood of Christ, and that this is to be understood not merely in a subjective way but ontologically? We can understand it as a change in the thinghood or reality of the bread and wine, where "thinghood" is taken to be constituted by having a place in a meaningful world, as has been explained above. The change or conversion takes place when the bread and wine are shifted out of one world of discourse into another, for this constitutes an ontological change.

It happened at the last supper of Christ with his disciples, when he transformed the passover meal into the prototype of the Christian eucharist by declaring the bread and wine to be his body and blood. It happens in every eucharist where the priest takes the bread and wine of ordinary human life and consecrates them to be for the eucharistic community the body and blood of Christ. We could say that the sentences "This is my body" and "This is my blood" are instances of what J. L. Austin called "performative" language, that is to say, language which does not merely describe but actually does something and brings about a new state of affairs.[37] In the eucharist, the language is not to be separated from the action, for the command is to *do* this, not to *say* this. The effect of the language in that context of action is to shift the elements out of one region of signification into another—from the everyday world into the setting of the eucharistic community. This is not a subjective view of presence, if one accepts that significance enters into the ontological constitution of a thing; but neither is it an objective view, as if the body and blood of Christ existed outside the context of the eucharistic community, which is also his body. Even when the sacrament is reserved after the action of the eucharist is over, it continues to be the body and blood within the context of the eucharistic community.

The understanding of eucharistic presence set forth here is close to what some modern Roman Catholic theologians have called "transignification," a view which they have developed on the basis of philosophical categories similar to those underlying the present work. Strictly speaking, transignification is not a *rival* view to transubstantiation in its austere classical form; but it is a *different* view because it employs quite different

---

[37] *How to Do Things with Words*, p. 6.

categories. It must be stressed, however, that no theology of the eucharist, whether transubstantiation or transignification or any other view, finally "explains" the mystery of Christ's sacramental presence. That mystery, like the related mystery of the incarnation, depends ultimately on the *potestas divina*, the power which manifests itself chiefly in Being's gracious making itself present in the beings.

So the eucharist re-presents Christ's saving work, communicates his presence to us, and incorporates us with him. It thus continues and establishes the work begun in baptism, and stands as the center and paradigm of the sacramental life of the community of faith.

83. OTHER SACRAMENTS

We have already discussed baptism and the eucharist, the two preeminent sacraments of the Christian Church; and with them, we have also said something about confirmation, because of its close connection with baptism. However, it will be remembered that we saw no reason for withholding the name of "sacrament" from the seven rites that have for long been so designated, so that we have still to take note of the remaining four. Of these four, two, ordination and matrimony, can be treated very briefly here, because they get discussed elsewhere in the book. Thus only penance and unction will receive detailed attention in this section.

We have already seen the importance of ordination, and considered the various grades of the ministry. What has since been said about baptism corroborates the comparison that was drawn earlier between ordination and baptism. Just as baptism confers the general ministry of the Church, so the various ordinations confer the special ministries. Like baptism, ordination to any particular order of the ministry is given once only, but the *caveat* which we uttered against too facile a conception of a once-for-all status must be repeated here, as applying to ordination just as much as to baptism. Ordination does indeed confer a status, but its vows have to be continually renewed and its grace continually bestowed.

In the context of the other sacraments, we are able to obtain a fuller understanding of ordination and the function of the ministry. We spoke of this as the ministry of the word and sacraments. The ministry of the word implies not only the instruction and edification of the community of faith, but also the speaking of the prophetic word as a word of judgment in the general human society, and the defense and communication of the faith to those who are outside of the community. The ministry of the sacraments is primarily the cure of souls, the carrying out of Christ's injunction to St. Peter, "Feed my sheep." [38] We have already seen how the Christian sacraments, beginning with baptism, cover the whole span of human life and provide a framework for the nurture of that life at every stage by divine grace. The sacrament of ordination has a special place within the sacramental structure as a whole, for it confers the authority and grace for the ministration of all the other sacraments by those who are called to a special ministry in the Church and to whom is entrusted the care of souls. It is right that the modern priest should, so far as possible, acquire a knowledge of psychology, sociology, and other disciplines that impinge upon his own sphere, and it is right that he should learn how best to cooperate with psychiatrists, social workers, and others. But there is no need for him to become an amateur psychiatrist or social worker, or to attempt to do work for which he has not been trained. Occasionally we have the pathetic spectacle of a minister trying to do this, though it means that he has in fact ceased to believe in the significance of his own work as a Christian minister. The danger is much greater in Protestant groups that have lost much of the sacramental structure of the ministry, than in those branches of the Church where the sacraments are given a fuller role; though it should be added that sometimes the ministry of the word together with the personal qualities of the minister and his individual capacity for pastoral care can make up for the lack of sacramental forms. Nevertheless, the great vehicle for the cure of souls is the sacramental structure. It provides for every stage of life, for health and sickness, for guilt and estrangement. With this entrusted to him, the priest need not become an imitator of the secular social worker. The priest brings something that no one else can give—the means of divine grace, the vehicles for the divine presence. If we believe this, then we see his uniqueness and irreplaceability. If we do not believe this, then we have to regard him as just a purveyor of psychological comfort through outmoded means, and we have in fact tacitly abandoned Christianity as a faith and a religion, and reduced it to a humanistic ethic or a harmless custom.

Like ordination, marriage is treated in another part of this book,[39] though this still lies ahead of us. At this stage, we simply drawn attention to the complete appropriateness of bringing marriage within the sacramental structure. It is one of the high moments in the life of the individ-

[38] John 21:17.
[39] See below, pp. 513–515.

ual; it is the foundation of the family, the basic unit of human social life; it is the form that protects and controls the sexual instinct, one of the strongest human drives. In bringing marriage into the sacramental structure, the Church declares that divine grace belongs to and is required at this vital center of social existence. Grace is not just something to fall back on in moments of guilt, sickness, and the like. Its place is at the center and the foundation of daily life. But of these matters, we shall have more to say at a later stage.

We pass on to the sacrament of penance. In some ways, this does not look like a sacrament, because it does not have the outward and visible elements or actions that normally belong to a sacrament. On the other hand, as we have noted, this sacrament might well claim to share with baptism and the eucharist the distinction of having been in an explicit way dominically instituted. In several passages of the New Testament, Jesus entrusts to his disciples the authority to forgive sins, or to withhold forgiveness.[40] Whether or not we think that Jesus actually spoke the words attributed to him in these cases (or, for that matter, in the cases where he institutes baptism and the last supper), there can be no doubt that the New Testament Church firmly believed that he had bequeathed to his followers the power, exercised by himself, of forgiving sins. For instance, apart from explicit statements entrusting this power to the apostles, such a story as the healing of the paralytic[41] connects our Lord's forgiving of sins with his healing miracles, and, if we follow Bultmann's analysis, constitutes a claim on behalf of the Church to have received both of these powers; for the Church "demonstrates by her possession of healing powers that she has the right to forgive sins."[42]

It is indeed in connection with healing, understood in the widest sense of reconciliation, that we must look upon this sacrament of penance. Of course, like every act of grace, it may also be considered an act of judgment, and it belongs to the discipline of the Church. If the community is to maintain its being as the community of Christian faith, it must make certain demands on its members. It may be that a member who rejects these demands, or even a whole group of the membership (like those churches or congregations, mentioned earlier, that practice racial discrimination), estrange themselves by their conduct from the body of Christ. They must then be subject to judgment and discipline, though the end of

[40] Matt. 16:19; John 20:23.
[41] Mark 2:2–12.
[42] *History of the Synoptic Tradition*, p. 16.

such discipline must always be the hope that the offenders will confess their sins and return in penitence to the body from which they had cut themselves off.

Of course, every member of the body of Christ is still subject to sin, and every day he estranges himself in greater or less degree from the body of Christ and from God himself. It is important not to exaggerate guilt feelings or to suppose that every action demands discipline or specific sacramental action. St. Paul bids us examine ourselves,[43] and there is obviously an important place for self-examination and self-discipline in the responsible Christian community, without introducing some specific disciplinary or sacramental action of the Church at all. But on the other hand, it seems unwise to leave so much to self-examination and self-discipline as is usually done in Protestant churches. If too much reliance on the sacrament of penance can lead to scrupulosity, too little opportunity for it can lead to a great deal of unresolved guilt feelings, and to lack of guidance which people have a right to expect from the Church. Perhaps we should not pay too much attention to pragmatic considerations, but we can hardly ignore the fact, attested by Jung and other psychoanalysts, that Protestants are much more likely to end up on the psychiatrist's couch than Catholics who practice the sacrament of penance.

Perhaps the best arrangement is the one which prevails in the Anglican communion. Much is left to individual responsibility and self-discipline, and everyday matters are taken care of in the practices of general confession and general absolution. But if there is anyone who "cannot quiet his own conscience" by self-examination and self-discipline, then the opportunity of the sacrament of penance is offered. And certainly it should be offered, for presumably most people will find occasions when they do desire to make confession and receive absolution. This is part of the reconciling ministry of the Church, begun in baptism when original sin is forgiven. The sacrament of penance has therefore a valuable place within the whole sacramental structure.

Mention has been made of the communal dimension that is usually present in the sacraments, though more obviously in some than in others. It may be noted that recently attempts have been made to bring a more evidently communal character into the sacrament of penance. It can too easily be misunderstood as the individual's making his private peace with God, whereas it is also the reconciliation of the individual to the body of

---

[43] I Cor. 11:28.

Christ, from which his sin had separated him. So we now find that sometimes those who desire to receive this sacrament first assemble together for the ministry of the word, prayer, and self-examination, then make their private confessions, and finally come back for a general absolution and a common act of thanksgiving and reconciliation. At the same time, we must not let the desirability of communal expression obscure the fact that there is also an individual pole to our existence and an individual responsibility, and that the Church has to minister to the individual in his specific guilt and weakness, and to give him specific absolution and guidance, though it will always best strengthen him by binding him more closely to the body of Christ.

Finally, something is to be said about the sacrament of holy unction. Here we have an outward sacramental form—anointing with oil or, as an alternative, laying on of hands. And here again we have a sacrament that was practiced in the New Testament Church, as is clear from various references.[44] This was originally part of the Church's healing ministry, but we have seen the close connection between the healing of sickness and the forgiving of sins, and we have also noted that in the widest sense, the ministry of healing merges into the ministry of reconciliation. Thus holy unction is still another form in which the Church seeks to fulfill its mission of bringing wholeness to mankind.

With the revival of interest in the ministry of healing and the recognition that many diseases have a psychosomatic character, there has also been an increased interest in this ancient rite of unction. It provides an "objective" form for the ministry to the sick and dying, which can sometimes place an almost intolerable burden on the minister, if it depends only on his personal gifts. The sacramental form of unction does not annul these gifts, but rather provides a focus for them, and it also provides a recognized way of approach to the sick for those ministers whose personal gifts may not have equipped them so well for this particular duty.

The sacrament of holy unction has been particularly associated with the approach of death. There is no reason why it should be reserved for this extremity, but on the other hand we must not fall into the idea that all ministration to the sick should be aimed at recovery. Death belongs to the finitude of our existence, and this sacrament of unction can be understood as the bringing of the grace in which to face death, as well as the bringing of the courage which may sometimes be a factor in recovering from sick-

---

[44] Mark 6:13; James 5:14.

ness. Since death isolates the individual as no other event does, this sacrament is peculiarly directed to the individual. Yet at the same time it has its communal character, for it brings to the individual, whether in sickness or at the approach of death, the assurance that he is one with the whole body of Christ. He is therefore incorporated through Christ into the very structure of Being, and the destiny that awaits him is to be given a still fuller share in the life of Being.

Thus the sacramental structure of the Church ends only with the termination of the life of the individual member. It has embraced the whole of that life, and sustained it at every point, aiming to conform it to the life of Christ and to fit it for life in God. As reaching into the past and making-present Christ, and as reaching into the future and making-present the eschatological goal, the sacraments both reflect and transcend the pattern of authentic selfhood, and point to the completion of selfhood in the wider context of Being.

20 | Worship and Prayer

84. WORSHIP AND EXISTENCE

Every religion has its worship or cult, and this indeed constitutes the most obvious outward expression of the religion. The character of the worship and its importance vary greatly from one religion to another. The worship may be simple or elaborate; it may be frequent or infrequent, participation in it may be obligatory upon the adherents of the particular religion, or they may take part in it only sporadically.

The need for worship has become problematical in the modern world. Even those who hold strongly to the Christian faith sometimes question the relevance and value of worship, and we have already had occasion to note the extreme developments of this attitude among some of those who advocate a "religionless" Christianity and who interpret this as meaning the elimination of the traditional cultic expressions of faith. We have made clear our objections to such extreme points of view and shown how they fail to take account of the actual embodied condition of historical human existence. Yet we have also conceded that these protests have their elements of truth, wherever there is a danger that the cult comes to be prized for its own sake. These questions must now be looked at from still another angle. We must try to work out a theology of worship that will retain what is of value in the cultic side of religion—what, indeed, is not only of value, but is imperatively demanded by the factical conditions of our existence—while at the same time we seek to avoid the errors against which the advocates of "religionless" Christianity have legitimately protested.

At first sight, worship seems to be something that man himself does, and of course the belief that this is the case has been one of the reasons for the suspicion of worship among those who still want to retain faith. They think of it as a kind of survival of magic, perhaps an attempt to manipulate the world and to obtain benefits for the worshippers by occult means. It need not be denied that such misunderstandings of worship and prayer are still prevalent among those who take part in them, and deserve to be severely criticized. However, we have already pointed to the perfectly clear distinction between magic and religion,[1] and this distinction arises again in connection with the question of worship. Even if worship often appears to be a purely human activity, and even if in fact many persons participate in it with a mentality that has not been freed from magical and mythical presuppositions, the true worship or the worship that is "in spirit and in truth" [2] is, like all "true" religion and "true" faith, a happening in which God comes to men, and the initiative is God's. As Hugh Blenkin has well said, "God can never be the object of man's worship; he is always the subject—that is to say, it is he who initiates within the heart of man the desire for union with himself." [3] This writer goes on immediately to mention the Holy Spirit, and we have seen that the Holy Spirit is unitive Being, so that the spring and source of worship (at least, of such worship as is "in spirit and in truth") is nothing less than the unitive action of Being.

The fundamental motives of worship are nowhere better set forth than in the *Book of Common Prayer* where we are said to "assemble and meet together to render thanks for the great benefits we have received at his hands, to set forth his most worthy praise, to hear his most holy word, and to ask those things which are requisite and necessary, as well for the body as the soul"; and it should not be forgotten that these intentions are coupled with the priest's invitation "humbly to acknowledge our sins before God." [4] As expressed in these classic words, the character of worship is clearly one of response to the God who has first drawn near to us and addressed us; yet the response is on the personal level, for we are free existents. Worship is not a homage that is exacted from us, but our free response to God's action upon us and in us. So we see in worship the same kind of relation that we have found in revelation, in faith, and in many of the other topics we have considered; there is indeed the divine initiative,

---

[1] See above, p. 160.
[2] John 4:23–24.
[3] *Immortal Sacrifice*, p. 30.
[4] Orders for Morning and Evening Prayer.

but it completes and realizes itself only in the free cooperative response of the human existent.

With this in mind, we come back to the point that there is a human contribution in worship. In the more elaborate kinds of worship, this contribution may be considerable. Buildings, furniture, music, ceremonial, lights, incense—the whole range of human skills and human experience seems to be brought to the act of worship. The very breadth and richness of this contribution is a recognition that man's response to God must be a total response and one that extends over the whole range of existence. We have already noted the importance of this, in considering how the sacraments affect the senses as well as the understanding. However, this very richness of the human contribution in worship has its own dangers. Worship may come to be prized for itself, as an esthetic enjoyment. Worse still, it may degenerate into an idolatry. We have seen that idolatry is the basic sin, and that the temptation to it is never far away. Worship becomes idolatrous when it is no longer a response to the divine initiative but has become the projection of human achievements and self-centered aspirations. It is against this kind of worship that one must protest, for its effects can be disastrous. False worship can be only distorting for the existences of those who engage in it.

But provided that there is no infringement upon the divine initiative and no attempt to suppress the note of judgment which is an ever-present aspect of this initiative, there is no reason for not permitting the human contribution in worship to be as rich as we can make it. Certainly, the puritanical demand for "simplicity" in worship is no safeguard against idolatrous worship, but is more frequently itself an even subtler kind of idolatry and self-righteousness. Man rightly brings to his worship his highest achievements, and we shall see later what is the specific justification for this in Christian worship. But from the earliest times and in all religions, worship and the arts have been closely allied. Architecture, painting, sculpture, music, poetry—these have all been closely associated with worship, not by usurping its function as a response to God, but as ancillary to that function and as themselves informed and inspired by the meaning of worship. Here we are concerned only with the theology of worship. A complete study of the subject would have to move into the fields of esthetics, of psychology, of the history of forms. Yet such a study must always come back to its theological foundation, since worship is above all the response to God's approach and action. If this basic point about worship is kept in mind, namely, that God comes first to us and we respond to him, then we must welcome the fullest and richest contribution that man's arts and skills can make to worship, seeing in this contribution an index of the total response which God demands.

But if we have seen that cult and worship are not to be dismissed as man-centered or as magical or as immature attempts to accommodate the world to our wishes, we still have some further objections to consider. We are told that worship and the services of the Church become a substitute for action, and that they are a kind of escape by which we conceal from ourselves the real demands of Christian faith. Again, one can sympathize with this kind of criticism and the accompanying demand for a "religionless" Christianity. Worship can become a separate self-contained department of life, and when this happens, it deserves censure. If the cult or the building in which it takes place or the community which engages in it is a separate realm of the sacred to which we withdraw from the demands of everyday life, then there would seem to be nothing to commend it. This kind of worship is roundly condemned in the Bible, by the Hebrew prophets and then by Jesus and the New Testament writers. But Jesus speaks also of "true" worship. If there is a false worship, this should not lead us to condemn all worship. We have already seen that the true worship is the kind in which the initiative lies with God. To this we must now add the further claim that the true worship is continuous with all of life. It is no compartment, no special area of the sacred, no escape from the real world. This indeed follows, if the divine initiative in worship is not suppressed. For if worship is the point at which God or Being touches our lives and makes impact upon them, this must be the very center of life, and no corner or point out on the periphery. Worship is not a temporary withdrawal from life, but rather the concentration of life, its "recollection" in the sense of its gathering together.

I do not profess to know precisely what Bonhoeffer had in mind when he talked about "religionless" Christianity, but when he says that God must grasp us at the center of life rather than at its edges,[5] I do not only agree with this but would maintain that this is exactly what happens in worship. That is to say, I intend that the word "concentration," which I used in the last paragraph, should be taken in a fairly literal sense. Worship, in which God comes among us, is the center of existence, and could not be anything else, since this very existence of ours flows from God, as the mystery of Being. From this center, there move out concentric rings,

[5] *Letters and Papers from Prison*, p. 165.

as it were, through all the concerns of life to its very boundaries. The whole of life is thus conformed to the center, and we shall see more clearly what this means when we come to discuss the specific form of Christian worship.[6]

Most of what has so far been said about worship in this section would be descriptive of any true worship whatsoever. Such worship is to be understood as a focalizing, as it were, of the divine presence. In genuine worship, the divine initiative is not obscured, but recognized so that the presence of God is experienced as both judgment and grace; and moreover this worship is experienced as continuous with the whole of life, the center which influences and informs all the concerns of life, out to the most peripheral. But now we must consider how these general characteristics of worship appear in specifically Christian worship.

In discussing the sacraments, we asserted that all Christian worship centers in the Holy Eucharist, and that this is the norm for worship. Can we now develop this assertion further, so as to reach a more comprehensive understanding of Christian worship—and perhaps, though this is not our concern here, of worship in general?

I believe that we can. From our earlier discussion of the eucharist, let us recall the remarkable way in which it reaches out through different dimensions of time. On the one hand, it is a memorial, by which we remember the work of Christ. On the other hand, the eucharist has its eschatological character, as something that we do "until he comes," so that we not only remember but anticipate. Above all, however, the eucharist is a making-present, bringing both the past event and the future consummation into the sacramental act.

But this bringing into unity the three dimensions of temporality recalls our earlier discussion about the realization of selfhood. What constitutes a self is precisely the same kind of remarkable relationship among the dimensions of temporality that we see in the eucharist. This enables us still better to understand what was meant when we said that worship is a kind of concentration of life. It is the realization in a particularly intense way of the unity of the dimensions of temporality; and since it is this unity which constitutes selfhood, then we can make the further claim that worship is creative of selfhood.

Yet another point emerges. The achieving of selfhood is a work of grace. Authentic selfhood is not ego-centered so that it prizes and seeks

[6] See below, pp. 499–502.

to preserve its own being; rather, authentic selfhood goes out beyond itself, and find its highest fulfillment in letting-be. It does this not of itself, but by letting itself be caught up into the movement of Being, that is to say, of the absolute letting-be of God. We have already seen that the formation of selfhood in the human existent through the unifying of the dimensions of temporality affords a faint analogy to the way in which Being reaches through and unifies the dimensions of time. In worship, the existent is incorporated into this vaster movement of Being, and in this way his selfhood is strengthened and his capacity for letting-be increased.

To speak in more specifically Christian and eucharistic terms, worship is a conformation to Christ. This helps us to see the place of the human contribution in worship. It is something like the offertory in the eucharist —man brings his gifts and offers them with Christ, so that they and all else that he has and is may be conformed to Christ. But since Christ, in turn, is like to God, that is to say, the particular being in whom expressive Being has most perfectly expressed itself, conformation to Christ means conformation to Being, in the sense that the particular being becomes more transparent to Being and is thus fulfilled in his being. This is that transfiguration of humanity, of which we have spoken, and which the patristic writers boldly called "deification" ($\theta\epsilon o\pi o\iota\eta\sigma\iota s$), incorporation into God. The threefold character of the eucharist as remembering, anticipating, and making-present gathers up in the participant the three temporal dimensions that constitute selfhood, but both of these threefold schemes belong ultimately within the great all-embracing threefold movement of Being as creation-reconciliation-consummation.

Let us remember too that all that has been described takes place in the context of the community, the body of Christ. It is "when we assemble and meet together" that the transfiguring movement from an egocentric existence to the authentic selfhood of letting-be can take place. The individual is one with the worshipping congregation, the congregation is one with the whole Church, while the Church, as we have seen, merges with the wider community of faith and eschatologically identifies itself with all humanity. Our claim then that worship is the center of existence is well founded, for it *concentrates* the movement that goes on throughout the whole realm of beings—the movement of creation-reconciliation-consummation.

With this analysis of worship in relation to existence, we leave the topic for the moment in order to turn to the question of prayer. But we shall come back shortly to consider more closely how the forms of worship can best promote that conformation of the worshipper to Christ, which is an essential character of Christian worship.

85. PRAYER

Prayer is a universal phenomenon in the life of faith, and it would be hard to imagine any faith or religion without prayer, or something like prayer. Obviously, prayer is very close to worship, and many of the things said about worship would apply also to prayer. However, prayer is not identical with worship but rather an element in it. Specifically, when we talk of "prayer," we have in mind ways in which the worshipper expresses himself verbally. It is true that we sometimes talk of "silent prayer," but such silence, like silence in music or a significant silence in conversation, has meaning only in a context that can be heard and understood.

This is to say that prayer, including its silences, is a mode of discourse. As a mode of discourse, we would expect it to have the characteristics which we earlier claimed to belong to all discourse—expression, referring, communication. It is not too hard to see how prayer exhibits the first and second of these characteristics. All prayer expresses, and perhaps it expresses some of the deepest moods and aspirations of which man is capable. All prayer refers—there is hardly any situation that cannot be brought within the scope of prayer. But can prayer communicate? We have seen that the condition for communication is a shared universe of discourse, a common stock of ideas and presuppositions. Without such a shared background, discourse cannot communicate, or rather, there cannot be discourse. Often enough, communication breaks down between human existents, because they do not have the shared background that makes communication possible. How then could we possibly think of communication with God or Being? It seems clear that we do not have a shared background of ideas with God—the very suggestion is absurd.

Prayer, then, is no ordinary kind of discourse, yet we must not conclude too hastily that it just is not discourse at all. Certainly, it is more than a mere inarticulate yearning or beseeching. The use of words in prayer gives it a distinctively human character. An animal can beseech, but prayer seeks to lift the deepest desires of our human existence to an explicit level.

If we cannot suppose that prayer is a kind of conversation between man and God or that the usual conditions for communication can obtain in this case, nevertheless we have been committed throughout this book to the idea that there is some affinity between God and man, on the basis of which some kind of communion is possible. This affinity has been expressed in a great many ways. We saw it in the *fascinans* aspect of the holy, an aspect that is just as fundamental as the *tremendum;* we saw it in the notion of revelation, in which, it was claimed, God "addresses" man and opens himself to him, though the "address" is not words and sentences; we saw it in the notion of expressive Being, the Word or *Logos,* whereby primordial Being moves out into the openness of the creation; above all, we saw it in the doctrine of the incarnation, whereby God expresses himself in a particular being. Admittedly, in all these cases, it is God who communicates himself to us. But then, we must say of prayer as we have said of worship, that God himself is its author. It is unitive Being (the Holy Spirit) that moves us to prayer, in response to the self-communication of Being, a communication that is possible because Being is immanent in every being. Is it then surprising that if we are moved to respond to the self-communication of Being, our response is the distinctively human form of words? We are not so foolish as to imagine that we can speak to God as we speak to one another. But language is the way by which we can give shape to our deepest desires, aspirations, and concerns, and, as it were, hold them up in the presence of holy Being, so that they may be submitted both to the grace and judgment of Being.

I will not repeat points that were made in the section on worship, though clearly some of these apply with equal force in the case of prayer. In prayer as in worship, the divine initiative is always to be recognized, so that what we do or say has the character of response; and prayer, again like worship, is not some special department of life, but continuous with all our activities. Understood in this way, we can see prayer as a very special form of discourse, giving shape and definiteness to that mysterious communion between God and man which is founded on the very structure of our existence as beings whom Being has not only let-be but has made open in their being so that they can be understanding, answering, and responsible.

The foregoing remarks on prayer do give some account of various kinds of prayer. Prayers of confession, or prayers in which the believer explicitly places his existence in the light of Being, subjecting himself to judgment; prayers of supplication, in which aspirations for a better life are laid out in the presence of holy Being; prayers of thanksgiving, in which the worshipper responds in devotion to the grace of Being—in sum, all those prayers that have an inward and meditative character can be fairly well understood in terms of the description we have given. We can see how such prayers have their part in the process of conformation to Christ, as the mediator of Being; and this is something that is recognized in the custom of ending Christian prayers with some such phrase as "through Jesus Christ, our Lord."

But what are we to say about the kind of prayers that are directed outward, such as intercessions for other people? Are we perhaps being evasive in our account of prayer? We seem to be taking as the norm the prayers of saints and mystics, and ignoring prayer as it is commonly understood and practiced by ordinary Christians. Surely they understand prayer as asking God to do quite specific actions in the world, such as healing a sick person or sending rain in a drought or preventing the outbreak of war or whatever it may be.

Let us at once agree that we cannot run away from the problems presented by these petitionary and intercessory forms of prayer. Let it also be made clear that we must stand consistently by all that we have said already on the subjects of miracle, providence, divine action, and the like. This means that all magical ideas of prayer must be rejected, and of course they ought to be. Religion and faith have nothing to do with attempts to manipulate the world by occult means.

Perhaps the first point to be made about petitions offered to God is that many of them wither away when they are really brought before God and exposed to the judgment of holy Being. We see that they are egocentric, and our prayer becomes rather one for grace to accept the existing state of affairs. Even our prayers for objects that transcend our personal interests may often have egocentric motives mixed in with them. However, when all egocentric and magical forms of petitionary and intercessory prayer have been eliminated, there still remain prayers of this kind that can and indeed should be presented to God. It is surely right, for instance, to pray for peace; and it is certainly right, in a more general way, to obey Christ's own bidding and pray for the doing of God's will on earth and the coming of his kingdom.[7]

Of course, such prayers, like worship, have to be continuous with the rest of life if they are to have any value or significance. A prayer for peace is worthless if its motive is simply that the person who offers it does not want the disturbance and inconvenience of war. It becomes meaningful if he is also actively concerning himself with reconciliation and the

---

[7] Matt. 6:10.

removal of injustices. Petitionary prayer makes sense if we are committing ourselves to what we are praying for, and if we can hold up this kind of commitment in the light of holy Being.

Are we then simply saying that prayers of this kind have only a kind of psychological value, in so far as they strengthen commitment on the part of the persons who offer them? Is even the prayer that seems to reach out beyond the inward needs of the believers into the world at bottom subjective, a kind of exercise to produce a right frame of mind in those who engage in such prayer? It seems to me that few Christians would be satisfied with this answer. In any case, it rests on much too individualistic a view of the human existent. Prayer takes place in the context of the community, and beyond that, in the context of Being. It seems to me that without falling into any magical or fanciful notions on the subject, one may readily admit that prayer has repercussions beyond the life of the person or persons who actually offer the prayer. Let us think for a moment of the prayer for the coming of the kingdom. While on the one hand this prayer may be a strengthening of one's own commitment to Christ's kingdom, may we not also believe that the sincere prayer of faith is a strengthening of the movement of Being itself in its threefold action of creation-reconciliation-consummation? For this, as we have seen, is not something that proceeds just automatically, but something that needs man's free response and cooperation. So where one person or group of persons pray for the coming of the kingdom and commit themselves more deeply in faith, this means an "objective" strengthening of the kingdom beyond the lives of the actual persons concerned.

We may put the same point somewhat differently by saying that petitionary prayer, rightly understood, is never an attempt to manipulate God (that is precisely magic!) or an attempt to persuade him to do what he might not otherwise have done. Rather, we have to begin from the idea that God is already aiming at the highest good of all his creatures. What hinders the fulfilling of his love in them is the resistance offered by human wills, exercising their limited freedom to impede the work of creation-reconciliation-consummation. When we pray therefore for the realization of some goal, we are not trying to bend God's will to ours but, on the contrary, to bend our wills to his and to remove the resistances that are standing in the way of his love. It is for this reason that those who have advanced furthest in prayer recognize that it is not so much a case of their praying to God as of the Holy Spirit praying in them, striving with them for their cooperation. And because of that solidarity, already noted, of all human beings with each other, the prayers of an individual or a group afford a way of ingress for the unitive Spirit into the closely knit texture of human society, so that the effects of the prayer may be experienced far beyond the lives of those who are consciously and explicitly engaged in prayer.

Something may be said here also about the relation between prayers of asking (petitions and intercessions) and prayers which are meditative or contemplative. It is the latter kinds of prayer that immerse the believer in the mind of Christ, so that his petitions are formed by that mind and he learns to ask aright. All this, in turn, takes place in the context of the community.

The need to see prayer in the context of the community of faith is also the best safeguard against egocentric aberrations in prayer. No doubt there is a place for private prayer, yet such prayer must be subordinated to common prayer, and the individual experience submitted to the wider experience and wisdom of the community. Within the community, classic forms of prayer have been developed that express its mind as it responds to the advent of God in grace and judgment. In the Christian community, we give pride of place to the Lord's Prayer, and then to the classic prayers and liturgies of the Church. The individual need not indeed confine himself to these prayers, and sometimes he will feel the need for some spontaneous expression suited to his particular situation. But the common prayers of the community remain as guidelines and norms to protect against egocentricity and occultism.

86. VARIETIES OF SPIRITUALITY

The eucharist is the center of Christian prayer and worship, but it has become surrounded by many other acts of prayer and devotion. These are designed to extend the pattern of the eucharist into all of life. There are the other sacraments, the daily offices built up of psalms, scripture lessons, and prayers, together with many special devotions that have developed in the Church. These constitute a structure that reinforces the pattern of the Christian life in the existence of those who engage in them. At this point we touch on the border of a special discipline without seeking to invade it—the discipline of ascetical theology which studies the development and deepening of the spiritual life through the practices of prayer, worship, and self-discipline.

The word "spirituality" is commonly used for the process of learning by which the disciple becomes more proficient in the Christian life and advances along the way of sanctification. But it is important to guard against common misunderstandings of what is intended. Spirituality is not a retreat or escape into an inner world, for spirit is precisely the capacity to go out, and the truly spiritual person is the one who is able to go out or to *exist* in the full dynamic sense. Furthermore, although we have called spirituality a process of learning, the disciple is not aiming directly at sanctification, as if this were a human work or achievement. He is learning to look consistently beyond himself, even to forget himself. Only a perverted spirituality is concerned with one's own condition, and true sanctification comes as a gift to those who have been reaching out to God and their neighbors.

Every individual human being is a unique creation, and so there must be many patterns of spirituality to suit the many needs and temperaments. A minority in the Church will devote themselves almost exclusively to contemplative prayer. "The monk," wrote Thomas Merton, "is one who is called to give himself exclusively to the one thing necessary for all men —the search for God." [8] Since the Church is a differentiated body or people, there is certainly a place within it for the religious life of prayer, and those who are praying, it must be remembered, pray on behalf of all, just as the Church itself can be considered representative of all. Even within the religious life itself there are, of course, different emphases and different ways of dividing the day. Another minority group is constituted by the Christian mystics. They have often been suspect because, in their claim to have a direct vision of God, they seem to have bypassed the normal Christian channels of worship; or again because their sometimes elaborate methods seem too much like an attempt to take away the initiative from God. But the best of them escape these criticisms and have brought great enrichment to Christianity. Their importance today lies not least in the fact that the mystic way affords a link with Eastern religions. At the opposite extreme is another minority group—the activists who see little point in spending time in prayer and meditation, and claim that their prayer takes the form of service to the neighbor. But the great majority of Christians follow none of these minority ways. The majority lives in the alternation of prayer and action, though these are not separated. Prayer, we have seen, is the concentration in explicit moments of that which is supportive of all of life, while action is in turn suffused with

[8] *The Silent Life*, p. viii.

prayer. But the modes and times of prayer, and the balance of prayer and action, are matters which each has to work out for himself.

The aim of all is the vision of God and communion with God—or rather, we should say an ever-deepening vision and communion, for we have seen that the Christian pilgrimage does not come to an end but always keeps its dynamic character. We would agree with St. Gregory of Nyssa: "The perfect life is the one whose progress into perfection is not limited by any boundary." [9] And he gave a very good reason for his teaching: God is inexhaustible, and there can be no end to our participation and exploration in him.

There are many ways toward the vision, but the vision itself is one and exercises a control over the plurality of spiritual disciplines. There is something like a classic pattern of prayer, worship, and spiritual progress.

87. THE SHAPE OF CHRISTIAN WORSHIP

The last section ended by stressing the normative value of the classic forms of prayer, and something further will now be said about the importance of form in worship and prayer generally. Again, let it be said that we do not intend to be drawn into the special field of liturgics, which involves questions of history, psychology, esthetics, and other matters besides theology. But it is part of the business of theology to indicate its own contribution toward the problems of liturgics, and of course this theological contribution is a fundamental one.

Here, as in the other themes treated under the heading of "applied theology," we have the tension between fixed forms on the one hand and spontaneity on the other. A too rigid formalism can imprison and even kill that authentic worship that is "in spirit and in truth." Thus within the Christian Church there have been revolts against liturgical forms, and attempts to practice a worship that is "free" and that will more truly express the spontaneity of man's response to God. But even these nonliturgical kinds of prayer and worship tend to develop a form of their own. Our own attitude in this matter is like the one we have adopted in connection which the Church, the ministry, and the sacraments—that is to say, we stress the need for definite forms, yet recognize that there must be sufficient diversity and flexibility in these forms to preserve the spontaneity and richness of prayer and worship. We believe that liturgical

[9] *Vita Moysi*, II, 306.

forms, and especially those classic forms that the Church has developed over the centuries, are the best protection for the authentic but delicate movements of Christian prayer and worship. These forms preserve their communal character and safeguard against individual aberrations and perversions. Yet on the other hand the forms must be subordinated to the matter for which they are the vehicles, and certainly they must not become so rigid and immutable as to stifle the inward significance of prayer and worship.

For the fundamental shape of Christian worship, we turn again to the eucharist, as the norm of such worship. The variety of eucharistic rites is itself an evidence of the flexibility which Christian worship exhibits in the face of the variety of human needs and the variety of ways in which man responds to God. Nevertheless, it seems to me that throughout all these varieties of the eucharistic rite, a definite form or sequence is discernible. There are three elements in this. The first is the approach to God through penitence. In some rites, this may be the first part of the actual public office. In other cases, it may be a preparation that is undertaken by the worshippers before the office begins—and probably there will be such preparation even when this mood of penitence is summed up again in the opening phase of the office. This penitential approach corresponds to St. Paul's recommendation of self-examination before receiving communion.[10] We have already seen that where self-examination still leaves a troubled conscience, the Church offers the sacrament of penance.[11] The penitential approach is reflected too in the ancient custom of coming to communion fasting. The second element is the ministry of the word, the first half of the main part of the eucharistic office, after the opening phase. In the ministry of the word, the scriptures are read, usually a homily is preached, and the people respond in the reciting of the creed. This is the bringing to them of the good news, and the renewal and confirming of their faith. The third part is the eucharist proper—the consecration and offering of the sacramental body and blood of Christ, and the receiving of them by the faithful. This third and culminating element is incorporation.

The three elements then are the penitential approach, instruction and commitment in faith, and incorporation into the body of Christ. It is not hard to recognize in this a kind of summary or compression of the Chris-

---

[10] I Cor. 11:28.
[11] See above, p. 484.

tian life, for it will be remembered that this was described in terms of conviction of sin and repentance, election and justification by faith, and sanctification in the fellowship of the Holy Spirit.[12] If we want a convenient terminology in which to speak of the three elements that have been mentioned, it is not, I think, inaccurate to view them as corresponding to the three "ways" of the Christian life described by mystical writers —the purgative way, the illuminative way, and the unitive way.

What we are saying then is that eucharistic worship compresses the Christian life into the action of the liturgy. This is a further illustration of our point that worship (and especially eucharistic worship) "concentrates" existence. On this occasion, our analysis differs from the earlier one because we are now concerned with form and order, whereas then we were concerned with content. The two analyses, however, complement one another. Worship concentrates existence by creating selfhood and conforming the existent to Christ; and this process of conformation is promoted by the summing up in the act of worship of the form and order of the Christian life.

The shape of Christian worship is further expanded in the cycle of the Christian year. The penitential seasons of Advent and Lent lead the worshippers along the purgative way. The remembering and proclaiming of God's mighty acts in Christ and the new life which they open to mankind is the illuminative way that instructs and confirms the worshippers in faith. And the so-called "green Sundays" that follow the feasts of Whitsunday and Trinity Sunday are the period of growth and sanctification when the unitive action of the Spirit builds up the Church, so that we can speak of the unitive way.

Of course, these indications of shape and form are not to be taken too strictly, as if one could sharply distinguish them, either in the mass or in the Christian life or in the liturgical year. We have deliberately avoided any talk of "stages," and it will be remembered from our discussion of the Christian life that it was insisted that one does not go through stages once for all, but that the process is repeated again and again, though presumably with deepening effect and with an overall movement toward the goal. This is recognized in the cyclic character of Christian worship, each little cycle recurring within a greater one.

We have seen then how prayer and worship lie at the center of Christian existence, and how they build up selfhood, authentic community,

---

[12] See above, pp. 337–350.

and ultimately (such is the Christian hope) the kingdom of God. But while we have spoken of the center and of the concentration of human existence at that point where God's advent and epiphany take place, where his grace and judgment are opened to us, we have said little so far about the spread from the center through the various concentric areas of our existence. We have indeed insisted that the center must be continuous with all the rest of existence, out to its very periphery, and that this center is not a separate region of the "sacred." If faith is indeed an overarching commitment, as we saw it to be in the early parts of this book, then it must be formative for the whole of life. If the presence of God, known in worship, is more than a luxury or an esthetic enjoyment, the pattern which it forms must spread into all the concerns of life. So this brings us to the final theme in applied theology—the relation of Christian faith to conduct and ethics.

21 | Christianity in the World

88. CHRISTIANITY AND ETHICS

The theme of the present chapter is beautifully summed up in a sentence of W. Adams Brown: "The sense of God's presence, which is the crown of the religious life, reaches over into the sphere of ethics and glorifies it."[1] I say that this sums up the theme to be unfolded in the present chapter, and it does so for two reasons. The quotation recognizes, as we have done in the earlier parts of this book, that the heart of religion is the awareness of the divine presence, so that this awareness will be the determinative factor in any distinctively Christian understanding of ethics; and the quotation further recognizes, as we have consistently done, that the Christian contribution is continuous with our "natural" endowment, for the sense of God's presence does not create a new ethic but rather "glorifies" the ethic that is already there—and the expression seems to mean that we are enabled to understand the moral life in a new light and a new depth.

We have been brought to consider the implications of Christian theology for the moral life by our study of the sacraments and worship which, we have claimed, put the presence of God and the process of conformation to Christ at the center of life, so that from this center the transforming influence of the divine grace must spread out even to our most peripheral interests. But not only the past two or three chapters, but our whole study of Christian theology has led us up to this point of considering its application to the daily problems of human existence. We took our

[1] *Christian Theology in Outline*, p. 391.

start from an analysis of this existence itself, as it is disclosed generally in the very act of existing. Now that we have studied this existence in the light of the Christian revelation, we come back to it, hoping to see it in a new depth and to have fresh light on its problems.

But the unbroken connection from first to last stresses our point that we make no sharp separation between man's natural understanding of himself and the understanding that is given in revelation, or between the understanding that we find in the Christian religion and that which is attained in other faiths. To use the expression which we have used so often and which we have tried to explain in various connections, the difference between "natural" and "revealed" is not that the latter sees anything different or anything additional, but the same things are seen "in depth," that is to say, in the light and transparency of Being. This continuity is nowhere more obvious than in the field of ethics. The great world religions come nearer to each other in their moral teaching than anywhere else, and unite in demanding of their adherents love, compassion, altruism; and in this respect, they stand nearest also to the best secular ethics. Nothing could be more arrogant than the absurd claim that Christianity has some kind of monopoly of the good life, though, regrettably, this claim is sometimes made. Yet, on the other hand, the Christian understanding of existence and Being is bound to have a very profound effect on the way in which adherents of the Christian faith conceive the good life, and I certainly wish to maintain that the moral life is in a very significant way illuminated in new depth by the Christian faith.

In the field of ethics, as in the other fields we have considered, it is necessary to maintain that dialectical tension which is so characteristic of Christian theology. The understanding of the moral life in Christian faith is, on the one hand, continuous with the understanding that belongs to human existence as such; yet, on the other hand, this faith "glorifies" or gives new depth to our "natural" morality. Although I shall stress the continuity of the Christian ethic with man's natural moral aspirations, I hope to do justice also to the distinctive quality of a morality that is informed by grace and revelation, so that the Christian ethic is not presented only in terms of continuity, but in terms of a genuine transfiguration. This is surely in line with all that has already been said about our human existence in this world. If we take seriously sin and the need for repentance and justification, then we have already denied a *mere* continuity; and if we go on to visualize the Christian life as man's cooperation in the divine work of letting-be, then we are seeing his moral aspirations "glorified" or "transfigured," and given a new seriousness and dignity beyond what "natural" morality discloses.

We have already had an interesting illustration of the kind of thing that we have in mind, when we took note of the deepening of the conception of sin in the light of Christian teaching. We began with that uneasy sense that existence is not in order—a sense that belongs to the "natural" man, that is to say, to all human existence in virtue of its basic existentiality; then we found that our understanding of sin was deepened and enlarged when we saw it in the light of the biblical doctrines of creation and providence; but even this was still an interim understanding of sin, and its full depth was seen only in the light of the atonement, with its dual aspects of grace and judgment.[2]

There has been a similar progression on the positive side. At an early stage of our inquiry, we met the phenomenon of conscience, as a kind of synoptic self-knowing belonging to existence as such; conscience was in turn seen to be associated with the quest for selfhood, a quest which is likewise intrinsic to existence itself; then the doctrine of creation showed how the kind of being that opens up as the potentiality for the human existent is characterized by letting-be; and finally, this upper level toward which human existence tends as the fulfillment of its potentialities was illuminated in terms of christhood and sonship.[3]

These successive analyses, which moved from the general disclosedness of existence without a radical break into the sharper definitions that come out of the Christian revelation, established the case for what has been traditionally known as "natural law." We are not to think of this as some basic, unchanging *corpus* of commands and prohibitions. Our conception of man as "existing," that is to say, as not having a fixed "nature" but standing in the openness of possibility, rules out the idea of an unchanging law based on an unchanging "nature." If there is any unchanging formulation of natural law, it could be only in the most general, and therefore the emptiest, of terms, as, for instance, St. Thomas' formulation of the first precept of the natural law: "Good is to be done and promoted, and evil is to be avoided." [4] This, of course, can become the basis for more detailed formulations, and we might understand the Ten Commandments as an attempt to formulate some of the basic features of the natural law. Yet even a formulation so simple and universal in its appeal as the Deca-

[2] See above, pp. 68–73, 259–267, 338–339.
[3] See above, pp. 63–64, 231, 300.
[4] *Summa Theologiae*, Ia IIae, q. 94, a. 2.

logue is shaped by particular historical and cultural conditions. If we are to talk of "natural law" (as I believe we should) as meaning the moral awareness that belongs to man in virtue of the existentiality into which he has been created, we must at the same time avoid the error of suggesting an unchanging body of clearly formulated precepts, based on a supposedly unchanging nature. We must look in the direction suggested by J. V. Langmead Casserley: "The natural law for men must necessarily grow and expand as man's potentialities and responsibilities are deepened and widened through his gradual fulfillment of God's purpose in creating him. Natural law doctrine is not conservative. . . . We might even describe 'natural law' as an existential concept. Natural law is the *insurgent authenticity*."[5]

We have seen in the doctrine of creation how man, in his freedom and responsibility, has a share of creativity and cooperates with God in the shaping of the world. More and more, man takes over the direction of "nature"—both external nature and his own nature, that is to say, those elements of his being that are simply "given." As this process goes on, it is clear that "natural law," in the sense explained above, must have flexibility. What might have been against natural law at one time may not still be against it as man, fulfilling his destiny, reshapes his own "nature" or develops it or reduces the area of the "given" by bringing more of his being under his conscious responsible will. One obvious controversial example of these matters is the question of contraception or birth control. On the one hand, man has, by better health arrangements, extended his life-span and his chances of survival far beyond what was once "natural," that is to say, simply given. No one condemns this. On the other hand, then, surely it is equally in order to take over from nature control of procreation, and to achieve in a responsible way by suitable techniques that balance between new life and death which was once regulated by the merely "given" factors in both man and his environment, for some such regulation is required if we are to have regard to the quality of existence and not just to the biological (and probably miserable) proliferation of life.

Of course, there are terrible risks lying all along the way. But these are the risks inherent in creation itself, and man cannot back away from the demand that he take over control more and more. We hear of responsibilities in the future that frighten us, such as the possibility of so-

---

[5] "Liberal Catholicism," in *The American Church Quarterly*, vol. V, p. 87 (italics mine).

called "genetic engineering." There will be those who will think of this as a kind of usurping of divine prerogatives, and the assuming of godlike powers by man. But we have seen that it is man's destiny to be godlike. There is no usurpation of the divine, if the taking over of new powers is done not with proud autonomy but with a sense of stewardship and a consciousness of the divine grace and judgment over man. Certainly I cannot see that any supposed unchanging natural law could be invoked against such developments, or that it would be likely to halt them.

Thus, as we understand the expression "natural law," it lies beyond any formulation except the simplest and emptiest, and the word "natural" points only to what belongs universally to man's existentiality. We mean the tendency toward fulfillment that is intrinsic to existence itself. This is the tendency to actualize selfhood, but since there cannot be selfhood without community, it is also the tendency toward authentic community. In terms of our existential-ontological approach, we may say that the natural law directs toward letting-be, which is both the highest potentiality for the existent and is also the essence of Being (God). It is entirely in line with our general approach to theology to hold that the specific task of a Christian ethic or moral theology is to help us to understand in the depth and fullness of the Christian revelation the tendencies, aspirations, and obligations that already belong to us in virtue of the "natural law."

Just as some Protestant theologians hold that there is no continuity between the Christian revelation and what they regard as the merely human wisdom of philosophy or of the non-Christian faiths, so they deny any continuity between the Christian ethic and natural law. We must therefore spend some time in defending the case for continuity in ethics, just as we have defended continuity elsewhere. Moreover, as we discuss these matters, it will become clearer what is meant by the "depth" or "illumination" which, we have claimed, the Christian revelation brings to man's "natural" moral strivings; and in the end, it is the distinctive Christian contribution that we wish to bring out.

It seems to me that both continuity and a new depth can be clearly illustrated from Jesus' own ethical teaching. On the one hand, there is surely no question about the continuity of his teaching with Old Testament ethics and so with the "natural law." However revolutionary he may have been, Jesus understood himself as standing in the Hebrew tradition. His aim, he says, is to fulfill the law, not to destroy it.[6] It is true that he is

[6] Matt. 5:17.

strongly opposed to all legalism and self-righteousness. Apparently, too, he had little use for minute regulations concerning the sabbath and the like. He befriended sinners and outcasts. He strongly asserted the primacy of love and charity. He showed extraordinary freedom toward the law, especially in the so-called "antitheses" where he radically reinterprets the traditional laws.[7] Yet all this need not be understood as destroying continuity. Actually, we know that many of Jesus' sayings can be paralleled from the words of other Jewish teachers; and although Christian apologists sometimes set up a sharp contrast between "Jewish legalism" and the ethic of Jesus, what they represent as "Jewish legalism" is often a mere caricature. We can learn from such Jewish writers as Martin Buber or, for that matter, from the Hebrew scriptures themselves, that inwardness, charity, and humanity were by no means foreign to the law. The Hebrew ideal of the righteous man, as depicted in Job,[8] is no narrowly legalistic one. Buber, pointing out that *"torah"* means not "law" but "instruction," claims that Jesus and Judaism (both biblical and post-biblical) have been at one in fighting against the perversion of *torah* into a merely external legalism, and have sought rather "to extend the hearing of the word to the whole dimension of human existence."[9]

Yet while we recognize this continuity, we have also to acknowledge or rather to assert that in a signal way Jesus lets us see the law in a new depth. He directs attention away from overt behavior as the fulfilling (or not fulfilling) of laws, to existential attitudes. These attitudes are what determines conduct, and since these attitudes in turn constitute the faith (or lack of faith) by which selfhood is formed (or missed), conduct is firmly linked to the formative influences of faith. In stressing the existential basis of conduct, Jesus also directs attention to the concrete situation rather than to general rules. This comes out above all in his conception of the "neighbor," the person with whom we are in direct confrontation.[10] Most strikingly of all, there is the radicalizing of the moral demand, which gets expressed in extreme and apparently "impractical" formulations, such as that we should not resist evil or that we should love our enemies.[11] Here, it might seem, there is no longer any continuity with "natural law" but rather a complete reversal of its promptings. But the full significance

[7] Matt. 5:21ff.
[8] Job 31:1ff.
[9] *Two Types of Faith*, p. 58.
[10] Luke 10:29ff.
[11] Matt. 5:39, 44.

of this demand for "radical obedience" (as Bultmann has called it) is to be seen in the career of Jesus himself, as the one who was obedient even to the cross.[12] We have seen that it was this self-emptying, this absolute letting-be, that constitutes Jesus the Christ, so that we confess him as the incarnate Word.[13] Yet however far this christhood is from the imperfect humanity that we see every day in ourselves, we nevertheless perceived that because humanity is not something fixed but stands in the openness of possibility, this very humanity is at its upper limit continuous with christhood—if, indeed, we are not going to think of Christ in docetic terms. So the radical obedience which Christ both demanded and exemplified is after all, and despite the fact that the connection has been so sadly obscured by sin, continuous with the "natural law," that is to say, with those potentialities for fulfillment that God placed in man at creation. Jesus' ethical teaching reveals the obscured and forgotten depths.

In the ethical teaching of St. Paul, one can likewise trace both the notion of continuity with "natural law" and the novel depth that had been given to the moral situation by the Christian revelation. On the one hand, he has something like an explicit conception of natural law, for he talks of the Gentiles as having a "law written in their hearts," [14] and apparently thinks of the content of this law as similar to the content of the law of Israel. This natural law is also associated with conscience, and St. Paul is the first Christian writer to use the term "conscience." St. Paul is indeed critical of the law conceived as a way to salvation. He seems to think that both the natural law and the law of Israel simply reveal man's sinfulness and his impotence to fulfill the demands intrinsic to his own existence. This in turn points to the need for grace, and for justification by faith. But we have seen already that justification is not to be separated from sanctification.[15] Having established faith, and with it, hope and love, as the foundations of Christian existence, St. Paul still sees the law as providing the guidelines for our life on earth. The law is not "made void" by grace, but "established." [16] The point he is making is that self-sufficient moral endeavor will not lead to salvation, but that entry upon the Christian way of salvation brings moral renewal as part of that whole "new creation" which is Christian existence and yet which, we must say, is also

[12] Phil. 2:8.
[13] See above, pp. 302–303.
[14] Rom. 2:15.
[15] See above, p. 343.
[16] Rom. 3:31.

the fulfilling of the potentialities of creation. The "new creation" is the man "in Christ," the man whose life is conformed in the body of Christ to the dying and rising of Christ, and in which therefore love is paramount.[17]

The manner in which the Christian ethic combines continuity with distinctiveness gets its classic illustration in the history of theology from St. Thomas' treatment of the virtues.[18] He brings together the four "cardinal virtues" of classical philosophy and the three "theological virtues" of the New Testament. The four cardinal virtues may be taken as summing up man's "natural" aspirations for the good, that is to say, the tendencies toward fullness of being that are intrinsic to existence. The three theological virtues are not, strictly speaking, additional virtues, but rather they supply an additional dimension to the moral life, so that it is seen in a new depth.

We have already said something about faith, hope, and love as basic characteristics of the Christian life.[19] Here it will be sufficient to add a few remarks on their significance for ethics.

Faith, as acceptance and commitment, is fundamental to the realization of selfhood. We are concerned, however, not with any and every faith or with a merely formal conception of faith, but with specifically Christian faith. This is directed to Jesus Christ, the incarnate Word, the particular being in whom expressive Being has most fully expressed itself. The center of this Christian faith is therefore the incarnation, the presence and manifestation, or the advent and epiphany, of Being among the beings. Thus, as was stated at the beginning of the present section, the awareness of the divine presence becomes the determinative factor in any distinctively Christian understanding of ethics. Differently stated, this means an extension of the sacramental principle to the whole of life, the movement out from the center of which we have already spoken. How this movement occurs, we shall see later. But for the present, it is enough to note that the faith that holy Being presents and manifests itself in the neighbor and even in material things lends a new depth to the world and profoundly influences behavior in it.

Hope belongs to the eschatological dimension of the Christian life and, from the ethical point of view, provides a dynamic to action. Many moral philosophers have noted that if moral ideals have to be realized in an alien or indifferent world, then the moral task is a harsh and discouraging

[17] II Cor. 5:17; etc.
[18] *Summa Theologiae*, Ia IIae, qq. 61-62.
[19] See above, pp. 345-350.

one; while, on the other hand, if the very structure of Being supports moral aspirations, then one can embark on the moral life with an enthusiasm and confidence that would be hard to attain otherwise. We are not concerned here with any "moral arguments" for the existence of God or with the question of whether morality needs to be "completed" or filled out by religion. After all, it may be the case that morality and human existence with it just do not make sense. Yet even to say this is to indicate the difference which the Christian hope makes in the human approach to morality. A philosophy which takes existence (and *a fortiori* morality) to be absurd is surely less likely to spur moral endeavor than the faith that creation is good and moves toward the good. Of course, if this were simply a fatalistic belief, then again it might produce indifference and inaction. But if it is understood in Christian terms as the coworking of divine grace and human endeavor, then it would be difficult to imagine any more powerful moral dynamic.

Finally, the good, or the goal of moral striving, is exhibited with a new clarity and depth as Christian love—that is to say, not any and every love, but the love revealed in Jesus Christ as absolute letting-be. The good is fullness of being, and this in turn is letting-be. The whole Christian interpretation of the world as creation-reconciliation-consummation points to the end, or *summum bonum*, as that perfect community of love in God which we call the "kingdom of God," and it already sees the actualizing of this in the incarnation and in the extension of the incarnation in the Church. Yet the vision extends far beyond the borders of the recognizably Christian Church to embrace all men and all beings.

An attempt has been made in the foregoing paragraphs to delineate some of the basic considerations that will shape a Christian view of morality, and to show how such a view is both continuous with "natural law" and yet makes its own very distinctive contribution. The working out in detail of the principles of Christian behavior belongs to moral theology, and like the other specialized studies on which we have impinged in our discussions of "applied theology," moral theology involves not only theological questions but questions belonging to other disciplines that make a study of human behavior in its many activities. We do not intend therefore to invade the field of the moral theologian, but are only concerned to draw such implications from our general theology as may be helpful toward the work of those who make a special study of Christian ethics. Nevertheless, there are some matters that it is legitimate for us to pursue further, and among other things, we have still to fulfill our promise of showing how the center of worship moves out to shape all the activities of life.

89. THE TRANSFIGURATION OF THE WORLD

In our discussion of the sacraments and of worship, we found ourselves led to make the claim that these constitute a center of existence, and that through this concentration or intensification, existence is brought to fuller levels of being, so that there are actualized authentic selfhood and authentic community. We have expressed the same processes in more specifically Christian language as conformation to Christ and incorporation into Christ. But this center, it was asserted, becomes formative for the whole existence out to its periphery, and it was here that we saw the relevance to ethics. The whole of life and existence is to be penetrated by the grace of Being, and the entire creation is to be transfigured in the direction of that goal when its fullest potentialities for being will have been realized. Yet this process can go on only through the free cooperation of those responsible agents that have been brought forth in creation. Between where we now are and the eschatological transfiguration of the world lies the sphere of ethical action. The community of faith, as the spearhead of God's acting in the world, should also be in the van of ethical action, because ethics, as we have seen, takes on a new depth and seriousness in the community of faith. Response to the moral demand, as seen in the light of revelation, is the step by which the community of faith cooperates in its present situation with the action of Being for the penetration of all creation by the grace of Being, and makes its indispensable contribution toward the eschatological transfiguration of creation.

But this doctrine of the relevance of worship and the sacraments to the ethical tasks of mankind stands in need of fuller support than we have so far provided. To many people, worship and the sacraments appear as merely survivals with no relevance to the problems of the contemporary world, or perhaps at best they may appear as props for the weak-minded and to have little contribution to offer. This is far from our own assertion of their centrality, and it is this assertion that we have to vindicate.

It seems to me that if we look again at the Christian sacramental structure, we can see that it does in a very remarkable way establish its relevance to everyday life, and itself provides a channel for continuity between the worshipping center of life and the bewildering range of problems that confront man in the many areas in which he has to live out his life in the world. This sacramental channel is the one sacrament which we did not discuss in the earlier chapters but have deferred to the present—the sacrament of holy matrimony. In taking marriage into its sacramental structure, the Church breaks down the barrier between the sacred and the secular, declares its concern with our worldly, embodied existence, and provides for the impact of the divine grace upon our everyday activities. At first sight, it may seem strange that matrimony is reckoned a sacrament at all. Yet the recognition of its sacramental character forms an indispensable link between worship and life, and Christian marriage becomes the gateway through which the grace of holy Being made present in the sacraments can penetrate the wider world of human relationships.

Marriage, of course, is a "natural" institution as well as being a Christian sacrament, and as a natural institution, it is a far wider phenomenon. Here we must recognize the continuity between the natural institution and the Christian sacrament. The relation between them is to be understood in the way outlined in the preceding section. The so-called "natural" institution already contains *in nuce* that which is unfolded and understood in new depth in the light of the Christian revelation. At a very early stage of this book we already indicated what is the "natural" or the universal existential content of this particular phenomenon, when we said that sex is the most obvious indicator of the fundamentally communal character of human existence, no single existent being complete in himself or herself.[20] Marriage is the institutional form which protects and stabilizes the sexual relation. But this means that in the "natural" order, marriage is the simplest and most fundamental form of human community. For this reason alone, marriage is well fitted to be taken into the sacramental structure of the Christian religion and made the gateway whereby divine grace can enter and penetrate the whole complex structure of man's communal life.

But if we agree that marriage as a natural institution has the character of the simplest and most fundamental human community, what are we to say about the distinctively Christian understanding of marriage? What depth does the Christian revelation bring to the understanding of marriage, and what does it mean to recognize its sacramental character? The answer to these questions is surely to be found in the parallel which the New Testament draws between the marriage bond and the relation between Christ and his Church. On the one hand, marriage—and this is true of marriage as a "natural" institution—is contrasted as a personal, loving

[20] See above, pp. 66–67.

relationship of the sexes with undisciplined sexual lust as something that is destructive of selfhood and community.[21] On the other hand, marriage is presented distinctively in terms of Christ's love for the Church.[22] Christ "loved the Church" and "gave himself for it"; he lets it be, and the Church in turn is his body and the extension of his incarnation. The Church is incorporated into Christ, and thus becomes the community of Being, where existence is brought to the fulfillment of its potentialities. This high doctrine of Christ and the Church becomes the paradigm for understanding the relation of those who are made "one flesh" in Christian marriage.

To attempt to draw out all the implications of this parallel and to point to its limitations as well as to its positive contribution would take us beyond what is required for our theological argument. For a brief but sufficient statement of this understanding of marriage sacramentally in terms of the relation of Christ and his Church, I can do no better than quote a sentence or two from Karl Rahner: "This representative function has to be exercised not only by Christians inasmuch as they are human beings, but in a higher degree through their being Christians and members of the Church. . . . Marriage is the smallest community, but, for all that, a genuine community of the redeemed and sanctified—the smallest of local churches, but a true one, the Church in miniature." [23]

A special significance, I would suggest, attaches to the words "the Church in miniature." The natural institution of marriage is the basic form of community, while Christian marriage transforms this basic community into a community of faith. In many ways, it is this "natural" form of community, marriage, that is ideally fitted to become the prototype of the community of faith, the fellowship of the Spirit, the body of Christ. The "natural" community of marriage is essentially a self-transcending community, a community the very purpose of which is to let-be and to pass over into the larger community of the family. This prefigures the Church, or community of faith, which does not exist for its own sake but in order that, through its ministry of reconciliation, it may eventually lose itself in the wider all-embracing eschatological community.

We can now see much more clearly why marriage is reckoned among the sacraments of the Church, and why it is the channel that links the whole sacramental structure with everyday life and so with the problems of ethics. We can see too why the Church has always laid stress on the

---

[21] Eph. 5:1–12.

[22] Eph. 5:22–33.

[23] *Inquiries*, pp. 292, 294.

importance of marriage and the family, and why it has sought to protect these by sometimes stringent rules. If prayer, worship, and the sacraments form the center of Christian life, then it must be said that the first concentric ring as one moves out from the center is the area of sex, marriage, and family life. The Church has rightly seen that this area provides a bridgehead into the world, and that if these most intimate communal relations can be "sanctified," that is to say, made whole and healthy, then a decisive step has been taken toward eventually sanctifying the larger social relations that lie beyond.

Actually, it is not hard to see the immediate outreach of the sacramental idea beyond marriage and the family. The Christian doctrines of creation and incarnation, by recognizing the divine presence in the world and our own responsibility to cooperate with this presence in its work of creation-reconciliation-consummation, enable us to see the world and our policies of action in it with a new clarity and seriousness. The other person is seen as the neighbor, destined to have his place in the family of God. Even material things are to be seen in the light of Being and of our own status as stewards or shepherds or guardians of Being. All this, of course, is clearly stated in one way or another in the New Testament.

In the contemporary world, however, these remarks may seem very naive. Modern society is complicated far beyond anything of which the New Testament or, for that matter, the Church through most of its history, ever dreamed. Perhaps in the past one could claim for marriage and the family the key position which, as we have seen, seems to be assigned to them in the Christian Church, and one could visualize them as having a formative influence for the wider social patterns that lay beyond them, but were still not too distant or too much lacking in concreteness. But what seem to be the formative influences in our life today? Must we not say science and technology, the political machinery of the modern state, the web of international relations, the immensely complex economic system? These are things that seem to be beyond the reach of the little areas that we have talked about—indeed, in all kinds of ways (urbanization, mobility, techniques of contraception, and the like) they seem to have reacted upon family life itself, so that instead of the world being penetrated by love and personal values, these very things are in peril of being destroyed by the world. The situation becomes even more frightening when we ask about the control of these things. When we ask who is responsible, the answer must often be a vague "they"—the "they" of which Heidegger has so revealingly written, the "they" that is everybody and nobody. We talk nowadays of "escalation," a word which we have ourselves used earlier in this book to describe runaway situations when circumstances have taken over and we find ourselves being hustled along, whether we like it or not. The frightening thing is that in many areas of contemporary life (the most obvious example is war, but it is not the only one) impersonal factors can take over, and we are dragged along behind them. Of course, some people still have momentous decisions to make—statesmen, industrialists, and others. They may have to make decisions that will affect millions of other people. Yet often their decisions seem to be really forced on them. To some extent, however, this has always been the case. The possibilities of existence are always narrowed down by the facticity of the situation. But there is always some area for responsible decision.

Has Christianity anything to say in this new situation, or is it hopelessly outmoded? I believe that it still has its important contribution to make. It has to strive for the maintenance of personal values and for the supreme importance of love in a world where these are gravely threatened. Moreover, the account we have given of the penetration of the world through marriage and the family is still fundamentally sound, and there is no substitute for this sacramental channel in the Christian outreach into the world. I think this has been well shown by G. R. Dunstan in his study of the family in the industrial and urban setting of today. He recognizes the revolutionary changes that are going on in the world, but also that some of the basic desires and possibilities of our human existence remain, including our "capacity for God"; he recognizes too that although many of the old patterns of marriage and the family, as "subtly and deeply intertwined with the life of society," have been disrupted by change, new and in some respects better patterns are emerging. He sees the family as "often a base from which its members give generous service to the community," and his careful analysis should certainly prevent anyone from writing off the importance of marriage and the family, either in the modern world or in the Christian dispensation.[24]

But we still have the problem of how Christian grace is to reach out from the more immediate and personal areas of life to those areas which, to the ordinary man, seem so frighteningly distant. Government departments, economic corporations, trade unions, international organizations—these are indispensable organs of our mass society, they cannot be assimi-

[24] *The Family is not Broken*, pp. 40, 62, 91.

lated to family patterns, and yet somehow they must be humanized, personalized, christianized, if anything like an authentic existence is to be left to man.

Christianity and the Christian virtues seem to be so closely related to the personal and interpersonal areas of life that it is hard to see how they are relevant to the large-scale structures of a modern society, and unfortunately Christian pronouncements on political and social issues are frequently simplistic. But we cannot accept that Christianity is irrelevant when we move from individuals and small groups to the large-scale social and political questions, and certainly we are still dealing with human beings. Nevertheless, the relation between the small-scale and the large-scale is a very complex one. For instance, if love is the fundamental Christian virtue in the realm of personal relations, one might say that peace is the corresponding global virtue. But if peace is to be more than simply the absence of overt violence (and that might be only a sham peace), it demands vast resources of technical knowledge quite as much as goodwill, and it is founded as much in justice as in love. In turn, justice itself is a virtue with obviously both individual and social dimensions, and these are complementary.

Just as moral philosophy is complemented by political philosophy, so moral theology needs the complement of a political or social theology. Political theology has been described by Johannes Metz as a "critical corrective" aimed at what he calls the "deprivatizing" of Christianity.[25] To be sure, there is the danger that Christianity might be transformed into a political ideology, or made subservient to one. There is the more subtle danger that Christianity begins to use the methods of secular society and forgets its true mission. Yet the dangers must be risked if Christian faith and life are to engage seriously with the actual world. The dialectic of this situation was well understood by Ritschl when he wrote that to say Christ's kingdom is not of this world cannot possibly mean that it has nothing to do with our life here, but only that it works in quite other ways from the claims and counterclaims of secular societies.[26] We can agree with Jürgen Moltmann that "political hermeneutics of faith is not a reduction of the theology of the cross to a political ideology, but an interpretation of it in political discipleship."[27]

How this happens in detail will vary very much from one situation to

[25] *Theology of the World*, p. 108.
[26] *Justification and Reconciliation*, p. 433.
[27] *The Crucified God*, p. 318.

another, and there could be no question of tying Christianity to some particular political or social ideology. But I shall make two general points about the way in which Christianity may impinge on the structures of society.

The first is the need for a stronger sense among Christians of the Church as, on the one hand, the spearhead of God's letting-be in the world, and, on the other, as an historical, embodied social entity—an "association," in the sense explained earlier.[28] Such an association can exercise its influences and pressures on other associations, and so society as a whole. So far as the Church is really exhibiting genuine community and making-present something of the kingdom of God (and, of course, it will do so only in a degree), then it has to society at large a relation closely analogous to that which conscience (as the call of authentic existence) bears to actual existence. There are many fields, such as race relations, where a Church alive to its responsibilities and actualizing genuine community could be the "conscience" of society. The relation of Church and state will vary in different countries according to their histories and the religious and ethnic composition of their populations, but whatever the relation may be, even if it is one where the state persecutes the Church, the function of conscience seems a possible one for the Church, if it is indeed spearheading the kingdom of God. But here I repeat a point made earlier, namely, that the witnessing of the Church will best be done by communions having an interracial and international character, and the Church should not allow itself to be divided along lines that conform to the "worldly" divisions of race or nation, divisions which ought to be overcome in the Church. Thus the developing and strengthening in mutual responsibility of international communions, such as the Roman and Anglican communions, is a more urgent task than what has hitherto been the ideal of many Protestant ecumenists, namely, the formation of national united churches.

The second point to be made is also a restressing of something said earlier, though this time we apply it to the special problem of ethics. What we have in mind is the apostolate of the laity. In our complex modern world with all its specialization, it is doubtful if the clergy or even the moral theologians can have enough acquaintance with all the different areas of human activity to be able to reach solutions of the moral problems raised in these areas. But the laity of the Church are directly involved

[28] See above, p. 375.

in all of these areas, and often at the decision-making level. We have seen that every member of the Church has, by his baptism, the ministry of reconciliation entrusted to him.[29] We have seen also that this ministry is not some pale imitation of the clergy's ministry but a "secular" ministry of letting-be, that is to say, of safeguarding and encouraging potentialities for fuller existing and being. The responsibility for this ministry lies upon laymen in government, industry, technology and other spheres, but an equally heavy responsibility lies upon the clergy and educators of the Church who must support these men, giving them the nurture and training in the faith and its application that they need if they are to carry out an effective ministry of reconciliation.

I have spoken of the penetration of the world by divine grace, and I have stressed especially the notion of sacramental presence. The picture would be unbalanced if we did not remember also the transcendence of Being, and the inseparability of grace and judgment. The eschatological consummation of the kingdom of God is a mystery to be realized by the movement of Being, not by creaturely striving, even if this makes an indispensable contribution. We delude ourselves if we think that some ideal state of affairs is attainable on earth, or that the main business of Christianity is to establish a super welfare state. Enough has been said in earlier sections about the ambiguity of the world and about the need for the Christian to maintain a dialectical attitude toward it.

This however can now be given its specific ethical application by the recognition that there always will be a place in the Church for the so-called "religious" life, that is to say, for those whose vocation leads them to world-renunciation, in varying measures. In this section, we have stressed marriage, involvement in the world, and the penetration of its affairs. But Christianity is not a mere worldliness, but a holy worldliness; as we learned from the temptations of Jesus, Christianity is grievously reduced if it is turned into a mere social gospel. The concern of Christianity is less for the quantity of life than for its quality, not that men should live biologically but that they should *exist*. Precisely because of the current stress on worldly Christianity, it is necessary that some should witness to the transcendent element in faith and remind us of the need to maintain a dialectical attitude to the world. For the majority, the Christian vocation lies in the world, and this is not a "lower" vocation than the "religious" life. But neither is it a "higher" one, and we need those who

[29] See above, pp. 421–422.

choose the way of poverty, celibacy, and obedience to remind us that the aim of Christianity is not just universal affluence and enjoyment of life. Those witnesses, moreover, are not confined to the religious orders. One of the most instructive examples is Kierkegaard, admittedly an "exceptional" man but one who surely taught us something of the depths of the Christian faith.

90. LAW AND GOSPEL

We have just been saying something of the ambiguities of the world, and of our action in it, and this theme needs to be expanded to complete our discussion of Christianity in the world. The ambiguity runs all through the problems of ethics, and appears in many forms, such as the dichotomy of aspiration and obligation, the pursuit of the good and the fulfillment of obligation, or again, the dichotomy of law and gospel, the imperative and the indicative.

Let us begin with the contrast between an ethic of aspiration and an ethic of obligation, a contrast which is well known on the level of "natural" mortality. It may well be that the contrast is not an absolute one. The two paths seem to lead toward the same goal, and it is not always possible to distinguish them sharply—for instance, most moral philosophers would agree with Sir W. D. Ross that beneficence is among our *prima facie* duties,[30] but who would be willing to say just where the *duty* of beneficence ends and there begins the pursuit of the other's good, beyond what duty demands? Yet even if one cannot always draw the distinction sharply, the two ways of conceiving moral action can be fairly well separated. The pursuit of the good reflects man's innate quest for fullness of existence, his "original righteousness," as we called it in an earlier discussion.[31] It is to this pursuit of the good that we have chiefly devoted attention in what has been said about ethics so far. But this pursuit of the good is a fitful matter in human existence, and over against it we have to set the fact of human sinfulness, the disorder, alienation, and imbalance that affect existence. We have already seen that this basic awareness of the disorder of existence belongs to "natural" existence, though it is sharpened and deepened by the Christian revelation. It is because of sin and the fact that man does not pursue the good that alongside the morality of aspira-

[30] *The Right and the Good*, p. 21.
[31] See above, p. 267.

tion we find the morality of obligation. The natural law that directs toward the good is formulated in terms of concrete commands and prohibitions that sometimes lay upon man obligations to contribute toward
the realizing of the good, and sometimes simply try to contain and minimize his deviations from the path that leads to the good.

In society, many of these obligations are enforced by the state. Presumably, if human society were not fallen and sinful, there would be no need
of the state. However, its laws and the machinery for enforcing them are
indispensable in the actual condition of mankind. On the whole, the laws
of the state have their roots in the natural law, so that they protect and
encourage the pursuit of the good. For this reason, the New Testament
clearly teaches obedience to the civil power,[32] and most theologians have
followed the New Testament in this. If some of them have recognized
that there may be exceptional cases where the law should be disobeyed,
they have done so only reluctantly, for in sinful human society, anarchy
is likely to be even more destructive of human well-being than tyranny.
On the whole, the civil law provides at least a minimal level of order and
justice that makes possible the pursuit of the good. Of course, the modern
state goes far beyond this minimal provision, and tends increasingly to
provide for the good of its citizens in many areas of life.

The need for law in the secular order and the Christian's duty to support the forces of justice is paralleled within the Church itself. While we
have spoken of the specifically Christian conception of the good and of
the pursuit of this good in the life of the Christian community, we have
to remember that the Christian is still a sinner. He will, it is hoped, be in
process of sanctification, but so many of the things of which we speak
—conformation to Christ, sonship with God, incorporation, radical obedience—are only to be realized at the end, and are certainly far from being
realized in the middle of our earthly existence, whether as individuals or
as a community of faith. Just as we had to remember that the Church on
earth is not to be confused with the eschatological kingdom of God, so
we have to remember that Christian action reflects only in a very imperfect way that ideal in which the natural virtues are raised to a new level
by faith, hope, and love.

This means that the Church too must have laws and rules that it lays
upon its members. This necessity follows from the facticity of Christian
existence. The Christian is always already in a situation where his choices

[32] Rom. 13:1ff.

are, in part at least, determined by the sinfulness of human society, perhaps by his own past sins or by the sins of others. Perhaps the best he can do is to contain and minimize the evil. The Church has to provide guidelines for its members as they confront the problems of how to act, and sometimes these guidelines may be simply prohibitions to keep them from wandering too far. The famous doctrine of the just war, for instance, recognizes realistically that in our sinful world, justice has sometimes to be upheld by force, but it hedges round with restrictions the cases where force may be used, so that the evil is as far as possible reduced. In other cases, the laws of the Church may seem to lay down the very minimal standards of conduct for the individual Christian. But here it has to be remembered that a man does not automatically become a moral hero through joining the Christian community. The goal of Christian life is self-giving love, but Reinhold Niebuhr realistically reminds us that this is "a moral ideal scarcely possible for the individual and certainly not relevant to the morality of self-regarding nations." [33]

Every pastor knows that the first task of the Christian may be the relatively lowly one of overcoming some of his sinful tendencies. Sanctification may be a slow process, and its end is always ahead. We have to be careful also not to be too individualistic in our view of these matters. Sanctification belongs to the community, as the body of Christ and the fellowship of the Spirit, and within that community there must be room for "weaker brethren" who are sustained by the whole body.

For these reasons, it is hard to understand the antinomian tendencies that sometimes powerfully express themselves in the Church. Some extreme existential interpretations of Christianity tell us that there can be no rules of conduct for the Christian, for every situation is unique, and our duty is to respond to the unique demand of love in that situation. Likewise they deny any value to habitual action, claiming again that every situation demands a new decision. Others, claiming that "persons are more important than principles," seem to understand by this the abolition of all principles of action.

Such views are surely much exaggerated, and are also far too individualistic. They fail to recognize that all Christians have not reached the same level of moral maturity, and that even those with most insight often need the guidance of the Church's collective wisdom, as expressed in her rules for her members. They fail also to recognize that even if there can be

[33] *Man's Nature and his Communities*, p. 42.

deadening habits that make conduct mechanical, there is a place for the stabilizing of character, and that there is a kind of habit-formation that can protect us from our own weaknesses—for instance, it would be reckless and presumptuous for anyone to insist on undergoing an agonizing struggle in every situation where he was exposed to the temptation of a besetting sin, if he could be protected from it by the formation of a good habit. Like attacks on institutional religion, attacks on rules, laws, and precepts do not sufficiently consider the embodied, historical condition of man, the relativities and ambiguities of his situation, the differences between individuals and the need for training. Those existentialists who deny any place to law or habit make a great point of the *possibilities* of human existence; but they commit the error of not recognizing what the best existential analyses take into account as equally characteristic of human existence—its *facticity*.

We have seen already from the ethical teaching of both Jesus and St. Paul that the Christian gospel does not abolish the law. It does indeed oppose all narrow legalism and it asserts the primacy of love. But Christianity is too realistic to suppose that men in this world can get along without rules to guide them, or that the community of faith can function without some minimal law for its membership.

The tension of law and gospel, and what it means to speak of Christian freedom in relation to the law, is admirably treated by Bernhard Häring in the context of a renewed catholic moral theology. He departs from the legalistic character of much traditional moral theology and stresses the understanding of the moral life as man's response to God's call within a personal community. He acknowledges that a situational ethic (*Situationsethik*) has something in common with this view, in so far as it represents a reaction against a too rigid ethic that deals in terms of unchanging essences and immutable laws. But he rejects an extreme situational ethic (that is to say, one that sets aside all laws or norms and thinks of the demand of each moment as absolutely unique). His rejection is based on the fact that by making each moment of decision a unique and independent occasion, the continuity of personal life is dissolved into a series of acts. This argument must obviously carry weight with our own point of view, which has stressed the formation of unified selfhood. But what chiefly interests us is Häring's way of talking about the law, if we neither take it in a narrowly legalistic way nor yet are prepared to reject all law in order to rely on the insight of the moment. "Our whole relation to the law," he declares, "has to be considered in terms of Christ. What is most essential

for the Christian disciple is that Christ does not command him from outside, as does a human lawgiver, and as did the law of Moses, to the extent
it was viewed in terms of the letter rather than of the spirit. But Christ
commands from within, through our living incorporation in him." [34]

Law is like the other earthly institutional forms we have considered in
the course of our remarks on applied theology. Though law can become
hardened and distorted, it is intended to protect and advance the way of
life which it enshrines, and to promote the pursuit of the good. Like all
earthen vessels of this kind, law is imperfect, and sometimes its incidence
in particular situations and on particular individuals may be harsh. Yet
without the protection of laws, the delicate life which they guard could
perhaps scarcely survive in a sinful world and a pilgrim Church. One
thinks, for instance, of the laws that have been devised to protect Christian
marriage. There may be cases where these laws seem harsh, and yet without such laws the Christian ideal of marriage would soon become debased.
Like the institutional structure of the Church, like the sacraments, the
ministry, the liturgy, it is clear that the laws which the Church may impose are not to be made so rigid that they become an end in themselves
and may threaten to stifle rather than protect the Christian way of life.
There are perhaps few immutable laws, and such as there are will be the
most general and empty of specific content. Laws must always be subject
to love, and there must be room for ethical creativity in new situations,
especially in our rapidly changing world. All this can be freely conceded,
or rather, asserted. But here, as in the whole field of applied theology, we
need stability as well as flexibility. The place of law in the Christian life
is not to be despised. To be incorporated into the body of Christ is to be
subject to the law of Christ, and this must have some concrete formulations. These formulations will indeed be subject to revision in the light of
changing conditions, but such revisions will be agreed by the whole body
as illuminated by the Spirit, and there would soon be chaos if every individual member of the body claimed the right to obey the law or to set it
aside from one situation to another. In any case, we have to remember
again that individual Christians vary in their maturity and that many of
them need the guidance of laws, and become confused if they see these
laws disregarded by other members of the body to which they all belong.

In the end, the Church, her laws, her forms of worship, her institutions
and ceremonies, will become one with the world in the eschatological

---

[34] *Das Gesetz Christi*, p. 278.

consummation. But we are not yet at the end. For the present, we have to live in the tension of Church and world, law and gospel, form and content, facticity and possibility. If we are going to be realistic, then we have also to be patient, and to act where we are with the means that we have, even if some of these means are sadly imperfect. But this is a realism guided and strengthened by the Christian hope—the hope that all things will come to their destined fulfillment in God:

UNTO WHOM,
FATHER, SON AND HOLY SPIRIT,
BE GLORY FOR EVER.

INDEX

The Crime of Julian Wells

Thomas H. Cook

W F HOWES LTD

This large print edition published in 2012 by
W F Howes Ltd
Unit 4, Rearsby Business Park, Gaddesby Lane,
Rearsby, Leicester LE7 4YH

1 3 5 7 9 10 8 6 4 2

First published in the United Kingdom in 2012
by Head of Zeus Ltd.

A CIP catalogue record for this book is available
from the British Library

ISBN 978 1 47121 303 8

Typeset by Palimpsest Book Production Limited,
Falkirk, Stirlingshire
Printed and bound in Great Britain
by MPG Books Ltd, Bodmin, Cornwall

For the women of Maui:
Ann Hood, Diane Lake, Annie LeClaire,
Jacquelyn Mitchard, Deborah Todd, and
Sara Young.

And in loving memory of Heiman Zeidman.

The Curfew tolls the Knell of parting Day,
The lowing Herd winds slowly o'er the Lea,
The Plow-man homeward plods his weary Way,
And leaves the World to Darkness, and to me.

Thomas Gray, *Elegy Written in a Country*
Church-Yard

BEFORE

He folds the map and puts it on the table beside his chair. Beyond the window, he sees the flat gray waters of the pond. The boat, its yellow paint long faded, rests beneath a weeping birch.

He rises, walks to the window, and looks out.

In the distance, a small breeze rustles the leaves of the birch and skirts along the green lawn and gently rocks the purple irises that grow beside the water. He has seen so many grasses, so many flowers. The lavender fields of France, the cloud-berries of the Urals with their little orange petals, the feather grasses of the pampas swaying like dancers.

He will miss these things.

He considers the act, then its consequences.

He will make it clean.

There will be no fuss.

He turns and gives a final glance at the map. He has studied so many maps. He thinks of the water bearers of the world, almost always women, hauling their jerry jars to the river or the lake. His mind is like those jars, worn and dusty, scarred by use, but still able to hold its heavy store of memory.

And yet there is something he forgot.

He walks to the small desk in the corner, opens the notebook, and tears out the top sheet. He folds it carefully, without hurry, then sinks it deep into his pocket.

It is disturbance you must look for, the old trackers told him. Not prints. Not trails. But disturbance in the spear grass, a sense of reeds askew. Those will lead you to the one you seek.

He looks about the room for any hint of such disturbance, finds none, and with that assurance, walks to the door, then passes through it, and moves out onto the lawn. He feels the breeze whose movement he had sensed before, cool upon his face, a pressure on his shirt, a gentle movement in his hair.

He hears a bird call, glances up, and sees a gull as it crosses the lower sky. When was it he first saw the sunbirds of the Sudan, their sun-streaked, iridescent feathers?

He shakes his head. It doesn't matter now.

He draws down his gaze and with a steady stride makes his way to the boat. It is heavy, and he has been weakened, though less by his final work than by this final decision.

But the decision has been made.

The boat is weighty but he pulls it into the water. What was the lightest he ever knew? Oh yes, it was made of bulrushes. And what was the other word for bulrushes? Oh yes, it was **tule**.

The boat rocks violently as he climbs in, but he rights himself, grabs an oar, and pushes out into the water.

How far to go?

The center of the pond. Far enough that he will appear small and indistinct in the distance so that his sister cannot tell what he is doing, nor get to him before he can complete the task.

Seventy feet from shore now. Perhaps eighty. He has not rowed in a long time. Even now his arms are aching. But that will be over soon. He knows that he has grown weak in the Russian wastes, but he is surprised by just how weak he is. Or has his secret always worked upon him like a withering disease?

One hundred feet out from shore.

Enough.

He takes the folded paper from his pocket and sinks it into the water.

Done.

He sits quietly for a moment, then with his old resolve, he begins the process. First he rolls up his sleeves. For a few seconds he pumps his fist, squeezing in and out. The blue veins rise as if to his command.

He leans forward and picks up the knife. Its serrated edge will hurt, but he has all his life known pain.

No mess.

No fuss.

He holds one arm over the pale yellow port side and with a single slice opens up his vein. The blood flows down his hand and along his fingers in a steady stream that reddens the water below them. He brings the other arm and hangs it over the water, takes the knife with his bloodied hand and makes a second motion.

It is done.

At least the first phase.

Now there is only the will to wait.

He releases the knife and watches it splash into the red water.

The wait is not long.

Soon he begins to lean forward as life flows out of him. He will think no more of sunbirds and bulrushes.

Finally, he droops over the port side, his arms now deep in the water.

Seconds later he is gone.

The wait was not long, but its solitariness is unimaginable.

Oh, if I had but been there, my dear friend.

Oh, if I had but been there in the boat with you.

Knowing what I know now.

PART I

THE TORTURES OF CUENCA

CHAPTER 1

There is no more haunting story than that of an unsolved crime, Julian had once written, but solutions, I was to discover, can be haunting, too.

To know the world, one must travel it in the third-class carriage, and I had little doubt that that was surely how Julian had come to know it. He was one of those for whom the usual comforts meant nothing. If the water was yellow, the walls laced with mold, if the sink was ringed in rust, or even if there was no sink at all, if the mosquito net was ripped and the cloaca full, it was the same to Julian. The deeds that drew him were the darkest that we know, and he'd pursued them with the urgency of a lover.

From his first trip abroad, I'd had little doubt that he would remain an expatriate all his life, which made it all the stranger that, in the end – that terrible, lonely end – he had died at home.

Now my thought, growing more insistent by the hour, was how I might have saved him.

'He was wizened,' his sister, Loretta, said to me. 'If you can say that about a man who was only in his fifties.' She took a sip from her drink. 'It's hard to imagine that he's gone.'

We sat at a small square table in a quiet corner of what was still called an actors' bar, though now it catered mostly to Broadway tourists. I presumed that Loretta had chosen it because it returned her to the days when she'd struggled to be an actress, trudged that dreary path from audition to audition until rejection's blade had whittled away the last of that youthful hope. I'd seen her in two productions, both pretty far off Broadway. In the first, she'd played the object of desire in *A View from the Bridge*. In the second, the title role in *Hedda Gabler*. In both cases her talent had impressed me, especially the uneasy balance of pathos and simmering violence she'd brought to Hedda, which had also frightened me a little. She'd had every right to succeed on the stage, but hadn't. Watching her now, I decided that there was perhaps no ash quite so cold as the one left by an unrealized ambition, particularly an artistic one. But then, I thought, there is no such thing as a truly fulfilled ambition, is there? At twenty-three, Alexander the Great had bemoaned the fact that there were no more worlds for him to conquer. It seemed to me that we were all like poor thwarted Alexander, unsatisfied in one way or another. Some were dissatisfied with their choice of careers, others with their choice of mates, still others with their lack of money. My chief dissatisfactions were

4

childlessness and widowhood, to which had now been added my failure to save my one true friend.

'Some people, when they die, bring more than themselves to an end,' Loretta said. 'The books I copyedit now are mostly happy talk. Tips on how to avoid thinking about the only things Julian ever thought about.' She shook her head. 'Half the time, I feel like a whore.' Her smile carried the dogged effort of a lost cause. 'Have you seen the new rewrite of *The Great Gatsby* for teen readers? It's sixty-seven pages long, and it seems that Fitzgerald intended the book to have a happy ending.'

She was in her early fifties now, but her eyes were as sparkling as they'd ever been. In Egypt, Flaubert had encountered a woman whose exquisite beauty was marred only by that one bad incisor. I could find no such flaw in Loretta. She wore the beauty of her maturity as she had worn the beauty of her youth – easily, almost unconsciously, and with breathtaking grace. Time would do what time always does, but there would be no Botox in Loretta's future, no facelifts. She would move through the remaining seasons of her life as easily as she moved through the stages of a single day.

'Julian was an artist,' Loretta said firmly.

An artist, yes, but with a curious obsession.

I thought of how he'd spent his last six years following the Russian serial killer Andrei Chikatilo's path through countless dismal towns, sleeping in the same railway stations, eating black bread and cheese, eyeing the vagabond children who had been Chikatilo's prey, *becoming* him, as Julian always seemed to do while writing about such villains.

'The last book really took it out of him,' Loretta added. 'But it wasn't just exhaustion.'

'What was it?'

She thought a moment, then said, 'He was like a man in a locked room, trying to get out.'

Perhaps, but even so, Julian's mood hadn't troubled me, because I'd always thought that studying atrocities and detailing the outrages of serial killers would be a labor he would at some point seek to escape. Perhaps, at last, he was breaking free of all that, for there were times, such as when he described a sunset on the Atlas Mountains or a rainstorm in the Carpathians, when his love of the world cut through the darkness and he seemed, at least briefly, to soar above the grim nature of his subject matter. At such moments his spirits would lift, only to be dragged down again, as if by some invisible weight. Oh, what can you do, I had often thought, what can do you do with such a man?

'I had no inkling he might do what he did,' Loretta said.

Nor had I, though only a week before, Julian had canceled a trip into the city. Two days after that, Loretta had called to say that he'd been unusually agitated. For that reason, she'd been surprised when she'd seen him calmly make his way toward the

6

small pond that bordered the house, even more surprised that he'd climbed into the little boat the two of them had used as a child, and rowed away. A few minutes later she'd noticed the boat drifting toward shore with Julian leaning over the port side, his bare arms dangling in the water.

'I knew instantly that he was dead,' Loretta said. 'And that he'd done it to himself.' She took another sip of wine. 'But why?'

The tone of her question was quite different from any I'd heard in her voice before. She gave off the air of a person going through someone else's old papers, looking not for deeds or insurance policies but for the small journal with its cracked leather binding and rusty latch – an item of no value whatsoever, save that it was there, written on some faded page, that the dreadful secret lay.

But had Julian actually had any such dreadful secret? I had no idea. We'd lived very different lives, after all: he, the expatriate writer; I, the stay-at-home literary critic, whose primary gift was in dissecting novels that, no matter how awful, were certainly beyond my own creative powers. He'd settled in Paris, if you could call the apartment in Pigalle that he rarely used his permanent residence. But even when I'd met him in Paris, or London, or Madrid, he'd had the air of a man briefly stranded in a railway station. For Julian, the road was home, and he'd trudged down some of the worst ones on earth, writing articles about plague and famine and holocaust in addition to his five books. And his writing had been exquisite. Like Orpheus, he had brought music into hell, and like him, he had died in a world that no longer wished to hear it.

'I sometimes think of him as a fictional character,' Loretta said. 'An immortal detective in pursuit of some equally immortal arch villain.' Something in her eyes shattered. 'But he will be forgotten, won't he?'

'Probably,' I answered frankly.

'Each book was like a nail in his coffin,' Loretta said. 'Even that first one.'

She meant *The Tortures of Cuenca*, Julian's study of a fabled injustice that had been committed in Spain, in 1911. He'd never really returned after that book, save for short periods, during which he would search for his next book or article. After *Cuenca*, the pattern was always the same. Go away. Write. Return. Go away. Write. Return. I could not recall just how many times he'd left the Montauk farmhouse he and Loretta had inherited, then come back to it out of nowhere and with no advance word, like a body washed up onshore.

'He was already planning the next one, you know,' Loretta said. 'In a way, that's what threw me off, because Julian was the same as always. Sitting in the sunroom, planning his next move.'

'Planning it how?' I asked.

'By studying a map,' Loretta answered. 'That's how he always began working on his next piece, by studying a map of the country he was going to. Then he'd start reading books about the place.'

As a result of that research, there'd always been considerable sweep to Julian's work, as his friendlier reviewers had sometimes pointed out. No crime floated freely. It was always part of a larger disorder, one fiber sprung from a hideous cloth. In a passage on Henri Landru, for example, he'd managed to connect the serial killer's murders in Paris to the nearby slaughter on the Somme, and this while writing a curious meditation on one of Gilles de Rais's blood-spattered minions.

'It was going the way it always had, the circle of Julian's life,' Loretta said. 'Then suddenly he was dead.'

I felt an inner jolt, not only at Julian's death, but at my own inevitable demise and everyone else's, the wheel of time, that ceaselessly revolving door that ushers you out and brings the one behind you in, life itself, the killer we can't catch.

'I keep imagining myself in the boat with him,' I said. 'I'm completely silent, but I'm searching for what I could say to him that would change his mind.'

'Do you find the words?' Loretta asked.

I shook my head. 'No.'

Loretta cocked her head slightly, the way she did when an idea hit her. 'Do you suppose he had a wife somewhere? Or a lover? Someone we should notify?'

The question took me off guard. I'd never considered such a thing.

'I would certainly doubt it,' I answered, though it was conceivable that a rootless man might eventually have sunk secret roots.

'I always hoped that he had someone,' Loretta said. 'Some whore in Trieste, if nothing more. Just someone he was growing old with, someone who might comfort him.'

'Then perhaps you should believe he did,' I said.

Loretta's eyes flashed. 'Is that what gets you through the night, Philip?' she asked. 'Choosing to believe something, whether it's true or not?'

'In one way or another, Loretta, isn't that what gets everyone through the night?' I asked.

'You don't think he ever fell in love?' Loretta asked.

'No, I don't think he ever fell in love,' I answered, and again felt the pain of losing my wife three years before, a hole in my heart I could find no way to heal.

Loretta reached for her drink but only stared into it. 'It was Argentina,' she said, her tone quite thoughtful. 'The map Julian was looking at the day he died. Maybe he was thinking about that trip the two of you made down there.'

'That was thirty years ago, Loretta,' I said. 'Why would he have been thinking about that?'

She released a breath that was like a tired breeze, driven too far over rough terrain. 'Like the winds from off the Karst,' as Julian had once written in one of his college essays, 'thirsting for the Adriatic.' Such had been his style in the high days of his youth, his language predictably stilted, cluttered with allusions to places he'd never been. So different from what his work later became, those emaciated sentences, so darkly spare.

'A map of Argentina,' Loretta said softly, almost to herself. 'Do you think he was on the trail of something down there?'

'It's possible, I suppose.'

But on the trail of what? I wondered, though there seemed no way to know in what direction Julian was heading when he decided to go to the pond instead.

'By the way,' I said, 'have you read the manuscript Julian brought back?'

'No,' Loretta said as if my question had only drawn her deeper into Julian's mystery. 'He cut out their eyes, you know, that Russian horror. And that's not all, of course.'

'Yes, I know what Chikatilo did,' I said with a wave of the hand.

Loretta's attention drifted toward the window. 'We were in Rome, Julian and I. Just children. We were in that little piazza, the Campidoglio. He said it looked perfectly square because Michelangelo had designed it to look perfectly square by widening it here and elongating it there. It wasn't actually square at all. It was a masterful trick of perspective. "It's distortion that creates perfection, Loretta," he said.'

11

She turned toward me and I saw a subtle shift in the mosaic of this woman, and with that shift I realized just how deeply Loretta had loved Julian, and that she always would. He'd been the older brother who had taken time with her, who had offered her his thoughts, his feelings, and then, for some reason she would never know, had chosen to remove himself for years on end, one of life's true vagabonds.

'Julian was good,' she said softly. 'That's what I'll miss. His goodness.'

I felt a scuttling movement in the place where my youth lay like a discarded old traveling case, timeworn and battered, layered in gray dust. I glanced at my watch. 'I'm sorry, but I have to look in on my father.'

Loretta nodded. 'How is he?'

For the first time in a long time, I felt an uneasy loosening in the grip I was careful to maintain upon myself.

'Fading,' I said. I looked toward the window, where the rain had not let up. 'Bad night.' I rose, grabbed my coat, and drew it on. 'Well, I'll see you at the service on Friday.'

Loretta stared at her now-empty glass. 'Do you think you knew him, Philip?'

'Not enough to have saved him, evidently,' I answered. 'Which means I'll always be silent in that boat.'

She looked up at me. 'I guess we all leave a trail of little pebbles scattered on the forest floor,' she said. 'But I'll always wonder where those pebbles would have led to with Julian.'

I had no answer to this question, nor ever expected to have one. She saw my retreat, and so offered her own admittedly inadequate one.

'Just to more pebbles, I suppose,' she added with a small, sad smile.

I gathered up my coat. 'I'm afraid so.'

I expected this to be the end of it, but something behind Loretta's eyes darkened. 'I'm silent in that boat, too, you know,' she said.

The feeling I saw rise in her at that moment was striking in its subdued passion. She had worked at home for years and years, while nursing Colin through his long dying, and yet, for all that, something still sparkled in her, a fierce curiosity.

'And if I never find those words, I feel that I'll live a bit like poor Masha,' she said. 'Dressed in black, in mourning for my life.'

They were dramatic words, of course, but the moment was dramatic, too, I thought, and in its aftermath, as I stepped outside and hailed a cab, it struck me that both for her and for me, what she'd said was true. A man we'd both loved had taken his own life. He had done so alone and had given neither of us a chance to stop him.

There are times when the very earth seems poised to move against us, and at that instant, I recalled Julian at Two Groves, playing croquet with my father, while Loretta and I looked on. He'd hit the ball with both verve and confidence, which had given his game a dead-on accuracy that even then I suspected he would later apply to whatever he chose to do. Upon his inevitable victory, he had leaped into a shimmering summer air that had seemed to embrace him.

How, from so bright a beginning, I wondered, had the world conspired to bring him to so black an end?

CHAPTER 2

There are some bridges you cannot cross again, and so your only choice is simply to make the best of the shore you have chosen. And so, in the taxi, heading toward my father's apartment, I concentrated on my life's many satisfactions. The smaller ones, like good food, and the larger ones, like the years I'd had with my wife – comforts that Julian had not found in his youth and later chose not to seek.

For some reason, these thoughts brought to mind a passage from one of Julian's books, his description of Henri Landru. He'd written that the famous French serial killer had begun to talk as his date with the guillotine grew near, even going so far as to make a crude drawing of the kitchen where the bodies had been burned. Death's approach had turned him quite gossipy, Julian said, so that in the last days, Landru had been less the condemned man silently brooding on his crimes than a washerwoman chatting in the market square.

Not so Julian, I thought now, and instantly imagined him alone on the sunporch with his map of Argentina and God only knew what grim thoughts in his mind. Had he, in his last hours, inexplicably returned to the first tragedy that touched him? And if so, why?

There could be no answer to these questions, of course, so rather than pursue a fruitless trail, I drifted through the mundane details of Julian's early life.

He was born upper-middle-class, his father a State Department official who'd been one of my father's closest friends. His mother had died giving birth to Loretta, and after that Julian and his sister had been overseen by a series of nannies. By the time Julian and Loretta were in grade school, James Wells had retired because of a heart condition. A few years later, he'd bought the Montauk farmhouse, in which he had died at age fifty-five.

That death had devastated Julian, and something of his lost father settled over him for many months, a lingering presence, like the ghost of Hamlet's father, which is exactly how Julian once described it. In the wake of his father's death, he seemed ever more determined to make a mark in life. Even so, the space his father had occupied remained empty, a void never filled. 'A little boy needs a hero,' he once said to me, though without adding what I knew was on his mind, the fact that with his father gone, he'd lost that hero in his own life.

A cautious man, Julian's father had left his two children, Julian, fifteen, and Loretta, twelve, well fixed, mostly by means of a substantial life insurance policy, the proceeds from which had retired

16

the Montauk mortgage. A bachelor uncle had promptly moved into the house and from there attempted to assume the role of father. Boarding school had taken up the remaining slack. College tuitions had later absorbed what was left of the inheritance, so that by the time Julian graduated from Columbia and Loretta from Barnard, only the Montauk house remained.

The surprise in all this was that despite the loss of his father and the rather haphazard and emotionally flat nature of his later upbringing, Julian had emerged with so solid, even sterling, a personal character. He had not received the intense moral education my father had provided for me – his many lectures on charity as the greatest of all virtues, his compassion for the poor and the disinherited, his deathless hope that the meek might one day inherit some portion of the earth. And yet, Julian appeared to have taught himself those very lessons, so that by the time he began to spend summers with me, he seemed already primed to receive the finishing touches of my father's table talk – that is to say, his ancestral tales of men who'd fought under the banner of some universal goodness.

But why was I recounting Julian's personal history? I wondered. What good would it do now?

None whatsoever, of course, and so I had no explanation for this bend in my mind, except that something in my latest exchange with Loretta had set me to considering Julian's life in the way a

17

detective might, as if he were a mystery whose disparate clues I was now trying to puzzle out. No, not a detective exactly, I decided, more like a writer seized by a mysterious purpose: Charles Latimer in *A Coffin for Dimitrios* listening as Colonel Haki describes the nefarious career of a strange Greek swindler, wondering what he really was, this dead Dimitrios, and as he listens, growing slowly, haltingly, and against his own better judgment, ever more determined to find out.

I thought again of the summers Julian had spent at our home in Virginia while Loretta either attended a theater camp in upstate New York or stayed at her aunt's house in Connecticut. Those had been hot, languid days at Two Groves, days of fishing in the pond, canoeing down the river, reading together in the study, or listening as my father talked, mostly to Julian, about having a career in the State Department, one he expected to be very different from his own, Julian more what he called 'the James Bond type' than he had ever been.

And this was true enough. There'd been a genuinely dashing quality to Julian. It was easy to imagine him swinging a polo mallet or leaping hedges on a black stallion. He had an ear for classical music and an eye for painting, but even these less muscular attributes did not detract from how very male he was. Both men and women loved him, and that, as my father once noted, cannot be said of many men. Sometimes he reminded me of

Sebastian in *Brideshead Revisited*, equally favored by the stars. But Sebastian had lost himself to drink and thus lived his life in a blur of attenuated afternoons. Julian on the other hand was strictly spit-and-polish, ready to work and quick to pitch in, a young man who drank very little and whom I often found alone in our orchard, his back pressed against the trunk of a pecan tree, studying, it seemed, the crazy patchwork of the limbs.

From my great store of memories, I suddenly drew out the one of Julian visiting me at Princeton. It was a memory that lifted me, as if on the swell of some elegiac refrain, then drew me down again like sand in a wave, so that I was once again seated on my dormitory bed, alone, reading, of all things, *A Sentimental Journey*.

'Sterne hated Smollett, you know,' Julian informed me as he swung a chair around and sat down before me. 'He said his travel writing was all "spleen and jaundice."'

Tall and slender, he wore dark, well-pressed pants and a white shirt with both sleeves rolled up to just below the elbow. He'd done his share of sports at school, but what he gave off, more than health and raw competitiveness, was that confident American sense of not only getting what you want, but of getting it easily and, in a way, deservedly, as if it had been awaiting you all along.

'Are you really going to major in English, Philip?' he asked.

I turned to face him. 'What's wrong with studying English?'

'Nothing at all,' Julian answered. 'But your life will be rather sedentary, don't you think?'

And so it had turned out, I thought now, my life just the sort Julian had never contemplated for himself any more than he would have contemplated the darker one that had come to him after Argentina.

After Argentina.

Had it begun there, I asked myself, the downward spiral of Julian's life?

The question brought up one of Julian's abiding themes, the fact that in each life there are confluences, currents, and undercurrents, and that in some swim the Graces – Splendor, Mirth, and Good Cheer – while in others there are surely monsters. So it was in much of Julian's writing, a chance encounter, a hastily spoken word, some idle conversation that might seem of no importance but which, for better or worse, changes a life forever. In *The Tortures of Cuenca*, it is the mundane selling of a lamb that ignites suspicions that ultimately lead to a great crime.

Crime, I repeated in my mind, then cut off any further thought along such lines as the corner of West End and Seventy-eighth Street came into view.

'That awning there,' I said. 'The blue one.'

The cab drifted forward a few more yards, then stopped. I paid and got out. The building's uniformed doorman nodded as he approached. 'How's your father?' he asked.

20

'Holding his own,' I answered.

'Give him my regards.'

The elevator was old and elegant, all dark paneling and brass, and in that way it struck me as oddly military, a device meant to convey the high command to some tower from which a general could survey the field. Curiously, this thought again returned me to Julian. This time it was his description of Waterloo, the day we'd walked the field together under the unblinking eyes of the Lion Monument. As we walked, he'd recounted the descriptions various travelers had written a few days after the battle, the field littered with bits of white paper, the stationery of two armies. They'd found blood-spattered love letters and letters to children, Julian told me, letters written by hands now severed by flashing sabers and cannon fire, a juxtaposition of images that suggested what his later writing would be like, slaughters, sometimes massive ones, described with a haunting poignancy.

This flash of memory made me briefly wonder if I were becoming a character out of Proust, poor melancholic Swann biting into a madeleine or tripping on an uneven paving stone and by that taste and brief imbalance propelled backward to times past. If so, I felt the need to shake it off, because at a certain point memory becomes a beach strewn with landmines, all life's many losses buried in those sands.

★   ★   ★

21

My father was seated by the window, peering down at the rain-soaked street when I stepped into the living room. If he heard the jangle of keys as I entered the apartment, he gave no sign of it. His body remained still, his shoulders squared, his head upright, his eyes flashing with their customary fire.

'You're tardy, Philip,' he said.

Tardy was one of those quaint words my father refused to jettison. To do so, he said, would be to surrender language to the whims of mere novelty. It was important to keep old things, he insisted, because it was through them alone that new things could be judged. He said this without rancor, and nothing in his demeanor suggested the crankiness of some old geezer bemoaning the loss of the five-cent cigar. Yet he was someone who fancied himself a defender of ancient values, and he'd often spoken of such things to Julian during those evenings when the two of them smoked cigars and drank port in the library at Two Groves, my father in full Socratic pose, despite the fact that he was hardly a man of great intellect.

But the wish to be wise is almost as valuable in a man as wisdom itself, and so I'd always admired my father's goodness. Julian, more than anyone, had known the depth of my love for him. Once, as the two of us had walked the grounds of Two Groves, he'd slung a brotherly arm over me. 'You're lucky to feel the way you do about your father, Philip,' he said to me. 'A man needs to revere someone.' Years later, in Salzburg, he talked about Mozart's contempt for lesser talents: 'A man with no one to revere, Julian said, is a man alone.' At that moment, he seemed to consider such loneliness the worst of fates, a sentence he would not have imposed upon the vilest man on earth. And yet, at times, I thought now, he had seemed to impose that very loneliness upon himself.

'So why were you late?' my father asked.

'I was with Loretta,' I explained. 'We met for a drink.'

My father nodded softly. 'So sad about Julian. Please give her my best at the service.'

He had decided not to attend the upcoming memorial, and given his many aches and pains, I didn't press the issue, since I knew that his arthritis would make the ride to Montauk difficult for him.

'Did you hear what happened today?' my father asked. 'More bombings in Europe. It's the price of colonialism. You should never invade another people's country if you don't expect to be invaded in return.'

My father had toiled his life away as a State Department bureaucrat, his eyes forever glancing wistfully at the oversized globe he'd hauled from office to office during his long tenure in the old gray C Street building rightly situated, he'd once joked, in an area of the capital known as Foggy Bottom.

'When the Soviet Union fell, I thought we might have a few years of actual peace,' he added. He shook

23

his head in grim frustration. 'But humanity isn't made for peace. It finds a hundred ways to keep itself riled up.'

He'd hoped to devote his life to peace, an ambition that had foundered on the banks of Foggy Bottom at least in part because as a young man he'd made the mistake of joining a few ultraliberal organizations, though that was but the first of many problems that had stymied his career. Succinctly put, he'd had a warm heart during a Cold War, and for that reason he'd been shuttled from desk to desk, his hopes for an appointment that would give him genuine authority forever thwarted by his own fierce feeling that the human interest was larger than the national interest, a view that had won him many friends among the radical reformers of the Third World, but none in Washington.

It was a failure that struck deep, all the more so given that his own forefathers had been robust men of affairs, both soldiers and diplomats. Portraits of those men now lined the walls of his apartment, men in uniforms and formal dress who with equal courage had faced bullets on the field and bullying at the negotiating table.

Given the blighted nature of his career, I'd assumed that retirement would be a good thing for my father, but he hadn't taken to it very well. Certainly, he had not wanted to move to New York, but the last of his old friends had died, and he'd been left alone in his Tidewater house. At last he'd acquiesced to my repeated entreaties for him to move north, where he could enjoy the many diversions of the city, along with the company of his son. Nor did he seem to regret this move, though there were times when the pall of loneliness came over him and he stared out at a skyline he probably found as foreign as the minarets of Cairo.

'So how are you feeling?' I asked.

'Good enough,' my father answered.

I glanced at the array of pill containers that sprouted like sickly orange growths from the top of the small, wooden table beside my father's chair. It's not that we grow old, I thought, but that we grow old in decline and discomfort, and these hardships are made worse by the awareness that nothing will improve. No coming days will dawn brighter than the last that dawned, and this sorrow is further deepened by a fear of death – one that I could on occasion see in my father's eyes. Those same eyes had some years before begun to fail, so he had given up reading spy novels and Westerns for watching movies of the same ilk, John Wayne and Gary Cooper the unlikely heroes of his waning years.

'Loretta and I talked about Julian, of course,' I said. 'She thought he was already planning his next book.'

'Already at work on the next one?' my father asked. 'I thought he'd just come back from Russia.'

'He had, but rest was never Julian's thing,' I said.

'So, once he'd finished the book on Chikatilo, I suppose he just began to research the next one.'

'Chikatilo?' my father asked. 'Who is that?'

'A Russian serial killer.'

My father shook his head. 'I don't know how Julian lived with such people in his head.'

'For some people, bad things are alluring, I suppose,' I said. 'Chekhov went all the way to Sakhalin, and Robert Louis Stevenson—'

'Well, it's unhealthy, if you ask me,' my father interrupted with a quick wave of his hand. 'Unhealthy to sink into that mire.' He leaned forward and massaged one of his knees. 'I remember that first summer when Julian came to stay with us. We fished all day, remember?'

I nodded. 'Loretta stayed with an aunt that summer. In Chicago.'

'But Julian came to Two Groves,' my father said. His spirit lifted on a memory. 'We took long walks in the orchard.'

It was a fine house, to say the least, set upon substantial acreage, but hardly the Tara of *Gone with the Wind* that its grand title suggested. Still, Julian had made considerable sport of Two Groves before his visit there. 'We come from houses that have addresses,' he would tell some recent acquaintance, 'but Philip here comes from TWO GROVES!'

'Julian saved your life that summer,' my father added.

I saw him dive cleanly into the water, then swim furiously toward me. I'd tried to swim too far and

26

had exhausted myself. Had Julian not been there, I would most certainly have drowned. Over the years, my father had mentioned this incident many times. Julian, of course, never had.

'Do you think he would have risen to the top at the State Department?' I asked.

'Probably not,' my father answered. On that word, his mood abruptly soured. 'Well, I should be off to bed now, Philip.'

He rose with the help of a cane that was itself a part of his regalia, dark wood, with a brass eagle's head grip. Using it, he stood very erect, and in that proud stance, made his way slowly across the room, I at his side, but careful not to extend my hand or offer any unnecessary physical support. That would come at some point, I knew, but not yet, and as long as my father could make his way without assistance, I let him do so.

We were halfway down the corridor when he stopped and nodded toward a photograph of his father in his doughboy uniform.

'Julian noticed that picture,' he said. 'It was hanging in the library at Two Groves, and he asked me if my father had ever killed a man. I said he probably had, but that he'd been an artillery officer in the Great War, so he probably never saw the people he killed. I remember that Julian said he thought it must be quite different to kill close up, looking your victim directly in the eye.'

'He described just that sort of close-up murder once,' I said. 'It's in *The Tortures of Cuenca*. He has a sister imagine the killing of her brother, how the murderer must have actually felt her brother's dying breath. On his face, I mean. I remember the phrase he used. He called it "the last moist breath of life."'

'Moist,' my father whispered. 'How would Julian have known that a last breath is moist?'

He moved forward again before he stopped, turned back and looked at me, a glance that alerted me that I'd unaccountably remained behind.

'Are you all right, Philip?' he asked.

'Yes, why?' I asked.

'You look odd, that's all.'

I shook my head. 'Not at all,' I assured him. 'I was just thinking of Julian, how deeply he sank into the crimes he described.'

'Julian had a lot of feeling,' my father said, 'but too much of it was morbid.'

He turned and made his way into the bedroom, I now at this side. He was already in his pajamas, and so, after taking off his robe, he eased himself into the bed, all of this done without my assistance, but under my watchful eye.

My mind was still on Julian. 'He was like Mephistopheles,' I said. 'He took hell with him wherever he went.'

My father waved his hand by way of dismissing such literary notions. He had always been impatient with my bookish talk, bookish ways, bookish life, so different from the one he'd sought but never achieved.

'It's a pity about Julian,' he said softly and sadly. 'No wife. No children. A wasted life in some ways.' He shook his head at the hopeless extent of that waste. 'Darkness was the only thing he knew.'

CHAPTER 3

A man is made by the questions he asks, and I found myself increasingly questioning my father's statement regarding Julian, that he had known only darkness. For I could remember my friend in the bright days of his youth, when he'd gone full speed at life. Like my father, he'd wished to change the world for the better. He'd known about history's many horrors, of course, but he hadn't focused on them. Life had seemed manageable to him then, its evils visible because they were so large: poverty, oppression, and the like. It was against these forces he would take up arms, a young Quixote. He'd been naive, of course, but that had made him genuine. He'd known that he was good, and this had been enough to make him happy.

When the best man you'd ever known, the one you'd loved the most, and of all the people you'd ever known, the one who'd had the greatest capacity for true achievement, when such a man later trudges to a pond, climbs into a boat, rows a hundred feet out into the water, rolls up his sleeves, and cuts his wrists, are you not called upon to ask what you might have said to him in that boat, how you might have saved him?

And if you do not ask this question, are you not, yourself, imperiled?

I would later consider the unsettling tremor I'd felt when I asked myself those very questions. It was as if I'd suddenly felt the bite of a blade, the warmth of my own blood now spilling down my arm.

Outside the building, the doorman was leaning against the wall, smoking a cigarette. 'Rain's stopped,' he said.

I stepped from beneath the awning and looked into a quickly clearing sky. There were wisps of dispersing clouds, and here and there the flicker of a star, a rare sight in Manhattan.

'Yes, it's quite nice now,' I said. 'I think I'll walk.'

'They've already warned me,' the doorman whispered with a sly wink and something vaguely sneering in his voice.

'Warned you?' I asked as if he'd just heard a sinister aside.

'About me smoking,' the doorman explained. 'The board don't like it when I smoke.'

'Oh,' I said.

He laughed. 'But I do it out in the open, so the union says I can smoke if I want to.'

'Yes, of course,' I said. 'Well, good night.'

I walked to Broadway, then turned south, a route I'd taken many times, so the sights of this section of the world's longest street were familiar to me.

And yet I felt that something had been minutely altered, and that this change had occurred in some part of me that I'd thought impenetrable since my wife's death, a wound I'd covered with a thick scar tissue that nothing had pierced until now.

Clearly Julian's death, the dread manner and heartbreaking loneliness of it, had opened me up both to questions and to memories, one of which came to me now.

We were in Greece, where Julian had come across the case of Antonis Daglis, the otherwise nondescript truck driver who had murdered several prostitutes. For Julian, such ordinary murderers were of no interest. Tracing their crimes, he said one day while we drank ouzo in an Athens taverna, was like following a shark through murky waters, dully recording that it ate this fish, then that one. It was evil he was after, I could tell, some core twist in the scheme of things.

In the end, Julian found nothing to write about in Greece, but while in the country, we wandered through various remote areas, notably the Mani. He was reading the great travel writer Patrick Fermor at the time, and one night, as we tented on a rocky cliff overlooking the Aegean, he told me about a funeral Fermor had attended in the same area. At the funeral, the dead man's soul had been commended to the Virgin Mary in strict Christian fashion, but a coin had also been placed in his coffin as payment to Charon for ferrying the dead man's soul across the Styx. To this incident Julian added a comment that now echoed through my mind: *All excavations lead to hell.*

Had Julian been clawing toward some fiery pit during those last days in the sunroom? I wondered.

This question, along with the memory that had just summoned it, added to the feeling of unease that was steadily gathering around me, and which I experienced as a shift in the axis of my life or, more precisely, as a faint, somewhat ghostly color added to a spectrum. It was as if Julian's death now called my own life into question, threw it off balance, so that I had to confront the stark fact of how little I had known the man I thought I'd known the most.

On that thought, another memory came to me, this time of Julian and me walking in Grosvenor Square in London. Julian had suddenly stopped and pointed up ahead. 'That's where Adlai Stevenson died,' he said.

He went on to tell me that Stevenson had been strolling with an acquaintance at the time, feeling old, talking of the war. 'How many secrets must have died with him,' Julian said.

Had secrets died with Julian, too?

I thought again of the agitation Loretta had noticed in him and that she'd previously described: Julian sleepless, pacing, a man who seemed not so much depressed as hounded. In every way, until that last moment, she told me, Julian had appeared less a man determined to die than one ceaselessly searching for a way to live.

I reached Lincoln Center a few minutes later and, still curiously unready to go directly to my apartment, sat down on the rim of the circular fountain and watched as the last of those bound for the symphony or the theater made their way across the plaza. It was here I'd met Julian a week after we'd graduated from college. He'd already sent in an application to work at the State Department, and I'd expected him to tell me a little more about the ground-level job he hoped to get, but instead he said, 'I want to go somewhere, Philip. Out of the country. And not Europe. Someplace that feels different.'

'Where do you have in mind?'

Without the slightest hesitation, he said, 'Your father suggested Argentina. He said I should see a country where the political situation is dangerous. Get a feel for what it's like to live in a place where everything is at risk.'

I was, of course, aware that Argentina was still in the midst of very dark political repression, and for that reason, if for no other, it hadn't been on my 'must-see' list.

'I'm not sure going to Argentina is a good thing,' I said. 'Or even a safe one.'

'Do you always want to play it safe, Philip?'

'Yes,' I answered.

'Oh, come on,' Julian said. 'You have a month before you start your job.'

34

I remained unconvinced.

'Philip, for God's sake,' Julian said. 'Don't measure out your life in coffee spoons.'

His allusion to poor, pathetic J. Alfred Prufrock was clearly meant to shock me into acquiescing to his idea of an Argentine adventure, but now, when I recalled that moment, it was Julian's energy and self-confidence rather than my hesitation that struck me, the sense that he could walk through a hail of bullets and emerge unscathed. He was rather like Aiden Pyle in *The Quiet American*, young and inexperienced in anything beyond the well-ordered life of a privileged American. Julian Wells, conqueror of worlds, shielded by his many gifts, destined for greatness. Like his country, invulnerable.

How quickly all that had changed. All of it. After Argentina.

I knew that in a novel it would be a woman who caused this change. But Julian hadn't fallen in love with the woman we'd met there. Even so, her sudden disappearance had turned our Argentine holiday into a bitter experience, one I'd long ago managed to put behind me, but which had lingered in Julian, so that over the years he often returned to it in our conversation. I thought of the map he'd laid on the little table in the sunroom. In his last hours had he been thinking of Argentina again?

I rose from the fountain and made my way to my apartment.

It was in a prewar building with high ceilings,

one of the few such buildings whose upper floors still provided a view of Central Park. Once there, I dropped into a chair and let my gaze roam among the shelves of books that stood across from me until my attention was drawn to where Julian's books were arranged chronologically, beginning with *The Tortures of Cuenca*.

I drew the book from the shelf, opened it, and read the book's dedication: *For Philip, sole witness to my crime.*

The 'crime,' I always thought, was Julian's decision to write about what had happened in Cuenca, an effort I disparaged at the time because I could see no need to retell a story already well known. It would be a *crime* to waste his time on such a book, I told him, advice he'd obviously not taken, and of which his dedication had been meant to remind me.

I'd read this dedication many times, of course, always with a knowing smile, but now it returned me to the brief few days Julian and I had spent together in Cuenca. We'd met in Madrid, where Julian had been living, doing odd jobs, picking up the first of his many languages. We'd then driven around Spain for several days before reaching the town. Our month in Argentina was more than a year behind us by then, but Julian was still laboring under the effects of what he'd experienced there, all of which I'd expected to dissipate in time.

We'd arrived at Cuenca about midday, strolled the town's streets, then taken a table at a small café on the village square. Though a matter of dark renown in Spain, neither of us had ever heard of the crime that had occurred there some seventy years before. As I later discovered, it was briefly mentioned in the guidebook I'd bought in the airport before leaving New York, a book I'd intended to read on the flight but hadn't. In any event, an English-speaking former magistrate had given us the details, an old man who'd claimed to have seen the actual figures in the story – the guards, the prisoners, even the prosecutor.

'No one thought anything about the crime of Cuenca,' he said. 'I mean, that it would take so strange a turn.'

The old man had then gone through the details of what had happened there, a story he told quite well but from which he drew a somewhat banal conclusion.

'So you see, it's quite possible for a person to disappear,' he said.

I glanced at Julian and saw that he was deep in thought. 'Yes,' he said quietly, 'It's quite possible.'

The old man glanced about the village square, his gaze captured by a group of unruly teenagers, all of them speaking in loud voices, heedless of the disturbance they caused.

'*Vivíamos mejor cuando vivía Franco*,' he said, almost to himself, reverting to Spanish. 'We lived better when Franco lived.' With that he rose, bid us a polite good-bye, and left.

Seconds later, I noticed that Julian's attention

was focused on two Guardia Civil lounging at the entrance to one of the town's official buildings, tall and dark, wearing their curiously winged black caps. It was such men as these who'd carried out the tortures of Cuenca, and for a moment Julian simply stared at them quietly.

Then, quite suddenly, a thought appeared to seize him.

'Let's go,' he said.

We paid the bill, then rose, and moved along the town's dusty streets. The evening shade was descending, the first lights coming on.

'Someone once said to me that it's not what a man feels before he first wields the whip,' Julian said as we closed in on the road that let out of the town, 'it's what he feels after it.' He stopped and looked at me. 'But it's really what the person being whipped feels that matters. Guilt is a luxury, Philip.'

I thought of a French painter, James Tissot, the way he'd portrayed the scourging of Christ from different angles, the faces of the men who'd beaten him, obscured in one, revealed in the other.

I described these paintings to Julian, then said, 'The guilt of whipping a great man would be terrible.'

'Or an innocent one,' Julian said.

We continued on, now down the hill and toward the bridge below the town. I kept quiet for a time, but finally made an attempt to lighten the mood that had descended upon us.

'So, when are you coming back to the States?' I asked.

'Never,' Julian answered so abruptly that I wondered if he had only just made that stark decision. 'At least not to live.'

And so there would be no brilliant career? No rising through the ranks of government? He would never be secretary of state? Wild and unreal as those dreams had been, were they truly to be abandoned now?

All of this I voiced in a simple question.

'Are you sure, Julian?'

He stopped and looked at me. 'Yes.'

His gaze had something in it that chilled me, something I expected him to voice, so that it surprised me when he said nothing more as we descended the slope that led to the river and the bridge.

I was still reliving that long-ago moment when the phone rang.

It was Loretta.

'Harry called,' she said.

She meant Harry Gibbons, Julian's editor.

'We've agreed that you should deliver the eulogy at Julian's memorial service,' Loretta said.

She repeated what she'd told me earlier: that it was to be a quiet affair, just a few friends and associates.

'Anyway, Harry has a few things you might want to include,' she added. 'He thought the two of you should discuss it at his office tomorrow afternoon.'

'Okay,' I said.

A pause, then, 'Are you all right, Philip?'

It was the same question my father had asked only an hour or so before, and I gave the same answer. 'I'm fine.'

'You seem so . . . quiet.'

'It's how I grieve, I suppose.'

'Yes, I can see that in you,' Loretta told me. A brief silence, then, 'Well, good night, Philip.'

'Good night.'

I hung up the phone, glanced down at the book in my lap. *The Tortures of Cuenca* with its stark cover, a drawing of the two hapless victims of that crime huddled in the dusty corner of a Spanish prison, shackled hand and foot, waiting, as they eternally would be in this rendering, for the torturer's approach. I'd found the cover quite disturbing and said so to Julian. He'd replied with the tale of Ned Kelly's execution, how the murderous rogue had stood on his Australian gallows, peered down at the reveling crowd, then turned to the hangman and, with a shrug, uttered his last words. 'Such is life.'

I peered into the frightened eyes of these baffled and despairing men a moment longer. Had this, in the end, been Julian's only view of life?

I drew my gaze back to the window. The park beyond it was well lighted, as it had always been, a fact that made me wonder why its reaches seemed so much darker to me now.

Darker to me now?

Heavy-handed, I decided, now in critical judgment of my own last thought. Too much foreshadowing. In a novel, as the last line of a chapter, it would make a wary reader groan.

CHAPTER 4

'When Bernal Díaz first came with Cortés to the central market in Mexico City, he found little bowls of human feces for sale,' Harry said. 'They were used in tanning leather, and Díaz said that the tanners were going around sniffing at these bowls to find the very best of the lot.'

We were sitting in Harry's office on Sixth Avenue. It was spacious with a large window overlooking the street. From such a vantage point, I thought, you could actually think of yourself as a prince of the city, something Harry clearly did.

'That has always been my view of Julian,' Harry continued. 'That he was a very fine craftsman who worked with disgusting materials.'

'Did you ever tell him that?' I asked.

'Of course not,' Harry answered. 'It wouldn't have mattered anyway. After that book about Cuenca, Julian never considered writing anything but that grim stuff.' He shook his head as if in the face of such repellent work. 'Like that African piece.'

'The one he wrote about Swaziland,' I said. 'Yes, that was quite horrifying.'

'No, not that one,' Harry said. 'The one about that French bastard.' He shivered. 'Julian really made you feel the misery in that one.'

He meant Julian's account of Paul Voulet's vicious trek into the African interior.

'But at least that piece had a hero,' Harry added.

This was true, and Julian had written quite beautifully of Lieutenant Colonel Klobb, the man who'd gone after Voulet, trailed him from one outrage to the next, an archipelago of razed villages, slaughtered men, women, and children, some still alive when Voulet hung them from trees low enough for the hyenas to eat their feet. Klobb emerged at last as a paragon of courage and nobility, and his death at the hands of Voulet's men generated a final scene of inevitable tragedy, life having once again turned its back upon the good.

Harry leaned back in his chair and folded his hands over a stomach much rounded by Grey Goose martinis. 'I was quite shocked by Julian's death, of course,' he said. 'I suppose you were, too.'

I nodded.

Harry drew in a somewhat labored breath and leaned back in his chair. 'And so we have seen the last of Julian.'

I found myself wary of closing the book on Julian so decisively, suspecting, as Loretta had, that the map of Argentina suggested a project Julian had been considering, but which he had, in the strongest possible terms, decided to abandon.

'Do you have any idea what his next book was going to be about?' I asked.

'No,' Harry answered. 'He hadn't mentioned any new ideas to me. Why do you ask?'

'He was looking at a map of Argentina,' I said. 'Loretta told me that this was the way he always began to research his next book.'

Harry cocked his head to the right. 'Why would the subject of Julian's next book matter now?'

'I don't know that it matters,' I admitted. 'But he seemed very agitated during those last days, and I can't help wondering what might have been on his mind. I suppose I've come to think of the map as a clue.'

'A clue?' Harry asked. 'You're a critic, Philip, not a detective. Julian's next book went with him.' He clearly saw that I would not be so easily deterred. 'All right, look,' he said, 'I have no idea why Julian was looking at a map of Argentina, but he might have been thinking about a book on Pedro Lopez, the "Monster of the Andes." Three hundred little girls, can you imagine?'

'When did this happen?' I asked.

'It may still be happening,' Harry answered. 'Because this Lopez fiend is still at large. So, maybe – perhaps like you, Philip – Julian had begun to fancy himself a detective, rather than a writer.' He released the breath of someone chronically frustrated by an author whose unprofitable direction

44

had never changed. 'Now, let's forget about what Julian's next book might have been and focus on what will surely be his last one. He worked his ass off on it, after all, and it's going to be published posthumously, so we need to give it a little push.' He looked at me pointedly. 'And try not to make the book sound too grim. People don't like reading dark stuff.'

'That's too bad,' I said. 'Because they're missing something.'

'Really? What?'

'The gravity of life.'

Harry sat back and folded his arms over his chest. 'What's bothering you, Philip? Clearly something is.'

With Harry's question, the actual nature of what was bothering me came clear for the first time.

'It bothers me that there might have been something Julian never told me,' I said, 'and that if he had, I might have saved his life.'

But this was a notion I couldn't prove, and I had a job to do, so when I got back to my apartment, I considered what I could say at Julian's memorial service that might help him matter, at least in the eyes of those in attendance. It would need to be something unique to Julian, or at least some gift he'd used uniquely.

But what?

I didn't know, and so I let my mind drift toward other aspects of my remarks.

I'd need to mention the Russian book, of course.

Harry had been right about that. I knew that people liked anecdotes at memorial services, and this realization allowed my mind to range without limit or direction over the years of my friendship with Julian. But soon I realized that to have such liberty was not altogether helpful in terms of organizing a eulogy, so I began to divide his life into the usual chronological segments: boyhood, early manhood, and the like. This was not helpful either, and in the end I found myself dividing Julian's life into the parts represented by his books. To prepare my talk, I decided to peruse them in hopes of finding something cogent to say about each one. This would allow me to end my talk by giving a plug to the Russian book, Julian's last and as yet unpublished work.

Later that evening, after I'd let time calm my mood a little more, I sat down in my favorite chair and again drew down the first of Julian's books.

The Tortures of Cuenca.

The facts of the crime had been well known long before Julian had written his book, but I'd forgotten most of them, so I took a few minutes to familiarize myself with them again:

On August 21, 1911, a man by the name of José Maria Lopez Grimaldos, twenty-eight, was seen walking alone on the road between Osa de la Vega, a small town, and the nearby village of Tresjuncos in the Spanish province of Cuenca. Grimaldos was known as 'El Cepa,' which means 'the strain,' an

46

odd nickname, all but untranslatable, as Julian had noted, but it evidently referred to the fact that Grimaldos was short and something of a dullard, thus, presumably, a 'strain' on those who knew him.

On that day in August, Grimaldos had been seen on the road that led from the farm of Francisco Ruiz, where he sometimes worked, to his small house. He never got home, however, and the following day, his sister reported his disappearance to the authorities. Her brother had sold a few sheep on the day of his disappearance, she told them, and at least two men would have been aware that he was in possession of the proceeds from that sale. Their names were Valero and Sanchez, and it just so happened that they had often treated Grimaldos quite badly, ridiculing and bullying him. Was it not possible that they had robbed and killed him, too?

An investigation ensued, with other witnesses also focusing the investigators" attention on Valero and Sanchez, but in the absence of Grimaldos's body or any actual proof of his murder, the case had been closed in September of 1911.

There is no more haunting story than that of an unsolved crime.

Thus Julian had declared in the first line of his first book, and thus it had proved for the Grimaldos family.

Julian's account of their relentless struggle for justice was the best part of the book, and as I read

47

it again, I realized that it was there that Julian had found the beating heart of his narrative. It had not been in the aerial view of Spain with which he'd begun, suggestive though it was of his later sweep. Nor had it been in his meticulous rendering of the Spanish legal system, for that had been overelaborated and had at last grown rather tedious. It had not even been in Julian's rendering of the fierce emotions that had seethed beneath Cuenca's monochromatic landscape.

According to Julian, those emotions had been unearthed not only by the haunting nature of an unsolved crime, but because, for the people of Cuenca, all mysteries had to be solved, else demons would rule the world.

Armed by their unwavering faith, the Grimaldos family had refused to forget poor, lowly El Cepa. Holding him in their memory and seeking justice for his murder became their sole obsession, a work of the soul carried out in countless acts of remembrance, El Cepa the persistent subject of their daily conversation. But Julian had also recorded the family's endless chores – planting and harvesting, sweeping, washing, trudging to the well and back again, the backbreaking work their bodies had endured even as their minds continued to be ceaselessly tormented by their brother's vanishing – and with each day they grew more convinced that Valero and Sanchez, still their neighbors and men they saw each day, had murdered him.

They watched and waited, and in 1913, when a new judge was appointed over Cuenca, they seized the moment and drew their swords again, now hopeful that the earlier judge's dismissal of the case against Valero and Sanchez for lack of evidence might be overturned.

The new judge was young and zealous, and the specter of an unsolved crime, as Julian wrote, worked like a rattle in his brain.

Valero and Sanchez were rearrested, and this time the Guardia Civil was determined that the killing of José Maria Lopez Grimaldos, as well as the obvious torment it had caused his family, would not go unavenged.

The torture inflicted upon Valero and Sanchez was hideous, and Julian's account of it was highly detailed. Initial reviews of the book had noted, not always approvingly, the graphic nature of his description, but reading it now, I was struck by the fact that Julian had written of those torments through the eyes of the men who'd suffered them. In Cuenca, I had told him about a painting of men scourging Christ, the expressions on their faces as they'd tormented him. Julian had placed his emphasis on the suffering of the victims, and in reading it again, I found myself admiring how he made the lashes fly so that I heard their crack and felt their terrible bite as if entirely encased within the very flesh they tore.

Had this been Julian's greatest gift, I wondered, that he had been able to describe with such terrible depth, wounds he had neither felt himself nor inflicted upon another?

I wasn't sure, but for my little talk at Julian's memorial ceremony, it would have to do.

CHAPTER 5

'It wasn't Julian's hard work that made him singular,' I said. 'Nor was it even the depth of his research. It was the way he made the reader feel the sting of the lash, the blunt force of the truncheon, the point of the knife. His books are the echoing cries of those whom time has silenced. He never turned away from pain, or cheapened it, or added to it the slightest degree of false amelioration. The purpose of an artist is to convey the harder truths so that we may understand them and learn from them and be less baffled by life. This is what Julian did because he was an artist.'

Thus, with a thud, my little talk ended.

The people assembled beneath the white tent Loretta had had erected on the lawn of the Montauk house had listened respectfully, but they were clearly happy I was done. They'd thought me a windbag, I knew, and a boring one at that.

I glanced to the left, where the pond winked in the light, the yellow boat beside it.

I had failed Julian once again.

I recalled Harry's request for a plug.

51

'*The Commissar*, Julian's study of Andrei Chikatilo, will be published next fall,' I added. 'I hope you all will read it.'

I waited a beat, added the required 'Thank you,' then stepped away from the lectern.

I was the last to speak, so the people now rose and made their way out of the tent and into the house, where Loretta had food and wine waiting for them. I trailed after the group, but stopped at the entrance of the tent and glanced back toward the lectern. Loretta had placed large photographs of Julian to the right and left of where I'd just spoken. The one to the right was of Julian standing in the snow, the great wall of the Kremlin rising behind him. In the photograph he wore a huge overcoat and an *ushanka*, a Russian fur cap with large flaps to cover the ears. In one of his letters, Julian had informed me that *ushanka* meant literally 'ear cap.' This had been typical of Julian. He'd known the word for the hippopotamus skin whip with which the Belgians had flayed open the backs of the Congolese, *chicotte*, and the word for the labyrinthine mines dug in search of water in the Sahara, *foggara* – words that had given his books a rare authenticity.

'Good job, Philip.'

I turned to find Harry standing next to me, grinning cheerfully, clearly long past our difficult last encounter.

'And thanks for plugging the Russian book,'

Harry added. 'Loretta finally sent it to me. It's pretty strange.'

'In what way?' I asked.

'In that Julian focused on Chikatilo's fantasies,' Harry said. 'The way he assumes the part of a patriot when he kills these kids. They were spies. They were traitors. They had to be destroyed to protect Mother Russia.' He glanced toward the house and now clearly wanted to push this unpleasantness aside. 'So, you coming?' he asked.

'In a minute,' I said, then turned back toward the front of the tent, my gaze now focused on the photograph to the left of the lectern.

I had no trouble placing the photo, of course. I'd taken it when we were in Buenos Aires, the Río de la Plata behind him, the two of us about to take a boat to Montevideo with our guide. I'd left Argentina a week later, but Julian had stayed on.

For the first time in a long time, I thought of the grave purpose that had kept Julian in Argentina, the many leads he'd followed, the growing sense of futility as each led nowhere. He had looked everywhere, but had failed to find her. Had he been thinking of that failure while he studied the map of Argentina on that last day? Had he still been thinking of it as he later walked to that little yellow boat?

Loretta had thrown open the windows of the sunroom, and I could hear the white noise of muffled voices, along with the strains of Mahler's

Kindertotenlieder, which Julian had first heard at Two Groves and he later called the saddest music in the world.

For the next hour or so I mingled with the guests, most of whom were friends of Loretta's who'd come to pay their respects to her departed brother but hadn't actually known Julian.

By evening everyone had left, so Loretta and I sat alone, still in the sunroom but no longer in the sun. Loretta lit a few candles. They aged the air to a pale yellow, rather than turning the atmosphere romantic. But this perception, I thought, was actually a misperception, a little elegiac twist of mind.

'Julian liked candles,' she said as she poured herself a scotch. 'Scotch for you, too, Philip?'

'No, I still have a little wine,' I said.

While Loretta poured herself a drink, I let my eyes roam the bookshelves that lined the adjoining room, the library she'd built some years before. They were filled with books on every imaginable subject, and in that way they suggested the range of Loretta's mind. For most of her life she'd worked as a freelance copy editor while taking care of her son, Colin, who had died at sixteen from the degenerative disease he'd been born with and which had slowly removed first his ability to stand, then to walk, then to speak, and at last, to breathe. Her husband had left her not long after Colin's birth, and after that, she'd moved into the Montauk house.

'Did Harry give you Julian's latest?' she asked as she took a seat across from me.

'No, but he's sending it to me.'

Loretta lifted her glass. 'Well, to Julian's last book,' she said.

A thought occurred to me. 'Do you have the map?' I asked. 'The one Julian was looking at before he died?'

'Of course,' Loretta said.

'May I see it?'

She gave me a quizzical look, then got to her feet, walked over to a nearby table, and drew the map from one of its drawers.

'Argentina, like I said,' she said, handing it to me.

I took the map from her and unfolded it.

'What are you looking for?' Loretta asked.

'I'm not sure,' I admitted.

I did not have to be Sherlock Holmes to see that Julian had focused his attention quite narrowly on a small area of Argentina, the sparsely populated region tucked near the conjoining borders of Paraguay and Brazil, very near the great falls at Iguazú. In pencil, he'd traced a route from the falls to the small village of Clara Vista, which he'd circled, and which lay just across the Paraguayan border. It was a town I'd never heard of and we hadn't visited it during our trip to Argentina.

'He may simply have been reminiscing,' Loretta said. 'It wasn't all bad, his time in Argentina. He always described Buenos Aires as quite beautiful. And, of course, there was that guide who so impressed him.'

I glanced up from the map and for the first time in many years, said her name.

'Marisol.'

Loretta nodded softly. 'By the way, I called René today,' she said.

She meant René Brossard, who had served in one way or another as Julian's assistant, first as his French interpreter, then by means of small tasks, collecting his mail and paying the bills on the apartment in Paris during the long periods when Julian was away.

'I'd already told him about Julian, of course,' Loretta said. 'But today I told him that I wanted him to have something of Julian's. Just a little token. His pen.'

'I'm sure René will appreciate that.'

'And I have something for you,' Loretta said.

With that, she rose and left the room. I heard her footsteps as she made her way up the stairs to the little room that had been Julian's office.

She came back down the stairs a few minutes later, carrying an old leather briefcase.

'It was Julian's one true traveling companion,' she said as she handed it to me. 'It went all over the world with him.'

The briefcase was old and discolored, its seams frayed here and there, and it gave off a powerful sense of Julian's life, how he'd lived it like a man on the run.

'Thank you, Loretta,' I said as I took it from her. 'I will treasure it, believe me.'

*   *   *

Later, back at my apartment, I put Julian's brief-case beside my reading chair, then picked up *The Tortures of Cuenca*, determined, perhaps as a final act of homage to my best friend's life and work, to finish it before going to bed.

Under torture, Valero and Sanchez had confessed to killing José Grimaldos and destroying his body. Oddly, they'd been unable to designate where his body lay, a fact, as Julian noted, that should have called their confessions into question, but which, in a strange reversal, had served instead as further evidence of their guilt:

> *Valero and Sanchez had refused to locate the body because the death of Grimaldos had been long and terrible, so the town believed. They had refused because, once unearthed, Grimaldos's body would reveal what had been inflicted upon it while poor, bullied El Cepa had still lived: a body beaten, slashed, burned, with eyes plucked out and ears cut off, with knees bashed and fingers severed, and every-where, everywhere, sliced-away flaps of skin. So runs the imagination, as greater guilt is made certain by the uncertainty of the evidence. By this means, the lack of a body merely deepened the crime of Cuenca, multi-plied its offense, and made Grimaldos's murder yet more cruel, sprouting new snakes from Medusa's head.*

For these many crimes, the prosecuting attorney asked for the death penalty, but the case dragged on through the labyrinthine chambers of the Spanish judicial system, until, in 1918, the accused were at last sentenced, each to eighteen years.

They were released six years later, and two years after that, in the spring of 1926, as Julian wrote, 'poor, bullied El Cepa, so long assumed hideously murdered, suddenly appeared.'

He had been living in a nearby village all those many years, and in the final passage of his book, Julian takes his readers from the eagle-eye roost of the Casas Colgadas, over the twining river and scrub brush and the bare rocks of the plain, then eastward, toward the coast, along the shabby roads of rural Spain, on and on, until he brings them to the flowered streets of Valencia and at last into the shadowy interior of a small kiosk, where . . .

> . . . during the last years of his life, El Cepa, the unmurdered, toiled in his tiny, suffocating space, remembering or not the dusty streets of Cuenca, and selling lottery tickets for life's least deadly game of chance. And thus did he remain, El Cepa, still undead, but locked in the casket of his booth, and with each hot breath, struggling in that darkness to outlive his crime.

I closed the book and recalled that when I'd first read it all those many years ago, I'd found nothing particularly striking in that final passage. For that reason it seemed strange to me that these same stark words now quite inexplicably moved me. For here was Julian's sense of life's cruel randomness, life a lottery upon whose uncontrollable outcome everything depended, how because this streetcar stopped on this particular corner at this particular moment, nothing for this particular human being would ever be the same.

But was this all that was to be found at the end of Julian's first book?

I considered all the books and articles that had followed *The Tortures of Cuenca*, a life's work whose dark subject matter I had always laid at the foot of some mental oddity little different from the obsession of stamp collectors or people who grow orchids.

Loretta had once said that Julian's books always ended like the tolling of a bell. But had that really been his concluding mood? Or was it rather, as it seemed at the end of *The Tortures of Cuenca*, a sense of life as a grim trickster whose cruel twists and turns none of us can avoid.

I closed the book, then, on impulse opened it again, this time to the dedication Julian had written so many years before: *For Philip, sole witness to my crime*. I had always thought this entirely tongue-in-cheek. But now, given the life that had subsequently come to my friend, and the terrible way by which he'd ended it, I couldn't help but wonder if this strange dedication, haunting as it seemed to me now, pointed to some different, darker, and perhaps still-unsolved crime.

I recalled the final passage once again, my mind now focused on its concluding line: *to outlive his crime*.

In the book's dedication I'd been singled out as the sole witness to Julian's crime, but I could think of no such offense, no crime I'd ever witnessed. But had there been one that I hadn't recognized or discovered, a crime that Julian, too, had struggled to outlive but failed?

PART II

THE EYES OF ORADOUR

CHAPTER 6

'I can't stop thinking about Julian,' I told Loretta. She'd come into the city as she always did on the anniversary of her son's death. He'd loved Central Park, and during the earlier stages of his illness, before he'd been confined to a wheelchair, they'd sometimes come here to sit and watch passersby, and even from time to time, when he'd still been able to do it, to stroll around the pond, as Loretta and I were now doing.

'It feels like I'm always in the presence of an unquiet ghost,' I added as we walked over to a nearby bench and sat down.

'Well, he was unquiet, that's for sure,' Loretta said. 'Usually he came home quite tired, but this time was different. It was as if some vicious little animal were clawing around inside him.'

I glanced out into the park, where scores of strollers were making their way along its deeply shaded paths. 'My mind keeps bringing things to the surface. Little bits of memory that swirl and coalesce and pick up other little bits.'

She clearly saw the troubling aspect of this. 'What little bits?' she asked.

'That dedication in his first book, for example,' I said. 'That I was the "sole witness" to his crime.' I shrugged. 'I don't remember witnessing any crime. I thought he meant his writing of the book, which I'd advised against. But now, I'm not so sure that that's the "crime" Julian meant.'

This last remark clearly connected to something in Loretta's mind.

'You know, it's strange, but for all the dreadful acts Julian wrote about, I don't think he ever witnessed a crime of any sort.' Her gaze drifted over to one of the great gray stones of the park, children scooting down its smoothly rounded surface. 'I wonder how he would have reacted if he'd ever actually seen an atrocity like the one at Oradour.' She looked at me. 'Psychologically, he might not have been able to survive it. Primo Levi killed himself, remember? Tadeusz Borowski, too.'

'But they were the victims of a great crime,' I reminded her. 'Not people who had done some awful thing. They didn't die of guilt. They died because they were unable to bear the suffering they'd seen.'

'Well, Julian had certainly seen plenty of suffering,' Loretta said. 'But I don't think that was the source of his agitation.'

'Then what was?' I asked.

Loretta remained silent for a time, thinking something through. Then she said, 'Julian and I were sitting in the yard at Montauk a few days before he died. I looked over at him. Looked closely at his face. There were these deep lines. And his eyes looked sunken. I said, "You know, Julian, the crimes you've written about are carved into your face."'

Loretta was right. Julian's features did seem to bear the imprint of Cuenca and Oradour, the castle ruins of Brittany and Čachtice, the bleak wastes of the Ukraine.

'His response was strange,' Loretta said. 'He said, "No, only the one I'll never write about."'

As if once again on that rainy street, I saw Julian turn up his collar, pull down his hat, and wave me under the awning of a small store on Avenida de la Republique. He'd grasped my arm fiercely, then asked if I'd heard from Marisol.'

'Do you suppose it could have been Marisol's disappearance?' I asked. 'I mean, he was looking at a map of Argentina, after all.'

'I suppose that could have been the crime,' Loretta said.

'But what would keep him from writing about that?' I asked.

Loretta's look reminded me of a fictional detective in some old noir classic.

'Did Julian love her?' she asked.

'No,' I answered. 'He cared for her, certainly. But he didn't fall in love with her.'

'Did you?'

'No,' I said.

With that answer, I heard Marisol's voice again:

Our time on earth is divvied out like stolen things, a booty of nights and days.

'But there was something compelling about her,' I added.

'That Julian saw?'

'Yes, of course,' I said. 'And he did everything he could to find her. But people simply vanished in those days.'

Vanished, yes, I thought, but why had she vanished? For me, this had always been the mysterious part of Marisol's disappearance, that it had remained so thoroughly unaccountable. Her body had never been found, and thus it was unlikely that she'd been the victim of an ordinary murder. But neither would she have been a likely target of the country's political repression. What had she done, after all, except work as a guide and study dress design and occasionally express some opinion about a writer or a style of dance? Of all the people I had ever known, she had seemed to me the most innocent.

'The thing about Marisol,' I said, 'is that she wasn't at all political. She was smart and ambitious, a hard worker. She had a way about her, a knowingness, but in every other way, there were thousands like her in Buenos Aires at that time.'

'Thousands who were like her but who didn't disappear,' Loretta said.

I nodded. 'Yes.'

With that answer, there seemed little to do but change the subject.

'Anything more from René?' I asked.

'Yes,' Loretta said. 'An e-mail, if you can believe it. I never met him, but Julian's description didn't suggest a man who's ever been computer savvy.' She looked somewhat puzzled. 'He wasn't at all surprised by Julian's death. That he killed himself. René likes to use English phrases. He said Julian was "a burned-out case."'

Suddenly, I felt somewhat like one myself, a man who'd lost his wife to disease and his friend to suicide, both irreplaceable, a childless man whose father would soon be passing, a man with a small apartment who practiced a dying profession.

I tried to shrug off the darkness that settled over me with these thoughts. 'So, what else did René say?'

'He wanted to know what he should do with Julian's stuff,' Loretta answered. 'Whatever he had in his apartment.'

The thought of René rifling through Julian's possessions struck me as profoundly wrong. Should it not be someone else, someone close to Julian, who did this? These were the personal possessions of a very private person, after all, a man I'd loved and whose work I'd admired and with whom I'd traveled some small portion of the world.

'Would you mind if I did it?' I asked Loretta.

She leaned back slightly. 'You mean go to Paris?'

I nodded. 'René will just throw everything into the garbage,' I said. 'And somehow that just doesn't seem the right end for Julian's things.'

Loretta smiled softly. 'You truly loved him, didn't you?' she asked.

A fierce emotion stirred in me.

'I did, yes,' I said. 'And more than anything, Loretta, I wish I could have been with him in that little boat.'

'I'm going to Paris,' I told my father the next day.

The two of us were sitting at the small breakfast table over morning coffee.

'I need to go through Julian's things,' I added.

It surprised me that in response to this, my father abruptly sank directly back to his own past.

'I never got to travel much in my job,' he said quietly, then drew in a long breath and released it slowly, 'but I did find myself at the Nile Hotel once. In Kambala. Idi Amin was still in power in those days.'

Something in his recollection of that time clearly pained him, but he faced it bravely and went on.

'Everybody knew that Amin had several suites in the hotel,' he said. 'Some were for his whores. Others were torture chambers.'

It was the latter rooms he appeared to visualize now, and I found myself seeing them, too: walls splattered with dried blood, a straight-back chair, a naked lightbulb hanging from a black cord, a metal table fitted with drains. Hell is not other people, I thought, in opposition to Sartre's famous line; it is what we do to other people.

'I was at the hotel when he put Archbishop

68

Luwum on trial there,' my father continued. 'I tried to get my superiors to intervene, but they said it was none of our affair, and besides, dreadful as Amin was, he was no different from others. "The Africans don't have presidents," one of them told me. "They have chiefs." Mobutu said that, too, by the way, as justification for his own slaughters.' He shrugged. 'Well, Amin charged Luwum with smuggling guns, if you can believe that, and tried him out in the open, African-style, in the courtyard of the hotel. He'd filled the place with his rabble of soldiers. They were drinking whiskey and chewing khat, and they kept screaming, "Kill him! Kill him!" Luwum just stood there, not saying a word, just staring that fat, whoremongering Kakwa thug right in the eye.' His gaze intensified and bore into me. 'That's what Julian should have looked for and written about, Philip,' he said. 'Men like Luwum. Men who were doing some good in the world.' He shrugged. 'Julian's tragedy is that he only looked at the dark side, and it weakened him and made him sick.'

My father had never indicated such qualms about Julian's work, so it had never occurred to me that he thought it so misdirected.

'In my opinion, it's the good people who deserve to be written about,' he added softly.

This called into question the whole of Julian's work, how relentlessly dark it had been. I recalled an article on bastinado he'd once written, the beating of the feet, its different names, *falanga, falaka,* where and when it had been practiced, and with what instruments. He'd even meticulously described the physical structure of the feet, the large number of small bones, the nerves that cluster in the soles, how painful it must be to suffer such assault.

My father shrugged. 'But that was Julian,' he said in a way that made it clear he had no intention of dwelling further on the grim nature of his books. 'So you'll be going away.'

'For a little while,' I said. 'But I'll stay in touch. With Skype, we can even see each other. And if anything . . . comes up, I can fly back in no time.'

'Of course,' my father said, though he was clearly reticent to see me go, feeling vulnerable as old people inevitably do.

'I have to do this, Dad,' I said.

My father smiled, then reached over and touched my hand. 'I can see that,' he said. Something inexpressibly sad drifted into his eyes. 'It's a good thing to have a mission.'

I considered all the futile missions my father had undertaken. He'd worked for fresh water in lands ravaged by cholera, for regional clinics in jungle redoubts, for irrigation in regions made barren by drought. In every case, as he'd long ago admitted, he'd been thwarted by the 'big picture' at the State Department, global strategies of containment, domino theories, the specter of mutually assured destruction.

'Yes,' I said, then changed the subject, and for

the next hour or so we talked of old films he'd watched on television lately. In addition to Westerns and spy movies, he'd begun to watch the noir movies of the forties, Humphrey Bogart and Alan Ladd, and when he spoke of them I could hear a strange longing in his voice, his old desire to be a man of action still pursuing him and accusing him and tainting his memory with failure.

'Do you want to watch a movie?' I asked in hopes of stopping the downward slant of his mood.

'No,' my father answered. He seemed to go deep inside himself, then return slowly, like a diver resurfacing. 'It's the dusty people, Philip, too small for us to notice,' he said, 'the little dusty people who bear the brunt of our mistakes.'

His mood was quite obviously descending, so I gently urged him toward his youth, and for the next few minutes he talked rather nostalgically about his own father, then his college years, then about my mother, who, like my own wife, had died before her time.

'You should be getting home now,' he said at last. 'I could go on for hours.'

'Yes, I probably should,' I said.

My father looked like one who'd once been offered a mission not unlike my own, but had either refused it or failed to achieve it. 'Good luck,' was all he said.

CHAPTER 7

There is no substitute for meaning, and the luckiest of us are those who have felt the spur of a grave commitment. I couldn't possibly include myself among the men who hung in dark frames from the walls of my father's apartment. They had been warriors and diplomats, and a few, as my father had once reluctantly admitted, had been spies. I knew that my own life would never be as charged with mission as theirs. Even so, that map of Argentina, the grim fact of Marisol's disappearance, and finally Julian's curious mention of some crime I had witnessed – *his* crime – had joined together to provide a purpose to my going to Paris that was larger than any I had known in a long time.

This purpose was still in my mind when I got back to my apartment.

I poured a glass of brandy, took my usual seat at the window, and looked out over the park, a glance into the night that loosened the bonds of recollection, and took me back to Berlin with Julian more than twenty years before.

He'd gone there in an effort to track down and

interview some of the surviving German soldiers who had massacred the villagers of Oradour-sur-Glane in June of 1944. He had decided to write an account of this atrocity, and on the train from Paris to Berlin, he'd gone through its terrible details.

He was twenty-seven at the time, and although we had regularly exchanged letters, it had been well over a year since I'd seen him. By then, a certain texture had been added to him by his travels and his studies, and his voice bore a gravity that I associated with the knowledge and experiences he had accumulated since last we'd met.

'So, how is the new book coming?' I asked him.

'Oradour is hard to write about,' he said.

His eyes were still blue, but their shade seemed deeper, though I doubt their color had actually changed. Still, there was an incontestable depth in those eyes, something that spoke of the charred village whose tragedy he had chosen as the subject of his next book.

'Yes, it was terrible what happened at Oradour,' I said.

'I don't mean that it's hard to write about in that way,' Julian said. 'It's that there's a kind of voyeurism involved, a peep-show quality.'

I looked at him, puzzled, and at that instant, the train entered a tunnel that threw us into shadow, so that we sat in silence, rumbling on, until the train passed out of the darkness and we were bathed in light again.

Something in Julian's face had changed. It was as if, during the brief darkness of the tunnel, some other, deeper darkness had fallen upon him.

'The pain of others should not be made thrilling,' he said softly. 'There should be no intellectual sadism in reading about Oradour.'

Had that been the moment when it first occurred to him to write his book as he'd later written it? I wondered now.

One thing was clear: *In The Eyes of Oradour*, Julian had focused exclusively on the victims, all 642 of them, each given a single page to bear witness, a kind of *Spoon River Anthology* for the members of that murdered village. That was the magisterial oddity of the book, the way Julian had managed to see the massacre through the eyes of those who'd suffered it. To write of the atrocity at Oradour in so strange a way had been a brave choice, and at times – when a little girl used her own body to shield her doll from the attack, for example – he had brought a heartrending vividness to the victims' deaths.

But in that same narrative, he'd refused to name either the men who ordered the massacre or those who carried it out. Even as unnamed figures, the Germans are glimpsed only at quick moments when the crowd breaks and the back of a soldier, or perhaps only a boot or uniformed leg, is glimpsed in what amounts to a photo flash. At other times the soldiers are disembodied voices, shouting

74

commands or gently deceiving the villagers of Oradour as to their real intent. In other instances, they appear only as the blurry hint of a figure, a brushstroke of helmeted gray.

On the whole, I thought the book extraordinarily accomplished, worthy of the many years it had taken Julian to write it, though a few reviewers had complained that he had concealed the methodical human agency behind the massacre too much, making the innocent of Oradour seem less like the victims of actual cruelty than of the touching down of a storm.

At the time, even though I greatly admired the book, I also thought this criticism not altogether unfair. It was a monumental crime, after all, and Julian had determinedly concealed the men who had carried it out.

Why had he done that?

We were sitting on a bench behind the great library on Fifth Avenue when I posed that very question. It was winter, and we were both wrapped in our overcoats. It had snowed the day before, and the bare limbs of the trees were laced in white. Julian remained silent for a long time before explaining why he hadn't identified any of the German soldiers. 'They deserve to be forgotten,' he said, as if shielding the murderers had been one of the book's metaphorical devices. 'It's the innocent who deserve to be remembered.'

'But don't you think the perpetrators need to be remembered, too?' I asked.

He turned to me and something in his eyes told me that this was a subject that pained him.

'What would be the point of telling some little boy that on a particular day, in a particular place, his father was complicit in a terrible crime?' he demanded. 'What good would come of it?'

'But otherwise the father would get away with it,' I answered. 'And a man who does a terrible thing should be identified.'

Julian gave no response, so I hammered home the point.

'Like whoever killed Marisol,' I added because the unsolved crime of her disappearance suddenly occurred to me. 'He got away with it.'

One of Julian's gloved hands wrapped around the other. 'Yes,' he muttered.

He seemed so abruptly moved by the mention of Marisol that I quickly added, 'You did your best to find her, Julian.'

Then, to change the subject, I glanced at the book peeking out from the pocket of his coat.

'What are you reading?' I asked. He drew the book from his pocket and I looked at the title, quite surprised by what I saw.

'Eric Ambler, I see. So, you're reading spy fiction now?'

'It helps to pass the time,' Julian said.

'Betrayal and false identities,' I said jokingly. 'People who are not what they appear. Thrilling stuff,' I added with a laugh, 'but not the stuff of great literature.'

'You might be surprised,' Julian said softly. 'Life is a shadow game, after all.'

I absently opened the book and saw that he'd underlined its most famous line. 'It's not who fires the shot,' I read, 'but who pays for the bullet.'

He removed the book from my hands and returned it to his pocket. 'It helps to pass the time,' he repeated. 'And I don't read Borges anymore.'

Borges, I thought, and felt the dust of the Chaco settle over us once again, a place I'd never seen, but which our guide had called home.

Borges.

A sure sign, I knew, that Julian's mind remained on Marisol.

CHAPTER 8

In the great tales, she is always beautiful, of course, the one whose loss torments a man. Since Helen walked the ramparts of Sparta and equally dazzled the men of two opposing armies, we have given little value, in literature at least, to a plain-looking girl.

That is not to say that Marisol was plain, but simply to say that she was by no means a dazzling Helen or a fiery Antigone. She was Cordelia, the loyal daughter of King Lear, quiet, modest, motionless at her center, a pendulum at rest.

She came into the lobby of the hotel like a small breeze off the pampas, the sort that barely moves the grasses.

'I am Marisol,' she said in her softly accented English. 'I am pleased to meet with you.' Her eyes were black, but striking, and her skin brown, but with a golden undertone, so that in a certain light, as Julian once observed, she seemed carved from a muted amber.

A week before, my father had contacted the American consulate in Buenos Aires, and someone in that office had recommended Marisol as a guide. She was fluent in English, according to the consulate, and others had been satisfied with her services. With a slightly comic edge, my father had added that Marisol had been properly vetted by the consulate, which meant, of course, that she was no female Che Guevara.

On that first morning, she wore a dark gray skirt that fell just below the knee, with a matching jacket. Her blouse was white, with a tailored collar, and she wore it open at the throat. The shoes were black and well polished, with a modest, business-like heel. But such gestures toward urbanity did not conceal the depth of her indigenous roots. These were in the oval shape of her eyes and the width of her nose and the black panther sheen of her hair. Europe had made no invasion of her blood. For that reason one sensed in her, as I'm sure Julian did, a strange and unconquerable purity.

'I welcome you to Buenos Aires,' she added with a quick smile.

Where many of the women of the city wore a crucifix on a gold or silver chain, Marisol wore a simple string of wooden beads. From the beginning, Julian said, there was a no-nonsense quality about her, something steady, down-to-business, and in a way profoundly conservative, a brick in the sturdy wall, as he would later write of those who resist the excesses of revolutionary fervor, that slows the violent winds of change.

Julian offered his hand. 'I'm Julian Wells, and this is Philip Anders.'

79

'*Un placer*,' Marisol said as she shook our hands. 'I will teach you a little Spanish while you are here.' She gave each of us an evaluating glance. 'That is okay?'

'Absolutely,' Julian told her. 'Right, Philip?'

'Of course.'

She swept her arm toward the entrance to the hotel. 'Come then. There is much to see in Buenos Aires.'

The day's tour began with a long walk that took us from Casa Rosada all the way to La Boca, by which Marisol hoped, as she said in one of her rare misuses of English, 'to integrate us.'

She was a woman of extended silences, I noticed, and she said very little as we walked the streets of La Boca, looking at its brightly colored houses. It was as if she understood that quiet observation was the key to knowing a place, perhaps even the key to life. In any event, she was careful to allow space for standing, sitting, seeing, so that we never felt rushed. Nor did she engage in the guidebook patter that can be so annoying. Marisol, as I would come to understand, was a shaded pond, calm and unruffled.

By evening we had found our way back to the hotel. The restaurant, Marisol said, had a good reputation, though she had never eaten there.

We took a table outside. It was early evening, that twilight interval between a city's working day and its nocturnal life.

80

'By the way, where are you from?' Julian asked her at one point.

'I was always moving between Argentina and Paraguay,' Marisol answered. 'I crossed this border many times as a child.'

'Why?' I asked.

'When my mother died, I was sent to my father in Paraguay,' Marisol answered. 'At this moment, my father died, and I was sent to an aunt back in Argentina. When she was also dying, she took me to a priest, and it was this man who cared for me.'

The priest had lived in a part of northern Argentina that bordered on the Gran Chaco.

'It is very dry, with nothing, and for many years no one cared about it,' Marisol informed us. 'Then they found oil.'

It was the struggle to possess this oil that had generated the Chaco War, she said, a conflict that had been unimaginably brutal.

'They died in great numbers, the soldiers,' she said. 'So much sickness, and no doctors. You have not heard of it, this war?'

'No,' Julian answered.

Marisol didn't seem surprised. 'We are unknown to you, we who live down here,' she said. 'To you, we are fallen off the earth.'

A silence settled over her, both somber and serene, from which emerged what seemed to be the central hope she had for her people, their one quite justified aim.

'All we want is a fighting chance,' she added softly.

Then her eyes abruptly brightened and she was our professional guide again.

'You must have a taste of Argentina,' she said. 'Of our wine. It is called Malbec, and the difference in taste between the cheap and the not cheap, it is not so big.' She smiled softly, but it seemed an actress's smile. 'You will like it, I think. But just in case, you should order the cheap one.'

Only once more during that day did Marisol again leave her role as cheerful, uncomplicated guide. It was in answer to Julian's question about her feelings concerning the current state of Argentina, then in the final throes of its Dirty War.

In response, Marisol's gaze grew tense. 'Here we say that Argentina *es un país perdido*,' she said softly. 'A lost country.' She shrugged. 'And we have another saying. A funny answer when we are asked how we are doing.' She glanced about to make sure she could not be heard, then whispered, '*Jodido pero contento*.'

'What does that mean?' I asked.

She was suddenly hesitant. 'I do not wish to be vulgar.'

'Oh, come on, Marisol,' Julian said. 'We're all adults here.'

'Okay,' she said, then laughed. 'It means "screwed but happy."'

We parted at around nine that evening, then met again the next morning, mostly for a tour of various museums, during which Marisol was very much the professional guide, talking of this artist

82

or that one in the fashion of a museum brochure. There were also walks along the canals, a visit to Teatro Colón, Buenos Aires's famed opera house. Our third day involved a ferry to Montevideo followed by a boat ride to the estuary where the Germans had scuttled the *Graf Spee* in December of 1939. Marisol was surprisingly knowledgeable and knew the exact coordinates beneath which the doomed vessel lay.

'The English tourists like to come here,' she told Julian by way of explanation. 'Sometimes the Germans, too. So I discovered where it is and we are now exactly at this place.' She smiled brightly. 'Knowing such a thing makes me a better guide, no?'

On the fourth day Marisol took us to the cemetery in Recoleta.

'This is a very quiet place,' Marisol said as she led us beneath the dazzlingly white arched entrance.

For a time we wandered silently among the mausoleums, moving slowly, but without a stop, until we reached Evita's tomb.

'Eva Perón was a poor girl,' Marisol said softly when we paused before it. 'Just another poor girl from Los Toldos.'

'Would you have voted for her?' Julian asked.

Marisol shrugged. 'Now there is no voting here,' she said. 'It is only between two bad things that we must choose.' She peered at the small plaque attached to the tomb. 'Sometimes, when I bring the people here, I tell them what Borges said about life,' she went on. 'This adds to me as a guide.'

'What did Borges say?' Julian asked.

Marisol, honest to the quick, said, 'The English, it is not my translation.'

'Still, I'd like to hear it,' Julian insisted.

Marisol summoned this translation that was not hers, then said, 'Okay, Borges said: "Our time on earth is divvied out like stolen things: a booty of nights and days."'

Her eyes darkened slightly, and then, as if by an act of will, they brightened again, though this time something behind them remained in shadow. 'Come,' she said. Then, very quickly, she turned and headed out among the tombs. 'Come,' she repeated as she waved us forward. 'A guide should be always smiling.'

She had only contracted for a set number of hours each day, but she went off the clock at six that evening, so we remained in the restaurant for a long time. We had dinner, then strolled along Calle Florida for a time, where we stopped to watch a couple of street performers dance the tango.

Marisol watched them for a little while, and during that interval I noticed her mood descending. 'I do not like the tango,' she said as she turned and led us away from the dancers. 'The man rushes forward. The woman pushes him away, then turns her back to him. The man rushes to her again and jerks her around with violence. It is disturbing to me, this

84

dance. It is not romantic. It is – what is the English word? – prelude. Yes, it is the prelude to a beating.'

We returned to the hotel at around eight in the evening. I was tired, but Julian was full of energy, so we went to the lounge for a nightcap, where he talked of nothing but Marisol. He had seldom traveled since his father's death, and I could see that her foreignness appealed to him: the fact that she was bilingual, which he was not, and perhaps even her indigenous facial features.

'Do you suppose she really isn't political?' he asked. 'That business of having only two bad things to choose from?'

'That's what she said.'

'But coming from that poor background, she must hate the junta,' Julian said.

'Yes, but maybe she's one of those people who look within themselves for a way out of oppression,' I told him. 'That's why they get on boats and sail to new worlds.'

Julian hesitated briefly, then said, 'If someone like Marisol doesn't have a fighting chance, then something's very wrong, Philip.'

I smiled. 'You'll fix that when you're secretary of state,' I assured him.

I'd meant this only half jokingly for at that moment it seemed quite possible.

'That's not for me,' Julian said. 'It's all politics. Your father knows that. He's had plenty of experience with it. You want to do good, but the policy is evil, and you must serve the policy.'

'What then?' I asked. 'You have to do something with your life.'

'Something behind the scenes, I guess,' Julian said. 'The secret gears.'

'The secret gears?' I asked, rather amused by how vague, yet adventurous it seemed. 'You mean dark alleys and notes slipped into drop boxes? That's the work of spies, Julian.'

'I suppose it is,' Julian said. 'But it would be better than an office at Foggy Bottom.'

'It would also be more dangerous,' I reminded him.

'More dangerous, yes,' Julian agreed. 'But only for me.'

And with that, he laughed.

CHAPTER 9

'Laughed?' Loretta asked when I told her this.

It was the day I was to leave for Paris, and she'd insisted on taking me to the airport. She'd arrived late in the afternoon, dressed in a dark green pants suit and looking so surprisingly rested that I'd have sworn she'd spent time in a spa.

'Laughed, yes,' I told her. 'So I didn't take him seriously.'

She was seated by the window, the park to her back, the light quite bright, so that she was half in silhouette. 'Julian would have made a good spy,' she said. 'That's clear from his books, how good he was at integrating information, making connections, seeing the big picture.'

'That's true,' I said. 'He did that in *The Eyes of Oradour*. In one passage you're not even in France. He takes you to the sarcophagi of Cozumel, describes how small the people of that island were, and from there to how small all the Indians of South America must have seemed to the likes of Cortés and Pizarro.'

'It's a great skill, putting such details together,' Loretta said. 'And of course the clandestine part of it would have appealed to Julian when he was a young man, the secret devices.'

Like one seated in a dark movie house, I unexpectedly imagined Julian as precisely that, a figure in a rainy alleyway, dressed in a trench coat, the brim of his hat pulled low, smoking a Gauloise as he waited for his beautiful female contact.

No, that would not have been it, I thought.

Julian would have been waiting for something else.

But what?

On the heels of that question, a strange anxiety swept down upon me, and as if from a great height, I saw Julian lean over the side of the boat and make those two horrible motions, and then a circle of blood sweep out from the boat, deep and red, flowing out and widening until the whole pond was a deep, thick, impenetrable red.

Loretta's voice suddenly brought me back.

'I have something for you,' she said, then reached into her pocket, drew out a photograph, and handed it to me. 'It was in Julian's notebook. The one I gave him the morning he died. I found this picture tucked inside, so I think he must have been thinking of that first trip.'

In the photograph Julian and Marisol were posed before the Obelisk, a place we'd often used as a point of rendezvous. It was around noon, the sun directly overhead so that it hardly cast a shadow.

88

Marisol stood to Julian's left, and he'd put his arm around her waist and was gently drawing her toward him.

'You took that picture, didn't you, Philip?' Loretta asked.

'Yes,' I answered. 'It was our last day together.' I stared at the picture a moment longer, then looked at Loretta.

'How very odd,' she said. 'Julian had the same expression on his face as the one you just had.'

'What expression?'

'Dread,' Loretta answered. 'We were having dinner three days before he died. I'd been editing a book on Soviet espionage. There was an agent with the code name Beaker, quite a clever agent. He was a double agent, actually, working for one side while pretending to work for the other. Beaker was a very gifted little actor, but at one point, when he is sitting with another agent, he knows this other agent is trying to determine if Beaker, himself, is a spy. So Beaker is trying very hard to appear completely nonchalant, give no hint that he even knows that this other guy is out to get him. In the past he has always been able to completely conceal his terror of being discovered, but this time, his nerves give way . . . and he turns the corner of napkin. It's a tiny little movement, but it's a nervous movement, and at that moment Beaker knows absolutely that the other guy has seen it, and has read it for what it is.' She smiled, but cheerlessly. 'It was as if a tiny bead of sweat

89

had just popped onto his brow, but it was enough for the other man to see the jumpy little spy beneath the mask.'

'It's almost comic,' I said.

'I thought so, too,' Loretta said. 'But it wasn't comic to Julian. I could tell by the look on his face. His mind was going somewhere. And one thing was clear. He understood Beaker. I could see that. He understood how his nerves had cracked. He didn't talk for a second or two, then he said, "When your life is a lie, the truth has high stakes."'

We watched each other silently for a moment, a time during which a dark cord seemed to draw us closer to each other.

'One more thing,' she said. 'Another little anecdote. Then you'll have all I have to give you about Julian.'

She appeared somewhat reluctant to tell me the story.

'The day before he died, he went into the sunroom after dinner,' she said. 'There was a notebook on the little table beside his chair. I saw him take it up and write something in it. Then he put it back down and after a while he dozed off. When I went in to wake him, I saw what he'd written. A single sentence, but I remember it because it was so strange.'

Briefly she seemed captured in that very strangeness.

'He'd written, "Life is, at last, a Saturn Turn."'

I had no idea what this meant, and told her so.

'I have no idea either,' Loretta said. 'But it must have meant something to Julian, because after his death, when I found that little notebook, I saw that he'd torn out that page. I couldn't find it anywhere, and it was summer, so there was no fire. I looked in all the places he might have tried to discard or hide it. I never found it, so there was only one place he could have put it.'

'The pond,' I said.

She nodded. 'Hiding that note was his penultimate act.'

'And it was an act of subterfuge,' I added. 'Of concealment.' I felt the soft click of a tumbler. 'One of his themes.'

Now the dread that had earlier marked Julian's face, and more recently my own, settled upon Loretta's features, too.

'Julian once told me about a myth he'd come across,' she said. 'It came from the Pacific Islands. It was called the "Myth of the Reeds." It says that at death, the soul of each man is bound by his hidden crimes, each one wrapped around him like a reed. And it is only as these crimes are solved that he is freed.' She let this settle in before she added, 'I sometimes thought that Julian was tangled up in a reed.'

'And died that way?' I asked.

'Unless that's what he was cutting,' Loretta said. 'Metaphorically, at least.'

I could find nothing illuminating to add to this,

and so we talked of other things until the hour came, and we set off for the airport.

Evening was beginning to drift down over the city by then, lights coming on, both in the buildings and in the traffic. The time had come for me to leave.

At the airport, I pulled my luggage from the back of the car.

'When will you be back?' Loretta asked.

'I haven't booked the return yet,' I answered.

'Does that feel good?' Loretta asked.

'I suppose it does, but at the same time I know that I'm a little at sea in all this,' I admitted. 'Let's face it, I was never trained in finding anything but metaphors and symbols.'

She smiled. 'Julian used to say that you find more when you don't know what you're looking for.'

I felt a wave of admiration for my lost friend, the random riches of his work. Harry had often complained that he could not be categorized. Was he writing about crime or was he writing about history? Did you put him in 'General Nonfiction' or did you put him in 'True Crime'? His books had been strewn with little nuggets of everything: history, science, philosophy, a vast number of quotations, all of which made it nearly impossible for booksellers to find a slot on the shelf. I'd even found his books tucked hopelessly in 'Travel' and even once in 'Vampires.'

'He found a great deal,' I said.

'And so will you, Philip,' Loretta assured me.

I thought of all the many years during which she had accumulated her own great store of knowledge and experience, all she had read and all she had endured, a bounty I found myself wanting to share.

'I hope so,' I told her, 'because I think something very important depends upon it.'

'What?' she asked.

'Us,' I answered softly, and knew that in some inexpressible way this was true.

Loretta came forward and kissed me on the cheek. 'Julian could not have had a better friend,' she said.

CHAPTER 10

But Julian had had perhaps as good a friend in René Brossard.

They'd met in Africa, when Julian was researching the Paul Voulet outrages, and had subsequently traveled together to some of the remote outposts where those atrocities had been committed. According to Julian, Brossard had a lingering aura of old crimes, though the nature of those crimes had never been revealed. Even so, there was a hint of violence both suffered and inflicted, Brossard's one of those lives that had both struck and received a blow.

I'd met him in Julian's company a few times, though he'd made certain to remain in the background on those occasions. Whether this had been the product of Gallic manners or simply that he was slow to warm to strangers had never been clear. Of course, it might equally have been the outward evidence of some inner furtiveness, for there was surely something veiled about Brossard.

He had aged quite a bit during the intervening years. Where before his hair had been sprinkled with gray, it had now gone white. His eyes were

94

more webbed and the lines in his long face had deepened. The muted light of Charles de Gaulle Airport added a layer of grayness to his unexpected pallor.

'I was very sad to hear of Julian,' he said as he offered his hand.

'It came as quite a shock.'

'Hmm,' René said.

We exchanged a few pleasantries, then René led me to his car, and we set off for Paris, where I'd booked a small hotel not far from l'Opéra.

It was early in the morning, but I'd slept on the plane, so rather than bid René a quick farewell and go up to bed, I asked him to join me for a cup of coffee so that we could begin to discuss whatever itinerary he thought appropriate for my stay.

'I am sorry to say, but there is a delay in getting you into Julian's apartment,' he informed me. 'It is my fault that I did not tell you before, but I did not learn of it until this morning.'

'What's the problem?' I asked.

'The one who owns the building, he has gone from the city for a few days, and I cannot get the key,' René said. He shrugged. 'I only come to the building to get Julian's mail. I never have a key to go inside.' He smiled. 'Perhaps he was not so good at the keeping house.' He drew a pack of cigarettes from his jacket pocket, thumped one out, and lit it. 'But he was a good writer, Julian. Very good.' He seemed at the end of what he knew of Julian. 'Always writing. Tap, tap, tap. Day and night.'

'But no one can write twenty-four hours a day,' I said. 'He must have gone out from time to time.'

'Sometimes, yes,' René said. 'Mostly to this little bar, Le Chapeau Noir. In Pigalle.'

'Yes, I remember Julian writing about that place,' I said. 'He seems to have gone there quite a lot.'

'It has cheap wine, and Julian was always lacking in the money,' René told me. 'But, me, I do not like it. It is full of refugees and émigrés. Africans and Arabs, people on the run from bad things.'

'What kind of bad things?' I asked.

'Crimes,' Brossard answered. 'There were such places in Algiers. Criminals are like chickens, they crowd in upon each other. In a place like Le Chapeau Noir, there is blood on every hand.'

'Except for Julian's, of course,' I said.

'Except for Julian's, yes,' Brossard agreed.

'Then why did he choose such a place?' I asked.

'It was near his apartment,' Brossard said. 'Perhaps it was the first door that opened to him.' He shrugged. 'He was a sad man, Julian. They are often in this way, such people. I saw it early. He was drawn to darkness. This I saw at Oradour.'

'Oradour,' I said as an idea occurred to me. 'Since I can't get into Julian's apartment, would you mind taking me there?'

'It is only a destroyed village,' René said. 'But, okay, when do you want to go?'

'Tomorrow morning?'

'So fast? You are not wanting to sleep tomorrow, for the jet lag?'

'No,' I answered. 'I'll be rested by morning.'

'Okay, tomorrow we go to Oradour,' René said. He took a draw on his cigarette, then crushed it out. 'I remember that Julian, he was not so interested in the Germans. But the Malgré-nous, these interested him.'

He saw that I did not speak a word of French.

'It means "despite ourselves." The Malgré-nous were from Alsace, these men, but the Germans drafted them. A few were at Oradour, and so they were made to do what they did, as they say, "despite themselves."'

It struck me that this was one of Julian's abiding themes, the sudden intervention of some event that without warning reveals a previously hidden element of character and by that means leaves a man forever the victim of a dark surprise.

'He talked to a few of them,' René continued. 'Old men. Dead now.' His smile was wily, a ferret's grin. 'It would be just so in one of those books, no? A thriller? The hero seeks a witness, but when he finds him, this witness is dead?'

'In pulp fiction, yes,' I said. 'But about that bar, the one Julian frequented, was there anyone he spent time with?'

René thought a moment, then said, 'A priest. They spoke Spanish. This man, he was from Argentina. Julian said that he had been to his country during a bad time.'

'The Dirty War, yes,' I said.

René nodded. 'I remember one night, Julian

97

spoke of a woman he met there. He was very moved by this woman. Julian did not often show his feelings, but this night, I saw that for this one, a pain was left with him.'

'Her name was Marisol,' I told René. 'She disappeared while Julian and I were in Buenos Aires.'

René shrugged. 'Lots of women disappeared during that time, no?'

'Yes, but they were kidnapped by the junta,' I told him. 'Marisol, on the other hand, wasn't in the least political.'

René laughed at what he seemed to consider my naïveté. 'Not political? How do you know?'

The question was simple, but it surprised me anyway, for, in fact, I didn't know whether Marisol had or had not been political. At least, not for sure.

With that recognition, a small crack appeared in the wall of what I'd always assumed about her. True, she'd only once mentioned the situation in Argentina, and even then only generally: *Argentina es un país perdido.*

But in what way had she thought it lost? I wondered now.

Marisol had never said.

One thing was clear, however. Although she always listened attentively when Julian spoke, it had been with an air of critical attunement, as if, because he was a privileged American, she should be wary of him and his worldview.

It was a distrust that surfaced one afternoon as we

strolled down Calle Florida. Julian had begun to talk about the many far-flung places he hoped to visit in the future, one of which was Calcutta.

'The Black Hole of Calcutta is one of the places I'd like to see,' he said. 'I always thought that phrase referred to the city itself, that it was hopeless and impoverished. A pit.'

Marisol listened to him in that highly attentive way of hers, as if seeking to understand not only the words, but what might lie between them, in the manner of a translator always in search of some new idiom or nuance in a language not yet fully mastered.

'But it was really an event,' Julian added. 'A mass murder, really.'

Then, with characteristic detail, giving the precise date and location, Julian told us how Indian troops had crammed scores of British subjects into an unventilated room, where they'd died of suffocation or been trampled to death during one long night's ordeal.

'What did the British do after that?' Marisol asked.

'They decided that the Indians were savages,' Julian answered. 'And the subjugation of India became less—'

'Gentle?' Marisol interrupted softly.

I'd never heard her interrupt anyone. It simply wasn't her style. There was an unmistakable edge in her tone, too, though one so subtle I couldn't tell if it reflected anything more than the general anticolonialism any young person might have embraced at the time. Certainly it was not enough for me to conclude that Marisol was political in the sense that I'd used the word with René, something that would have caused her to be a target of the Dirty War.

René was quiet for a time after I related this small exchange to him. Then he said, 'Anyway, you were safe. You and Julian, I mean. He made much of this, that despite all that was going on in Argentina, the two of you were safe.'

'Yes, Julian and I were safe,' I said, and thought of the legions of the disappeared, the marches their mothers made each day in the Plaza de Mayo. Still, I could not place the Marisol I'd known – so very quiet and lacking any visible political position – among the ranks of those who'd later been caught up in the Dirty War's repression. From those clutches, she'd always seemed as safe as Julian and I, and because of that, it had never occurred to me that she might have ended up in some dank cell, bruised and battered and lying in her own excrement, listening, with whatever consciousness remained to her, for the dreadful footfall of her torturer's approach.

'You have been silent for a long time,' René said.

His voice seemed to come to me from a far less perilous world.

'Really?' I said. 'I didn't realize.'

René drained the rest of his coffee. 'Tomorrow we go to Oradour.'

*　　*　　*

We left Paris the next morning, a warm day but rainy, the city streets shrouded in a gray mist that gradually dissipated, so that we were in bright sun within an hour or so.

The way to Oradour was south from Paris, and it led into the heart of what had once been Vichy France, where the French had been permitted to rule – or pretend to rule – during the German occupation. Here Pierre Laval had signed the infamous order deporting non-French Jews to their deaths, for which, among other of his collaborationist acts, he had been executed by firing squad after the war.

Julian had touched on all this in a letter written while working on Oradour, and in recounting Laval's death, he had offered an unexpectedly sympathetic portrait of Laval's final hours, how he'd bungled a suicide attempt by not shaking the bottle before drinking the poison it contained, the way he'd worn a tricolor scarf to the execution site in a twelfth-hour effort to grasp the laurel of patriotism, his final love-of-country declaration, shouted just before the shots rang out: *Vive la France!*

It was the seamless combination of scope and detail that Julian brought to all his later books, and thinking of it as we closed in upon Oradour, it renewed my admiration for him as a writer, one all the more fortified by what I'd learned from René the day before: the solitary life Julian had led in France, the habitué of a seedy bar in Pigalle,

101

the way he'd made himself companion to the alien and the lost.

We reached Oradour in the early afternoon. My plan was to walk through it slowly, absorbing the place in increments as the day waned, so that I would reach the end of my tour at the very time of day when, according to the final passage of his book, Julian had left it for the last time, his research completed, his many hours of interviews and of walking the town's ghostly streets finally come to their end.

We parked just outside the town by the visitors' center, and for the next few hours I carried Julian's book with me as I slowly ambled among its ruined streets, René at my side, looking faintly bored. Along with a scattering of other tourists, we strolled among the shattered buildings and stood in the charred nave of the church in which so many had been burned alive, the rest shot as they attempted to escape. I paused at Hotel Avril, where the three Pinède children had hidden, their village burning around them, its smoke and fire finally driving them from their hiding places. Behind the hotel, I saw where, in the midst of their flight, they had encountered an SS soldier who had unaccountably permitted them to escape.

Toward the end of my walk, I paused at the well into which the bodies of several villagers had been tossed. Julian had no doubt stood here, and so I tried to imagine what he might have been thinking as from this vantage point his own eyes had observed the ruins of Oradour.

Surely he would have considered how, for a few hours on June 10, 1944, Oradour had truly been a hell on earth, for in his account of it nothing of that horror had been lost. He'd tried to see the tragedy from 642 angles, but it was his own eyes, at the end of the book, that had seen the town in its grief-stricken repose. That final view had been glimpsed on the Champ de Foire, so when I at last came to that part of town, I opened Julian's book and read, softly but aloud, its concluding passage:

Twilight fell on the Champ de Foire. The car Dr Desourteaux drove into Oradour that afternoon still rests where he left it, though no longer in the same state. Time has stripped away its paint and its metal has gone to rust, for even a ruin cannot be spared the assault of further ruin. So also fade the killing sites, the barns at Laudy, Milord, and Bouchole, the Beaulieu forge, the Desourteaux garage, the little wine store on the road to St Junien, the church where the women and children were gathered, and whose shattered belfry still looks down upon the road that, but for the terrors of that day, those same women and children might later have taken to distant, spared Limoges. The signs that designate these once unheralded spots have begun to peel and soon must be repainted. The bolts that hold them to Oradour's stone walls will likewise need to be replaced. For ruins, too, must be restored, and with every restoration, Oradour, the town, slips further into Oradour, the event, a process that will reach its end when the last of those who survived those fearful hours pass beyond all further restoration, and the last eyes to have seen Oradour as something other than a martyred village will at last be closed.

After a dramatic pause, I closed the book and looked at René.

'Okay,' he said. 'So, we go now?'

A few minutes later we reached the hotel René had booked for us. It was in a neighboring village, small, quiet, with a restaurant that served us politely, though the waitress appeared somewhat surprised when René, so thoroughly French, asked for ketchup for his *pommes frites*.

'A self-conscious American in France would never do that,' I told him.

He laughed. 'Yes, but I am French, so I can do what I want.'

He ate with great relish, like a man accustomed to answering his appetites without reserve, and in that way quite the opposite of Julian, who had lived a far more Spartan life.

'Did you ever see Julian happy?' I asked. 'Did you ever see him laugh uncontrollably?'

'He had only black thoughts,' René answered. 'That was his nature.'

'No, it wasn't,' I said. 'When he was a young man, he was happy and self-confident. He had lots of romances. He would horse around like anyone else.'

'Horse around?'

'Joke with people, that sort of thing.'

'This is what it means, "horse around"?'

'Yes.'

René took out a pad and made a note. 'Julian, yes, you are right, he did not, as you say, "horse around,"' he said as he returned the pad to his pocket. 'Only sometimes he went to Le Chapeau Noir.' He placed the bowl of his glass between his large hands and rolled it back and forth. 'It is like a place from a movie, this bar,' he said.

'In what way?' I asked.

The glass stilled, as did René's usually darting eyes. 'If you go there, you will see,' he said.

CHAPTER 11

But why should I go there? Julian had never written about Le Chapeau Noir in any of his books. From time to time it had made an appearance in his letters, though rather sketchily, a line here, a line there. Still, he'd written about it enough for me to have gathered that it was typical of Pigalle, that is to say, rather seedy. I'd imagined it with a cement floor, its tables and chairs a mismatched assemblage. Julian had once described its clientele as a ragged array of expatriates. He'd probably said other things about it, too, though only one of them had stuck, the fact that it was the sort of place where, even when men talk of love, they seem to talk of murder. That had been a telling phrase, which no doubt accounted for the fact that I'd remembered it.

Clearly, Julian had gone to Le Chapeau Noir quite often, and perhaps for that reason, I found myself imagining him as a lone figure, dressed in a worn trench coat, moving down a deserted, rain-slicked street, the lights of Pigalle's famous windmill shining dimly through a mist.

This was a purely fanciful portrait, of course,

and yet, in imagining such a scene, my curiosity was heightened, particularly as to why Julian had described Le Chapeau Noir in a way that was so incontestably sinister, a bar where love and murder mingled with the smoke, curled and twined and became entangled.

'It was like places in those spy books he was reading,' René told me when I mentioned this to him the next morning over breakfast. 'There was still the Cold War in those days, and this bar, it was maybe a little like Vienna in that movie.' He began to hum the theme of *The Third Man*. 'And now you are maybe a little like the American in that movie, no?' he asked with a short laugh. 'Searching for your dead friend?'

I'd never thought of myself as a character in a film, especially one written by Graham Greene, and yet, I had to admit that I did feel a little like Martins in *The Third Man*. I wasn't a penniless pulp writer, as he'd been, and I didn't expect to meet a mysterious woman in a cemetery, but, as a man who'd lived a relatively safe life, experienced only the most commonplace adventures, risked nothing except on the stock market, there was something in Martins's steadily intensifying investigation of the mysterious Harry Lime that was not unlike my own.

But I could also feel Martins's confidence that no matter what he discovered about Harry Lime, it would do nothing to undermine his love or admiration for him. Anna Schmidt had assured him of exactly that in one of the movie's most quoted lines: 'A person doesn't change just because you find out more.' I felt no doubt that it would be the same with Julian, for it seemed to me at the time that the goodness of a man was like a vein of gold that only widens as it deepens, then dazzles at the core.

My walk through Oradour had only increased my confidence in his essential goodness because it was here that Julian had made innocents the focus of his art by giving them voice, while at the same time, in a single, extraordinary artistic choice, he had denied any voice to their tormenters, so that while the villagers had emerged as individuals, the Germans had all but disappeared.

Disappeared.

Strange how that word brought Marisol back into my mind, she whose disappearance had so disturbed Julian, his search for her one of his life's distinct failures, a dark end to his Argentine adventure that could not have been predicted by its bright beginning.

And it had been very bright, indeed, that beginning. We were often together, the three of us a faintly *Jules and Jim* trio of young people, though it was never a love triangle.

But though Julian was not in love with Marisol in that fiercely romantic way, he had certainly searched for her as if she'd been a lost lover, journeying all the way to the Chaco to see the priest who'd raised her.

108

He was in his midsixties, this priest, but he looked much older. His hair was gray, his face deeply lined, so that upon first impression he seemed to be as weathered as the destitute parish in which he'd labored all his life.

'He was already old when my aunt brought me to him,' Marisol said as we made our way to meet him that afternoon. 'But he took in this little girl he did not know.'

She was dressed less stylishly than usual and had added a small white flower to her hair, a touch of the indigene that you never saw in worldly Buenos Aires. A nod to the priest, I supposed, proof that her heart – or at least part of it – remained with him in the Chaco.

The old priest was sitting alone on a bench as we approached him. He did not see us but continued to stare straight ahead while he fingered a wooden rosary.

'It is Father Rodrigo who sent me to Buenos Aires,' Marisol said, her gaze more intently on Julian than on me. 'He is the saint of the Chaco.'

He was now only a few feet away, and it seemed to me that he was older than the color of his hair or the texture of his skin suggested. There was a spiritual quality to his agedness, a sense that he was as old as his faith, a witness to that first crucifixion.

We were almost upon him before he caught Marisol in his eye and struggled to his feet.

'Ah, my sweet daughter,' he said as he drew her into his arms.

She kissed him on both cheeks, then turned and introduced us.

The priest shook Julian's hand first, then turned to me.

'I have heard of your father,' he said. He stretched his hand toward me and I took it. 'He is said to be a good American. A friend. *Hermano en la lucha.*'

'I don't know what that means,' I confessed.

'A brother in the struggle,' Marisol informed me.

Brother in the struggle?

I couldn't imagine what Father Rodrigo was talking about.

'He is a man of the people, your father,' Rodrigo added. 'This is what I have heard. He is known as our friend in your capital. The poor do not have many friends there.'

He had been gently pumping my hand during all this, and only now released it. 'So, how do you know my Marisol?'

Though the question had been addressed to me, it was Julian who answered it.

'By way of the American consulate,' he said.

Father Rodrigo's expression soured as he turned toward Julian. 'They are working with the bad men of this country,' he said firmly, then looked at Marisol. 'Be careful what you say, my child. It is known that they are spies.'

Spies. The word clearly caught Julian's attention.

110

'Really?' he asked. 'Spies for whom?'

'For Casa Rosada,' Rodrigo answered. 'They give them names. Then these people disappear.' He looked at Marisol and placed a single, jagged finger at his lips. 'Careful,' he said, then glanced toward a nearby bench. 'Come, let us sit down.'

Once seated, Father Rodrigo took a moment to observe his surroundings. 'Ah, how beautiful is San Martín. I have not seen it since I was a boy.'

He meant Plaza San Martín, a lovely park in the heart of the city, where Marisol had earlier instructed us to meet her. It was close to Retiro Station, she said, and Father Rodrigo was scheduled to leave the city that evening. I'd had little interest in coming, but Julian had insisted. Clearly he had indicated to Marisol that he considered it important to meet this old priest.

At rest, Father Rodrigo seemed even older, but also he looked neglected. His clerical collar was slightly frayed and there were a few small tears in his cassock. This suggested that no help was being provided to him, no Gran Chaco equivalent to those formidable ladies of my boyhood parish, women who kept their priests tidy down to the neatly folded underwear.

My father had explained that South American clergy who subscribed to revolution theology were being punished by what he called 'the powers that be,' but on Father Rodrigo such imposed deprivations had created an aura of saintliness. Here was the Church as it should be, I thought, not a thing clothed in robes and adorned by jewels and housed in splendid cathedrals, but a country priest in a worn cassock.

'So,' Father Rodrigo said, glancing first to Julian, then back to me, 'has Marisol told you of the place where she grew up?'

She had, as a matter of fact, but for the next few minutes, we listened politely as Father Rodrigo detailed the sad life of the Chaco, the poverty and poor education, young lives doomed to nothing else. It was this doom that he'd wanted Marisol to escape. He'd seen her intelligence, her will, the fact that she would grasp whatever opportunity came her way.

'Which she has done,' he said proudly, then drew Marisol beneath his arm. 'She is no longer a girl from the Chaco.'

Marisol plucked the small white flower from her hair and gave it to Rodrigo. 'I will always be a girl from the Chaco,' she said.

By then, night had begun to fall over Plaza San Martín. Father Rodrigo struggled to his feet.

'I must go now,' he said. 'The bus home leaves soon.'

Marisol tucked her hand beneath the old man's arm. 'I will go with you to the station,' she said.

'I'll come, too,' Julian volunteered immediately.

'No,' Marisol said softly. 'It is for me to do this.'

And I thought, here is the soul of goodness: love, duty, sacrifice, and atonement, all combined to form something for which no word exists in English, save perhaps *grace*.

'No, I want to go with you,' Julian said insistently, like one who wished to share this service with Marisol.

Marisol appeared uncertain of accepting Julian's offer and surprised by his adamance.

'Let these good boys come with us,' Father Rodrigo said to Marisol. He pressed his sunbaked hand against her immaculate skin. 'We must learn the many roads into each other.'

Had it not been for the utter sincerity in the old man's eyes, I would have thought that final line scripted, a homily only a Barry Fitzgerald could have delivered without provoking laughter. As a statement, it was at once profound and corny, as true as it was impossible, and yet, as an expression of the old man's Christian perfectionism, it seemed entirely sincere.

The old man smiled. 'Come then,' he said, now looking at Julian and me and nodding forward, his signal that we were to come with them to the station.

It was only a short distance to the train station, but much of it was down a long sweep of concrete stairs, which made our progress slow and halting, Father Rodrigo somewhat unsteady on his feet, so that often Marisol took one arm and Julian the other.

At Retiro, crowds of people gathered in great, noisy throngs. Some carried cardboard boxes tied with twine rather than luggage, but this was Buenos Aires in the eighties, not some distant jungle outpost of a century before, and so the vast majority carried simple, battered suitcases and valises not very different from what would have been seen in any American bus station.

If the bus to the Chaco was different from the others, it was only in that those who waited for it looked poorer and more resigned than those on their way to less distant and impoverished shores. They were farmworkers, as Father Rodrigo noted, toilers in soy and sorghum and maize.

The bus pulled in after a few minutes.

Father Rodrigo got to his feet. 'God be with you all,' he said, then turned to Marisol, and drew out a strand of dark beads. 'I brought these from the Chaco,' he said.

Marisol took the beads and hung them around her neck. 'I will wear them every day,' she said.

The old priest smiled. 'Be kind to yourself, my daughter,' he said to her, 'and remember me.'

Marisol faced the bus as it pulled away, her hand raised, waving, craning her neck, trying for one last glimpse of Father Rodrigo. But he had taken a seat on the opposite side, and so she did not see him again, though she didn't give up her effort until the bus had disappeared into the night.

'He could easily be arrested,' Julian said firmly and in a way that gave his words a distinct authority. Then he looked at Marisol pointedly. 'Talking the way he does about spies in the American consulate.

114

If there were such people, spying for Casa Rosada, they might feel threatened.'

Marisol's eyes shot over to Julian, and I could see that his remark had struck her as very serious indeed.

'Threatened? But he is just a country priest,' she said. She began to toy with the beads the old priest had just given her. 'He is nothing to the ones in Casa Rosada. Who would listen to a priest from the Chaco? He is dust to them.'

Julian's voice was full of warning. 'Even dust gets trampled,' he said. He looked out toward the distant and still-departing bus. 'No one is too small to be noticed by the generals at Casa Rosada,' he added.

He spoke with great authority, as if he had knowledge of secret connections between the American consulate and the masters of Casa Rosada, which, of course, he did not have. And yet, as I could see, Marisol took his words to heart, though she added nothing to the exchange that had just taken place and instead nodded toward the stairs that led back to San Marco.

'There is a nice little restaurant there,' she said. 'It is called La Flora.'

A few minutes later we were seated at an outdoor table of the little café she'd mentioned. For no apparent reason, Julian began to talk about a book I was reading, arguing with me over a certain point. He was almost never wrong in such matters, but on this point I knew he was, which rather pleased me, and so to prove that I was right, I went back to the hotel to get the book. It was a chance, however juvenile, to one-up my always completely confident friend. The hotel was only a block away, so I was back very quickly, moving briskly toward the café because I knew I was right and couldn't wait to prove it. But as I closed in upon their table, I saw that Julian and Marisol were talking very intently. Julian was leaning forward, and Marisol looked extraordinarily grave, like one who's just been given a dreadful warning. They both shrugged off this seriousness as I approached, however, and it wasn't until after Marisol had left us that I brought the scene up with Julian.

'What were you talking about with Marisol?' I asked.

'Nothing,' Julian answered.

He said nothing more, but the troubled mood of that earlier conversation returned and seemed to haunt him, and he appeared to be questioning himself rather like a little boy who'd done something wrong.

'Marisol loves Father Rodrigo,' he said.

'Yes, she does,' I said. 'I hope he's not in danger. But who knows? You're right, they could do anything to a man like Rodrigo.' I looked out over the street. 'It's a lost country, just like Marisol says. Because if it gained power, the left would be just as oppressive as the right is now.'

Julian nodded softly.

'Marisol's right to stay out of it,' I said. 'Because they're crazy on both sides.'

We sat in silence for a time, Julian's gaze curiously unsettled, like a man trying to find his way in a dark wood.

Finally, I said, 'What's the matter, Julian?'

He looked at me and his lips parted, but he didn't speak. Instead, he turned away again, now looking out in the night-bound depths of San Martín.

'Nothing,' he said softly.

I sensed that if I chose to pursue the matter, Julian would probably tell me what was on his mind. But it had been a long day and I was tired.

'Well, I'm heading for bed,' I said.

Julian continued to face the park. 'Good night,' he said.

I went to my room and prepared for bed, but just before climbing into it, I glanced out the window, down to the little bar seven flights below. Julian was still sitting, just as he'd been when I left him, still peering out toward San Martín. Even from that distance, I could sense that something was troubling him.

I thought now, I should have gone down to him. If life knew only happy endings, a friend would have done just that. He would have looked down from the window, seen his friend in the shadowy light, understood, if not the cause of his trouble, then at least the fact that the trouble was there. He would have looked at his bed and felt a great need to climb into it. He would have thought of the soft pillows and the caressing sheets. He would have yearned for sleep and dreams and in his bone tiredness, he would have recognized his need for both. But in the end, this friend would have dressed himself and gone back downstairs, taken a seat at his friend's table and said to him, simply, 'Tell me.' He would have done all this because despite his youth and inexperience, he would have understood that sometimes it is simply such a gesture that makes the difference.

I knew that in any view of life designed to put a better face on man, this friend would have known these things and done them.

But I had not.

Now, however, with that scene playing in my mind, the question rose again as to whether Julian had been right in thinking that Father Rodrigo was going to be arrested. Therefore, when I got back to Paris, I decided to see if I could answer it.

CHAPTER 12

I dialed the number almost immediately after returning to my hotel in Paris, then waited the usual protracted amount of time it took my father to answer, longer this time than when I'd called him on my first night in Paris.

But at last he appeared on my computer screen, already dressed for bed, though it was late afternoon in New York.

'I can see you very clearly,' I told him.

He smiled. 'You, too. It's really quite amazing.'

We talked about trivial matters for a time, the weather in New York and Paris, a smattering of world and national news, then on to my impression of René and our visit to Oradour-sur-Glane.

At last I said, 'Do you remember that when Julian and I were in Buenos Aires we met an old priest named Father Rodrigo?'

'Of course,' my father answered. 'You said he'd heard of me. I was surprised by that.'

'Do you have any idea whatever happened to him?'

'Only that when Julian went down to the Chaco, he was no longer there,' my father answered. 'But I'm sure Julian told you that.'

'Another of the disappeared,' I said.

'So Julian thought,' my father answered.

'He spoke to you about it?'

'Yes,' my father answered. 'Evidently this priest had said some fairly dangerous things when they met. Julian told me what he'd said, but I didn't see it as all that dangerous. It was common knowledge, after all, that we were more or less in cahoots with the junta.'

'But what else could explain the fact that Rodrigo went missing?' I asked.

'Well, sometimes people vanish of their own accord,' my father told me. 'In a place like Argentina at that time, there were many reasons a man might want to make himself scarce.'

'What would have made Father Rodrigo leave Argentina?' I asked.

'Nothing, if he was what he seemed,' my father said.

'A country priest, you mean?'

My father nodded. 'Even one with a loose tongue.'

'You're saying Father Rodrigo might have been more than that?' I asked.

'I'm saying it's possible that in Argentina at that time such a priest might have been used.'

'By whom?'

'The Montoneros, of course,' my father answered. 'Lots of priests were working for the Montoneros.'

He saw that I had no idea what he was talking about.

'They were pretty much finished by the time you went to Argentina,' he explained. 'But before the junta, they murdered anyone who opposed them. And if Rodrigo were a Montonero, and he got wind that he had been discovered or was about to be discovered, then he might have found it a very good idea to leave the country.'

'How could he have escaped?' I asked. 'He was a poor parish priest.'

'Yes, but if he were a Montonero, they could have financed his departure from Argentina,' my father told me.

'What money would the Montoneros have had?'

'They would have had the millions they got from kidnappings and bank robberies,' my father answered. 'One kidnapping alone brought in sixty million dollars. It was the largest ransom ever paid. It's in the *Guinness Book of Records*.'

'Would Julian have known any of this?' I asked.

'I doubt it,' my father answered. 'Why do you ask?'

'Because he seemed to think that Rodrigo was going to be arrested,' I answered. 'He told this to Marisol.'

My father suddenly grew very still. 'I didn't know that,' he said quietly, and for a moment looked like a man sitting in a darkened theater, awaiting a film whose story he dreaded.

'He never mentioned it?' I asked. 'Not even after he got back from Argentina?'

My father shook his head. 'Of course, we rarely talked after that.'

This was true. Julian had but rarely seen my father after Argentina, and even then only at what were more or less public gatherings, Loretta's wedding, for example, and Colin's funeral.

'Good people like this Father Rodrigo can be manipulated, Philip,' my father said quietly, like a man considering the treacheries of life.

'But Julian couldn't have known that Rodrigo might be a Montonero operative,' I said.

'That's true,' my father said firmly. 'The only way he could have had intelligence of that sort was if he had some contact at Casa Rosada.'

'Which, of course, he didn't,' I said.

'No, of course not,' my father said. 'They were absolute evil.' His eyes appeared to see that evil quite clearly. 'They tortured people mercilessly.'

I saw that his mood was blackening, so I moved to change the subject.

'You know, it's interesting to think that Rodrigo might still be alive,' I said, almost lightly. 'And if the Montoneros wanted to get him out of Argentina, he could be anywhere.'

Now my mind fixed on the shadowy priest with whom Julian had often been seen at Le Chapeau Noir. 'Anywhere at all,' I said, almost to myself.

'Anywhere at all,' my father repeated. The darkness fell upon him again. 'It's a twisted world, Philip,' he said, 'the one you're touching now.'

'At the end of the conversation, my father said that I was getting into a twisted world,' I told Loretta when I called her later that night.

She had listened silently, and when I finished, she took a moment before she spoke.

'Do you think that priest might actually have been a Montonero?' she asked.

'I don't know,' I said, though I immediately began to consider the possibility. Certainly it was possible that Rodrigo might have gotten carried away with some form of revolutionary theology, agreed to help the Montoneros in some way, and then, with the junta on his trail, found it necessary to flee the country.

I shared this with Loretta, then added as if I half believed it, 'He might even be in Paris. Maybe even at this little bar Julian frequented. René said that Julian often talked with a priest there.'

I said this jokingly, as if describing the elements of a potboiler plot, but Loretta's tone turned serious.

'Your father's right,' she said. 'It is a twisted world.' A pause, then, 'Be careful, Philip.'

Some warnings come like the tolling of a bell, and thus it was with Loretta's.

For that reason, if for no other, I should have heeded what she said to me and thus anticipated the terrors that awaited. But the Saturn Turn twists for all, as Julian had already learned, and so I moved unknowingly ahead.

PART III

THE TERROR

CHAPTER 13

In *The Terror,* Julian's curious meditation on one of Gilles de Rais's awful minions, he wrote:

The route to moral horror is never direct. There are always ramps and stairs, corridors and tunnels, the secret chamber forever concealed from those who would be appalled by what they found there.

We all had secret chambers, I thought, though most chambers probably harbored nothing more fearful than some peculiar desire, or if not that, then perhaps simply the sad awareness of an inexplicable inadequacy we dared not reveal. Even so, Julian would have been the last I'd have suspected of having such a place. At his father's death, he had been deeply stricken, but he had rallied even from this loss, regained his footing, and proceeded on, his confidence returning with each passing day, so that within a month or so, he seemed once again the boy of old, though perhaps even more determined to make a mark in the world.

For his spiritual resilience alone, I had admired

him. But later, as his life took shape, I had also thought him physically brave. He'd been an intrepid traveler, after all, with the courage to cross fields so foreign he must have thought himself on the moon at times. Rimbaud, stranded in Egypt, had written stinging letters of regret, his pen crying out, *why, oh why, am I here?* I had little doubt that Julian had often found himself floating in some similar sea of strangeness, isolated, friendless, knowing little of the language and customs, short of money, with only history's most vile miscreants to occupy his mind. It takes courage to roam the world in that way, and roam it Julian certainly had.

But this same physical courage had sometimes struck me as reckless and foolhardy. I'd seen scars on his arms, bruises on his body. He never mentioned these injuries, but on one occasion, I got a hint about how he'd received them.

We were walking in Chueca, at that time one of Madrid's most dangerous neighborhoods, when two young men staggered out of a bar, headed for the bright lights of Gran Via. On the way, they came across a young gypsy woman crumpled against a building in a common beggarly pose. Normally such people were passed without a nod, but on this occasion, the men stopped to taunt her. 'Look at this gitana,' they said. 'Can you smell this filthy whore?'

By the time Julian and I reached them, the insults had escalated into a physical assault, one of the men lifting his leg to press the toe of his shoe against the woman's breast while calling her names – *puta, coño,* and the like.

In Spanish, Julian said, 'Leave her alone.'

He said it quietly, but before the man could draw back his foot, Julian rushed forward and plowed into him, and they both went sprawling into the street. I didn't try to intervene, but neither did the other man's friend, so Julian and the man simply rolled around for a bit before getting to their feet, the Spaniard muttering curses as he staggered away.

That night, Julian emerged more or less unharmed, and we went on our way. But I suspected that on other occasions he'd done the same and gotten a thorough beating as a result. I idealized those confrontations in a way that ennobled Julian, cast him as a selfless defender of the weak, and yet, at the same time, I sometimes wondered what his motives were. Was he driven to test his courage? Had he decided that the grand work he once dreamed of could only be realized in small acts of self-sacrifice? I knew that martyrdom was sometimes less the product of saintliness than of spiritual ambition, so had Julian from time to time felt the pinch of his own shrunken hope of doing some great work and for that reason lashed out in acts of reckless altruism?

I had no answer to this question, of course. Yet, the more I pondered it, the more I felt that something was buried in Julian, a need, a remorse, something that held the key to him. I had no place to go for an answer, but nevertheless I decided to drop in on Le Chapeau Noir. Perhaps, with a little luck, I might run into the man Julian had spoken with there, the one with whom he appeared to have discussed Marisol.

René was right, as it turned out. Le Chapeau Noir was indeed a good deal like the sort of place one would find in novels of intrigue. In fact, it was less a place than an atmosphere, and even if its shadowy interior were not clouded with cigarette smoke, you would add this smoke to any description of it. You would also include a dim, oddly undulating light that throws this mysterious figure into half shadow, that one into silhouette, by turns revealing or concealing a forehead, a jaw, an eye with a patch, each face broken into puzzle pieces. You would add a random arrangement of wooden tables, and over there, huddled in a corner, you would put two men in linen suits, one with a very thin moustache, the other clean shaven, wearing a panama hat. Snatches of many languages would come at you like bats. Spanish answered by Greek, a hint of German from behind a curtain, Turkish over there, where a man in a red fez drinks tea from a white china cup. To his left, an Englishman in evening dress, come to sample the demimonde after a dazzling night at the embassy. No doubt there'd be an American, too, wearing a dark suit, off in a distant corner, seemingly naive and deceptively trusting, but with a revolver close at hand.

That would be me, I thought, as I slouched, minus the revolver, in a distant corner and silently watched the regulars at Le Chapeau Noir.

René had told me that the place was dead until around midnight, so I'd dutifully showed up at just after twelve. By then, a few of the tables were taken, though hardly by the throng of shady characters I'd anticipated. True, the majority of the customers were foreigners, just as René had described, but of these, only a few looked like thieves or black marketers. There were a few Algerians, but they were off by themselves, closely huddled around a small table. A tight group of East Indians had claimed the far end of the bar, their eyes glancing about rather nervously, though it was unclear whether it was the police or the Algerians they feared. The rest were French or Eastern Europeans, though at one point I thought I heard a bit of German.

Le Chapeau Noir was, of course, a thoroughly landlocked bar, and yet something about it had the moldering dankness of a harbor. I might have thought of Marseille or Naples, but for some reason – perhaps it was the presence of those few North Africans – I found myself associating it in full literary fashion with ancient Cádiz, known by the Phoenicians, an immemorial coastal trading post, populated by every kind of adventurer and deserter, safe haven for the criminal flotsam of

131

two continents; perhaps in all the world, the first true city of intrigue.

I'd come here in hopes of encountering the priest with whom Julian had often been seen in what René called – with his usual melodrama and showy English – 'dark conclave.' With a little probing, René had gone on to describe the man and even volunteered to accompany me to the bar, for which I thanked him but declined. I needed to be alone, I thought, to experience Le Chapeau Noir in the solitary way I assumed Julian must first have encountered it. I suppose that I'd come to feel that I needed to see what Julian had seen, talk to the people he'd talked to, go where he'd gone, *become* him in the way he sought to become the great criminals he studied. Such a route is always dangerous, of course, like shooting the rapids of another's neural pathways. And yet, step by step, I'd come to feel myself drawn – perhaps lured – deeper and deeper into Julian's mind and character. It was as if I were once again following him into the caves we'd sometimes explored in the hills around Two Groves, Julian always in the lead, beckoning me forward with an 'Oh, come on, Philip, what's to fear?' I dragging reluctantly behind him, refusing to give the answer that came to me: 'Everything.'

Suddenly I felt that I was once again trailing after him in just that way, going deeper and into yet more narrow spaces, caverns that were dark and cramped and airless, and in that way not unlike Le Chapeau Noir.

132

No one spoke to me, of course, but that hardly mattered, because my French was very bad, and so it would have been impossible for me to have a conversation with any of the bar's clientele, save to inform them that *'le plume est sur la table.'*

Even so, I felt that my nights at Le Chapeau Noir provided a feeling for the dispossessed that was akin to Julian's. For there was something about this bar that gave off an aura of precious things irretrievably lost. For some it had been a homeland, for others, a political ideal. For yet others, it was some romantic dream the intransigent facts of life had indefinitely deferred.

Without telling me, René had been more practical in his research, and he had located the priest Julian had sometimes spoken with at Le Chapeau Noir, a man who had recently been detained for what René called 'a document problem.' He was now at liberty, however, and René assured me that he would appear at the bar the following night.

And so he did.

After talking with my father, I'd actually entertained the faint hope that this priest might be Father Rodrigo, a hope encouraged by René's description of an old man with leathery brown skin, very thin, quite stooped. Such a person might turn out to be Marisol's beloved priest, now in his eighties, and perhaps, if my father's vague suggestion turned out to be true, still withdrawing modest sums from God knows how much Montonero money. I imagined him as essentially unchanged, except physically, and therefore, with secular communism now in tatters, still dreamily devoted to some Christian version of the same radical, and to my mind naive, egalitarianism.

But the man I met at Le Chapeau Noir that evening was considerably younger than Rodrigo would have been. He was shorter than Rodrigo, too, and a tad rounder, with dark skin and black hair that had thinned a great deal and which he parted on the left side just above his ear.

'Ah, so you are a friend of Julian,' he said as I approached him.

His accent was predominately Spanish, though there were hints of other lands, which gave the impression that he'd lived somewhat nomadically, his speech now marked with the fingerprints of his travels.

'When I met him, he had just returned from Bretagne,' the man said.

He offered a smile that was rather rueful and suggested that his journey through life had been a difficult one, a smile that ran counter to his eyes.

'Julian noticed that I was drinking Malbec, the wine of Argentina,' the man said. 'He came to me and introduced himself.' He thrust out his hand. 'I am Eduardo.'

'Philip Anders,' I said, hoping to elicit Eduardo's last name.

He did not respond, however, and we took our seats at a small table near the back of the bar, Eduardo quick to position himself with his back to the wall, clearly a man long accustomed to keeping an eye on both the front door and the exits.

'We talked first of Cuenca,' Eduardo said. 'Julian had spent much time in that part of Spain.' His smile was quite warm, but that warmth ran counter to what he said next. 'Years before, when I was young and angry, I had gone to Cuenca to kill a man. He had wronged my sister in Zaragoza. He brought drugs into her life, and they killed her. Everywhere he spread this poison. Pity another's knife found his heart before mine could. I wanted my face to be the last he saw.' He waved to the barman and ordered a bottle of wine, though not a Malbec. When it came, he poured each of us a round, then lifted his glass. 'Do you know the fascist toast?'

'I'm afraid not.'

'It comes from the Spanish Civil War,' Eduardo said. 'It was first made in Salamanca. Imagine that? Spain's ancient seat of learning. In the presence of Miguel de Unamuno, our country's greatest philosopher. Made by a one-eyed, one-armed general of Franco's army.' He touched his glass to mine. 'Long live death.'

It was not a pleasing toast, but I drank to it anyway.

'He was an interesting man, Julian,' Eduardo said as he set down his drink. 'I enjoyed very much talking to him.'

'What did you talk about?' I asked.

Eduardo smiled. 'Many things. Julian was very learned. He had read a great deal. But, at the time, he was mostly thinking about evil women.'

I thought of the evil women Julian had written about: La Meffraye, Countess Báthory.

'Yes,' I said, 'he wrote about such women.'

'This he did, yes, but the one he spoke of most, this woman he never wrote about,' Eduardo said. 'But he was much interested in her and often he spoke of this woman.'

'Who?'

'Her name was Ilse Grese.'

When he saw that I'd never heard the name he said, 'She was a guard at Ravensbrück.'

'The concentration camp?'

Eduardo nodded. 'Yes.'

Irma Ida Ilse Grese, I found out later, was born in Wrechen, Germany, in 1923. Her father was a dairy worker who joined the Nazi Party early and, presumably, passed his political views on to his young daughter. At fifteen, she quit school as a result of poor grades and because she'd been bullied, particularly for her already fanatical devotion to the League of German Girls, a Nazi youth organization. After leaving school, she worked as an assistant nurse at an SS sanatorium. Later, she tried to apprentice as a nurse but was blocked by the German Labor Exchange, so she worked as a shop girl for a time, then drifted through a series of lowly agricultural jobs until she found her true calling as a guard, first at Ravensbrück, then at

136

Auschwitz, where, given more power than a lowly milkmaid could ever imagine, she added her own peculiar heat to that hell.

'She was very cruel, this woman,' Eduardo went on to say. 'Julian told me of the many terrible things she did. How she wore heavy boots and carried a riding crop. She starved her dogs until they were crazed with hunger, he said, and then she set them on her prisoners. She enjoyed their pain. A true monster, this woman.'

'Why did he never write about her?' I asked.

Eduardo shrugged. 'Perhaps she was too simple. He said that she was just a thug. It was the other one who had captured him by then. The one he called "The Terror."'

Her real name was Perrine Martin, but she was known as La Meffraye, which in French means 'the terror.' Julian described her as being an old woman and longtime assistant to the serial killer Gilles de Rais. In his service, she proved herself very adept at procuring young children, despite her vaguely sinister clothing – a long gray robe with a black hood. Her actual involvement in the many murders recounted in Gilles's trial was, according to Julian's book, perhaps as much dark fairy tale as truth, but his writing suggested that she possessed demonic qualities well beyond her crimes – chief among them, I remembered now, was her capacity for deception.

Still, it was for murder that she was arrested and to which she later confessed, giving some of the most graphic and horrifying testimony of Gilles de Rais's trial. After that, she was imprisoned in Nantes, where, presumably at a very old age, she died. Thus her story ended, at least as far as Julian had followed it in his book.

'This woman who was a terror,' Eduardo said, 'Julian had a big interest in her.'

'He did, yes,' I agreed. 'But in the book he some-times seemed less concerned with her crimes than in the clever way she disguised herself.'

Eduardo laughed. 'A nice old grandmother, yes. You are right, it was in this that Julian found her true evil. This is what he said to me. Before the crime, there was the disguise.'

'Disguise,' I repeated softly, and with that word recalled something Julian had written in his book on La Meffraye, the telling phrase he'd used, how the woman's kindness, simplicity, devotion, and humility were nothing more than serrated notches in the blade she held.

Eduardo seemed to glimpse the dark and unset-tling recollection that had suddenly come into my mind. 'It sometimes caused me to wonder if perhaps someone had deceived Julian in his youth,' he said. 'Could this be so? Was there such a one?'

'Not that I know of,' I said, then added what seemed to me an ever-deepening truth. 'But I suppose there's a lot about Julian that I don't know.'

We talked on for a time, and as we did, it became clear that Julian had shared a great deal with

Eduardo: his early life, his father's death, the great emptiness he'd felt at this loss, and how, from then on, he believed that to kill a father was to a kill a son. He had also related a few stories about his travels with Loretta and his days at Two Groves.

By then I'd learned a few things about Eduardo, as well, most notably that he had never been a priest but had used that disguise, along with false papers, to move more or less undetected throughout Europe. Those movements had interested Julian, he said, and he had questioned him about them quite relentlessly. It was during those conversations that Eduardo had inquired about Julian's earliest travels. In response, Julian had first described the happy journeys he'd taken with his father and Loretta; then, quite reluctantly, according to Eduardo, he had at last spoken of Argentina.

'It was not a happy place for Julian,' Eduardo told me. 'He told me that Buenos Aires was a place that swarmed with agents and secret agents.'

'That's true,' I said. 'The Dirty War was still going on when we were there.'

Eduardo nodded. 'Julian said a bad thing happened there. It was to a woman he knew.'

'Our guide, yes,' I said. 'While we were in Buenos Aires, she disappeared. She was never found.'

'And Julian loved this woman?' Eduardo answered.

'No,' I answered. 'At least not romantically. But he cared for her.'

Eduardo looked puzzled. 'Then there was perhaps another woman in his life?'

139

'Not one he ever spoke of,' I said. 'Why do you ask?'

'Because Julian seemed like a man betrayed,' Eduardo said.

'In what way?' I asked.

'In the way of one who cannot forget his betrayal,' Eduardo said. 'For most men, it is a woman who leaves this stain. Perhaps this was not so with Julian.'

He was silent for a moment, clearly thinking of Julian. At last he said, 'Julian told me that on the walls of Russian prison cells, the prisoners of the gulag had written one word more than any other. It was not what you would expect it to be, this word. It was not *mother or father or God*.' He seemed once again to be with my old friend, peering into the gravity of his face. 'It was *zachem*.'

'What does *zachem* mean?' I asked.

'It means "why."' Eduardo answered. His gaze became quite quizzical, but with a somberness that deepened it. 'I think this was written also in Julian's mind. And that it was written there by betrayal.'

CHAPTER 14

Later that night, sleepless in my bed, I remembered Julian during our flight to Buenos Aires, how boyishly excited he was at the time, and how different from the man he later became, isolated and reclusive, the habitué of a Pigalle bar, talking of evil women who brilliantly disguised their vile crimes, with *zachem*, as Eduardo said, somehow carved into his mind.

Now, recalling the eerie sensation I felt at his mention of this word, I remembered my first meeting with Julian after he returned from France with the completed manuscript of *The Terror* and, in particular, a remark he made during our conversation, the fact that he considered deception to be life's cruelest act. El Cepa had deceived his neighbors into believing he was dead. The German soldiers had deceived the villagers of Oradour into believing they were only to have their identities checked. La Meffraye had deceived the children she brought to Gilles de Rais for slaughter.

'So is that your theme, Julian?' I asked him. 'Deception?'

I sensed a defensive hardening within him at that

moment, a wall going up. He glanced about and looked at his hands before he said, 'I often think of something Thoreau wrote, that although children kill frogs in play, the frogs die in earnest.'

Odd though this remark was, it seemed like an opening up, a chance to speak of whatever was so clearly troubling him, but in a moment of supreme insensitivity, I became pedantic.

'Thoreau took that from Plutarch,' I told him in a little show of erudition, 'who took it from Bion.'

Julian nodded. 'We're all thieves, I suppose,' he said. 'Spies and secret agents.'

'Magicians of manipulation,' René said the next morning when we had breakfast together in the hotel dining room. 'That's what Julian called spies and secret agents.'

'He told Eduardo that Buenos Aires had been full of such people when we were there,' I said. 'Which it probably was, though Julian couldn't have known much about such things.'

'Then why does what he said trouble you?' René asked. 'I can see that it does.'

And he was right. Even now, I suddenly felt a twinge of uneasiness, the sense that I could no longer be certain of what Julian had or had not known about anything.

'It troubles me because Julian seems to have believed that he was betrayed at some point in his life,' I said. 'At least that's what Eduardo told me. And he seemed quite sure of it.'

I related the memory that had returned to me the night before, the vaguely enigmatic conversation I'd had with Julian the day he turned in the manuscript of *The Terror*, how troubled he looked when he talked briefly about deception as the chief of crimes, the way it seemed to open the door into some darker room.

'He never worked on a book about spies, did he?' I asked. 'I mean, for all his talk about spies and agents, he never wrote about them.'

'No, he didn't,' René said. He lit his usual after-breakfast cigarette. 'I think he was not so much interested in spies. But, as you say, perhaps in disguise he was interested. We spoke of this from time to time. Deception was something I knew about from my time in Algiers. They were great deceivers, those terrorists in Algeria. I told Julian this. They passed codes during prayers, reciting the Koran but making a mistake. The mistake was the code.' He laughed. 'And sometimes even their ailments they used as code. A stomach problem was a man who got scared and had to drop out of a plot. A headache was a new development or maybe some technical matter that had to be figured out before those fucking bastards could blow up the next building or shoot the next policemen.'

He laughed. 'Half the time, it seemed like child's play.'

'Child's play,' I repeated, struck by the fact that so dangerous an endeavor could be thought of in such a way.

René took a long draw on his cigarette. 'Child's play, yes,' he said. 'Julian knew this. He even spoke of Mata Hari in this way. That she was just a woman playing a game. Until they shot her, of course. He said once, "But it is no longer a game when the bullet strikes."' He looked at me quite starkly. 'Julian believed they do many horrible things, the ones who don't grow up. Not to grow up, he said, was a kind of crime.'

'What did he mean by that?'

René crushed out his cigarette with a violence that seemed to come from something deep within him. 'We were talking about Algeria, those girls who planted bombs. I say to him, they were like kids in a playground, those terrorists. Only throwing bombs instead of balls.'

Suddenly, he stopped, and I saw that this memory had brought something abruptly to mind.

'What is it, René?' I asked.

With a curious gravity, René said, 'He looked very strange, Julian. When I said this to him. He looked like maybe this was a truth he knew and which he did not like.'

'What did he say?'

'The thing I told you, that not to grow up was maybe also a crime,' René answered.

He sat back, lit another cigarette, and drew in several deep puffs before speaking. 'He was a sad fellow, Julian.'

'Maybe he was a classic romantic,' I said. 'In his youth, he wanted to change the world.'

René shook his head. 'No, Julian had clear eyes. Once he said to me, "Do you know what love is, René? A failure of perspective."' He shifted slightly. 'Such things are not said by romantics.'

I considered how very dark this remark was, the notion that no love could withstand the inquiry of clear minds, love itself a clever deceiver.

'He thought we all dangled in a great web of illusion, didn't he?' I asked.

René nodded.

'Illusions we had to have in order to be happy,' I added.

René stared at the tip of his cigarette for a moment, then looked up at me. 'These he hid from you, his sad truths.'

A somewhat painful recognition hit me. 'Perhaps he thought I was too soft to bear them.'

René smiled. 'He said to me once, "It is not what you tell a friend but what you refrain from telling him that shows your love for him."'

A single strand broke in the web that I had perhaps long dangled in.

'So Julian would deceive his friend,' I said. 'For his own good.'

René shrugged, took a final puff of his cigarette. 'So,' he said. 'He is back now in Paris, the landlord.'

I looked at him quizzically.

'To Julian's apartment,' René explained.

'Oh.'

René watched me darkly. 'You do not want this

145

key?' he asked. 'Perhaps you do not wish to go through Julian's things?'

'Why wouldn't I?' I asked.

René shrugged. 'In a man's room, there are always secrets. I learned this in Algeria. Always secret things, and some of them, not so nice.'

I waved my hand. 'I'm not afraid of anything I might find in Julian's room. Besides, it's the reason I came to Paris.'

René crushed out his cigarette like a man who'd given his prisoner one last opportunity to avoid a grim fate. 'Okay,' he said. 'You have made your choice.'

'But, you know, at that moment, I wasn't sure I truly wanted to go to Julian's room or go through his things,' I confessed to Loretta when I called her that same night, recounted my conversations with Eduardo and the one I subsequently had with René, his final warning, all of it oddly disturbing.

'And yet, at the same time, I can't stop myself from taking a look inside Julian's apartment,' I added. 'I see him in that boat, and that compelling urge comes over me again, the need to stop him, to find out if there was some way I could have stopped him.'

'You're like one of those obsessed detectives searching through a cold-case folder,' Loretta said. 'Only with you, the file you're looking through has Julian's name written on it.'

146

'Yes,' I said. 'That's exactly how I feel. But all this talk of deception, of hiding things from his friends, it's very disquieting, Loretta.' I smiled, but edgily. 'In a thriller it would be others who are trying to keep me from finding things out. They'd be shooting at me or trying to run me down in a car. But in this case, it seems to be Julian who's covering his tracks.' I considered what I just said, then asked, 'Did he ever mention a woman named Ilse Grese?'

'No,' Loretta said.

'He never wrote about her, but he seems to have been quite interested in her,' I said. 'She was a guard at Ravensbrück. A very cruel one.'

Loretta said nothing, but I sensed a troubling ripple in her mind.

'He once talked about what he called "beautiful beasts,"' she said. 'Women who used their beauty or their innocence to deceive people.'

I thought again of Julian's interest in Ilse Grese and others like her, women who'd committed their crimes partly by means of clever disguises. In *The Terror*, he had digressed into a discussion of Charlotte Corday, the murderer of Marat, her certainty that by killing one man she had saved a hundred thousand. He'd made similar points about Mata Hari in that same book, with lengthy discourses on women as revolutionaries, assassins, and spies – in every case, deceptive women. Women who had hidden their true motives, often behind masks of beauty, but sometimes behind masks of kindness, simplicity, innocence. Women who, for all their evil, appeared to be no more dangerous than a . . .

The name that suddenly popped into my mind stopped me cold.

Marisol.

CHAPTER 15

It struck me as quite strange that late in the night when I thought of Marisol again, it was not Argentina that came to mind but a scene in *The Terror*, one I later looked up to make sure I'd remembered it correctly.

La Meffraye stands beside a forest woodshed, watching as a small boy skips playfully down a narrow, overgrown path. She is carrying a basket filled with baked goods, and as the boy draws near, she uncovers them just enough to release their fragrance into 'the famished air.' She does not let go of the cloth, however, but holds it – 'with fingers not yet talons' – ready to cover the cakes, and in that gesture make it plain that she will offer none of her sweets to this little boy. For a single, heart-stopping instant, the cloth remains as suspended as her goodness, for this is the first of La Meffraye's potential victims. She wavers as the boy grows near, thinking now that it is only a game, that she will offer the sweet, but the boy will refuse. She convinces herself that this is true, and with that conviction she draws back the cloth and stretches out her hand and offers a sweet, which the boy

149

immediately takes. At that moment, it is life itself that appears to betray La Meffraye by concealing the moral precipice even as she approaches it, a deception that continues until the instant of her fall.

The passage was primarily about La Meffraye, of course, but rereading it I found myself putting Julian in the place of the little boy she coaxes to his death. It was a nightmare scenario that had no doubt been generated by Loretta's mention of 'beautiful beasts' and probably would have tormented me all night had I not finally escaped into a book I'd been asked to review. To my great relief, it was something entirely the opposite of Julian's dark tomes, sweet and light and at last uplifting, something completely forgettable, about a blind schoolteacher and a talking dog.

'When can we get into Julian's apartment?' I asked René the next morning when we met at the tiny breakfast room where the hotel served its far from well-heeled guests weak coffee and an even worse bread.

It was the bread René eyed suspiciously. 'I would not have thought it possible to find bad bread in Paris,' he said. 'Perhaps it comes from England?' He stirred a coffee he also appeared to find far from his liking. 'We can go today.'

I took a sip of coffee. 'This morning?'

'If you wish,' René said.

'I presume Julian's things are still there?'

'Where else would they be?' René said. 'It is on Rue Saint-Denis, as you must know.' He smiled. 'Julian was always near the prostitutes, but I don't think he enjoyed their pleasures.'

'You obviously think he should have,' I said. 'Why?'

René considered my question for a moment, then lifted his right hand and curled his fingers into a fist. 'When you are with your wife, your children, even your friends, you are like this,' he said. 'But when you are with a whore, you are like this.' He opened his hand like one freeing a caged bird. 'You can say to her the truths you hide from others. That you hate your life, that your friends are stupid, that your work destroys you, that you are a joke to yourself.' A vague sorrow swam into his eyes. 'Julian understood this. "With the fallen," he said to me once, "you can be fallen, too."' He drew his fingers once again into a fist. 'But even so, Julian was always like this, clenched, holding on to himself.'

René's observation was like him, I thought, a tad over-the-top, and yet I couldn't help but wonder if it truly might be the thing that Julian held within the tightly curled fist of himself that had finally drawn the blade across his veins.

We arrived at Julian's apartment an hour later. René had arranged for the owner of the building to leave the key with an old woman who lived on the first floor. She was North African, and I could see that René immediately regarded her with suspicion, as if he were still in Algiers, where every woman carried a bomb in her basket.

'Okay, we can go up now,' he said as he ushered me toward the stairs. 'But be careful. As we say, "Napoleon pissed here." You cannot trust the wood.'

Despite my earlier reservations, I now felt a curious anticipation as I mounted the stairs, a sense that I was coming nearer to Julian. For it was to this one space on earth that, after all his many and extended travels, he had always been drawn back.

So why, I asked myself, as I stepped inside it, did it feel so lost and cheerless, so devoid of the homey quality one associates with decades of living in a space? In this room I'd expected to glimpse at least some small aspect of the devotion I thought Julian must have had for his work. Instead, I saw only evidence of his loneliness and isolation. There were no pictures to brighten the room's dim light, nor even so much as a calendar by which he might have recorded an upcoming rendezvous. There was no radio or television. Evidently, he did not listen to music either while he worked or to relax when his work was done.

What I found was a garret five floors above a dismal street. It had small windows kept tightly shuttered for so long that I had trouble prying them open. When I did, the light revealed the full austerity of the room, the iron bed, the small wooden desk, no element of which was in the least unexpected. Julian had lived like a monk, and on that thought I remembered the day we visited Mont Saint-Michel. We had climbed the stairs to its uppermost tower, where the monks had once sat exposed to the frigid winds of the Normandy coast. In that icy, windswept scriptorium, they'd spent their lives copying manuscripts, using small metal rods to break the ice-encrusted ink, and in this one, almost as uncomfortable and psychologically no less isolated, Julian, the secular anchorite, had written his dark books.

The materials he used in his research filled the bookshelves that covered almost every wall. There were probably around five hundred books, most of them about the eras during which the crimes he studied had taken place. There were books on Spain when the crime of Cuenca had occurred, and on the rest of Europe, particularly Germany and France, at the time of Oradour. Several shelves were devoted to his study of La Meffraye, and he had grouped a number of biographies of Elizabeth Báthory together, along with general histories of Hungary at the time of her crimes, though there were far fewer research materials having to do with her case. One bookcase held works that dealt with Andrei Chikatilo, interspersed with books on Russia during the time of the killer's life span, the dark age of Stalinism.

'Was this the only place Julian had?' I asked René, hoping that perhaps somewhere on earth Julian had found a less gloomy place to live.

'The only one I know about,' René answered. He glanced about, clearly repulsed by the bleakness of the room.

'What's in there?' I asked.

He looked at the squat metal filing cabinet I indicated and shrugged.

I was not amused by René's indifference, so I ignored him and walked over and opened the cabinet's only drawer.

In a novel it would be Julian's 'secret chamber' I found inside the drawer, and in a single, riveting instant, everything would be revealed, and I would subsequently return to New York knowing what I should have known to save Julian from himself.

But life holds its trump cards more closely to the vest, and what I found was five folders, each identified by a location: Cuenca, Oradour, Brittany, Čachtice, Rostov, places that like dark magnets had irresistibly drawn Julian to them. A sixth file lay beneath the others, but without an identifying label.

I turned to René. 'You don't have to stay while I go through this,' I told him.

René plopped down in one of the room's two chairs. 'I can wait.'

'Okay,' I said, and with that I took the folders over to the desk and turned the switch on the small lamp I found there, though I expected that René had already arranged for the electricity to be turned off, since Julian had been gone for well over a month by then. But the light came on and in its dim glow I opened the first of the files.

There were mostly photographs Julian had taken in and around Cuenca of the various locations he would later describe in his book, pictures of its dusty plaza, the bridge, the roads that led out of the town, along with various municipal buildings. There was one of the two of us, as well. It had been taken by a passerby, and in the picture Julian was curiously focused, his gaze drawn, as I now recalled, to the Guardia Civil officer who was standing a few feet away talking to a well-dressed American whom we had encountered only minutes before. It was the only photograph with either of us in it, and I could find no reason, save sheer accident, that it had been included with the others. It was also the only picture Julian had failed to identify in his usual way by writing the name of the place on the back.

The photographs in the file marked 'Oradour' were of the same sort, all of them taken at the site of the massacre and clearly meant to jog Julian's memory as he wrote. I had not gone with Julian to the town, so there could be no pictures of the two of us there. Nor were there any photographs of Julian himself or of René, who had accompanied him there several times during the years he'd been writing his book on the massacre. Instead, there was a photograph of a man in his midseventies, dressed in the clothes of a rural laborer and standing beside a horse-drawn cart, with a grove of trees behind him. It was not a particularly striking picture; it was slightly out of focus and no attempt had been made to frame it in an interesting way.

Following Oradour and his work in Bretagne, Julian had gone to Hungary, where he'd spent a considerable amount of time in the area over which the castle of Countess Báthory loomed. In the file marked 'Čachtice,' as in the others, there were only pictures, and as before, most were of the castle ruins in which her crimes had been committed. But there were also views of the landscape that fell away on every side from the castle mount, and of the small villages that dotted the area, from which many of Elizabeth's victims had been drawn. The only difference in this case was that he had included four portraits that he'd evidently photocopied from various sources; one of them I recognized as the countess, and the other three Julian had identified on the back of the photocopies. The first portrait was of Dorottya Szentes, called 'Dorka,' according to Julian's note. The others were identified as Ilona Joo and János Ujvary, known as 'Ficko.' All had been accomplices in the crimes, and on the back of each photocopy Julian had noted their punishments. Dorka and Ilona had each had their fingernails ripped out before being burned alive. Ficko had simply been beheaded.

The fourth file contained exactly what I expected, a short stack of photographs of what were obviously the train and railway stations where Andrei Chikatilo had identified his victims, usually teenage runaways, both boys and girls, of which a collapsing Soviet Union had provided a continuous supply.

Julian had not identified the fifth file, but given what I found inside, its label instantly occurred to me: *Argentina*.

Marisol was in each of the photographs I found inside this file, and in each she was the same age she'd been during our time in Buenos Aires, her hair the same length, and she was even wearing, in one of the photographs, the same clothes she'd worn on the day she first met us.

None of the photographs was the sort normally taken by tourists. Save for one, they were all black-and-white and appeared to have been shot from a considerable distance, no doubt by someone who did not want to be seen, and clearly without Marisol's knowledge.

The exception, in color and quite the sort one would expect from a tourist, was a picture I'd taken in San Martín. In the photograph Marisol was seated next to Father Rodrigo. The two of them appeared to be locked in an intense conversation. Rodrigo had his hand in the air, his finger pointed upward, as if making a crucial point. I had taken it as Julian and I closed in upon them and had only gotten it developed after returning home. When I showed it to Julian, he peered at it for a long time, then said simply, 'May I have this?' I'd given it to him, of course, and had never seen it again until now.

I had no idea who might have taken the remaining pictures.

In the first, Marisol is alone, this time in the Plaza de Mayo, the Casa Rosada behind her. In the picture she stares off to the right. Her expression is curiously troubled, and anxiety shows in her posture, suggesting that she might have been waiting for someone who had not appeared.

The second photograph shows Marisol on what is clearly a different day. It is raining and she is drawing in her umbrella as she prepares to board a bus.

In the third photograph Marisol is sitting with a young man near the entrance to Recoleta. His features are indigenous, like Marisol's. But his hair is black and curly, and even though he is sitting, it is obvious that he is quite tall. He is wearing jeans and a sweatshirt, and something in his manner seems wary. Marisol is leaning toward him, the black beads Father Rodrigo had given her hanging loosely from her throat. Her lips are at the young man's ear, parted slightly, so that she is clearly speaking. When I turned it over, I found a typed inscription: *Marisol Menendez y Emilio Vargas.*

'Look at these,' I said to René.

He stepped over and looked at the pictures I'd spread out before him.

'I took that one,' I told him, 'but I don't know where the others came from. The young woman is Marisol. She was our guide in Argentina, the young woman who disappeared.'

'Ah,' René said softly. 'Pretty, but not my type.' He smiled. 'Too small. Not enough meat. Who is the guy?'

'Someone named Emilio Vargas,' I said. 'At least that's what it says on the back of the picture.'

René continued to stare at the pictures. 'They look like surveillance photographs,' he said. 'They remind me of the old days in Algiers.' He took out a cigarette and lit it. 'There are eyes upon these two.'

'Police surveillance, you mean,' I said.

'Police, army, intelligence operatives,' René said. 'What's the difference?' He smiled, but rather mirthlessly, like one recalling a memory that still troubled him. 'There was a young woman in Algiers,' he said. 'Her name was Khalida. It means "eternal" in Arabic, but it didn't turn out to be so with this girl.' Something in René's eyes shifted to the dark side. 'By what you call coincidence, one of our men—'

'Our men?' I interrupted.

'A cop, like me,' René answered casually, then continued. 'Anyway, he took a picture outside the Milk Bar Café a few minutes before the bombing. Khalida was in this picture, standing a few feet from the door, looking nervous.' He tapped the face of Emilio Vargas in the photograph. 'Like this one. You can see it in his eyes. He is not at rest, this fellow. His mind is busy. With Khalida, we thought she was this way because she knew about the bomb, that she was maybe a lookout, waiting for the man who was to bring it, but it turned out to be a boy she was waiting for, a boy her father didn't like.' He shrugged. 'But it was too late before we found this out.'

That outcome seemed to strike René as one of life's cruel turns, a twist in events that had swept poor innocent Khalida into the maelstrom of the Algerian revolt.

René laughed, but dryly. 'In those days, we did what we did to whoever we thought deserved it.' He laughed again, no less humorlessly. 'Revolution is not a kind mother to its children.'

'What happened to Khalida?' I asked.

'We followed her,' René answered. 'We thought maybe she would lead us to the big boss. But this girl, she goes to the casbah to buy vegetables; then she goes home with her little basket. She lives with her stupid father, who fills her mind with the massacre at Setif, how the Pieds-Noirs must all be killed, the usual "Allahu Akbar" bullshit.'

'She told you what her father said to her?' I asked.

'Not for a while,' René answered with a casual shrug of the shoulders. 'But like I said, we did what we did. And by the time we finished, it was too late for little Khalida.' He picked up the picture of Marisol and Emilio Vargas and looked at it closely. 'Their hands are touching.'

I glanced at the photograph, and it was true. On the bench between them, they'd rested their hands in such a way that their fingers touched.

René continued to stare at the picture. 'Betrayal

160

is like a landslide in your soul, no?' he said. 'After it, you cannot regain your footing.' When I gave no response to this, he looked at me. 'Perhaps this boy was Marisol's lover,' he said. 'It is an old story, no? The secret lover. It would have made Julian very jealous, no?'

I shook my head. 'Not at all, because Julian was never in love with Marisol,' I said. 'You've read too many bodice rippers, René.'

He was clearly puzzled by the phrase. 'Bodice rippers?'

'Romance novels,' I explained.

René dutifully drew out his notebook and added the phrase to it. 'Very good,' he said with small laugh. 'I like the English language.' His lingering smile coiled into a grimace. 'The people, not so much.'

CHAPTER 16

We left Julian's place a few minutes later. René had obviously found Julian's apartment depressing. But so had I, and thus, with no reason to linger, I had already returned to my hotel later that afternoon when the phone rang.

'Philip Anders?'

'Yes.'

'My name is Walter Hendricks. Your father asked me to call you. He said that you were investigating a friend of yours.'

Investigating?

Was that truly what I was doing now? I asked myself.

'Your friend was Julian Carlton Wells, I believe?' Hendricks asked.

He had pronounced Julian's full name in the way of a man reading it from a dossier, but I only said, 'Yes.'

'I live in London now,' Hendricks said. 'But in the early eighties I was stationed in Buenos Aires. Your father thought I might be of help since I was in charge of the Argentine desk at the time that

162

Mr Wells became involved with a young woman who worked as a guide for the consulate.'

'Marisol,' I said. 'What do you mean by "became involved"?'

'Well, at least to the extent that after her disappearance, he inquired about her at Casa Rosada,' Hendricks said.

'Julian went to Casa Rosada? I didn't know that.'

'It's a matter of record,' Hendricks said.

'What kind of record?'

'Well, I'm sure you're aware that dictatorships keep good records on people who visit the seat of government.'

'Yes, of course.'

'They record their names, their addresses, and if a flag is raised, they investigate them.'

'Did Casa Rosada investigate Julian?' I asked.

'No, he wasn't investigated,' Hendricks said. 'But he was noted. Anyone connected to Ms Menendez would have been noted.'

'Anyone connected with Marisol?' I asked. 'Why?'

'Because she had gotten the government's attention, evidently,' Hendricks replied. 'At least enough for them to have done a background check on her.'

'But she seemed so uninvolved in politics,' I said. 'She seemed quite innocent, actually.'

Hendricks laughed. 'Well, there's an old line in intelligence work,' he said lightly. 'Play the kitten. Conceal the tigress.' He seemed rather like a man who had completed a small task and was now anxious to move on. 'In any event, Casa Rosada had a report on Marisol. There was nothing of intelligence value in it. Hundreds, perhaps thousands, of such reports were compiled during the Dirty War. Marisol's is no different from the others.'

'May I see it?' I asked cautiously.

'I see no reason why not,' Hendricks said. 'But you'd have to come here. It's not something I could just put in the mail.' He offered a small laugh. 'It's of no importance to anyone, but procedure is a form of paranoia, as I'm sure you know.'

'Of course,' I said. 'I could be in London by Monday if that's convenient for you.'

'Monday is fine,' Hendricks said. 'If you're sure you want to make that effort.'

He seemed genuinely surprised that I would pursue the matter any further.

'You thought I wouldn't want to see the report?' I asked.

'Frankly, yes,' Hendricks answered.

'Why?'

'Oh, nothing, really,' Hendricks said. 'Just something your father said.'

'Which was?'

'That you were the opposite of Julian.'

'In what way?'

'That you had no taste for the "cloak-and-dagger" life,' Hendricks said.

'And Julian did?' I asked.

'Your father seemed to think so,' Hendricks admitted.

164

'But Julian was just a writer,' I said.

This was clearly a line of conversation that Hendricks had no interest in pursuing. 'So, I'll see you in London, on Monday, right?' he asked.

'Yes.'

'Meet me in the bar at Durrants Hotel,' Hendricks said, and gave me the address. 'Say four in the afternoon?'

'See you on Monday,' I said firmly, then, rather than dwell on my father's curious comment about Julian, I decided to go out into the Parisian night, where I found a small café, took a table outside, and ordered a glass of red wine.

It was a warm summer evening, and given my visit to Julian's garret earlier in the day, it inevitably reminded me of Buenos Aires, the similar nights I spent there, often at an outdoor café, all of us talking about whatever came to mind, but almost never politics. It was the one subject Marisol carefully avoided, though at the time I noticed that Julian often tried to move the topic of conversation in that direction. Why had he done that? I wondered now, and on that thought, I recalled the few occasions when he abruptly canceled meeting me at one place or another, times when I didn't know where he was, and during which I now imagined him skulking behind some street kiosk, taking pictures of Marisol.

It was an almost comic notion of Julian as a spy, but a tiny shift in perception can sometimes bring about a seismic shift in suspicion, and in thinking through all this, I felt just such a shift and remembered a particular evening when we were all seated at a small café.

It was more or less at the corner of Avenida de Mayo and the wide boulevard of 9 de Julio, the obelisk at Plaza de la República rising like a gigantic needle in the distance. The night before, one of the junta's notorious Ford Falcon trucks had screeched to a halt before the obelisk. According to several witnesses, four men had leaped out, seized a young couple who were standing at the monument, thrown them into the back, and then jumped in after them as the truck sped away.

The abduction was so blatant, and occurred in the presence of so many witnesses, that the government had issued a statement decrying the kidnapping, though everyone knew that the government's own paramilitary thugs had carried it out and that these latest victims of the repression would likely never be seen again.

'But where do they take them?' Julian asked. 'I mean, in the middle of a huge city, hundreds of people will see them.'

'And hundreds will say nothing, so some little house in La Boca will do,' Marisol answered in that nonpolitical way of hers, as if it were merely a matter of convenience that such people might disappear into one of Buenos Aires's most colorful neighborhoods.

'But they have to take them somewhere,' Julian insisted.

'But why to some secret place?' Marisol said. 'If they can take them in the middle of a city in the middle of the day, why should they need some cave in a faraway place to put them in?'

She saw that Julian was taken aback by what she said.

'It is before such men have the power that your courage should make you act,' she said. 'Once they have the power, your fear will control you.'

'So you would do nothing to find this young man and woman?' Julian demanded, as if now accusing her of complicity in these crimes.

In response, and for the first and only time, Marisol's eyes flashed with anger, and with the force of a wind she shot forward.

'How would you find these two people, Julian?' she fired back. 'Would you take some other man or woman from the street? Would you bring them to some place and torture them or maybe torture their children before their eyes? For, this you would have to do. Do you know why this is true? It is because once a monster has the power, to destroy this monster, you must become a monster, too.'

With that, she sat back and with an unexpected violence drained the last of the wine. 'There is no blood in your politics. But down here, it is always blood.'

Julian said nothing as Marisol drew her hands from the table and let them fall into her lap, a gesture that told me she regretted her outburst because it was not how a guide should act.

Yes, Julian said nothing, but now I recalled that something in his eyes had glimmered darkly, as if, deep inside some secret chamber, a door had opened up.

I had taken the photographs of Marisol that I'd found in Julian's garret with me, and now I drew them from my jacket pocket and looked through them again. The one on top was the one I'd taken, and for a moment, I studied Marisol's face, her quiet features, her gentle eyes.

Play the kitten, conceal the tigress, I heard Hendricks say, and with those words I drew my gaze away from Marisol's face and settled it on her hands. To me, they seemed soft and delicate. I could not imagine them with claws.

PART IV

THE TIGRESS

CHAPTER 17

We must imagine a little girl looking up from her manacled hands, seeing a woman approach, and believing in that instant that she is surely saved. For this woman is the mistress of the castle, she whose delicate white fingers hold authority over the secret chambers of Čachtice. With a gesture, she can open every barred door, pull down all the ropes and chains, order Ficko to the gallows and Dorottya to the pyre for what they have done: stripped her naked, forced her onto this sticky straw mat, and placed the manacles on her wrists and ankles, crimes for which she knows they will now be punished. It is beautiful Elizabeth she sees enter her cell, approach her, and, after a short pause and with a gaze no innocent should ever face, bid Ficko fetch her whip.

It was not Julian's words that awakened me, but my visualization of what the passage described: I'd seen Countess Báthory in her gown, weighted with jewels, her fingers sprouting precious stones, drawing nearer to me, her deception so perfect and so humbling. I'd glanced down, like one presented to royalty.

I was not prone to nightmares. In fact, I couldn't remember the last time one had shaken me from sleep. But this one had been extraordinarily vivid, and I'd felt the manacles around my wrists, the gummy straw beneath my feet.

In memory, I thought the scene was much longer and more detailed, but in one of Julian's surprises, as I saw when I found the passage in the book, he had cut it short, then gone into a brief meditation on the added horror, as he supposed it, of being tortured by a woman rather than a man, the ordeal intensified, he said, by a horrifying turn in which humanity's oldest vision of female comfort is suddenly and terrifyingly reversed.

René arrived at the hotel just after nine, looking quite rested, clearly a man who never did battle with himself or questioned his past deeds, even the dark ones he'd probably committed in Algeria.

'You look like Julian,' he said when I joined him at the little outdoor café not far from my hotel. 'In the morning, he looked like a man who'd spent his night being chased by dogs.'

'This happened often?' I asked.

'Many nights, yes,' René answered. 'Nightmares.' He lit his breakfast cigarette, though I suspected it was not his first of the day. There'd probably been one when he rose, one before he shaved and one after, one before he dressed, one on the way out into the morning light. 'Julian had terrible ones.'

'I had a nightmare of my own last night,' I told him. 'It had to do with Julian's book *The Tigress*. The scene where we see the countess through one of the girls' eyes, a girl she is about to torture and murder.'

'Julian was always doing that,' René said absently. 'Putting himself in the place of the victim.' He glanced toward the street and seemed to lose himself in the traffic, until he said, 'Perhaps he did not like to live in his own skin.' He shrugged. 'But we can live only in the one we have, no?'

The question was so rhetorical I felt no need to answer it.

'Last night, I got a call from a man in London,' I told him. 'He had a file on Marisol. He implied – well, a bit more than implied – that Marisol was something more than a guide.'

René blew a column of smoke out of the right side of his mouth. 'Perhaps a dangerous woman? We had one in Algeria. She was called "the Blade," and we feared her more than any of the men.'

'Feared that she would do to you what you did to Khalida?' I asked cautiously.

'Algeria was a bad place, and in such places, bad things happen,' René said. He looked at the lit end of his cigarette like one considering an ember from hell. 'She was a torturer and an assassin, this one. These things she did, as you say in English, "by night."' He smiled as if admiring of her cunning. 'By day, she was an ordinary woman. A teacher in a school.' His smile widened and became more cutting. 'She deceived everyone. Only her lover knew. And he was as bad as she was. They were – what do you say – "partners in crime"?'

I thought of the pictures of Marisol that Julian had placed in that unmarked file, Marisol looking entirely unaware, going about her business, except when she was with Emilio Vargas. In that picture she had looked quite intense. Had she lived a secret life? I wondered, with Emilio Vargas her partner?

I left Paris by way of Gare du Nord the next morning. On the high-speed train it was a journey of a little more than two hours, a pleasant ride through the French countryside, then under the channel and on to London. On the way, I thought of nothing but Marisol, though it was one particular memory that triumphed over all the rest.

Julian and I had gone to the Gran Café Tortini to meet her. It was on one of Avenida de Mayo's busy corners and had been long favored by Argentina's greatest artists and performers. Before more or less leaving the country, Borges had been a frequent visitor, along with a number of playwrights and actresses less well known to the outside world. The tavern had even gone so far as to commission wax figures of its most famous customers, so there was Borges, frozen in time, seated at a small table, in conversation with Carlos Gardel, the renowned tango singer, the great writer rendered so peacefully that I could hardly imagine him in the Argentina that now swirled around this serene representation of himself, the violence and the chaos, his beloved country very much in the turmoil my father had recommended that we see.

Marisol, so very punctual on all other occasions, was late. Her failure to appear shook Julian in a way that surprised me, and he'd begun to fidget and glance about.

'She's always on time,' he said.

'She's only five minutes late,' I reminded him.

'But she's always on time.'

'I think you're overreacting a little, Julian,' I said. 'It's only five minutes.'

'Yes,' Julian said pointedly, 'but it's five minutes in Argentina.'

He meant in a country where anything could happen, of course, where a couple could be seized in broad daylight at the obelisk, where in La Plata ten high school students could be kidnapped, raped, and tortured, as they had been some years before in what was known as 'The Night of the Pencils.'

'Borges at first favored the junta,' I said, 'but now he attacks it. Usually from Europe.'

'Where it's safe,' Julian said. He peered out over the avenue, searching the morning crowds for Marisol.

'Sometimes that's the only choice,' I said. 'What would be the point of staying here?'

'To fight,' Julian answered in a way that made me wonder if he'd begun to entertain the romantic notion of adopting Argentina, making its struggle his struggle, Julian a one-man international brigade.

I might have said something to that effect, but then Marisol came rushing up from behind us, looking a bit in disarray, but with her customary energy and good cheer.

'Ah,' she said brightly, but with a smile that seemed painted on. 'So we have arrived at the cultural center of the city.' She glanced toward the wax figures, Borges, blind, holding his cane, and with that glimpse, an uncharacteristic shadow passed over her. 'He wrote once that "the present is alone,"' she said, then looked about at the other customers, most of them well dressed, smoking quietly, sipping coffee. 'He was not so blind that he could not see the junta's knife coming for him.'

Never until that moment had I seen a trace of mockery in Marisol, and although she quickly brushed it aside and assumed her apolitical station as a cheerful guide, her disdain for Argentina's greatest living writer was clear.

'He wrote that kindness is not what a dagger wants,' Julian said, his gaze quite intense.

Marisol looked at him in a way that suggested she had never seen him in exactly the same light. 'You are reading Borges?' she asked.

'After you quoted him in Recoleta, how could I not?' Julian said.

'What did you read last?' Marisol asked.

'A short story called "The Zahir,"' Julian answered.

Then he smiled softly and repeated a line from

the story: 'In the drawer of my writing table, among draft pages and old letters, the dagger dreams over and over its simple tiger's dream.'

Tiger.

Dagger.

What in the name of heaven, I wondered as my train hurtled toward London, did any of it mean?

CHAPTER 18

It was around noon when I arrived in London, several hours before I was scheduled to meet Hendricks at Durrants, the small hotel he'd recommended because it was near the American embassy. Durrants had often been used by American officials during the war, a time, spy novelists often pointed out, when the line between the good guys and the bad guys was clearly drawn.

London had changed considerably since my last visit, the influx of immigrants having put its mark on such places as Oxford Street, where Middle Eastern men now smoked hookahs in sidewalk cafés and women strolled about in full burkas. These were changes that gave the city a deeper sense of intrigue, or so it seemed. For I couldn't be sure that my present view of London as a place of plots and counterplots came from the actual changes I noted in the city itself or from the troubling details that were emerging from Julian's life – especially the preoccupation with betrayal that marked both his books and his conversation.

Durrants was on a side street not far from Hyde Park. By the time I got there, one of London's famous drizzles had settled in, along with a touch of fog. Beyond the bar's small windows, I could see black umbrellas sprouting like dark flowers on the street.

'You must be Philip.'

I turned from the window to see a man standing at my table.

'Walter Hendricks,' he said. 'I trust your father is well?'

'As well as can be expected,' I told him.

'For a man his age, you mean,' Hendricks said with a knowing grin. 'And mine, too, for that matter.'

Hendricks, however, appeared far less frail than my father. In fact, there was something rough-and-tumble about him, a sense that he could still handle other men with a sure hand. His accent was Southern, of the type that held the soft twang of the Appalachians rather than the rounded *o*'s of the Tidewater. Here was one whose ancestors had fought under Lee, rather than beside him, I thought, men who staggered back from Pickett's charge to hear their general's apology while trying hard not to notice that there was no blood on his sleek lapels.

'I would have expected you and Julian to have gone on the grand tour after college,' he said as he sat down opposite me. 'Argentina always seemed to be an odd choice.' He smiled quite warmly. '"The dusty places," your father used to call them. He had a soft spot for the people of those regions.'

His smile grew into a soft chuckle. 'I told him that he should spend some time in Timbuktu, where even the food tastes like dirt.'

'I'm sure he would have loved a posting like that,' I said in defense of my father. 'To face that kind of reality.'

Hendricks's laughter trailed away. 'Not for long,' he said with the certainty of one who'd experienced such places. 'No one likes that kind of reality for long.'

He glanced about the bar. 'Have you ever been here?'

'No.'

He smiled. 'Well, my guess is that many a plot was hatched in this place,' he said. We were sitting at a small, round table clearly meant to accommodate drinks only. 'It wouldn't surprise me if Reilly, Prince of Spies, once sat right in this corner, at this little table, and wondered if it might be possible to have Lenin assassinated.'

Even in such casual conversation, Hendricks's eyes remained penetrating, the gaze of a man to whom one should not lie.

'I love history,' he added. 'It's the reason I retired to London, the sheer history of the place. I read history all the time. Probably as much as your father reads spy novels. He seemed to live in books back then.' He laughed. 'He was reading *The Thirty-Nine Steps* the day I met him.'

'He doesn't read now,' I said. 'He watches old movies. Black-and-white mostly. From the forties.'

'Yes,' Hendricks said. 'That would be his type.' His smile bore the usual indulgence that men of the world accord their dreamier compatriots, and in it I saw the most that was likely ever given to my father by the sturdier and far less idealistic souls who'd pulled the strings at Foggy Bottom. 'Stories about lone heroes. That was what he wanted to be, I think.'

'But instead he lived his life behind a desk,' I said.

Hendricks nodded. 'That's true,' he admitted. 'But I'm not sure your father would have functioned very effectively beyond a desk.'

'Really?'

Hendricks nodded. 'As a matter of fact, he sometimes reminded me of what Trotsky said about Czar Nicholas.'

'Which was?'

'That he should have been a kindly neighborhood grocer or something of that sort,' Hendricks said. 'A simple tradesman, invisible to history. But your father not only wanted to change the world, he wanted to do it by means of derring-do.' He laughed. 'In C Building, he was the resident Walter Mitty.'

The resident Walter Mitty.

That was both the saddest and truest thing anyone had ever said about my father, that he had lived his life behind a desk while watching spy movies and reading spy books and dreaming of the romantic secret-agent life he would never have.

To think of my father in such a way pained me, so I turned the conversation away from him.

'So, the report on Marisol,' I said as a reminder of why I'd come to London.

'Marisol, yes,' Hendricks said. 'I have to say that I am a bit curious as to why you're so interested in your friend's quixotic effort to find this young woman.'

'Was it quixotic?' I asked.

'I would call it that, yes,' Hendricks answered flatly. 'He was trying to find someone he didn't know much about in a country about which he knew even less. He had no connections in Argentina and no authority to conduct any sort of inquiry into this young woman's whereabouts. And yet, he felt that he could simply and quite brazenly walk into Casa Rosada and ask whatever questions he liked.' He shook his head gravely. 'Such a little boy.'

I recalled something Julian had said many years before. I'd been talking about Mussolini, how amazingly childlike he'd been, his love for mounting white horses and prancing about, his comical strut. The whole story had seemed to darken Julian's mood, his voice very serious when he said, 'He wasn't funny to the Ethiopians.' With that, he'd shaken his head softly, then added, 'Men with power shouldn't be little boys.'

Hendricks's gaze took on an added seriousness. 'How could he have possibly expected anyone in authority to tell him anything? Not only where

Marisol was or what had happened to her, but who she was?'

'Who she was?' I asked by way of directing the conversation back to her.

Hendricks smiled. 'Nowadays they'd call her a "person of interest,"' he said.

'To Casa Rosada,' I added.

'Yes.'

'Why?'

'Because she was evidently working for a well-known Montonero named Emilio Vargas,' Hendricks answered matter-of-factly.

I tried to conceal my surprise. 'Julian had a picture of Marisol with him,' I said. 'Where would he have gotten it?'

'Perhaps he was more successful at Casa Rosada than I thought,' Hendricks answered with a shrug. 'Anyway, as to Vargas. He was called "the Hook." It was his method of choice. To hang people on meat hooks.'

I remembered an atrocity Julian had once mentioned, an entire Balkan village rounded up and loaded onto trucks, then transported to the local abattoir, where every man, woman, and child was put through all the stages of animal slaughter. He had described the process so vividly and with such detail that I'd finally skipped ahead.

'Vargas was as vicious as they come,' Hendricks said. 'Names were given to him and he had those people kidnapped. Their children, too, sometimes. Torturing them was Vargas's specialty. He would

183

have justified it, of course. And it's true, there are people who can't be broken by torture. But when they see their children, naked, strapped to a bed beside a small electric generator . . .' He stopped. 'I'm sure you get the picture.'

I nodded.

'He operated a torture farm in the Chaco,' Hendricks added.

'That's where Marisol was from,' I told him.

Hendricks nodded. 'Yes. I saw that when I read the report.'

'What happened to Vargas?' I asked.

'He was shot eventually,' Hendricks answered. 'It was quite clear that before he died, he'd been rather badly treated.'

'What does that mean?'

'That he'd been tortured for a long time,' Hendricks said. 'Missing some important parts, if you know what I mean.' A smile slithered onto his face. 'He deserved every cut, if you ask me.'

'Where was he found?'

'Floating in the Plata,' Hendricks answered.

'I can't imagine Marisol having anything to do with a man like that,' I said.

'Then how do you explain the picture?' Hendricks asked. 'I don't know how Julian got that picture, but I do know this: Casa Rosada had come to suspect that Marisol was a spy for Vargas and that she was primarily trying to find information while working as a guide for the American consulate.'

I had briefly imagined Marisol in this

cloak-and-dagger role, skulking in the shadows of the consulate, pressing her ears against a door or her eyes to a keyhole.

'Of course, that might only have been her cover,' Hendricks added.

He saw that I didn't understand this.

'It's called the double take,' Hendricks explained. 'The agent allows herself to be revealed as a little, insignificant operative in order to conceal the fact that she is actually a very important one. So you have to look again. Hence, the double take.'

'But there's no evidence that Marisol was . . .' My question trailed off.

'No, but there was an intelligence report on her,' Hendricks answered. 'It didn't say a lot, but it didn't have to, because what it says emphatically just by existing is that Marisol was a person of considerable interest to Casa Rosada.' He shrugged. 'As I'm sure you know, Buenos Aires was a nest of vipers in those days. On both sides, people were being tortured, killed. For most people in the world, politics is not a game.'

There was more than a hint of condescension in Hendricks's last remark, the implication that in Argentina Julian and I were playing hopscotch in a torture chamber.

Hendricks placed his briefcase on the table. 'Was Julian political?' he asked.

'Political,' I repeated. 'Do you mean was he an idealist, some kind of an ideologue?'

'Those two are very different,' Hendricks said.

185

'In what way?'

'An idealist is a man with blinders,' Hendricks answered. 'An ideologue is a man who's blind.' He looked at me gravely. 'Which was Julian?'

'I'm not sure he was either one,' I said. 'I don't think he had time to be before . . .'

'Before what?'

'Before Marisol disappeared,' I said. 'And after that, as you know, he did nothing but look for her.'

Hendricks nodded. 'Look for her, yes.'

Now his eyes gave off the sense of a man who'd seen too much and who regarded those who hadn't as little more than children.

'Who did this friend of yours think he was, hmm?' he asked. 'Some superhero? The type your father dreamed of being?' He looked at me as if the bloom of youth were still on my cheeks. 'Grow up, please.'

He paused a moment, then leaned forward in a way that was decidedly avuncular.

'Do you know what real warriors say about a fictional creation like Rambo?' he asked. 'That he would be dead in five minutes. But that during the course of those fateful five minutes, his bullshit heroics would kill every soul under his command.'

He watched me for a moment, like a man looking for a hidden motive; then he leaned forward and looked at me as though certain of one thing: that for all my privilege, all my expensive education, I could still stand another lesson.

186

'You cannot know a people if you do not share their pain,' he said, 'and Julian knew nothing about what was going on in Argentina. He was just a tourist who happened to stick his toe into a river of blood.'

He drew an envelope from his briefcase.

'Be glad you've lived a cautious life, Philip,' he said. 'Because the reckless die young.' The envelope slid toward me. 'And they kill young, too.'

CHAPTER 19

In literature, the unopened envelope occupies a privileged place. Most famous, perhaps, is the one Angel does not find in *Tess of the d'Urbervilles*, and the lack of its discovery causes a deeper tragedy to unfold.

As I began to read it, I couldn't help wonder if a further tragedy might also unfold in the report Hendricks had given me.

It was seventeen pages long. It had originally been written in Spanish, but Hendricks had gone to the trouble of having it translated.

The first pages were dully biographical. They recounted the date and place of Marisol's birth, the deaths of her parents, her subsequent border crossings from Argentina to Paraguay, and her final settlement at age six, now an orphan, in the charge of Father Rodrigo, whose parish 'presided over various charitable affairs within the region of Gran Chaco.'

On page 3, Marisol arrives in Buenos Aires. She is fourteen years old, the recipient of a small scholarship at a Catholic academy, one arranged by Father Rodrigo 'as a result of her intelligence and ambition.' Marisol continues in this school for the next four years, chalking up impressive grades and glowing testimonials from the nuns, who find her dutiful, obedient, and 'quick to take advantage of any opportunity to please.' She studies English more assiduously than any other subject.

On page 9, Marisol graduates from the academy, then begins to take courses at a vocational school that focuses on various aspects of what the report calls 'clothing.' While at the school, she focuses on design.

To support herself, Marisol takes several jobs, all of the sort traditionally opened to the penniless. For a time she is a waitress, but she also serves as an usher at the opera house and as a clerk in its gift shop. She works as a tour guide at one of the city's art museums. While working at the museum, her proficiency in English is noticed, and she makes a little extra money by leading English-speaking tours.

Throughout this time in her life, Marisol continues to take courses at the vocational school. In this way, she is like hundreds of other young women in the city. But now, and for the first time, something ominous appears in the report: 'Subject makes contact with the American consulate in Buenos Aires and is employed as a guide.'

I knew that it did not take much to fall under the eye of the junta, but Marisol's work as a guide struck me as so unlikely to yield useful information that it would hardly have been worth it for them to keep track of her, much less bother to kidnap and 'disappear' her. I found no evidence that she'd made any effort to cozy up to any particular person, some high civilian or military official she might seduce, and from whom, during an evening of sex-hazed pillow talk, she might garner a bit of useful intelligence. In fact, she had never even served as a guide to anyone who could have been remotely considered a conduit for vital information.

The final two pages of the report provided both a chronology that succinctly recorded the previous events and a complete list of the people to whom Marisol had been recommended by the consulate, along with their professions, and their reasons for being in Argentina. Almost all of them were businessmen or people connected in one form or another to cultural exchange. Among the people for whom Marisol had served as a guide, there were no military personnel listed, no diplomats, no high officials from any government. Instead, Marisol appeared to have spent most of her time escorting members of various religious organizations who moved in steady caravans through whatever region was perceived rich in desperate souls, along with low-level representatives from a few small charities. It was such modest figures who made up Marisol's list of clients, hardly the sort that might interest a spy.

So if she had indeed been a Montonero operative, what information had she brought to Vargas,

I wondered, and from whom had she received it? The answer was that her information would have been of little value and she herself of little importance as a spy.

Such is what any Casa Rosada agent would have seen on first glancing at Marisol.

But what might he have seen, I wondered, if he'd done a double take?

The Skype screen flickered slightly, but I could see my father quite clearly. He was wearing a burgundy robe with a velvet lapel, and it struck me that he looked much more like some retired CIA chief than a lowly State Department functionary. Because of that, I wondered if he might sometimes still be captured by the Walter Mitty fantasies Hendricks had mentioned, a man who, in his private moments, assumed an imaginary role far more important than any he'd ever actually had.

'I spoke to your friend, Hendricks,' I told my father. 'He thinks that Marisol might have been a Montonero operative of some sort.'

I half expected my father to laugh at this, but instead he only nodded. 'Well, it can be seductive,' he said. 'The world of intrigue.'

I took him through the details of my talk with Hendricks, Casa Rosada's suspicions that Marisol was a spy who had kept her ears open while working for the American consulate. Then I added the odder supposition that she might have been a far more important figure, her lowly guide job merely a mask.

'What might she have been?' he asked.

'She seems to have been associated with a very bad guy,' I said. 'His name was Emilio Vargas. He was from the Chaco, like Marisol.'

My father didn't seem at all surprised by what to me still seemed an outrageous conjecture.

'It's easy to get caught up in a revolution,' he said in his most worldly tone. 'It's a very heady business. Especially for the young. You start to imagine yourself a Mao or a Lenin, the savior of your country.'

I recalled what Harry had said about Julian's book on Chikatilo, how he'd gone to some lengths to detail the killer's elaborate fantasies, the serial killer and sexual psychopath as savior of Mother Russia.

'It has a terrible allure, being part of a secret army,' my father added. 'It's possible that Marisol could have been swept into something like that. Youth is a minefield, after all. Even Julian was attracted to the idea of being a secret agent.'

This was true, of course. Even before our trip to Argentina, he mentioned 'secret gears,' which I took to mean some sort of intelligence work. But he appeared to drop any interest in such a life after Argentina.

'What part of that sort of work interested him?' I asked.

'Deception,' my father answered matter-of-factly.

'Disinformation, that sort of thing. Playing psychological games. He thought himself quite clever, you know.'

'Very clever, yes,' I said.

'He thought he would be best at winning someone's confidence,' my father added. 'Particularly in a one-on-one situation.'

I thought of the times I arrived at the exact time and place of rendezvous only to find Julian and Marisol already waiting for me, sitting at some little table, their glasses half-empty, so it was obvious that they'd been there for quite a while.

'Hendricks gave me the report Casa Rosada had on Marisol,' I said. 'It makes it pretty clear that Marisol never had contact with anyone who would been of interest to the Montoneros while she worked as a guide for the American consulate.'

I stopped cold as the thought hit me, worked it through, then stated it.

'No one except for me, that is,' I told my father. 'And Julian.'

'Why would the Montoneros have had any interest in you or Julian?' my father asked.

'Because we were connected to you, Dad,' I answered.

My father said nothing, but I could see his mind turning this over.

'We would have been the perfect targets, wouldn't we?' I asked. 'If Marisol had actually been a spy.'

'But how would she have known that you and Julian were connected to me?' my father asked.

'Well, for one thing, she heard Father Rodrigo mention you,' I answered. 'And beyond that, I once heard Julian describe you as something of a mentor. As a matter of fact, he even suggested that you were a little higher up in the department than you were.'

'Did he?' my father asked softly.

'Yes, and I also remember him telling her about our house,' I added. 'He described it pretty grandly, so she might have gotten the idea that you were quite powerful, the center of an influential circle.'

'How ironic,' my father said quietly. 'Since I was never anything but—'

'Julian had a picture of Marisol with Emilio Vargas,' I interrupted. 'Where would he have gotten it?'

'From someone in Casa Rosada, I suppose,' my father answered. He appeared to run a curious possibility through his mind. 'He might have gotten it from my contact there.'

'You had a contact in Casa Rosada?' I asked, surprised that he'd even lightly touch such cloak-and-dagger operations.

'She was only a clerk,' my father added quickly. 'She's in her eighties now.'

'So no longer a Casa Rosada functionary, of course.'

'Not for many years,' my father said.

'Where is she now?'

'Why do you want to know that, Philip?'

'Because this contact of yours might have some idea of who Marisol was, what she was doing,' I answered. 'She might know if any of this is true about her, that she was . . . a deceiver.'

My father drew in a long, slow breath. 'She went back to Hungary,' he said. 'You should be aware that hers was not a clean record. You've probably never heard of the Maros Street hospital massacre.'

It occurred in Budapest, he went on to tell me, a peculiarly monstrous incident during the last-ditch effort by the collaborationist Arrow Cross to annihilate the few Jews not yet deported from Hungary. Having taken control of the city in the wake of the retreating Germans, the men of the Arrow Cross Party went on a rampage, and among the victims were the most helpless of the city's remaining Jews. The poorhouse on Alma Street was attacked, as well as the hospital on Városmajor. But it was the patients, doctors, and nurses at the Jewish hospital on Maros Street who suffered the full brunt of Arrow Cross cruelty, a full day of slaughter that included torture and murder.

'My contact played a part in it,' my father said at the end of this narrative. 'She never denied this. At least that was to her credit.'

'What happened to her after she left Casa Rosada?'

'She returned to Budapest,' my father answered. 'She got a job with the American consulate.'

'Her reward for being a spy?' I asked.

My father didn't answer, but I saw the answer in his eyes, all the dirty little deals he'd known about but never approved of, the ratlines and secret bombings and clandestine overthrows.

'Do you know where she is?' I asked.

'She retired and moved into a small town in what is now Slovakia.'

I was surprised that my father knew this, as he could tell from my expression.

'We were . . . friends briefly,' he told me. 'Your mother died long before.'

'I see,' I said.

'We met in a restaurant on one of my few trips to Buenos Aires,' he added. 'Each time I went there, I saw her. It was never love.' He shrugged. 'But she worked in Casa Rosada, and so I . . .'

'Played the secret agent?' I asked.

My father nodded with the sadness of one who had run out of fantasies, a Walter Mitty no longer inclined to daydream.

'Foolish,' he said softly. 'It was all very foolish.'

For a moment he seemed lost in thought. Then, quite suddenly, like one who sensed himself rather under surveillance, he said, 'Anyway, since she was my only contact, I sent Julian to her when he was looking for Marisol.'

'It was you who sent him to Casa Rosada?' I asked, surprised that he'd never mentioned this.

'It was a fool's errand,' my father said. 'But he seemed desperate to find this young woman. She'd gotten under his skin somehow. He was really quite determined. I thought my contact might help him solve the mystery of her disappearance.'

'Would she talk to me, this contact of yours?' I asked.

'I'm sure she would,' my father said. 'For old times' sake, as they say.'

'Who did this woman work for?'

'A colonel by the name of Ramírez,' my father answered. 'Juan Ramírez. He ran a few of the junta's *escuelitas*.'

He saw that I didn't understand the word.

'The "little schools,"' my father said. 'There were a great many of them in Argentina at that time. They were places where the enemies of Casa Rosada were taken to be reeducated. That is to say, where they were tortured.' He appeared to consider his next move with a strange seriousness. 'I could write to her if you like. I'm sure she'd been willing to talk to you.'

'Yes, do that,' I said. 'I'll follow up with a letter of my own.' I reached for a paper and pen. 'What's her name, your contact?'

'Irene.'

'And her last name?'

'Jóság,' my father answered. 'It's Hungarian, of course. It means "goodness."'

Goodness.

How bright a word, I would later realize, to have given so dark a new direction to my tale.

CHAPTER 20

When I later located Irene Jóság's village on a map, I saw that it was quite near to Čachtice, where the Bloody Countess had lived and in whose looming castle she had carried out her many torture-murders, her life and crimes the subject of Julian's fourth book, *The Tigress*.

The countess was born in Nyirbator, Hungary, in 1560, the daughter of one of that country's ruling families, and according to Julian, nothing in her early life suggested the monster she would become. Rather, she was quite studious, and by the time of her marriage, she had mastered Latin, German, and Greek, and had read a great deal in science and astronomy – learning that Julian portrayed as part of her perfect disguise.

At the age of fifteen, she married the son of another equally favored family, and in 1575, the presumably happy couple took up residence at Varanno, a small palace, before moving to a larger one at Sárvár, and finally to the castle that was her wedding gift, the looming, often fogbound Čachtice.

The war to defend Europe against the Ottoman encroachment would last until 1606, and during all that time it fell to Elizabeth not only to manage but to defend her holdings against the ever-threatening Ottomans. This she did with great skill and vigor. But it was not all she did, for although the outer walls of Čachtice remained strong, something was crumbling inside them; it was during this period that loneliness began to weather Elizabeth's carefully constructed edifice and, in that weathering, reveal what lay beneath. With her husband at his studies in Vienna, Elizabeth now, for the first time in her life, had real power, that is to say, power on the scale of a man's. She was the lady of the estate, her authority absolute, and like Ilse Grese at Ravensbrück, she began to wield a whip.

It was a weapon she could use with complete impunity, as it turned out, because her husband had by then become chief commander of Hungarian troops in the western war against the Ottoman Empire, a campaign that removed him for months at a time. Thus, with no one to stay her hand, she began first to berate and then to slap her servants, each attack fueling the next, until at last she drew blood and later found that where this drop had fallen on her cheek, the flesh beneath had seemed to bloom. In the blood of servants, she had miraculously discovered youth's eternal fountain.

More of this restorative blood was easy to find, of course, and in the coming months and years,

Elizabeth found plenty of it. Enough first to taste, then to sip, then to drink. Enough first to dot her finger, then to cover her face, then to coat her body.

But even the walls of Čachtice were not thick enough to hide what was going on there. The first rumors began to circulate as early as 1602, and by 1604, when Elizabeth's husband died, they could no longer be dismissed, for they were not rumors of infidelity or even of odd sexual practices, both of which were common among the nobility of the time.

It was a Lutheran minister who finally raised his voice so loudly that the authorities were forced to hear it. Even then, however, they were slow to act, and it was not until 1610 that an investigation was ordered, which resulted in Elizabeth's being caught in the act of beheading a teenage girl.

Elizabeth, being of such high birth, was put under house arrest, where she remained until her death in 1614.

During those intervening years, the investigation continued and more than three hundred victims were discovered, Julian reported, though the exact number of young girls who lost their lives in the secret chambers of Čachtice could never be known.

Julian had not been reticent to detail the horrors of Čachtice. There'd been whippings and mutilations. Elizabeth had bitten off parts of her victims' faces and other body parts. She'd taken some of

200

the girls out into the snow and watched them freeze to death. She'd performed surgery and other medical procedures upon them as well. She'd observed the stages of starvation before death. She'd used needles and hot irons. There seemed no end to her cruel ingenuity.

But in Julian's account, the countess's crimes, horrible as they were, were in some sense less cruel than her deceits, her great show of piety, her many gifts to the Church, the changing aspects of her mask. For Julian, it seemed, of all creatures great and small, it was the chameleon that should be most feared, particularly – I thought of both the Terror, La Meffraye, and the Tigress, Countess Báthory – when deceit took the shape of a woman.

On the map, a jagged road led from the countess's castle to what I imagined to be the far more modest abode of Irene Jóság, and I found myself imagining Julian driving down it, bleary-eyed from another sleepless night, his head spilling over with the horrors of Čachtice.

I could have simply corresponded with Irene Jóság, of course, but by then I'd come to think of myself as something of a detective, and in that guise I entertained the hope that by actually talking to her I might learn something that would clear up the great bramble I'd stumbled into, a thicket of intrigue in which identities changed as well as motives, where I could no longer tell what Marisol had been or whether Julian had ever guessed that she was something other than she seemed.

'You'll miss Paris,' Loretta said when I told her that I was heading for Hungary. 'Everyone does.'

I told her that I was going to Hungary because my father had given me the name of someone who was at Casa Rosada when Julian was in Argentina. Now I added, 'Julian went to Casa Rosada looking for Marisol.'

'Why would he have gone there?' Loretta asked. 'I thought Marisol had nothing to do with politics.'

'That's not so clear anymore,' I said, then related what Hendricks had told me in London, along with my subsequent conversation with my father, the result being that I was now quite uncertain about who Marisol had been.

'So she might have been anything,' Loretta said at the end of my account.

'Yes,' I said.

For the first time, I felt a turn in the narrative I'd been living through.

It was clear that Loretta had noticed a dark undertow in my answer.

'Do you think Julian ever knew any of this?' she asked.

'I don't know,' I answered.

For a moment I felt that we were both fixed in a space no one else could share.

'Philip, are you still there?' Loretta asked.

Her tone was troubled, and I realized that I'd

been silent for a long time, and the silence alarmed her.

'Yes,' I said.

There was a brief pause, then Loretta said, 'Would you mind if I joined you, Philip? Could you use a traveling companion?'

It struck me that Julian had never had such a companion, and that perhaps this, too, had served to doom him.

Might it doom me, too?

With that question I felt myself curiously imperiled, like a man moving down a river, into a darkness, now afraid that at the end of the journey there might be revelations as fatal to me as they had been for Julian, terrors that he had faced in solitude and isolation but that I had not the courage to face alone.

'Yes,' I said, like a man reaching for a life rope. 'Yes, I could.'

She arrived in Budapest a week later, dressed in a dark red blouse and floral skirt, glancing swiftly here and there, until she saw me in the waiting crowd.

'Welcome,' I said when she came over to me, and meant it.

Even so, she looked at me doubtfully. 'Really, Philip?'

'Yes, really,' I assured her. 'As you guessed, I could use some company.'

'But you've always seemed quite self-contained.'

'We're not always how we seem,' I said.

'Almost never, in fact,' Loretta said.

Something in her gaze took hold of me so that I felt exactly as Charles feels when he sees Emma Bovary, how dark her eyes are and how marked with fearless candor.

The intense feeling that swept over me at that moment had to be diverted, so I nodded toward where I had a car waiting.

On the drive into the city, Loretta kept her eyes keenly fixed on the new surroundings. In that keenness, that hunger for things she had not seen before, I glimpsed the young girl she had once been, the one who had traveled with Julian, two brilliant children facing their father's camera as they stood at the bottom of the Spanish Steps or at the Eiffel Tower, pictures she'd framed and hung in the Montauk house. There'd been other pictures, too, those same children walking through the butterfly house in Salzburg or along the shaded trails of the Vienna Woods. They had also strolled Barcelona's Ramblas together and paused to marvel at Sagrada Família.

In each photograph, they appeared splendidly happy, children endowed with as much good fortune as anyone could wish.

Those two bright young faces had changed quite a bit over the years, but it was Julian's that changed the most, and at our last meeting I'd gotten the feeling that it was not just exhaustion that plagued him but some tumorous mental growth that had at last broken through the surface.

When I said this to Loretta, she considered it a moment, then said, 'You know, he said something quite disturbing a couple of days before he went out in the boat. He was sitting by the pond. I went out to him. He had that look in his eye, like he was deep in thought. Just as a matter of conversation I said, "So, how are you doing, Julian?" I expected him to answer the way he usually did, something like, "I'm fine, Loretta, how are you?" But instead he quoted that line from *The Rime of the Ancient Mariner*. You know, the one where he says, "A thousand slimy things lived on and so did I." I took it for a little joke and made nothing of it. Julian often said things like that. Self-deprecating things. But this time, I should have known that he was in a very bad place.'

'We let a lot go by, didn't we?' I asked. 'There were signs we didn't read.'

She nodded. 'Yes, there were.'

When we reached the hotel, Loretta stepped out of the car and looked at its ornate facade. I could see that she recognized it.

'Julian mentioned this hotel,' she said. 'I remember it from his letters. "It has beautiful Zsolnay tiles," he said.'

'They're in the bathhouse,' I told her. 'In the old days, it was used by the Soviets. It's where they met their agents. Or at least that's what the hotel manager told me. In any event, it gives the place some history.'

Seconds later we were in the lobby. I nodded toward the bar. 'Maybe a drink before you go up?'

'Yes, that would be nice.'

We were soon seated at a small table in the bar, drinks in hand, Loretta casting her eyes about the room with what still seemed like a hint of childlike wonder.

'Very dark here,' she said. 'Thick curtains.'

'It looks like a place where "certain documents" might have been exchanged,' I said, rather as a joke.

'Julian described it in one of his letters,' Loretta said. 'He said that it looked like an old man still concealing his crime.' She took a sip of her drink. 'Do you think he came upon this hotel by accident?'

I shrugged. 'I suspect the bullet holes near the door and around the first-floor windows might have gotten his attention,' I answered. 'The manager here speaks English quite well, so I've listened to his history of the place. I asked him about the bullet holes. They're from when the Arrow Cross – the Hungarian fascist party that collaborated with the Nazis – defended the city against the Russians. The Germans had abandoned it by then.'

Loretta reached into her bag and retrieved a single photograph. 'I thought you might want to see this,' she said as she handed it to me.

In the photograph, Julian is seated at the little office alcove on the second floor of the Montauk house, a large window behind him, the pond shimmering in the background. He is holding a book whose title I can't make out, but which seems as battered as the man holding it. His hair is slightly mussed, as it often was in the morning, and he is wearing the blue robe I gave him as a welcome-home gift upon his return from Russia.

'Why this picture?' I asked.

'I thought of it after I talked to you,' Loretta said. 'It's the last picture of Julian. He set up the camera and took it himself.'

'It's an odd self-portrait,' I said. 'Not very flattering.'

'I didn't know he'd taken it,' Loretta said. 'But when I started to put the camera away, I noticed it and printed it out.' She drew the picture from me and looked at it very intently. 'It's a warning, a picture like that: "Don't end up like me."' She handed the photograph back to me, then looked toward the window, out at the busy street life. 'I've often thought that if life were fair, we'd be given a picture of where we'll end up if we continue down the road we're on.' She turned, and the smile she offered quickly faded. 'That might be enough to save us.'

For a time, she was silent, then she said, 'So, what's your theory about Julian at the moment, Philip?'

'I don't have one,' I admitted.

'I don't either,' Loretta said. 'I simply think Julian

was a condemned man, a man who was sentenced to some sort of inner life imprisonment.'

'But for what crime?' I asked.

'That would be the question, wouldn't it?' Loretta asked. She took another sip from her drink. 'The crime of Julian Wells,' she added. 'Still unsolved.' She seemed suddenly to shuffle off the weariness of her long flight, perhaps even some part of the long aridity that had marked her life since Colin's death. 'So,' she said, 'where do we begin?'

CHAPTER 21

All literature skirts the otherwise insurmountable issue of man's many different languages. Fictional characters roam from country to country miraculously speaking whatever language they encounter. The fictional character is sent from London to Istanbul and gets off the train in a city in which everyone speaks English. Throughout the fictional world, the Tower of Babel ever lies in ruins, so that upon first encounter with an African bushman or a Bedouin trader, all indecipherability vanishes, and our hero immediately engages in a profound discussion of life, death, and eternity, when, in actuality, he would have been struggling to locate the nearest watering hole.

This is to say that it was not within my power or Loretta's to simply head out of Budapest and locate Irene Jóság somewhere in the wilds of Slovakia without assistance. Arrangements had to be made, and several days were required to make them, a time during which Loretta and I strolled the streets of the city, took in its churches and museums and monuments.

By then I'd spoken often enough with the hotel

manager to have gained some slight knowledge of the city, at least enough to add a bit of local history to our strolls about the city.

'After the fall of the Soviet Union, the Russians were required to take away all the other monuments they'd erected to themselves in Budapest,' I told Loretta. 'All the plaques and red stars, everything.' I pointed to a pedestal upon which rested a single pair of boots. 'Of course the Hungarians had already beheaded the statue of Stalin. In fact, they cut him all the way down to his boots.'

We turned and walked on for a time, now closing in upon the Danube.

'I remember something Julian once told me,' I said. 'He said that a traveler enters the world into which he travels, but a tourist brings his own world with him and never sees the one he's in.'

'Where did he say this?' Loretta asked.

'In Buenos Aires,' I answered.

She walked on without speaking until she suddenly stopped and said, 'Then Julian must, at some point, have no longer thought of himself as a tourist there.'

'But that's what he was,' I told her, then returned to my meeting with Hendricks, how he'd seemed contemptuous of Julian's 'quixotic' effort to find Marisol. 'And in a way, I think Hendricks was right about Julian,' I said. 'Because in a sense, he was a tourist. How could he have been anything else?'

'By being drawn into the turmoil,' Loretta answered.

'How might that have happened?'

Her expression was pure collusion, as if we two were now in league, testing the same conjectures, exploring the same possibilities.

'I've been thinking of something you said the night you called me and told me you were going to Hungary,' Loretta answered. 'It was about the report on Marisol, the fact that she might have been a spy. You mentioned that she hadn't been with anyone important as a guide but that she might have gotten the idea that you or Julian could have known something.'

'Or some*one* – namely, my father,' I said.

'Yes,' Loretta said. Her gaze became quite intense. 'And I thought, if she actually was a spy, she might have had a completely different idea about Julian. Not as someone who knew something but as someone who might later be in a position to know something.'

'I'm not sure where you're headed.'

'That she might have thought he had access to information,' she answered. 'Or at least that he could gain access to it. Information from your father, for example. And so, for that reason, she might have tried to turn Julian. That's the term, isn't it? To "turn" someone?'

'You mean Marisol might have tried to turn Julian into a traitor?'

She saw how unlikely I thought that was.

211

'It's the oldest turn there is, Philip,' she reminded me. 'As a matter of fact, it goes back to Eve.'

There was Jezebel, too, and Delilah. The list of female deceivers is very long indeed. Could Marisol have been such a woman? If so, her disguise was quite brilliant, for I had no inkling that she was anything other than an admirable young woman, dutiful and striving, who simply wanted a fighting chance.

And yet, the photograph I'd found in Julian's apartment couldn't be denied. Marisol seated with Emilio Vargas, leaning toward him, whispering in his ear. Might she have targeted a young man who was naive and inexperienced in the ways of intrigue, one already determined to do some great good in the world, romantic and idealistic, a well-connected young American she could 'turn'?

I thought again of the photograph, Marisol's lips at Vargas's ear.

Might she have been whispering the name of this young man?

It was only a question, and yet I could almost hear the name she whispered.

Julian, I thought, and on that name, I once again recalled the time he got into an argument with me over some small detail, how uncharacteristically wrong he was, and how, to prove him so, I rushed back to my room to find the evidence. It was just after Father Rodrigo's departure, and I'd left him with Marisol at a small café near San Martín. I'd returned to find them talking very somberly, and at

212

that moment, as I thought now, they had truly looked like two conspirators caught in a moment, to use René's phrase, 'of dark conclave.'

As if it were a surveillance photograph, I saw Julian at the instant he suddenly caught me in his eye, his expression not unlike that of a little boy caught in a disreputable act.

Had I caught him? I wondered now.

And had the 'crime' he'd long ago claimed that I had witnessed been his treason?

There are times when no alternate route presents itself, so that your only choice is to continue down the road you're on. Now that road led out of Budapest.

By the time I took it, I'd secured the service of a guide. His name was Dimitri, and he was quite young and eager, utterly unlike René. On the way to Irene Jóság's village, he spoke of his great love of English, how assiduously he read the great writers of that language. He was astonishingly impressed to learn that I was a critic and that Loretta was the sister of what he called a 'real writer,' though he was quick to admit, not without apology, that he'd never heard of her brother.

'What is again the name of your brother?' he asked as he pulled out a small notebook.

'Julian Wells.'

'I am sorry to say that I have not read his books,' Dimitri told her, 'but I am certain that I will very soon search for them.'

Loretta promised to send him some of Julian's books when she returned to the States, and when we stopped for lunch, Dimitri responded by gathering her a bundle of wildflowers.

After that we drove on, now through a countryside that felt increasingly dense.

'There's Čachtice,' I said when it came into view. 'Countess Báthory's torture chamber.'

Loretta's gaze grew more intense as she peered at it, but the intensity was combined with noticeable dread.

'Are you sure you want to go to the castle?' I asked cautiously.

To my surprise she was, so Dimitri drove up the winding road that led to the ruin.

It was not overwhelmingly large, and as in the case of many such places, the walls had long ago been pulled down. The tower still stood, however, along with an imposing foundation whose broken stones we walked together, the great sweep of the countryside stretching below us as far as we could see.

It was within these now-crumbled walls that countless agonies had been inflicted upon the countess's victims, Elizabeth growing steadily more vicious as one year quite literally bled into another. Here she had starved and beaten and burned and slashed the bodies of innumerable innocents, while screaming obscenities so vile they shocked even the blood-spattered minions who helped carry out her tortures.

At one of Gilles de Rais's castles, no less a literary figure than Anthony Trollope had paused to reflect upon the screams of the victims, even claiming that they could still be heard, as if sound waves do not dissipate. But dissipate they do, as Julian had pointed out in *The Tigress*, such that the wintry trees that had gathered around the body of yet another child had remained silent and unhelpful while the magistrate's men searched for clues, as if they were bribed witnesses into whose snow-encrusted hands the countess had placed a few silver coins.

'It's creepy here, don't you think?' Loretta asked.

'Yes,' I said.

During the remainder of our walk about the grounds and rubble of Čachtice, Loretta appeared quite thoughtful. She gave no hint of what her thoughts were, however, though I suspected that she was considering the terrible possibility that Julian had, in fact, been turned by Marisol, and thus, for a brief time, might have proved himself a traitor. Still, I didn't press her. And it was not until we'd returned to the car and were headed toward Irene Jóság that she opened up to me.

'I remember one day when Julian and I were in that little boat I found him in,' she said. 'He'd come home after writing *The Tigress* but hadn't started *The Commissar*. We were talking about when we were children. Our travels. How fearless we were in those days. At one point I said that the things I feared most now were the things

215

everyone feared. Getting old. Getting sick. Dying. I could tell that he didn't fear any of those things. So I asked him what he was afraid of. He said that he wasn't afraid of anything anymore. It was the "anymore" that seemed strange to me, because the way he said it, he seemed to be telling me that he'd already confronted the thing he most feared.'

'And triumphed over it?' I asked.

Loretta shook her head. 'No, only that he'd confronted it.' She glanced up toward the broken towers of Čachtice. 'And after that, he was like those ruins. Beyond repair.'

Beyond repair.

Since we had no way of pursuing this point, Loretta and I simply continued on, and we reached Irene Jóság's house about an hour after leaving Čachtice.

It was very modest, and with all the growth around it, the tall grass and twining vines, it was barely visible from the road.

'Are you sure this is it?' I asked Dimitri.

'I am sure,' he answered.

We got out of the car and approached the house by means of a broken walkway overgrown with weeds and clogged with shrubs that seemed as swollen, as Julian might have written, as bodies in the sun.

I knocked at the door and heard a shuffle of feet inside the house. Then the door opened, and a very small woman appeared. She was dressed plainly, her hair streaked a yellowish white. Her eyes were startlingly blue, and there was a quickness to them that suggested what I had little doubt was a very high intelligence. She didn't wear the usual country clothes of Hungary, but a black dress with lace at the sleeves, so that she looked like a Spanish matron. Clearly she'd dressed for the occasion, and I even noticed a touch of blush on her cheeks along with some bright red lipstick that had missed its mark in one corner of her mouth.

'Ah,' she said in an English whose accent was far more Spanish than Eastern European, 'the Americans are arrived.'

She stepped back rather shakily, waved us in, and directed us to chairs in her small living room.

'You would like something to drink?' she asked.

'No, thank you,' I said.

With that, she slowly eased herself into a small wooden chair, and the usual niceties commenced. She asked about our hotel in Budapest but was more interested in my having come from Paris, a city she had romanticized but never seen, and now would never see, which brought us to her various ailments, bad joints and hearing loss, failing eyesight, the travails of old age, a subject that finally turned her mind toward my father.

'Your father is doing well?' she asked me.

'Not altogether well, no,' I answered. 'The same problems you've mentioned. Aches and pains.'

'I'm sorry,' she said. 'It is better to be young.'

We talked at some length about the work she'd done for the Americans, by way of my father, whom she described as having always been very kind to her. He had acted like a gentleman, without airs, she said, a man capable of speaking quite candidly to a simple clerk. She had either read or been told that 'the great George Marshall' had had such qualities, and after the arrogance of the big men at Casa Rosada, my father's modesty had been much more than simply refreshing. She gave no hint of the somewhat more intimate relationship to which my father had quite clearly alluded, so I made no mention of it either.

At the end of this tale, she drew in a long breath, then glanced at Loretta. 'I did not expect a second guest. This is your lovely wife?'

I had introduced Loretta at the door, but this appeared to have escaped the old woman's attention.

'No, this is Loretta Wells,' I reminded her. 'Julian's sister.'

'Ah, yes,' Irene said. 'Julian's sister. My mind fades, no? Ah, yes, Julian.' She drew her attention over to me. 'The reason you have come, as your father told me in his letter. Julian. What a sad young man.'

This seemed as good a segue into the purpose of our visit as any, and so I said, 'My father tells me that you worked at Casa Rosada in the early eighties.' I looked at the notes I'd taken during the conversation with my father. 'For a Colonel Juan Ramírez?'

Irene nodded. 'He was a ladies' man, Juan,' she said. 'Very handsome. He many times wished to take me to his hideaway in Puerto Madero.' She smiled. 'He was a true fascist. "You do not live with the Reds," he said to me. "You live under the Reds, or you do not live at all." He would have done anything to save Argentina from the Reds. In fact, he did what all fascists do, which is the same as Reds.' She clearly held the two groups in the same disdain. 'He was always after the Montoneros. Those he dreams about at night. Killing every one of them. It is for this he lived. He wanted to hunt them down like a fox would hunt a rabbit. With his nose to the ground until he found them. Then he rips them apart.'

'But how did he find them?' I asked.

'Names came to him,' Irene said.

'From informants?'

She nodded. 'He had many people, but it was the big fish, a Montonero, who gave him the big names. Where they lived, too, these other Montoneros hiding in their caves. Even the names of their children he gave to Juan.'

'Ramírez turned a high-ranking Montonero?' Loretta asked.

'Yes,' Irene answered. She appeared to see this informant in her mind. 'Very tall, but an indigene. He was from the Chaco.'

'Emilio Vargas?' I blurted.

Irene's eyes widened. 'You have heard of this one?'

'Yes,' I said. 'He was a Montonero torturer.'

Irene laughed. 'This he did to show how bad he was,' she said. 'It is sometimes necessary to do this. This shows you hate the enemy, that you are ruthless. When he did this, the others say to themselves, "See how he hates. See how much he is with us."' She laughed again. 'Cruelty was his disguise.' Her eyes twinkled with a curious admiration. 'But it was only one of his disguises.'

For a moment she looked like a little girl watching shapes change in a funhouse mirror.

'Because he had a disguise for Juan as well,' she added.

'Why would he need another disguise?' I asked.

'Because he was never really turned,' Irene said. 'He was always a crazy Montonero.'

'Vargas was a double agent?' I asked.

'Yes,' Irene said. 'Juan was suspicious of this. This is why he puts much pressure on Vargas to prove himself. It is what Juan always did. He works like a thumbscrew, tighter, tighter until his people break. For this reason, Vargas tries to give Juan better and better information.'

Her features suddenly grew tense, as if she were afraid that she was being watched even now.

'But it was never good enough for Juan,' she said. 'So he always asks Vargas to prove his loyalty. He threatens to cut off Vargas's ears, cut out his tongue. This he would do if Vargas does not deliver him the goods. And by this he means people.'

'People?' I asked.

'Juan wanted to scare Vargas into giving up a big-time Montonero. So he makes Vargas like a man in the ocean who sees the shark coming toward him. He does not have time to get out of the water, so he takes some smaller man and puts this man between himself and the shark.' She laughed. 'Juan loved this game. He said to me, "Vargas will pluck out his own eyes and cut off his ears. He will give me the name of this woman by the time I am finished with him."'

'Woman?' I asked.

Irene nodded. 'A real she-devil, this is what Juan called her. She had kidnapped some children of the junta. She would lure them with little candies. There would be a van, and very quick, they were gone, these kids. She was good at this. She sent them back torn and burned. It was very bad. The eyes gone. More than anyone, the big men at Casa Rosada wanted this woman for what she had done to these children. And it was this woman Juan wished to get from Vargas because it would be a big catch for him, and he would get a big promotion if he found her.'

'How did you happen to know so much about what Ramírez was doing?' Loretta asked.

'He wants me in his bed, so he makes himself a big man to me,' Irene answered. 'He tells me everything, his many stories of the spies and agents. He does this more when he has too much wine.' Her eyes squeezed together, as if I were a distant object she was trying to bring into focus.

221

'But he was a clever man, Juan. And when the house was on fire, he got out through a little hole.' Her smile was pure contempt. 'He speaks only Spanish, and so he goes to Spain. He sits in the park and talks to the old men of the Falange.' An odd defeat settled over her. 'There is always a place for such men.'

She paused like one exhausted by history, then continued with what seemed to be considerable effort, determined to complete her tale. 'But enough of this,' she said finally. She waved her hand as if to wipe the whole dark era from her mind. 'So, Julian. Your father says to me that you want to know what I say to Julian when he comes to Casa Rosada, no?'

'Yes,' Loretta answered quietly.

'Well, he comes to look for this woman,' Irene said. 'Excuse me, please, but I do not remember her name.'

'Marisol,' I told her.

Irene glanced toward Loretta, then turned to me. 'Julian comes to Casa Rosada to find this Marisol.' She looked at Loretta. 'I am sorry to hear of his death. Such a young man. It is always a tragedy when death comes so soon.' With that, Irene turned her attention back to me. 'Your father sends Julian to me, but I know nothing of this girl.'

'You knew nothing at all?' I asked. 'I thought you might have given him a picture of Marisol with Emilio Vargas. I found it in his room in Paris.'

The old woman shook her head. 'No, I do not

give Julian such a picture. I go to Juan. I ask about this girl who has disappeared. I can see he knows this girl, but he tells me nothing.'

'I thought he told you everything,' I said.

'This I also think,' Irene said. 'But about this one, he is silent.'

'He said nothing at all?' I asked doubtfully.

'He says to me, "Irene, to know about this one, this is not for your ears." And he will say nothing more about her. He tells me if this American comes again, to tell him to go home and forget about this girl.'

'So who was she?' Loretta asked. 'Marisol.'

Irene shrugged. 'This Juan never tells me, but I think she is big fish, because after a while, he is very big man at Casa Rosada.' She smiled. 'All of this I would have told Julian when he came here, but he did not ask about this girl.'

'Julian came here?' Loretta asked.

'Yes,' Irene answered. 'Just for one afternoon. We have cold drinks, and talk of the old days.'

'And during that time, Julian didn't mention Marisol?' I asked.

'No, nothing of this girl.' She looked oddly puzzled that this was the case. 'So, I think maybe he knows already what happened to her.'

My lips parted in dark amazement.

'Knew already?' I asked. 'But he couldn't have known.'

'This is how it seems me, yes,' Irene told me. 'That he has no more questions about this girl.'

223

For the first time, Loretta looked skeptical, though she had perhaps been so all along. But now she made no pretense of believing the old woman's story.

'Then why did he come here?' she asked.

'He comes here to – how I should say? – to say good-bye,' Irene answered. 'He wished to thank me for talking with him back in the old time, when he came to Casa Rosada.' She faced Loretta. 'He has much trouble, your brother. There is a heavy weight on him. This I can see. And so I tell him that I know this weight.'

She turned her gaze to an old album that lay on a nearby table. 'You can hand this to me, please?' she asked.

I stood, walked over to the table, retrieved the book, and gave it to her.

'There is the bad thing I show to Julian and speak to him about,' she said as she opened the book and began leafing through its ragged pages.

'Ah, here it is,' she said as she motioned Loretta and me to come forward and look at it.

In the photograph, a young woman with a rifle, wearing an Arrow Cross armband, stands beside a priest, staring down at the sprawled bodies of a group of men and women, all of them in civilian clothes.

'That is Father Kun,' she said. 'He is a priest, but it is his fantasy to be a soldier. He wears always a gun in his cassock and he lines up the Jews and he draws this gun and he says to us, the ones with

224

rifles, he says, "In the name of Christ, FIRE!"'
She looked up from the photograph. 'And so I did.' She closed the book. 'This is my confession, and I tell it to Julian.' She smiled. 'He says good-bye. He kisses my hand. He says he goes soon to Rostov.'

'Because that's where Andrei Chikatilo lived,' I said.

Irene clearly did not recognize the name.

'A Russian serial killer,' I told her.

She shook her head. 'Julian says nothing of this killer,' she said. 'He is going to Rostov to say also a good-bye to this man from many years before. I know his name from my time in Argentina. He was a Russian agent there.'

'Julian was in contact with a Russian agent while he was in Argentina?' I asked.

'Yes,' Irene said. 'This is what he tells to me. He met with this man many times, he says to me. He was a man who knew many secrets from the bad times in Argentina.'

'Who was this Russian?' Loretta asked.

'His name is Mikhail Soborov,' she answered without the slightest hesitation. 'Juan had much fear of him.'

'Why?'

She laughed. 'Because he is one – as we say here – he is one who knows where the knife is.' She sat back slightly. 'Did Julian meet with him in Rostov?'

'I don't know,' I answered.

Irene shook her head softly and, with that gesture, appeared to slip into some former life. 'There was something about Julian that made you wish to speak with him the things you do not speak about with others. When I make my confession to him he tells me that he also has known bad things. He says he is like me.'

'Like you in what way?' I asked.

'In his crime,' Irene answered.

'Murdering innocent people?' I asked.

Irene shrugged. 'This I do not know.'

'He said nothing about what this crime was?' Loretta asked.

'No,' Irene answered. 'But it had made him tired, I think. He tells me that he wants someday to go home.'

'Home,' Loretta repeated softly.

'Home, yes,' Irene said. 'He wants to find peace there.' She smiled softly. 'He said there is a pond.'

PART V

THE COMMISSAR

CHAPTER 22

There is a scene in *The Commissar* where
Julian imagines Chikatilo's wife – the
mother of his children, the woman who
had lived with him all the many years during which
he had secretly ridden the desolate rails of a crumbling Soviet Union – at the moment she begins
to suspect that poor, pathetic Andrei is something
other than he seems:

*She recalled that cold December day, so near
to Christmas, when Yelena Zakotnova had first
gone missing. Had she ever seen Yelena walking
the streets of the village? In the papers she was
a pretty girl, only nine, with dark hair cut
short. From a distance, Chikatilo's wife said to
herself, her killer might have thought she was
a boy. 'Her killer,' she repeated in her mind,
now with a chill colder than any winter she'd
endured in Shankty, because at the very
moment she silently pronounced the words 'her
killer,' she envisioned Andrei and immediately
recalled the spots of blood she'd seen trailing
along the side of the house she shared with him,*

the dim light of that shared bedroom, her empty bed during the long absences of this man, the knife he packed with his black bread and cheese.

I mentioned this scene to Loretta over dinner, then added, 'It's in all Julian's books. Deceit. The moment when the face of someone you thought you knew changes, and you suspect that there's something terrible behind the mask.'

'And you're thinking that Marisol wore this mask,' Loretta said, 'that she was the "she-devil" Vargas gave to Ramírez – actually a terror, like La Meffraye, or a tigress, like Countess Báthory.'

During the drive back to Budapest, I'd actually envisioned Marisol in this dreadful role, her eyes glittering in the dark way Julian described the eyes of Countess Báthory.

'There are such women, after all,' I added. 'René mentioned one in Algiers. She was called "the Blade," and according to him, she scared the hell out of everybody. Marisol would have been even more frightening because she seemed so completely innocent.'

Loretta took a sip from her glass and cast her eyes about the lobby of the hotel.

'So it's a question of moral betrayal,' I went on. 'Marisol presents herself as this simple girl from the Chaco. She claims that all she wants is an opportunity to better herself. By day she quotes Borges and guides Julian and me around Buenos

Aires. By night she goes to some dungeon and becomes a monster for the Montoneros.'

Something about this scenario clearly troubled Loretta.

'If any of that is true, then Julian truly had stepped into that world your father warned you about,' Loretta said. 'That shadow world. Agents, double agents, triple agents. He wasn't used to that kind of complexity. But he would have begun to worry about it, don't you think, if he'd gotten wind of any of what we've found out? He'd have begun to ask himself the same questions about her that we're asking. He would have wanted to know not only where she was but who she was. Because he wouldn't have been sure of anything anymore. Was she a girl with no politics? Was she a Montonero? He might even have come to think that she could be a double agent working for the junta.'

'Working for the junta?' I asked.

'Working to catch Vargas, or something like that,' Loretta said. 'Julian would have begun to consider all kinds of deception.'

All kinds of deception.

With those words, I felt life turn again, and on that turn, Marisol became an ever-changing shape. Could it be, I wondered, that the many faces of female evil that Julian had drawn were merely his multiple attempts to capture the yet more elusive moral nightmare that was Marisol?

I thought all this through for a moment, then

said, 'But if Marisol worked for the junta, why did she disappear?'

Loretta appeared surprised that I'd taken her latest conjecture seriously. At the same time, she clearly began to considerer such a possibility.

'The most obvious reason would be that her cover was close to being blown,' she answered. 'For that reason her "handlers" took her out of the game.'

'So, in this scenario, Marisol was never kidnapped or murdered at all?' I asked.

It was a dark twist that now produced yet another wholly unexpected turn in my mind.

'That would mean that Julian was looking for a woman who had never been kidnapped at all,' I said.

I could scarcely imagine the betrayal he would have felt if he had unearthed such a grim truth about Marisol, how deep it might have been, how thoroughly it might have unraveled him.

The grave effect of that thought must have shown in my features, because I could see it reflected in Loretta's.

'Of course, we have no idea what Julian finally came to think about Marisol,' she reminded me.

True enough, I thought, and yet I remembered a night when Julian and I were in La Boca. Julian had stopped suddenly in front of one of the neighborhood's characteristically bright-colored houses. He gave a slight nod toward the back of the house, where an old car rested near a basement window.

232

Its hood was up, and a set of long black cables ran from its battery down into the cellar.

'That's one of the places where the junta takes people,' Julian said quietly. 'It's a little torture chamber.'

'How do you know that?' I asked.

'Marisol pointed it out one afternoon,' Julian answered. 'She says everyone knows what happens there.'

But had everyone truly known that, I wondered now, or was it only Marisol who'd known?

And had Julian, in some dreadful moment of awful recognition, discovered this grim truth?

There is always a moment when the various elements of a mystery must be gathered together like puzzle pieces and rearranged upon the table, each piece seeking its place in the slowly emerging picture. I knew that it was time for the pieces of my story to arrange themselves for that final 'reveal,' but instead of reaching illumination, I faced an even darker world of shifting loyalties and identities, one in which Julian, so young and naive, could easily have been ensnared.

'What are you thinking, Philip?' Loretta asked.

'I was thinking about Julian,' I answered. 'That the world had become very dark to him by the time he left Argentina. And that if we keep pursuing this, it may become very dark to us, as well.'

'So, do you want to stop looking?' Loretta asked.

'No,' I answered. 'But I don't know why.'

She reached over and touched my hand. 'It's

because curiosity is the hungriest of beasts,' she said. 'And so we have no choice but to go on.' Her smile had an element of old tragedies about it. 'We're like Nick and Nora, Philip. Only a much darker version.'

Her touch was soft and warm, and I had not felt such a touch in many years.

'Yes,' I said. 'We are.'

CHAPTER 23

We arrived in Rostov early in the morning. Our guide, Yuri Kasov, looked to be around fifty, and had served as Julian's guide and interpreter, as well.

'No problem,' he assured us by phone. 'I do everything.'

True to his word, he subsequently made all the plans necessary to get Loretta and me to Rostov-on-Don, which, despite its rustic name, turned out to be a bustling city of more than a million.

At the airport, Yuri whisked us off to a surprisingly modern hotel, where we treated him to dinner. Loretta struck up a curiously intense interrogation that began with Yuri's first meeting with Julian, progressed through Julian's research, and moved rapidly until she reached her intended point.

'Do you remember Julian meeting a man named Mikhail Soborov?' Loretta asked. 'He lives here in Rostov, I believe.'

'Yes, I went with him to this man,' Yuri answered in an English that became more offbeat by the minute. 'At first beginning they are trying to speak

Spanish, but the old man, he was no longer to speak it.' His smile betrayed a carefully honed cleverness. 'I never have expect that Julian to look for such a one as Mikhail Soborov.'

'Such a one?' Loretta asked.

'Old-time KGB,' Dimitri answered.

'What did they talk about?' Loretta asked.

'I don't know,' Dimitri said. 'They will not talk in front of me. Once Julian, he is said something in Spanish, and the old man, he is getting up and push me out of the room and close the door.'

Why? I wondered, but there was no point in asking, since the conversation moved to other topics until the meal came to an end.

But the notion of Julian having some secret conversation with a Russian agent continued to trouble me, and later that night, tossing sleeplessly in my bed, I decided to take a walk.

Outside the hotel, the charmless streets of Rostov swept outward toward the distant Don, a river that did indeed, as Sholokhov said in the title of his famous novel, flow quietly to the sea.

It was mostly a cheerless place, architecturally boring, yet its streets had been walked by an extraordinary number of Russia's great literary figures. Pushkin had a boulevard named after him; Chekhov and Solzhenitsyn had also spent time in Rostov; and a young Gorky had worked on its docks. A city with such rich literary history appealed to me, of course, but I saw little evidence that it had done the same for Julian. In *The*

Commissar, he had painted it as a warren of all but indistinguishable streets, a gray labyrinth fed by a gray stream, through which Chikatilo, 'the Red Ripper,' had made his way like a blind horse, sensing corners, alleys, and dead ends, and always, always, the presence of a waylaid child.

It was the route of this devouring monster that Julian had relentlessly followed. He had written of Chikatilo's birth in the tiny village of Yablochnoye, a little boy whose mother had filled his mind with tales of the Great Famine, including the hideous story that Chikatilo's own brother had been kidnapped and eaten by neighbors. Meticulously, Julian had detailed the emergence of this wounded boy into a biologically complete but inwardly crippled adult, a man who married and became the father of two children by the time he took a teaching job in Novoshakhtinsk, the one from which he was later dismissed amid charges of child molestation.

Julian had spent time in both those places, as was clear from *The Commissar*, but it was in Shakhty (Russian for 'mine shaft,' as Julian pointed out) that he had stayed the longest, as if attempting to unearth what it was about this grim little town that finally tempted Chikatilo to commit his first murder.

She was only nine years old, and Chikatilo lured her to an old house that he'd bought for the purpose; thus it was a crime, as Julian wrote in one of his stark phrases, 'as premeditated by his reason as it was preordained by his madness.'

It was the blood of this child that Chikatilo's wife found in the snow in front of her own house and that generated the suspicions she would harbor for decades, little noises that continually sounded like a footfall outside her window.

But loyal wife that she was, Fayina kept her silence as the years passed and the body count rose in towns and villages along railway lines, riverbanks, and the many forests of the Don.

It was here, in Rostov, that Chikatilo had killed two women in Aviator Park, then gone on to kill again in Novoshakhtinsk and from there back to Shakhty, then back to Rostov, where yet another body was found in Aviator Park.

Julian had pointed out Andrei Chikatilo's extraordinary recklessness, the careless abandon with which he murdered, the public arenas that were both his killing fields and his dumping grounds, as if he had come to believe, as all madmen do, that he was in league with the sun and the moon, protected by the elements themselves, shrouded by fog and veiled by rain, perhaps feeling the added pleasure of believing that in all the world he would be the last person suspected of his crimes.

In fact, Chikatilo's only precaution, though Julian came to doubt that even this was a conscious act of evasion, was that he'd finally begun to enlarge the murderous circle that had earlier enclosed him, killing outside Moscow, then in Revda, Zaporizhya, Krasny Sulin, and as far afield as Leningrad.

Julian had visited every murder site, his book made clear, but it was here, in Rostov, that he'd lived during most of his time in Russia, and it was here that he'd written a good deal of it while holed up in a small apartment off Ulyanovskaya Street.

I knew the address because I'd written him many e-mails, encouraging him in his research and subject matter, always adding that one day I thought his accomplishment would be clear. I never knew how he received my encouragement because he never once responded to it. Rather, his next communication would detail some new idiom he'd learned or some new author, usually Russian, whom he'd discovered.

Late in the evening I came to the little street where Julian had lived for many years. It was quite dark by then, but Rostov's reliable street lamps offered sufficient light for me to see the windows on the third floor. How many times Julian must have stood at those windows, I thought, stood and stared cheerlessly out over this deeply foreign city.

The expatriate is well established in literature, of course, but usually the portrayal is romantic – Lord Byron in Italy, for example. One sees the desolate exile less often, and yet when I considered Julian's time in Rostov, I thought of Ovid's banishment to bleak, impoverished Tomis. 'My punishment,' love's great poet wrote, 'is the place.' It was unimaginable to me that Rostov and Shakhty and Revda had not been similar punishments for Julian, and had I begun to write about him when

239

I returned to my room later that night, I would certainly have made some comparison between his life in Rostov and Ovid's in Tomis, how isolated Julian must have felt in Russia, and how incalculably alone. The difference was that Julian's exile was self-imposed – thus another sign that he had inflicted some strange punishment upon himself by living in desolate places and filling his mind with torture and murder, by choosing as his sole companions the great demons of the world. In that way, too, I supposed, he wasn't just a good man, but a great one, not just an artist, but one whose art had imposed exile and solitude. Ovid had been forced to live in dreadful Tomis, after all, while Julian, at least, had chosen it.

I said this to Loretta the next morning, and in response she glanced out over the spare little dining room our hotel provided, most of the tables occupied, the air filled with the soft Slavic murmur of the other guests.

'This must have been the loneliest place Julian ever lived,' she said. 'With no one who spoke English. Or any other language he knew.'

At Loretta's mention of Julian's languages, I found myself thinking of the first one he'd learned, Spanish, then of the first country in which he had encountered it.

I thought of Julian and Marisol in a sun-drenched Buenos Aires. But now Marisol was less fixed in my mind, an identity that had been in continual revision, first as businesslike guide, then as spy, then as an Argentine version of La Meffraye, working either for the Montoneros or the junta, but equally evil in either capacity.

It was no doubt my continual reimagining of Marisol that took me back to a particular moment only a few days before I left Buenos Aires. It was my only time alone with her, and she seemed curiously preoccupied. It didn't surprise me when she said, 'There are days when one falls out of love with one's life.'

'Months and years, if you're not lucky,' I told her.

'Why do you say this?'

'Because it happened to my father. He regrets everything.'

'And you?'

'My regret is not with anything I've done,' I told her. 'But sometimes I'm not altogether happy with what I am.'

'What makes you unhappy in this way?'

'Well, it's mostly the fact that I don't have any talent,' I answered. 'I don't sing or act or play a musical instrument. I've read the great books, but I couldn't write even a bad one. Julian, on the other hand, has talent in great abundance.' Then, for the first time, I gave full voice to the truth. 'I would like to be more like him.'

She glanced away, as if from a subject she didn't want to discuss. 'And what is Julian?'

I found that I had no answer for her, and this

241

surprised me, the fact that I couldn't pin Julian down, that something about him remained in flux, unsettled.

'He is very smart,' Marisol said, then looked out into the traffic. 'This much is true.' She turned to face me. 'But he is like his country. He isn't finished yet. And in many ways, he is still a little boy.'

She added a quick smile to this last remark, so that it seemed not a criticism of 'his country' but a curiously affectionate statement instead. For that reason, I let it pass and went on to another subject. But now, sitting at a breakfast table in Rostov, it returned to me insistently, and I related the exchange to Loretta.

'Still a little boy,' Loretta said. 'You know what's clear when a woman says that about a man? That she knows she's superior to him.' She seemed briefly to consider Marisol with an added complexity she was still struggling to grasp. Finally she said, 'Do you know the moment when Sherlock Holmes realizes that Irene Adler has seen through his disguise?'

I had never read Conan Doyle, so I said, 'No, I don't know any of those stories.'

'There is a moment when their eyes lock, Holmes and Irene Adler, and at that moment, the great detective knows, without doubt, that this one woman has fooled him.'

I imagined Julian in the shock of that recognition, coldly aware that he'd been played for a fool.

'You know,' I said, 'if Julian ever found out that he was fooled by Marisol, fooled into believing that she was this innocent girl from the Chaco when she was something different, a spy, a torturer, a double agent, it would have wounded his self-confidence, his entire sense of himself.'

Loretta nodded. 'Yes, it would have.'

'Would he have sought revenge?' I asked.

Loretta considered my question for a time before she spoke.

'You've stumbled upon another turn, you know,' she said. 'The idea that when Julian was looking for Marisol, it wasn't in order to find out what had happened to her or even who she really was.' Her gaze revealed something menacing. 'Because he already knew.'

I immediately grasped where she was headed.

'And so he went looking for Marisol because he intended to . . .,' I said, then stopped because I felt compelled to resist saying what had come into my mind.

I could have resisted it, almost on principle, but I would have had to ignore Loretta's eyes, how very intense they were, filled with the sudden dread that rises when you sense that you are closing in upon a horrible truth.

'Because he intended to kill her,' I said. I felt a shudder. 'Was that his crime?'

I saw Loretta entertain this possibility, then just as quickly reject it.

'But how could that have been Julian's crime?'

243

she asked. 'Because he said that you witnessed his crime, remember?' She smiled at the wrong turn my latest conjecture had made. 'Julian murder Marisol?' She smiled in utter confidence of the next thing she said. 'Surely, Philip, you did not see that.'

CHAPTER 24

Mikhail Soborov's residence was more of a cottage than a house, and it was in an area that was mostly rural, a part of the Ukraine that had once blossomed with small, independent farmers, the famed kulaks that Stalin had so despised and all but exterminated through planned famine. Julian had made the point that Chikatilo was beaten for bedwetting and for almost every other offense, but the Great Famine was the traumatic event in the Rostov Ripper's life; its tales of cruelty and cannibalism were ones to which the young Andrei responded not with horror or repulsion, but with a vicarious throb of pleasure and excitement that surely must have flooded his soul with dark surprise.

There was nothing at all surprising about Mikhail Soborov, however. In fact, he looked so much the way I expected that in a book he would have been a caricature of the boisterous, big-bellied Slav, hard-drinking and jolly, a Russian version of Falstaff.

'Thanks for talking to us,' I said as I took the hand he quite cheerfully offered.

The old man laughed robustly. 'In old days, I would have hidden in the woodshed,' he said, 'or had you killed en route.'

'In that case, I'm pleased that things have changed,' I said.

'Oh, yes, they have changed,' Soborov said with an air of jollity that now struck me as somewhat false, something other than Santa Claus underneath the bright red coat. 'In those days my ideals were young, and a man takes on the look of the god he worships, is that not so?'

Rather than wait for me to answer, he turned swiftly to Loretta. 'Now, here we have one who has not been aged by disenchantment,' he said as he took Loretta's hand and gallantly kissed it. 'Now, please. We shall have vodka, the three of us.'

But before reaching for the vodka, he cast a hard look at Yuri. 'We don't need extra set of ears,' he said sternly, and with that closed the door in his face.

When he turned back to us, he was frowning. 'They say we are free now in Russia to say what we wish, but I do not trust such "guides" as this one who comes here with you.'

'Why would they want an agent with us now?' I asked Soborov once we'd taken seats in his small living room.

'Because repression is a snake that grows back its head,' Mikhail answered in a way that clearly closed the subject. 'So, what did Julian tell you about me?'

'Nothing at all,' I answered. 'I learned about you from Irene, as I said in my letter.'

'Irene, yes,' Soborov said. 'You know that in Budapest, during the war, she shot Jews in hospital beds, no?'

'My father hinted at something like that,' I answered. 'And when we met her, she showed us a picture. It was quite sad. She feels—'

'Guilt, yes,' Soborov interrupted. 'Julian once called it the false consolation of those not really harmed.'

'What an unforgiving thing to say,' I told him.

'For most, time wears guilt away, like wind and water,' Soborov said, 'but perhaps time more forgiving than should be, yes?'

'Perhaps,' I said, since I could think of nothing else.

Soborov peered at me closely. 'We never meet, you and I?'

'No,' I answered. 'At least, I don't think so.'

Soborov laughed. 'Too bad. You might have learned one of our tricks.'

I looked at him quizzically.

'How to make meeting look not planned,' Soborov said. 'This how it looks with Julian and me. I am just a man at next table. I rise to leave, but I leave keys on table. Julian picks up keys and gives to me. I take keys and say to him that I am like Borges. Blind, like old poet.' He laughed. 'Code is passed, just like in movies.' He looked at me with an almost impish expression. 'Too much like in movies, yes?' He waved his hand as if dismissing the subject, and with that gesture, his features became more serious. 'This not how I meet Julian, of course.'

'How did you meet him?' I asked.

The old man smiled widely. 'You always in big hurry, you Americans, but we have not yet had vodka.'

With that he left the room, then returned to it a few seconds later with the glasses and a bottle encased in a square of ice.

'Do you know what we say in Russia?' he asked.

We shook our heads.

'That drink only second most important thing in life,' Soborov said. 'Of first importance is breathe.' He laughed loudly. 'You get it, yes?'

We nodded.

He poured each of us a glass, then offered his toast. 'To peace.'

We touched our glasses, and with that the old man sat down in a large chair opposite us.

'So, to Julian,' he said. 'Because you are Americans, I will tell you quickly. He came to Soviet consulate. He was looking for girl. She had disappeared and he was looking for her. He gets nothing from Casa Rosada, and so he comes to us.' His smile was that of an old man being mischievous. 'The Reds.' He shrugged. 'We did not know where this woman is, but perhaps we know someone who does.' He appeared briefly reluctant to say more and waved his hand. 'Ah, what difference does it make now?'

With this Soborov clapped his hands together.

'All right, then,' he said. 'So. Have you ever heard of the Dogo Córdoba?'

I had no idea what this was and said so.

'It is dog,' Soborov told me. 'Especially bred in Argentina.' He leaned forward and rubbed his hands together vigorously. 'It is fighting dog that is famous for not to back down. The Dogo Córdoba bred to endure great pain. They are champions in the dogfights.'

'What does this have to do with Julian?' Loretta asked.

'Because this is where we send him,' Soborov answered. 'To a dogfight.'

I could scarcely imagine Julian at such an event, but by then there were many aspects to Julian's life that were equally hard to imagine.

'They illegal, these fights,' Soborov continued, 'but there are places, hidden places, or maybe not hidden, but protected by police.' His smile was incongruously warm. 'And we know what Argentine police doing in other places, no? Things that make dogfights look like country dance.' He drew out a handkerchief and swabbed his neck, as if he had returned to the heat and humidity of an Argentine summer. 'It was July,' he said. 'Very hot.' Now he turned to Loretta. 'They very secretive, of course, the people who go to Dogo Córdoba fights. It is like a secret society. Important people in Argentina come to these special fights. High in government. But also thugs, and of these thugs there is one we keep eye on. He is called El Árabe.'

'The Arab?' I asked.

'That is what he is called, yes,' Soborov said. 'Because he is brown, almost like the peasants. He was very low sort of fellow. He had not much intelligence, but low cunning, this he had much. In this way, like Stalin. He had worked himself into a good job running whole network of *escuelitas*. We knew that some of our people were in his custody, but we did not know where they were. El Árabe was very hard man, maybe impossible to break, we thought, even under stress. But he had weakness.' He laughed at the nature of this weakness, then revealed it. 'He was like little child when it comes to Americans. A young man like Julian would attract his attention. This is what we think. A young American. Smart. Good-looking. Maybe with money, maybe from good family. We know that such a one would appeal to El Árabe.'

Loretta looked as if suddenly struck by a cold breeze. 'You tried to recruit Julian as a spy?'

'Not at first, because we think maybe he is spy, or maybe he is "spy who comes in from cold."' He laughed. 'Either way we wish to keep eye on him.'

Soborov paused to take another sip of vodka.

'There was Dogo Córdoba fight in little town outside Buenos Aires,' Soborov continued. 'In pampas, but not far from city. We know El Árabe will be there because he is great lover of these fights. Can you believe this? After day of torture, this

250

is what he does in order to relax, watch dogs tear each other apart.'

He looked at Loretta.

'And so we send your brother there,' he told her. 'We give him money and he bet like rich man, and this, too, we know, will catch eye of El Árabe.'

Now his gaze returned to me.

'I was Julian's "handler,"' he said, 'and so I go with him there because I want to see if he makes contact and report to my superiors if this American has talent for deception we might later use.' His face soured. 'It was dreadful place, where we went that night. Very dreadful place.'

Soborov described the event, how it had been conducted in the sweltering interior of a large shed, the dogs brought in on chains and lashed to the sides of a circular pit whose walls were made of corrugated tin, unpainted and splattered with the blood of previous combats. The crowd was washed with sweat and beer and they screamed to the dogs and across the pit to one another, yelling taunts and bragging about their picks of the night, waving money and sometimes knives.

'It is from hell, this scene,' Soborov said, 'and at center of pit, there is El Árabe, with his black hair plastered down, yelling at dogs, laughing, and drinking beer.'

I recalled a scene in *The Commissar*, a moment when Julian has Chikatilo dream of being a pit master at an orgy of torture, moving about with a riding crop, dressed in a red jacket and high

251

black boots, orchestrating the terrible performance as he strides from ring to ring.

'Julian has been shown photographs of this stupid little bastard,' Soborov went on, 'and he make it his business to get near him, waving money like the others, but speaking only good American English, which catches ear of El Árabe.'

In my mind, I saw this 'stupid little bastard' turn at the sound of Julian's voice, his gaze drinking in this young American as if he were a movie star.

'I am across pit, but I see El Árabe speak to Julian, and Julian speak back, then El Árabe turn back to pit and give signal with a big wave of hand for fight to begin.'

What happened after that was a fierce struggle between two Dogo Córdobas, white dogs, Soborov told us, and so the blood that swept over their spinning flanks and dripped from their mouths and coated their teeth and ran down their throats was vivid red.

'The Dogo Córdoba is extinct now,' Soborov said at the end of this description of the fight, 'because so many die in the pit and because they become so unstable, cannot be with another dog without killing it. Because of this they disappear.' He offered a rueful smile. 'Life cannot be sustained by ferocity alone.' He explained: 'I hear this and I like it.'

He was silent for a time, as if his last remark had come to him unexpectedly and was still resonating through his own long memory.

'Anyway, Julian meet El Árabe many times after this,' Soborov said, 'in the bars and in dance halls of the tango. He is good at pretending friendship. He can make anyone believe he loves them.' He shrugged. 'Once he say to me, "All you can offer to those who love you is the pretense that you love them back."'

Even for Julian, this struck me as an infinitely sad pronouncement, and to avoid its sting I rushed ahead.

'Did you help him find out what happened to Marisol?' I asked.

'No,' Soborov said, 'but I think perhaps El Árabe did, because Julian must have discovered something very bad. I believe this because he suddenly change. He has been a good-looking young man; then overnight he is old and looks like one who has, as we say, crossed the Styx. He still has this look when I see him last.' His gaze darkened. 'A very bad man, El Árabe. Very bad. He feels no guilt, this man. Even after the junta fall, he offers no apology for his little schools. To this day, he is sometimes on television in Argentina, regretting nothing, saying that he enjoyed every minute of it.'

'Did he go to prison?' Loretta asked.

'For few years,' Soborov said. 'Then he is released and after that he is home to his village near Iguazú.'

I recalled the town Julian had circled on the map he was looking at on the day he died. 'Clara Vista?'

Soborov nodded. 'He lives there still, makes

253

interviews, laughs in the faces of those who still seek the disappeared.'

He let this settle in. Then, as if trying to lighten the atmosphere, he smiled quite brightly and said, 'By the way, did Julian ever finish the book on Chikatilo?'

'Yes,' I answered. 'It'll be published next year. He called it *The Commissar*, and it's the most thorough account of Andrei Chikatilo yet written.'

'Good,' Soborov said. 'He was a hard worker, Julian. This much can be said of him, and it is not a small thing. I would like to receive a copy of this book when it is published.'

'I'll make sure you do,' I promised him.

Soborov smiled. 'So, have I said to you what you wished to know about Julian?'

'Not really,' Loretta answered bluntly.

Soborov was clearly surprised by this answer.

'Irene said that when Julian came to see her a few years ago, he already knew what happened to Marisol,' Loretta added. 'You're saying that it was this El Árabe who told him?'

Soborov nodded. 'Who else could? He was Julian's last contact in Argentina.'

'When Julian came here, did you talk about Argentina?' Loretta asked.

'Yes,' Soborov said. 'We talked of the dogs, and of that girl, the one who disappeared. He said that he found her.'

'Found her?' I asked. 'He found Marisol?'

254

'Yes,' Soborov answered. 'It was the Arab who led him to her, but he did not tell me how.'

'Did Julian say anything about who Marisol was or might have been?' Loretta asked.

Soborov looked puzzled. 'Might have been?'

'A Montonero, for example.'

Soborov shook his head.

'What did he say about her?' Loretta asked.

Soborov considered his answer for a moment, then said, 'He said only that a trick is played upon her.'

'What kind of trick?' I asked.

Soborov took a surprisingly casual sip from his glass. 'He was always speaking in . . . what is the word when it is about a little thing, but it is really about big things . . . what is the word for speaking in this way?'

'Metaphorically?' I asked.

'That is it, yes,' Soborov said. 'Not really about one thing, about many things.' Now he shrugged. 'So when I ask him what is this trick, he does not answer me directly. It is something he cannot speak about, he tell me.' He put down his glass. 'So all I know is that he has a name for this trick.' His smile bore the weight of the dark view of things he seemed to have glimpsed in Julian's eyes at that long-ago moment. 'It is called "the Saturn Turn."'

PART VI

THE SATURN TURN

CHAPTER 25

'The Saturn Turn,' Loretta repeated quietly. We were seated in a small park near our hotel. It was late in the afternoon and there were few people around. Children were in school and workers were at their jobs. A few older people walked about, along with an occasional mother pushing a stroller. Overall, the scene was quite peaceful, and this allowed my mind to roam rather freely until, for some reason, I hit upon Aeschylus, of all people. It was not a line from any of his plays that came to me, however, but the fact that he had written his own obituary and how odd that obituary was. In it, Aeschylus mentioned nothing of his fame, nothing of his plays, nothing even of his life, except that as a young man he had fought at Marathon. That, it seemed, was the thing of which he was most proud, the one thing about himself that he wanted remembered.

Julian, of course, had left no obituary, much less an explanation of why he had chosen to take his own life. Stranger still, while Aeschylus had proudly noted his fighting at Marathon, Julian had chosen to destroy the last words he'd ever written, as if dreading their meaning.

When she spoke, it was clear that Loretta's mind was tending in a completely different direction.

'I was just remembering something Julian once said,' she told me. 'He had just gotten back from Swaziland, where he'd gone to write an article. We were looking through the photographs he'd taken there. People in terrible conditions, all of them man-made. He looked up from one particularly grim picture and he said, "It all comes down to people in the end, Loretta. All the global policies and grand schemes. They all come down to what we do to people, whether we help or harm them."'

On that thought, I was with Julian again, sitting in Grosvenor Park, peering up at the great eagle that was mounted at the top of the American embassy. He was staring at that eagle when he spoke.

'Ambrose Bierce called diplomacy the art of manufacturing a plausible lie,' he said.

I laughed at this, but Julian didn't. Instead, his gaze darkened and a shadow settled over him. 'To play that trick really well, Philip,' he added, 'is a master crime.'

I related this odd exchange to Loretta, who listened to it very carefully, as if combing each word for some telling detail.

'Maybe Julian learned that in Argentina,' I added.

Loretta nodded and touched my hand. 'On to El Árabe,' she said.

★ ★ ★

For the next few days, we turned the small desk in my hotel room into a makeshift research center. Loretta's Spanish was far better than mine, though neither of us was in any sense fluent. Still, by working together, and despite online translations that were often close to indecipherable themselves, we got the gist of the many articles we found on El Árabe.

Just as Soborov had told us, El Árabe was anything but shy when it came to publicity. He'd been sentenced to ten years for his *escuelitas* activities and had served seven before being released.

Upon release, he'd moved to the small town near the great falls at Iguazú, an area of Argentina where it is possible not only to see both Paraguay and Brazil but to easily slip across their borders. He had not been shy about stating the obvious:

> *I wanted to be close to the border in case the little men of Casa Rosada want to try me again on some trumped-up charge. I live here in peace. I do not hurt a cat. I sit on my little porch and I say to the world, 'I take the dirty name you call me with pride, for I am El Árabe, and I regret nothing.'*

As became clear from the many interviews that Hernando Vilario – which was El Árabe's real name – had granted in the days following his release, he not only had no regrets, but he was actually proud of what he'd done.

You only have to look at Russia under the Reds to know what men like me saved Argentina from. The people of Argentina should put statues of us in the park, because we are the reason they do not live under the Red flag. Would they like it better under Castro? With the old cars and the falling-down capital and the eight-hour speeches in the hot Havana sun? They should thank men like me, the men who saved them from such a thing. Instead they put us in prison, and we are made to fall on our knees and deny the great thing we did. We stopped the Reds in their tracks, and for this all Argentina should be grateful to us.

He had repeated these pronouncements in almost every interview since his release. He had also appeared on radio and television, and with each appearance, according to one editorial, 'he becomes more bold and outrageous. He grows fat on ill repute and displays his crimes like medals.'

As the years passed, less and less notice was paid to him, though he clearly took every opportunity to regain the public eye. Once, he even ran for election in the small district in which he lived. He was soundly beaten, but his campaign of 'blood and fire' was vociferous enough to get him yet another brief burst of attention.

After this election, Loretta and I discovered, he had more or less faded from public attention until another series of articles appeared in a paper called

Hoy, a small Buenos Aires weekly. They were written by one David Leon, and their tone, though not sympathetic, was curiously tinged with what Loretta called 'a little mist of understanding.' Not enough to obscure El Árabe's deeds, she went on to tell me, but careful to place them within the context of Argentina's tumult, the raging battles that had rocked the country, the kidnappings and assassinations, the economic instability, all of which had combined, he wrote, 'to inject in every vein a liquid, icy fear.'

'This is our man,' Loretta said as she handed me the first of Leon's articles. 'This is the man who can help us meet El Árabe.'

In the photograph on the front page of Leon's series of articles, Hernando Vilario stood on a large veranda, his back to a sprawling jungle, naked to the waist and staring straight into the camera as if it were a gun. The brutality that came from him seemed the sort that must have been forged in man's early caves, hard beyond measure, merciless, and without remorse. But to this otherwise dreadful portrait, he had added a string of wooden beads. They hung from his neck, so brightly polished they glinted in the sunlight.

They might have come from anywhere, but the last time I had seen such beads, they had belonged to Marisol.

I didn't mention this to Loretta, however, because I saw no reason to. Even had I known absolutely that they were the same beads Marisol had worn so many years before, I still had no idea whether El Árabe had violently yanked them from her neck or whether she'd given them to him sweetly, tenderly, her eyes glittering with their shared work, a little gift in appreciative commemoration of their partnership in crime.

CHAPTER 26

We arrived in Buenos Aires on a clear, bright day, not unlike my first visit. That was many years before, but as the cab made its way down Avenida 9 de Julio, I recalled that time not as something that had vanished, but as a time whose still-obscure events were now adding a fierce purpose to my life. Of course, I also knew that part of that new purpose involved Loretta, who sat beside me, gazing out at the streets of the city.

'You look like you did the first time I saw you,' I told her now.

She looked at me. 'Hardly.'

'No, seriously,' I said. 'I once read that fear is the last reflex to leave us, but with you, I think it will be curiosity.'

She studied me a moment, then said, 'You know, Philip, I think that's the nicest thing anyone ever said to me.'

We reached the hotel a few minutes later. It was on San Martín, the plaza where Julian and I had often awaited Marisol and down whose wide stairs we had escorted Father Rodrigo to his bus.

'We should take a walk once we're settled in,' I told Loretta.

'Yes, let's.'

And so we did.

It was late in the afternoon and the air was turning cool and the shadows in the park were deepening. The lights had already been turned on. Not far away we could see the bus station.

'It's the same everywhere,' Loretta said. 'The orphaned poor gather in train and bus and subway stations. Julian said that he thought they unconsciously hovered near some means of escape.'

Below, I could see the same dusty boys who had huddled in those same littered corners the day we saw Father Rodrigo off to the Chaco, where undoubtedly yet more such children were to be found.

'I gave Julian a copy of *The Wretched of the Earth* the night he left for Argentina,' Loretta said. 'Franz Fanon's classic. Then I told him something an old African man had once said to a friend of mine. They'd met at one of those desert refugee camps that had cropped up all over Africa. The old man had lived all his life in the bush. He was missing several fingers. He'd amputated them himself, he said, with a machete. He held up the stubs and wiggled them a little in my friend's face. Then he said, "Do not avoid suffering." That was the message I had for Julian, that he should not avoid suffering.'

I smiled sadly. 'And as it turned out, he didn't.'

Loretta returned an errant strand of hair to its place. 'Just for the record, and because we must surely be near the end of this, I want you to know that I've enjoyed being with you, Philip. I've enjoyed traveling with you and talking with you and listening to you.'

'I feel the same, of course.'

She laughed. 'You know, in a book, this scene would be quite a maudlin moment, don't you think?'

'Yes, it would,' I said softly. 'But in life, those moments are often the best.'

The next morning we ate breakfast, then made our way to the address David Leon had given us for *Hoy*.

Loretta had gotten in touch with him while we were still in Budapest. She had found their exchanges quite warm, Leon more than willing to speak with us about El Árabe, a man he described as not only a sociopath but one who thought everyone else a sociopath, too.

The oddity in Leon's description of El Árabe, however, was the fact that he appeared to be extremely intelligent. Soborov had portrayed him as something of a buffoon, capable of low cunning, but little else. Leon's articles presented a far different assessment, one in which El Árabe seemed much closer to the Mr Kurtz of *Heart of Darkness*: keen-minded, resolute, with something curiously immortal in the nature of his malice.

David Leon was younger than I'd expected, a man in his thirties, tall, lean, with jet black hair that almost perfectly matched his glasses. He was dressed in a white shirt, jeans, and an olive green corduroy jacket.

'Good to see you after so many e-mails,' he said to Loretta when we arrived at *Hoy*, then turned and offered his hand to me. 'And you must be Philip?'

I took his hand. 'Thanks for seeing us,' I told him.

His office was a cubicle in a sea of cubicles, and so he suggested that we move to a conference room down the hall.

'It is more private there,' he said.

The conference room was also rather small, with a square table, scarred with use, and dotted with coffee rings.

'It is a historical artifact,' Leon said as he ran his fingers on the table. 'It belonged to José de Costa. He was imprisoned by the junta. A great reporter. One of the disappeared. It was while I was seeking to discover his fate that I came across El Árabe. He knew nothing of José, but he spoke of many other things. He is a great river of talk.'

'So it seems,' Loretta said.

We all took seats at the table. I had brought Julian's old briefcase, and while Loretta and Leon continued to speak, mostly about their earlier correspondence, I took out a paper and pen.

'You are a journalist?' Leon asked me.

'No,' I answered, then started to say that I was a book reviewer, but found that I could no longer describe myself in that way. What was I? For the first time in my life, I didn't know, an unexpected fact I found curiously exhilarating.

'As I told you in my first e-mail, my brother was going to write a book about his experience in Argentina,' Loretta said, clearly in an effort to get me off the hook. 'He evidently ran into Hernando Vilario at that time.'

She had already told him a great deal, I knew. In her correspondence with Leon, she'd described Julian's life and work, how he'd searched for Marisol after the disappearance, contacted both Casa Rosada and the Russians. She'd also told him that Julian was studying a map of Argentina before his death and that he'd circled the very village in which El Árabe now lived. She'd related the details of our talk with Soborov, as well – everything he'd revealed about his interaction with Julian and Julian's subsequent meeting with El Árabe.

Now, she said, 'So, as you know, we're here because we want to talk to him.'

'As I told you, this is not difficult,' Leon said. 'Hernando loves the attention. Especially from Americans. He is a big fan of the American Western. There is a picture of John Wayne in his house. I have already arranged for you to see him. You could fly there or take a bus. It is a long ride by bus, but not a bad trip. You will see our beautiful countryside.'

'We want to be well prepared before we talk to him,' Loretta said, 'so we'd appreciate anything you could add that you think we should know.'

'Know?' Leon asked. 'He is a monster. This you already know. But he is a monster who is at least without deceit. When he was arrested, he spit in the face of the government. At his trial, he spit at the judges and made no apologies for his *escuelitas*.'

Leon walked to a metal cabinet and withdrew an ancient carousel projector.

'It was El Árabe's. He took many pictures,' he said. 'He was proud of them. "My gift to you," he told me.'

Leon walked to the front of the room, pulled down a screen, turned off the room's overhead light, returned to his seat, and reached for the button that controlled the carousel.

'This will not be easy,' he said.

When the lights went on again, I felt that I had been gutted both spiritually and physically. In fact, mine had been a reaction so visceral that I'd had to hold my stomach and close my throat. At the end of it I was pale and felt that my legs had gone numb beneath me. There is a kind of revulsion that moves you beyond what some men do, to what some men are, and it is that that drains and exhausts you and leaves you with nothing but a need to escape the whole human race.

'So,' Leon said as he turned on the light. 'That is El Árabe. Do you still want to meet him?'

'It isn't a question of wanting to meet him,' I said. 'We need to meet him.'

Leon rose, walked to the front of the room, and drew up the screen, all of it done quite thoughtfully, as though he was turning something over his mind.

When he returned to his seat, he folded his hands together on the table, fingers laced, like a man with a pronouncement. 'Steel yourselves, then,' he said. 'For, no matter what evil you have known before, you have not known such a one as El Árabe.' He turned to Loretta. 'It is strange, is it not, that your brother was associated with such a man?'

With Leon's question, how little I still knew of Julian struck hard. But truth is truth, and the fact remained that the pieces of Julian's story were still scattered. It was as if Loretta had been right long ago when she'd said that the pebbles Julian had strewn along the forest floor might lead only to more pebbles.

'El Árabe will be expecting you,' Leon said as he turned to me. 'Good luck.'

Leon had wished me good luck quite cheerfully, but as Loretta and I left his office I found something final in his good wishes. For it was luck I would need, surely. In fact, it was all I had left, because I'd reached the very end of what I could discover of Julian beyond what was in his books.

271

I had read and reread those books, along with his notes and letters. I had gone to Paris, Oradour, London, Budapest, Čachtice, Rostov, and now Buenos Aires. I had interviewed the slender list of people who seemed to have made a contribution to Julian's work, his guides and his sources. I had talked to my father and to Loretta and even to myself, surely the three people, other than Marisol, who had most figured in his life. I had done all this, but I still had not cracked the door to my friend's most secret chamber or gained any notion of why he had rowed out to the center of the pond, nor what I might have said to stop him from what he eventually did.

'So,' I said to Loretta wearily, like an old gumshoe on his way to a final rendezvous, 'the last witness.'

CHAPTER 27

Our meeting with Hernando Vilario was not scheduled until the day after our arrival at Iguazú, and so Loretta and I decided to visit the great falls. I'd made the same trip with Julian years ago, the two of us flying out of Buenos Aires on a stormy afternoon. We'd stayed in Iguazú a couple of days, then returned to the capital.

A good deal had changed at Iguazú since then, changes no doubt necessary in order to make the place more attractive to tourists. Now a small train took visitors into the jungle that surrounded the falls. As we disembarked, I noticed that they were playing the theme from *The Mission*, a film whose dramatic opening scene had ended with the startling image of a crucified priest being swept over the Devil's Throat.

For a time we walked silently through a jungle that was now equipped with cement walkways and steel railings, safe for old people and children.

'The music back at the train reminds me of what Julian said about the difference between tourists and travelers,' I said.

Loretta peered out to where the roiling waters of Iguazú could be heard but not yet seen.

'This is the last time he was a tourist,' I said. 'When we got back to Buenos Aires, Marisol was waiting for us. We all went to a restaurant in La Boca and had dinner and wine. Julian had never looked more delighted with his life. Everything had come so easily to him.'

A thought appeared to strike Loretta. 'I know you felt rather dull in comparison to Julian. We both did. But were you jealous of him, too?'

It is strange what can be unearthed if the time is right and the inquisitor is dear, and at that moment I felt it rise like a gorge in my throat, the awful truth of things.

'Yes,' I said, and with that admission I felt a crack run through the portrait of my long friendship with Julian. I recalled all the times I might have influenced him, might have taken advantage of his weariness, his long bouts of despair, and even his penury – I might have used all that to nudge him in a different direction. I had even silenced any criticism of his work that might have made it leaner and sharper or reined in the wild sprawl that had sometimes marred his books. He might not have listened, but the fact remained that I had never offered him the slightest direction. With Loretta's question, I had to wonder if I had done this not because I thought it would do no good, but because I'd preferred him to remain where he was, tucked into a shadowy corner of the literary world, preferred him to remain what he was, a writer whose subject matter would doom him to an inconsequential place. Had I said nothing because I secretly delighted in all the now-darkened lights that had once shone on him, took pleasure in his failure?

'My God, Loretta,' I breathed. 'Was I not his friend?'

She saw my eyes glisten as all the many deceiving layers of my feigned friendship fell away.

She drew me into her arms. 'Now you are,' she said.

CHAPTER 28

The road to El Árabe led out of the bustling little town that bordered Iguazú and into the deepening jungle that surrounded it, burrowing into the depths in a way that did indeed remind me of Conrad's *Heart of Darkness*. Kurtz had gone far upriver, to the Inner Station, as Conrad had so metaphorically called it, deep into the savage heart of things, and there, amid that splendor, created a landscape that in all the world had most resembled hell.

I was busily going on about this when Loretta finally stopped me.

'Julian said something about goodness,' she told me. 'I hadn't thought of it before, but it was actually the last thing he said to me.'

She had gone down to the sunroom, where she found him in his chair, with the map of South America spread open on his lap. She asked him what he was doing and he said that he was remembering a place where he learned something about evil.

He had a pen in his hand, she said, the point touching the map, where, as she later saw, he'd circled the village of Clara Vista.

276

She asked him what it was that he had learned. His answer was surprisingly simple, though ultimately unrevealing. 'That goodness is evil's best disguise,' he said and added nothing else.

'Goodness is evil's best disguise,' I repeated as we moved ever deeper into the Paraguayan jungle from which El Árabe had made his many cruel pronouncements. I found myself imagining that his house was similar to the ravaged abode of Mr Kurtz, surrounded by a fence of bare wooden poles topped with dried-out human heads.

El Árabe's home was not emblematic of the dead soul who lived inside it, however. In fact, it looked more like a small woodland cottage of the sort one might see in more temperate climates. The vines that would otherwise have hung like thick green drapery from the roof had been cut back, and no vegetation crawled up the walls or slithered up the supporting posts of the side porch. For this reason, the cottage appeared curiously European in the way that any sense of wildness had been clipped away.

I could see three wicker chairs and a brightly colored hammock that took up almost the entire width of the porch. The windows were large, and their orange shutters were open; inside I could see unexpectedly feminine curtains, white and lacy, softly undulating in the warm, lazy air.

The house itself was built from concrete blocks,

painted to a glossy sheen. There was no front porch, just an earthen walkway leading to a door bordered by an assortment of plants potted in identical terra-cotta pots. A short storm fence stretched around the back of the house. Over the fence, I could see an old woman busy at a clothesline, hanging T-shirts, jeans, and a few oversized dresses with large floral patterns of the type I'd seen on the women in the town.

I glanced toward the front of the house. So the moment has come, I thought. I looked at Loretta. 'Ready?'

She nodded. 'Ready.'

And thus did we close in upon the Inner Station.

We had gotten only halfway up the dirt walkway that led to the house when the door suddenly swung open and a short, round man stepped out into the bright sun. He was perhaps seventy years old, but with jet black hair, quite obviously dyed, combed straight back and glinting in the sunlight.

'So the Eagle has landed,' he said with a laugh.

He was wearing light blue Bermuda shorts and no shirt, and his nearly hairless belly shook with quick spasms as he laughed. 'Welcome to my house. As we say, and I hear often said also in the American movies, *"Mi casa es su casa."'*

With that, El Árabe thrust out his large hand. 'I am a great fan of American movies and John Wayne. Come, you will see.' He stepped aside and waved us in. 'Please, come, come. I will have my housekeeper make drinks for us. You like mai tai? Margarita?'

I could not imagine having a drink with this man, and yet I could find no way to refuse it. He was my last contact, the end of the line, and if I learned nothing further, I could go no further.

'Whatever you have,' I said, and glanced at Loretta.

'Yes,' she said with a quick smile. 'Whatever you have.'

'Ah, good, we shall have drinks, then,' El Árabe said as if he was certain we would refuse them and now felt relieved that we hadn't. He walked to the window and called out to the old woman in the back, 'Vaya. Los invitados quieren algo de tomar. Margaritas para todos, por favor. With that he turned back to us. 'She is slow, poor thing,' he added sorrowfully. 'But in time the drinks will come.' He swept his arm out toward an adjoining veranda. 'Out there it is cool. We sit and talk and wait forever for the drinks.' He laughed heartily. 'You like my house?'

The living room was small, and El Árabe had decorated its walls with pictures not only of John Wayne but perhaps twenty other American movie stars, their studio photographs in cheap plastic frames. I caught Humphrey Bogart, Spencer Tracy, Alan Ladd, and John Wayne as I made my way outside.

'No women,' I said to him as I stepped out onto

279

the veranda. 'I would have expected, say, Veronica Lake or Ava Gardner.'

El Árabe waved his hand. 'I am a man of action,' he said with another broad laugh. 'I admire other such men. Men with, what do you call it, the steely stare.' He laughed again. 'I would wish to be the strong silent type. The Gary Cooper. But, as you see, I talk too much.' He grinned impishly. 'And I am not tall.' He indicated the wicker chairs. 'Please, rest. It is a long way from Buenos Aires. Did you fly?'

'Yes,' I answered. 'But once in Iguazú, we rented a car.'

'Iguazú, yes,' El Árabe said. 'So not a long drive this morning. Was it easy to find your way?'

'There aren't many roads, so it's hard to get lost,' I said.

'Not many roads,' El Árabe said. 'Not like in America, with the many, many highways.'

'No, not like America,' I said.

Out of the blue, El Árabe asked. 'So, my English is good, no?'

'It's very good,' I told him.

'From the American movies,' El Árabe said. 'I watched them when I was a kid. I still watch them. I like to practice all the time my English. But here it is hard. Here there is nothing. I am surrounded by such ignorant ones. They vote always for the Reds.' He leaned back slightly. 'Do you speak Spanish?'

'I'm afraid not,' I answered.

His gaze slid over to Loretta. 'And you, señora?'

'Only enough to get by,' Loretta said. 'My brother spoke it quite well.'

'Your brother, yes,' El Árabe said. 'You have come to speak of him. I understand this from Leon. He has died, your brother.'

'Yes,' Loretta said.

'So young,' El Árabe said sympathetically. 'Unusual in America. But here, they die like flies. We know death. We know pain. It is never far from us. At night we hear its voice in the undergrowth. There is much devouring one of the other here.' He turned to Loretta. 'As your brother knew.'

El Árabe looked like an actor who'd blown a line, and who, in doing so, had skipped ahead in the play, dropping five pages from the script and thus arriving too early at a place too far along.

'Margaritas!' he called, and looked back at us. 'She is slow, as I said. But she is good at the few little things she does. In Buenos Aires, they would not tolerate so slow a servant. But here, time has almost stopped, and we move slowly, like the sun.' His grin was rapier thin. 'I am also philosopher. I have many thoughts. But no one wishes to hear them.' He laughed. 'The world would have to change too much to give me honors. El Árabe is despised. El Árabe is a murderer, a rapist, a torturer.' For the second time, his gaze hardened. 'But who did I do these things to, eh? I will tell you. To people who would have done the same to me, to you.' He waved his hand. 'Even now, they

281

wear the T-shirts with the face of Che. Who was a murderer, this famous Che, with the movie-star face and the movie-star fame, a man who would have caused the deaths of millions.'

He didn't wait for this to settle in before he surged on, his eyes fiercely widening as he continued. 'And you have read what Castro said to Khrushchev?' His gaze leaped from me to Loretta, then back to me. 'You have read this? During the crisis with Cuba? With the missiles? He told that fat old Russian to kill all the Americans. To drop all the bombs. He said he would sacrifice Cuba for such an annihilation.'

He shook his head at the monstrousness of it. 'I am what you call "small potatoes" compared to this one who would have killed millions. As Stalin did. And Mao.' He thumped his chest. 'I, El Árabe, was never such a killer as these two Reds.'

It would have been a passionate attack on ideological extremism had El Árabe's own hideous acts not been equally extreme, but I felt it prudent to say nothing about this.

'I gather that you know why we've come here,' I said.

El Árabe nodded, then looked at Loretta. 'Leon told me about your brother. He said you believed he was perhaps going to write about me in his next book.'

'Perhaps,' Loretta said. 'Just before he died, he took out a map of Argentina. He had even circled the name of this village.'

This information seemed not to surprise El Árabe in the least.

'As you see, I am not hard to find,' he said. 'I hide from no one. I wish only that those Reds who now stink up the halls of Casa Rosada do not cross the border.' He pointed to an old hunting rifle that leaned against the far wall. 'I would fight, but I have nothing but this – what do you call it? – this . . . popgun. Even so, they do not come. Even so, they fear me. Do you know why? Because I know their secrets, these men at Casa Rosada. I know they are not so holy as they say they are. They know my crimes because I have not hidden them. But I know the crimes they hide.'

He smiled in the way of one who could easily prove his point. 'Guilt makes men tired and skinny.' He patted his full belly. 'I have no such problem.'

A rattle of pots and pans came from the other room.

El Árabe shook his head. 'It is hard to think with such commotion,' he said.

I glanced toward the kitchen, where I could see the woman stumbling about, her hands shaking violently.

'She probably has Parkinson's disease,' I said. 'Or something like it.'

El Árabe waved his hand; then his eyes shot over to Loretta. 'Your brother had come to me before. Back in the old days. He was looking for a girl. He thought I might know where she was.' He stopped and stared at me sullenly and with such

283

a sense of volcanic violence that I felt a cold streak of genuine fear.

Now he burst into a raucous laugh.

'See what I can do?' he asked. 'An old man, and I can still fill a heart with fear.' He laughed again, a great, self-satisfied laugh that shook his belly violently. 'With this look, too,' he said and seemed to clamp down upon me with his eyes, so that I felt like little more than a small animal in a steel trap. 'This one could really shut them up. Even when they were screaming, it would shut them up.'

He laughed again, and quite suddenly his entire demeanor changed. It was as if a cloud had parted to reveal a wholly different person, one whose every aspect had been clothed in shadow but which now became clear in the light.

'Shall I speak French to you, my American friends?' he asked in perfect English. 'Should I speak German?'

The transformation continued, and all the earlier features of his disguise fell away; he was no longer the slick-haired thug but was what he immediately claimed to be.

'Better that I should speak the Spanish of Castile,' he said, 'for I am Spanish, and this peasant patois I speak to such a one as that wretch in the kitchen is not my native tongue.'

'I see,' I said quietly.

'As Julian knew, a great spy must be a spy from birth,' El Árabe said. 'He must have played a role all his life.'

He was now as refined a worldling as could be imagined in any novel of intrigue. All his boorishness and vulgarity had simply dropped away like pieces of an old costume. Beneath it, there was no swagger, no bravado. I could almost imagine him in evening dress, having brandy and a cigar in the staterooms of Madrid, exactly the sort of suave foreign agent my father had dreamed of being.

'It takes intelligence to play a buffoon, and I fooled them all. Even Julian was fooled by my disguise. But those days are gone and there is no need for me to play this trick.' His laugh was no longer of the belly-jerking sort but was now the soft chuckle of a man in his club. 'Julian. You have come to speak of Julian. What a naive young man he was, looking for this girl.' Now his laughter turned cold and mirthless. 'He came to me because the Reds had sent him. They had told him I was in charge of many evil things, and so I perhaps might know of this missing girl.' He cocked his head and glanced from one side to the other. 'Shall I tell you about your friend, your brother?' he asked. 'He was looking for this girl, but shall I tell you what he found?'

Warily I nodded, and Loretta whispered, 'Yes, tell us.'

And so he did.

CHAPTER 29

At the end of *Heart of Darkness*, Marlow is drained by the tale he has just related, emptied not of energy but of belief. It is as if the darkness he describes has dialed down the light in his soul.

So it seemed also with Loretta, at the close of El Árabe's tale, and so it certainly was with me.

'Do you believe what he told us?' she asked a few minutes into our drive back to town. We had been facing the road in complete silence.

'Every word,' I answered.

She looked at me. 'Why?'

'Because it fits,' I said.

I thought of a moment in *The Secret Chamber*, when La Meffraye stands on the ramparts at Machecoul, staring down at the thirty men that the Bishop of Nantes has sent to arrest her master. From that height she considers the crimes in which she was complicit, and their consequences, and she knows, absolutely, that she is bound for hell.

'Julian could see nothing but darkness after that,' I said softly, now thinking of how hideous it must

286

have been for him, the scene he'd witnessed at El Sitio.

'I remember something I said earlier,' Loretta said. 'That if Julian ever saw an atrocity, it would have unstrung him.'

'And it did,' I said.

Loretta clearly understood that something had also unstrung me as well.

'El Árabe's last question,' she said.

With that simple reminder, I was there again, sitting on the veranda, listening to El Árabe. But now there was the added element of foreknowledge, and I found myself imagining as much as recalling his narrative, tasting the dust in the air, seeing the swirl of the dogs as they tore into each other, feeling the small droplets of blood that shot out from the ring, and hearing Julian's voice over the roar of the crowd.

'That one is a killer.'

El Árabe turned to him. 'American?'

Julian nodded, smiled. 'A bankrupt one if I keep betting on the wrong dog.'

El Árabe grinned, pulled a red handkerchief from his pocket, and swabbed his bare chest. 'Bet on John Wayne in the next match. With him you will get back your money.'

Julian laughed. 'John Wayne, really?'

'He is my dog. I am big fan for John Wayne.' He swayed slightly and hitched his pants. 'Howdy, Pilgrim,' he said, and offered his hand.

'Julian Wells,' Julian said as he took it.

'Where you are from?' El Árabe asked between swigs of beer.

'New York.'

El Árabe reached for a bottle, opened it, and thrust it toward him. 'We drink to friendship, eh? America and Argentina.' He pounded his chest with his right fist. 'Brothers.'

Julian took a long pull on the bottle. 'Brothers,' he said.

They were two actors, I thought, playing out the scene in my mind: Julian, the naive American with a vague lust for adventure; El Árabe, the crude peasant infatuated with American cowboys. Encased in their roles, they acted their way through the next few hours, Julian betting on El Árabe's dogs and almost always winning, so that as the evening deepened, his roll of cash grew thicker, a fact El Árabe was careful to notice because he needed Julian to think him not only a peasant buffoon, easily outwitted, but also a man who could no less easily be bribed.

'You got much money now, coño,' El Árabe cried over the noise of the crowd. 'You should be careful you don't lose it.' Julian laughed. 'How would I lose it?'

'Not lose, maybe. Someone take it. Not everyone is a brother. Not in this bad place.'

Julian swayed slightly, as if drunk. 'It doesn't look so bad here.'

El Árabe wagged his finger. 'Very bad. Very bad people in this place. You maybe not go back to Buenos Aires tonight.'

'I have to. I have no place to stay.'

'You stay with me. I protect you. Morning, you go back to Buenos Aires.' He threw his arm over Julian's shoulder. 'You safe with me. Brothers, no?'

Julian's head lolled to the left. 'Too much beer.'

El Árabe laughed. 'We go home now,' he said.

I imagined them almost as comic characters in a melodrama, the tall young American and the squat little Argentine, a drunken Don Quixote and a malignant Sancho Panza struggling toward the old truck where El Árabe had already caged the few dogs that had survived the fights – 'quick killers,' as he called the ones that emerged from their struggles with treatable rather than fatal wounds.

In the truck, Julian had fallen asleep, or pretended to, and I saw him slumped in the dusty darkness, his body jerking with the bump and sway of the road.

'Okay, we are home now,' El Árabe said. He opened the door and drew Julian out into the weedy driveway of his house. 'You never sleep in hammock before, no? You like it. Very good. Stars. Cool air.'

289

Either passed out or feigning unconsciousness, Julian had slumped into the hammock that hung on the wide porch of El Árabe's house, arisen groggily the next morning, reached for his money, and found it missing.

'I know what you look for,' El Árabe said with a loud laugh. 'You think maybe I steal money from you, no?' He reached into the pocket of his soiled jeans and pulled out a roll of cash. 'I keep it for you. We are brothers, no? We do not steal from each other.' He laughed again. 'Maybe from others we steal, and maybe to others we do bad things, but I do nothing bad to Pilgrim, and Pilgrim, he does nothing bad to El Árabe.'

Thus was sealed a bond that deepened over the next few weeks as both Julian and El Árabe continued to perfect their roles, playing off each other with such skill that there were times when the subtext of deception seemed almost to disappear, nights of less drinking and more talk, which at last brought them each the long-sought moment.

'It's all just a way of forgetting,' Julian said quietly. He took out a cigarette and lit it. 'All this drinking.' He drew in a long breath and released it slowly. 'It is because of a woman. She is missing.'

'You will find another,' El Árabe said. 'You must think of something else.'

'I can't.'

Then, in a sudden burst that El Árabe found either absolutely brilliant if meant to deceive him or absolutely stupid if it was real, Julian had revealed everything: how he had met Marisol, her work as a guide, how she had later disappeared, his long effort to find her, how he'd gone first to Casa Rosada, then to the Russians, who had set him up to meet El Árabe, all of it in a cataract of impassioned narrative that had finally impressed El Árabe in its anguished sincerity.

El Árabe remained silent for a time, then quite softly he said, 'It is possible this one you spoke of, this missing woman, it is possible she is still alive, no?'

'No, it's not possible,' Julian said. 'We both know what happens to these women.'

'Not to all, maybe,' El Árabe said. 'Maybe some of them are kept.'

'Kept?'

El Árabe shrugged. 'To some men, it is a waste to kill such a woman,' he said. 'Better to keep her for a while.'

Julian's gaze glimmered with hope. 'Keep her where?'

El Árabe smiled. 'They are called "escuelitas."'
He offered Julian a look that could not have

been mistaken. 'Perhaps she is still at one of these places. Do you wish I look for her?'

'Yes.'

'And if I find her, do you wish to go to this place?'

'Yes,' Julian answered. 'Yes, I want to go there.'

Time passed, and during that time Julian had revealed ever-deeper confidences. He had come to Argentina, he said, in search of a life's work. Such had been his chief hunger when he came here, he told El Árabe, a furious need to do some great good work, a need his host had found both naive and comical. But Julian's sincerity had won El Árabe over. He'd been a fool, but a lovable fool, a man who wanted to help the ones who live in the dust. More than anything, he now sought Marisol.

'Because you fuck her, no?' El Árabe asked. 'Those little indigenes, they fuck hard and fast.'

'I never touched her.'

El Árabe laughed. 'You think she is so innocent, this woman?' He drained the last beer of the evening. 'Maybe not so innocent, my friend. If she was so innocent, she would not have disappeared.'

'No, she was absolutely innocent,' Julian insisted. 'There was no reason for her to have been taken. She wasn't involved in politics. All

292

she wanted . . . and she said this to me . . .
all she wanted was a fighting chance.'

'If this is so, I will find her for you,' El Árabe
said.

It took him only a week to find the *escuelita* to
which Marisol had been taken, and though she
was no longer there, he felt certain that by talking
to the commissar of the camp, he would be able
to find her.

And he did.

'Okay, so we go there tomorrow,' El Árabe said.
'Where is it?' Julian asked,
'There is a dog farm on the pampas. They
breed there the Dogo Córdoba. They have also
a barn and stalls. This they have made into
an escuelita.'

They left Buenos Aires the next morning, driving
first along the wide boulevards, then out into the
suburbs, and finally down a dirt road to a location
El Árabe called El Sitio, which means only 'the
place.'

It was a farmhouse of sorts, though it was unclear
whether it had once been occupied or whether it
had been constructed only for its current purpose.
Its windows were boarded up and left unpainted,
which made the structure seem like an immense
crate. It had a corrugated roof that was streaked
with rust.

'They keep them here,' El Árabe said with a crude smile, 'the ones they are educating.'

The heat inside this building was stifling, of course, and so, El Árabe explained with a wink and a grin, there was no need for the women to have clothes.

Julian remained in the truck, El Árabe said, while he went in search of the commissar, who was in a nearby shed where preparations for 'the day's lessons' were under way. Those preparations involved hooks and ropes and the fetching of the commissar's favored whip, a *chicotte*, made of rhinoceros hide and imported from the Congo.

From his place inside the truck, Julian had a clear view of the farmhouse and the line of upright wooden poles, each fitted with handcuffs, that stood to the side of it, and toward which, while El Árabe discussed the whereabouts of Marisol with the commissar, a naked woman was pushed and shoved and prodded by two men in green uniforms, each wielding a *chicotte*.

I could only imagine Julian's thoughts at that moment, how he must surely have realized that the same outrage had been committed upon Marisol. Naked and caked in her own filth, she must have been led to those same poles, cuffed and left to bake in the sun, while the men took their lunch break under the nearby trees. Like the woman he watched from the interior of El Árabe's truck, Marisol must have waited as the minutes passed and the men leisurely smoked their cigarettes, then rose and came toward her, as these men now did toward this unknown woman, slapping their *chicottes* against their dusty brown boots and, as the whipping commenced, beginning to laugh.

The beating lasted for several minutes, El Árabe said, with long pauses during which the woman was left to hang in the sun. Through it all Julian sat in the stillness of the truck, staring through its dusty windows as the whips sang in the air, along with the cries of the woman and the laughter of the men.

'She was covered in blood by the time I got back to the truck,' El Árabe told us. 'She was hanging down so low her long hair almost touched the ground, and her back, legs, and arms were raw. The whips almost skinned her.'

But it was what El Árabe saw inside the truck that chilled the air around me as I listened. He had passed the bloody girl who slumped almost to the ground, her wounds now boiling in the noonday sun, and given the scene hardly any notice. He had, after all, attended many such sessions. Nor had he paid any mind to the second woman, also naked and filthy, who was at that very moment being led out by two other men. He had noticed the commissar strolling toward the broken-down corral, but that had had no interest for him, since he had already ascertained Marisol's whereabouts. It was Julian, and only Julian, upon whom El Árabe, with an unexpected feeling, had fixed his attention.

'He was sitting exactly where I'd left him a half hour before,' El Árabe told us. 'He said only, "Was this done to Marisol?"'

From the corner of my eye, I saw a terrible question form on Loretta's lips. 'Had it been?' she asked.

El Árabe nodded. 'And worse,' he said. 'But I did not tell this to Julian. I told him she was simply brought here and shot. It would have been a bad thing to tell him more than this. He was blaming himself. He was saying it was his fault she was dead. I could not tell him more. This would have made it worse for him. So I told him only that she was dead. "They dumped her," I said to him. "She is dust."'

Julian had gone quiet, El Árabe told us.

'Pain can make men wail like women,' he said. 'But in Julian, there was only silence. He was alive, but he was dead. I took him back to Buenos Aires. All the way, he did not speak. I left him at his hotel. He never came to me again.'

For a time, no one spoke, and we heard nothing but the woman still fumbling about in the kitchen, along with the occasional bark of a dog or the call of a bird.

Finally, I said, 'So Julian never saw Marisol?'

El Árabe shook his head. 'And this is good, for it was very bad, what had been done to her. Very bad, the torture. Even the ones who live do not recover.'

Another stark silence followed. Neither Loretta

nor I had been able to move, so we were still frozen in place when the woman at last came out onto the veranda, dragging one foot behind her, causing the tray that bore our drinks to jerk as it trembled in her shaking hand. Her head was down, her hair was unkempt and streaked with dull gray. It was long enough to shield her face, but suddenly, with a wildly trembling hand, she drew it back to reveal the only thing I might recognize among the web of wrinkles and behind the drooping eyelids: her startlingly black eyes.

In a novel, it would have been Marisol, of course, this sadly broken woman. And I would have risen and gathered her into my arms and brought her to some safer, kinder place. There she would have lived out her days, sitting beneath a mango tree, enjoying the breeze from off La Plata. I would have occasionally come back to see her, and at some point she would have recalled Julian in his youth, our bright days in Buenos Aires, and together, as the sun set over the great trees of San Martín, we would have found the small measure of peace this life affords.

All these sweet, consoling things would have happened in a book, but as Julian knew, life takes a different turn.

'Maria,' El Árabe said, 'say hello to my guests.'

She gave no response, but merely placed the drinks on the little wooden table in front of us, spilling them slightly as she did so. Then she turned and struggled back into the house.

When she'd finally disappeared into the shadowy interior of the house, I drew my eyes over to El Árabe.

'Why was Marisol disappeared?' I asked. 'Was she a Montonero?'

El Árabe shook his head. 'No. She was a nothing, just a girl from the Chaco.'

'Then why was she taken?'

El Árabe grinned. 'It was a mistake, but life, it is full of little twists and turns, no?'

'That's not an answer,' I said firmly. 'Why was Marisol taken?'

El Árabe shrugged. 'She was betrayed,' he said. 'A boy she grew up with in the Chaco. In that orphanage there. They have a picture of those two together, those two indigenes. Marisol and that other flat-nosed peasant.'

'Emilio Vargas?' I asked.

El Árabe nodded. 'He was a weasel, that Red. And he lied about this girl. She was just a guide or something. But this Vargas, he feeds her to the wolves. Who knows why? Perhaps he is getting even with her because she does not fuck him in the old days. Men are scum in this way. One thing I know, he was there when it was done. Laying it on her himself. Making a big show of it.' He shrugged. 'It was Vargas who caused Marisol to be killed. But that is not how Julian saw it. And for that reason he thought himself her murderer.'

'Why would Julian have felt responsible for what happened to Marisol?' I asked.

'This he told me, and this I know.'

'What did he tell you?'

El Árabe appeared quite amused by the tricks embedded in the scheme of things, and I could see the true cruelty of this man, how he loved, more than anything, to watch a helpless creature dangle.

'Tell me what Julian told you,' I demanded.

His smile was a paper cut. 'Perhaps you should ask your father.'

CHAPTER 30

*M*y *father?*
　　　　This could not be the ending, I thought. In a novel of intrigue it would be too obvious – the story of a son's quest to find out what he could have done to prevent his friend's suicide ends up circling back to the father. As a literary route toward dark discoveries this one was way too familiar, trod, as it were, by Oedipus.

Yet, I could see the question that remained open each time I looked into Loretta's eyes: *What did your father do?*

I had considered what I was going to say to him many times on the flight back home with Loretta. During that time, the stakes had steadily increased for both of us, Loretta needing to know what Julian had discovered, I needing to know the part my father had played in whatever that discovery had been. Life was a warren of secret chambers, I decided, everyone on the plane a harbor for dark things. All the old clichés of spy fiction took on a hard reality: hall of mirrors, nest of vipers. My father had always wanted to be a character in a tale of intrigue. Now he was.

'He doesn't have to tell you the truth,' Loretta warned me when we parted at the airport. 'He doesn't have to tell you anything.'

'I know.'

'So be careful, Philip,' she added. Her tone was tense and her eyes held a feline sharpness. It was clear how much all this had come to matter to her, our search, now in dead earnest, for Julian's crime.

'Because in a way, this is an interrogation,' she added.

This was true, of course, and if my father chose to remain silent, then the story would end with an ambiguity no novel of intrigue, or even the cheapest thriller, could permit. We would know what happened to Marisol. But we would never know why it had happened, or why Julian had blamed himself for it, or why at the end of his life he'd still been wanting to confess to a crime for which he had long ago pronounced himself guilty.

But what was Julian's crime?

And why had he died without revealing it?

The answer to those questions now lay with my father.

He looked much weaker than when I'd last seen him, and in the flesh, rather than on a computer screen, he seemed far more frail.

'Ah, Philip,' he said. 'Welcome home.'

He was sitting in his chair when I arrived, as upright as possible, and as he watched me settle

301

into the chair that faced him, his mood seemed one of cheerful expectation.

'So,' he said, 'tell me about your adventures.'

All my life I had wanted him to be eager to hear my tale. All my life I had felt somewhat inadequate for never having one to tell him. Now the one I brought him was incomplete, with missing pieces he alone could provide.

'Well?' my father said eagerly. 'You must surely have some stories.'

I felt like a man who had reached the final chapter of a book he had been reading for a long time, one of those vast nineteenth-century tomes in which many fates shift and veer, only to reach what in the last pages seems to be their predestined ends.

'Yes, I do,' I said quietly.

Then, like a wily cop in a bleak interrogation room, I laid the groundwork for what was to come. I offered a brief summation of the route I'd traveled, through Julian's books, then on to the places I'd gone and the people I'd met, first René and Oradour, then on to Irene in Budapest and Soborov in Rostov, a trail that finally wound its way back to Argentina, where I'd confronted El Árabe in a little house tucked into a corner of Paraguay near Iguazú Falls.

The last of my tale had taken me to the brink, but I found that I could not cross it, and only said, 'He was a cruel man, El Árabe.'

'They come out of the woodwork in a place like

302

Argentina during a time like the Dirty War,' my father said. He appeared to grow somber for a moment, then, by act of will, to lift his own heavy spirits. 'But you've had quite a time of it,' he said. 'Travel to exotic locales. Talks with various odd ducks, even a Russian spy. It's like the books I used to read.'

'A lot can be learned from those books, I suppose,' I said, rousing myself for another reluctant effort to confront my father. 'Deception, for one. False identities and wrong turns. That one may smile and smile and be a villain.' I paused, then added, 'That goodness is evil's best disguise. Julian said that. In fact, it was the last thing he said.'

My father stared at me silently for a moment, then said with perfect calm, 'What do you suppose he meant by that?'

'I don't know,' I said, now moving with small steps toward the trapdoor, the steps beneath it, 'but I think it was something he learned in Argentina.'

'Yes, he did change after that.' His gaze dropped to his hands, then lifted slowly up toward me. 'That girl who disappeared.'

'Marisol,' I said.

The trapdoor opened and I took one step down.

'We found out what happened to her, you know,' I told my father. 'She was arrested by the junta. She was tortured, then killed.'

'I thought as much,' my father said.

'But we never found out why,' I said as I made my slow descent. 'She wasn't political after all. That much is clear. She was just a girl from the country.'

My father said nothing, but I thought I saw a sad glimmer in his eyes, and with that I made the rest of my journey down.

'Julian thought it was his fault,' I said. 'He blamed himself for her death.'

'Why?'

'I don't know,' I answered. 'And when I tried to get that particular answer from El Árabe, he said I should ask you.'

My father's body tensed. 'Me? Why would he say that?'

'I don't know that either,' I told him.

He looked at me closely. 'But you think I know, don't you, Philip?'

When I didn't answer, he sat back slightly, as if some invisible interrogator had pushed him.

'Do you think I was working for the junta, Philip?' he asked. 'That I was one of their agents? Because I'd have to have been one, wouldn't I, in order to know why Marisol was killed?'

'I suppose you would have, yes,' I admitted.

'Is that what you think?' my father demanded sharply.

'I only know that Julian blamed himself,' I said, 'and that when I tried to find out why, El Árabe—'

'Pointed his finger at me,' my father interrupted. 'Yes, you said that, Philip.'

304

He was clearly offended, and in the grip of that offense, he lifted his head like a proud but wounded warrior and glared at me.

'Do you know why she was killed?' I asked flatly.

'No, I don't,' my father answered sternly. 'How could I?' His eyes sparkled with affront. 'I was nothing!' he cried. 'You may have some fantasy that I was the puppet master in Argentina and that Julian was – what? – my pawn?' A hot breath blasted from him. 'But I was nothing! I have always been nothing. Why else would I have played that silly little trick with Julian?'

There are moments in life that resemble the sound of wood cracking beneath you, and I had reached such a moment.

'What trick?' I asked.

My father seemed caught in a seizure of self-loathing. 'Passed over and passed over. Again and again.'

'What trick, Dad?'

'The butt of jokes,' my father hissed vehemently.

'What silly little trick with Julian?' I demanded more firmly.

'Like some character in a novel,' my father raged on. He paused for a long moment, drew in a smoldering breath, then stared at me coldly. 'But life is not a novel, Philip. Do you know why?'

'Because people die,' I said, paused a single, lethal second, then added, 'especially people like Marisol.'

My father's expression suddenly turned grave. 'What are you talking about?' he asked. 'Why do you keep going back to this girl?'

For the first time, he appeared to glimpse a dark shadow moving toward him, that pale rider we all fear, not the one that brings our death, but the one that brings the truth about our lives.

'What are you talking about, Philip?' he asked again, and it seemed clear to me that he honestly did not know.

'Something Julian once said just came back to me,' I answered. 'A thought from Thoreau. That although the little boys kill frogs in play, the frogs die in earnest.'

My father stared at me silently, waiting, with some small but building hint of foreboding in his eyes.

I leaned forward slightly.

'Julian wanted to know why Marisol had been arrested,' I said. 'He wanted to know what evidence they had that Marisol was anything but a young woman who was just a guide.' I paused, then released the arrow that contained all I knew. 'El Árabe told Julian what that evidence was. It had come to Casa Rosada by way of an agent named Emilio Vargas. A double agent, actually, because Vargas was pretending to work for Casa Rosada, but in fact he was working for the Montoneros. He was also a friend of Marisol's from childhood, from the Chaco. He was under surveillance when Marisol went to him. I saw a picture of them together, but I have no idea why she went to him, because evidently she hadn't been in touch with him for many years.'

'Then suddenly she went to him?' my father asked.

'Yes.'

'When?'

'Not long after we met Father Rodrigo,' I answered. 'I know it was right after that because in the picture she is wearing a bead necklace that Rodrigo gave her.'

I could see my father's mind working desperately, though it seemed less in an effort to get off the road we were on than to move farther down it.

'Of course,' he said, as if some dark veil had torn. 'Of course that's what she did.'

For a moment, neither of us spoke. But during that time, though he said nothing, I saw a frightening change come over my father, saw the stony facade crumble, his mask fall away, so that he suddenly looked like what he was, a man in the act of loosening the cord that had bound his soul for so long.

Finally, my father said, 'Julian felt responsible for what happened to Marisol because he was responsible, Philip.' He straightened himself slightly, like a man before the bugle sounds, prepared, as his forebears had been prepared, to receive the blow.

'And so was I,' he added. He seemed to rethink some painful issue of his own. 'I've always believed

307

that only the bravest of us have the courage to confront our wrongs.' He stared at me brokenly. 'Like Julian did.' He let this final thought rest a moment, then added, 'And the time has come for me to confront mine.'

It had begun with the most innocent of inquiries, my father told me, one made when he and Julian walked the grounds of Two Groves one morning. Julian had come downstairs early and found my father alone at the kitchen table, drinking coffee. With his usual perceptiveness, Julian had found the scene quite sad and pointedly suggested an early morning stroll. With that, the two of them made their way out of the house and into the small orchard that surrounded it. After a few minutes of inconsequential conversation, Julian asked, 'Do you think one person can change things?'

'It was a silly question,' my father told me, 'and at first I didn't take it seriously. It was a young man's question, and a very naive young man's at that.'

But as the talk progressed, Julian's seriousness became increasingly obvious.

'He wanted to do something great,' my father said. 'To use that shopworn phrase, he wanted to "make a difference."' He shrugged. 'Because he knew how my own career had gone, he doubted that he could do anything truly good at, say, the State Department. He wondered if there might be some other way. He was simply exploring things with me, considering different avenues. That's when I said, "Well, perhaps you should become a spy."'

To my father's complete surprise, the idea appeared to catch.

'Maybe it was the romance of it,' my father said. 'Or maybe he truly began to think that somehow, in the secret corridors, he would be able to learn things that would eventually allow him to do some important good in the world.' My father lifted his hands in a gesture of helplessness. 'It appealed to me, how much Julian ached to do something good.'

His gaze suddenly became quite intense. 'A man shouldn't grow old wanting vengeance against his life, but that's exactly what had happened to me and I knew it. I didn't want it to happen to Julian. I didn't want him to be consumed by the raging disappointment that was consuming me.'

It was an anger he had fiercely repressed, of course, though there'd been moments when I'd seen it in the way he grappled with a tangled coat hanger as if it were alive and thwarting him, as if to kill it.

'I was a little man trapped behind a desk,' my father said, 'dreaming my secret-agent dream.'

'Walter Mitty,' I said softly.

My father nodded. 'And so I suggested Argentina as a place Julian should visit. I did this for the right reasons. I wanted him to see the real world. Get out of the cocoon his intelligence and good looks had provided for him.' He sat back slightly and passed his hand over the blanket that covered his legs. 'And given what Julian had said about being a spy, it was also a place where we could play a little game.'

He stopped and looked at me brokenly.

'It was never more than a game, Philip,' he said, pleading his case before he'd even made it, 'a little boys' game.'

He decided to give Julian a harmless cloak-and-dagger assignment, he told me. If Julian liked the taste of the work, then perhaps he could pursue it. And if he didn't, then it might at least cool his zeal for whatever he thought the life of a secret agent was.

'Part of that assignment, of course, was to tell no one,' my father said. The sadness in his voice deepened. 'We swore this to each other, and clearly Julian kept his promise. Now I am breaking mine.'

My father had considered several small tasks Julian might carry out while in Buenos Aires. None of them appealed to Julian, however, and so he pressed my father until he finally came up with a mission that had a suggestion of romance in it.

'Simply because – stupid, stupid – simply because it involved a woman.'

Here he paused like a man at the jagged edge of a bottomless abyss.

'Marisol,' I said, and with that word, I pushed him over it.

My father nodded. 'Julian was so young, you see,' he explained in a tone that now seemed stripped of all but regret. 'So, in my own stupid way, I thought, What could be more thrilling than a secret assignment involving a young woman?' He seemed now on the brink of his own devastating revelation. 'She was just a guide,' he added. 'Just a young woman with a job, who wanted . . .

'A fighting chance,' I said.

My father drew in a long breath, then continued.

'It was just a little exercise in deceit,' he said. 'It had nothing to do with Marisol.'

My father could see that I had no idea where he was going with this.

'The idea was for Julian to try his hand at acting,' he told me, 'like Loretta on the stage. Julian was to test himself, to see how good he was at . . .' His eyes took on a terrible sense of his own foolishness. 'To spy, you must make the target trust you and believe you. You must be able to make a lie credible, so your target will accept the lie you tell.'

'And Julian's target was Marisol,' I said.

My father nodded. 'Because she was innocent, you see. She wasn't in the least political. She'd been vetted by the consulate. They knew she was just a simple country girl. And so it was safe.'

'What was safe?'

'It was safe to deceive her.'

Julian was to pick his time, my father said, and pass on a bit of information, something she would find doubtful but which he would make her believe.

For Philip, sole witness to my crime.

I recalled the meeting with the old priest, Julian's remark about the likelihood of his being arrested, then the far more intense conversation I'd later come upon, Julian and Marisol in that little outdoor café, Julian animated, Marisol grave. I never knew the substance of what had passed between them. Now I did.

'Julian told Marisol that he had information about Father Rodrigo, didn't he?' I asked. 'That he was going to be arrested. Not just a suspicion, but actual information from the consulate, as if he were a secret agent.'

My father's sad smile held nothing but the dreadful fact of his own great miscalculation.

'Yes,' he said. 'And I'm sure that Julian had no idea that she would tell anyone. It was just a game.' He shook his head despairingly. 'Little boys. We didn't think that she would tell anyone other than Rodrigo, and that would not have mattered. What was the worst that could happen? She would believe a harmless lie and nothing would happen to anyone.'

'But she told Emilio Vargas.'

My father nodded. 'Evidently, yes.'

'She loved that old priest, and so she went to someone she thought could help him,' I said.

My father lifted his arms and gripped the arms of his chair. 'An old friend from her childhood, apparently,' he said. 'Someone she thought she could trust as much as . . .'

'Julian?'

My father looked like what he was, a man confronting the wrong Julian had faced so many years before.

'Until you mentioned this man, Vargas, I'd never heard of him,' he said. 'But now that you've told me about him, I know exactly what happened because I've known other men in his situation. You have to deflect attention away from yourself. And because you are a traitor, you have to give up someone else as a traitor. When Marisol went to him and told him what Julian had said, he saw his chance. He could finger her as a "source" at the American consulate, say that she'd come to him as a fellow Montonero, and then he could turn her over to Casa Rosada.'

He eased back into his chair and, with that movement, seemed to deflate.

'It's a classic play, Philip,' he told me. 'The trick is to make sure that the one you give up is as innocent as a child, one who can be devoured like Saturn devoured his children, without their ever knowing why.' He paused, then added, 'That's why, as a ploy, it's called the Saturn Turn.'

These two little boys, my father and my best friend, had played a lethal trick, but Marisol had died in earnest.

'Julian never forgave himself,' I told my father 'He was good in that way. He thought only of the consequences of his acts, never of their intention.'

'I hope you can forgive me, Philip,' my father said.

313

'I do,' I assured him. 'But as Julian must have known, it's Marisol who can't.'

When he gave no response to this, I said, 'But then it's always like that, isn't it? You said so yourself.'

I was surprised that I felt neither ire nor bitterness as I quoted him: 'It's always the little people, too small for us to see, the little, dusty people, who pay for our mistakes.'

I left him a few minutes later, expecting to face the night alone, but to my immense relief, I found Loretta waiting in the lobby of my building.

'It's a lovely evening,' she said. 'How about a walk through the park?'

We left the building and headed out into the night. She could see that I was shaken, but she asked no questions, and thus left it to me to decide when and where to speak.

We had already walked some distance into the park and taken a seat on one of its benches before I did.

'One night I came upon Julian and my father at Two Groves,' I began. 'They were alone for a long time in the study. It was very late and I'd gone upstairs to bed. But later I came down again and found them there, talking. They both looked rather surprised, and a little jarred, by my sudden appearance. They waved me in and we all talked a while, and I went back up to bed soon after. But it was in their eyes, Loretta. Conspiracy.' I drew in an unsteady breath. 'It was just a game,' I said, then

314

in a sudden rush, I related everything that my father had just told me. 'He and my father promised each other never to mention Argentina. Like little boys with their blood oaths. And so he never did.' I shrugged. 'And I suppose that's what he couldn't bear any longer, the fact that he had this crime bottled up inside him and couldn't release it.'

Loretta looked doubtful. 'That's why he never confessed? Because he promised your father?'

Her question stopped me cold. No, of course not, I thought. Julian would not have held to such a childish oath. Nor would my father have cared if he'd broken it. After all, my father had just confessed his own complicity in Julian's crime.

So why had Julian never confessed, and why had he chosen death over that confession?

I recalled how, in light of his own father's death, Julian said that a little boy required a hero, someone he could look up to, someone who could guide him. Later still, he had concealed the identities of the men who massacred the villages of Oradour. When I asked him why he'd done this, his answer was simple. What would be the good, he asked, of telling some little boy that on a particular day in a particular place his father had been complicit in a great crime?

Had I been that little boy?

'No, Julian didn't confess because of me,' I said to Loretta. 'He didn't confess because I was still a little boy to him.'

Then I told her how I'd reached this conclusion, the fact that Julian must have been profoundly influenced by his own father's death, how he must have come to think of my father as central to my life, how he'd known that he could not confess his crime without revealing my father's complicity in it. He had protected me as he'd protected the children of the soldiers who massacred the villagers of Oradour. It was all of a piece, I told her.

At the end of this, Loretta simply stared at me doubtfully.

'It's all too neat, Philip,' she said. 'And it's all too simple. That's natural, of course, because when a man you love kills himself, you want it to be about one thing. Just one thing you could have changed. But for some people, it's not one thing. It's everything.' She looked at me pointedly. 'Julian killed himself because he was like Marisol,' she told me, 'the victim of a Saturn Turn.'

When she saw I didn't understand this, she continued.

'His simple goodness turned on him,' she said. 'Life used it against him in the same way Vargas used Marisol's innocence against her.' She shrugged. 'The meek never inherit the earth, Philip.'

I thought of poor, benighted Swaziland, Africa's last kingdom. Julian had gone there some years before, then written an article about the conditions he'd found, how, while their king ordered fleets of luxury cars and flew about in a private jet, the people lay on their stomachs lapping water from

316

fetid pools, picked chicken heads and pig's feet from the dumping grounds of the nearest abattoir, and brought this muck back home to cook in battered pails – a people whose life expectancy was thirty-one. In the final passage of his essay, Julian had written of the red-dirt townships and the plywood shanties, the motionless pools of poisoned water, the mud hovels and rusty sheds, where life comes for the people of Swaziland, as it has always come for the truly innocent, 'with a knife in its hand.'

As Loretta had now made it clear, that same life, fixed in a Saturnine gaze, had at last come for Julian.

'I don't want to be alone tonight, Loretta,' I confessed.

If she'd had the smallest hesitation, the look in her eyes would have betrayed it. But I saw only that she'd grasped the full meaning of what I'd said.

'Perhaps not ever,' she said.

I knew that it was not an ending Jane Austen would have written, orchestrated by the peal of marriage bells, all happiness assured, but even so, I took Loretta's hand.

'Perhaps not ever,' I repeated.

She smiled. 'Do you know what you would have said to him if you'd been in the boat?' she asked.

I shook my head. 'Not yet,' I told her.

But by the time we reached home, I did.

AFTER

He folds the map and puts it on the table beside his chair. Beyond the window, he sees the flat gray waters of the pond. The boat, its yellow paint long faded, rests beneath a weeping birch.

He rises, walks to the window, and looks out.

In the distance, a small breeze rustles the leaves of the birch and skirts along the green lawn and gently rocks the purple irises that grow beside the water. He has seen so many grasses, so many flowers. The lavender fields of France, the cloudberries of the Urals with their little orange petals, the feather grasses of the pampas swaying like dancers.

He will miss these things.

He considers the act, then its consequences.

He will make it clean.

There will be no fuss.

He turns and gives a final glance at the map. He has studied so many maps. He thinks of the water bearers of the world, almost always women, hauling their jerry jars to the river or the lake. His mind is like those jars, worn and dusty, scarred by use, but still able to hold its heavy store of memory.

319

And yet there is something he forgot.

He walks to the small desk in the corner, opens the notebook, and tears out the top sheet. He folds it carefully, without hurry, then sinks it deep into his pocket.

It is disturbance you must look for, the old trackers told him. Not prints. Not trails. But disturbance in the spear grass, a sense of reeds askew. Those will lead you to the one you seek.

He looks about the room for any hint of such disturbance, finds none, and with that assurance, walks to the door, then passes through it, and moves out onto the lawn. He feels the breeze whose movement he had sensed before, cool upon his face, a pressure on his shirt, a gentle movement in his hair.

He hears a bird call, glances up, and sees a gull as it crosses the lower sky. When was it he first saw the sunbirds of the Sudan, their sun-streaked, iridescent feathers?

He shakes his head. It doesn't matter now.

He draws down his gaze and with a steady stride makes his way to the boat. It is heavy, and he has been weakened, though less by his final work than by this final decision.

But the decision has been made.

The boat is weighty but he pulls it into the water. What was the lightest he ever knew? Oh yes, it was made of bulrushes. And what was the other word for bulrushes? Oh yes, it was tule.

The boat rocks violently as he climbs in, but he rights himself, grabs an oar, and pushes out into the water.

How far to go?

The center of the pond. Far enough that he will appear small and indistinct in the distance so that she cannot tell what he is doing, nor get to him before he can complete the task.

Seventy feet from shore now. Perhaps eighty. He has not rowed in a long time. Even now his arms are aching. But that will be over soon. He knows that he has grown weak in the Russian wastes, but he is surprised by just how weak he is. Or has his secret always worked upon him like a withering disease?

One hundred feet out from shore.

Enough.

He takes the paper from his pocket, unfolds it, and reads what he has written.

'It's your final dark conclusion, isn't it?' I ask. 'And it was going to be the first line of your next book.'

He turns to face me. His features bear the mark of life's many cruel tricks.

'Because there is no answer to our *zachem*,' I add.

He nods.

'Write it,' I tell him softly. 'Go home and write it.'

He remains silent, still.

'The world has plenty of noise, Julian, but not many voices.'

He watches me steadily.

'And because there are so few, each one matters.'

I lean toward him, hoping for more persuasive words. When none comes to me, I shrug. 'That's my argument. The simple fact that we need people who remind us of the darkness.'

His smile is slight and, like everything else, difficult to read, impossible to know.

'That is your job, Julian,' I add. 'And you need to do it.'

With a curiously resolved movement, the renewal of some almost vanished strength, Julian returns the paper to his pocket and once again takes up the oars. I know, because I know him, that he is thinking of his book.

The wind touches the far trees. On the near bank, a dragonfly shoots over the still waters.

I follow the soft beat of the oars.

Second by second, the house grows nearer.

Even so, I cannot be sure that he will make it home.

For life, as Julian knew and his life and words and crime declared, is, at last, a Saturn Turn.